# Historic Documents
## on the
## Presidency: 1776-1989

# Historic Documents on the Presidency: 1776-1989

**Michael Nelson**

*Editor*

Washington, D.C.

# Congressional Quarterly Inc.

Congressional Quarterly Inc., an editorial research service and publishing company, serves clients in the fields of news, education, business, and government. It combines Congressional Quarterly's specific coverage of Congress, government, and politics with the more general subject range of an affiliated service, Editorial Research Reports.

Congressional Quarterly publishes the *Congressional Quarterly Weekly Report* and a variety of books, including college political science textbooks under the CQ Press imprint and public affairs paperbacks on developing issues and events. CQ also publishes information directories and reference books on the federal government, national elections, and politics, including the *Guide to the Presidency,* the *Guide to Congress,* the *Guide to the U.S. Supreme Court,* the *Guide to U.S. Elections, Politics in America,* and *Congress A to Z: CQ's Ready Reference Encyclopedia.* The *CQ Almanac,* a compendium of legislation for one session of Congress, is published each year. *Congress and the Nation,* a record of government for a presidential term, is published every four years.

CQ publishes *The Congressional Monitor,* a daily report on current and future activities of congressional committees, and several newsletters including *Congressional Insight,* a weekly analysis of congressional action, and *Campaign Practices Reports,* a semimonthly update on campaign laws.

An electronic online information system, Washington Alert, provides immediate access to CQ's databases of legislative action, votes, schedules, profiles, and analyses.

Copyright © 1989 Congressional Quarterly Inc.
1414 22nd Street N.W., Washington, D.C. 20037

Printed in the United States of America

**Library of Congress Cataloging-in-Publication Data**
Historic documents of the presidency / [edited by] Michael Nelson.
    p.      cm.
    Includes bibliographical references.
    ISBN 0-87187-518-7
    1. Presidents--United States--History--Sources.  I. Nelson, Michael, 1949-  . II. Congressional Quarterly, inc.
    JK511.H57 1989                    89-22161
    353.03'13'09--dc20                  CIP

*Project Editor:* Margaret Seawell Benjaminson
*Production Assistant:* Jamie R. Holland
*Proofreaders:* Denise L. Hubbard, Bonnie Moore, Tracy W. Villano
*Indexer:* Patricia R. Ruggiero
*Cover Designer:* Ron Silberberg

# Table of Contents

# *Preface*

The reader of this unique one-volume collection of documents on the presidency is bound—and entitled—to assume that the editor's selections from the long history of the office are, by some useful standard, the most important ones. The reader also deserves to know what the editor's standard is for judging a document to be important.

In part, I have striven to include documents that embody the most memorable and significant activities of *individual presidents*. The presidents whom historians celebrate as "great," for example, are represented by as many as seven documents each. Ironically, because of the scandals that marked their administrations, some of the outright "failures" are heavily represented as well.

More important, however, is the emphasis I have placed on the development of the *presidency as an institution*. The documents trace in particular:

~ *origins and development* of the office, including three plans of government that were proposed at the Constitutional Convention, the Constitution itself, and *Federalist* Nos. 69 and 70, which deal with the presidency

~ *relations with the Supreme Court*, such as *Ex Parte Milligan, Humphrey's Executor v. United States, United States v. Nixon, Immigration and Naturalization Service v. Chadha,* and Franklin D. Roosevelt's "Court-packing" plan

~ *relations with Congress*, including the Pendleton Act, the Teapot Dome Resolution, the War Powers Resolution, and the articles of impeachment against Andrew Johnson and those proposed against Richard Nixon

~ *evolution of presidential power*, as demonstrated in George Washington's first inaugural address, the Monroe Doctrine, Abraham Lincoln's first message to Congress, the exchange between former presidents Theodore Roosevelt and William Howard Taft, and the Brownlow Commission report

~ *vice-presidential landmarks*, including Nixon's "Checkers" speech and Spiro T. Agnew's attack on the media

~ *presidential elections*, such as the Tennessee legislature's protest against "King Caucus," the first Kennedy-Nixon debate, and George Bush's acceptance speech at the 1988 Republican convention.

These documents also extensively cover the prominent leadership roles that, constitutionally and otherwise, the president has come to perform:

~ *commander in chief*, including the war messages of James Madison, James K. Polk, Franklin Roosevelt, and Harry S Truman; Lyndon B. Johnson's call for the Gulf of Tonkin resolution; Nixon's "silent majority" address on Vietnam; and Ronald Reagan's Grenada speech

~ *chief diplomat*, such as Washington's Farewell Address, Woodrow Wilson's "Fourteen Points" speech, Franklin Roosevelt's "Four Freedoms" speech, the Truman Doctrine, the Camp David accords, Nixon's China trip announcement, and the INF treaty

~ *chief legislator,* including Andrew Jackson's veto of the bank bill, Wilson's first State of the Union address, Truman's Point Four message, Jimmy Carter's "malaise" speech, and Reagan's economic plan speech.

The documents have been edited for clarity, but not at the expense of completeness. In addition, each document is introduced by a headnote that places it into its contemporary setting, into broad historical context, and, through cross-references to other documents, into the structure of the volume. Taken together, the headnotes constitute a virtual short history of the presidency.

One point of caution. Careful readers will note that individual documents are characterized variously as messages, ad-

dresses, and speeches. These are not the editor's categories but the labels each document has acquired in historical usage. Inconsistencies abound. For example, one presidential address will be written, the next spoken; one will be formal, another informal; and so on.

I am grateful to David R. Tarr, director of the Book Department, for his enthusiastic support for this book; to Jamie R. Holland, production assistant, whose research and organizational skills helped to ensure the accuracy of the material and keep the project on track; and, especially, to Margaret Seawell Benjaminson, project editor, whose professional skill and personal grace are unmatched by any editor I know. I also—and always—thank my wife, Linda E. Nelson, and my sons, Michael, Jr., and Samuel, for their steadfast love and encouragement.

Michael Nelson

# Declaration of Independence (1776)

On September 4, 1774, in response to a call by the Virginia and Massachusetts legislatures, a Continental Congress consisting of representatives of nearly all the British colonies in America assembled in Philadelphia, Pennsylvania, to demand fairer treatment from the government of Great Britain. Unsuccessful in their efforts, the colonists convened the Second Continental Congress (also in Philadelphia) on May 10, 1775. A congressionally enacted petition to King George III asking for "a happy and permanent reconciliation" was greeted on August 23, 1775, with a royal proclamation that a state of rebellion existed in the colonies.

On June 11, 1776, the responsibility to "prepare a declaration" of independence was assigned by Congress to a five-member committee of its members: John Adams of Massachusetts, Benjamin Franklin of Pennsylvania, Thomas Jefferson of Virginia, Robert Livingston of New York, and Roger Sherman of Connecticut. Impressed by his talents as a writer, the committee asked the thirty-three-year-old Jefferson to compose a draft, which he did. Jefferson's draft was modified by the committee and turned over to Congress on June 28. (One of the modifications that Congress made was to strike out a denunciation of the British slave trade.) On July 2 Congress voted to declare independence; two days later,

on the evening of July 4, it approved the Declaration of Independence by a near-unanimous vote.

The Declaration is best remembered for its ringing preamble, which affirms the "self-evident" truths that "all men are created equal, that they are endowed by their Creator with certain unalienable Rights, that among these are Life, Liberty and the pursuit of Happiness." But at the time, the more important part of the declaration was what followed the preamble: the list of "a long train of abuses and usurpations" against the American colonists by the British government. The charges contained in the list detailed the abuses that made it "necessary for one people [the Americans] to dissolve the political bands which have connected them with another [the British]."

Although many of the more than two dozen alleged British abuses were acts of Parliament, all were attributed to King George III. In general, the king was charged with "seeking the establishment of absolute Tyranny over these States." Among the specific complaints were these: he had vetoed "wholesome and necessary" laws, prevented elected colonial legislatures from meeting, quartered troops in the homes of colonists, and "erected a multitude of New Offices, and sent hither swarms of Officers to harass our People, and eat out their substance."

*The indictment of George III—and the Declaration of Independence as a whole—contributed to the idea that a strong executive threatened the fundamental liberties of the people. Perhaps the greatest obstacle the framers of the Constitution were to confront eleven years later in creating an effective presidency was the widespread fear that they were planting the seeds for another, equally threatening monarchy.*  ~

## In Congress, July 4, 1776, The Unanimous Declaration of the Thirteen United States of America,

When in the Course of human events, it becomes necessary for one people to dissolve the political bands which have connected them with another, and to assume among the Powers of the earth, the separate and equal station to which the Laws of Nature and of Nature's God entitle them, a decent respect to the opinions of mankind requires that they should declare the causes which impel them to the separation.

We hold these truths to be self-evident, that all men are created equal, that they are endowed by their Creator with certain unalienable Rights, that among these are Life, Liberty and the pursuit of Happiness. That to secure these rights, Governments are instituted among Men, deriving their just powers from the consent of the governed. That whenever any form of Government becomes destructive of these ends, it is the Right of the People to alter or to abolish it, and to institute new Government, laying its foundation on such principles and organizing its powers in such form, as to them shall seem most likely to effect their Safety and Happiness. Prudence, indeed, will dictate that Government long established should not be changed for light and transient causes; and accordingly all experience hath shown, that mankind are more disposed to suffer, while evils are sufferable, than to right themselves by abolishing the forms to which they are accustomed. But when a long train of abuses and usurpations, pursuing invariably the same Object evinces a design to reduce them under absolute Despotism, it is their right, it is their duty, to throw off such Government, and to provide new Guards for their future security.—Such has been the patient sufferance of these Colonies; and such is now the necessity which constrains them to alter their former Systems of Government. The history of the present King of Great Britain is a history of repeated injuries and usurpations, all having in direct object the establishment of an absolute Tyranny over these States. To prove this, let Facts be submitted to a candid world.

He has refused his Assent to Laws, the most wholesome and necessary for the public good.

He has forbidden his Governors to pass Laws of immediate and pressing importance, unless suspended in their operation till his Assent should be obtained; and when so suspended, he has utterly neglected to attend to them.

He has refused to pass other Laws for the accommodation of large districts of people, unless those people would relinquish the right of Representation in the Legislature, a right inestimable to them and formidable to tyrants only.

He has called together legislative bodies at places unusual, uncomfortable, and distant from the depository of their Public Records, for the sole purpose of fatiguing them into compliance with his measures.

He has dissolved Representative Houses repeatedly, for opposing with manly firmness his invasions on the rights of the people.

He has refused for a long time, after such dissolutions, to cause others to be elected; whereby the Legislative Powers, incapable of Annihilation, have returned to the People at large for their exercise; the State remaining in the mean time exposed to all the dangers of invasion from without, and convulsions within.

He has endeavored to prevent the population of these States; for that purpose obstructing the Laws of Naturalization of Foreigners; refusing to pass others to encourage their migration hither, and raising the conditions of new Appropriations of Lands.

He has obstructed the Administration of Justice, by refusing his Assent to Laws for establishing Judiciary Powers.

He has made Judges dependent on his Will alone, for the tenure of their offices, and the amount and payment of their salaries.

He has erected a multitude of New Offices, and sent hither swarms of Officers to harass our People, and eat out their substance.

He has kept among us, in times of peace, Standing Armies without the Consent of our legislature.

He has affected to render the Military independent of and superior to the Civil Power.

He has combined with others to subject us to a jurisdiction foreign to our constitution, and unacknowledged by our laws; giving his Assent to their acts of pretended legislation:

For quartering large bodies of armed troops among us:

For protecting them, by a mock Trial, from Punishment for any Murders which they should commit on the Inhabitants of these States:

For cutting off our Trade with all parts of the world:

For imposing taxes on us without our Consent:

For depriving us in many cases, of the benefits of Trial by Jury:

For transporting us beyond Seas to be tried for pretended offences:

For abolishing the free System of English Laws in a neighbouring Province, establishing therein an Arbitrary government, and enlarging its Bound-

aries so as to render it at once an example and fit instrument for introducing the same absolute rule into these Colonies:

For taking away our Charters, abolishing our most valuable Laws, and altering fundamentally the Forms of our Governments:

For suspending our own Legislature, and declaring themselves invested with Power to legislate for us in all cases whatsoever.

He has abdicated Government here, by declaring us out of his Protection and waging War against us.

He has plundered our seas, ravaged our Coasts, burnt our towns, and destroyed the lives of our people.

He is at this time transporting large armies of foreign mercenaries to compleat the works of death, desolation and tyranny, already begun with circumstances of Cruelty & perfidy scarcely parallel in the most barbarous ages, and totally unworthy the Head of a civilized nation.

He has constrained our fellow Citizens taken Captive on the high Seas to bear Arms against their Country, to become the executioners of their friends and Brethren, or to fall themselves by their Hands.

He has excited domestic insurrections amongst us, and has endeavoured to bring on the inhabitants of our frontiers, the merciless Indian Savages, whose known rule of warfare, is an undistinguished destruction of all ages, sexes and conditions.

In every stage of these Oppressions We have Petitioned for Redress in the most humble terms: Our repeated Petitions have been answered only by repeated injury. A Prince, whose character is thus marked by every act which may define a Tyrant, is unfit to be the ruler of a free People.

Nor have We been wanting in attention to our British brethren. We have warned them from time to time of attempts by their legislature to extend an unwarrantable jurisdiction over us. We have reminded them of the circumstances of our emigration and settlement here. We have appealed to their native justice and magnanimity, and we have conjured them by the ties of our common kindred to disavow these usurpations, which would inevitably interrupt our connections and correspondence. They too have been deaf to the voice of justice and of consanguinity. We must, therefore, acquiesce in the necessity, which denounces our Separation, and hold them, as we hold the rest of mankind, Enemies in War, in Peace Friends.

We, therefore, the Representatives of the United States of America, in General Congress, Assembled, appealing to the Supreme Judge of the world for the rectitude of our intentions, do, in the Name, and by Authority of the good People of these Colonies, solemnly publish and declare, That these United Colonies are, and of Right ought to be Free and Independent States; that they are Absolved from all Allegiance to the British Crown, and that all political connection between them and the State of Great Britain, is and ought to be totally dissolved; and that as Free and Independent States, they have full Power to levy War, conclude Peace, contract Alliances, establish Commerce, and to do all other Acts and Things which Independent States may of right do. And for the support of this Declaration, with a firm reliance on the Protection of Divine Providence, we mutually pledge to each other our Lives, our Fortunes and our sacred Honor.

JOHN HANCOCK.

| | |
|---|---|
| **New Hampshire:** | Josiah Bartlett, William Whipple, Matthew Thornton. |
| **Massachusetts-Bay:** | Samuel Adams, John Adams, Robert Treat Paine, Elbridge Gerry. |
| **Rhode Island:** | Stephen Hopkins, William Ellery. |
| **Connecticut:** | Roger Sherman, Samuel Huntington, William Williams, Oliver Wolcott. |
| **New York:** | William Floyd, Philip Livingston, Francis Lewis, Lewis Morris. |
| **Pennsylvania:** | Robert Morris, Benjamin Harris, Benjamin Franklin, John Morton, George Clymer, James Smith, George Taylor, James Wilson, George Ross. |
| **Delaware:** | Caesar Rodney, George Read, Thomas McKean. |
| **Georgia:** | Button Gwinnett, Lyman Hall, George Walton. |
| **Maryland:** | Samuel Chase, William Paca, Thomas Stone, Charles Carroll of Carrollton. |
| **Virginia:** | George Wythe, Richard Henry Lee, Thomas Jefferson, Benjamin Harrison, Thomas Nelson Jr., Francis Lightfoot Lee, Carter Braxton. |
| **North Carolina:** | William Hooper, Joseph Hewes, John Penn. |
| **South Carolina:** | Edward Rutledge, Thomas Heyward Jr., Thomas Lynch Jr., Arthur Middleton. |
| **New Jersey:** | Richard Stockton, John Witherspoon, Francis Hopkinson, John Hart, Abraham Clark. |

# Articles of Confederation (1781)

On June 11, 1776, the same day that it created a committee to draft the Declaration of Independence, the Continental Congress appointed a thirteen-member committee (one member from each state) to draft a "plan of confederation." The two actions were closely connected: a new and independent nation needed a government of some sort. The committee, relying heavily upon a draft prepared by one of its members, John Dickinson of Delaware, recommended the Articles of Confederation and Perpetual Union to the Continental Congress on July 12, 1776. Congress adopted the plan on November 15, 1777. Although unanimous ratification by the states did not come until March 1, 1781, the Articles served as the ad hoc basis for a national government during most of the revolutionary war. They were replaced by the Constitution in 1789.

Written at a time when public hostility to a strong central government (the British) and executive power (the king and his royal governors in each colony) was at its height, the Articles, not surprisingly, provided for a weak central government with no executive at all. Congress—a unicameral, or one-house, body in which each state was represented equally—was the sole organ of the new national government. It had no power to levy taxes or to enforce the laws that it passed. Even the powers that it did have—such as to declare war, to enter treaties and alliances, to raise an army and navy, to regulate coinage and borrow money, and to adjudicate disputes among the states—were hard to exercise, because any proposed law required a two-thirds majority (nine of thirteen votes) for passage. To amend the Articles required unanimity.

By empowering Congress to appoint civil officers to manage the affairs of the United States, the Articles did leave room for a modified executive branch to develop. Congress chose to exercise this power in 1781, naming Robert Livingston of New York to be secretary of foreign affairs, Gen. Benjamin Lincoln of Massachusetts as secretary of war, and Robert Morris of Pennsylvania as superintendent of finance. The historian Merrill Jensen has described Morris as the most powerful person in the United States.

The Articles of Confederation provided a barely adequate framework for fighting and winning the revolutionary war: the presence of a common enemy fostered a certain amount of unity among the states. But when the British were defeated in 1783, the national government found it increasingly difficult to unite the country to confront the new challenges of peace. Overlapping claims to western lands brought states into sometimes violent conflict. The nation's *enormous foreign and domestic debts went unpaid, damaging the economy. The government was powerless to enforce either British or American rights under the Treaty of Paris, which ended the American Revolution in 1783. U.S. borders were under siege, mainly from the British in the North and the Spanish in the West and South.* ~

To all to whom these Presents shall come, we the undersigned Delegates of the States affixed to our Names send greeting. Whereas the Delegates of the United States of America in Congress assembled did on the fifteenth day of November in the Year of our Lord One Thousand Seven Hundred and Seventy seven, and in the Second Year of the Independence of America agree to certain articles of Confederation and perpetual Union between the States of Newhampshire, Massachusetts-bay, Rhodeisland and Providence Plantations, Connecticut, New York, New Jersey, Pennsylvania, Delaware, Maryland, Virginia, North-Carolina, South-Carolina and Georgia in the Words following, viz. "Articles of Confederation and perpetual Union between the states of Newhampshire, Massachusetts-bay, Rhodeisland and Providence Plantations, Connecticut, New-York, New-Jersey, Pennsylvania, Delaware, Maryland, Virginia, North-Carolina, South-Carolina and Georgia.

**Article I.** The Stile of this confederacy shall be "The United States of America."

**Article II.** Each state retains its sovereignty, freedom and independence, and every Power, Jurisdiction and Right, which is not by this confederation expressly delegated to the United States, in Congress assembled.

**Article III.** The said states hereby severally enter into a firm league of friendship with each other, for their common defence, the security of their Liberties, and their mutual and general welfare, binding themselves to assist each other, against all force offered to, or attacks made upon them, or any of them, on account of religion, sovereignty, trade, or any other pretence whatever.

**Article IV.** The better to secure and perpetuate mutual friendship and intercourse among the people of the different states in this union, the free inhabitants of each of these states, paupers, vagabonds and fugitives from Justice excepted, shall be entitled to all privileges and immunities of free citizens in the several states; and the people of each state shall have free ingress and regress to and from any other state, and shall enjoy therein all the privileges of trade and commerce, subject to the same duties, impositions and restrictions as the inhabitants thereof respectively, provided that such restriction shall not extend so far as to prevent the removal of property imported into any state, to any other state of which the Owner is an inhabitant; provided also that no imposition, duties or restriction shall be laid by any state, on the property of the united states, or either of them.

If any Person guilty of, or charged with treason, felony, or other high misdemeanor in any state, shall flee from Justice, and be found in any of the united states, he shall upon demand of the Governor or executive power, of the state from which he fled be delivered up and removed to the state having jurisdiction of his offence.

Full faith and credit shall be given in each of these states to the records, acts and judicial proceedings of the courts and magistrates of every other state.

**Article V.** For the more convenient management of the general interests of the united states, delegates shall be annually appointed in such manner as the legislature of each state shall direct, to meet in Congress on the first Monday in November, in every year, with a power reserved to each state, to recall its delegates, or any of them, at any time within the year, and to send others in their stead, for the remainder of the Year.

No state shall be represented in Congress by less than two, nor by more than seven Members; and no person shall be capable of being a delegate for more than three years in any term of six years; nor shall any person, being a delegate, be capable of holding any office under the united states, for which he, or another for his benefit receives any salary, fees or emolument of any kind.

Each state shall maintain its own delegates in a meeting of the states, and while they act as members of the committee of the states.

In determining questions in the united states, in Congress assembled, each state shall have one vote.

Freedom of speech and debate in Congress shall not be impeached or questioned in any Court, or place out of Congress, and the members of congress shall be protected in their persons from arrests and imprisonments, during the time of their going to and from, and attendance on congress, except for treason, felony, or breach of the peace.

**Article VI.** No state without the Consent of the united states in congress assembled, shall send any embassy to, or receive any embassy from, or enter into any conference, agreement, or alliance or treaty with any King, prince or state; nor shall any person holding any office of profit or trust under the united states, or any of them, accept of any present, emolument, office or title of any kind whatever from any king, prince or foreign state; nor shall the united states in congress assembled, or any of them, grant any title of nobility.

No two or more states shall enter into any treaty, confederation or alliance whatever between them, without the consent of the united states in congress assembled, specifying accurately the purposes for which the same is to be entered into, and how long it shall continue.

No state shall lay any imposts or duties, which may interfere with any stipulations in treaties, entered into by the united states in congress assembled, with any king, prince or state, in pursuance of any treaties already proposed by congress, to the courts of France and Spain.

No vessels of war shall be kept up in time of peace by any state, except such number only, as shall be deemed necessary by the united states in congress assembled, for the defence of such state, or its trade; nor shall any body of forces be kept up by any state, in time of peace, except such number only, as in the judgment of the united states, in congress assembled, shall be deemed requisite to garrison the forts necessary for the defence of such state; but every state shall always keep up a well regulated and disciplined militia, sufficiently armed and accoutred, and shall provide and constantly have ready for use, in public stores, a due number of field pieces and tents, and a proper quantity of arms, ammunition and camp equipage.

No state shall engage in any war without the consent of the united states in Congress assembled, unless such state be actually invaded by enemies, or shall have received certain advice of a resolution being formed by some nation of Indians to invade such state, and the danger is so imminent as not to admit of a delay, till the united states in congress assembled can be consulted: nor shall any state grant commissions to any ships or vessels of war, nor letters of marque or reprisal, except it be after a declaration of war by the united states in congress assembled, and then only against the kingdom or state and the subjects thereof, against which war has been so declared, and under such regulations as shall be established by the united states in congress assembled, unless such state be infested by pirates, in which case vessels of war may be fitted out for that occasion, and kept so long as the danger shall continue, or until the united states in congress assembled shall determine otherwise.

**Article VII.** When land-forces are raised by any state for the common defence, all officers of or under the rank of colonel, shall be appointed by the legislature of each state respectively by whom such forces shall be raised, or in such manner as such state shall direct, and all vacancies shall be filled up by the state which first made the appointment.

**Article VIII.** All charges of war, and all other expences that shall be incurred for the common defence or general welfare, and allowed by the united states in congress assembled, shall be defrayed out of a common treasury, which shall be supplied by the several states, in proportion to the value of all land within each state, granted to or surveyed for any Person, as such land and the buildings and improvements thereon shall be estimated according to such mode as the united states in congress assembled, shall from time to time direct and appoint. The taxes for paying that proportion shall be laid and levied by the authority and direction of the legislatures of the several states within the time agreed upon by the united states in congress assembled.

**Article IX.** The united states in congress assembled, shall have the sole and exclusive right and power of determining on peace and war, except in the cases mentioned in the sixth article—of sending and receiving ambassadors—entering into treaties and alliances, provided that no treaty of commerce shall be made whereby the legislative power of the respective states shall be restrained from imposing such imposts and duties on foreigners, as their own people are subjected to, or from prohibiting the exportation or importation of any species of goods or commodities whatsoever—of establishing rules for deciding in all cases, what capture on

land or water shall be legal, and in what manner prizes taken by land or naval forces in the service of the united states shall be divided or appropriated—of granting letters of marque and reprisal in times of peace—appointing courts for the trial of piracies and felonies committed on the high seas and establishing courts for receiving and determining finally appeals in all cases of captures, provided that no member of congress shall be appointed a judge of any of the said courts.

The united states in congress assembled shall also be the last resort on appeal in all disputes and differences now subsisting or that hereafter may arise between two or more states concerning boundary, jurisdiction or any other cause whatever; which authority shall always be exercised in the manner following. Whenever the legislative or executive authority or lawful agent of any state in controversy with another shall present a petition to congress, stating the matter in question and praying for a hearing, notice thereof shall be given by order of congress to the legislative or executive authority of the other state in controversy, and a day assigned for the appearance of the parties by their lawful agents, who shall then be directed to appoint by joint consent, commissioners or judges to constitute a court for hearing and determining the matter in question: but if they cannot agree, congress shall name three persons out of each of the united states, and from the list of such persons each party shall alternately strike out one, the petitioners beginning, until the number shall be reduced to thirteen; and from that number not less than seven, nor more than nine names as congress shall direct, shall in the presence of congress be drawn out by lot, and the persons whose names shall be so drawn or any five of them, shall be commissioners or judges, to hear and finally determine the controversy, so always as a major part of the judges who shall hear the cause shall agree in the determination: and if either party shall neglect to attend at the day appointed, without shewing reasons, which congress shall judge sufficient, or being present shall refuse to strike, the congress shall proceed to nominate three persons out of each state, and the secretary of congress shall strike in behalf of such party absent or refusing; and the judgment and sentence of the court to be appointed, in the manner before prescribed, shall be final and conclusive; and if any of the parties shall refuse to submit to the authority of such court, or to appear to defend their claim or cause, the court shall nevertheless proceed to pronounce sentence, or judgment, which shall in like manner be final and decisive, the judgment or sentence and other proceedings being in either case transmitted to congress, and lodged among the acts of congress for the security of the parties concerned: provided that every commissioner, before he sits in judgment, shall take an oath to be administered by one of the judges of the supreme or superior court of the state, where the cause shall be tried, "well and truly to hear and determine the matter in question, according to the best of his judgment, without favour, affection or hope of reward:" provided also that no state shall be deprived of territory for the benefit of the united states.

All controversies concerning the private right of soil claimed under different grants of two or more states, whose jurisdictions as they may respect such lands, and the states which passed such grants are adjusted, the said grants or either of them being at the same time claimed to have originated antecedent to such settlement of jurisdiction, shall on the petition of either party to the congress of the united states, be finally determined as near as may be in the same manner as is before prescribed for deciding disputes respecting territorial jurisdiction between different states.

The united states in congress assembled shall also have the sole and exclusive right and power of regulating the alloy and value of coin struck by their own authority, or by that of the respective states—fixing the standard of weights and measures throughout the united states—regulating the trade and managing all affairs with the Indians, not members of any of the states, provided that the legislative right of any state within its own limits be not infringed or violated—establishing and regulating post-offices from one state to another, throughout all the united states, and exacting such postage on the papers passing thro' the same as may be requisite to defray the expences of the said office—appointing all officers of the land forces, in the service of the united states, excepting regimental officers—appointing all the officers of the naval forces, and commissioning all officers whatever in the service of the united states—making rules for the government and regulation of the said land and naval forces, and directing their operations.

The united states in congress assembled shall have authority to appoint a committee, to sit in the recess of congress, to be denominated "A Committee of the States," and to consist of one delegate from each state; and to appoint such other committees and civil officers as may be necessary for managing the general affairs of the united states under their direction—to appoint one of their number to preside, provided that no person be allowed to serve in the office of president more than one year in any term of three years; to ascertain the necessary sums of Money to be raised for the service of the united states, and to appropriate and apply the same for defraying the public expences—to borrow money, or emit bills on the credit of the united states, transmitting every half year to the respective states an account of the sums of money so borrowed or emitted,—to build and equip a navy—to agree upon the number of land forces, and to make requisitions from each state for its quota, in proportion to the number of white inhabitants in such state; which requisition shall be binding, and thereupon the legislature of each state shall appoint the regimental officers, raise the men and cloath, arm and equip them in a soldier like manner, at the expence of the united states, and the officers and men so cloathed, armed and equipped shall march to the place appointed, and within the time agreed on by the united states in congress assembled: But if the united states in congress assembled shall, on consideration of circumstances judge proper that any state should not raise men, or should raise a smaller number than its quota, and that any other state should raise a greater number of men than the quota thereof, such extra number shall be raised, officered, cloathed, armed and equipped in the same manner as the quota of such state, unless the legislature of such state shall judge that such extra number cannot be safely spared out of the same, in which case they shall raise, officer, cloath, arm and equip as many of such extra number as they judge can be safely spared. And the officers and men so cloathed, armed and equipped, shall march to the place appointed, and within the time agreed on by the united states in congress assembled.

The united states in congress assembled shall never engage in a war, nor grant letters of marque and reprisal in time of peace, nor enter into any treaties or alliances, nor coin money, nor regulate the value thereof, nor ascertain the sums and expences necessary for the defence and welfare of the united states, or any of them, nor emit bills, nor borrow money on the credit of the united states, nor appropriate money, nor agree upon the number of vessels of war, to be built or purchased, or the number of land or sea forces to be raised, nor appoint a commander in chief of the army or navy, unless nine states assent to the same: nor shall a question on any

other point, except for adjourning from day to day be determined, unless by the votes of a majority of the united states in congress assembled.

The congress of the united states shall have power to adjourn to any time within the year, and to any place within the united states, so that no period of adjournment be for a longer duration than the space of six Months, and shall publish the Journal of their proceedings monthly, except such parts thereof relating to treaties, alliances or military operations as in their judgment require secresy; and the yeas and nays of the delegates of each state on any question shall be entered on the Journal, when it is desired by any delegate; and the delegates of a state, or any of them, at his or their request shall be furnished with a transcript of the said Journal, except such parts as are above excepted, to lay before the legislatures of the several states.

**Article X.** The committee of the states, or any nine of them, shall be authorised to execute, in the recess of congress, such of the powers of congress as the united states in congress assembled, by the consent of nine states, shall from time to time think expedient to vest them with; provided that no power be delegated to the said committee, for the exercise of which, by the articles of confederation, the voice of nine states in the congress of the united states assembled is requisite.

**Article XI.** Canada acceding to this confederation, and joining in the measures of the united states, shall be admitted into, and entitled to all the advantages of this union: but no other colony shall be admitted into the same, unless such admission be agreed to by nine states.

**Article XII.** All bills of credit emitted, monies borrowed and debts contracted by, or under the authority of congress, before the assembling of the united states, in pursuance of the present confederation, shall be deemed and considered as a charge against the united states, for payment and satisfaction whereof the said united states, and the public faith are hereby solemnly pledged.

Article XIII. Every state shall abide by the determinations of the united states in congress assembled, on all questions which by this confederation are submitted to them. And the Articles of this confederation shall be inviolably observed by every state, and the union shall be perpetual; nor shall any alteration at any time hereafter be made in any of them; unless such alteration be agreed to in a congress of the united states, and be afterwards confirmed by the legislatures of every state.

And Whereas it has pleased the Great Governor of the World to incline the hearts of the legislatures we respectively represent in congress, to approve of, and to authorize us to ratify the said articles of confederation and perpetual union. Know Ye that we the undersigned delegates, by virtue of the power and authority to us given for that purpose, do by these presents, in the name and in behalf of our respective constituents, fully and entirely ratify and confirm each and every of the said articles of confederation and perpetual union, and all and singular the matters and things therein contained: And we do further solemnly plight and engage the faith of our respective constituents, that they shall abide by the determinations of the united states in congress assembled, on all questions, which by the said confederation are submitted to them. And that the articles thereof shall be inviolably observed by the states we respectively represent, and that the union shall be perpetual. In Witness whereof we have hereunto set our hands in Congress. Done at Philadelphia in the state of Pennsylvania the ninth Day of July in the Year of our Lord one Thousand seven Hundred and Seventy-eight, and in the third year of the independence of America.

| | |
|---|---|
| **New Hampshire:** | Josiah Bartlett, John Wentworth Jr. |
| **Massachusetts:** | John Hancock, Samuel Adams, Elbridge Gerry, Francis Dana, James Lovell, Samuel Holten. |
| **Rhode Island:** | William Ellery, Henry Marchant, John Collins. |
| **Connecticut:** | Roger Sherman, Samuel Huntington, Oliver Wolcott, Titus Hosmer, Andrew Adams. |
| **New York:** | James Duane, Francis Lewis, William Duer, Gouverneur Morris. |
| **New Jersey:** | John Witherspoon, Nathaniel Scudder. |
| **Pennsylvania:** | Robert Morris, Daniel Roberdeau, Jonathan Bayard Smith, William Clingan, Joseph Reed. |
| **Delaware:** | Thomas McKean, John Dickinson, Nicholas Van Dyke. |
| **Maryland:** | John Hanson, Daniel Carroll. |
| **Virginia:** | Richard Henry Lee, John Banister, Thomas Adams, John Harvie, Francis Lightfoot Lee. |
| **North Carolina:** | John Penn, Cornelius Harnett, John Williams. |
| **South Carolina:** | Henry Laurens, William Henry Drayton, John Mathews, Richard Hutson, Thomas Heyward Jr. |
| **Georgia:** | John Walton, Edward Telfair, Edward Langworthy. |

# Three Plans of Government (1787)

*Frustrated by the inadequacies of the national government, Congress voted on February 21, 1787, to call "a Convention of delegates who shall have been appointed by the several states to be held in Philadelphia for the sole and express purpose of [making recommendations for] revising the Articles of Confederation." Every state but Rhode Island sent delegates to the Constitutional Convention, which convened in late May.*

*During the convention, one or more delegates proposed plans of government. Three of the most important and interesting plans were the Virginia Plan of Union, the New Jersey Plan, and the Hamilton Plan.* ~

## The Virginia Plan of Union

*Convinced that the United States needed a strong national government, James Madison of Virginia worked hard to persuade Congress to call the Constitutional Convention. He also arrived in Philadelphia several days before the convention was scheduled to begin and drafted a proposed plan of government to lay before the delegates. Madison, who was only thirty-six years old and lacked a strong national reputation, persuaded the governor of his state, Edmund Randolph, to introduce*

*the plan on May 29, the convention's first day of substantive business.*

*The Virginia Plan of Union proposed a radical departure from the Articles of Confederation—a three-branch national government whose powers would make it superior to the states. The legislature would have two houses, not one, and would be apportioned according to population, not state equality. In addition, the new government would have an executive and a judicial branch. The executive would be chosen by the legislature but otherwise was largely undefined in the plan.*

*Despite its plain intention to replace, not merely revise, the Articles, the Virginia Plan was endorsed in principle by the delegates at the start of the convention. It provided a working agenda for their deliberations.* ~

1. Resolved that the Articles of Confederation ought to be so corrected and enlarged as to accomplish the objects proposed by their institution; namely "common defence, security of liberty and general welfare."

2. Resolved therefore that the rights of suffrage in the National Legislature ought to be proportioned to the Quotas of contribution, or to the number of free inhabitants, as the one or the other rule may seem best in different cases.

3. Resolved that the National Legis-

lature ought to consist of two branches.

4. Resolved that the members of the first branch of the National Legislature ought to be elected by the people of the several States every        for the terms of    ; to be of the age of      years at least, to receive liberal stipends by which they may be compensated for the devotion of their time to public service, to be ineligible to any office established by a particular State, or under the authority of the United States, except those peculiarly belonging to the functions of the first branch, during the term of service, and for the space of       after its expiration; to be incapable of reelection for the space of       after the expiration of their term of service, and to be subject to recall.

5. Resolved that the members of the second branch of the National Legislature ought to be elected by those of the first, out of a proper number of persons nominated by the individual Legislatures, to be of the age of      years at least; to hold their offices for a term sufficient to ensure their independency; to receive liberal stipends, by which they may be compensated for the devotion of their time to public service; and to be ineligible to any office established by a particular State, or under the authority of the United States, except those peculiarly belonging to the functions of the second branch, during the term of service, and for the space of       after the expiration thereof.

6. Resolved that each branch ought to possess the right of originating Acts; that the National Legislature ought to be impowered to enjoy the Legislative Rights vested in Congress by the Confederation and moreover to legislate in all cases to which the separate States are incompetent, or in which the harmony of the United States may be interrupted by the exercise of individual Legislation; to negative all laws passed by the several States, contravening in the opinion of the National Legislature the articles of Union; and to call forth the force of the Union against any member of the Union failing in its duty under the articles thereof.

7. Resolved that a National Executive be instituted; to be chosen by the National Legislature for the term of       years; to receive punctually, at stated times, a fixed compensation for the services rendered, in which no increase or diminution shall be made so as to affect the Magistracy, existing at the time of the increase or diminution, and to be ineligible a second time; and that besides a general authority to execute the National laws, it ought to enjoy the Executive rights vested in Congress by the Confederation.

8. Resolved that the Executive and a convenient number of the National Judiciary, ought to compose a Council or revision with authority to examine every act of the National Legislature before it shall operate, and every act of a particular Legislature before a Negative thereon shall be final; and that the dissent of the said Council shall amount to a rejection, unless the Act of the National Legislature be passed again, or that of a particular Legislature be again negatived by       of the members of each branch.

9. Resolved that a National Judiciary be established to consist of one or more supreme tribunals, and of inferior tribunals to be chosen by the National Legislature, to hold their offices during good behavior; and to receive punctually at stated times fixed compensation for their services, in which no increase or diminution shall be made so as to affect the persons actually in office at the time of such increase or diminution. That the jurisdiction of the inferior tribunals shall be to hear and determine in the first instance, and of the supreme tribunal to hear and determine in the dernier resort, all piracies and felonies on the high seas, captures from an enemy; cases in which foreigners or citizens of other States applying to such jurisdictions may be interested, or which respect the collection of the National rev-

enue; impeachments of any National officers, and questions which may involve the national peace and harmony.

10. Resolved that provision ought to be made for the admission of States lawfully arising within the limits of the United States, whether from a voluntary junction of Government and Territory or otherwise, with the consent of a number of voices in the National legislature less than the whole.

11. Resolved that a Republican Government and the territory of each State, except in the instance of a voluntary junction of Government and territory, ought to be guaranteed by the United States to each State.

12. Resolved that provision ought to be made for the continuance of Congress and their authorities and privileges, until a given day after the reform of the articles of Union shall be adopted, and for the completion of all their engagements.

13. Resolved that provision ought to be made for the amendment of the Articles of Union whensoever it shall seem necessary, and that the assent of the National Legislature ought not to be required thereto.

14. Resolved that the Legislative, Executive and Judiciary powers within the several States ought to be bound by oath to support the articles of Union.

15. Resolved that the amendments which shall be offered to the Confederation, by the Convention ought at a proper time, or times, after the approbation of Congress to be submitted to an assembly or assemblies of Representatives, recommended by the several Legislatures to be expressly chosen by the people, to consider and decide thereon.

## The New Jersey Plan

*Not everyone at the convention was satisfied with the Virginia Plan. One plank of the plan was especially controversial—the provision that both houses of the national legislature would be apportioned according to population. This proposal alienated delegates from the smaller states, who feared that they would be outnumbered in Congress and preferred that the "one state, one vote" rule of the Articles of Confederation be continued. The small states responded to the Virginia Plan with a sweeping counterproposal of their own. It was introduced to the convention on June 15 by William Paterson of New Jersey.*

*The New Jersey Plan was a series of amendments to the Articles rather than a new constitution. It proposed two new branches in the national government— a plural (committee-style) executive, to be elected by Congress, and a Supreme Court, to be appointed by the executive. It also empowered Congress to regulate commerce and impose taxes. The plan became the main alternative to the Virginia Plan but was rejected on June 19.* ~

1. Resolved that the Articles of Confederation ought to be so revised, corrected, and enlarged as to render the federal Constitution adequate to the exigencies of Government, and the preservation of the Union.

2. Resolved that in addition to the powers vested in the United States in Congress, by the present existing articles of Confederation, they be authorized to pass acts for raising a revenue, by levying a duty or duties on all goods or merchandizes of foreign growth or manufacture, imported into any part of the United States, by Stamps on paper, vellum or parchment, and by a postage on all letters or packages passing through the general post-office, to be applied to such federal purposes as they shall deem proper and expedient; to make rules and regulations for the collection thereof; and the same from time

to time, to alter and amend in such manner as they shall think proper: to pass Acts for the regulation of trade and commerce as well with foreign nations as with each other; provided that all punishments, fines, forfeitures and penalties to be incurred for contravening such acts rules and regulations shall be adjudged by the Common law Judiciaries of the State in which any offence contrary to the true intent and meaning of such Acts rules and regulations shall have been committed or perpetrated, with liberty of commencing in the first instance all suits and prosecutions for that purpose, in the superior common law Judiciary in such state, subject nevertheless for the correction of errors, both in law and fact in rendering Judgement, to an appeal to the Judiciary of the United States.

3. Resolved that whenever requisitions shall be necessary, instead of the rule for making requisitions mentioned in the articles of Confederation, the United States in Congress be authorized to make such requisitions in proportion to the whole number of white and other free citizens and inhabitants of every age sex and condition including those bound to servitude for a term of years and three fifths of all other persons not comprehended in the foregoing description, except Indians not paying taxes; that if such requisitions be not complied with, in the time specified therein, to direct the collection thereof in the non-complying States and for that purpose to devise and pass acts directing and authorizing the same; provided that none of the powers hereby vested in the United States in Congress shall be exercised without the consent of at least States, and in that proportion if the number of Confederated States should hereafter be increased or diminished.

4. Resolved that the United States in Congress be authorized to elect a federal Executive to consist of persons, to continue in office for the term of

years, to receive punctually at stated times a fixed compensation for their services, in which no increase or diminution shall be made so as to affect the persons composing the Executive at the time of such increase or diminution, to be paid out of the federal treasury; to be incapable of holding any other office or appointment during their time of service and for        years thereafter; to be ineligible a second time, and removeable by Congress on application by a majority of the Executives of the several States; that the Executives besides their general authority to execute the federal acts ought to appoint all federal officers not otherwise provided for, and to direct all military operations; provided that none of the persons composing the federal Executive shall on any occasion take command of any troops so as personally to conduct any enterprise as General or in other capacity.

5. Resolved that a federal Judiciary be established to consist of a supreme tribunal the Judges of which to be appointed by the Executive, and to hold their offices during good behaviour, to receive punctually at stated times a fixed compensation for their services in which no increase or diminution shall be made so as to affect persons actually in office at the time of such increase or diminution; that the Judiciary so established shall have authority to hear and determine in the first instance on all impeachments of federal officers, and by way of appeal in the dernier resort in all cases touching the rights of Ambassadors, in all cases of captures from an enemy, in all cases of piracies and felonies on the high Seas, in all cases in which foreigners may be interested, in the construction of any treaty or treaties, or which may arise on any of the Acts for regulation of trade, or the collection of the federal Revenue: that none of the Judiciary shall during the time they remain in office be capable of receiving or holding any other office or

appointment during the time of services or for thereafter.

6. Resolved that all acts of the United States in Congress made by virtue and in pursuance of the powers hereby and by the articles of Confederation vested in them, and all Treaties made and ratified under the authority of the United States, shall be the supreme law of the respective States so far forth as those Acts or Treaties shall relate to the said States or their Citizens, and that the Judiciary of the several states shall be bound thereby in their decisions, any thing in the respective laws of the Individual States to the contrary notwithstanding; and that if any State, or any body of men in any State shall oppose or prevent carrying into execution such acts or treaties, the federal Executive shall be authorized to call forth the power of the Confederated States, or so much thereof as may be necessary to enforce and compel an obedience to such Acts or an observance of such Treaties.

7. Resolved that provision be made for the admission of new States into the Union.

8. Resolved the rule for naturalization ought to be the same in every State.

9. Resolved that a Citizen of one State committing an offence in another State of the Union, shall be deemed guilty of the same offence as if it had been committed by a Citizen of the State in which the offence was committed.

## The Hamilton Plan

*Alexander Hamilton of New York worked shrewdly with James Madison to persuade Congress to call the 1787 convention. After the convention was over, he and Madison again joined forces to campaign brilliantly for ratification of the proposed Constitution.*

*During the convention itself, however, the main contribution from the thirty-two-year-old Hamilton was an intriguing but extreme proposal for an executive-dominated national government.*

*Hamilton delivered his proposal in a four- to six-hour speech to the convention on June 18. Under the Hamilton Plan, the national government would be all-powerful: state governors would be appointed by the national government and empowered to veto any laws passed by the state legislatures. The national executive (called "Governor") would be chosen by electors for a lifetime term and granted vast powers, including both an absolute veto on laws passed by the national legislature and the exclusive right to appoint the other members of the executive branch. Much admired for its brilliance by some of his fellow delegates, Hamilton's plan was politically unacceptable. Having won its independence from Great Britain, the United States was hardly about to adopt a British-style government.* ～

1. The Supreme Legislative power of the United States of America to be vested in two distinct bodies of men; the one to be called the Assembly, the other the Senate who together shall form the Legislature of the United States with power to pass all laws whatsoever subject to the Negative hereafter mentioned.

2. The Assembly to consist of persons elected by the people to serve for three years.

3. The Senate to consist of persons elected to serve during good behaviour; their election to be made by electors chosen for that purpose by the people. In order to this, the States to be divided into election districts. On the death, removal or resignation of any Senator his place to be filled out of the district from which he came.

4. The supreme Executive authority

of the United States to be vested in a Governor, to be elected to serve during good behaviour—His election to be made by Electors chosen by electors chosen by the people in the Election Districts aforesaid; or by electors chosen for that purpose by the respective Legislatures—provided that if an election be not made within a limited time, the President of the Senate shall be the Governor. The Governor to have a negative upon all laws about to be passed—and the execution of all laws passed—to be the Commander-in-Chief of the land and naval forces and of the militia of the United States—to have the entire direction of war when authorized or begun—to have, with the advice and approbation of the Senate, the power of making all treaties—to have the appointment of the heads or chief officers of the departments of finance, war, and foreign affairs—to have the nomination of all other officers (ambassadors to foreign nations included) subject to the approbation or rejection of the Senate—to have the power of pardoning all offences but treason, which he shall not pardon without the approbation of the Senate.

5. On the death, resignation, or removal of the Governor, his authorities to be exercised by the President of the Senate (until a successor be appointed).

6. The Senate to have the sole power of declaring war—the power of advising and approving all treaties—the power of approving or rejecting all appointments of officers except the heads or chiefs of the departments of finance, war, and foreign affairs.

7. The supreme judicial authority of the United States to be vested in twelve judges, to hold their offices during good behaviour, with adequate and permanent salaries. This court to have original jurisdiction in all causes of capture, and an appellate jurisdiction (from the courts of the several States) in all causes in which the revenues of the General Government or the citizens of foreign nations are concerned.

8. The Legislature of the United States to have power to institute courts in each State for the determination of all causes of capture and of all matters relating to their revenues, or in which the citizens of foreign nations are concerned.

9. The Governor, Senators, and all officers of the United States to be liable to impeachment for mal and corrupt conduct, and upon conviction to be removed from office, and disqualified for holding any place of trust or profit. All impeachments to be tried by a court, to consist of the judges of the Supreme Court, chief or senior judge of the Superior Court of law of each State—provided that such judge hold his place during good behaviour and have a permanent salary.

10. All laws of the particular States contrary to the Constitution or laws of the United States to be utterly void. And the better to prevent such laws being passed the Governor or President of each State shall be appointed by the General Government, and shall have a negative upon the laws about to be passed in the State of which he is Governor or President.

11. No State to have any forces, land or naval—and the militia of all the States to be under the sole and exclusive direction of the United States, the officers of which to be appointed and commissioned by them.

# United States Constitution (1789)

The Constitutional Convention completed its labors on September 17, 1787. Nine states (the number the Constitution itself stipulated as sufficient) ratified the document by June 21, 1788. The outgoing Congress declared that the new plan of government would go into effect on March 4, 1789, replacing the Articles of Confederation. (See "Articles of Confederation," p. 5.)

The presidency is the most original feature of the Constitution. Described mainly in Article II, it was created as a strong, unitary office, in contrast to the weak office of governor that most of the state constitutions provided and to the nonexistent executive of the Articles of Confederation. The president was to be elected by an electoral college to a four-year term and was empowered, among other things, to recommend and veto congressional acts, to appoint judges and executive officials, to command the army and navy, to negotiate treaties, and to issue pardons. Congress could impeach and remove a president for committing acts of treason, bribery, or "other high Crimes and Misdemeanors." Other provisions of Article II included qualifications for president, a presidential oath, and a restriction on the ability of Congress to change the salary of an incumbent president.

The Constitution also created the vice presidency and charged the vice president (the second-place finisher in the presidential election) to be president of the Senate and standby successor to the president.

Although James Madison often is referred to as "the father of the Constitution," his paternity did not extend to the presidency. Madison's views about the national executive were vague and variable. Like most of the delegates, he feared both executive power and executive weakness, looking upon the former as the seed of tyranny and the latter as the wellspring of anarchy. Other delegates—notably James Wilson and Gouverneur Morris, both of Pennsylvania—took the lead in persuading the convention to create a strong presidency. The near-certain knowledge that George Washington (who presided over the convention) would be the first president was a source of reassurance to many at the convention.

Numerous constitutional amendments have dealt with the presidency and vice presidency. The Twelfth Amendment (1804) adapted the electoral college to the rise of political parties by separating the balloting for president and vice president. The Twentieth Amendment (1933) advanced the start of the president's term from March 4 to January 20. The Twenty-second Amendment (1951) imposed a two-term limit on the president.

*(The framers had felt strongly that there should be no limit on the president's ability to seek reelection.) The Twenty-fifth Amendment (1967) empowered the president, with confirmation by Congress, to appoint a vice president when the vice presidency became vacant. It also created procedures to govern situations of presidential disability. Other constitutional amendments have affected the circumstances under which presidents are elected, such as the Fifteenth (1870), Nineteenth (1920), and Twenty-sixth (1971) amendments, which extended the right to vote to blacks, women, and eighteen-year-olds, respectively.* ~

We the People of the United States, in Order to form a more perfect Union, establish Justice, insure domestic Tranquility, provide for the common defence, promote the general Welfare, and secure the Blessings of Liberty to ourselves and our Posterity, do ordain and establish this Constitution for the United States of America.

## Article I

**Section 1.** All legislative Powers herein granted shall be vested in a Congress of the United States, which shall consist of a Senate and House of Representatives.

**Section 2.** The House of Representatives shall be composed of Members chosen every second Year by the People of the several States, and the Electors in each State shall have the Qualifications requisite for Electors of the most numerous Branch of the State Legislature.

No Person shall be a Representative who shall not have attained to the age of twenty five Years, and been seven Years a Citizen of the United States, and who shall not, when elected, be an Inhabitant of that State in which he shall be chosen.

[Representatives and direct Taxes shall be apportioned among the several States which may be included within this Union, according to their respective Numbers, which shall be determined by adding to the whole Number of free Persons, including those bound to Service for a Term of Years, and excluding Indians not taxed, three fifths of all other Persons.][1] The actual Enumeration shall be made within three Years after the first Meeting of the Congress of the United States, and within every subsequent Term of ten Years, in such Manner as they shall by Law direct. The Number of Representatives shall not exceed one for every thirty Thousand, but each State shall have at Least one Representative; and until such enumeration shall be made, the State of New Hampshire shall be entitled to chuse three, Massachusetts eight, Rhode-Island and Providence Plantations one, Connecticut five, New-York six, New Jersey four, Pennsylvania eight, Delaware one, Maryland six, Virginia ten, North Carolina five, South Carolina five, and Georgia three.

When vacancies happen in the Representation from any State, the Executive Authority thereof shall issue Writs of Election to fill such Vacancies.

The House of Representatives shall chuse their Speaker and other Officers; and shall have the sole Power of Impeachment.

**Section 3.** The Senate of the United States shall be composed of two Senators from each State, [chosen by the Legislature thereof,][2] for six Years; and each Senator shall have one Vote.

Immediately after they shall be assembled in Consequence of the first Election, they shall be divided as equally as may be into three Classes. The Seats of the Senators of the first Class shall be vacated at the Expiration of the second Year, of the second Class at the Expiration of the fourth Year, and of the third Class at the Expiration of the sixth Year, so that one third may be chosen every second Year; [and if Vacancies happen by Resignation, or otherwise, during the Recess of the Legislature of any State, the Executive thereof may make temporary Appointments until the next Meeting of the Legislature, which shall then fill such Vacancies.][3]

No Person shall be a Senator who shall not have attained to the Age of thirty Years, and been nine Years a Citizen of the United States, and who shall not, when elected, be an Inhabitant of that State for which he shall be chosen.

The Vice President of the United States shall be President of the Senate, but shall have no Vote, unless they be equally divided.

The Senate shall chuse their other Officers, and also a President pro tempore, in the Absence of the Vice President, or when he shall exercise the Office of President of the United States.

The Senate shall have the sole Power to try all Impeachments. When sitting for that Purpose, they shall be on Oath or Affirmation. When the President of the United States is tried the Chief Justice shall preside: And no Person shall be convicted without the Concurrence of two thirds of the Members present.

Judgment in Cases of Impeachment shall not extend further than to removal from Office, and disqualification to hold and enjoy any Office of honor, Trust or Profit under the United States: but the Party convicted shall nevertheless be liable and subject to Indictment, Trial, Judgment and Punishment, according to Law.

**Section 4.** The Times, Places and Manner of holding Elections for Senators and Representatives, shall be prescribed in each State by the Legislature thereof; but the Congress may at any time by Law make or alter such Regulations, except as to the Places of chusing Senators.

The Congress shall assemble at least once in every Year, and such Meeting shall [be on the first Monday in December],[4] unless they shall by Law appoint a different Day.

**Section 5.** Each House shall be the Judge of the Elections, Returns and Qualifications of its own Members, and a Majority of each shall constitute a Quorum to do Business; but a smaller Number may adjourn from day to day, and may be authorized to compel the Attendance of absent Members, in such Manner, and under such Penalties as each House may provide.

Each House may determine the Rules of its Proceedings, punish its Members for disorderly Behaviour, and, with the Concurrence of two thirds, expel a Member.

Each House shall keep a Journal of its Proceedings, and from time to time publish the same, excepting such Parts as may in their Judgment require Secrecy; and the Yeas and Nays of the Members of either House on any question shall, at the Desire of one fifth of those Present, be entered on the Journal.

Neither House, during the Session of Congress, shall, without the Consent of the other, adjourn for more than three days, nor to any other Place than that in which the two Houses shall be sitting.

**Section 6.** The Senators and Representatives shall receive a Compensation for their Services, to be ascertained by Law, and paid out of the Treasury of the United States. They shall in all Cases, except Treason, Felony and Breach of the Peace, be privileged from Arrest during their Attendance at the Session of their respective Houses, and in going to and returning from the same; and for any Speech or Debate in either House, they shall not be questioned in any other Place.

No Senator or Representative shall, during the Time for which he was elected, be appointed to any civil Office under the Authority of the United

States, which shall have been created, or the Emoluments whereof shall have been encreased during such time; and no Person holding any Office under the United States, shall be a Member of either House during his Continuance in Office.

**Section 7.** All Bills for raising Revenue shall originate in the House of Representatives; but the Senate may propose or concur with amendments as on other Bills.

Every Bill which shall have passed the House of Representatives and the Senate, shall, before it become a Law, be presented to the President of the United States; If he approve he shall sign it, but if not he shall return it, with his Objections to that House in which it shall have originated, who shall enter the Objections at large on their Journal, and proceed to reconsider it. If after such Reconsideration two thirds of that House shall agree to pass the Bill, it shall be sent, together with the Objections, to the other House, by which it shall likewise be reconsidered, and if approved by two thirds of that House, it shall become a Law. But in all such Cases the Votes of both Houses shall be determined by yeas and Nays, and the Names of the Persons voting for and against the Bill shall be entered on the Journal of each House respectively. If any Bill shall not be returned by the President within ten Days (Sundays excepted) after it shall have been presented to him, the Same shall be a Law, in like Manner as if he had signed it, unless the Congress by their Adjournment prevent its Return, in which Case it shall not be a Law.

Every Order, Resolution, or Vote to which the Concurrence of the Senate and House of Representatives may be necessary (except on a question of Adjournment) shall be presented to the President of the United States; and before the Same shall take Effect, shall be approved by him, or being disapproved by him, shall be repassed by two thirds of the Senate and House of Representatives, according to the Rules and Limitations prescribed in the Case of a Bill.

**Section 8.** The Congress shall have Power To lay and collect Taxes, Duties, Imposts and Excises, to pay the Debts and provide for the common Defence and general Welfare of the United States; but all Duties, Imposts and Excises shall be uniform throughout the United States;

To borrow Money on the credit of the United States;

To regulate Commerce with foreign Nations, and among the several States, and with the Indian Tribes;

To establish an uniform Rule of Naturalization, and uniform Laws on the subject of Bankruptcies throughout the United States;

To coin Money, regulate the Value thereof, and of foreign Coin, and fix the Standard of Weights and Measures;

To provide for the Punishment of counterfeiting the Securities and current Coin of the United States;

To establish Post Offices and post Roads;

To promote the Progress of Science and useful Arts, by securing for limited Times to Authors and Inventors the exclusive Right to their respective Writings and Discoveries;

To constitute Tribunals inferior to the supreme Court;

To define and punish Piracies and Felonies commited on the high Seas, and Offences against the Law of Nations;

To declare War, grant Letters of Marque and Reprisal, and make Rules concerning Captures on Land and Water;

To raise and support Armies, but no Appropriation of Money to that Use shall be for a longer Term than two Years;

To provide and maintain a Navy;

To make Rules for the Government and Regulation of the land and naval Forces;

To provide for calling forth the Militia to execute the Laws of the Union, suppress Insurrections and repel Invasions;

To provide for organizing, arming, and disciplining, the Militia, and for governing such Part of them as may be employed in the Service of the United States, reserving to the States respectively, the Appointment of the Officers, and the Authority of training the Militia according to the discipline prescribed by Congress;

To exercise exclusive Legislation in all Cases whatsoever, over such District (not exceeding ten Miles square) as may, by Cession of Particular States, and the Acceptance of Congress, become the Seat of the Government of the United States, and to exercise like Authority over all Places purchased by the Consent of the Legislature of the State in which the Same shall be, for the Erection of Forts, Magazines, Arsenals, dock-Yards, and other needful Buildings; — And

To make all Laws which shall be necessary and proper for carrying into Execution the foregoing Powers, and all other Powers vested by this Constitution in the Government of the United States, or in any Department or Officer thereof.

**Section 9.** The Migration or Importation of such Persons as any of the States now existing shall think proper to admit, shall not be prohibited by the Congress prior to the Year one thousand eight hundred and eight, but a Tax or duty may be imposed on such Importation, not exceeding ten dollars for each Person.

The Privilege of the Writ of Habeas Corpus shall not be suspended, unless when in Cases of Rebellion or Invasion the public Safety may require it.

No Bill of Attainder or ex post facto Law shall be passed.

No capitation, or other direct, Tax shall be laid, unless in Proportion to the Census of Enumeration herein before directed to be taken.[5]

No Tax or Duty shall be laid on Articles exported from any State.

No Preference shall be given by any Regulation of Commerce or Revenue to the Ports of one State over those of another; nor shall Vessels bound to, or from, one State, be obliged to enter, clear or pay Duties in another.

No Money shall be drawn from the Treasury, but in Consequence of Appropriations made by Law; and a regular Statement and Account of the Receipts and Expenditures of all public Money shall be published from time to time.

No Title of Nobility shall be granted by the United States: And no Person holding any Office of Profit or Trust under them, shall, without the Consent of the Congress, accept of any present, Emolument, Office, or Title, of any kind whatever, from any King, Prince or foreign State.

**Section 10.** No State shall enter into any Treaty, Alliance, or Confederation; grant Letters of Marque and Reprisal; coin Money; emit Bills of Credit; make any Thing but gold and silver Coin a Tender in Payment of Debts; pass any Bill of Attainder, ex post facto Law, or Law impairing the Obligation of Contracts, or grant any Title of Nobility.

No State shall, without the Consent of the Congress, lay any Imposts or Duties on Imports or Exports, except what may be absolutely necessary for executing it's inspection Laws: and the net Produce of all Duties and Imposts, laid by any State on Imports or Exports, shall be for the Use of the Treasury of the United States; and all such Laws shall be subject to the Revision and Controul of the Congress.

No State shall, without the Consent of Congress, lay any Duty of Tonnage, keep Troops, or Ships of War in time of Peace, enter into any Agreement or Compact with another State, or with a foreign Power, or engage in War, unless actually invaded, or in such imminent Danger as will not admit of delay.

## Article II

**Section 1.** The executive Power shall be vested in a President of the United States of America. He shall hold his Office during the Term of four Years, and, together with the Vice President, chosen for the same Term, be elected, as follows.

Each State shall appoint, in such Manner as the Legislature thereof may direct, a Number of Electors, equal to the whole Number of Senators and Representatives to which the State may be entitled in the Congress: but no Senator or Representative, or Person holding an Office of Trust or Profit under the United States, shall be appointed an Elector.

[The Electors shall meet in their respective States, and vote by Ballot for two Persons, of whom one at least shall not be an Inhabitant of the same State with themselves. And they shall make a List of all the Persons voted for, and of the Number of Votes for each; which List they shall sign and certify, and transmit sealed to the Seat of the Government of the United States, directed to the President of the Senate. The President of the Senate shall, in the Presence of the Senate and House of Representatives, open all the Certificates, and the Votes shall then be counted. The Person having the greatest Number of Votes shall be the President, if such Number be a Majority of the whole Number of Electors appointed; and if there be more than one who have such Majority, and have an equal Number of Votes, then the House of Representatives shall immediately chuse by Ballot one of them for President; and if no Person have a Majority, then from the five highest on the list the said House shall in like Manner chuse the President. But in chusing the President, the Votes shall be taken by States, the Representation from each State having one Vote; a quorum for this Purpose shall consist of a Member or Members from two thirds of the States, and a Majority of all the States shall be necessary to a Choice. In every Case, after the Choice of the President, the Person having the greatest Number of Votes of the Electors shall be the Vice President. But if there should remain two or more who have equal Votes, the Senate shall chuse from them by Ballot the Vice President.][6]

The Congress may determine the Time of chusing the Electors, and the Day on which they shall give their Votes; which Day shall be the same throughout the United States.

No Person except a natural born Citizen, or a Citizen of the United States, at the time of the Adoption of this Constitution, shall be eligible to the Office of President; neither shall any Person be eligible to that Office who shall not have attained to the Age of thirty five Years, and been fourteen Years a Resident within the United States.

In Case of the Removal of the President from Office, or of his Death, Resignation, or Inability to discharge the Powers and Duties of the said Office,[7] the Same shall devolve on the Vice President, and the Congress may by Law provide for the Case of Removal, Death, Resignation or Inability, both of the President and Vice President, declaring what Officer shall then act as President, and such Officer shall act accordingly, until the Disability be removed, or a President shall be elected.

The President shall, at stated Times, receive for his Services, a Compensation, which shall neither be encreased nor diminished during the Period for which he shall have been elected, and he shall not receive within that Period any other Emolument from the United States, or any of them.

Before he enter on the Execution of his Office, he shall take the following Oath or Affirmation: —"I do solemnly swear (or affirm) that I will faithfully execute the Office of President of the United States, and will to the best of my Ability, preserve, protect and defend the Constitution of the United States."

**Section 2.** The President shall be Commander in Chief of the Army and Navy of the United States, and of the Militia of the several States, when called into the actual Service of the United States; he may require the Opinion, in writing, of the principal Officer in each of the executive Departments, upon any Subject relating to the Duties of their respective Offices, and he shall have Power to grant Reprieves and Pardons for Offenses against the United States, except in Cases of Impeachment.

He shall have Power, by and with the Advice and Consent of the Senate, to make Treaties, provided two thirds of the Senators present concur; and he shall nominate, and by and with the Advice and Consent of the Senate, shall appoint Ambassadors, other public Ministers and Consuls, Judges of the supreme Court, and all other Officers of the United States, whose Appointments are not herein otherwise provided for, and which shall be established by Law: but the Congress may by Law vest the Appointment of such inferior Officers, as they think proper, in the President alone, in the Courts of Law, or in the Heads of Departments.

The President shall have Power to fill up all Vacancies that may happen during the Recess of the Senate, by granting Commissions which shall expire at the End of their next Session.

**Section 3.** He shall from time to time give to the Congress Information of the State of the Union, and recommend to their Consideration such Measures as he shall judge necessary and expedient; he may, on extraordinary Occasions, convene both Houses, or either of them, and in Case of Disagreement between them, with Respect to the Time of Adjournment, he may adjourn them to such Time as he shall think proper; he shall receive Ambassadors and other

public Ministers; he shall take Care that the Laws be faithfully executed, and shall Commission all the Officers of the United States.

**Section 4.** The President, Vice President and all Civil Officers of the United States, shall be removed from office on Impeachment for, and Conviction of, Treason, Bribery, or other high Crimes and Misdemeanors.

# Article III

**Section 1.** The judicial Power of the United States, shall be vested in one supreme Court, and in such inferior Courts as the Congress may from time to time ordain and establish. The Judges, both of the supreme and inferior Courts, shall hold their Offices during good Behaviour, and shall, at stated Times, receive for their Services, a Compensation, which shall not be diminished during their Continuance in Office.

**Section 2.** The judicial Power shall extend to all Cases, in Law and Equity, arising under this Constitution, the Laws of the United States, and Treaties made, or which shall be made, under their Authority; —to all Cases affecting Ambassadors, other public Ministers and Consuls; —to all Cases of admiralty and maritime Jurisdiction; —to Controversies to which the United States shall be a Party; —to Controversies between two or more States; —between a State and Citizens of another State;[8] —between Citizens of different States; —between Citizens of the same State claiming Lands under Grants of different States, and between a State, or the Citizens thereof, and foreign States, Citizens or Subjects.[9]

In all Cases affecting Ambassadors, other public Ministers and Consuls, and those in which a State shall be Party, the supreme Court shall have original Jurisdiction. In all the other Cases before mentioned, the supreme Court shall have appellate Jurisdiction, both as to Law and Fact, with such Exceptions, and under such Regulations as the Congress shall make.

The Trial of all Crimes, except in cases of Impeachment, shall be by Jury; and such Trial shall be held in the State where the said Crimes shall have been committed; but when not committed within any State, the Trial shall be at such Place or Places as the Congress may by Law have directed.

**Section 3.** Treason against the United States, shall consist only in levying War against them, or in adhering to their Enemies, giving them Aid and Comfort. No Person shall be convicted of Treason unless on the Testimony of two Witnesses to the same overt Act, or on Confession in open Court.

The Congress shall have Power to declare the Punishment of Treason, but no Attainder of Treason shall work Corruption of Blood, or Forfeiture except during the Life of the Person attainted.

## Article IV

**Section 1.** Full Faith and Credit shall be given in each State to the public Acts, Records, and judicial Proceedings of every other State. And the Congress may by general Laws prescribe the Manner in which such Acts, Records and Proceedings shall be proved, and the Effect thereof.

**Section 2.** The Citizens of each State shall be entitled to all Privileges and Immunities of Citizens in the several States.

A Person charged in any State with Treason, Felony, or other Crime, who shall flee from Justice, and be found in another State, shall on Demand of the executive Authority of the State from which he fled, be delivered up, to be removed to the State having Jurisdiction of the Crime.

[No Person held to Service or Labour in one State, under the Laws thereof, escaping into another, shall, in Consequence of any Law or Regulation

therein, be discharged from such Service or Labour, but shall be delivered up on Claim of the Party to whom such Service or Labour may be due.][10]

**Section 3.** New States may be admitted by the Congress into this Union; but no new State shall be formed or erected within the Jurisdiction of any other State; nor any State be formed by the Junction of two or more States, or Parts of States, without the Consent of the Legislatures of the States concerned as well as of the Congress.

The Congress shall have Power to dispose of and make all needful Rules and Regulations respecting the Territory or other Property belonging to the United States; and nothing in this Constitution shall be so construed as to Prejudice any Claims of the United States, or of any particular State.

**Section 4.** The United States shall guarantee to every State in this Union a Republican Form of Government, and shall protect each of them against Invasion; and on Application of the Legislature, or of the Executive (when the Legislature cannot be convened) against domestic Violence.

## Article V

The Congress, whenever two thirds of both Houses shall deem it necessary, shall propose Amendments to this Constitution, or, on the Application of the Legislatures of two thirds of the several States, shall call a Convention for proposing Amendments, which, in either Case, shall be valid to all Intents and Purposes, as Part of this Constitution, when ratified by the Legislatures of three fourths of the several States, or by Conventions in three fourths thereof, as the one or the other Mode of Ratification may be proposed by the Congress; Provided [that no Amendment which may be made prior to the Year One thousand eight hundred and eight shall in any Manner affect the first and fourth Clauses in the Ninth

Section of the first Article; and]¹¹ that no State, without its Consent, shall be deprived of its equal Suffrage in the Senate.

## Article VI

All Debts contracted and Engagements entered into, before the Adoption of this Constitution, shall be as valid against the United States under this Constitution, as under the Confederation.

This Constitution, and the Laws of the United States which shall be made in Pursuance thereof; and all Treaties made, or which shall be made, under the Authority of the United States, shall be the supreme Law of the Land; and the Judges in every State shall be bound thereby, any Thing in the Constitution or Laws of any State to the Contrary notwithstanding.

The Senators and Representatives before mentioned, and the Members of the several State Legislatures, and all executive and judicial Officers, both of the United States and of the several States, shall be bound by Oath or Affirmation, to support this Constitution; but no religious Test shall ever be required as a Qualification to any Office or public Trust under the United States.

## Article VII

The Ratification of the Conventions of nine States, shall be sufficient for the Establishment of this Constitution between the States so ratifying the Same. Done in Convention by the Unanimous Consent of the States present the Seventeenth Day of September in the Year of our Lord one thousand seven hundred and Eighty seven and of the Independence of the United States of America the Twelfth. In witness whereof We have hereunto subscribed our Names, George Washington, President and deputy from Virginia.

| | |
|---|---|
| **New Hampshire:** | John Langdon, Nicholas Gilman. |
| **Massachusetts:** | Nathaniel Gorham, Rufus King. |
| **Connecticut:** | William Samuel Johnson, Roger Sherman. |
| **New York:** | Alexander Hamilton. |
| **New Jersey:** | William Livingston, David Brearley, William Paterson, Jonathan Dayton. |
| **Pennsylvania:** | Benjamin Franklin, Thomas Mifflin, Robert Morris, George Clymer, Thomas FitzSimons, Jared Ingersoll, James Wilson, Gouverneur Morris. |
| **Delaware:** | George Read, Gunning Bedford Jr., John Dickinson, Richard Bassett, Jacob Broom. |
| **Maryland:** | James McHenry, Daniel of St. Thomas Jenifer, Daniel Carroll. |
| **Virginia:** | John Blair, James Madison Jr. |
| **North Carolina:** | William Blount, Richard Dobbs Spaight, Hugh Williamson. |
| **South Carolina:** | John Rutledge, Charles Cotesworth Pinckney, Charles Pinckney, Pierce Butler. |
| **Georgia:** | William Few, Abraham Baldwin. |

[The language of the original Constitution, not including the Amendments, was adopted by a convention of the states on Sept. 17, 1787, and was subsequently ratified by the states on the following dates: Delaware, Dec. 7, 1787; Pennsylvania, Dec. 12, 1787; New Jersey, Dec. 18, 1787; Georgia, Jan. 2, 1788; Connecticut, Jan. 9, 1788; Massachusetts, Feb. 6, 1788; Maryland, April 28, 1788; South Carolina, May 23,

1788; New Hampshire, June 21, 1788.

Ratification was completed on June 21, 1788.

The Constitution subsequently was ratified by Virginia, June 25, 1788; New York, July 26, 1788; North Carolina, Nov. 21, 1789; Rhode Island, May 29, 1790; and Vermont, Jan. 10, 1791.]

# Amendments

## Amendment I
### *(First ten amendments ratified December 15, 1791.)*

Congress shall make no law respecting an establishment of religion, or prohibiting the free exercise thereof; or abridging the freedom of speech, or of the press; or the right of the people peaceably to assemble, and to petition the Government for a redress of grievances.

## Amendment II

A well regulated Militia, being necessary to the security of a free State, the right of the people to keep and bear Arms, shall not be infringed.

## Amendment III

No Soldier shall, in time of peace be quartered in any house, without the consent of the Owner, nor in time of war, but in a manner to be prescribed by law.

## Amendment IV

The right of the people to be secure in their persons, houses, papers, and effects, against unreasonable searches and seizures, shall not be violated, and no Warrants shall issue, but upon probable cause, supported by Oath or affirmation, and particularly describing the place to be searched, and the persons or things to be seized.

## Amendment V

No person shall be held to answer for a capital, or otherwise infamous crime, unless on a presentment or indictment of a Grand Jury, except in cases arising in the land or naval forces, or in the Militia, when in actual service in time of War or public danger; nor shall any person be subject for the same offence to be twice put in jeopardy of life or limb; nor shall be compelled in any criminal case to be a witness against himself, nor be deprived of life, liberty, or property, without due process of law; nor shall private property be taken for public use, without just compensation.

## Amendment VI

In all criminal prosecutions, the accused shall enjoy the right to a speedy and public trial, by an impartial jury of the State and district wherein the crime shall have been committed, which district shall have been previously ascertained by law, and to be informed of the nature and cause of the accusation; to be confronted with the witnesses against him; to have compulsory process for obtaining witnesses in his favor, and to have the Assistance of Counsel for his defence.

## Amendment VII

In Suits at common law, where the value in controversy shall exceed twenty dollars, the right of trial by jury shall be preserved, and no fact tried by a jury, shall be otherwise re-examined in any Court of the United States, than according to the rules of the common law.

## Amendment VIII

Excessive bail shall not be required, nor excessive fines imposed, nor cruel and unusual punishments inflicted.

## Amendment IX

The enumeration in the Constitution, of certain rights, shall not be construed to deny or disparage others retained by the people.

## Amendment X

The powers not delegated to the United States by the Constitution, nor prohibited by it to the States, are reserved to the States respectively, or to the people.

## Amendment XI
### (Ratified February 7, 1795)

The Judicial power of the United States shall not be construed to extend to any suit in law or equity, commenced or prosecuted against one of the United States by Citizens of another State, or by Citizens or Subjects of any Foreign State.

## Amendment XII
### (Ratified June 15, 1804)

The Electors shall meet in their respective states and vote by ballot for President and Vice-President, one of whom, at least, shall not be an inhabitant of the same state with themselves; they shall name in their ballots the person voted for as President, and in distinct ballots the person voted for as Vice-President, and they shall make distinct lists of all persons voted for as President, and of all persons voted for as Vice-President, and of the number of votes for each, which lists they shall sign and certify, and transmit sealed to the seat of the government of the United States, directed to the President of the Senate; —The President of the Senate shall, in the presence of the Senate and House of Representatives, open all the certificates and the votes shall then be counted; —The person having the greatest number of votes for President, shall be the President, if such number be a majority of the whole number of Electors appointed; and if no person have such majority, then from the persons having the highest numbers not exceeding three on the list of those voted for as President, the House of Representatives shall choose immediately, by ballot, the President. But in choosing the President, the votes shall be taken by states, the representation from each state having one vote; a quorum for this purpose shall consist of a

member or members from two-thirds of the states, and a majority of all the states shall be necessary to a choice. [And if the House of Representatives shall not choose a President whenever the right of choice shall devolve upon them, before the fourth day of March next following, then the Vice-President shall act as President, as in the case of the death or other constitutional disability of the President—][12] The person having the greatest number of votes as Vice-President, shall be the Vice-President, if such number be a majority of the whole number of Electors appointed, and if no person have a majority, then from the two highest numbers on the list, the Senate shall choose the Vice-President; a quorum for the purpose shall consist of two-thirds of the whole number of Senators, and a majority of the whole number shall be necessary to a choice. But no person constitutionally ineligible to the office of President shall be eligible to that of Vice-President of the United States.

## Amendment XIII
### (Ratified December 6, 1865)

**Section 1.** Neither slavery nor involuntary servitude, except as a punishment for crime whereof the party shall have been duly convicted, shall exist within the United States, or any place subject to their jurisdiction.

**Section 2.** Congress shall have power to enforce this article by appropriate legislation.

## Amendment XIV
### (Ratified July 9, 1868)

**Section 1.** All persons born or naturalized in the United States and subject to the jurisdiction thereof, are citizens of the United States and of the State wherein they reside. No State shall make or enforce any law which shall abridge the privileges or immunities of citizens of the United States; nor shall any State deprive any person of life, liberty, or property, without due process of law; nor deny to any person within its jurisdiction the equal protection of the laws.

**Section 2.** Representatives shall be apportioned among the several States according to their respective numbers, counting the whole number of persons in each State, excluding Indians not taxed. But when the right to vote at any election for the choice of electors for President and Vice President of the United States, Representatives in Congress, the Executive and Judicial officers of a State, or the members of the Legislature thereof, is denied to any of the male inhabitants of such State, being twenty-one years of age,[13] and citizens of the United States, or in any way abridged, except for participation in rebellion, or other crime, the basis of representation therein shall be reduced in the proportion which the number of such male citizens shall bear to the whole number of male citizens twenty-one years of age in such State.

**Section 3.** No person shall be a Senator or Representative in Congress, or elector of President and Vice President, or hold any office, civil or military, under the United States, or under any State, who, having previously taken an oath, as a member of Congress, or as an officer of the United States, or as a member of any State legislature, or as an executive or judicial officer of any State, to support the Constitution of the United States, shall have engaged in insurrection or rebellion against the same, or given aid or comfort to the enemies thereof. But Congress may by a vote of two-thirds of each House, remove such disability.

**Section 4.** The validity of the public debt of the United States, authorized by law, including debts incurred for payment of pensions and bounties for services in suppressing insurrection or rebellion, shall not be questioned. But neither the United States nor any State shall assume or pay any debt or obligation incurred in aid of insurrection or rebellion against the United States, or

any claim for the loss or emancipation of any slave; but all such debts, obligations and claims shall be held illegal and void.

**Section 5.** The Congress shall have power to enforce, by appropriate legislation, the provisions of this article.

### Amendment XV
### *(Ratified February 3, 1870)*

**Section 1.** The right of citizens of the United States to vote shall not be denied or abridged by the United States or by any State on account of race, color, or previous condition of servitude.

**Section 2.** The Congress shall have power to enforce this article by appropriate legislation.

### Amendment XVI
### *(Ratified February 3, 1913)*

The Congress shall have power to lay and collect taxes on incomes, from whatever source derived, without apportionment among the several States, and without regard to any census or enumeration.

### Amendment XVII
### *(Ratified April 8, 1913)*

The Senate of the United States shall be composed of two Senators from each State, elected by the people thereof, for six years; and each Senator shall have one vote. The electors in each State shall have the qualifications requisite for electors of the most numerous branch of the State legislatures.

When vacancies happen in the representation of any State in the Senate, the executive authority of such State shall issue writs of election to fill such vacancies: *Provided,* That the legislature of any State may empower the executive thereof to make temporary appointments until the people fill the vacancies by election as the legislature may direct.

This amendment shall not be so construed as to affect the election or term of any Senator chosen before it becomes valid as part of the Constitution.

[Amendment XVIII
*(Ratified January 16, 1919)*

Section 1. After one year from the ratification of this article the manufacture, sale, or transportation of intoxicating liquors within, the importation thereof into, or the exportation thereof from the United States and all territory subject to the jurisdiction thereof for beverage purposes is hereby prohibited.

Section 2. The Congress and the several States shall have concurrent power to enforce this article by appropriate legislation.

Section 3. This article shall be inoperative unless it shall have been ratified as an amendment to the Constitution by the legislatures of the several States, as provided in the Constitution, within seven years from the date of the submission hereof to the States by the Congress.][14]

## Amendment XIX
*(Ratified August 18, 1920)*

The right of citizens of the United States to vote shall not be denied or abridged by the United States or by any State on account of sex.

Congress shall have power to enforce this article by appropriate legislation.

## Amendment XX
*(Ratified January 23, 1933)*

Section 1. The terms of the President and Vice President shall end at noon on the 20th day of January, and the terms of Senators and Representatives at noon on the 3d day of January, of the years in which such terms would have ended if this article had not been ratified; and the terms of their successors shall then begin.

Section 2. The Congress shall assemble at least once in every year, and such meeting shall begin at noon on the 3d day of January, unless they shall by law appoint a different day.

Section 3.[15] If, at the time fixed for the beginning of the term of the President, the President elect shall have died, the Vice President elect shall become President. If a President shall not have been chosen before the time fixed for the beginning of his term, or if the President elect shall have failed to qualify, then the Vice President elect shall act as President until a President shall have qualified; and the Congress may by law provide for the case wherein neither a President elect nor a Vice President elect shall have qualified, declaring who shall then act as President, or the manner in which one who is to act shall be selected, and such person shall act accordingly until a President or Vice President shall have qualified.

Section 4. The Congress may by law provide for the case of the death of any of the persons from whom the House of Representatives may choose a President whenever the right of choice shall have devolved upon them, and for the case of the death of any of the persons from whom the Senate may choose a Vice President whenever the right of choice shall have devolved upon them.

Section 5. Sections 1 and 2 shall take effect on the 15th day of October following the ratification of this article.

Section 6. This article shall be inoperative unless it shall have been ratified as an amendment to the Constitution by the legislatures of three-fourths of the several States within seven years from the date of its submission.

## Amendment XXI
*(Ratified December 5, 1933)*

Section 1. The eighteenth article of amendment to the Constitution of the United States is hereby repealed.

Section 2. The transportation or importation into any State, Territory or possession of the United States for delivery or use therein of intoxicating liquors, in violation of the laws thereof, is hereby prohibited.

Section 3. This article shall be inoperative unless it shall have been ratified as an amendment to the Constitution by conventions in the several States, as provided in the Constitution, within seven years from the date of the submission hereof to the States by the Congress.

## Amendment XXII
### *(Ratified February 27, 1951)*

**Section 1.** No person shall be elected to the office of the President more than twice, and no person who has held the office of President, or acted as President, for more than two years of a term to which some other person was elected President shall be elected to the office of the President more than once. But this Article shall not apply to any person holding the office of President when this Article was proposed by the Congress, and shall not prevent any person who may be holding the office of President, or acting as President, during the term within which this Article becomes operative from holding the office of President or acting as President during the remainder of such term.

**Section 2.** This Article shall be inoperative unless it shall have been ratified as an amendment to the Constitution by the legislatures of three-fourths of the several States within seven years from the date of its submission to the States by the Congress.

## Amendment XXIII
### *(Ratified March 29, 1961)*

**Section 1.** The District constituting the seat of Government of the United States shall appoint in such manner as the Congress may direct:

A number of electors of President and Vice President equal to the whole number of Senators and Representatives in Congress to which the District would be entitled if it were a State, but in no event more than the least populous State; they shall be in addition to those appointed by the States, but they shall be considered, for the purposes of the election of President and Vice President, to be electors appointed by a State; and they shall meet in the District and perform such duties as provided by the twelfth article of amendment.

**Section 2.** The Congress shall have power to enforce this article by appropriate legislation.

## Amendment XXIV
### *(Ratified January 23, 1964)*

**Section 1.** The right of citizens of the United States to vote in any primary or other election for President or Vice President, for electors for President or Vice President, or for Senator or Representative in Congress, shall not be denied or abridged by the United States or any State by reason of failure to pay any poll tax or other tax.

**Section 2.** The Congress shall have power to enforce this article by appropriate legislation.

## Amendment XXV
### *(Ratified February 10, 1967)*

**Section 1.** In case of the removal of the President from office or of his death or resignation, the Vice President shall become President.

**Section 2.** Whenever there is a vacancy in the office of the Vice President, the President shall nominate a Vice President who shall take office upon confirmation by a majority vote of both Houses of Congress.

**Section 3.** Whenever the President transmits to the President pro tempore of the Senate and the Speaker of the House of Representatives his written declaration that he is unable to discharge the powers and duties of his office, and until he transmits to them a written declaration to the contrary, such powers and duties shall be discharged by the Vice President as Acting President.

**Section 4.** Whenever the Vice President and a majority of either the principal officers of the executive departments or of such other body as Congress may by law provide, transmit to the

President pro tempore of the Senate and the Speaker of the House of Representatives their written declaration that the President is unable to discharge the powers and duties of his office, the Vice President shall immediately assume the powers and duties of the office as Acting President.

Thereafter, when the President transmits to the President pro tempore of the Senate and the Speaker of the House of Representatives his written declaration that no inability exists, he shall resume the powers and duties of his office unless the Vice President and a majority of either the principal officers of the executive department or of such other body as Congress may by law provide, transmit within four days to the President pro tempore of the Senate and the Speaker of the House of Representatives their written declaration that the President is unable to discharge the powers and duties of his office. Thereupon Congress shall decide the issue, assembling within forty-eight hours for that purpose if not in session. If the Congress, within twenty-one days after receipt of the latter written declaration, or, if Congress is not in session, within twenty-one days after Congress is required to assemble, determines by two-thirds vote of both houses that the President is unable to discharge the powers and duties of his office, the Vice President shall continue to discharge the same as Acting President; otherwise, the President shall resume the powers and duties of his office.

## Amendment XXVI
### (Ratified July 1, 1971)

**Section 1.** The right of citizens of the United States, who are eighteen years of age or older, to vote shall not be denied or abridged by the United States or by any State on account of age.

**Section 2.** The Congress shall have power to enforce this article by appropriate legislation.

## Notes

1. The part in brackets was changed by section 2 of the Fourteenth Amendment.
2. The part in brackets was changed by section 1 of the Seventeenth Amendment.
3. The part in brackets was changed by the second paragraph of the Seventeenth Amendment.
4. The part in brackets was changed by section 2 of the Twentieth Amendment.
5. The Sixteenth Amendment gave Congress the power to tax incomes.
6. The material in brackets has been superseded by the Twelfth Amendment.
7. This provision has been affected by the Twenty-fifth Amendment.
8. This clause was affected by the Eleventh Amendment.
9. This clause was affected by the Eleventh Amendment.
10. This paragraph has been superseded by the Thirteenth Amendment.
11. Obsolete.
12. The part in brackets has been superseded by section 3 of the Twentieth Amendment.
13. See the Twenty-sixth Amendment.
14. This Amendment was repealed by section 1 of the Twenty-first Amendment.
15. See the Twenty-fifth Amendment.

# The Federalist Papers, Nos. 69-70 (1788)

Article II of the proposed Constitution posed a political problem to those who were trying to persuade the states to vote for ratification. Not only was the presidency the most obvious innovation in the new plan of government, but its unitary nature and strong powers roused fears of the most horrifying specter most Americans could imagine—an all-powerful monarchy like the one they had overthrown in the revolutionary war. Opponents of the Constitution—called "Anti-Federalists"—effectively fanned these fears.

Proponents of the Constitution at the state ratifying conventions—the "Federalists"—answered their critics by stressing both the virtues of the presidency and the restraints that the Constitution placed upon the office. In doing so they relied to some degree on the explanations and defenses of the Constitution that Alexander Hamilton, James Madison (a Virginian), and John Jay (like Hamilton, a New Yorker) were putting forth in a series of eighty-five newspaper articles that Hamilton had commissioned. These articles, later gathered together in a book called The Federalist Papers, appeared pseudonymously under the name "Publius" in several New York newspapers and were widely circulated around the country.

Hamilton wrote more than fifty of the Federalist Papers, including Nos. 69-77, the articles that dealt with the presidency. No. 69 squarely addressed the Anti-Federalist charge that the presidency was a latent monarchy. Hamilton argued that in contrast to the British king, who secures his office by inheritance and serves for life, the president is freely elected for a limited term. The president may be impeached and removed from office; the king may not be. The king has an absolute veto over laws passed by the legislature; the president's vetoes may be overridden. The king can both declare war and raise an army and navy; the president can do neither. The king can create offices and appoint people to fill them; the president cannot create offices and can fill those that Congress creates only after securing the approval of the Senate.

Federalist No. 70, less defensive in tone than the first article, described the virtues of the presidency. Its theme was "energy," a quality that, according to Hamilton, is essential to the defense of the nation and the steady administration of the laws. In the government created by the Constitution, energy was to be provided by the presidency, mostly because of its unitary character. Unity imbues the presidency with a whole host of virtues—"decision, activity, secrecy, and dispatch . . . vigor and expedition."

In Federalist Nos. 71-77, Hamilton

*dealt with the specific features of the presidency in detail, defending the office's four-year term, eligibility for re-election, fixed salary, and each of its enumerated powers. The great irony of these essays is that Hamilton, who would have preferred that the Constitution create a much stronger presidency than it did, became the office's most effective defender.* ~

## *Federalist* No. 69

I proceed now to trace the real characters of the proposed executive, as they are marked out in the plan of the convention. This will serve to place in a strong light the unfairness of the representations which have been made in regard to it.

The first thing which strikes our attention is that the executive authority, with few exceptions, is to be vested in a single magistrate. This will scarcely, however, be considered as a point which any comparison can be grounded; for if, in this particular, there be a resemblance to the king of Great Britain, there is not less a resemblance to the Grand Seignior, to the khan of Tartary, to the Man of the Seven Mountains, or to the governor of New York.

That magistrate is to be elected for *four* years; and is to be re-eligible as often as the people of the United States shall think him worthy of their confidence. In these circumstances there is a total dissimilitude between *him* and a king of Great Britain, who is an *hereditary* monarch, possessing the crown as a patrimony descendible to his heirs forever; but there is a close analogy between *him* and a governor of New York, who is elected for *three* years, and is re-eligible without limitation or intermission. If we consider how much less time would be requisite for establishing a dangerous influence in a single State than for establishing a like influence throughout the United States, we must conclude that a duration of *four* years for the Chief Magistrate of the Union is a degree of permanency far less to be dreaded in that office, than a duration of *three* years for a corresponding office in a single State.

The President of the United States would be liable to be impeached, tried, and, upon conviction of treason, bribery, or other high crimes or misdemeanors, removed from office; and would afterwards be liable to prosecution and punishment in the ordinary course of law. The person of the King of Great Britain is sacred and inviolable; there is no constitutional tribunal to which he is amenable; no punishment to which he can be subjected without involving the crisis of a national revolution. In this delicate and important circumstance of personal responsibility, the President of Confederated America would stand upon no better ground than a governor of New York, and upon worse ground than the governors of Virginia and Delaware.

The President of the United States is to have power to return a bill, which shall have passed the two branches of the legislature, for reconsideration; but the bill so returned is not to become a law unless, upon that reconsideration, it be approved by two thirds of both houses. The king of Great Britain, on his part, has an absolute negative upon the acts of the two houses of Parliament. The disuse of that power for a considerable time past does not affect the reality of its existence and is to be ascribed wholly to the crown's having found the means of substituting influence to authority, or the art of gaining a majority in one or the other of the two houses, to the necessity of exerting a prerogative which could seldom be exerted without hazarding some degree of national agitation. The qualified negative of the President differs widely from this absolute negative of the British sovereign and tallies exactly with the revisionary authority of the council of revision of this State, of which the governor is a constituent part. In this respect the power of the President would exceed that of the governor of New York, because the former would possess, singly, what the latter shares with the chancellor and judges; but it would be precisely the same with that of the governor of Massachusetts, whose constitution, as to this article, seems to have been the original from which the convention have copied.

The President is to be the "commander-in-chief of the army and navy of the United States, and of the militia of the several States, when called into the actual service of the United States. He is to have power to grant reprieves and pardons for offenses against the United States, *except in cases of impeachment;* to recommend to the consideration of Congress such measures as he shall judge necessary and expedient; to convene, on extraordinary occasions, both houses of the legislature, or either of them, and, in case of disagreement between them *with respect to the time of adjournment,* to adjourn them to such time as he shall think proper; to take care that the laws be faithfully executed; and to commission all officers of the United States." In most of these particulars, the power of the President will resemble equally that of the king of Great Britain and of the governor of New York. The most material points of difference are these:—*First.* The President will have only the occasional command of such part of the militia of the nation as by legislative provision may be called into the actual service of the Union. The king of Great Britain and the governor of New York have at all times the entire command of all the militia within their several jurisdictions. In this article, therefore, the power of the President would be inferior to that of either the monarch or the governor. *Second.* The President is to be commander-in-chief of the army and navy of the United States. In this respect his authority would be nominally the same with that of the king of Great Britain, but in substance much inferior to it. It would amount to nothing more than the supreme command and direction of the military and naval forces, as first general and admiral of the Confederacy; while that of the British king extends to the *declaring* of war and to the *raising* and *regulating* of fleets and armies—all which, by the Constitution under consideration, would appertain to the legislature.[1] The governor of New York, on the other hand, is by the constitution of the State vested only with the command of its militia and navy. But the constitutions of several of the States expressly declare their governors to be commanders-in-chief, as well of the army as navy; and it may well be a question whether those of New Hampshire and Massachusetts, in particular, do not, in this instance, confer larger powers upon their respective governors than could be claimed by a President of the United States. *Third.* The power of the President, in respect to pardons, would extend to all cases, *except those of impeachment.* The governor of New York may pardon in all cases, even in those of impeachment, except for treason and murder. Is not the power of the governor, in this article, on a calculation of political consequences, greater than that of the President? All conspiracies and plots against the government which have not been matured into actual treason may be screened from punishment of every kind by the interposition of the prerogative of pardoning. If a governor of New York, therefore, should be at the head of any such conspiracy, until the design had been ripened into actual hostility he could insure his accomplices and adherents an entire impunity. A President of the Union, on the other hand, though he may even pardon treason, when prosecuted in the ordinary course of law, could shelter no offender, in any degree, from the effects of impeachment and conviction. Would not the prospect of a total indemnity for all the preliminary steps be a greater temptation to undertake and persevere in an enterprise against the public liberty, than the mere prospect of an exemption from death and confiscation, if the final execution of the design, upon an actual appeal to arms, should miscarry? Would this last expectation have any influence at all, when the probability was computed that the person who was to afford that exemption might himself be involved in the consequences of the measure, and might be incapacitated by his agency in it from affording the desired impunity? The better judge of this matter, it will be necessary to recollect that, by the proposed Constitution, the offense of treason is limited "to levying war upon the United States, and adhering to their enemies, giving them aid and comfort"; and that by the laws of New York it is confined within similar bounds. *Fourth.* The President can only adjourn the national legislature in the single case of disagreement about the time of adjournment. The British monarch may prorogue or even dissolve the Parliament. The governor of New York may also prorogue the legislature of this State for a limited time; a power which, in certain situations, may be employed to very important purposes.

The President is to have power, with the advice and consent of the Senate, to make treaties, provided two thirds of the senators present concur. The king of Great Britain is the sole and absolute representative of the nation in all foreign transactions. He can of his own accord make treaties of peace, commerce, alliance, and of every other description. It has been insinuated that his authority in this respect is not conclusive, and that his conventions with foreign powers are subject to the revision, and stand in need of the ratification, of Parliament. But I believe this doctrine was never heard of until it was broached upon the present occasion.

Every jurist[2] of that kingdom, and every other man acquainted with its Constitution knows, as an established fact, that the prerogative of making treaties exists in the crown in its utmost plenitude; and that the compacts entered into by the royal authority have the most complete legal validity and perfection, independent of any other sanctions. The Parliament, it is true, is sometimes seen employing itself in altering the existing laws to conform them to the stipulations in a new treaty; and this may have possibly given birth to the imagination that its co-operation was necessary to the obligatory efficacy of the treaty. But this parliamentary interposition proceeds from a different cause: from the necessity of adjusting a most artificial and intricate system of revenue and commercial laws, to the changes made in them by the operation of the treaty; and of adapting new provisions and precautions to the new state of things, to keep the machine from running into disorder. In this respect, therefore, there is no comparison between the intended power of the President and the actual power of the British sovereign. The one can perform alone what the other can only do with the concurrence of a branch of the legislature. It must be admitted that in this instance the power of the federal executive would exceed that of any State executive. But this arises naturally from the exclusive possession by the Union of that part of the sovereign power which relates to treaties. If the Confederacy were to be dissolved, it would become a question whether the executives of the several States were not solely invested with that delicate and important prerogative.

The President is also to be authorized to receive ambassadors and other public ministers. This, though it has been a rich theme of declamation, is more a matter of dignity than of authority. It is a circumstance which will be without consequence in the administration of the government; and it was far more convenient that it should be arranged in this manner than that there should be a necessity of convening the legislature, or one of its branches, upon every arrival of a foreign minister, though it were merely to take the place of a departed predecessor.

The President is to nominate, and, *with the advice and consent of the Senate,* to appoint ambassadors and other public ministers, judges of the Supreme Court, and in general all officers of the United States established by law, and whose appointments are not otherwise provided for by the Constitution. The king of Great Britain is emphatically and truly styled the fountain of honor. He not only appoints to all offices, but can create offices. He can confer titles of nobility at pleasure, and has the disposal of an immense number of church preferments. There is evidently a great inferiority in the power of the President, in this particular, to that of the British king; nor is it equal to that of the governor of New York, if we are to interpret the meaning of the constitution of the State by the practice which has obtained under it. The power of appointment is with us lodged in a council, composed of the governor and four members of the Senate, chosen by the Assembly. The governor *claims,* and has frequently *exercised,* the right of nomination, and is *entitled* to a casting vote in the appointment. If he really has the right of nominating, his authority is in this respect equal to that of the President, and exceeds it in the article of the casting vote. In the national government, if the Senate should be divided, no appointment could be made; in the government of New York, if the council should be divided, the governor can turn the scale and confirm his own nomination.[3] If we compare the publicity which must necessarily attend the mode of appointment by the President and an entire branch of the national legislature, with the privacy in the mode of appointment by the governor of New York, closeted in a secret apartment with at most four, and frequently with only two persons; and if we at the same time consider how much more easy it must be to influence the small number of which council of appointment consists than the considerable number of which the national Senate would consist, we cannot hesitate to pronounce that the power of the chief magistrate of this State, in the disposition of offices, must, in practice, be greatly superior to that of the Chief Magistrate of the Union.

Hence it appears that, except as to the concurrent authority of the President in the article of treaties, it would be difficult to determine whether that magistrate would, in the aggregate, possess more or less power than the governor of New York. And it appears yet more unequivocally that there is no pretense for the parallel which has been attempted between him and the king of Great Britain. But to render the contrast in this respect still more striking, it may be of use to throw the principal circumstances of dissimilitude into a closer group.

The President of the United States would be an officer elected by the people for *four* years; the king of Great Britain is a perpetual and *hereditary* prince. The one would be amenable to personal punishment and disgrace; the person of the other is sacred and inviolable. The one would have a qualified negative upon the acts of the legislative body; the other has an *absolute* negative. The one would have a right to command the military and naval forces of the nation; the other, in addition to this right, possesses that of *declaring* war, and of *raising* and *regulating* fleets and armies by his own authority. The one would have a concurrent power with a branch of the legislature in the formation of treaties; the other is the *sole possessor* of the power of making treaties. The one would have a like concurrent authority in appointing to offices; the other is the sole author of all appointments. The one can confer no privileges whatever; the other can make denizens of aliens, noblemen of commoners; can erect corporations with all the rights incident to corporate bodies. The one can prescribe no rules concerning the commerce or currency of the nation; the other is in several respects the arbiter of commerce, and in this capacity can establish markets and fairs, can regulate weights and measures, can lay embargoes for a limited time, can coin money, can authorize or prohibit the circulation of foreign coin. The one has no particle of spiritual jurisdiction; the other is the supreme head and governor of the national church! What answer shall we give to those who would persuade us that things so unlike resemble each other? The same that ought to be given to those who tell us that a government, the whole power of which would be in the hands of the elective and periodical servants of the people, is an aristocracy, a monarchy, and a despotism.

PUBLIUS

### Notes

1. A writer in a Pennsylvania paper, under the signature of Tamony, has asserted that the king of Great Britain owes his prerogative as commander-in-chief to an annual mutiny bill. The truth is, on the contrary, that his prerogative in this respect is immemorial, and was only disputed "contrary to all reason and precedent," as Blackstone, vol. i, page 262, expresses it, by the Long Parliament of Charles I; but by the statute the 13th of Charles II, chap. 6, it was declared to be in the king alone, for that the sole supreme government and command of the militia within his Majesty's realms and dominions, and of all forces by sea and land, and of all forts and places of strength, *ever was and is* the undoubted right of his Majesty and his royal predecessors, kings and queens of England, and that both or either house

of Parliament cannot nor ought to pretend to the same.

2. *Vide* Blackstone's *Commentaries*, Vol. I., p. 257.

3. Candor, however, demands an acknowledgment that I do not think the claim of the governor to a right of nomination well founded. Yet it is always justifiable to reason from the practice of a government till its propriety has been constitutionally questioned. And independent of this claim, when we take into view the other considerations and pursue them through all their consequences, we shall be inclined to draw much the same conclusion.

---

## *Federalist* No. 70

There is an idea, which is not without its advocates, that a vigorous executive is inconsistent with the genius of republican government. The enlightened well-wishers to this species of government must at least hope that the supposition is destitute of foundation; since they can never admit its truth, without at the same time admitting the condemnation of their own principles. Energy in the executive is a leading character in the definition of good government. It is essential to the protection of the community against foreign attacks; it is not less essential to the steady administration of the laws; to the protection of property against those irregular and high-handed combinations which sometimes interrupt the ordinary course of justice; to the security of liberty against the enterprises and assaults of ambition, of faction, and of anarchy. Every man the least conversant in Roman history knows how often that republic was obliged to take refuge in the absolute power of a single man, under the formidable title of dictator, as well against the intrigues of ambitious individuals who aspired to the tyranny, and the seditions of whole classes of the community whose conduct threatened the existence of all government, as against the invasions of external enemies who menaced the conquest and destruction of Rome.

There can be no need, however, to multiply arguments or examples on this head. A feeble executive implies a feeble execution of the government. A feeble execution is but another phrase for a bad execution; and a government ill executed, whatever it may be in theory, must be, in practice, a bad government.

Taking it for granted, therefore, that all men of sense will agree in the necessity of an energetic executive, it will only remain to inquire, what are the ingredients which constitute this energy? How far can they be combined with those other ingredients which constitute safety in the republican sense? And how far does this combination characterize the plan which has been reported by the convention?

The ingredients which constitute energy in the executive are unity; duration; an adequate provision for its support; and competent powers.

The ingredients which constitute safety in the republican sense are a due dependence on the people, and a due responsibility.

Those politicians and statesmen who have been the most celebrated for the soundness of their principles and for the justness of their views have declared in favor of a single executive and a numerous legislature. They have, with great propriety, considered energy as the most necessary qualification of the former, and have regarded this as most applicable to power in a single hand; while they have, with equal propriety, considered the latter as best adapted to deliberation and wisdom, and best calculated to conciliate the confidence of the people and to secure their privileges and interests.

That unity is conducive to energy will not be disputed. Decision, activity, secrecy, and dispatch will generally characterize the proceedings of one man in a much more eminent degree than the proceedings of any greater number; and

in proportion as the number is increased, these qualities will be diminished.

This unity may be destroyed in two ways: either by vesting the power in two or more magistrates of equal dignity and authority, or by vesting it ostensibly in one man, subject in whole or in part to the control and cooperation of others, in the capacity of counselors to him. Of the first, the two consuls of Rome may serve as an example; of the last, we shall find examples in the constitutions of several of the States. New York and New Jersey, if I recollect right, are the only States which have intrusted the executive authority wholly to single men.[1] Both these methods of destroying the unity of the executive have their partisans; but the votaries of an executive council are the most numerous. They are both liable, if not equal, to similar objections, and may in most lights be examined in conjunction.

The experience of other nations will afford little instruction on this head. As far, however, as it teaches anything, it teaches us not to be enamored of plurality in the executive. We have seen that the Achaeans, on an experiment of two Praetors, were induced to abolish one. The Roman history records many instances of mischiefs to the republic from the dissensions between the consuls, and between the military tribunes, who were at times substituted for the consuls. But it gives us no specimens of any peculiar advantages derived to the state from the circumstance of the plurality of those magistrates. That the dissensions between them were not more frequent or more fatal is matter of astonishment, until we advert to the singular position in which the republic was almost continually placed, and to the prudent policy pointed out by the circumstances of the state, and pursued by the consuls, of making a division of the government between them. The patricians engaged in a perpetual struggle with the plebeians for the preservation of their ancient authorities and dignities; the consuls, who were generally chosen out of the former body, were commonly united by the personal interest they had in the defense of privileges of their order. In addition to this motive of union, after the arms of the republic had considerably expanded the bounds of its empire, it became an established custom with the consuls to divide the administration between themselves by lot—one of them remaining at Rome to govern the city and its environs, the other taking command in the more distant provinces. This expedient must no doubt have had great influence in preventing those collisions and rivalships which might otherwise have embroiled the peace of the republic.

But quitting the dim light of historical research, and attaching ourselves purely to the dictates of reason and good sense, we shall discover much greater cause to reject them to approve the idea of plurality in the executive, under any modification whatever.

Whenever two or more persons are engaged in any common enterprise or pursuit, there is always danger of difference of opinion. If it be a public trust or office in which they are clothed with equal dignity and authority, there is peculiar danger of personal emulation and even animosity. From either, and especially from all these causes, the most bitter dissensions are apt to spring. Whenever these happen, they lessen the respectability, weaken the authority, and distract the plans and operations of those whom they divide. If they should unfortunately assail the supreme executive magistracy of a country, consisting of a plurality of persons, they might impede or frustrate the most important measures of the government in the most critical emergencies of the state. And what is still worse, they might split the community into the most violent and irreconcilable factions, adhering differently to the different individuals who composed the magistracy.

Men often oppose a thing merely because they have had no agency in planning it, or because it may have been planned by those whom they dislike. But if they have been consulted, and have happened to disapprove, opposition then becomes, in their estimation, an indispensable duty of self-love. They seem to think themselves bound in honor, and by all the motives of personal infallibility, to defeat the success of what has been resolved upon contrary to their sentiments. Men of upright, benevolent tempers have too many opportunities of remarking, with horror, to what desperate lengths this disposition is sometimes carried, and how often the great interests of society are sacrificed to the vanity, to the conceit, and to the obstinacy of individuals, who have credit enough to make their passions and their caprices interesting to mankind. Perhaps the question now before the public may, in its consequences, afford melancholy proofs of the effects of this despicable frailty, or rather detestable vice, in the human character.

Upon the principles of a free government, inconveniences from the source just mentioned must necessarily be submitted to in the formation of the legislature; but it is unnecessary, and therefore unwise, to introduce them into the constitution of the executive. It is here too that they may be most pernicious. In the legislature, promptitude of decision is oftener an evil than a benefit. The differences of opinion, and the jarring of parties in that department of the government, though they may sometimes obstruct salutary plans, yet often promote deliberation and circumspection, and serve to check excesses in the majority. When a resolution too is once taken, the opposition must be at an end. That resolution is a law, and resistance to it punishable. But no favorable circumstances palliate or atone for the disadvantages of dissension in the executive department. Here they are pure and unmixed. There is no point at which they cease to operate. They serve to embarrass and weaken the execution of the plan or measure to which they relate, from the first step to the final conclusion of it. They constantly counteract those qualities in the executive which are the most necessary ingredients in its composition—vigor and expedition, and this without any counterbalancing good. In the conduct of war, in which the energy of the executive is the bulwark of the national security, everything would be to be apprehended from its plurality.

It must be confessed that these observations apply with principal weight to the first case supposed—that is, to a plurality of magistrates of equal dignity and authority, a scheme, the advocates for which are not likely to form a numerous sect; but they apply, though not with equal yet with considerable weight to the project of a council, whose concurrence is made constitutionally necessary to the operations of the ostensible executive. An artful cabal in that council would be able to distract and to enervate the whole system of administration. If no such cabal should exist, the mere diversity of views and opinions would alone be sufficient to tincture the exercise of the executive authority with a spirit of habitual feebleness and dilatoriness.

But one of the weightiest objections to a plurality in the executive, and which lies as much against the last as the first plan, is that it tends to conceal faults and destroy responsibility. Responsibility is of two kinds—to censure and to punishment. The first is the more important of the two, especially in an elective office. Men in public trust will much oftener act in such a manner as to render them unworthy of being any longer trusted, than in such a manner as to make them obnoxious to legal punishment. But the multiplication of the executive adds to the difficulty of detection in either case. It often becomes impossible, amidst mutual accusations, to determine on whom the blame or the punishment of a pernicious measure, or series of pernicious measures, ought really to fall. It is shifted from one to another with so much dexterity, and under such plausible appearances, that the public opinion is left in suspense about the real author. The circumstances which may have led to any national miscarriage or misfortune are sometimes so complicated that where there are a number of actors who may have had different degrees and kinds of agency, though we may clearly see upon the whole that there has been mismanagement, yet it may be impracticable to pronounce to whose account the evil which may have been incurred is truly chargeable.

"I was overruled by my council. The council were so divided in their opinions that it was impossible to obtain any better resolution on the point." These and similar pretexts are constantly at hand, whether true or false. And who is there that will either take the trouble or incur the odium of a strict scrutiny into the secret springs of the transaction? Should there be found a citizen zealous enough to undertake the unpromising task, if there happened to be a collusion between the parties concerned, how easy it is to clothe the circumstances with so much ambiguity as to render it uncertain what was the precise conduct of any of those parties.

In the single instance in which the governor of this State is coupled with a council—that is, in the appointment to offices, we have seen the mischiefs of it in the view now under consideration. Scandalous appointments to important offices have been made. Some cases, indeed, have been so flagrant that *all parties* have agreed in the impropriety of the thing. When inquiry has been made, the blame has been laid by the governor on the members of the council, who, on their part, have charged it upon his nomination; while the people remain altogether at a loss to determine by whose influence their interests have been committed to hands so unqualified and so manifestly improper. In tenderness to individuals, I forbear to descend to particulars.

It is evident from these considerations that the plurality of the executive tends to deprive the people of the two greatest securities they can have for the faithful exercise of any delegated power, *first,* the restraints of public opinion, which lose their efficacy, as well on account of the division of the censure attendant on bad measures among a number as on account of the uncertainty on whom it ought to fall; and, *second,* the opportunity of discovering with facility and clearness the misconduct of the persons they trust, in order either to their removal from office or to their actual punishment in cases which admit of it.

In England, the king is a perpetual magistrate; and it is a maxim which has obtained for the sake of the public peace that he is unaccountable for his administration, and his person sacred. Nothing, therefore, can be wiser in that kingdom than to annex to the king a constitutional council, who may be responsible to the nation for the advice they give. Without this, there would be no responsibility whatever in the executive department—an idea inadmissible in a free government. But even there the king is not bound by the resolutions of his council, though they are answerable for the advice they give. He is the absolute master of his own conduct in the exercise of his office and may observe or disregard the counsel given to him at his sole discretion.

But in a republic where every magistrate ought to be personally responsible for his behavior in office, the reason which in the British Constitution dictates the propriety of a council not only ceases to apply, but turns against the institution. In the monarchy of Great Britain, it furnishes a substitute for the prohibited responsibility of the Chief Magistrate, which serves in some degree as a hostage to the national justice for his good behavior. In the American republic, it would serve to destroy, or would greatly diminish, the intended and necessary responsibility of the Chief Magistrate himself.

The idea of a council to the executive, which has so generally obtained in the State constitutions, has been derived from that maxim of republican jealousy which considers power as safer in the hands of a number of men than of a single man. If the maxim should be admitted to be applicable to the case, I should contend that the advantage on that side would not counterbalance the numerous disadvantages on the opposite side. But I do not think the rule at all applicable to the executive power, I clearly concur in opinion, in this particular, with a writer whom the celebrated Junius pronounces to be "deep, solid, and ingenious," that "the executive power is more easily confined when it is one"; [2] that it is far more safe there should be a single object for the jealousy and watchfulness of the people; and, in a word, that all multiplication of the executive is rather dangerous than friendly to liberty.

A little consideration will satisfy us that the species of security sought for in the multiplication of the executive is unattainable. Numbers must be so great as to render combination difficult, or they are rather a source of danger than of security. The united credit and influence of several individuals must be more formidable to liberty than the credit and influence of either of them separately. When power, therefore, is placed in the hands of so small a number of men as to admit of their interests and views being easily combined in a common enterprise, by an artful leader, it becomes more liable to abuse, and more dangerous when abused, than if it be lodged in the hands of one man, who, from the very circumstance of his being alone, will be more narrowly watched and more readily suspected, and who cannot unite so great a mass of influence as when he is associated with others. The decemvirs of Rome, whose name denotes their number,[3] were more to be dreaded in their usurpation than any *one* of them would have been. No person would think of proposing an executive much more numerous than that body; from six to a dozen have been suggested for the number of the council. The extreme of these numbers is not too great for an easy combination; and from such a combination America would have more to fear than from the ambition of any single individual. A council to a magistrate, who is himself responsible for what he does, are generally nothing better than a clog upon his good intentions, are often the instruments and accomplices of his bad, and are almost always a cloak to his faults.

I forbear to dwell upon the subject of expense; though it be evident that if the council should be numerous enough to answer the principal end aimed at by the institution, the salaries of the members, who must be drawn from their homes to reside at the seat of government, would form an item in the catalogue of public expenditures too serious to be incurred for an object of equivocal utility.

I will only add that, prior to the appearance of the Constitution, I rarely met with an intelligent man from any of the States who did not admit, as the result of experience, that the UNITY of the executive of this State was one of the best of the distinguishing features of our Constitution.

PUBLIUS

## Notes

1. New York has no council except for the single purpose of appointing to offices; New Jersey has a council whom the governor may consult. But I think, from the terms of the Constitution, their resolutions do not bind him.
2. De Lolme.
3. Ten.

# George Washington's First Inaugural Address (1789)

The Constitution makes no provision for presidential inaugurations, requiring only that the new president repeat the oath stated in Article II, section 1, clause 8: "I do solemnly swear (or affirm) that I will faithfully execute the Office of President of the United States, and will to the best of my Ability preserve, protect and defend the Constitution of the United States." Tradition is the wellspring of every other aspect of inaugural ceremonies. The inauguration of George Washington as the first president began many of these traditions, such as swearing the oath on the Bible, delivering an inaugural address, and holding a public celebration afterward.

Washington was elected president on February 4, 1789. The election was organized by the outgoing Congress that existed under the Articles of Confederation. After declaring that the Constitution was ratified in July 1788, Congress had passed a resolution on September 13 that each state should appoint presidential electors on the first Wednesday in January 1789 (January 7). When these electors (who were chosen by the various state legislatures) convened in their state capitals on the first Wednesday in February (February 4), they voted unanimously for Washington. They also elected John Adams of Massachusetts as vice president.

Although the old Congress had set the first Wednesday in March (March 4) as the day the new government of the Constitution was supposed to begin, not enough members of Congress arrived in New York City (then the U.S. capital) to constitute a quorum. Thus, the electoral votes for president were not opened and Washington declared elected until April 6. The president-elect, waiting at Mount Vernon, his Virginia home, was officially informed by messenger of his election on April 14. Washington proceeded slowly northward to New York by coach. He was greeted by ecstatic crowds, pealing church bells, and cannon salutes at every stop along the way. On April 30 Washington arrived in New York to be sworn in as president.

Washington took the constitutional oath of office on the outdoor balcony of New York's Federal Hall before an exuberant crowd. Observing the oath-taking custom of the time, he placed his left hand on the Bible and his right hand heavenward and added the words "so help me God" to the official language of the Constitution. The first president then went inside to the Senate chamber to deliver an inaugural address.

Washington's address sounded two themes that have characterized the inaugural addresses of most subsequent presidents. First, he paid "homage to *the Great Author of every public and private good," both noting the benign workings of "providential agency" in the birth of the United States and urging Congress and the American people to earn "the propitious smiles of Heaven" by acting with justice and magnanimity. Second, Washington spoke of national unity and dedication to the Constitution.*

*The final event of the first presidential inauguration was a public fireworks display. After it was over, the new president walked to his new home.*   ~

Fellow-Citizens of the Senate and of the House of Representatives:

Among the vicissitudes incident to life no event could have filled me with greater anxieties than that of which the notification was transmitted by your order, and received on the 14th day of the present month. On the one hand, I was summoned by my country, whose voice I can never hear but with veneration and love, from a retreat which I had chosen with the fondest predilection, and, in my flattering hopes, with an immutable decision, as the asylum of my declining years—a retreat which was rendered every day more necessary as well as more dear to me by the addition of habit to inclination, and of frequent interruptions in my health to the gradual waste committed on it by time. On the other hand, the magnitude and difficulty of the trust to which the voice of my country called me, being sufficient to awaken in the wisest and most experienced of her citizens a distrustful scrutiny into his qualifications, could not but overwhelm with despondence one who (inheriting inferior endowments from nature and unpracticed in the duties of civil administration) ought to be peculiarly conscious of his own deficiencies. In this conflict of emotions all I dare aver is that it has been my faithful study to collect my duty from a just appreciation of every circumstance by which it might be affected. All I dare hope is that if, in executing this task, I have been too much swayed by a grateful remembrance of former instances, or by an affectionate sensibility to this transcendent proof of the confidence of my fellow-citizens, and have thence too little consulted my incapacity as well as disinclination for the weighty and untried cares before me, my error will be palliated by the motives which mislead me, and its consequences be judged by my country with some share of the partiality in which they originated.

Such being the impressions under which I have, in obedience to the public summons, repaired to the present station, it would be peculiarly improper to omit in this first official act my fervent supplications to that Almighty Being who rules over the universe who presides in the councils of nations, and whose providential aids can supply every human defect, that His benediction may consecrate to the liberties and happiness of the people of the United States a Government instituted by themselves for these essential purposes, and may enable every instrument employed in its administration to execute with success the functions allotted to his charge. In tendering this homage to the Great Author of every public and private good, I assure myself that it expresses your sentiments not less than my own, nor those of my fellow-citizens at large less than either. No people can be bound to acknowledge and adore the Invisible Hand which conducts the affairs of men more than those of the United States. Every step by which they have advanced to the character of an independent nation seems to have been distinguished by some token of providential agency; and in the important revolution just accomplished in the system of their united government the tranquil deliberations and voluntary consent of so many distinct communities from which the event has resulted can not be compared with the means by which most governments have been established without some return of pious gratitude, along with an humble anticipation of the future blessings which the past seem to presage. These reflections, arising out of the present crisis, have forced themselves too strongly on my mind to be suppressed. You will join with me, I trust, in thinking that there are none under the influence of which the proceedings of a new and free government can more auspiciously commence.

By the article establishing the executive department it is made the duty of the President "to recommend to your consideration such measures as he shall judge necessary and expedient." The circumstances under which I now meet you will acquit me from entering into that subject further than to refer to the great constitutional charter under which you are assembled, and which, in defining your powers, designates the objects to which your attention is to be given. It will be more consistent with those circumstances, and far more congenial with the feelings which actuate me, to substitute, in place of a recommendation of particular measures, the tribute that is due to the talents, the rectitude, and the patriotism which adorn the characters selected to devise and adopt them. In these honorable qualifications I behold the surest pledges that as on one side no local prejudices or attachments, no separate views nor party animosities, will misdirect the comprehensive and equal eye which ought to watch over this great assemblage of communities and interests, so, on another, that the foundation of our national policy will be laid in the pure and immutable principles of private morality, and the preeminence of free government be exemplified by all the attributes which can win the affections of its citizens and command the respect of the world. I dwell on this prospect with every satisfaction which an ardent love for my country can inspire, since there is no truth more thoroughly established than that there exists in the economy and course of nature an indissoluble union between virtue and happiness; between duty and advantage; between the genuine maxims of an honest and magnanimous policy and the solid rewards of public prosperity and felicity; since we ought to be no less persuaded that the propitious smiles of Heaven can never be expected on a nation that disregards the eternal rules of order and right which Heaven itself has ordained; and since the preservation of the sacred fire of liberty and the destiny of the republican model of government are justly considered, perhaps, as deeply, as finally, staked on the experiment intrusted to the hands of the American people.

Besides the ordinary objects submitted to your care, it will remain with your judgement to decide how far an exercise of the occasional power delegated by the fifth article of the Constitution is rendered expedient at the present juncture by the nature of objections which have been urged against the system, or by the degree of inquietude which has given birth to them. Instead of undertaking particular recommendations on this subject, in which I could be guided by no lights derived from official opportunities, I shall again give way to my entire confidence in your discernment and pursuit of the public good; for I assure myself that whilst you carefully avoid every alteration which might endanger the benefits of an united and effective government, or which ought to await the future lessons of experience, a reverence for the characteristic rights of freemen and a regard for the public harmony will sufficiently influence your deliberations on the question how far the former can be impregnably fortified or the latter be safely and advantageously promoted.

To the foregoing observations I have

one to add, which will be most properly addressed to the House of Representatives. It concerns myself, and will therefore be as brief as possible. When I was first honored with a call into the service of my country, then on the eve of an arduous struggle for its liberties, the light in which I contemplated my duty required that I should renounce every pecuniary compensation. From this resolution I have in no instance departed; and being still under the impressions which produced it, I must decline as inapplicable to myself any share in the personal emoluments which may be indispensably included in a permanent provision for the executive department, and must accordingly pray that the pecuniary estimates for the station in which I am placed may during my continuance in it be limited to such actual expenditures as the public good may be thought to require.

Having thus imparted to you my sentiments as they have been awakened by the occasion which brings us together, I shall take my present leave; but not without resorting once more to the benign Parent of the Human Race in humble supplication that, since He has been pleased to favor the American people with opportunities for deliberating in perfect tranquility, and dispositions for deciding with unparalleled unanimity on a form of government for the security of their union and the advancement of their happiness, so His divine blessing may be equally conspicuous in the enlarged views, the temperate consultations, and the wise measures on which the success of this Government must depend.

# George Washington's Farewell Address (1796)

George Washington had hoped to retire from public life at the end of his first term as president—he even asked James Madison to draft a farewell address in 1792—but was prevailed upon to serve another term. In 1796 Washington resolved to retire after his second term expired in 1797. Weaving together Madison's draft, a new draft by Alexander Hamilton, and his own words and ideas, Washington wrote (the address was never spoken to an audience) a long address directed to his "friends and fellow citizens" (not Congress) and released it to the Daily American Advertiser, a Philadelphia newspaper, where it was published on September 19, 1796. Newspapers around the country reprinted what soon became known as the "farewell address," setting off a national wave of tributes and expressions of thanks. By disseminating word of his decision to retire three months before the presidential election, Washington forestalled any effort to reelect him.

Voluntary retirement after two terms was one precedent Washington established for future presidents, although his main reason for leaving office seems to have been more personal (he said in the Farewell Address that he longed for "the shade of retirement") than political. Washington also formed the heads of the departments into a cabinet of advisers; established

the principle of presidential leadership of the executive branch, including the right to remove officials from office without consulting the Senate; and, especially through his 1793 proclamation that the United States would remain neutral between Great Britain and France, asserted the president's primacy in foreign affairs.

In one area of presidential leadership, however, Washington's effort to establish a precedent failed. Although Washington tried to govern in a nonpartisan style, his eight-year administration was marked by developing differences between the pro-British, pro-national-government Federalist party, led by Secretary of the Treasury Hamilton, and the pro-French, pro-local-government Democratic-Republican party, led by Secretary of State Thomas Jefferson.

The Farewell Address reviewed Washington's career of public service, then looked ahead to the long-term future of the new nation. Washington was especially concerned about threats to national unity. He dwelled at length on two such threats—the "Spirit of Party" and the inclination among Americans to choose sides in disputes between Great Britain and France.

Washington intended not only that the Farewell Address mark his retirement from the presidency but also that it "terminate the career of my public *life." In 1798, however, he was called back into service by his successsor as president, John Adams. Fears of a French invasion in the aftermath of a diplomatic imbroglio prompted Adams to name Washington lieutenant general and commander in chief of the army. The invasion never occurred. Washington died in 1799.*  ~

Friends, and Fellow-Citizens:

The period for a new election of a Citizen, to administer the Executive Government of the United States, being not far distant, and the time actually arrived, when your thoughts must be employed in designating the person, who is to be clothed with that important trust, it appears to me proper, especially as it may conduce to a more distinct expression of the public voice, that I should now apprise you of the resolution I have formed, to decline being considered among the number of those, out of whom a choice is to be made. . . .

The acceptance of, and continuance hitherto in, the office to which your suffrages have twice called me, have been a uniform sacrifice of inclination to the opinion of duty, and to a deference for what appeared to be your desire.—I constantly hoped, that it would have been much earlier in my power, consistently with motives, which I was not at liberty to disregard, to return to that retirement, from which I had been reluctantly drawn.—The strength of my inclination to do this, previous to the last election, had even led to the preparation of an address to declare it to you; but mature reflection on the then perplexed and critical nature of our affairs with foreign Nations, and the unanimous advice of persons entitled to my confidence, impelled me to abandon the idea.—

I rejoice that the state of your concerns, external as well as internal, no longer renders the pursuit of inclination

incompatible with the sentiment of duty, or propriety; and am persuaded, whatever partiality may be retained for my services, that in the present circumstances of our country, you will not disapprove my determination to retire.

The impressions, with which I first undertook the arduous trust, were explained on the proper occasion.—In the discharge of this trust, I will only say, that I have, with good intentions, contributed towards the organization and administration of the government, the best exertions of which a very fallible judgment was capable.—Not unconscious, in the outset, of the inferiority of my qualifications, experience in my own eyes, perhaps still more in the eyes of others, has strengthened the motives to diffidence of myself; and every day the increasing weight of years admonishes me more and more, that the shade of retirement is as necessary to me as it will be welcome.—Satisfied, that, if any circumstances have given peculiar value to my services, they were temporary, I have the consolation to believe, that, while choice and prudence invite me to quit the political scene, patriotism does not forbid it. . . .

Here, perhaps, I ought to stop.—But a solicitude for your welfare, which cannot end but with my life, and the apprehension of danger, natural to that solicitude, urge me on an occasion like the present, to offer to your solemn contemplation, and to recommend to your frequent review, some sentiments; which are the results of much reflection, of no inconsiderable observation, and which appear to me all-important to the permanency of your felicity as a People.— These will be offered to you with the more freedom, as you can only see in them the disinterested warnings of a parting friend, who can possibly have no personal motive to bias his counsels.—Nor can I forget, as an encouragement to it your indulgent reception of my sentiments on a former and not dissimilar occasion.

Interwoven as is the love of liberty with every ligament of your hearts, no recommendation of mine is necessary to fortify or confirm the attachment.—

The Unity of Government which constitutes you one people, is also now dear to you.—It is justly so;—for it is a main Pillar in the Edifice of your real independence; the support of your tranquility at home; your peace abroad; of your safety; of your prosperity; of that very Liberty, which you so highly prize.— But as it is easy to foresee, that from different causes, and from different quarters, much pains will be taken, many artifices employed, to weaken in your minds the conviction of this truth;—as this is the point in your political fortress against which the batteries of internal and external enemies will be most constantly and actively (though often covertly and insidiously) directed, it is of infinite moment, that you should properly estimate the immense value of your national Union to your collective and individual happiness;—that you should cherish a cordial, habitual, and immoveable attachment to it; accustoming yourselves to think and speak of it as of the Palladium of your political safety and prosperity; watching for its preservation with jealous anxiety; discountenancing whatever may suggest even a suspicion that it can in any event be abandoned, and indignantly frowning upon the first dawning of every attempt to alienate any portion of our Country from the rest, or to enfeeble the sacred ties which now link together the various parts. . . .

. . . Let me now . . . warn you in the most solemn manner against the baneful effects of the Spirit of Party, generally.

This Spirit, unfortunately, is inseparable from our nature, having its root in the strongest passions of the human mind.—It exists under different shapes in all Governments, more or less stifled, controuled, or repressed; but, in those of the popular form, it is seen in its greatest rankness, and is truly their worst enemy. . . .

It serves always to distract the Public Councils, and enfeeble the Public administration.—It agitates the community with ill-founded jealousies and false alarms, kindles the animosity of one part against another, foments occasionally riot and insurrection.—It opens the doors to foreign influence and corruption, which find a facilitated access to the Government itself through the channels of party passions. Thus the policy and the will of one country, are subjected to the policy and will of another.

There is an opinion that parties in free countries are useful checks upon the Administration of the Government, and serve to keep alive the Spirit of Liberty.—This within certain limits is probably true—and in Governments of a Monarchical cast, Patriotism may look with indulgence, if not with favour, upon the spirit of party.—But in those of the popular character, in Governments purely elective, it is a spirit not to be encouraged.—From their natural tendency, it is certain there will always be enough of that spirit for every salutary purpose,—and there being constant danger of excess, the effort ought to be, by force of public opinion, to mitigate and assuage it.—A fire not to be quenched; it demands a uniform vigilance to prevent its bursting into a flame, lest, instead of warning, it should consume. . . .

Observe good faith and justice towards all Nations. Cultivate peace and harmony with all.—Religion and Morality enjoin this conduct; and can it be that good policy does not equally enjoin it?—It will be worthy of a free, enlightened, and, at no distant period, a great nation, to give to mankind the magnanimous and too novel example of a People always guided by an exalted justice and benevolence.—Who can doubt that in the course of time and things, the fruits of such a plan would richly repay any temporary advantages, which might be lost by a steady adherence to it? Can it be, that Providence has not connected the permanent felicity of a Nation with its virtue? The experiment, at least, is recommended by every sentiment which ennobles human nature.—Alas! is it rendered impossible by its vices?

In the execution of such a plan nothing is more essential than that permanent, inveterate antipathies against particular nations and passionate attachments for others should be excluded; and that in place of them just and amicable feelings towards all should be cultivated.—The Nation, which indulges towards another an habitual hatred or an habitual fondness, is in some degree a slave. It is a slave to its animosity or to its affection, either of which is sufficient to lead it astray from its duty and its interest.—Antipathy in one nation against another disposes each more readily to offer insult and injury, to lay hold of slight causes of umbrage, and to be haughty and intractable, when accidental or trifling occasions of dispute occur.—Hence frequent collisions, obstinate, envenomed and bloody contests.—The Nation promoted by ill-will and resentment sometimes impels to War the Government, contrary to the best calculations of policy.—The Government sometimes participates in the national propensity, and adopts through passion what reason would reject;—at other times, it makes the animosity of the Nation subservient to projects of hostility instigated by pride, ambition, and other sinister and pernicious motives.—The peace often, sometimes perhaps the Liberty, of Nations has been the victim. . . .

The great rule of conduct for us, in regard to foreign Nations, is, in extending our commercial relations, to have with them as little *Political* connection as possible.—So far as we have already formed engagements, let them be fulfilled with perfect good faith.—Here let us stop. . . .

In offering to you, my Countrymen, these counsels of an old and affectionate friend, I dare not hope they will make the strong and lasting impression, I could wish,—that they will controul the usual current of the passions, or prevent our Nation from running the course which has hitherto marked the destiny of Nations.—But if I may even flatter myself, that they may be productive of some partial benefit; some occasional good; that they may now and then recur to moderate the fury of party spirit, to warn against the mischiefs of foreign intrigue, to guard against the impostures of pretended patriotism, this hope will be a full recompense for the solicitude for your welfare, by which they have been dictated.—

How far in the discharge of my official duties, I have been guided by the principles which have been delineated, the public Records and other evidences of my conduct must witness to You, and to the World.—To myself, the assurance of my own conscience is, that I have at least believed myself to be guided by them. . . .

. . . With me, a predominant motive has been to endeavour to gain time to our country to settle and mature its yet recent institutions, and to progress without interruption to that degree of strength and consistency, which is necessary to give it, humanly speaking, the command of its own fortunes.

Though, in reviewing the incidents of my Administration, I am unconscious of intentional error—I am nevertheless too sensible of my defects not to think it probable that I may have committed many errors.—Whatever they may be I fervently beseech the Almighty to avert or mitigate the evils to which they may tend.—I shall also carry with me the hope that my country will never cease to view them with indulgence; and that after forty-five years of my life dedicated to its service, with an upright zeal, the faults of incompetent abilities will be consigned to oblivion, as myself must soon be to the mansions of rest.

Relying on its kindness in this as in other things, and actuated by that fervent love towards it, which is so natural to a man, who views in it the native soil of himself and his progenitors for several generations;—I anticipate with pleasing expectation that retreat, in which I promise myself to realize, without alloy, the sweet enjoyment of partaking, in the midst of my fellow-citizens, the benign influence of good Laws under a free Government,—the ever favourite object of my heart, and the happy reward, as I trust, of our mutual cares, labours, and dangers.

# Thomas Jefferson's
# First Inaugural Address (1801)

Despite George Washington's warnings about the dangers of party strife, his retirement from the presidency in 1797 loosed spirits of angry partisanship in the land. The Federalist party, which won the election of 1796, passed laws (notably the Alien and Sedition acts of 1798) to stifle public criticism of the government and thus undermine the opposition Democratic-Republican party. In response, the Democratic-Republicans quickly passed resolutions in Kentucky and Virginia to deny the federal government's right to impose its laws on resisting states.

In a rematch of the 1796 presidential election, Thomas Jefferson, the Democratic-Republican candidate, ran against the Federalist president John Adams in 1800—this time Jefferson won. But the very act of tallying the votes aggravated partisan tensions. Under the Constitution, electors did not vote separately for president and vice president; instead, they cast two votes for president, with the candidate who received the most electoral votes elected as president and the runner-up as vice president. The anomalous consequence of this system in 1800 was that when all seventy-three Democratic-Republican electors cast their two votes for Jefferson and for Aaron Burr of New York, the party's vice-presidential nominee, the result was recorded as a tie vote for president

between Jefferson and Burr.

Constitutionally, the House of Representatives is charged to choose the president in the event of a tie vote. Federalist mischief-makers, who still had a majority in the House, delayed Jefferson's election through thirty-six ballots. Finally, at the behest of Federalist leader Alexander Hamilton, who feared for both the reputation of his party and the stability of the still-fragile constitutional government he had worked so hard to help create, the House chose Jefferson.

Under the circumstances, the very fact of Jefferson's inaugural address on March 4, 1801, was significant—it marked the first peaceful transfer of power from one political party to another in the new nation. (It also was the first inauguration to take place in the new capital city of Washington.)

In addition to the occasion itself, however, Jefferson's address was significant because of what he said. Resisting the temptation to proclaim a partisan triumph, the new president insisted that "every difference of opinion is not a difference of principle. We have called by different names brethren of the same principle. We are all Republicans, we are all Federalists."

As president, Jefferson worked to undo some Federalist policies (the Alien and Sedition acts were repealed, for example), but he preserved many *others. His administration is best remembered for the Louisiana Purchase of 1803, a remarkable assertion of presidential power that nearly doubled the size of the United States by acquiring French territory west of the Appalachian Mountains. Jefferson retired as president in 1809, stating publicly that no president should serve more than two terms.*

*In 1804 Congress passed and the states ratified the Twelfth Amendment, which separated the voting for president and vice president. The amendment preserved the electoral college but ensured that no recurrence of the 1800 election could take place.*    ~

Friends and Fellow-Citizens:

Called upon to undertake the duties of the first executive office of our country, I avail myself of the presence of that portion of my fellow-citizens which is here assembled to express my grateful thanks for the favor with which they have been pleased to look toward me, to declare a sincere consciousness that the task is above my talents, and that I approach it with those anxious and awful presentiments which the greatness of the charge and the weakness of my powers so justly inspire. A rising nation, spread over a wide and fruitful land, traversing all the seas with the rich productions of their industry, engaged in commerce with nations who feel power and forget right, advancing rapidly to destinies beyond the reach of mortal eye—when I contemplate these transcendent objects, and see the honor, the happiness, and the hopes of this beloved country committed to the issue and the auspices of this day, I shrink from the contemplation, and humble myself before the magnitude of the undertaking. Utterly, indeed, should I despair did not the presence of many whom I here see remind me that in the other high authorities provided by our

Constitution I shall find resources of wisdom, of virtue, and of zeal on which to rely under all difficulties. To you, then, gentleman, who are charged with the sovereign functions of legislation, and to those associated with you, I look with encouragement for that guidance and support which may enable us to steer with safety the vessel in which we are all embarked amidst the conflicting elements of a troubled world.

During the contest of opinion through which we have passed the animation of discussions and of exertions has sometimes worn an aspect which might impose on strangers unused to think freely and to speak and to write what they think; but this being now decided by the voice of the nation, announced according to the rules of the Constitution, all will, of course, arrange themselves under the will of the law, and unite in common efforts for the common good. All, too, will bear in mind this sacred principle, that though the will of the majority is in all cases to prevail, that will to be rightful must be reasonable; that the minority possess their equal rights, which equal law must protect, and to violate would be oppression. Let us, then, fellow-citizens, unite with one heart and one mind. Let us restore to social intercourse that harmony and affection without which liberty and even life itself are but dreary things. And let us reflect that, having banished from our land that religious intolerance under which mankind so long bled and suffered, we have yet gained little if we countenance a political intolerance as despotic, as wicked, and capable of as bitter and bloody persecutions. During the throes and convulsions of the ancient world, during the agonizing spasms of infuriated man, seeking through blood and slaughter his long-lost liberty, it was not wonderful that the agitation of the billows should reach even this distant and peaceful shore; that this should be more felt and feared by some and less by others, and should divide opinions as to measures of safety. But every difference of opinion is not a difference of principle. We have called by different names brethren of the same principle. We are all Republicans, we are all Federalists. If there be any among us who would wish to dissolve this Union or to change its republican form, let them stand undisturbed as monuments of the safety with which error of opinion may be tolerated where reason is left free to combat it. I know, indeed, that some honest men fear that a republican government can not be strong, that this Government is not strong enough; but would the honest patriot, in the full tide of successful experiment, abandon a government which has so far kept us free and firm on the theoretic and visionary fear that this Government, the world's best hope, may by possibility want energy to preserve itself? I trust not. I believe this, on the contrary, the strongest Government on earth. I believe it the only one where every man, at the call of the law, would fly to the standard of the law, and would meet invasions of the public order as his own personal concern. Sometimes it is said that man can not be trusted with the government of himself. Can he, then, be trusted with the government of others? Or have we found angels in the forms of kings to govern him? Let history answer this question.

Let us, then, with courage and confidence pursue our own Federal and Republican principles, our attachment to union and representative government. Kindly separated by nature and a wide ocean from the exterminating havoc of one quarter of the globe; too high-minded to endure the degradations of the others; possessing a chosen country, with room enough for our descendants to the thousandth and thousandth generation; entertaining a due sense of our equal right to the use of our faculties, to the acquisitions of our own industry, to honor and confidence from our fellow-citizens, resulting not from birth, but from our actions and their sense of them; enlightened by a benign religion, professed, indeed, and practiced in various forms, yet all of them inculcating honesty, truth, temperance, gratitude, and the love of man; acknowledging and adoring an overruling Providence, which by all its dispensations proves that it delights in the happiness of man here and his greater happiness hereafter—with all these blessings, what more is necessary to make us a happy and a prosperous people? Still one thing more, fellow-citizens—a wise and frugal Government, which shall restrain men from injuring one another, shall leave them otherwise free to regulate their own pursuits of industry and improvement, and shall not take from the mouth of labor the bread it has earned. This is the sum of good government, and this is necessary to close the circle of our felicities.

About to enter, fellow-citizens, on the exercise of duties which comprehend everything dear and valuable to you, it is proper you should understand what I deem the essential principles of our Government, and consequently those which ought to shape its Administration. I will compress them within the narrowest compass they will bear, stating the general principle, but not all its limitations. Equal and exact justice to all men, of whatever state or persuasion, religious or political; peace, commerce, and honest friendship with all nations, entangling alliances with none; the support of the State governments in all their rights, as the most competent administrations for our domestic concerns and the surest bulwarks against antirepublican tendencies; the preservation of the General Government in its whole constitutional vigor, as the sheet anchor of our peace at home and safety abroad; a jealous care of the right of election by the people—a mild and safe corrective of abuses which are lopped by the sword of revolution where peaceable remedies are unprovided; absolute acquiescence in the decisions of the majority, the vital principle of republics, from which is not appeal but to force, the vital principle and immediate parent of despotism; a well-disciplined militia, our best reliance in peace and for the first moments of war, till regulars may relieve them; the supremacy of the civil over the military authority; economy in the public expense, that labor may be lightly burthened; the honest payment of our debts and sacred preservation of the public faith; encouragement of agriculture, and of commerce as its handmaid; the diffusion of information and arraignment of all abuses at the bar of the public reason; freedom of religion; freedom of the press, and freedom of person under the protection of the habeas corpus, and trial by juries impartially selected. These principles form the bright constellation which has gone before us and guided our steps through an age of revolution and reformation. The wisdom of our sages and blood of our heroes have been devoted to their attainment. They should be the creed of our political faith, the text of civic instruction, the touchstone by which to try the services of those we trust; and should we wander from them in moments of error or of alarm, let us hasten to retrace our steps and to regain the road which alone leads to peace, liberty, and safety.

I repair, then, fellow-citizens, to the post you have assigned me. With experience enough in subordinate offices to have seen the difficulties of this the greatest of all, I have learnt to expect that it will rarely fall to the lot of imperfect man to retire from this station with the reputation and the favor which bring him into it. Without pretensions to that high confidence you reposed in our first and greatest revolutionary character, whose preëminent services had entitled him to the first place in his country's love and destined for him the fairest page in the volume of faithful history, I ask so much confidence only as may give firmness and effect to the legal administration of your affairs. I shall often go wrong through defect of judgment. When right, I shall often be thought wrong by those whose positions will not command a view of the whole ground. I ask your indulgence for my own errors, which will never be intentional, and your support against the errors of others, who may condemn what they would not if seen in all its parts. The approbation implied by your suffrage is a great consolation to me for the past, and my future solicitude will be to retain the good opinion of those who have bestowed it in advance, to conciliate that of others by doing them all the good in my power, and to be instrumental to the happiness and freedom of all.

Relying, then, on the patronage of your good will, I advance with obedience to the work, ready to retire from it whenever you become sensible how much better choice it is in your power to make. And may that Infinite Power which rules the destinies of the universe lead our councils to what is best, and give them a favorable issue for your peace and prosperity.

# James Madison's
# War Message to Congress (1812)

The Constitution empowers the president to be "the Commander in Chief of the Army and Navy of the United States, and of the Militia of the several States," but entrusts Congress with the responsibilities to "declare War," "raise and support Armies," and "provide and maintain a Navy." The War of 1812 was the first declared war in U.S. history. In June 1812, Congress voted by a margin of 79-49 in the House of Representatives (June 4) and 19-13 in the Senate (June 18) to go to war with Great Britain. Congress's action followed quickly on the heels of President James Madison's June 1 war message, which reviewed the history of U.S. grievances against Great Britain and encouraged Congress to consider and make such a declaration.

War sentiment had been aroused by British seizure of American ships and impressment (that is, conscription) of their crews, by evidence that the British were supplying hostile Indians on the American frontier with arms, and (to some degree) by a U.S. desire to acquire territory in British Canada and Spanish Florida. "War Hawks" (Democratic-Republican members of Congress from the South and West whose constituents were suffering from Indian attacks and falling agricultural prices) fanned the flames of anti-British feeling. New England Federalists, traditionally pro-British and commercially tied to Great Britain through shipping and trading, opposed war but were outnumbered.

Madison, himself a Democratic-Republican, was reluctant to accede to the congressional pressure to go to war. But when his diplomatic efforts with Great Britain failed and intraparty pressures jeopardized his renomination for president in 1812, Madison sent the war message to Congress.

The bulk of Madison's war message consisted of a close review of British abuses and of his administration's unsuccessful efforts to bring them to an end through diplomacy. The message concluded by saying that although Madison was "recommending" that war be declared, he regarded war making as "a solemn question which the Constitution wisely confides to the legislative department of the Government." Subsequent presidential war messages, which preceded the Mexican War (1846), the Spanish-American War (1898), World War I (1917), and World War II (1941), were less explicitly deferential to Congress's prerogatives in this regard than the message written by the "father of the Constitution."

The War of 1812 did not go well for the United States. Internally divided and militarily unprepared, the United States suffered a string of military defeats, including the capture and burn-

*ing of Washington, D.C., in August
1814. Madison, who was humiliatingly
forced to flee the capital for three days
until the British moved on, was widely
regarded, both by his contemporaries
and by historians, as an inept commander in chief. The war was concluded by the Treaty of Ghent on December 24, 1814. The treaty did little
more than restore relations between
the United States and Great Britain to
the prewar status quo.*            ~

To the Senate and House of Representatives of the United States:

I communicate to Congress certain
documents, being a continuation of
those heretofore laid before them on the
subject of our affairs with Great
Britain.

Without going back beyond the renewal in 1803 of the war in which Great
Britain is engaged, and omitting unre-
paired wrongs of inferior magnitude,
the conduct of her Government
presents a series of acts hostile to the
United States as an independent and
neutral nation.

British cruisers have been in the continued practice of violating the American flag on the great highway of nations, and of seizing and carrying off
persons sailing under it, not in the exercise of a belligerent right founded on
the law of nations against an enemy,
but of a municipal prerogative over
British subjects. British jurisdiction is
thus extended to neutral vessels in a
situation where no laws can operate but
the law of nations and the laws of the
country to which the vessels belong, and
a self-redress is assumed which, if British subjects were wrongfully detained
and alone concerned, is that substitution of force for a resort to the responsible sovereign which falls within the definition of war. Could the seizure of
British subjects in such cases be regarded as within the exercise of a belligerent right, the acknowledged laws of

war, which forbid an article of captured
property to be adjudged without a regular investigation before a competent tribunal, would imperiously demand the
fairest trial where the sacred rights of
persons were at issue. In place of such a
trial these rights are subjected to the
will of every petty commander.

The practice, hence, is so far from
affecting British subjects alone that,
under the pretext of searching for these,
thousands of American citizens, under
the safeguard of public law and of their
national flag, have been torn from their
country and from everything dear to
them; have been dragged on board ships
of war of a foreign nation and exposed,
under the severities of their discipline,
to be exiled to the most distant and
deadly climes, to risk their lives in the
battles of their oppressors, and to be
the melancholy instruments of taking
away those of their own brethren.

Against this crying enormity, which
Great Britain would be so prompt to
avenge if committed against herself, the
United States have in vain exhausted
remonstrances and expostulations, and
that no proof might be wanting of their
conciliatory dispositions, and no pretext
left for a continuance of the practice,
the British Government was formally
assured of the readiness of the United
States to enter into arrangements such
as could not be rejected if the recovery
of British subjects were the real and the
role object. The communication passed
without effect.

British cruisers have been in the
practice also of violating the rights and
the peace of our coasts. They hover over
and harass our entering and departing
commerce. To the most insulting pretensions they have added the most lawless proceedings in our very harbors,
and have wantonly spilt American
blood within the sanctuary of our territorial jurisdiction. The principles and
rules enforced by that nation, when a
neutral nation, against armed vessels of
belligerents hovering near her coasts

and disturbing her commerce are well known. When called on, nevertheless, by the United States to punish the greater offenses committed by her own vessels, her Government has bestowed on their commanders additional marks of honor and confidence.

Under pretended blockades, without the presence of an adequate force and sometimes without the practicability of applying one, our commerce has been plundered in every sea, the great staples of our country have been cut off from their legitimate markets, and a destructive blow aimed at our agricultural and maritime interests. In aggravation of these predatory measures they have been considered as in force from the dates of their notification, a retrospective effect being thus added, as has been done in other important cases, to the unlawfulness of the course pursued. And to render the outrage the more signal these mock blockades have been reiterated and enforced in the face of official communications from the British Government declaring as the true definition of a legal blockade "that particular ports must be actually invested and previous warning given to vessels bound to them not to enter."

Not content with these occasional expedients for laying waste our neutral trade, the cabinet of Britain resorted at length to the sweeping system of blockades, under the name of orders in council, which has been molded and managed as might best suit its political views, its commercial jealousies, or the avidity of British cruisers.

To our remonstrances against the complicated and transcendent injustice of this innovation the first reply was that the orders were reluctantly adopted by Great Britain as a necessary retaliation on decrees of her enemy proclaiming a general blockade of the British Isles at a time when the naval force of that enemy dared not issue from his own ports. She was reminded without effect that her own prior blockades, unsupported by an adequate naval force actually applied and continued, were a bar to this plea; that executed edicts against millions of our property could not be retaliation on edicts confessedly impossible to be executed; that retaliation, to be just, should fall on the party setting the guilty example, not on an innocent party which was not even chargeable with an acquiescence in it.

When deprived of this flimsy veil for a prohibition of our trade with her enemy by the repeal of his prohibition of our trade with Great Britain, her cabinet, instead of a corresponding repeal or a practical discontinuance of its orders, formally avowed a determination to persist in them against the United States until the markets of her enemy should be laid open to British products, thus asserting an obligation on a neutral power to require one belligerent to encourage by its internal regulations the trade of another belligerent, contradicting her own practice toward all nations, in peace as well as in war, and betraying the insincerity of those professions which inculcated a belief that, having restored to her orders with regret, she was anxious to find an occasion for putting an end to them.

Abandoning still more all respect for the neutral rights of the United States and for its own consistency, the British Government now demands as prerequisites to a repeal of its orders as they relate to the United States that a formality should be observed in the repeal of the French decrees nowise necessary to their termination nor exemplified by British usage, and that the French repeal, besides including that portion of the decrees which operates within a territorial jurisdiction, as well as that which operates on the high seas, against the commerce of the United States should not be a single and special repeal in relation to the United States, but should be extended to whatever other neutral nations unconnected with them may be affected by those decrees. And as an additional insult, they are called on for a formal disavowal of conditions and pretensions advanced by the French Government for which the United States are so far from having made themselves responsible that, in official explanations which have been published to the world, and in a correspondence of the American minister at London with the British minister for foreign affairs such a responsibility was explicitly and emphatically disclaimed.

It has become, indeed, sufficiently certain that the commerce of the United States is to be sacrificed, not as interfering with the belligerent rights of Great Britain; not as supplying the wants of her enemies, which she herself supplies; but as interfering with the monopoly which she covets for her own commerce and navigation. She carries on a war against the lawful commerce of a friend that she may the better carry on a commerce with an enemy—a commerce polluted by the forgeries and perjuries which are for the most part the only passports by which it can succeed.

Anxious to make every experiment short of the last resort of injured nations, the United States have withheld from Great Britain, under successive modifications, the benefits of a free intercourse with their market, the loss of which could not but outweigh the profits accruing from her restrictions of our commerce with other nations. And to entitle these experiments to the more favorable consideration they were so framed as to enable her to place her adversary under the exclusive operation of them. To these appeals her Government has been equally inflexible, as if willing to make sacrifices of every sort rather than yield to the claims of justice or renounce the errors of a false pride. Nay, so far were the attempts carried to overcome the attachment of the British cabinet to its unjust edicts that it received every encouragement within the competency of the executive branch of

our Government to expect that a repeal of them would be followed by a war between the United States and France, unless the French edicts should also be repealed. Even this communication, although silencing forever the plea of a disposition in the United States to acquiesce in those edicts originally the sole plea for them, received no attention.

If no other proof existed of a predetermination of the British Government against a repeal of its orders, it might be found in the correspondence of the minister plenipotentiary of the United States at London and the British secretary for foreign affairs in 1810, on the question whether the blockade of May, 1806, was considered as in force or as not in force. It had been ascertained that the French Government, which urged this blockade as the ground of its Berlin decree, was willing in the event of its removal to repeal that decree, which, being followed by alternate repeals of the other offensive edicts, might abolish the whole system on both sides. This inviting opportunity for accomplishing an object so important to the United States, and professed so often to be the desire of both the belligerents, was made known to the British Government. As that Government admits that an actual application of an adequate force is necessary to the existence of a legal blockade, and it was notorious that if such a force had ever been applied its long discontinuance had annulled the blockade in question, there could be no sufficient objection on the part of Great Britain to a formal revocation of it, and no imaginable objection to a declaration of the fact that the blockade did not exist. The declaration would have been consistent with her avowed principles of blockade, and would have enabled the United States to demand from France the pledged repeal of her decrees, either with success, in which case the way would have been opened for a general repeal of the belligerent edicts, or without success, in which case the United States would have been justified in turning their measures exclusively against France. The British Government would, however, neither rescind the blockade nor declare its nonexistence, nor permit its nonexistence to be inferred and affirmed by the American plenipotentiary. On the contrary, by representing the blockade to be comprehended in the orders in council, the United States were compelled so to regard it in their subsequent proceedings.

There was a period when a favorable change in the policy of the British cabinet was justly considered as established. The minister plenipotentiary of His Britannic Majesty here proposed an adjustment of the differences more immediately endangering the harmony of the two countries. The proposition was accepted with the promptitude and cordiality corresponding with the invariable professions of this Government. A foundation appeared to be laid for a sincere and lasting reconciliation. The prospect, however, quickly vanished. The whole proceeding was disavowed by the British Government without any explanations which could at that time repress the belief that the disavowal proceeded from a spirit of hostility to the commercial rights and prosperity of the United States; and it has since come into proof that at the very moment when the public minister was holding the language of friendship and inspiring confidence in the sincerity of the negotiation with which he was charged a secret agent of his Government was employed in intrigues having for their object a subversion of our Government and a dismemberment of our happy union.

In reviewing the conduct of Great Britain toward the United States our attention is necessarily drawn to the warfare just renewed by the savages on one of our extensive frontiers—a warfare which is known to spare neither age nor sex and to be distinguished by features peculiarly shocking to humanity. It is difficult to account for the activity and combinations which have for some time been developing themselves among tribes in constant intercourse with British traders and garrisons without connecting their hostility with that influence and without recollecting the authenticated examples of such interpositions heretofore furnished by the officers and agents of that Government.

Such is the spectacle of injuries and indignities which have been heaped on our country, and such the crisis which its unexampled forbearance and conciliatory efforts have not been able to avert. It might at least have been expected that an enlightened nation, if less urged by moral obligations or invited by friendly dispositions on the part of the United States, would have found in its true interest alone a sufficient motive to respect their rights and their tranquillity on the high seas; that an enlarged policy would have favored that free and general circulation of commerce in which the British nation is at all times interested, and which in times of war is the best alleviation of its calamities to herself as well as to other belligerents; and more especially that the British cabinet would not, for the sake of a precarious and surreptitious intercourse with hostile markets, have persevered in a course of measures which necessarily put at hazard the invaluable market of a great and growing country, disposed to cultivate the mutual advantages of an active commerce.

Other counsels have prevailed. Our moderation and conciliation have had no other effect than to encourage perseverance and to enlarge pretensions. We behold our seafaring citizens still the daily victims of lawless violence, committed on the great common and highway of nations, even within sight of the country which owes them protection. We behold our vessels freighted with the products of our soil and industry, or returning with the honest proceeds of them, wrested from their lawful destinations, confiscated by prize courts no longer the organs of public law but the instruments of arbitrary edicts, and their unfortunate crews dispersed and lost, or forced or inveigled in British ports into British fleets, whilst arguments are employed in support of these aggressions which have no foundation but in a principle equally supporting a claim to regulate our external commerce in all cases whatsoever.

We behold, in fine, on the side of Great Britain a state of war against the United States, and on the side of the United States a state of peace toward Great Britain.

Whether the United States shall continue passive under these progressive usurpations and these accumulating wrongs, or, opposing force to force in defense of their national rights, shall commit a just cause into the hands of the Almighty Disposer of Events, avoiding all connections which might entangle it in the contest or views of other powers, and preserving a constant readiness to concur in an honorable reestablishment of peace and friendship, is a solemn question which the Constitution wisely confides to the legislative department of the Government. In recommending it to their early deliberations I am happy in the assurance that the decision will be worthy the enlightened and patriotic councils of a virtuous, a free, and a powerful nation.

Having presented this view of the relations of the United States with Great Britain and of the solemn alternative growing out of them, I proceed to remark that the communications last made to Congress on the subject of our relations with France will have shewn that since the revocation of her decrees, as they violated the neutral rights of the United States, her Government has authorized illegal captures by its privateers and public ships, and that other outrages have been practiced on our vessels and our citizens. It will have been seen also that no indemnity had been provided or satisfactorily pledged for the extensive spoliations committed under the violent and retrospective orders of the French Government against the property of our citizens seized within the jurisdiction of France. I abstain at this time from recommending to the consideration of Congress definitive measures with respect to that nation, in the expectation that the result of unclosed discussions between our minister plenipotentiary at Paris and the French Government will speedily enable Congress to decide with greater advantage on the course due to the rights, the interests, and the honor of our country.

JAMES MADISON

# The Monroe Doctrine (1823)

President James Monroe, a Democratic-Republican from Virginia who
was elected president in 1816 and reelected without opposition in 1820, is
best known for the doctrine that bears
his name. Like President James Madison before him, Monroe faced an asser-
tive Congress that dominated his administration (and those of most
nineteenth-century presidents) in matters of domestic policy. In foreign affairs, however, Monroe reinforced the
constitutional right of the president to
take the initiative in setting U.S.
policy.

The Monroe Doctrine was proclaimed in response to two foreign policy disputes in which the United States
was involved during the early 1820s.
The first was a Russian claim of land
along the Pacific coast, from the Bering
Strait south to some unspecified location along the shore of the Oregon
territory. The other was a variety of
rumored European plans, most of them
involving France, to recolonize the
newly independent nations of previously Spanish South America.

After frequent consultations with the
cabinet and with former presidents
Madison and Thomas Jefferson during
the fall of 1823, Monroe and Secretary
of State John Quincy Adams resolved
to declare the "new world" of the
Americas off-limits to any attempts at
colonization by the "old world" of the
European powers.

The Monroe Doctrine was included
as part of Monroe's long annual message to Congress on December 23, 1823.
No consultation with Congress preceded the declaration, and some legislators believed that Monroe had over-
stepped the powers of his office by
unilaterally enunciating a major foreign policy on behalf of the U.S. government. Yet the doctrine stood as an
accomplished fact: Congress took no
action either to affirm or to repudiate
it. Public reaction around the country
was generally positive.

The Monroe Doctrine had little immediate practical effect. As it turned
out, Europe was not planning to recolonize South America; as for the Rus-
sians, they continued for a time their
efforts in the Pacific Northwest. Nonetheless, the doctrine was widely understood, both at home and abroad, to be a
bold assertion of U.S. government
power and of presidential control of
foreign policy within that government.

Around the turn of the century, the
Monroe Doctrine was officially endorsed by Congress (1899) and expanded by President Theodore Roosevelt. In 1904 Roosevelt declared in his
annual message to Congress that the
United States had the right to intervene if "chronic wrongdoing or impotence" in a country of the Western
Hemisphere seemed to require such in-

*tervention. Protest from Latin America itself led to the withdrawal of the Roosevelt Corollary in 1928.*

*In recent years, the Monroe Doctrine has seldom been explicitly invoked: even when Soviet nuclear missiles were introduced into Cuba in 1962, President John F. Kennedy demanded their withdrawal on other diplomatic grounds. (See "The Cuban Missile Crisis: President Kennedy's Letter to Khrushchev," p. 359.) The administration of President Ronald Reagan actually tilted toward Great Britain in its 1982 war with Argentina for possession of the Falkland Islands. Nonetheless, the United States has continued to regard Latin America as a sphere of influence, interfering both in its domestic politics and in its relations with other parts of the world when deemed necessary to protect American interests.* ～

Fellow Citizens of the Senate and House of Representatives:

. . . At the proposal of the Russian Imperial Government, made through the minister of the Emperor residing here, a full power and instructions have been transmitted to the minister of the United States at St. Petersburg to arrange by amicable negotiation the respective rights and interests of the two nations on the northwest coast of this continent. A similar proposal had been made by His Imperial Majesty to the Government of Great Britain, which has likewise been acceded to. The Government of the United States has been desirous by this friendly proceeding of manifesting the great value which they have invariably attached to the friendship of the Emperor and their solicitude to cultivate the best understanding with his Government. In the discussions to which this interest has given rise and in the arrangements by which they may terminate the occasion has been judged proper for asserting, as a principle in which the rights and interests of the

United States are involved, that the American continents, by the free and independent condition which they have assumed and maintain, are henceforth not to be considered as subjects for future colonization by any European powers. . .

It was stated at the commencement of the last session that a great effort was then making in Spain and Portugal to improve the condition of the people of those countries, and that it appeared to be conducted with extraordinary moderation. It need scarcely be remarked that the result has been so far very different from what was then anticipated. Of events in that quarter of the globe, with which we have so much intercourse and from which we derive our origin, we have always been anxious and interested spectators. The citizens of the United States cherish sentiments the most friendly in favor of the liberty and happiness of their fellow-men on that side of the Atlantic. In the wars of the European powers in matters relating to themselves we have never taken any part, nor does it comport with our policy to do so. It is only when our rights are invaded or seriously menaced that we resent injuries or make preparation for our defense. With the movements in this hemisphere we are of necessity more immediately connected, and by causes which must be obvious to all enlightened and impartial observers. The political system of the allied powers is essentially different in this respect from that of America. This difference proceeds from that which exists in their respective Governments; and to the defense of our own, which has been achieved by the loss of so much blood and treasure, and matured by the wisdom of their most enlightened citizens, and under which we have enjoyed unexampled felicity, this whole nation is devoted. We owe it, therefore, to candor and to the amicable relations existing between the United States and those powers to declare that we should consider any attempt on their part to extend their system to any portion of this hemisphere as dangerous to our peace and safety. With the existing colonies or dependencies of any European power we have not interfered and shall not interfere. But with the Governments who have declared their independence and maintained it, and whose independence we have, on great consideration and on just principles, acknowledged, we could not view any interposition for the purpose of oppressing them, or controlling in any other manner their destiny, by any European power in any other light than as the manifestation of an unfriendly disposition toward the United States. In the war between those new Governments and Spain we declared our neutrality at the time of their recognition, and to this we have adhered, and shall continue to adhere, provided no change shall occur which, in the judgment of the competent authorities of this Government, shall make a corresponding change on the part of the United States indispensable to their security.

The late events in Spain and Portugal shew that Europe is still unsettled. Of this important fact no stronger proof can be adduced than that the allied powers should have thought it proper, on any principle satisfactory to themselves, to have interposed by force in the internal concerns of Spain. To what extent such interposition may be carried, on the same principle, is a question in which all independent powers whose governments differ from theirs are interested, even those most remote, and surely none more so than the United States. Our policy in regard to Europe, which was adopted at an early stage of the wars which have so long agitated that quarter of the globe, nevertheless remains the same, which is, not to interfere in the internal concerns of any of its powers; to consider the government de facto as the legitimate government for us; to cultivate friendly

relations with it, and to preserve those relations by a frank, firm, and manly policy, meeting in all instances the just claims of every power, submitting to injuries from none. But in regard to those continents circumstances are eminently and conspicuously different. It is impossible that the allied powers should extend their political system to any portion of either continent without endangering our peace and happiness; nor can anyone believe that our southern brethren, if left to themselves, would adopt it of their own accord. It is equally impossible, therefore, that we should behold such interposition in any form with indifference. If we look to the comparative strength and resources of Spain and those new Governments, and their distance from each other, it must be obvious that she can never subdue them. It is still the true policy of the United States to leave the parties to themselves, in the hope that other powers will pursue the same course.

If we compare the present condition of our Union with its actual state at the close of our Revolution, the history of the world furnishes no example of a progress in improvement in all the important circumstances which constitute the happiness of a nation which bears any resemblance to it. At the first epoch our population did not exceed 3,000,000. By the last census it amounted to about 10,000,000, and, what is more extraordinary, it is almost altogether native, for the immigration from other countries has been inconsiderable. At the first epoch half the territory within our acknowledged limits was uninhabited and a wilderness. Since then new territory has been acquired of vast extent, comprising within it many rivers, particularly the Mississippi, the navigation of which to the ocean was of the highest importance to the original States. Over this territory our population has expanded in every direction, and new States have been established almost equal in number to those which formed the first bond of our Union. This expansion of our population and accession of new States to our Union have had the happiest effect on all its highest interests. That it has eminently augmented our resources and added to our strength and respectability as a power is admitted by all. But it is not in these important circumstances only that this happy effect is felt. It is manifest that by enlarging the basis of our system and increasing the number of States the system itself has been greatly strengthened in both its branches. Consolidation and disunion have thereby been rendered equally impracticable. Each Government, confiding in its own strength, has less to apprehend from the other, and in consequence each, enjoying a greater freedom of action, is rendered more efficient for all the purposes for which it was instituted. It is unnecessary to treat here of the vast improvement made in the system itself by the adoption of this Constitution and of its happy effect in elevating the character and in protecting the rights of the nation as well as of individuals. To what, then, do we owe these blessings? It is known to all that we derive them from the excellence of our institutions. Ought we not, then, to adopt every measure which may be necessary to perpetuate them?

JAMES MONROE.

# The Tennessee General Assembly's Protest against the Caucus System (1823)

The presidential selection process underwent some wrenching changes during the first few decades of the Constitution's existence. The delegates to the Constitutional Convention had explicitly rejected the simple expedient of having Congress elect the president, creating instead an electoral college in which the candidate who received the most electoral votes became president and the runner-up became vice president. The early rise of political parties that nominated both presidential and vice-presidential candidates upset this arrangement, causing a tie vote for president to occur between Thomas Jefferson and his running mate, Aaron Burr, in 1800 and prompting passage of the Twelfth Amendment to separate the balloting for president and vice president in 1804. (See "Thomas Jefferson's First Inaugural Address," p. 53.)

The rise of political parties also meant that a mechanism had to be developed to nominate the candidates who would represent each party in the election. Beginning in 1796, Federalist and Democratic-Republican party members in Congress met (or "caucused") separately every four years to choose their respective nominees. The Democratic-Republican caucus nominated Thomas Jefferson in 1796, 1800, and 1804, James Madison in 1808 and 1812, and James Monroe in 1816 and 1820. (It also chose their vice-presiden-

tial running mates.) The Federalist caucus nominated John Adams in 1796 and 1800 but soon fell into disuse as the party's fortunes in Congress drastically declined.

Almost from the beginning, "King Caucus," as its critics called it, was attacked by some as elitist and unrepresentative of the party rank and file. Indeed, any state or district that did not elect a party's candidate to Congress was left out of its nominating process entirely. When the Federalist party's demise before the 1820 election left the voters with only the Democratic-Republican ticket, these criticisms intensified. With just one party in the field, nomination by caucus was tantamount to election.

In late 1823, Tennessee felt particularly aggrieved by the caucus system because its candidate for president, Gen. Andrew Jackson, seemed unlikely to be nominated. On November 1, the state's General Assembly published a resolution that condemned the caucus for, among other things, violating "the spirit of the Constitution," which rejected congressional election of the president. Other states registered protests of their own.

The Democratic-Republican caucus that took place in mid-February 1824 was a disaster. Only 66 of 261 members of Congress attended. Their nominee, Secretary of the Treasury William

*Crawford of Georgia, ran a distant third in the presidential election, trailing both Jackson and Secretary of State John Quincy Adams. (Because neither Jackson, who finished first, nor Adams received a majority of electoral votes, the House of Representatives chose the winner, Adams.)*

*The 1824 election marked the demise of King Caucus. By the 1830s, political parties were nominating their candidates for president and vice president at national conventions. These conventions, consisting of delegates chosen by local party organizations all around the country, have taken place in presidential election years ever since.* ~

The General Assembly of the state of Tennessee has taken into consideration the practice which, on former occasions, has prevailed at the city of Washington, of members of the Congress of the United States meeting in caucus, and nominating persons to be voted for as President and Vice-President of the United States; and, upon the best view of the subject which this General Assembly has been able to take, it is believed that the practice of congressional nominations is a violation of the spirit of the Constitution of the United States.

That instrument provides that there shall be three separate and distinct departments of the government, and great care and caution seems to have been exercised by its framers to prevent any one department from exercising the smallest degree of influence over another; and such solicitude was felt on this subject, that, in the 2nd Section of the 2nd Article, it is expressly declared, "That no senator or representative, or person holding an office of trust or profit under the United States, shall be appointed an elector." From this provision, it is apparent that the Convention intended that the members of Congress should not be the principal and primary

agents or actors in electing the President and Vice-President of the United States; so far from it, they are expressly disqualified from being placed in a situation to vote for these high officers.

Is there not more danger of undue influence to be apprehended when the members of Congress meet in caucus and mutually and solemnly pledge themselves to support the individuals who may have the highest number of votes in such meeting than there would be in permitting them to be eligible to the appointment of electors? In the latter case, a few characters rendered ineligible by the Constitution might succeed; but, in the former, a powerful combination of influential men is formed, who may fix upon the American people their highest officers against the consent of a clear majority of the people themselves; and this may be done by the very men whom the Constitution intended to prohibit from acting on the subject.

Upon an examination of the Constitution of the United States, there is but one case in which the members of Congress are permitted to act, which is in the event of a failure to make an election by the electoral college; and then the members of the House of Representatives vote by states. With what propriety the same men, who, in the year 1825, may be called on to discharge a constitutional duty, can, in the year 1824, go into a caucus and pledge themselves to support the men then nominated, cannot be discerned, especially when it might so happen that the persons thus nominated could not, under any circumstances, obtain a single vote from the state whose members stand pledged to support them.

It is said that an election by the House of Representatives would be a dangerous occurrence which ought to be avoided. If so, let the Constitution be so changed as to avoid it; but so long as the Constitution directs one mode of electing officers, let not a different mode prevail in practice. When the history of the American government is looked into with an eye to this subject, the apprehended danger disappears. Experience long since pointed out the inconveniences of the original provision in the Constitution on this subject. An amendment, calculated, as was supposed, to remove every obstacle, was proposed by our wisest statesmen—it was adopted by the American people, and no difficulty has presented itself in subsequent practice. Shall a fear that the amendment made may fail to answer the end proposed by it induce us to adopt a course, or persist in a practice, which is manifestly an evasion of the Constitution and a direct infraction of the spirit of one of its most important provisions?

It has been said that the members of Congress in caucus only recommend to the people for whom to vote, and that such recommendation is not obligatory. This is true and clearly proves that it is a matter which does not belong to them —that, in recommending candidates, they go beyond the authority committed to them as members of Congress and thus transcend the trust delegated to them by their constituents. If their acts had any obligatory force, then the authority must be derived from some part of the Constitution of the United States and might be rightfully exercised; but when they say they only *recommend,* it is an admission, on their part, that they are acting without authority and are attempting, by a usurped influence, to effect an object not confided to them and not within their powers, even by implication.

It cannot be admitted that there is any weight in the argument drawn from the fact that both the parties, heretofore contending for the superiority in the United States, have, in former times, resorted to this practice. The actions of public or private men, heated by party zeal and struggling for ascendency and power, ought not to be urged as precedents when circumstances have

entirely changed. All political precedents are of doubtful authority and should never be permitted to pass unquestioned, unless made in good times and for laudable purposes. In palliation of the practice of resorting to caucus nominations in former times, it was said that each party must of necessity consult together in the best practicable way and select the most suitable persons from their respective parties so that the united efforts of all those composing it might be brought to bear upon their opponents. It is to be recollected that there is no danger of a departure from or violation of the Constitution, except when strong temptations are presented, and this will seldom occur, except when parties are arrayed against each other and their feelings violently excited.

The state of things, however, in the United States is entirely changed; it is no longer a selection made by members of Congress of different parties, but it is an election by the two houses of Congress, in which all the members must be permitted to attend and vote. It is not difficult to perceive that this practice may promote and place men in office who could not be elected were the constitutional mode pursued. It is placing the election of the President and Vice-President of the United States—an election in which all the states have an equal interest and equal rights—more in the power of a few of the most populous states than was contemplated by the Constitution. This practice is considered objectionable on other accounts: so long as Congress is considered as composed of the individuals on whom the election depends, the executive will is subjected to the control of that body, and it ceases, in some degree, to be a separate and independent branch of the government; and the expectation of executive patronage may have an unhappy influence on the deliberations of Congress.

Upon a review of the whole question, the following reasons which admit of much amplification and enlargement, more than has been urged in the foregoing, might be conclusively relied on to prove the impolicy and unconstitutionality of the congressional nominations of candidates for the presidency and vice-presidency of the United States: 1. A caucus nomination is against the spirit of the Constitution. 2. It is both inexpedient and impolitic. 3. Members of Congress may become the final electors and therefore ought not to prejudge the case by pledging themselves previously to support particular candidates. 4. It violates the equality intended to be secured by the Constitution to the weaker states. 5. Caucus nominations may, in time (by the interference of the states), acquire the force of precedents and become authoritative and, thereby, endanger the liberties of the American people.

This General Assembly, believing that the true spirit of the Constitution will be best preserved by leaving the election of President and Vice-President to the *people themselves,* through the medium of electors chosen by them, uninfluenced by any previous nomina-

tion made by members of Congress, have adopted the following resolutions:

1. *Resolved*, that the senators in Congress from this state be instructed, and our representatives be requested, to use their exertions to prevent a nomination being made during the next session of Congress, by the members thereof in caucus, of persons to fill the offices of President and Vice-President of the United States.

2. *Resolved*, that the General Assembly will, at its present session, divide the state into as many districts, in convenient form, as this state is entitled to electoral votes, for the purpose of choosing an elector in each to vote for the President and Vice-President of the United States.

3. *Resolved*, that the governor of this state transmit a copy of the foregoing preamble and resolutions to the executive of each of the United States, with a request that the same be laid before each of their respective legislatures.

4. *Resolved*, that the governor transmit a copy to each of the senators and representatives in Congress from this state.

# Andrew Jackson's
# First Message to Congress (1829)

Andrew Jackson may be fairly described as the first "outsider" president in U.S. history. He was the first president to lack extensive experience in national politics. Although briefly a member of Congress, he had made his reputation as the general who defeated the British in the Battle of New Orleans, the greatest U.S. victory in the War of 1812. Jackson also was a political outsider: he viewed the national government with suspicion, as a bastion of privilege for a ruling eastern and commercial elite. Finally, Jackson, a Tennessean, was the first president from west of the Appalachian Mountains. (Each of the first six presidents was from either Virginia or Massachusetts.)

In all of these characteristics, Jackson represented rising tendencies that were broadening the base of the U.S. political system. The system was becoming broader geographically: settlement in the West (the area roughly between the Appalachians and the Mississippi River) had almost doubled the number of states from thirteen in 1776 to twenty-four in 1828. The political system also was broader socially. Virtually every state had abandoned the traditional requirement that to vote one must own property. And the system had become broader politically. In the 1828 election, almost all presidential electors were selected by vote of the people, not of the state legislatures. (The Constitution allowed each state the right to choose its electors either way.) The total popular vote for president nearly tripled in just four years, from 365,833 in 1824 to 1,148,018 in 1828.

The 1828 election was a rematch between Jackson and President John Quincy Adams. In 1824 Jackson had won a plurality of ninety-nine electoral votes to eighty-four for Adams, forty-one for Secretary of the Treasury William Crawford of Georgia, and thirty-seven for Speaker of the House Henry Clay of Kentucky. (Jackson also won a plurality of 41 percent of the popular vote to Adams's 31 percent.) But because Jackson lacked a majority of electoral votes, the election was thrown into the House of Representatives. The House chose Adams, whom Clay had endorsed. When Adams named Clay to be secretary of state shortly after the election, Jackson's supporters angrily charged that their candidate had been cheated from the presidency by a "corrupt bargain."

Adams was an unpopular, politically ineffective president. Jackson easily defeated him in 1828 by an electoral vote margin of 178-83. (Adams swept New England and won some votes in the Middle Atlantic states, but Jackson carried the entire South and West.) Jackson's popular vote majority

*(56 percent to 44 percent) was built on the votes of those whom he called "the humble members of society," especially farmers and laborers.*

*An outsider president who was elected by a coalition of outsider voters, Jackson used his first message to Congress, sent on December 8, 1829, to state officially his view that "the first principle of our system" is that "the majority is to govern." Among other policies that he discussed in the message, Jackson announced that he intended for government jobs to be given to the common people who had supported him. Dubbed the "spoils system" by his opponents, Jackson defended the policy on grounds that it would foster "efficiency,... industry and integrity" in government.*   ～

Fellow Citizens of the Senate and of the House of Representatives:

It affords me pleasure to tender my friendly greetings to you on the occasion of your assembling at the Seat of Government, to enter upon the important duties to which you have been called by the voice of our countrymen. The task devolves on me, under a provision of the Constitution, to present to you, as the Federal Legislature of twenty-four sovereign States, and twelve millions of happy people, a view of our affairs; and to propose such measures as, in the discharge of my official functions, have suggested themselves as necessary to promote the objects of our Union.

In communicating with you for the first time, it is, to me, a source of unfeigned satisfaction, calling for mutual gratulation and devout thanks to a benign Providence, that we are at peace with all mankind; and that our country exhibits the most cheering evidence of general welfare and progressive improvement. Turning our eyes to other nations, our great desire is to see our brethren of the human race secured in the blessings enjoyed by ourselves, and advancing in knowledge, in freedom, and in social happiness....

I consider it one of the most urgent of my duties to bring to your attention the propriety of amending that part of our Constitution which relates to the election of President and Vice President. Our system of government was, by its framers, deemed an experiment; and they, therefore, consistently provided a mode of remedying its defects.

To the People belongs the right of electing their Chief Magistrate: it was never designed that their choice should, in any case, be defeated, either by the intervention of electoral colleges, or by the agency confided, under certain contingencies, to the House of Representatives. Experience proves, that, in proportion as agents to execute the will of the People are multiplied, there is danger of their wishes being frustrated. Some may be unfaithful: all are liable to err. So far, therefore, as the People can, with convenience, speak, it is safer for them to express their own will.

The number of aspirants to the Presidency, and the diversity of the interests which may influence their claims, leave little reason to expect a choice in the first instance: and, in that event, the election must devolve on the House of Representatives, where, it is obvious, the will of the People may not be always ascertained; or, if ascertained, may not be regarded. From the mode of voting by States, the choice is to be made by twenty-four votes; and it may often occur, that one of these will be controlled by an individual representative. Honors and offices are at the disposal of the successful candidate. Repeated ballotings may make it apparent that a single individual holds the cast in his hand. May he not be tempted to name his reward? But even without corruption—supposing the probity of the Representative to be proof against the powerful motives by which it may be assailed—the will of the People is still constantly liable to be misrepresented. One may err from ignorance of the wishes of his constituents; another, from a conviction that it is his duty to be governed by his own judgment of the fitness of the candidates: finally, although all were inflexibly honest—all accurately informed of the wishes of their constituents—yet, under the present mode of election, a minority may often elect the President; and when this happens, it may reasonably be expected that efforts will be made on the part of the majority to rectify this injurious operation of their institutions. But although no evil of this character should result from such a perversion of the first principle of our system—*that the majority is to govern*—it must be very certain that a President elected by a minority cannot enjoy the confidence necessary to the successful discharge of his duties.

In this, as in all other matters of public concern, policy requires that as few impediments as possible should exist to the free operation of the public will. Let us, then, endeavor so to amend our system, that the office of Chief Magistrate may not be conferred upon any citizen but in pursuance of a fair expression of the will of the majority.

I would therefore recommend such an amendment of the Constitution as may remove all intermediate agency in the election of President and Vice President. The mode may be so regulated as to preserve to each State its present relative weight in the election; and a failure in the first attempt may be provided for, by confining the second to a choice between the two highest candidates. In connexion with such an amendment, it would seem advisable to limit the service of the Chief Magistrate to a single term, of either four or six years. If, however, it should not be adopted, it is worthy of consideration whether a provision disqualifying for office the Representatives in Congress on whom such an election may have devolved, would not be proper.

While members of Congress can be constitutionally appointed to offices of trust and profit, it will be the practice, even under the most conscientious adherence to duty, to select them for such stations as they are believed to be better qualified to fill than other citizens; but the purity of our Government would doubtless be promoted, by their exclusion from all appointments in the gift of the President in whose election they may have been officially concerned. The nature of the judicial office, and the necessity of securing in the Cabinet and in diplomatic stations of the highest rank, the best talents and political experience, should, perhaps, except these from the exclusion.

There are perhaps few men who can for any great length of time enjoy office and power, without being more or less under the influence of feelings unfavorable to the faithful discharge of their public duties. Their integrity may be proof against improper considerations immediately addressed to themselves; but they are apt to acquire a habit of looking with indifference upon the public interests, and of tolerating conduct from which an unpractised man would revolt. Office is considered as a species of property; and Government, rather as a means of promoting individual interests, than as an instrument created solely for the service of the People. Corruption in some, and, in others, a perversion of correct feelings and principles, divert Government from its legitimate ends, and make it an engine for the support of the few at the expense of the many. The duties of all public officers are, or, at least, admit of being made, so plain and simple, that men of intelligence may readily qualify themselves for their performance; and I cannot but believe that more is lost by the long continuance of men in office, than is generally to be gained by their experience. I submit therefore to your consideration, whether the efficiency of the

Government would not be promoted, and official industry and integrity better secured, by a general extension of the law which limits appointments to four years.

In a country where offices are created solely for the benefit of the People, no one man has any more intrinsic right to official station than another. Offices were not established to give support to particular men, at the public expense. No individual wrong is therefore done by removal, since neither appointment to, nor continuance in, office, is a matter of right. The incumbent became an officer with a view to public benefits; and when these require his removal, they are not to be sacrificed to private interests. It is the People, and they alone, who have a right to complain, when a bad officer is substituted for a good one. He who is removed has the same means of obtaining a living, that are enjoyed by the millions who never held office. The proposed limitation would destroy the idea of property, now so generally connected with official station; and although individual distress may be sometimes produced, it would, by promoting that rotation which constitutes a leading principle in the republican creed, give healthful action to the system.

No very considerable change has occurred, during the recess of Congress, in the condition of either our Agriculture, Commerce, or Manufactures. . . .

In deliberating, therefore, on these interesting subjects, local feelings and prejudices should be merged in the patriotic determination to promote the great interests of the whole. All attempts to connect them with the party conflicts of the day are necessarily injurious, and should be discountenanced. Our action upon them should be under the control of higher and purer motives. Legislation, subjected to such influences, can never be just; and will not long retain the sanction of a People, whose active patriotism is not bounded

by sectional limits, nor insensible to that spirit of concession and forbearance, which gave life to our political compact, and still sustains it. Discarding all calculations of political ascendancy, the North, the South, the East, and the West, should unite in diminishing any burthen, of which either may justly complain.

The agricultural interest of our country is so essentially connected with every other, and so superior in importance to them all, that it is scarcely necessary to invite to it your particular attention. It is principally as manufactures and commerce tend to increase the value of agricultural productions, and to extend their application to the wants and comforts of society, that they deserve the fostering care of Government.

[The] state of the finances exhibits the resources of the nation in an aspect highly flattering to its industry; and auspicious of the ability of Government, in a very short time, to extinguish the public debt. When this shall be done, our population will be relieved from a considerable portion of its present burthens; and will find, not only new motives to patriotic affection, but additional means for the display of individual enterprise. The fiscal power of the States will also be increased; and may be more extensively exerted in favor of education and other public objects; while ample means will remain in the Federal Government to promote the general weal, in all the modes permitted to its authority.

After the extinction of the public debt, it is not probable that any adjustment of the tariff, upon principles satisfactory to the People of the Union, will, until a remote period, if ever, leave the Government without a considerable surplus in the Treasury, beyond what may be required for its current service. . . . It appears to me that the most safe, just, and federal disposition which could be made of the surplus revenue, would be its apportionment among the several States according to their ratio of representation; and should this measure not be found warranted by the Constitution, that it would be expedient to propose to the States an amendment authorizing it. I regard an appeal to the source of power, in cases of real doubt, and where its exercise is deemed indispensable to the general welfare, as among the most sacred of all our obligations. Upon this country, more than any other, has, in the providence of God, been cast the special guardianship of the great principle of adherence to written constitutions. If it fail here, all hope in regard to it will be extinguished. That this was intended to be a Government of limited and specific, and not general powers, must be admitted by all; and it is our duty to preserve for it the character intended by its framers. If experience points out the necessity for an enlargement of these powers, let us apply for it to those for whose benefit it is to be exercised; and not undermine the whole system by a resort to overstrained constructions. The scheme has worked well. It has exceeded the hopes of those who devised it, and become an object of admiration to the world. We are responsible to our country, and to the glorious cause of self-government, for the preservation of so great a good. The great mass of legislation relating to our internal affairs, was intended to be left where the Federal Convention found it—in the State Governments. Nothing is clearer, in my view, than that we are chiefly indebted for the success of the Constitution under which we are now acting, to the watchful and auxiliary operation of the State authorities. This is not the reflection of a day, but belongs to the most deeply rooted convictions of my mind. I cannot, therefore, too strongly or too earnestly, for my own sense of its importance, warn you against all encroachments upon the legitimate sphere of State sovereignty. Sustained by its healthful and invigorating influence, the Federal system can

never fall. . . .

I would suggest, also, an inquiry, whether the provisions of the act of Congress, authorizing the discharge of the persons of debtors to the Government, from imprisonment, may not, consistently with the public interest, be extended to the release of the debt, where the conduct of the debtor is wholly exempt from the imputation of fraud. Some more liberal policy than that which now prevails, in reference to this unfortunate class of citizens, is certainly due to them, and would prove beneficial to the country. The continuance of the liability, after the means to discharge it have been exhausted, can only serve to dispirit the debtor; or, where his resources are but partial, the want of power in the Government to compromise and release the demand, instigates to fraud, as the only resource for securing a support to his family. He thus sinks into a state of apathy, and becomes a useless drone in society, or a vicious member of it, if not a feeling witness of the rigor and inhumanity of his country. All experience proves, that oppressive debt is the bane of enterprise; and it should be the care of a Republic not to exert a grinding power over misfortune and poverty. . . .

The condition and ulterior destiny of the Indian Tribes within the limits of some of our States, have become objects of much interest and importance. It has long been the policy of Government to introduce among them the arts of civilization, in the hope of gradually reclaiming them from a wandering life. This policy has, however, been coupled with another, wholly incompatible with its success. Professing a desire to civilize and settle them, we have, at the same time, lost no opportunity to purchase their lands, and thrust them further into the wilderness. By this means they have not only been kept in a wandering state, but been led to look upon us as unjust and indifferent to their fate. Thus, though lavish in its expenditures upon the subject, Government has constantly defeated its own policy; and the Indians, in general, receding further and further to the West, have retained their savage habits. A portion, however, of the Southern tribes, having mingled much with the whites, and made some progress in the arts of civilized life, have lately attempted to erect an independent government, within the limits of Georgia and Alabama. These States, claiming to be the only Sovereigns within their territories, extended their laws over the Indians; which induced the latter to call upon the United States for protection.

Under these circumstances, the question presented was, whether the General Government had a right to sustain those people in their pretensions? The Constitution declares, that "no new State shall be formed or erected within the jurisdiction of any other State," without the consent of its legislature. If the General Government is not permitted to tolerate the erection of a confederate State within the territory of one of the members of this Union, against her consent; much less could it allow a foreign and independent government to establish itself there. Georgia became a member of the Confederacy which eventuated in our Federal Union, as a sovereign State, always asserting her claim to certain limits; which having been originally defined in her colonial charter, and subsequently recognised in the treaty of peace, she has ever since continued to enjoy, except as they have been circumscribed by her own voluntary transfer of a portion of her territory to the United States, in the articles of cession of 1802. Alabama was admitted into the Union on the same footing with the original States, with boundaries which were prescribed by Congress. There is no constitutional, conventional, or legal provision, which allows them less power over the Indians within their borders, than is possessed by Maine or New York. Would the

People of Maine permit the Penobscot tribe to erect an Independent Government within their State: and unless they did, would it not be the duty of the General Government to support them in resisting such a measure? Would the People of New York permit each remnant of the Six Nations within her borders, to declare itself an independent people under the protection of the United States? Could the Indians establish a separate republic on each of their reservations in Ohio? and if they were so disposed, would it be the duty of this Government to protect them in the attempt? If the principle involved in the obvious answer to these questions be abandoned, it will follow that the objects of this Government are reversed; and that it has become a part of its duty to aid in destroying the States which it was established to protect.

Actuated by this view of the subject, I informed the Indians inhabiting parts of Georgia and Alabama, that their attempt to establish an independent government would not be countenanced by the Executive of the United States; and advised them to emigrate beyond the Mississippi, or submit to the laws of those States.

Our conduct towards these people is deeply interesting to our national character. Their present condition, contrasted with what they once were, makes a most powerful appeal to our sympathies. Our ancestors found them the uncontrolled possessors of these vast regions. By persuasion and force, they have been made to retire from river to river, and from mountain to mountain; until some of the tribes have become extinct, and others have left but remnants, to preserve, for a while, their once terrible names. Surrounded by the whites, with their arts of civilization, which, by destroying the resources of the savage, doom him to weakness and decay; the fate of the Mohegan, the Narragansett, and the Delaware, is fast overtaking the Choctaw, the Cherokee, and the Creek. That this fate surely awaits them, if they remain within the limits of the States, does not admit of a doubt. Humanity and national honor demand that every effort should be made to avert so great a calamity. It is too late to inquire whether it was just in the United States to include them and their territory within the bounds of new States whose limits they could control. That step cannot be retraced. A State cannot be dismembered by Congress, or restricted in the exercise of her constitutional power. But the people of those States, and of every State, actuated by feelings of justice and a regard for our national honor, submit to you the interesting question, whether something cannot be done, consistently with the rights of the States, to preserve this much injured race?

As a means of effecting this end, I suggest, for your consideration, the propriety of setting apart an ample district West of the Mississippi, and without the limits of any State or Territory, now formed, to be guarantied to the Indian tribes, as long as they shall occupy it: each tribe having a distinct control over the portion designated for its use. There they may be secured in the enjoyment of governments of their own choice, subject to no other control from the United States than such as may be necessary to preserve peace on the frontier, and between the several tribes. There the benevolent may endeavor to teach them the arts of civilization; and, by promoting union and harmony among them, to raise up an interesting commonwealth, destined to perpetuate the race, and to attest the humanity and justice of this Government.

This emigration should be voluntary: for it would be as cruel as unjust to compel the aborigines to abandon the graves of their fathers, and seek a home in a distant land. But they should be distinctly informed that, if they remain within the limits of the States, they must be subject to their laws. In return for their obedience, as individuals, they will, without doubt, be protected in the enjoyment of those possessions which they have improved by their industry. But it seems to me visionary to suppose, that, in this state of things, claims can be allowed on tracts of country on which they have neither dwelt nor made improvements, merely because they have seen them from the mountain, or passed them in the chace. Submitting to the laws of the States, and receiving, like other citizens, protection in their persons and property, they will, ere long, become merged in the mass of our population. . . .

I now commend you, fellow-citizens, to the guidance of Almighty God, with a full reliance on his merciful providence for the maintenance of our free institutions; and with an earnest supplication, that, whatever errors it may be my lot to commit, in discharging the arduous duties which have devolved on me, will find a remedy in the harmony and wisdom of your counsels.

ANDREW JACKSON

# Andrew Jackson's
# Veto of the Bank Bill (1832)

Andrew Jackson's veto of the bill passed by Congress to renew the charter of the Second Bank of the United States was both politically important at the time and enduringly important as a bold assertion of presidential power.

Politically, Jackson believed strongly that the federal government had become a promoter of special privileges for the mainly eastern commercial and financial elite at the expense of southern and western farmers and laborers, whom he championed. Jackson regarded the bank not only as the leading institutional bastion of everything he found wrong in the government but also as an ally of the opposition National Republican (or Whig) party. Indeed, bank president Nicholas Biddle, encouraged by Sen. Henry Clay of Kentucky, the Whig candidate for president in 1832, asked Congress to renew the bank's charter four years before the old charter was scheduled to expire in 1836 because Clay thought that a veto by Jackson would be a good issue for the Whigs in the election. Despite Jackson's opposition, Congress acceded to Biddle's request.

Presidents from George Washington to John Quincy Adams had used their veto power sparingly: in forty years, they had vetoed nine bills, only three of them important. The belief of Federalist and Democratic-Republican presi-

dents alike had been that the veto should be reserved only for legislation that was of doubtful constitutionality.

Jackson regarded the veto power differently. He grounded his view in a new and expansive conception of the presidency that reflected in part the recent extension of the suffrage to those who did not own property, the near-universal selection of presidential electors by popular vote, and the dismantling of the congressional caucus as a device to nominate candidates for president. (See headnotes to "The Tennessee General Assembly's Protest against the Caucus System," p. 67, and "Andrew Jackson's First Message to Congress," p. 71.) The president, Jackson believed, was a truer representative of the people than even Congress. He was their "tribune," the only person in the government who had been elected by the entire country and who could claim to articulate the national interest accurately and completely. As a consequence, Jackson felt that if the president regarded an act of Congress as unwise public policy, that judgment was sufficient grounds for a veto.

On July 10, 1832, seven days after Congress voted to renew the charter of the national bank, Jackson sent his veto message to Capitol Hill. While claiming that the bank bill was unconstitutional, Jackson made clear that he regarded his dislike for it as reason enough to *cast a veto. This first departure from past presidential practice was accompanied by another. In the final paragraph of the veto message, Jackson appealed over the heads of Congress to the American people. With an eye to the coming election, Jackson wrote that "if sustained by his fellow citizens," he would be "grateful and happy."*

*Congress failed to override Jackson's veto of the bank bill. In the 1832 election, the president was resoundingly reelected over Clay by a margin of 219-49 in the electoral college. (Jackson's popular vote majority was 54-37 percent.)*

*Both the veto and the theory of the presidency that underlay it established precedents that were of lasting significance. In the short term, President John Tyler and Jackson's other immediate successors institutionalized his practice of vetoing bills on political grounds. In the long term, the attitude that the president is the people's main representative in government took root widely and deeply in the U.S. political system.* ∼

The bill "to modify and continue" the act entitled "An act to incorporate the subscribers to the Bank of the United States" was presented to me on the 4th July instant. Having considered it with that solemn regard to the principles of the Constitution which the day was calculated to inspire, and come to the conclusion that it ought not to become a law, I herewith return it to the Senate, in which it originated, with my objections.

A bank of the United States is in many respects convenient for the government and useful to the people. Entertaining this opinion, and deeply impressed with the belief that some of the powers and privileges possessed by the existing bank are unauthorized by the Constitution, subversive of the rights of the states, and dangerous to the liberties of the people, I felt it my duty at an early period of my administration to call the attention of Congress to the practicability of organizing an institution combining all its advantages and obviating these objections. I sincerely regret that in the act before me I can perceive none of those modifications of the bank charter which are necessary, in my opinion, to make it compatible with justice, with sound policy, or with the Constitution of our country.

The present corporate body, denominated the president, directors, and company of the Bank of the United States, will have existed at the time this act is intended to take effect twenty years. It enjoys an exclusive privilege of banking under the authority of the general government, a monopoly of its favor and support, and, as a necessary consequence, almost a monopoly of the foreign and domestic exchange. The powers, privileges, and favors bestowed upon it in the original charter, by increasing the value of the stock far above its par value, operated as a gratuity of many millions to the stockholders.

An apology may be found for the failure to guard against this result in the consideration that the effect of the original act of incorporation could not be certainly foreseen at the time of its passage. The act before me proposes another gratuity to the holders of the same stock, and in many cases to the same men, of at least $7 million more. This donation finds no apology in any uncertainty as to the effect of the act. On all hands it is conceded that its passage will increase at least 20 or 30 percent more the market price of the stock, subject to the payment of the annuity of $200,000 per year secured by the act, thus adding in a moment one-fourth to its par value. It is not our own citizens only who are to receive the bounty of our government. More than $8 million of the stock of this bank are held by foreigners. By this act the American republic proposes virtually to make them a present of some millions of dollars. For these gratuities to foreigners and to some of our own opulent citizens the act secures no equivalent whatever. They are the certain gains of the present stockholders under the operation of this act, after making full allowance for the payment of the bonus.

Every monopoly and all exclusive privileges are granted at the expense of the public, which ought to receive a fair equivalent. The many millions which this act proposes to bestow on the stockholders of the existing bank must come directly or indirectly out of the earnings of the American people. It is due to them, therefore, if their government sell monopolies and exclusive privileges, that they should at least exact for them as much as they are worth in open market. The value of the monopoly in this case may be correctly ascertained. The $28 million of stock would probably be at an advance of 50 percent and command in market at least $42 million, subject to the payment of the present bonus. The present value of the monopoly, therefore, is $17 million, and this the act proposes to sell for $3 million, payable in fifteen annual installments of $200,000 each.

It is not conceivable how the present stockholders can have any claim to the special favor of the government. The present corporation has enjoyed its monopoly during the period stipulated in the original contract. If we must have such a corporation, why should not the government sell out the whole stock and thus secure to the people the full market value of the privileges granted? Why should not Congress create and sell $28 million of stock, incorporating the purchasers with all the powers and privileges secured in this act and putting the premium upon the sales into the treasury?

But this act does not permit competition in the purchase of this monopoly. It seems to be predicated on the erroneous idea that the present stockholders have a prescriptive right not only to the favor but to the bounty of government. It appears that more than a fourth part of the stock is held by foreigners and the residue is held by a few hundred of our own citizens, chiefly of the richest class. For their benefit does this act exclude the whole American people from competition in the purchase of this monopoly and dispose of it for many millions less than it is worth. This seems the less excusable because some of our citizens not now stockholders petitioned that the door of competition might be opened and offered to take a charter on terms much more favorable to the government and country.

But this proposition, although made by men whose aggregate wealth is believed to be equal to all the private stock in the existing bank, has been set aside, and the bounty of our government is proposed to be again bestowed on the few who have been fortunate enough to secure the stock and at this moment wield the power of the existing institution. I cannot perceive the justice or policy of this course. If our government must sell monopolies, it would seem to be its duty to take nothing less than their full value, and, if gratuities must be made once in fifteen or twenty years, let them not be bestowed on the subjects of a foreign government nor upon a designated and favored class of men in our own country. It is but justice and good policy, as far as the nature of the case will admit, to confine our favors to our own fellow citizens and let each in his turn enjoy an opportunity to profit by our bounty. In the bearings of the act before me upon these points I find ample reasons why it should not become a law.

It has been urged as an argument in favor of rechartering the present bank that the calling in its loans will produce great embarrassment and distress. The time allowed to close its concerns is ample, and, if it has been well managed, its pressure will be light, and heavy only in case its management has been bad. If, therefore, it shall produce distress, the fault will be its own; and it would furnish a reason against renewing a power which has been so obviously abused. But will there ever be a time when this reason will be less powerful? To acknowledge its force is to admit that the bank ought to be perpetual, and as a consequence the present stockholders and those inheriting their rights as successors be established a privileged order, clothed both with great political power and enjoying immense pecuniary advantages from their connection with the government.

The modifications of the existing charter proposed by this act are not such, in my view, as make it consistent with the rights of the states or the liberties of the people. The qualification of the right of the bank to hold real estate, the limitation of its power to establish branches, and the power reserved to Congress to forbid the circulation of small notes are restrictions comparatively of little value or importance. All the objectionable principles of the existing corporation, and most of its odious features, are retained without alleviation. . . .

By documents submitted to Congress at the present session it appears that on the 1st of January, 1832, of the $28 million of private stock in the corporation, $8,405,500 were held by foreigners, mostly of Great Britain. The amount of stock held in the nine Western and Southwestern states is $140,200, and in the four Southern states is $5,623,100, and in the Middle and Eastern states is about $13,522,000. The profits of the bank in 1831, as shown in a statement to Congress, were about $3,455,598; of this there accrued in the nine Western states about $1,640,048; in the four Southern states about $352,507, and in the Middle and Eastern states about $1,463,041. As little stock is held in the West, it is obvious that the debt of the people in that section to the bank is principally a debt to the Eastern and foreign stockholders; that the interest they pay upon it is carried into the Eastern states and into Europe, and that it is a burden upon their industry and a drain of their currency, which no country can bear without inconvenience and occasional distress.

To meet this burden and equalize the exchange operations of the bank, the amount of specie drawn from those states through its branches within the last two years, as shown by its official reports, was about $6 million. More than $500,000 of this amount does not stop in the Eastern states but passes on to Europe to pay the dividends of the foreign stockholders. In the principle of taxation recognized by this act the Western states find no adequate compensation for this perpetual burden on their industry and drain of their currency. The branch bank at Mobile made last year $95,140, yet under the provisions of this act the state of Alabama can raise no revenue from these profitable operations, because not a share of the stock is held by any of her citizens. Mississippi and Missouri are in the same condition in relation to the branches at Natchez and St. Louis, and such, in a greater or less degree, is the condition of every Western state. The tendency of the plan of taxation which this act proposes will be to place the whole United States in the same relation to foreign countries which the Western states now bear to the Eastern. When by a tax on resident stockholders the stock of this bank is made worth 10 or 15 percent more to foreigners than to residents, most of it will inevitably leave the country.

Thus will this provision in its practical effect deprive the Eastern as well as the Southern and Western states of the means of raising a revenue from the extension of business and great profits of this institution. It will make the American people debtors to aliens in nearly the whole amount due to this bank, and send across the Atlantic from $2 million to $5 million of specie every year to pay the bank dividends.

In another of its bearings this provision is fraught with danger. Of the twenty-five directors of this bank, five are chosen by the government and twenty by the citizen stockholders. From all voice in these elections the foreign stockholders are excluded by the charter. In proportion, therefore, as the stock is transferred to foreign holders the extent of suffrage in the choice of directors is curtailed. Already is almost a third of the stock in foreign hands and not represented in elections. It is constantly passing out of the country, and this act will accelerate its departure. The entire control of the institution would necessarily fall into the hands of a few citizen stockholders, and the ease with which the object would be accomplished would be a temptation to designing men to secure that control in their own hands by monopolizing the remaining stock. There is danger that a president and directors would then be able to elect themselves from year to year and, without responsibility or control, manage the whole concerns of the bank during the existence of its charter. It is easy to conceive that great evils to our country and its institutions might flow from such a concentration of power in the hands of a few men irresponsible to the people.

Is there no danger to our liberty and independence in a bank that in its nature has so little to bind it to our country? The president of the bank has told us that most of the state banks exist by its forbearance. Should its influence become concentered, as it may under the operation of such an act as this, in the hands of a self-elected directory whose interests are identified with those of the foreign stockholders, will there not be cause to tremble for the purity of our elections in peace and for the independence of our country in war? Their power would be great when-

ever they might choose to exert it; but if this monopoly were regularly renewed every fifteen or twenty years on terms proposed by themselves, they might seldom in peace put forth their strength to influence elections or control the affairs of the nation. But if any private citizen or public functionary should interpose to curtail its powers or prevent a renewal of its privileges, it cannot be doubted that he would be made to feel its influence.

Should the stock of the bank principally pass into the hands of the subjects of a foreign country, and should we unfortunately become involved in a war with that country, what would be our condition? Of the course which would be pursued by a bank almost wholly owned by the subjects of a foreign power and managed by those whose interests, if not affections, would run in the same direction, there can be no doubt. All its operations within would be in aid of the hostile fleets and armies without. Controlling our currency, receiving our public moneys, and holding thousands of our citizens in dependence, it would be more formidable and dangerous than the naval and military power of the enemy.

If we must have a bank with private stockholders, every consideration of sound policy and every impulse of American feeling admonishes that it should be *purely American*. Its stockholders should be composed exclusively of our own citizens, who at least ought to be friendly to our government and willing to support it in times of difficulty and danger. So abundant is domestic capital that competition in subscribing for the stock of local banks has recently led almost to riots. To a bank exclusively of American stockholders, possessing the powers and privileges granted by this act, subscriptions for $200 million could be readily obtained. Instead of sending abroad the stock of the bank in which the government must deposit its funds and on which it must rely to sustain its credit in times of emergency; it would rather seem to be expedient to prohibit its sale to aliens under penalty of absolute forfeiture.

It is maintained by the advocates of the bank that its constitutionality in all its features ought to be considered as settled by precedent and by the decision of the Supreme Court. To this conclusion I cannot assent. Mere precedent is a dangerous source of authority and should not be regarded as deciding questions of constitutional power except where the acquiescence of the people and the states can be considered as well settled. So far from this being the case on this subject, an argument against the bank might be based on precedent. One Congress in 1791 decided in favor of a bank; another in 1811 decided against it. One Congress in 1815 decided against a bank; another in 1816 decided in its favor. Prior to the present Congress, therefore, the precedents drawn from that source were equal. If we resort to the states, the expressions of legislative, judicial, and executive opinions against the bank have been probably to those in its favor as four to one. There is nothing in precedent, therefore, which, if its authority were admitted, ought to weigh in favor of the act before me.

If the opinion of the Supreme Court covered the whole ground of this act, it ought not to control the coordinate authorities of this government. The Congress, the executive, and the court must each for itself be guided by its own opinion of the Constitution. Each public officer who takes an oath to support the Constitution swears that he will support it as he understands it and not as it is understood by others. It is as much the duty of the House of Representatives, of the Senate, and of the President to decide upon the constitutionality of any bill or resolution which may be presented to them for passage or approval as it is of the supreme judges when it may be brought before

them for judicial decision. The opinion of the judges has no more authority over Congress than the opinion of Congress has over the judges, and on that point the President is independent of both. The authority of the Supreme Court must not, therefore, be permitted to control the Congress or the executive when acting in their legislative capacities, but to have only such influence as the force of their reasoning may deserve.

But in the case relied upon, the Supreme Court have not decided that all the features of this corporation are compatible with the Constitution. It is true that the Court have said that the law incorporating the bank is a constitutional exercise of power by Congress; but, taking into view the whole opinion of the Court and the reasoning by which they have come to that conclusion, I understand them to have decided that, inasmuch as a bank is an appropriate means for carrying into effect the enumerated powers of the general government, therefore the law incorporating it is in accordance with that provision of the Constitution which declares that Congress shall have power "to make all laws which shall be necessary and proper for carrying those powers into execution." Having satisfied themselves that the word "necessary" in the Constitution means "needful," "requisite," "essential," "conducive to," and that "a bank" is a convenient, a useful, and an essential instrument in the prosecution of the government's "fiscal operations," they conclude that to "use one must be within the discretion of Congress" and that "the act to incorporate the Bank of the United States is a law made in pursuance of the Constitution"; "but," say they, *where the law is not prohibited and is really calculated to effect any of the objects entrusted to the government, to undertake here to inquire into the degree of its necessity would be to pass the line which circumscribes the judicial de-*

*partment and to tread on legislative ground."*

The principle here affirmed is that the "degree of its necessity," involving all the details of a banking institution, is a question exclusively for legislative consideration. A bank is constitutional, but it is the province of the legislature to determine whether this or that particular power, privilege, or exemption is "necessary and proper" to enable the bank to discharge its duties to the government, and from their decision there is no appeal to the courts of justice. Under the decision of the Supreme Court, therefore, it is the exclusive province of Congress and the President to decide whether the particular features of this act are necessary and proper in order to enable the bank to perform conveniently and efficiently the public duties assigned to it as a fiscal agent, and therefore constitutional, or unnecessary and improper, and therefore unconstitutional.

Without commenting on the general principle affirmed by the Supreme Court, let us examine the details of this act in accordance with the rule of legislative action which they had laid down. It will be found that many of the powers and privileges conferred on it cannot be supposed necessary for the purpose for which it is proposed to be created and are not, therefore, means necessary to attain the end in view, and consequently not justified by the Constitution.

The original Act of Incorporation, Section 21, enacts that "no other bank shall be established by any future law of the United States during the continuance of the corporation hereby created, for which the faith of the United States is hereby pledged: *Provided,* Congress may renew existing charters for banks within the District of Columbia not increasing the capital thereof, and may also establish any other bank or banks in said District with capitals not exceeding in the whole $6 million if they

shall deem it expedient." This provision is continued in force by the act before me fifteen years from the 3rd of March, 1836.

If Congress possessed the power to establish one bank, they had power to establish more than one if in their opinion two or more banks had been "necessary" to facilitate the execution of the powers delegated to them in the Constitution. If they possessed the power to establish a second bank, it was a power derived from the Constitution to be exercised from time to time, and at any time when the interests of the country or the emergencies of the government might make it expedient. It was possessed by one Congress as well as another, and by all congresses alike, and alike at every session. But the Congress of 1816 have taken it away from the successors for twenty years, and the Congress of 1832 proposes to abolish it for fifteen years more. It cannot be "necessary" or "proper" for Congress to barter away or divest themselves of any of the powers vested in them by the Constitution to be exercised for the public good. It is not "necessary" to the efficiency of the bank, nor is it "proper" in relation to themselves and their successors. They may *properly* use the discretion vested in them, but they may not limit the discretion of their successors. This restriction on themselves and grant of a monopoly to the bank is therefore unconstitutional.

In another point of view this provision is a palpable attempt to amend the Constitution by an act of legislation. The Constitution declares that "the Congress shall have power to exercise exclusive legislation in all cases whatsoever" over the District of Columbia. Its constitutional power, therefore, to establish banks in the District of Columbia and increase their capital at will is unlimited and uncontrollable by any other power than that which gave authority to the Constitution. Yet this act declares that Congress shall *not* increase the capital of existing banks, nor create other banks with capitals exceeding in the whole $6 million.

The Constitution declares that Congress *shall* have power to exercise exclusive legislation over this District *"in all cases whatsoever,"* and this act declares they shall not. Which is the supreme law of the land? This provision cannot be *"necessary"* or *"proper"* or *constitutional* unless the absurdity be admitted that whenever it be "necessary and proper" in the opinion of Congress they have a right to barter away one portion of the powers vested in them by the Constitution as a means of executing the rest.

On two subjects only does the Constitution recognize in Congress the power to grant exclusive privileges or monopolies. It declares that "Congress shall have power to promote the progress of science and useful arts by securing for limited times to authors and inventors the exclusive right to their respective writings and discoveries." Out of this express delegation of power have grown our laws of patents and copyrights. As the Constitution expressly delegates to Congress the power to grant exclusive privileges in these cases as the means of executing the substantive power "to promote the progress of science and useful arts," it is consistent with the fair rules of construction to conclude that such a power was not intended to be granted as a means of accomplishing any other end. On every other subject which comes within the scope of congressional power there is an ever living discretion in the use of proper means, which cannot be restricted or abolished without an amendment of the Constitution. Every act of Congress, therefore, which attempts by grants or monopolies or sale of exclusive privileges for a limited time, or a time without limit, to restrict or extinguish its own discretion in the choice of means to execute its delegated powers is equivalent to a legislative

amendment of the Constitution and palpably unconstitutional.

This act authorizes and encourages transfers of its stock to foreigners and grants them an exemption from all state and national taxation. So far from being *"necessary and proper"* that the bank should possess this power to make it a safe and efficient agent of the government in its fiscal operations, it is calculated to convert the Bank of the United States into a foreign bank, to impoverish our people in time of peace, to disseminate a foreign influence through every section of the republic, and in war to endanger our independence.

The several states reserved the power at the formation of the Constitution to regulate and control titles and transfers of real property, and most, if not all, of them have laws disqualifying aliens from acquiring or holding lands within their limits. But this act, in disregard of the undoubted right of the states to prescribe such disqualifications, gives to aliens stockholders in this bank an interest and title, as members of the corporation, to all the real property it may acquire within any of the states of this Union. This privilege granted to aliens is not *"necessary"* to enable the bank to perform its public duties, nor in any sense *"proper,"* because it is vitally subversive of the rights of the states.

The government of the United States have no constitutional power to purchase lands within the states except "for the erection of forts, magazines, arsenals, dockyards, and other needful buildings," and even for these objects only "by the consent of the legislature of the state in which the same shall be." By making themselves stockholders in the bank and granting to the corporation the power to purchase lands for other purposes, they assume a power not granted in the Constitution and grant to others what they do not themselves possess. It is not *necessary* to the receiving, safekeeping, or transmission of the funds of the government that the bank should possess this power, and it is not *proper* that Congress should thus enlarge the powers delegated to them in the Constitution. . . .

The government is the only "proper" judge where its agents should reside and keep their offices, because it best knows where their presence will be "necessary." It cannot, therefore, be "necessary" or "proper" to authorize the bank to locate branches where it pleases to perform the public service, without consulting the government and contrary to its will. The principle laid down by the Supreme Court concedes that Congress cannot establish a bank for purposes of private speculation and gain, but only as a means of executing the delegated powers of the general government. By the same principle a branch bank cannot constitutionally be established for other than public purposes. The power which this act gives to establish two branches in any state, without the injunction or request of the government and for other than public purposes, is not "necessary" to the due execution of the powers delegated to Congress.

The bonus which is exacted from the bank is a confession upon the face of the act that the powers granted by it are greater than are "necessary" to its character of a fiscal agent. The government does not tax its officers and agents for the privilege of serving it. The bonus of $1,500,000 required by the original charter and that of $3 million proposed by this act are not exacted for the privilege of giving "the necessary facilities for transferring the public funds from place to place within the United States or the territories thereof, and for distributing the same in payment of the public creditors without charging commission or claiming allowance on account of the difference of exchange," as required by the act of incorporation, but for something more beneficial to the stockholders.

The original act declares that it (the bonus) is granted "in consideration of the exclusive privileges and benefits conferred by this act upon the said bank," and the act before me declares it to be "in consideration of the exclusive benefits and privileges continued by this act to the said corporation for fifteen years, as aforesaid." It is therefore for "exclusive privileges and benefits" conferred for their own use and emolument and not for the advantage of the government, that a bonus is exacted. These surplus powers for which the bank is required to pay cannot surely be "necessary" to make it the fiscal agent of the treasury. If they were, the exaction of a bonus for them would not be "proper."

It is maintained by some that the bank is a means of executing the constitutional power "to coin money and regulate the value thereof." Congress have established a mint to coin money and passed laws to regulate the value thereof. The money so coined, with its value so regulated, and such foreign coins as Congress may adopt are the only currency known to the Constitution. But if they have other power to regulate the currency, it was conferred to be exercised by themselves and not to be transferred to a corporation. If the bank be established for that purpose, with a charter unalterable without its consent, Congress have parted with their power for a term of years, during which the Constitution is a dead letter. It is neither necessary nor proper to transfer its legislative power to such a bank, and therefore unconstitutional.

By its silence, considered in connection with the decision of the Supreme Court in the case of M'Culloch against the state of Maryland, this act takes from the states the power to tax a portion of the banking business carried on within their limits, in subversion of one of the strongest barriers which secured them against federal encroachments. Banking, like farming, manufacturing, or any other occupation or profession, is a business, the right to follow which is not originally derived from the laws. Every citizen and every company of citizens in all of our states possessed the right until the state legislatures deemed it good policy to prohibit private banking by law. If the prohibitory state laws were now repealed, every citizen would again possess the right. The state banks are a qualified restoration of the right which has been taken away by the laws against banking, guarded by such provisions and limitations as in the opinion of the state legislatures the public interest requires. These corporations, unless there be an exemption in their charter, are, like private bankers and banking companies, subject to state taxation. The manner in which these taxes shall be laid depends wholly on legislative discretion. It may be upon the bank, upon the stock, upon the profits, or in any other mode which the sovereign power shall will.

Upon the formation of the Constitution the states guarded their taxing power with peculiar jealousy. They surrendered it only as it regards imports and exports. In relation to every other object within their jurisdiction, whether persons, property, business, or professions, it was secured in as ample a manner as it was before possessed. All persons, though United States officers, are liable to a poll tax by the states within which they reside. The lands of the United States are liable to the usual land tax, except in the new states, from whom agreements that they will not tax unsold lands are exacted when they are admitted into the Union. Horses, wagons, any beasts or vehicles, tools, or property belonging to private citizens, though employed in the service of the United States, are subject to state taxation. Every private business, whether carried on by an officer of the general government or not, whether it be mixed with public concerns or not, even if it be carried on by the government of the United States itself, separately or in

partnership, falls within the scope of the taxing power of the state. Nothing comes more fully within it than banks and the business of banking, by whomsoever instituted and carried on. Over this whole subject matter it is just as absolute, unlimited, and uncontrollable as if the Constitution had never been adopted, because in the formation of that instrument it was reserved without qualification.

The principle is conceded that the states cannot rightfully tax the operations of the general government. They cannot tax the money of the government deposited in the state banks nor the agency of those banks remitting it; but will any man maintain that their mere selection to perform this public service for the general government would exempt the state banks and their ordinary business from state taxation? Had the United States, instead of establishing a bank at Philadelphia, employed a private banker to keep and transmit their funds, would it have deprived Pennsylvania of the right to tax his bank and his usual banking operations? It will not be pretended. Upon what principle, then, are the banking establishments of the Bank of the United States and their usual banking operations to be exempted from taxation?

It is not their public agency or the deposits of the government which the states claim a right to tax, but their banks and their banking powers, instituted and exercised within state jurisdiction for their private emolument— those powers and privileges for which they pay a bonus, and which the states tax in their own banks. The exercise of these powers within a state, no matter by whom or under what authority, whether by private citizens in their original right, by corporate bodies created by the states, by foreigners or the agents of foreign governments located within their limits, forms a legitimate object of state taxation. From this and like sources, from the persons, property, and business that are found residing, located, or carried on under their jurisdiction, must the states, since the surrender of their right to raise a revenue from imports and exports, draw all the money necessary for the support of their governments and the maintenance of their independence. There is no more appropriate subject of taxation than banks, banking, and bank stocks, and none to which the states ought more pertinaciously to cling.

It cannot be "necessary" to the character of the bank as a fiscal agent of the government that its private business should be exempted from that taxation to which all the state banks are liable, nor can I conceive it "proper" that the substantive and most essential powers reserved by the states shall be thus attacked and annihilated as a means of executing the powers delegated to the general government. It may be safely assumed that none of those sages who had an agency in forming or adopting our Constitution ever imagined that any portion of the taxing power of the states not prohibited to them nor delegated to Congress was to be swept away and annihilated as a means of executing certain powers delegated to Congress.

If our power over means is so absolute that the Supreme Court will not call in question the constitutionality of an act of Congress the subject of which "is not prohibited, and is really calculated to effect any of the objects entrusted to the government," although, as in the case before me, it takes away powers expressly granted to Congress and rights scrupulously reserved to the states, it becomes us to proceed in our legislation with the utmost caution. Though not directly, our own powers and the rights of the states may be indirectly legislated away in the use of means to execute substantive powers.

We may not enact that Congress shall not have the power of exclusive legislation over the District of Columbia, but

we may pledge the faith of the United States that as a means of executing other powers it shall not be exercised for twenty years or forever. We may not pass an act prohibiting the states to tax the banking business carried on within their limits, but we may, as a means of executing our powers over other objects, place that business in the hands of our agents and then declare it exempt from state taxation in their hands. Thus may our own powers and the rights of the states, which we cannot directly curtail or invade, be frittered away and extinguished in the use of means employed by us to execute other powers. That a bank of the United States, competent to all the duties which may be required by the government, might be so organized as not to infringe on our own delegated powers or the reserved rights of the states I do not entertain a doubt. Had the executive been called upon to furnish the project of such an institution, the duty would have been cheerfully performed. In the absence of such a call it was obviously proper that he should confine himself to pointing out those prominent features in the act presented which in his opinion make it incompatible with the Constitution and sound policy. A general discussion will now take place, eliciting new light and settling important principles; and a new Congress, elected in the midst of such discussion, and furnishing an equal representation of the people according to the last census, will bear to the Capitol the verdict of public opinion, and, I doubt not, bring this important question to a satisfactory result.

Under such circumstances the bank comes forward and asks a renewal of its charter for a term of fifteen years upon conditions which not only operate as a gratuity to the stockholders of many millions of dollars but will sanction any abuses and legalize any encroachments.

Suspicions are entertained and charges are made of gross abuse and violation of its charter. An investigation unwillingly conceded and so restricted in time as necessarily to make it incomplete and unsatisfactory discloses enough to excite suspicion and alarm. In the practices of the principal bank partially unveiled, in the absence of important witnesses, and in numerous charges confidently made and as yet wholly uninvestigated there was enough to induce a majority of the committee of investigation—a committee which was selected from the most able and honorable members of the House of Representatives—to recommend a suspension of further action upon the bill and a prosecution of the inquiry. As the charter had yet four years to run, and as a renewal now was not necessary to the successful prosecution of its business, it was to have been expected that the bank itself, conscious of its purity and proud of its character, would have withdrawn its application for the present and demanded the severest scrutiny into all its transactions. In their declining to do so there seems to be an additional reason why the functionaries of the government should proceed with less haste and more caution in the renewal of their monopoly.

The bank is professedly established as an agent of the executive branch of the government, and its constitutionality is maintained on that ground. Neither upon the propriety of present action nor upon the provisions of this act was the executive consulted. It has had no opportunity to say that it neither needs nor wants an agent clothed with such powers and favored by such exemptions. There is nothing in its legitimate functions which makes it necessary or proper. Whatever interest or influence, whether public or private, has given birth to this act, it cannot be found either in the wishes or necessities of the Executive Department, by which present action is deemed premature, and the powers conferred upon its agent not only unnecessary but dangerous to the government and country.

It is to be regretted that the rich and powerful too often bend the acts of government to their selfish purposes. Distinctions in society will always exist under every just government. Equality of talents, of education, or of wealth cannot be produced by human institutions. In the full enjoyment of the gifts of Heaven and the fruits of superior industry, economy, and virtue, every man is equally entitled to protection by law; but when the laws undertake to add to these natural and just advantages artificial distinctions, to grant titles, gratuities, and exclusive privileges, to make the rich richer and the potent more powerful, the humble members of society—the farmers, mechanics, and laborers—who have neither the time nor the means of securing like favors to themselves, have a right to complain of the injustice of their government. There are no necessary evils in government. Its evils exist only in its abuses. If it would confine itself to equal protection, and, as Heaven does its rains, shower its favors alike on the high and the low, the rich and the poor, it would be an unqualified blessing. In the act before me there seems to be a wide and unnecessary departure from these just principles.

Nor is our government to be maintained or our Union preserved by invasions of the rights and powers of the several states. In thus attempting to make our general government strong, we make it weak. Its true strength consists in leaving individuals and states as much as possible to themselves—in making itself felt, not in its power, but in its beneficence; not in its control, but in its protection; not in binding the states more closely to the center, but leaving each to move unobstructed in its proper orbit.

Experience should teach us wisdom. Most of the difficulties our government now encounters and most of the dangers which impend over our Union have sprung from an abandonment of the legitimate objects of government by our national legislation and the adoption of such principles as are embodied in this act. Many of our rich men have not been content with equal protection and equal benefits but have besought us to make them richer by act of Congress. By attempting to gratify their desires, we have in the results of our legislation arrayed section against section, interest against interest, and man against man, in a fearful commotion which threatens to shake the foundations of our Union.

It is time to pause in our career to review our principles and, if possible, revive that devoted patriotism and spirit of compromise which distinguished the sages of the Revolution and the fathers of our Union. If we cannot at once, in justice to interests vested under improvident legislation, make our government what it ought to be, we can at least take a stand against all new grants of monopolies and exclusive privileges, against any prostitution of our government to the advancement of a few at the expense of the many, and in favor of compromise and gradual reform in our code of laws and system of political economy.

# James K. Polk's
# War Message to Congress (1846)

During his two terms as president, Andrew Jackson transformed the Democratic party into the nation's majority party: from 1828 to 1856, Democrats won six of eight presidential elections. The party was deeply divided, however, by the petition of Texas, which had been Mexican territory until it declared its independence in 1836, to become part of the United States. Southerners wanted to admit Texas to the Union, but northerners objected to adding another slave state to the southern ranks in Congress and warned that to admit Texas might provoke an invasion by Mexico.

In 1844 a fractious Democratic convention nominated former Tennessee governor James K. Polk, a staunch Jacksonian, for president on the ninth ballot. Polk was a generally unknown, compromise candidate—indeed, he was the first nominee to whom the label "dark horse" was ever applied. But Polk, who favored annexing Texas, handily defeated his better-known, anti-annexation Whig opponent, Henry Clay. (The vote in the electoral college was 170-105.) Congress responded by voting to make Texas a state on March 1, 1845, three days before Polk was inaugurated.

In the spring of 1846, Polk ordered Gen. Zachary Taylor to deploy troops in a strip of land north of the Rio Grande that was claimed by both Texas and Mexico. Shots were fired between U.S. and Mexican soldiers on April 25. Polk received word of the skirmish on May 11; two days later he sent a war message to Congress declaring that Mexico had invaded U.S. territory and killed American soldiers. "War exists," Polk wrote, "and notwithstanding all our efforts to avoid it, exists by the act of Mexico itself."

In truth, Polk had wanted war (he saw it as a way to obtain New Mexico and California from Mexico) and had provoked it. But Congress responded to his message at once and declared war on May 13. The vote was 173-14 in the House and 40-2 in the Senate.

The second president to lead the United States into war, Polk was the first to exercise effectively the powers of his office as commander in chief. He insisted on being the decisive and controlling authority on all important military matters. Generals Taylor and Winfield Scott resented Polk's involvement because Polk lacked military experience and was a Democrat. (Taylor and Scott were experienced soldiers and politically ambitious Whigs). But the president had clear constitutional authority over the army and navy and generally exercised it well. Although the war became increasingly unpopular among Whigs and northerners (Rep. Abraham Lincoln of Illinois introduced an antiwar resolution in 1847), success

*on the battlefield enabled Polk to nego-*
*tiate a peace treaty with Mexico that*
*secured the Rio Grande boundary for*
*Texas and the purchase of New Mexico*
*and California for $15 million. Polk*
*submitted the Treaty of Guadalupe*
*Hidalgo to the Senate on February 23,*
*1848. It was ratified on March 10 by a*
*vote of 38-14.*

*In addition to invigorating the presi-*
*dent's powers as commander in chief,*
*Polk was the first president to play an*
*active, ongoing role as chief executive*
*of the departments. A stickler for fiscal*
*economy, he closely oversaw federal*
*spending. After the Mexican War*
*ended, for example, Polk forced his*
*reluctant secretary of war, William*
*Marcy, to restore military spending to*
*its prewar level.*           ~

To the Senate and House of Representatives:

The existing state of the relations
between the United States and Mexico
renders it proper that I should bring the
subject to the consideration of Congress. In my message at the commencement of your present session the state
of these relations, the causes which led
to the suspension of diplomatic intercourse between the two countries in
March, 1845, and the long-continued
and unredressed wrongs and injuries
committed by the Mexican Government
on citizens of the United States in their
persons and property were briefly set
forth. . . .

The strong desire to establish peace
with Mexico on liberal and honorable
terms, and the readiness of this Government to regulate and adjust our boundary and other causes of difference with
that power on such fair and equitable
principles as would lead to permanent
relations of the most friendly nature,
induced me in September last to seek
the reopening of diplomatic relations
between the two countries. Every measure adopted on our part had for its

object the furtherance of these desired
results. In communicating to Congress a
succinct statement of the injuries which
we had suffered from Mexico, and
which have been accumulating during a
period of more than twenty years, every
expression that could tend to inflame
the people of Mexico or defeat or delay
a pacific result was carefully avoided.
An envoy of the United States repaired
to Mexico with full powers to adjust
every existing difference. But though
present on the Mexican soil by agreement between the two Governments,
invested with full powers, and bearing
evidence of the most friendly dispositions, his mission has been unavailing.
The Mexican Government not only refused to receive him or listen to his
propositions, but after a long-continued
series of menaces have at last invaded
our territory and shed the blood of our
fellow-citizens on our own soil.

It now becomes my duty to state
more in detail the origin, progress, and
failure of that mission. In pursuance of
the instructions given in September
last, an inquiry was made on the 13th of
October, 1845, in the most friendly
terms, through our consul in Mexico, of
the minister for foreign affairs, whether
the Mexican Government "would receive an envoy from the United States
intrusted with full powers to adjust all
the questions in dispute between the
two Governments," with the assurance
that "should the answer be in the affirmative such an envoy would be immediately dispatched to Mexico." The Mexican minister on the 15th of October
gave an affirmative answer to this inquiry, requesting at the same time that
our naval force at Vera Cruz might be
withdrawn, lest its continued presence
might assume the appearance of menace and coercion pending the negotiations. This force was immediately withdrawn. On the 10th of November, 1845,
Mr. John Slidell, of Louisiana, was commissioned by me as envoy extraordinary
and minister plenipotentiary of the

United States to Mexico, and was intrusted with full powers to adjust both the questions of the Texas boundary and of indemnification to our citizens. The redress of the wrongs of our citizens naturally and inseparably blended itself with the question of boundary. The settlement of the one question in any correct view of the subject involves that of the other. I could not for a moment entertain the idea that the claims of our much-injured and long-suffering citizens, many of which had existed for more than twenty years, should be postponed or separated from the settlement of the boundary question.

Mr. Slidell arrived at Vera Cruz on the 30th of November, and was courteously received by the authorities of that city. But the Government of General Herrera was then tottering to its fall. The revolutionary party had seized upon the Texas question to effect or hasten its overthrow. Its determination to restore friendly relations with the United States, and to receive our minister to negotiate for the settlement of this question, was violently assailed, and was made the great theme of denunciation against it. The Government of General Herrera, there is good reason to believe, was sincerely desirous to receive our minister; but it yielded to the storm raised by its enemies, and on the 21st of December refused to accredit Mr. Slidell upon the most frivolous pretexts. These are so fully and ably exposed in the note of Mr. Slidell on the 24th of December last to the Mexican minister of foreign relations, herewith transmitted, that I deem it unnecessary to enter into further detail on this portion of the subject.

Five days after the date of Mr. Slidell's note General Herrera yielded the Government to General Paredes without a struggle, and on the 30th of December resigned the Presidency. This revolution was accomplished solely by the army, the people having taken little part in the contest; and thus the supreme power in Mexico passed into the hands of a military leader.

Determined to leave no effort untried to effect an amicable adjustment with Mexico, I directed Mr. Slidell to present his credentials to the Government of General Paredes and ask to be officially received by him. There would have been less ground for taking this step had General Paredes come into power by a regular constitutional succession. In that event his administration would have been considered but a mere constitutional continuance of the Government of General Herrera, and the refusal of the latter to receive our minister would have been deemed conclusive unless an intimation had been given by General Paredes of his desire to reverse the decision of his predecessor. But the Government of General Paredes owes its existence to a military revolution, by which the subsisting constitutional authorities had been subverted. The form of government was entirely changed, as well as all the high functionaries by whom it was administered.

Under these circumstances, Mr. Slidell, in obedience to my direction, addressed a note to the Mexican minister of foreign relations, under date of the 1st of March last, asking to be received by that Government in the diplomatic character to which he had been appointed. This minister in his reply, under date of the 12th of March, reiterated the arguments of his predecessor, and in terms that may be considered as giving just grounds of offense to the Government and people of the United States denied the application of Mr. Slidell. Nothing therefore remained for our envoy but to demand his passports and return to his own country.

Thus the Government of Mexico, though solemnly pledged by official acts in October last to receive and accredit an American envoy, violated their plighted faith and refused the offer of a peaceful adjustment of our difficulties. Not only was the offer rejected, but the indignity of its rejection was enhanced by the manifest breach of faith in refusing to admit the envoy who came because they had bound themselves to receive him. Nor can it be said that the offer was fruitless from the want of opportunity of discussing it; our envoy was present on their own soil. Nor can it be ascribed to a want of sufficient powers; our envoy had full powers to adjust every question of difference. Nor was there room for complaint that our propositions for settlement were unreasonable; permission was not even given our envoy to make any proposition whatever. Nor can it be objected that we, on our part, would not listen to any reasonable terms of their suggestion; the Mexican Government refused all negotiation, and have made no proposition of any kind.

In my message at the commencement of the present session I informed you that upon the earnest appeal both of the Congress and convention of Texas I had ordered an efficient military force to take a position "between the Nueces and the Del Norte." This had become necessary to meet a threatened invasion of Texas by the Mexican forces, for which extensive military preparations had been made. The invasion was threatened solely because Texas had determined, in accordance with a solemn resolution of the Congress of the United States, to annex herself to our Union, and under these circumstances it was plainly our duty to extend our protection over her citizens and soil.

This force was concentrated at Corpus Christi, and remained there until after I had received such information from Mexico as rendered it probable, if not certain, that the Mexican Government would refuse to receive our envoy.

Meantime Texas, by the final action of our Congress, had become an integral part of our Union. The Congress of Texas, by its act of December 19, 1836, had declared the Rio del Norte to be the boundary of that Republic. Its jurisdiction had been extended and exercised beyond the Nueces. The country between that river and the Del Norte had been represented in the Congress and in the convention of Texas, had thus taken part in the act of annexation itself, and is now included within one of our Congressional districts. Our own Congress had, moreover, with great unanimity, by the act approved December 31, 1845, recognized the country beyond the Nueces as a part of our territory by including it within our own revenue system, and a revenue officer to reside within that district had been appointed by and with the advice and consent of the Senate. It became, therefore, of urgent necessity to provide for the defense of that portion of our country. Accordingly, on the 13th of January last instructions were issued to the general in command of these troops to occupy the left bank of the Del Norte. This river, which is the southwestern boundary of the State of Texas, is an exposed frontier. From this quarter invasion was threatened; upon it and in its immediate vicinity, in the judgment of high military experience, are the proper stations for the protecting forces of the Government. In addition to this important consideration, several others occurred to induce this movement. Among these are the facilities afforded by the ports at Brazos Santiago and the mouth of the Del Norte for the reception of supplies by sea, the stronger and more abundant supply of provisions, water, fuel, and forage, and the advantages which are afforded by the Del Norte in forwarding supplies to such posts as may be established in the interior and upon the Indian frontier.

The movement of the troops to the Del Norte was made by the commanding general under positive instructions to abstain from all aggressive acts toward Mexico or Mexican citizens and to regard the relations between that Republic and the United States as peaceful unless she should declare war or commit acts of hostility indicative of a state of war. He was specially directed to protect private property and respect personal rights.

The Army moved from Corpus Christi on the 11th of March, and on the 28th of that month arrived on the left bank of the Del Norte opposite to Matamoras, where it encamped on a commanding position, which has since been strengthened by the erection of fieldworks. A depot has also been established at Point Isabel, near the Brazos Santiago, 30 miles in rear of the encampment. The selection of his position was necessarily confided to the judgment of the general in command.

The Mexican forces at Matamoras assumed a belligerent attitude, and on the 12th of April General Ampudia, then in command, notified General Taylor to break up his camp within twenty-four hours and to retire beyond the Nueces River, and in the event of his failure to comply with these demands announced that arms, and arms alone, must decide the question. But no open act of hostility was committed until the 24th of April. On that day General Arista, who had succeeded to the command of the Mexican forces, communicated to General Taylor that "he considered hostilities commenced and should prosecute them." A party of dragoons of 63 men and officers were on the same day dispatched from the American camp up the Rio del Norte, on its left bank, to ascertain whether the Mexican troops had crossed or were preparing to cross the river, "became engaged with a large body of these troops, and after a short affair, in which some 16 were killed and wounded, appear to have been surrounded and compelled to surrender."

The grievous wrongs perpetrated by Mexico upon our citizens throughout a long period of years remain unre-

dressed, and solemn treaties pledging her public faith for this redress have been disregarded. A government either unable or unwilling to enforce the execution of such treaties fails to perform one of its plainest duties.

Our commerce with Mexico has been almost annihilated. It was formerly highly beneficial to both nations, but our merchants have been deterred from prosecuting it by the system of outrage and extortion which the Mexican authorities have pursued against them, whilst their appeals through their own Government for indemnity have been made in vain. Our forbearance has gone to such an extreme as to be mistaken in its character. Had we acted with vigor in repelling the insults and redressing the injuries inflicted by Mexico at the commencement, we should doubtless have escaped all the difficulties in which we are now involved.

Instead of this, however, we have been exerting our best efforts to propitiate her good will. Upon the pretext that Texas, a nation as independent as herself, thought proper to unite its destinies with our own, she has affected to believe that we have severed her rightful territory, and in official proclamations and manifestoes has repeatedly threatened to make war upon us for the purpose of reconquering Texas. In the meantime we have tried every effort at reconciliation. The cup of forbearance has been exhausted even before the recent information from the frontier of the Del Norte. But now, after reiterated menaces, Mexico has passed the boundary of the United States, has invaded our territory and shed American blood upon the American soil. She has proclaimed that hostilities have commenced, and that the two nations are now at war.

As war exists, and, notwithstanding all our efforts to avoid it, exists by the act of Mexico herself, we are called upon by every consideration of duty and patriotism to vindicate with decision the honor, the rights, and the interests of our country.

Anticipating the possibility of a crisis like that which has arrived, instructions were given in August last, "as a precautionary measure" against invasion or threatened invasion, authorizing General Taylor, if the emergency required, to accept volunteers, not from Texas only, but from the States of Louisiana, Alabama, Mississippi, Tennessee, and Kentucky, and corresponding letters were addressed to the respective governors of those States. These instructions were repeated, and in January last, soon after the incorporation of "Texas into our Union of States," General Taylor was further "authorized by the President to make a requisition upon the executive of that State for such of its militia force as may be needed to repel invasion or to secure the country against apprehended invasion." On the 2d day of March he was again reminded, "in the event of the approach of any considerable Mexican force, promptly and efficiently to use the authority with which he was clothed to call to him such auxiliary force as he might need." War actually existing and our territory having been invaded, General Taylor, pursuant to authority vested in him by my direction, has called on the Governor of Texas for four regiments of State troops, two to be mounted and two to serve on foot, and on the Governor of Louisiana for four regiments of infantry to be sent to him as soon as practicable.

In further vindication of our rights and defense of our territory, I invoke the prompt action of Congress to recognize the existence of the war, and to place at the disposition of the executive the means of prosecuting the war with vigor, and thus hastening the restoration of peace. To this end I recommend that authority should be given to call into the public service a large body of volunteers to serve for not less than six or twelve months unless sooner discharged. A volunteer force is beyond question more efficient than any other description of citizen soldiers, and it is not to be doubted that a number far beyond that required would readily rush to the field upon the call of their country. I further recommend that a liberal provision be made for sustaining our entire military force and furnishing it with supplies and munitions of war.

The most energetic and prompt measures and the immediate appearance in arms of a large and overpowering force are recommended to Congress as the most certain and efficient means of bringing the existing collision with Mexico to a speedy and successful termination.

In making these recommendations I deem it proper to declare that it is my anxious desire not only to terminate hostilities speedily, but to bring all matters in dispute between this Government and Mexico to an early and amicable adjustment; and in this view I shall be prepared to renew negotiations whenever Mexico shall be ready to receive propositions or to make propositions of her own. . . .

JAMES K. POLK

# Abraham Lincoln's "House Divided" Speech (1858)

The slavery issue dominated national politics throughout the middle decades of the nineteenth century. Although most northerners were willing to tolerate the continued existence of slavery in the South, they strongly opposed its extension into the western territories that were preparing for statehood. Southern slaveowners, however, felt that if slavery were confined within its current borders, antislavery sentiment eventually would lead to its abolition by a Congress dominated by free states.

In 1854 Sen. Stephen Douglas of Illinois, a Democrat, persuaded Congress to pass the Kansas-Nebraska Act, which tried to skirt the slavery issue by stipulating that "popular sovereignty" (a vote by the settlers) would determine whether slavery would be allowed to exist in the Kansas and Nebraska territories after they were admitted as states. Violent conflict between supporters and opponents of slavery quickly ensued in Kansas. Then, in 1857, a crippling blow was dealt to popular sovereignty (and to antislavery sentiment in general) by the Supreme Court. The Court ruled in the case of Dred Scott v. Sanford that because slaves were the property of their owners, no government could restrict the right of slaveholders to take their slaves with them anywhere in the country.

Politically, the controversy over slavery destroyed one political party and gave rise to another. The antislavery, northern-based Republican party formed in 1854 mainly to replace the defunct Whig party, which had been torn apart by the conflict between its northern and southern wings. In 1856 the Republicans fielded a ticket in the presidential election. Although defeated, their nominee, Gen. John C. Fremont, ran a strong race against the Democratic candidate, former secretary of state James Buchanan of Pennsylvania.

In 1858 former Whig representative Abraham Lincoln was nominated by the Republican party of Illinois to challenge the author of the Kansas-Nebraska Act, Senator Douglas, for reelection. In conformance with the Constitution, senators still were elected by the state legislatures (direct election by the people came only with the enactment of the Seventeenth Amendment in 1913), but Lincoln and Douglas campaigned vigorously to try to influence the outcome of the state legislative elections. The Lincoln-Douglas debates, a series of joint appearances by the candidates around the state, set a standard for political discussion that seldom has been matched.

Lincoln began his senatorial campaign on June 16, 1858, with an acceptance speech to the Republican state *convention that nominated him for senator. The highly partisan address excoriated the Democrats in general and Douglas and the Supreme Court in particular for promoting policies that, Lincoln claimed, ultimately would prevent even northern free states from barring slavery. The speech is best remembered, however, for a keenly prophetic passage in the second paragraph. " 'A house divided against itself cannot stand,' " Lincoln said, quoting Jesus. "I believe this government cannot endure permanently, half slave and half free. . . . It will become all one thing, or all the other."*

*The Illinois legislature remained narrowly Democratic after the election and voted to return Douglas to the Senate for another term. But Lincoln's brilliant campaign won him national attention.*                                ~

Mr. President and Gentlemen of the Convention:

If we could first know where we are and whither we are tending, we could better judge what to do and how to do it.

We are now far into the fifth year since a policy was initiated with the avowed object and confident promise of putting an end to slavery agitation. Under the operation of that policy, that agitation has not only not ceased, but has constantly augmented. In my opinion it will not cease until a crisis shall have been reached and passed. "A house divided against itself cannot stand." I believe this government cannot endure permanently, half slave and half free. I do not expect the Union to be dissolved,—I do not expect the house to fall; but I do expect it will cease to be divided. It will become all one thing, or all the other. Either the opponents of slavery will arrest the further spread of it, and place it where the public mind shall rest in the belief that it is in the course of ultimate extinction; or its ad-

vocates will push it forward till it shall become alike lawful in the States, old as well as new, North as well as South.

Have we no tendency to the latter condition? Let any one who doubts, carefully contemplate that now almost complete legal combination—piece of machinery, so to speak—compounded of the Nebraska doctrine and the Dred Scott decision. Let him consider not only what work the machinery is adapted to do, and how well adapted; but also let him study the history of its construction, and trace, if he can, or rather fail, if he can, to trace the evidences of design and concert of action among its chief architects from the beginning.

The new year of 1854 found slavery excluded from more than half the States by State constitutions, and from most of the national territory by congressional prohibition. Four days later commenced the struggle which ended in repealing that congressional prohibition. This opened all the national territory to slavery, and was the first point gained.

But so far, Congress only had acted; and an indorsement by the people, real or apparent, was indispensable to save the point already gained and give chance for more.

This necessity had not been overlooked, but had been provided for, as well as might be, in the notable argument of *Squatter Sovereignty,* otherwise called *sacred right of self-government,* which later phrase, though expressive of the only rightful basis of any government, was so perverted in this attempted use of it, as to amount to just this: That if any one man choose to enslave another, no third man shall be allowed to object. That argument was incorporated into the Nebraska bill itself, in the language which follows: "It being the true intent and meaning of this act, not to legislate slavery into any Territory or State, nor to exclude it therefrom; but to leave the people thereof perfectly free to form and regulate their own way, subject only to the Constitution of the United States." Then opened the roar of loose declamation in favor of *Squatter Sovereignty* and sacred right of self-government. "But," said opposition members, "let us amend the bill so as to expressly declare that people of the Territory may exclude slavery." "Not we," said the friends of the measure, and down they voted the amendment.

While the Nebraska bill was passing through Congress a law case, involving the question of a negro's freedom, by reason of his owner having voluntarily taken him first into a free State and then into a Territory covered by the congressional prohibition, and held him as a slave for a long time in each, was passing through the United States Circuit Court for the District of Missouri; and both Nebraska bill and lawsuit were brought to a decision, in the same month of May, 1854. The negro's name was "Dred Scott," which name now designates the decision finally rendered in the case. Before the then next presidential election, the law case came to, and was argued in, the Supreme Court of the United States; but the decision of it was deferred until after the election. Still, before the election, Senator Trumbull, on the floor of the Senate, requested the leading advocate of the Nebraska bill to state his opinion whether the people of a Territory can constitutionally exclude slavery from their limits, and the latter answers: "That is a question for the Supreme Court."

The election came. Mr. Buchanan was elected, and the indorsement, such as it was, secured. That was the second point gained. The indorsement, however, fell short of a clear popular majority by nearly four hundred thousand votes, and so, perhaps, was not overwhelmingly reliable and satisfactory. The outgoing President, in his last annual message, as impressively as possible echoed back upon the people the weight and authority of the indorsement. The Supreme Court met again; did not announce their decision, but ordered a reargument. The presidential inauguration came, and still no decision of the Court; but the incoming President in his inaugural address fervently exhorted the people to abide by the forthcoming decision, whatever it might be. Then, in a few days, came the decision.

The reputed author of the Nebraska bill finds an early occasion to make a speech at this capitol, indorsing the Dred Scott decision, and vehemently denouncing all opposition to it. The new President, too, seizes the early occasion of the Silliman letter to indorse and strongly construe that decision, and to express his astonishment that any different view had ever been entertained!

At length a squabble springs up between the President and the author of the Nebraska bill, on the mere question of *fact* whether the Lecompton constitution was, or was not, in any just sense, made by the people of Kansas; and in that quarrel, the latter declares that all he wants is a fair vote for the people, and that he cares not whether slavery be *voted down* or *voted up*. I do not understand his declaration that he cares not whether slavery be voted down or voted up, to be intended by him other than as an apt definition of the policy he would impress upon the public mind,—the principle for which he declares he has suffered so much, and is ready to suffer to the end. And well he may cling to that principle. If he has any parental feeling, well he may cling to it. That principle is the only shred left of his original Nebraska doctrine. Under the Dred Scott decision, "squatter sovereignty" squatted out of existence, tumbled down like temporary scaffolding; like the mould at the foundry, it served through one blast, and fell back into loose sand,—helped to carry an election, and then was kicked to the winds. His late joint struggle with the Republicans against the Lecompton constitution involves nothing of the original Nebraska doctrine. That struggle was made on a point—the right of the people to make their own constitution—upon which he and the Republicans have never differed.

The several points of the Dred Scott decision in connection with Senator Douglas's "care not" policy constitute the piece of machinery in its present state of advancement. This was the third point gained. The working points of that machinery are:

*First:* That no negro slave, imported as such from Africa, and no descendant of such slave, can ever be a citizen of any State, in the sense of that term as used in the Constitution of the United States. This point is made in order to deprive the negro, in every possible event, of the benefit of that provision of the United States Constitution which declares that "the citizens of each State shall be entitled to all privileges and immunities of citizens in the several States."

*Secondly.* That "subject to the Constitution of the United States," neither Congress nor a territorial legislature can exclude slavery from any United States Territory. This point is made in order that individual men may fill up the Territories with slaves, without danger of losing them as property, and thus enhance the chances of permanency to the institution through all the future.

*Thirdly.* That whether the holding a negro in actual slavery in a free State makes him free as against the holder, the United States Courts will not decide, but will leave to be decided by the courts of any slave State the negro may be forced into by the master. This point is made, not to be pressed immediately; but if acquiesced in for a while, and apparently indorsed by the people at an election, then to sustain the logical conclusion that what Dred Scott's master might lawfully do with Dred Scott in the free State of Illinois, every other master may lawfully do, with any other one, or one thousand slaves in Illinois, or in any other free State.

Auxiliary to all this, and working hand-in-hand with it, the Nebraska doctrine, or what is left of it, is to educate and mould public opinion not to care whether slavery is voted down or voted up. This shows exactly where we now are, and partially, also, whither we are tending.

It will throw additional light on the latter, to go back, and run the mind over the string of historical facts already stated. Several things will now appear less dark and mysterious than they did when they were transpiring. The people were to be left "perfectly free," "subject only to the Constitution." What the Constitution had to do with it, outsiders could not then see. Plainly enough now: it was an exactly fitted niche for the Dred Scott decision to afterwards come in, and declare the perfect freedom of the people to be just no freedom at all. Why was the amendment expressly declaring the right of the people voted down? Plainly enough now: the adoption of it would have spoiled the niche for the Dred Scott decision. Why was the Court decision held up? Why even a Senator's individual opinion withheld till after the presidential election? Plainly enough now: the speaking out then would have damaged the perfectly free argument upon which the election was to be carried. Why was the outgoing President's felicitation on the indorsement? Why the delay of a reargument? Why the incoming President's advance exhortation in favor of the decision? These things look like the cautious patting and petting of a spirited horse, preparatory to mounting him, when it is dreaded that he may give the rider a fall. And why the hasty after-indorsement of the decision by the President and others?

We cannot absolutely know that all these adaptations are the result of pre-concert. But when we see a lot of framed timbers, different portions of which we know have been gotten out at different times and places, and by different workmen—Stephen, Franklin, Roger, and James, for instance—and when we see those timbers joined together, and see they exactly make the frame of a house or a mill, all the tenons and mortices exactly fitting, and all the lengths and proportions of the different pieces exactly adapted to their respective places, and not a piece too many or too few, not omitting even scaffolding—or if a single piece be lacking, we see the place in the frame exactly fitted and prepared yet to bring such piece in—in such a case, we find it impossible not to believe that Stephen and Franklin and Roger and James all understood one another from the beginning, and all worked upon a common plan or draft, drawn up before the first blow was struck.

It should not be overlooked that by the Nebraska bill the people of a State as well as Territory were to be left "perfectly free," "subject only to the Constitution." Why mention a State? They were legislating for Territories, and not for or about States. Certainly the people of a State are and ought to be subject to the Constitution of the United States; but why is mention of this lugged into this merely territorial law? Why are the people of a Territory and the people of a State therein lumped together, and their relation to the Constitution therein treated as being precisely the same? While the opinion of the Court by Chief Justice Taney, in the Dred Scott case, and the separate opinions of all the concurring judges, expressly declare that the Constitution of the United States neither permits Congress nor a territorial legislature to exclude slavery from any United States Territory, they all omit to declare whether or not the same Constitution permits a State or the people of a State to exclude it. *Possibly* this is a mere omission; but who can be quite sure if McLean or Curtis had sought to get into the opinion a declaration of unlimited power in the people of a State to exclude slavery from their limits,—just as Chase and Mace sought to get such declaration in behalf of the people of a Territory, into the Nebraska bill,—I ask who can be quite sure it would not have been voted down in the one case as it had been in the other? The nearest approach to the point of declaring the power of a State over slavery is made by Judge Nelson. He approaches it more than once, using the precise idea, and almost the language too, of the Nebraska act. On one occasion his exact language is "except in cases where the power is restrained by the Constitution of the United States, the law of the State is supreme over the subject of slavery within its jurisdiction." In what cases the power of the State is so restrained by the United States Constitution is left an open question, precisely as the same question, as to the restraint on the power of the Territories, was left open in the Nebraska act. Put this and that together, and we have another nice little niche, which we may, ere long, see filled with another Supreme Court decision, declaring that the Constitution of the United States does not permit a State to exclude slavery from its limits. And this may especially be expected if the doctrine of "care not whether slavery be voted down or voted up" shall gain the public mind sufficiently to give promise that such a decision can be maintained when made.

Such a decision is all that slavery now lacks of being alike lawful in all the States. Welcome or unwelcome, such decision is probably coming, and will soon be upon us, unless the power of the present political dynasty shall be met and overthrown. We shall lie down, pleasantly dreaming that the people of Missouri are on the verge of making their State free, and we shall awake to the reality instead, that the Supreme Court has made Illinois a slave State. To meet and overthrow the power of that dynasty is the work now before all those who would prevent that consummation. That is what we have to do. How can we best do it?

There are those who denounce us openly to their own friends, and yet whisper to us softly that Senator Douglas is the aptest instrument there is with which to effect that object. They wish us to infer all from the fact that he now has a little quarrel with the present head of the dynasty, and that he has regularly voted with us on a single point, upon which he and we have never differed. They remind us that he is a great man and that the largest of us are very small ones. Let this be granted. But "a living dog is better than a dead lion." Judge Douglas, if not a dead lion, for this work is at least a caged and toothless one. How can he oppose the advances of slavery? He don't care anything about it. His avowed mission is impressing the "public heart" to care nothing about it. A leading Douglas Democratic newspaper thinks Douglas's superior talent will be needed to resist the revival of the African slave-trade. Does Douglas believe an effort to revive that trade is approaching? He has not said so. Does he really think so? But if it is, how can he resist it? For years he has labored to prove it a sacred right of white men to take negro slaves into the new territories. Can he possibly show that it is a less sacred right to buy them where they can be bought cheapest? And unquestionably they can be bought cheaper in Africa than in Virginia. He has done all in his power to reduce the whole question of slavery to one of a mere right of property: and, as such, how can he oppose the foreign slave trade?—how can he refuse that trade in that property shall be "perfectly free,"

unless he does it as a protection to the home production? And as the home producers will probably not ask the protection, he will be wholly without a ground of opposition.

Senator Douglas holds, we know, that a man may rightfully be wiser today than he was yesterday—that he may rightfully change when he finds himself wrong. But can we, for that reason, run ahead, and infer that he will make any particular change, for which he himself has given no intimation? Can we safely base our action upon any such vague inference?

Now, as ever, I wish not to misrepresent Judge Douglas's position, question his motives, or do aught that can be personally offensive to him. Whenever, if ever, he and we can come together on principle, so that our cause may have assistance from his great ability, I hope to have interposed no adventitious obstacle. But, clearly, he is not now with us—he does not pretend to be—he does not promise ever to be.

Our cause, then, must be intrusted to, and conducted by, its own undoubted friends—those whose hands are free, whose hearts are in the work, who do care for the result. Two years ago the Republicans of the nation mustered over thirteen hundred thousand strong. We did this under the single impulse of resistance to a common danger, with every external circumstance against us. Of strange, discordant, and even hostile elements, we gathered from the four winds, and formed and fought the battle through, under the constant hot fire of a disciplined, proud, and pampered enemy. Did we brave all then to falter now?—now, when that same enemy is wavering, dissevered, and belligerent? The result is not doubtful. We shall not fail. If we stand firm, we shall not fail. Wise counsels may accelerate or mistakes delay it; but sooner or later the victory is sure to come.

# Abraham Lincoln's
# First Message to Congress (1861)

Abraham Lincoln's strong campaign in 1858 to become U.S. senator from Illinois helped to make him a presidential contender, as did some speeches he later gave. In 1860 he was nominated for president by the Republican party. Despite winning only 40 percent of the popular vote, Lincoln carried nearly every northern state (but none in the South) and triumphed over a Democratic party that was split among three candidates: Sen. Stephen Douglas of Illinois, the nominee of the northern Democrats; Vice President John C. Breckinridge of Kentucky, who was nominated by southern Democrats; and Tennessean John Bell of the newly formed Constitutional Union party.

Although Lincoln had pledged not to attack the rights of slaveowners in the South, his opposition to extending slavery beyond its existing borders prompted seven Deep South states to secede quickly from the United States and, on February 7, 1861 (nearly a month before Lincoln's inauguration), to form the Confederate States of America. In his March 4 inaugural address, Lincoln warned secessionists that they would not be allowed to leave the Union peacefully: "You have no oath registered in Heaven to destroy the government, while I shall have the most solemn one 'to preserve, protect, and defend' it. You can forbear the assault; I can not shrink from the defense of it."

Notwithstanding Lincoln's warning, rebel forces surrounded Fort Sumter, South Carolina, the next day. On April 12 they fired on the fort, which soon fell. On May 3 Lincoln issued a proclamation that called out the state militia and asked for seventy-five thousand volunteers to aid in executing the national laws. Four other southern states seceded and joined the Confederacy in short order. Border states, notably Kentucky and Maryland, considered secession seriously.

Although calling out the militia was clearly within the president's constitutional powers, other of Lincoln's actions during the spring of 1861 were not. With Congress not yet convened in Washington (and the president reluctant to summon them into special session before getting the war effort under way), Lincoln substantially increased the size of the army and navy, ordered a blockade of southern ports, suspended the writ of habeas corpus (the constitutional guarantee against detention without legal cause by government authorities) in certain militarily vital parts of the country, instructed the Treasury to pay $2 million to two secret agents to purchase military supplies, imposed new passport regulations on foreign visitors, and barred "treasonable correspondence" from being delivered by the Post Office.

On July 4 Congress convened at Lin-

*coln's instruction. In a written message sent to Congress on that day, the president defended his actions. Some of them, he said, were constitutional. For example, although the Constitution seems to assign the power to suspend* habeas corpus *to Congress by listing it in Article I (the legislative article), Lincoln argued that the framers must have intended that the president exercise this power when Congress was not in session. Other actions, Lincoln wrote, "whether strictly legal or not, were ventured upon what appeared to be a popular demand and a public necessity, trusting then, as now, that Congress would readily ratify them." Yet Lincoln did not shrink from the charge that he may have broken some laws: "Are all the laws* but one *to go unexecuted, and the Government itself go to pieces lest that one be violated?" In asking this question, Lincoln implied that when a national emergency threatens the nation's existence, the Constitution may implicitly empower the president to ignore specific constitutional provisions in order to defend the entire plan of union.* ～

Fellow Citizens of the Senate and House of Representatives:

Having been convened on an extraordinary occasion, as authorized by the Constitution, your attention is not called to any ordinary subject of legislation.

At the beginning of the present Presidential term, four months ago, the functions of the Federal Government were found to be generally suspended within the several States of South Carolina, Georgia, Alabama, Mississippi, Louisiana, and Florida, excepting only those of the Post-Office Department.

Within these States all the forts, arsenals, dockyards, custom-houses, and the like, including the movable and stationary property in and about them, had been seized and were held in open hos-tility to this Government, excepting only Forts Pickens, Taylor, and Jefferson, on and near the Florida coast, and Fort Sumter, in Charleston Harbor, South Carolina. The forts thus seized had been put in improved condition, new ones had been built, and armed forces had been organized and were organizing, all avowedly with the same hostile purpose.

The forts remaining in the possession of the Federal Government in and near these States were either besieged or menaced by warlike preparations, and especially Fort Sumter was nearly surrounded by well-protected hostile batteries, with guns equal in quality to the best of its own and outnumbering the latter as perhaps ten to one. A disproportionate share of the Federal muskets and rifles had somehow found their way into these States, and had been seized to be used against the Government. Accumulations of the public revenue lying within them had been seized for the same object. The Navy was scattered in distant seas, leaving but a very small part of it within the immediate reach of the Government. Officers of the Federal Army and Navy had resigned in great numbers, and of those resigning a large proportion had taken up arms against the Government. Simultaneously and in connection with all this the purpose to sever the Federal Union was openly avowed. In accordance with this purpose, an ordinance had been adopted in each of these States declaring the States respectively to be separated from the National Union. A formula for instituting a combined government of these States had been promulgated, and this illegal organization, in the character of Confederate States, was already invoking recognition, aid, and intervention from foreign powers.

Finding this condition of things and believing it to be an imperative duty upon the incoming Executive to prevent, if possible, the consummation of such attempt to destroy the Federal Union, a choice of means to that end became indispensable. This choice was made, and was declared in the inaugural address. The policy chosen looked to the exhaustion of all peaceful measures before a resort to any stronger ones. It sought only to hold the public places and property not already wrested from the Government and to collect the revenue, relying for the rest on time, discussion, and the ballot box. It promised a continuance of the mails at Government expense to the very people who were resisting the Government, and it gave repeated pledges against any disturbance to any of the people or any of their rights. Of all that which a President might constitutionally and justifiably do in such a case, everything was forborne without which it was believed possible to keep the Government on foot.

On the 5th of March, the present incumbent's first full day in office, a letter of Major Anderson, commanding at Fort Sumter, written on the 28th of February and received at the War Department on the 4th of March, was by that Department placed in his hands. This letter expressed the professional opinion of the writer that reenforcements could not be thrown into that fort within the time for his relief rendered necessary by the limited supply of provisions, and with a view of holding possession of the same, with a force of less than 20,000 good and well-disciplined men. This opinion was concurred in by all the officers of his command, and their memoranda on the subject were made inclosures of Major Anderson's letter. The whole was immediately laid before Lieutenant-General Scott, who at once concurred with Major Anderson in opinion. On reflection, however, he took full time, consulting with other officers, both of the Army and the Navy, and at the end of four days came reluctantly, but decidedly, to the same conclusion as before. He also stated at the same time that no such sufficient force was then at the control of the Government or could be raised and brought to the ground within the time when the provisions in the fort would be exhausted. In a purely military point of view this reduced the duty of the Administration in the case to the mere matter of getting the garrison safely out of the fort.

It was believed, however, that to so abandon that position under the circumstances would be utterly ruinous; that the *necessity* under which it was to be done would not be fully understood; that by many it would be construed as a part of a *voluntary* policy; that at home it would discourage the friends of the Union, embolden its adversaries, and go far to insure to the latter a recognition abroad; that, in fact, it would be our national destruction consummated. This could not be allowed. Starvation was not yet upon the garrison, and ere it would be reached *Fort Pickens* might be reenforced. This last would be a clear indication of *policy,* and would better enable the country to accept the evacuation of Fort Sumter as a military *necessity.* An order was at once directed to be sent for the landing of the troops from the steamship *Brooklyn* into Fort Pickens. This order could not go by land but must take the longer and slower route by sea. The first return news from the order was received just one week before the fall of Fort Sumter. The news itself was that the officer commanding the *Sabine,* to which vessel the troops had been transferred from the *Brooklyn,* acting upon some *quasi* armistice of the late Administration (and of the existence of which the present Administration, up to the time the order was dispatched, had only too vague and uncertain rumors to fix attention), had refused to land the troops. To now reenforce Fort Pickens before a crisis would be reached at Fort Sumter was impossible, rendered so by the near exhaustion of provisions in the latter-named fort. In precaution against such a conjuncture the Government had a few days before commenced preparing an expedition, as well adapted as might be, to relieve Fort Sumter, which expedition was intended to be ultimately used or not, according to circumstances. The strongest anticipated case for using it was now presented, and it was resolved to send it forward. As had been intended in this contingency, it was also resolved to notify the governor of South Carolina that he might expect an attempt would be made to provision the fort, and that if the attempt should not be resisted there would be no effort to throw in men, arms, or ammunition without further notice, or in case of an attack upon the fort. This notice was accordingly given, whereupon the fort was attacked and bombarded to its fall, without even awaiting the arrival of the provisioning expedition.

It is thus seen that the assault upon and reduction of Fort Sumter was in no sense a matter of self-defense on the part of the assailants. They well knew that the garrison in the fort could by no possibility commit aggression upon them. They knew—they were expressly notified—that the giving of bread to the few brave and hungry men of the garrison was all which would on that occasion be attempted, unless themselves, by resisting so much, should provoke more. They knew that this Government desired to keep the garrison in the fort, not to assail them, but merely to maintain visible possession, and thus to preserve the Union from actual and immediate dissolution, trusting, as hereinbefore stated, to time, discussion, and the ballot box for final adjustment; and they assailed and reduced the fort for precisely the reverse object—to drive out the visible authority of the Federal Union, and thus force it to immediate dissolution. That this was their object the Executive well understood; and having said to them in the inaugural address, "You can have no conflict without being yourselves the aggressors," he took pains not only to keep this declaration good, but also to keep the case so free from the power of ingenious sophistry as that the world should not be able to misunderstand it. By the affair at Fort Sumter, with its surrounding circumstances, that point was reached. Then and thereby the assailants of the Government began the conflict of arms, without a gun in sight or in expectancy to return their fire, save only the few in the fort, sent to that harbor years before for their own protection, and still ready to give that protection in whatever was lawful. In this act, discarding all else, they have forced upon the country the distinct issue, "Immediate dissolution or blood."

And this issue embraces more than the fate of these United States. It presents to the whole family of man the question whether a constitutional republic, or democracy—a government of the people by the same people—can or can not maintain its territorial integrity against its own domestic foes. It presents the question whether discontented individuals, too few in numbers to control administration according to organic law in any case, can always, upon the pretenses made in this case, or on any other pretenses, or arbitrarily without any pretense, break up their government, and thus practically put an end to free government upon the earth. It forces us to ask, Is there in all republics this inherent and fatal weakness? Must a government of necessity be too *strong* for the liberties of its own people, or too *weak* to maintain its own existence?

So viewing the issue, no choice was left but to call out the war power of the Government and so to resist force employed for its destruction by force for its preservation.

The call was made, and the response of the country was most gratifying, surpassing in unanimity and spirit the most sanguine expectation. Yet none of the States commonly called slave States, except Delaware, gave a regiment through regular State organization. A few regiments have been organized within some others of those States by individual enterprise and received into the Government service. Of course the seceded States, so called (and to which Texas had been joined about the time of the inauguration), gave no troops to the cause of the Union. The border States, so called, were not uniform in their action, some of them being almost *for* the Union, while in others, as Virginia, North Carolina, Tennessee, and Arkansas, the Union sentiment was nearly repressed and silenced. The course taken in Virginia was the most remarkable, perhaps the most important. A convention elected by the people of that State to consider this very question of disrupting the Federal Union was in session at the capital of Virginia when Fort Sumter fell. To this body the people had chosen a large majority of *professed* Union men. Almost immediately after the fall of Sumter many members of that majority went over to the original disunion minority, and with them adopted an ordinance for withdrawing the State from the Union. Whether this change was wrought by their great approval of the assault upon Sumter or their great resentment at the Government's resistance to that assault is not definitely known. Although they submitted the ordinance for ratification to a vote of the people, to be taken on a day then somewhat more than a month distant, the convention and the legislature (which was also in session at the same time and place), with leading men of the State not members of either, immediately commenced acting as if the State were already out of the Union. They pushed military preparations vigorously forward all over the State. They seized the United States armory at Harpers Ferry and the navy-yard at

Gosport, near Norfolk. They received—perhaps invited—into their State large bodies of troops, with their warlike appointments, from the so-called seceded States. They formally entered into a treaty of temporary alliance and cooperation with the so-called "Confederate States," and sent members to their congress at Montgomery; and, finally, they permitted the insurrectionary government to be transferred to their capital at Richmond.

The people of Virginia have thus allowed this giant insurrection to make its nest within her borders, and this Government has no choice left but to deal with it *where* it finds it; and it has the less regret, as the loyal citizens have in due form claimed its protection. Those loyal citizens this Government is bound to recognize and protect, as being Virginia.

In the border States, so called—in fact, the Middle States—there are those who favor a policy which they call "armed neutrality;" that is, an arming of those States to prevent the Union forces passing one way or the disunion the other over their soil. This would be disunion completed. Figuratively speaking, it would be the building of an impassible wall along the line of separation, and yet not quite an impassable one, for, under the guise of neutrality, it would tie the hands of the Union men and freely pass supplies from among them to the insurrectionists, which it could not do as an open enemy. At a stroke it would take all the trouble off hands of the secession, except only what proceeds from the external blockade. It would do for the disunionists that which of all things they most desire—feed them well and give them disunion without a struggle of their own. It recognizes no fidelity to the Constitution, no obligation to maintain the Union; and while very many who have favored it are doubtless loyal citizens, it is, nevertheless, very injurious in effect.

Recurring to the action of the Government, it may be stated that at first a call was made for 75,000 militia, and rapidly following this a proclamation was issued for closing the ports of the insurrectionary districts by proceedings in the nature of blockade. So far all was believed to be strictly legal. At this point the insurrectionists announced their purpose to enter upon the practice of privateering.

Other calls were made for volunteers to serve three years unless sooner discharged, and also for large additions to the Regular Army and Navy. These measures, whether strictly legal or not, were ventured upon under what appeared to be a popular demand and a public necessity, trusting then, as now, that Congress would readily ratify them. It is believed that nothing has been done beyond the constitutional competency of Congress.

Soon after the first call for militia it was considered a duty to authorize the Commanding General in proper cases, according to his discretion, to suspend the privilege of the writ of *habeas corpus,* or, in other words, to arrest and detain without resort to the ordinary processes and forms of law such individuals as he might deem dangerous to the public safety. This authority has purposely been exercised but very sparingly. Nevertheless, the legality and propriety of what has been done under it are questioned, and the attention of the country has been called to the proposition that one who is sworn to "take care that the laws be faithfully executed" should not himself violate them. Of course some consideration was given to the questions of power and propriety before this matter was acted upon. The whole of the laws which were required to be faithfully executed were being resisted and failing of execution in nearly one-third of the States. Must they be allowed to finally fail of execution, even had it been perfectly clear that by the use of the means necessary to their execution some single law,

made in such extreme tenderness of the citizen's liberty that practically it relieves more of the guilty than of the innocent, should to a very limited extent be violated? To state the question more directly, Are all the laws *but one* to go unexecuted, and the Government itself go to pieces lest that one be violated? Even in such a case, would not the official oath be broken if the Government should be overthrown when it was believed that disregarding the single law would tend to preserve it? But it was not believed that this question was presented. It was not believed that any law was violated. The provision of the Constitution that "the privilege of the writ of *habeas corpus* shall not be suspended unless when, in cases of rebellion or invasion, the public safety may require it" is equivalent to a provision—is a provision—that such privilege may be suspended when, in cases of rebellion or invasion, the public safety *does* require it. It was decided that we have a case of rebellion and that the public safety does require the qualified suspension of the privilege of the writ which was authorized to be made. Now it is insisted that Congress, and not the Executive, is vested with this power; but the Constitution itself is silent as to which or who is to exercise the power; and as the provision was plainly made for a dangerous emergency, it can not be believed the framers of the instrument intended that in every case the danger should run its course until Congress could be called together, the very assembling of which might be prevented, as was intended in this case, by the rebellion.

No more extended argument is now offered, as an opinion at some length will probably be presented by the Attorney-General. Whether there shall be any legislation upon the subject, and, if any, what, is submitted entirely to the better judgment of Congress.

The forbearance of this Government had been so extraordinary and so long continued as to lead some foreign nations to shape their action as if they supposed the early destruction of our National Union was probable. While this on discovery gave the Executive some concern, he is now happy to say that the sovereignty and rights of the United States are now everywhere practically respected by foreign powers, and a general sympathy with the country is manifested throughout the world.

The reports of the Secretaries of the Treasury, War, and the Navy will give the information in detail deemed necessary and convenient for your deliberation and action, while the Executive and all the Departments will stand ready to supply omissions or to communicate new facts considered important for you to know.

It is now recommended that you give the legal means for making this contest a short and a decisive one; that you place at the control of the Government for the work at least 400,000 men and $400,000,000. That number of men is about one-tenth of those of proper ages within the regions where apparently *all* are willing to engage, and the sum is less than a twenty-third part of the money value owned by the men who seem ready to devote the whole. A debt of $600,000,000 *now* is a less sum per head than was the debt of our Revolution when we came out of that struggle, and the money value in the country now bears even a greater proportion to what it was *then* than does the population. Surely each man has as strong a motive *now* to *preserve* our liberties as each had *then* to *establish* them.

A right result at this time will be worth more to the world than ten times the men and ten times the money. The evidence reaching us from the country leaves no doubt that the material for the work is abundant, and that it needs only the hand of legislation to give it legal sanction and the hand of the Executive to give it practical shape and efficiency. One of the greatest perplexi-

ties of the Government is to avoid receiving troops faster than it can provide for them. In a word, the people will save their Government if the Government itself will do its part only indifferently well.

It might seem at first thought to be of little difference whether the present movement at the South be called "secession" or "rebellion." The movers, however, well understand the difference. At the beginning they knew they could never raise their treason to any respectable magnitude by any name which implies *violation* of law. They knew their people possessed as much of moral sense, as much of devotion to law and order, and as much pride in and reverence for the history and Government of their common country as any other civilized and patriotic people. They knew they could make no advancement directly in the teeth of these strong and noble sentiments. Accordingly, they commenced by an insidious debauching of the public mind. They invented an ingenious sophism, which, if conceded, was followed by perfectly logical steps through all the incidents to the complete destruction of the Union. The sophism itself is that any State of the Union may *consistently* with the National Constitution, and therefore *lawfully* and *peacefully,* withdraw from the Union without the consent of the Union or of any other State. The little disguise that the supposed right is to be exercised only for just cause, themselves to be the sole judge of its justice, is too thin to merit any notice.

With rebellion thus sugar coated they have been drugging the public mind of their section for more than thirty years, and until at length they have brought many good men to a willingness to take up arms against the Government the day *after* some assemblage of men have enacted the farcical pretense of taking their State out of the Union who could have been brought to no such thing the day *before.*

This sophism derives much, perhaps the whole, of its currency from the assumption that there is some omnipotent and sacred supremacy pertaining to a *State*—to each State of our Federal Union. Our States have neither more nor less power than that reserved to them in the Union by the Constitution, no one of them ever having been a State *out* of the Union. The original ones passed into the Union even *before* they cast off their British colonial dependence, and the new ones each came into the Union directly from a condition of dependence, excepting Texas; and even Texas, in its temporary independence, was never designated a State. The new ones only took the designation of States on coming into the Union, while that name was first adopted for the old ones in and by the Declaration of Independence. Therein the "United Colonies" were declared to be "free and independent States;" but even then the object plainly was not to declare their independence of *one another* or of the *Union,* but directly the contrary, as their mutual pledge and their mutual action before, at the time, and afterwards abundantly show. The express plighting of faith by each and all of the original thirteen in the Articles of Confederation, two years later, that the Union shall be perpetual is most conclusive. Having never been States, either in substance or in name, *outside* of the Union, whence this magical omnipotence of "State rights," asserting a claim of power to lawfully destroy the Union itself? Much is said about the "sovereignty" of the States, but the word even is not in the National Constitution, nor, as is believed, in any of the State constitutions. What is a "sovereignty" in the political sense of the term? Would it be far wrong to define it "a political community without a political superior"? Tested by this, no one of our States, except Texas, ever was a sovereignty; and even Texas gave up the character on coming into the Union, by which act she acknowledged the Constitution of the United States and the laws and treaties of the United States made in pursuance of the Constitution to be for her the supreme law of the land. The States have their status in the Union, and they have no other legal status. If they break from this, they can only do so against law and by revolution. The Union, and not themselves separately, procured their independence and their liberty. By conquest or purchase the Union gave each of them whatever of independence and liberty it has. The Union is older than any of the States, and, in fact, it created them as States. Originally some dependent colonies made the Union, and in turn the Union threw off their old dependence for them and made them States, such as they are. Not one of them ever had a State constitution independent of the Union. Of course it is not forgotten that all the new States framed their constitutions before they entered the Union, nevertheless dependent upon and preparatory to coming into the Union.

Unquestionably the States have the powers and rights reserved to them in and by the National Constitution; but among these surely are not included all conceivable powers, however mischievous or destructive, but at most such only as were known as a governmental—as a merely administrative power. This relative matter of national power and State rights, as a principle, is no other than the principle of *generality* and *locality.* Whatever concerns the whole should be confided to the whole—to the General Government—while whatever concerns *only* the State should be left exclusively to the State. This is all there is of original principle about it. Whether the National Constitution in defining boundaries between the two has applied the principle with exact accuracy is not to be questioned. We are all bound by that defining without question.

What is now combated is the position that secession is *consistent* with the Constitution—is *lawful* and *peaceful*. It is not contended that there is any express law for it, and nothing should ever be implied as law which leads to unjust or absurd consequences. The nation purchased with money the countries out of which several of these States were formed. Is it just that they shall go off without leave and without refunding? The nation paid very large sums (in the aggregate, I believe, nearly a hundred millions) to relieve Florida of the aboriginal tribes. Is it just that she shall now be off without consent or without making any return? The nation is now in debt for money applied to the benefit of these so-called seceding States in common with the rest. Is it just either that creditors shall go unpaid or the remaining States pay the whole? A part of the present national debt was contracted to pay the old debts of Texas. Is it just that she shall leave and pay no part of this herself?

Again: If one State may secede, so may another; and when all shall have seceded none is left to pay the debts. Is this quite just to creditors? Did we notify them of this sage view of ours when we borrowed their money? If we now recognize this doctrine by allowing the seceders to go in peace, it is difficult to see what we can do if others choose to go or to extort terms upon which they will promise to remain.

The seceders insist that our Constitution admits of secession. They have assumed to make a national constitution of their own, in which of necessity they have either *discarded* or *retained* the right of secession, as they insist it exists in ours. If they have discarded it, they thereby admit that on principle it ought not to be in ours. If they have retained it, by their own construction of ours they show that to be consistent they must secede from one another whenever they shall find it the easiest way of settling their debts or effecting

any other selfish or unjust object. The principle itself is one of disintegration, and upon which no government can possibly endure.

If all the States save one should assert the power to *drive* that one out of the Union, it is presumed the whole class of seceder politicians would at once deny the power and denounce the act as the greatest outrage upon State rights. But suppose that precisely the same act, instead of being called "driving the one out," should be called "the seceding of the others from that one," it would be exactly what the seceders claim to do, unless, indeed, they make the point that the one, because it is a minority, may rightfully do what the others, because they are a majority, may not rightfully do. These politicians are subtle and profound on the rights of minorities. They are not partial to that power which made the Constitution and speaks from the preamble, calling itself "we, the people."

It may well be questioned whether there is to-day a majority of the legally qualified voters of any State, except, perhaps, South Carolina, in favor of disunion. There is much reason to believe that the Union men are the majority in many, if not in every other one, of the so-called seceded States. The contrary has not been demonstrated in any one of them. It is ventured to affirm this even of Virginia and Tennessee; for the result of an election held in military camps, where the bayonets are all on one side of the question voted upon, can scarcely be considered as demonstrating popular sentiment. At such an election all that large class who are at once *for* the Union and *against* coercion would be coerced to vote against the Union.

It may be affirmed without extravagance that the free institutions we enjoy have developed the powers and improved the condition of our whole people beyond any example in the world. Of this we now have a striking and an impressive illustration. So large an army as the Government has now on foot was never before known without a soldier in it but who had taken his place there of his own free choice. But more than this, there are many single regiments whose members, one and another, possess full practical knowledge of all the arts, sciences, professions, and whatever else, whether useful or elegant, is known in the world; and there is scarcely one from which there could not be selected a President, a Cabinet, a Congress, and perhaps a court, abundantly competent to administer the Government itself. Nor do I say this is not true also in the army of our late friends, now adversaries in this contest; but if it is, so much better the reason why the Government which has conferred such benefits on both them and us should not be broken up. Whoever in any section proposes to abandon such a government would do well to consider in deference to what principle it is that he does it; what better he is likely to get in its stead; whether the substitute will give, or be intended to give, so much of good to the people. There are some foreshadowings on this subject. Our adversaries have adopted some declarations of independence in which, unlike the good old one penned by Jefferson, they omit the words "all men are created equal." Why? They have adopted a temporary national constitution, in the preamble of which, unlike our good old one signed by Washington, they omit "We, the people," and substitute "We, the deputies of the sovereign and independent States." Why? Why this deliberate pressing out of view the rights of men and the authority of the people?

This is essentially a people's contest. On the side of the Union it is a struggle for maintaining in the world that form and substance of government whose leading object is to elevate the condition of men; to lift artificial weights from all shoulders; to clear the paths of laudable pursuit for all; to afford all an unfettered start and a fair chance in the race of life. Yielding to partial and temporary departures, from necessity, this is the leading object of the Government for whose existence we contend.

I am most happy to believe that the plain people understand and appreciate this. It is worthy of note that while in this the Government's hour of trial large numbers of those in the Army and Navy who have been favored with the offices have resigned and proved false to the hand which had pampered them, not one common soldier or common sailor is known to have deserted his flag.

Great honor is due to those officers who remained true despite the example of their treacherous associates; but the greatest honor and most important fact of all is the unanimous firmness of the common soldiers and common sailors. To the last man, so far as known, they have successfully resisted the traitorous efforts of those whose commands but an hour before they obeyed as absolute law. This is the patriotic instinct of plain people. They understand without an argument that the destroying the Government which was made by Washington means no good to them.

Our popular Government has often been called an experiment. Two points in it our people have already settled— the successful *establishing* and the successful *administering* of it. One still remains—its successful *maintenance* against a formidable internal attempt to overthrow it. It is now for them to demonstrate to the world that those who can fairly carry an election can also suppress a rebellion; that ballots are the rightful and peaceful successors of bullets, and that when ballots have fairly and constitutionally decided there can be no successful appeal back to bullets; that there can be no successful appeal except to ballots themselves at succeeding elections. Such will be a great lesson of peace, teaching men that what they can not take by an election neither can they take it by a war; teaching all the folly of being the beginners of a war.

Lest there be some uneasiness in the minds of candid men as to what is to be the course of Government toward the Southern States *after* the rebellion shall have been suppressed, the Executive deems it proper to say it will be his purpose then, as ever, to be guided by the Constitution and the laws, and that he probably will have no different understanding of the powers and duties of the Federal Government relatively to the rights of the States and the people under the Constitution than that expressed in the inaugural address.

He desires to preserve the Government, that it may be administered for all as it was administered by the men who made it. Loyal citizens everywhere have the right to claim this of their government, and the government has no right to withhold or neglect it. It is not perceived that in giving it there is any coercion, any conquest, or any subjugation in any just sense of those terms.

The Constitution provides, and all the States have accepted the provision, that "the United States shall guarantee to every State in this Union a republican form of government." But if a State may lawfully go out of the Union, having done so it may also discard the republican form of government; so that to prevent its going out is an indispensable *means* to the *end* of maintaining the guaranty mentioned; and when an end is lawful and obligatory the indispensable means to it are also lawful and obligatory.

It was with the deepest regret that the Executive found the duty of em-

ploying the war power in defense of the Government forced upon him. He could but perform this duty or surrender the existence of the Government. No compromise by public servants could in this case be a cure; not that compromises are not often proper, but that no popular government can long survive a marked precedent that those who carry an election can only save the government from immediate destruction by giving up the main point upon which the people gave the election. The people themselves, and not their servants, can safely reverse their own deliberate decisions.

As a private citizen the Executive could not have consented that these institutions shall perish; much less could he in betrayal of so vast and so sacred a trust as these free people had confided in him. He felt that he had no moral right to shrink, nor even to count the chances of his own life, in what might follow. In full view of his great responsibility he has so far done what he has deemed his duty. You will now, according to your own judgment, perform yours. He sincerely hopes that your views and your action may so accord with his as to assure all faithful citizens who have been disturbed in their rights of a certain and speedy restoration to them under the Constitution and the laws.

And having thus chosen our course, without guile and with pure purpose, let us renew our trust in God and go forward without fear and with manly hearts.

ABRAHAM LINCOLN.

# The Emancipation Proclamation (1863)

To Abraham Lincoln, the Civil War was a crusade not to end slavery but to preserve the Union: "If I could save the Union without freeing any slave, I would do it," he wrote in a letter to the New York Herald. In the face of more than a year of continuing Union frustration on the battlefield, however, Lincoln's hands-off policy regarding slavery jeopardized the support of northern abolitionists at home and of Great Britain and other European governments abroad.

During the summer of 1862, Lincoln resolved to move against slavery but heeded the advice of the cabinet that he wait until after the Union army had won a battle so that his action would not seem desperate or ineffective. A partial military victory at Antietam, Maryland (it helped to forestall a Confederate incursion into the North) in September was occasion enough; and on September 22, 1862, Lincoln issued a preliminary proclamation of emancipation. The rebellious states were told that unless they laid down their arms by January 1, 1863, the president would declare their slaves to be legally free.

Not surprisingly, the Confederacy ignored Lincoln's warning. Thus, on New Year's Day 1863, declaring that "I never, in my life, felt more certain that I was doing right than I do in signing this paper," Lincoln signed the Emancipation Proclamation at a White House ceremony. The proclamation freed "all persons held as slaves within any State or designated part of a State, the people whereof shall then be in rebellion against the United States." It maintained that the president's power as commander in chief authorized him to take this action, since to free slaves reduced the labor force of the South and, consequently, lessened its ability to continue the rebellion.

The Emancipation Proclamation was actually a moderate document. Abolitionists and their Radical Republican allies in Congress had hoped that the president would proclaim a comprehensive policy of emancipation. Yet Lincoln did not include even a condemnation of slavery or a pledge to abolish it entirely after the war was over. Conservatives fretted that to seize slaves or other property without due process or compensation violated either the Constitution, if southerners still were considered to be U.S. citizens, or international law, if they were considered enemy citizens. Few slaves were freed right away by the proclamation, since the only slaves to whom the proclamation applied were in states that the Confederacy controlled.

For all its limitations, the Emancipation Proclamation was a powerful first step against slavery. More than 100,000 freed slaves eventually became *part of the Union army. Others laid down their shovels and fled north. Perhaps most important, abolitionists and European public opinion rallied to the Union cause.*

*In the long run, slavery was ended as the Union army regained more and more southern territory. Lincoln pressed Congress to pass the Thirteenth Amendment to the Constitution, abolishing slavery "within the United States, or any place subject to their jurisdiction." The amendment cleared Congress on January 31, 1865, and was ratified by the necessary three-fourths of the states (excluding the by-then defeated Confederate states) on December 6, 1865.* ～

## By the President of the United States of America: A Proclamation.

Whereas on the 22d day of September, A.D. 1862, a proclamation was issued by the President of the United States, containing, among other things, the following, to wit:

"That on the 1st day of January, A.D. 1863, all persons held as slaves within any State or designated part of a State, the people whereof shall then be in rebellion against the United States shall be then, thenceforward, and forever free; and the executive government of the United States, including the military and naval authority thereof, will recognize and maintain the freedom of such persons and will do no act or acts to repress such persons, or any of them, in any efforts they may make for their actual freedom.

"That the executive will on the 1st day of January aforesaid, by proclamation, designate the States and parts of States, if any, in which the people thereof, respectively, shall then be in rebellion against the United States; and the fact that any State or the people thereof shall on that day be in good faith represented in the Congress of the United States by members chosen thereto at elections wherein a majority of the qualified voters of such States shall have participated shall, in the absence of strong countervailing testimony, be deemed conclusive evidence that such State and the people thereof are not then in rebellion against the United States."

Now, therefore, I, Abraham Lincoln, President of the United States, by virtue of the power in me vested as Commander-in-Chief of the Army and Navy of the United States in time of actual armed rebellion against the authority and government of the United States, and as a fit and necessary war measure for suppressing said rebellion, do, on this 1st day of January, A.D. 1863, and in accordance with my purpose so to do, publicly proclaim for the full period of one hundred days from the first day above mentioned, order and designate as the State and parts of States wherein the people thereof, respectively, are this day in rebellion against the United States the following, to wit:

Arkansas, Texas, Louisiana (except the parishes of St. Bernard, Plaquemines, Jefferson, St. John, St. Charles, St. James, Ascension, Assumption, Terrebonne, Lafourche, St. Mary, St. Martin, and Orleans, including the city of New Orleans), Mississippi, Alabama, Florida, Georgia, South Carolina, North Carolina, and Virginia (except the forty-eight counties designated as West Virginia, and also the counties of Berkeley, Accomac, Northhampton, Elizabeth City, York, Princess Anne, and Norfolk, including the cities of Norfolk and Portsmouth), and which excepted parts are for the present left precisely as if this proclamation were not issued.

And by virtue of the power and for the purpose aforesaid, I do order and declare that all persons held as slaves within said designated States and parts of States are, and henceforward shall be, free; and that the Executive Government of the United States, including the military and naval authorities thereof, will recognize and maintain the freedom of said persons.

And I hereby enjoin upon the people so declared to be free to abstain from all violence, unless in necessary self-defense; and I recommend to them that, in all cases when allowed, they labor faithfully for reasonable wages.

And I further declare and make known that such persons of suitable condition will be received into the armed service of the United States to garrison forts, positions, stations, and other places, and to man vessels of all sorts in said service.

And upon this act, sincerely believed to be an act of justice, warranted by the Constitution upon military necessity, I invoke the considerate judgment of mankind and the gracious favor of Almighty God.

# The Gettysburg Address (1863)

*On July 4, 1863, the Union army won two military victories that almost ensured that the North would prevail in the Civil War. In the West, the Confederate fortification at Vicksburg, Mississippi, fell to the forces of Gen. Ulysses S. Grant, bringing the strategically vital Mississippi River completely under northern control. In Gettysburg, Pennsylvania, Union forces beat back a Confederate incursion into the North led by Gen. Robert E. Lee.*

*On November 18 Abraham Lincoln rode a train from Washington to Gettysburg to attend the next day's dedication of a cemetery in which six thousand casualties of the Battle of Gettysburg were buried. Lincoln was not the main speaker at the dedication—that honor fell to former senator and renowned orator Edward Everett, who delivered a lengthy and moving address. Instead, Lincoln spoke briefly after Everett was finished.*

*The brilliance of the Gettysburg Address is that, in the space of around 250 words, it solemnly and honestly acknowledges the awful pain of "these honored dead" while placing the war in which they had fought into the context of the struggle to attain "government of the people, by the people, for the people." That government, which had begun "four score and seven years ago" in 1776, must, Lincoln urged, continue into "a new birth of freedom" so that* the fallen soldiers would not have "died in vain."  ~

Four score and seven years ago our fathers brought forth on this continent, a new nation, conceived in Liberty, and dedicated to the proposition that all men are created equal.

Now we are engaged in a great civil war, testing whether that nation or any nation so conceived and so dedicated, can long endure. We are met on a great battle-field of that war. We have come to dedicate a portion of that field, as a final resting place for those who here gave their lives that that nation might live. It is altogether fitting and proper that we should do this.

But, in a larger sense, we can not dedicate—we can not consecrate—we can not hallow—this ground. The brave men, living and dead, who struggled here, have consecrated it, far above our poor power to add or detract. The world will little note, nor long remember what we say here, but it can never forget what they did here. It is for us the living, rather, to be dedicated here to the unfinished work which they who fought here have thus far so nobly advanced. It is rather for us to be here dedicated to the great task remaining before us—that from these honored dead we take increased devotion to that cause for which they gave the last full measure of devotion—that we here highly resolve that these dead shall not have died in vain—that this nation, under God, shall have a new birth of freedom—and that government of the people, by the people, for the people, shall not perish from the earth.

# Abraham Lincoln's Plan of Reconstruction (1863)

*Success on the battlefield prompted President Lincoln and many Republican members of Congress to think seriously about the terms on which rebellious southern states would be allowed to return to full participation in the Union.*

*Lincoln and Congress generally agreed that two important characteristics of the old South would have to be eliminated: slavery and the prominent role played in southern state governments by secessionists. Beyond that, the president and his fellow Republicans on Capitol Hill had considerable differences.*

*One basic disagreement between Lincoln and Congress was philosophical in nature but highly political in its consequences. The president had never deviated from the theory that because secession is illegal the southern states had not really left the Union. Rebels had taken control of their state governments temporarily; the main task of reconstruction was to restore loyal leaders to power. Since the president has the constitutional authority to suppress insurrections, Lincoln argued, reconstruction was mainly a presidential responsibility.*

*In contrast, most Republicans in Congress subscribed to one version or another of the theory that, in seceding to form the Confederacy, southern states had forfeited their status as*

*states and would have to petition to regain statehood. According to this theory, Congress had primary jurisdiction over reconstruction because of its constitutional responsibility to set the conditions under which "territories" are governed and admitted as states.*

*Further complicating matters, congressional Republicans tended to regard the reconstruction of the South as a much more punitive process than did the president. If Lincoln had the father's attitude toward the prodigal son, Congress had the elder brother's.*

*Lincoln took the lead in the reconstruction process when, on December 8, 1863, he proclaimed formally that "whereas it is now desired by some persons heretofore engaged in said rebellion to resume their allegiance to the United States and to reinaugurate loyal State governments," he would pardon any rebel who would swear loyalty to the United States and to its policies concerning slavery. (This offer did not extend to Confederate military leaders and government officials.) When the number of persons taking the oath reached 10 percent of a state's voter turnout in the 1860 presidential election, they could form a loyal government that the president would recognize as the legitimate government of the state. Lincoln noted, however, that, constitutionally, Congress alone had the power to determine whether to admit a state's representatives and senators to legislative membership.*

*Congress judged Lincoln's plan to be too conciliatory. In 1864, loyalists in Louisiana, Arkansas, and Tennessee, using the "10 percent plan," established state governments, which Lincoln recognized. But Congress did not seat their legislators. In July 1864, Congress passed a reconstruction act that would have required 50 percent of a state's white male citizens to take a loyalty oath before it could form a new government. Although Lincoln pocketvetoed the bill, Congress clearly had indicated that reconstruction was still an unsettled issue, even as the Civil War was moving to a close.* ~

## Proclamation of Amnesty and Reconstruction

*Whereas* in and by the Constitution of the United States it is provided that the President "shall have power to grant reprieves and pardons for offenses against the United States, except in cases of impeachment;" and

*Whereas* a rebellion now exists whereby the loyal state governments of several States have for a long time been subverted, and many persons have committed and are now guilty of treason against the United States; and

*Whereas*, with reference to said rebellion and treason, laws have been enacted by Congress declaring forfeitures and confiscation of property and liberation of slaves, all upon terms and conditions therein stated, and also declaring that the President has thereby authorized at any time thereafter, by proclamation, to extend to persons who may have participated in the existing rebellion in any State or part thereof pardon and amnesty, with such exceptions and at such times and on such conditions as he may deem expedient for the public welfare; and

*Whereas* the congressional declaration for limited and conditional pardon accords with well-established judicial exposition of the pardoning power; and

*Whereas*, with reference to said rebellion, the President of the United States has issued several proclamations with provisions in regard to the liberation of slaves; and

*Whereas* it is now desired by some persons heretofore engaged in said rebellion to resume their allegiance to the United States and to reinaugurate loyal State governments within and for their respective States:

*Therefore*, I, Abraham Lincoln, President of the United States, do proclaim, ... to all persons who have, directly or by implication, participated in the existing rebellion, except as hereinafter excepted, that a full pardon is hereby granted to them and each of them, with restoration of all rights of property, except as to slaves and in property cases where rights of third parties shall have intervened, and upon the condition that every such person shall take and subscribe an oath and thenceforward keep and maintain said oath inviolate, and which oath shall be registered for permanent preservation and shall be of the tenor and effect following, to wit:

I, ___ ___, do solemnly swear, in presence of Almighty God, that I will henceforth faithfully support, protect, and defend the Constitution of the United States and the Union of the States thereunder; and that I will in like manner abide by and faithfully support all acts of Congress passed during the existing rebellion with reference to slaves, so long and so far as not repealed, modified, or held void by Congress or by decision of the Supreme Court; and that I will in like manner abide by and faithfully support all proclamations of the President made during the existing rebellion having reference to slaves, so long and so far as not modified or declared void by decision of the Supreme Court. So help me God.

The persons excepted from the benefits of the foregoing provisions are all who are or shall have been civil or diplomatic officers or agents of the so-called Confederate Government; all who have left judicial stations under the United States to aid the rebellion; all who are or shall have been military or naval officers of said so-called Confederate Government above the rank of colonel in the army or of lieutenant in the navy; all who left seats in the United States Congress to aid the rebellion; all who resigned commissions in the Army or Navy of the United States and afterwards aided the rebellion; and all who have engaged in any way in treating colored persons, or white persons in charge of such, otherwise than lawfully as prisoners of war, and which persons may have been found in the United States service as soldiers, seamen, or in any other capacity.

And I do further proclaim, declare, and make known that whenever, in any of the States of Arkansas, Texas, Louisiana, Mississippi, Tennessee, Alabama, Georgia, Florida, South Carolina, and North Carolina, a number of persons, not less than one-tenth in number of the votes cast in such State at the Presidential election of the year A.D. 1860, each having taken oath aforesaid, and not having since violated it, and being a qualified voter by the election law of the State existing immediately before the so-called act of secession, and excluding all others, shall re-establish a State government which shall be republican and in nowise contravening said oath, such shall be recognized as the true government of the State, and the State shall receive thereunder the benefits of the constitutional provision which declares that "the United States shall guarantee to every State in this Union a republican form of government and shall protect each of them against invasion, and, on application of the legislature, or the executive (when the legislature can not be convened), against domestic violence."

And I do further proclaim, declare, and make known that any provision which may be adopted by such State government in relation to the freed people of such State which shall recognize and declare their permanent freedom, provide for their education, and which may yet be consistent as a temporary arrangement with their present condition as a laboring, landless, and homeless class, will not be objected to by the National Executive.

And it is suggested as not improper that in constructing a loyal State government in any State the name of the State, the boundary, the subdivisions, the constitution, and the general code of laws as before the rebellion be maintained, subject only to the modifications made necessary by the conditions hereinbefore stated, and such others, if any, not contravening said conditions and which may be deemed expedient by those framing the new State government.

To avoid misunderstanding, it may be proper to say that this proclamation, so far as it relates to State governments, has no reference to States wherein loyal State governments have all the while been maintained. And for the same reason it may be proper to further say that whether members sent to Congress from any State shall be admitted to seats constitutionally rests exclusively with the respective Houses, and not to any extent with the Executive. And, still further, that this proclamation is intended to present the people of the States wherein the national authority has been suspended and loyal State governments have been subverted a mode in and by which the national authority and loyal State governments may be re-established within said States or in any of them; and while the mode presented is the best the Executive can suggest, with his present impressions, it must not be understood that no other possible mode would be acceptable.

Abraham Lincoln.

# Abraham Lincoln's
# Letter to A. G. Hodges (1864)

As a young member of the U.S. House of Representatives during the Mexican War, Abraham Lincoln, in a February 15, 1848, letter to his law partner in Illinois, William H. Herndon, denounced the expansive view of the president's war-making power that "places our President where kings have always stood." Sixteen years later, after three years of the Civil War, President Lincoln took a somewhat different view in a letter to Kentuckian A. G. Hodges.

In the letter, written on April 4, 1864, Lincoln argued that it made no sense to observe constitutional niceties while the ultimate purpose of the Constitution—to preserve the Union—was under siege. "Was it possible to lose the nation and yet preserve the Constitution?" Lincoln asked, rhetorically. "By general law, life and limb must be protected, yet often a limb must be amputated to save a life; but a life is never wisely given to save a limb." Defending the actions of his first few months in office and afterward (see headnote to "Abraham Lincoln's First Message to Congress," p. 103), Lincoln added: "I felt that measures otherwise unconstitutional might become lawful by becoming indispensable to the preservation of the Constitution through the preservation of the nation."

Although Lincoln did not mention John Locke, his letter to Hodges was reminiscent of the great seventeenth-century English philosopher's essay on prerogative, which is contained in the Second Treatise on Government. In the absence or sometimes in defiance of law, Locke had argued, an executive must obey "this fundamental law of nature and government, viz., that, as much as may be, all the members of society are to be preserved." Such is prerogative: "the people's permitting their rulers to do several things of their own free choice, where the law was silent, and sometimes, too, against the direct letter of the law, for the public good, and their acquiescing in it when so done." The check on executive power in such an instance is the elected legislature's subsequent decision to accept or reject the propriety of the executive's actions.

Certainly Lincoln could claim that, for the most part, his own exercises of prerogative had been vindicated. To be sure, Lincoln was denounced by some as a dictator. But in August 1861, after several weeks of debate, Congress voted that it regarded most of the president's early actions as "hereby approved and in all respects legalized and made valid, to the same effect as if they had been issued and done under the previous express authority and direction of the Congress of the United States." In 1862 and 1863, Congress retroactively validated other of Lincoln's actions.

*Not just Congress but the voters endorsed the president's unusual wartime leadership. Lincoln won 55 percent of the popular vote in his bid for reelection in November 1864.* ~

My dear Sir:

You ask me to put in writing the substance of what I verbally said the other day in your presence, to Governor Bramlette and Senator Dixon. It was about as follows:

"I am naturally antislavery. If slavery is not wrong, nothing is wrong. I cannot remember when I did not so think and feel, and yet I have never understood that the presidency conferred upon me an unrestricted right to act officially upon this judgment and feeling. It was in the oath I took that I would, to the best of my ability, preserve, protect, and defend the Constitution of the United States. I could not take the office without taking the oath. Nor was it my view that I might take an oath to get power, and break the oath in using the power. I understood, too, that in ordinary civil administration this oath even forbade me to practically indulge my primary abstract judgment on the moral question of slavery. I had publicly declared this many times, and in many ways. And I aver that, to this day, I have done no official act in mere deference to my abstract judgment and feeling on slavery. I did understand, however, that my oath to preserve the Constitution to the best of my ability imposed upon me the duty of preserving, by every indispensable means, that government—that nation, of which that Constitution was the organizing law. Was it possible to lose the nation and yet preserve the Constitution? By general law, life and limb must be protected, yet often a limb must be amputated to save a life; but a life is never wisely given to save a limb. I felt that measures otherwise unconstitutional might become lawful by becoming in- dispensable to the preservation of the Constitution through the preservation of the nation. Right or wrong, I assume this ground, and now avow it. I could not feel that, to the best of my ability, I had even tried to preserve the Constitution if, to save slavery or any minor matter, I should permit the wreck of government, country, and Constitution all together. When, early in the war, General Frémont attempted military emancipation, I forbade it, because I did not then think it an indispensable necessity. When, a little later, General Cameron, then Secretary of War, suggested the arming of the blacks, I objected because I did not yet think it an indispensable necessity. When, still later, General Hunter attempted military emancipation, I again forbade it, because I did not yet think the indispensable necessity had come. When in March and May and July, 1862, I made earnest and successive appeals to the border States to favor compensated emancipation, I believed the indispensable necessity to military emancipation and arming the blacks would come unless averted by that measure. They declined the proposition, and I was, in my best judgment, driven to the alternative of either surrendering the Union, and with it the Constitution, or of laying strong hand upon the colored element. I chose the latter. In choosing it, I hoped for greater gain than loss; but of this, I was not entirely confident. More than a year of trial now shows no loss by it in our foreign relations, none in our home popular sentiment, none in our white military force—no loss by it anyhow or anywhere. On the contrary it shows a gain of quite a hundred and thirty thousand soldiers, seamen, and laborers. These are palpable facts, about which, as facts, there can be no caviling. We have the men; and we could not have had them without the measure.

"And now let any Union man who complains of the measure test himself by writing down in one line that he is for subduing the rebellion by force of arms; and in the next, that he is for taking these hundred and thirty thousand men from the Union side and placing them where they would be but for the measure he condemns. If he cannot face his case so stated, it is only because he cannot face the truth."

I add a word which was not in the verbal conversation. In telling this tale I attempt no compliment to my own sagacity. I claim not to have controlled events, but confess plainly that events have controlled me. Now, at the end of three years' struggle, the nation's condition is not what either party, or any man, devised or expected. God alone can claim it. Whither it is tending seems plain. If God now wills the removal of a great wrong, and wills also that we of the North, as well as you of the South, shall pay fairly for our complicity in that wrong, impartial history will find therein new cause to attest and revere the justice and goodness of God. *Yours truly,*

A. Lincoln

# Abraham Lincoln's Second Inaugural Address (1865)

*In 1864 Abraham Lincoln became the first president to be renominated by his party for a second term since Martin Van Buren in 1840 and the first to be reelected since Andrew Jackson in 1832. Neither of Lincoln's victories was uncontested. To be renominated, he had to overcome Republican opposition to his Reconstruction policies. (See headnote to "Abraham Lincoln's Plan of Reconstruction," p. 119.) To be reelected against the Democrats, Lincoln had to defeat George B. McClellan, the general whom he had fired for lack of military boldness but who had always been popular with the troops. The Democrats campaigned by calling for a peace convention with the Confederacy to restore the Union and by criticizing Lincoln's violations of civil liberties and other allegedly unconstitutional actions as president.*

*For a time, Lincoln was so wary of defeat that in August 1864 he had the cabinet sign a pledge to cooperate in the transfer of power to the new president if, as "seems exceedingly probable . . . this Administration will not be reelected." Lincoln may have been unduly pessimistic: in any event, a series of substantial military victories by Gen. William Tecumseh Sherman in Georgia, Gen. Ulysses S. Grant in Virginia, and Gen. Philip H. Sheridan in the Shenandoah Valley undercut Democratic opposition to the war. In the*

*election, Lincoln carried every state in the Union but Delaware, Kentucky, and New Jersey to defeat McClellan by 212-21 votes in the electoral college.*

*Lincoln delivered his second inaugural address, which could not have lasted more than five minutes, on March 4, 1865, almost four years after the beginning of the Civil War. Six hundred thousand people had already died in the war, but it clearly was drawing to an end. Indeed, Confederate general Robert E. Lee surrendered to Grant at Appomattox Court House in Virginia only a month later, on April 9, 1865.*

*In style, Lincoln's second inaugural address is biblical—he quoted from the Old and New Testaments, described the hand of Providence in the war, and wrote in cadences reminiscent of the King James Version. In substance, the address was tolerant and conciliatory toward the almost-defeated South, whose people he referred to as "adversaries," not enemies. "[L]et us judge not that we be not judged . . .," Lincoln said, quoting Jesus, then concluded with words almost as well remembered as the first and last sentences of the Gettysburg Address: "With malice toward none; with charity for all; with firmness in the right, as God gives us to see the right, let us strive on to finish the work we are in; to bind up the nation's wounds; to care for him who shall have borne the battle, and for his widow, and his orphan—to do all which may achieve and cherish a just, and a lasting peace, among ourselves, and with all nations."*

*On April 14, 1865, while watching a play at Ford's Theater, Lincoln was shot by John Wilkes Booth, an actor and Confederate sympathizer. The president died early the next morning.* ～

Fellow-Countrymen:

At this second appearing to take the oath of the presidential office there is less occasion for an extended address than there was at the first. Then a statement somewhat in detail of a course to be pursued seemed fitting and proper. Now, at the expiration of four years, during which public declarations have been constantly called forth on every point and phase of the great contest which still absorbs the attention and engrosses the energies of the nation, little that is new could be presented. The progress of our arms, upon which all else chiefly depends, is as well known to the public as to myself, and it is, I trust, reasonably satisfactory and encouraging to all. With high hope for the future, no prediction in regard to it is ventured.

On the occasion corresponding to this four years ago all thoughts were anxiously directed to an impending civil war. All dreaded it, all sought to avert it. While the inaugural address was being delivered from this place, devoted altogether to *saving* the Union without war, insurgent agents were in the city seeking to *destroy* it without war— seeking to dissolve the Union and divide effects by negotiation. Both parties deprecated war, but one of them would *make* war rather than let the nation survive, and the other would *accept* war rather than let it perish, and the war came.

One eighth of the whole population

was colored slaves, not distributed generally over the Union, but localized in the southern part of it. These slaves constituted a peculiar and powerful interest. All knew that this interest was somehow the cause of the war. To strengthen, perpetuate, and extend this interest was the object for which the insurgents would rend the Union even by war, while the Government claimed no right to do more than to restrict the territorial enlargement of it. Neither party expected for the war the magnitude or the duration which it has already attained. Neither anticipated that the *cause* of the conflict might cease with or even before the conflict itself should cease. Each looked for an easier triumph, and a result less fundamental and astounding. Both read the same Bible and pray to the same God, and each invokes His aid against the other. It may seem strange that any men should dare to ask a just God's assistance in wringing their bread from the sweat of other men's faces, but let us judge not, that we be not judged. The prayers of both could not be answered. That of neither has been answered fully. The Almighty has His own purposes. "Woe unto the world because of offenses; for it must needs be that offenses come, but woe to that man by whom the offense cometh." If we shall suppose that American slavery is one of those offenses which, in the providence of God, must needs come, but which, having continued through His appointed time, He now wills to remove, and that he gives to both North and South this terrible war as the woe due to those by whom the offense came, shall we discern therein any departure from those divine attributes which the believers in a living God always ascribe to Him? Fondly do we hope, fervently do we pray, that this mighty scourge of war may speedily pass away. Yet, if God wills that it continue until all the wealth piled by the bondsman's two hundred and fifty years of unrequited toil shall be sunk, and until every drop of blood drawn with the lash shall be paid by another drawn with the sword, as was said three thousand years ago, so still it must be said, "The judgments of the Lord are true and righteous altogether."

With malice toward none; with charity for all; with firmness in the right as God gives us to see the right, let us strive on to finish the work we are in; to bind up the nation's wounds; to care for him who shall have borne the battle, and for his widow, and his orphan—to do all which may achieve and cherish a just, and a lasting peace, among ourselves, and with all nations.

# Ex Parte Milligan (1866)

Can the president legitimately claim emergency powers in wartime beyond those powers that are enumerated in the Constitution? The typical answer of the Supreme Court to this question, like that of many other Americans, has been variable: yes in the heat of war but no upon later, calmer reflection. This pattern of oscillation concerning the question of presidential war-making powers was established by the Court during the Civil War and its aftermath.

Midway through the Civil War, the Court was asked to rule on the legality of the naval blockade that President Abraham Lincoln had imposed on southern ports in 1861. The foreign owners of four captured vessels sued for redress (their ships and cargo had been sold at public auction) on the grounds that Congress had not declared war on the Confederacy.

The Court rejected this appeal in an 1863 decision, the Prize Cases. Writing for the majority, Justice Robert C. Grier explained that when U.S. territory is taken by hostile armies, the absence of a congressional declaration of war does not mean that a war does not exist. In such circumstances, the decision continued, "the President was bound to meet [the insurrection] in the shape it presented itself, without waiting for Congress to baptise it with a name; and no name given to it by him

or them could change that fact." Justice Grier went on to say that in crises such as the one Lincoln faced, the Court must defer to the president's judgment.

In 1866, with the Civil War over, the Court took a more critical view of another of Lincoln's wartime actions. Two years earlier, an outspoken southern sympathizer named Lambdin P. Milligan had been arrested in Indiana on charges of disloyalty. Even though the regular civil courts of Indiana were open and operating, Milligan was tried by a military commission that had been established by the president. (Lincoln had imposed martial law on some portions of northern states whose loyalty to the Union he did not trust.) The military commission found Milligan guilty and sentenced him to be hanged.

In the case of Ex Parte Milligan (1866), the Supreme Court ruled in Milligan's favor. Ordering Milligan released from prison, the Court condemned the president's assertion that he had the power, even in time of war, unilaterally to impose military trials on civilians while the regular courts were functioning.

Justice David Davis, a close friend of the late president, wrote the opinion of the Court, stating: "No doctrine involving more pernicious consequences was ever invented by the wit of man than *that any of the [Constitution's] provisions can be suspended during any of the great exigencies of war."*  ~

MR. JUSTICE DAVIS delivered the opinion of the court.

On the 10th day of May, 1865, Lambdin P. Milligan presented a petition to the Circuit Court of the United States for the District of Indiana, to be discharged from an alleged unlawful imprisonment. The case made by the petition is this: Milligan is a citizen of the United States; has lived for twenty years in Indiana; and, at the time of the grievances complained of, was not, and never had been in the military or naval service of the United States. On the 5th day of October, 1864, while at home, he was arrested by order of General Alvin P. Hovey, commanding the military district of Indiana; and has ever since been kept in close confinement.

On the 21st day of October, 1864, he was brought before a military commission, convened at Indianapolis, by order of General Hovey, tried on certain charges and specifications; found guilty, and sentenced to be hanged; and the sentence ordered to be executed on Friday, the 19th day of May, 1865.

On the 2d day of January, 1865, after the proceedings of the military commission were at an end, the Circuit Court of the United States for Indiana met at Indianapolis and empanelled a grand jury, who were charged to inquire whether the laws of the United States had been violated; and, if so, to make presentments. The court adjourned on the 27th day of January, having, prior thereto, discharged from further service the grand jury, who did not find any bill of indictment or make any presentment against Milligan for any offence whatever; and, in fact, since his imprisonment, no bill of indictment has been found or presentment made against him by any grand jury of the United States.

Milligan insists that said military commission had no jurisdiction to try him upon the charges preferred, or upon any charge whatever; because he was a citizen of the United States and the State of Indiana, and had not been, since the commencement of the late Rebellion, a resident of any of the States whose citizens were arrayed against the government, and that the right of trial by jury was guaranteed to him by the Constitution of the United States.

The prayer of the petition was, that under the act of Congress, approved March 3d, 1863, entitled, "An act relating to *habeas corpus* and regulating judicial proceedings in certain cases," he may be brought before the court, and either turned over to the proper civil tribunal to be proceeded against according to the law of the land or discharged from custody altogether.

With the petition were filed the order for the commission, the charges and specifications, the findings of the court, with the order of the War Department reciting that the sentence was approved by the President of the United States, and directing that it be carried into execution without delay. The petition was presented and filed in open court by the counsel for Milligan; at the same time the District Attorney of the United States for Indiana appeared, and, by the agreement of counsel, the application was submitted to the court. The opinions of the judges of the Circuit Court were opposed on three questions, which are certified to the Supreme Court:

1st. "On the facts stated in said petition and exhibits, ought a writ of *habeas corpus* to be issued?"

2d. "On the facts stated in said petition and exhibits, ought the said Lambdin P. Milligan to be discharged from custody as in said petition prayed?"

3d. "Whether, upon the facts stated in said petition and exhibits, the military commission mentioned therein had jurisdiction legally to try and sentence Milligan in manner and form as in said petition and exhibits is stated?"

The importance of the main question presented by this record cannot be overstated; for it involves the very framework of the government and the fundamental principles of American liberty.

During the late wicked Rebellion, the temper of the times did not allow that calmness in deliberation and discussion so necessary to a correct conclusion of a purely judicial question. *Then,* considerations of safety were mingled with the exercise of power; and feelings and interests prevailed which are happily terminated. *Now* that the public safety is assured, this question, as well as all others, can be discussed and decided without passion or the admixture of any element not required to form a legal judgment. We approach the investigation of this case, fully sensible of the magnitude of the inquiry and the necessity of full and cautious deliberation.

But, we are met with a preliminary objection. It is insisted that the Circuit Court of Indiana had no authority to certify these questions; and that we are without jurisdiction to hear and determine them.

The sixth section of the "Act to amend the judicial system of the United States," approved April 29, 1802, declares "that whenever any question shall occur before a Circuit Court upon which the opinions of the judges shall be opposed, the point upon which the disagreement shall happen, shall, during the same term, upon the request of either party or their counsel, be stated under the direction of the judges and certified under the seal of the court to the Supreme Court at their next session to be held thereafter; and shall by the said court be finally decided: And the decision of the Supreme Court and their order in the premises shall be remitted

to the Circuit Court and be there entered of record, and shall have effect according to the nature of the said judgment and order: *Provided,* That nothing herein contained shall prevent the cause from proceeding, if, in the opinion of the court, further proceedings can be had without prejudice to the merits."

It is under this provision of law, that a Circuit Court has authority to certify any question to the Supreme Court for adjudication. The inquiry, therefore, is, whether the case of Milligan is brought within its terms.

It was admitted at the bar that the Circuit Court had jurisdiction to entertain the application for the writ of *habeas corpus* and to hear and determine it; and it could not be denied; for the power is expressly given in the 14th section of the Judiciary Act of 1789, as well as in the later act of 1863. Chief Justice Marshall, in Bollman's case (4 Cranch, 75), construed this branch of the Judiciary Act to authorize the courts as well as the judges to issue the writ for the purpose of inquiring into the cause of the commitment; and this construction has never been departed from. But, it is maintained with earnestness and ability, that a certificate of division of opinion can occur only in a *cause;* and, that the proceeding by a party, moving for a writ of *habeas corpus,* does not become a cause *until after the writ has been issued and a return made.*

Independently of the provisions of the act of Congress of March 3, 1863, relating to *habeas corpus,* on which the petitioner bases his claim for relief, and which we will presently consider, can this position be sustained?

It is true, that it is usual for a court, on application for a writ of *habeas corpus,* to issue the writ, and, on the return, to dispose of the case; but the court can elect to waive the issuing of the writ and consider whether, upon the facts presented in the petition, the prisoner, if brought before it, could be discharged. One of the very points on which the case of Tobias Watkins, reported in 3 Peters (page 193), turned, was, whether, if the writ was issued, the petitioner would be remanded upon the case which he had made.

The Chief Justice, in delivering the opinion of the court, said: "The cause of imprisonment is shown as fully by the petitioner as it could appear on the return of the writ; consequently the writ ought not to be awarded if the court is satisfied that the prisoner would be remanded to prison."

The judges of the Circuit Court of Indiana were, therefore, warranted by an express decision of this court in refusing the writ, if satisfied that the prisoner on his own showing was rightfully detained.

But it is contended, if they differed about the lawfulness of the imprisonment, and could render no judgment, the prisoner is remediless; and cannot have the disputed question certified under the act of 1802. His remedy is complete by writ of error or appeal, if the court renders a final judgment refusing to discharge him; but if he should be so unfortunate as to be placed in the predicament of having the court divided on the question whether he should live or die, he is hopeless and without remedy. He wishes the vital question settled, not by a single judge at his chambers, but by the highest tribunal known to the Constitution; and yet the privilege is denied him; because the Circuit Court consists of two judges instead of one.

Such a result was not in the contemplation of the legislature of 1802; and the language used by it cannot be construed to mean any such thing. The clause under consideration was introduced to further the ends of justice, by obtaining a speedy settlement of important questions where the judges might be opposed in opinion.

The act of 1802 so changed the judicial system that the Circuit Court, instead of three, was composed of two judges; and, without this provision or a kindred one, if the judges differed, the difference would remain, the question be unsettled, and justice denied. The decisions of this court upon the provisions of this section have been numerous. In *United States* v. *Daniel* (6 Wheaton, 542), the court, in holding that a division of the judges on a motion for a new trial could not be certified, say: "That the question must be one which arises in a cause depending before the court relative to a proceeding belonging to the cause." Testing Milligan's case by this rule of law, is it not apparent that it is rightfully here; and that we are compelled to answer the questions on which the judges below were opposed in opinion? If, in the sense of the law, the proceeding for the writ of *habeas corpus* was the "*cause*" of the party applying for it, then it is evident that the "cause" was pending before the court, and that the questions certified arose out of it, belonged to it, and were matters of right and not of discretion.

But it is argued, that the proceeding does not ripen into a cause, until there are two parties to it.

This we deny. It was the *cause* of Milligan when the petition was presented to the Circuit Court. It would have been the *cause* of both parties, if the court had issued the writ and brought those who held Milligan in custody before it. Webster defines the word "cause" thus: "A suit or action in court; any legal process which a party institutes to obtain his demand, or by which he seeks his right, or supposed right"—and he says, "this is a legal, scriptural, and popular use of the word, coinciding nearly with case, from *cado,* and action, from *ago,* to urge and drive."

In any legal sense, action, suit, and cause, are convertible terms. Milligan supposed he had a right to test the validity of his trial and sentence; and the proceeding which he set in operation for that purpose was his "cause" or "suit." It was the only one by which he could recover his liberty. He was powerless to do more; he could neither instruct the judges nor control their action, and should not suffer, because, without fault of his, they were unable to render a judgment. But, the true meaning to the term "suit" has been given by this court. One of the questions in *Weston* v. *City Council of Charleston* (2 Peters, 449), was, whether a writ of prohibition was a suit; and Chief Justice Marshall says: "The term is certainly a comprehensive one, and is understood to apply to any proceeding in a court of justice by which an individual pursues that remedy which the law affords him." Certainly, Milligan pursued the only remedy which the law afforded him.

Again, in *Cohens* v. *Virginia* (6 Wheaton, 264), he says: "In law language a suit is the prosecution of some demand in a court of justice." Also, "To commence a suit is to demand something by the institution of process in a court of justice; and to prosecute the suit is to continue that demand." When Milligan demanded his release by the proceeding relating to *habeas corpus,* he commenced a suit; and he has since prosecuted it in all the ways known to the law. One of the questions in *Holmes* v. *Jennison et al.* (14 Peters, 540), was, whether under the 25th section of the Judiciary Act a proceeding for a writ of *habeas corpus* was a "suit." Chief Justice Taney held, that, "if a party is unlawfully imprisoned, the writ of *habeas corpus* is his appropriate legal remedy. It is his suit in court to recover his liberty." There was much diversity of opinion on another ground of jurisdiction; but that, in the sense of the 25th section of the Judiciary Act, the proceeding by *habeas corpus* was a suit, was not controverted by any except Baldwin, Justice, and he thought that

"suit" and "cause" as used in the section, mean the same thing.

The court do not say, that a return must be made, and the parties appear and begin to try the case before it is a suit. When the petition is filed and the writ prayed for, it is a *suit,*—the suit of the party making the application. If it is a suit under the 25th section of the Judiciary Act when the proceedings are begun, it is, by all the analogies of the law, equally a suit under the 6th section of the act of 1802.

But it is argued, that there must be *two* parties to the suit, because the point is to be stated upon the request of "either party or their counsel."

Such a literal and technical construction would defeat the very purpose the legislature had in view, which was to enable any party to bring the case here, when the point in controversy was a matter of right and not of discretion; and the words "either party," in order to prevent a failure of justice, must be construed as words of enlargement, and not of restriction. Although this case is here *ex parte,* it was not considered by the court below without notice having been given to the party supposed to have an interest in the detention of the prisoner. The statements of the record show that this is not only a fair, but conclusive inference. When the counsel for Milligan presented to the court the petition for the writ of *habeas corpus,* Mr. Hanna, the District Attorney for Indiana, also appeared; and, by agreement, the application was submitted to the court, who took the case under advisement, and on the next day announced their inability to agree, and made the certificate. It is clear that Mr. Hanna did not represent the petitioner, and why is his appearance entered? It admits of no other solution than this,— that he was informed of the application, and appeared on behalf of the government to contest it. The government was the prosecutor of Milligan, who claimed that his imprisonment was illegal; and sought, in the only way he could, to recover his liberty. The case was a grave one; and the court, unquestionably, directed that the law officer of the government should be informed of it. He very properly appeared, and, as the facts were uncontroverted and the difficulty was in the application of the law, there was no useful purpose to be obtained in issuing the writ. The cause was, therefore, submitted to the court for their consideration and determination.

But Milligan claimed his discharge from custody by virtue of the act of Congress "relating to *habeas corpus,* and regulating judicial proceedings in certain cases," approved March 3d, 1863. Did that act confer jurisdiction on the Circuit Court of Indiana to hear this case?

In interpreting a law, the motives which must have operated with the legislature in passing it are proper to be considered. This law was passed in a time of great national peril, when our heritage of free government was in danger. An armed rebellion against the national authority, of greater proportions than history affords an example of, was raging; and the public safety required that the privilege of the writ of *habeas corpus* should be suspended. The President had practically suspended it, and detained suspected persons in custody without trial; but his authority to do this was questioned. It was claimed that Congress alone could exercise this power; and that the legislature, and not the President, should judge of the political considerations on which the right to suspend it rested. The privilege of this great writ had never before been withheld from the citizen; and as the exigence of the times demanded immediate action, it was of the highest importance that the lawfulness of the suspension should be fully established. It was under these circumstances, which were such as to arrest the attention of the country, that this law was passed.

The President was authorized by it to suspend the privilege of the writ of *habeas corpus,* whenever, in his judgment, the public safety required; and he did, by proclamation, bearing date the 15th of September, 1863, reciting, among other things, the authority of this statute, suspend it. The suspension of the writ does not authorize the arrest of any one, but simply denies to one arrested the privilege of this writ in order to obtain his liberty.

It is proper, therefore, to inquire under what circumstances the courts could rightfully refuse to grant this writ, and when the citizen was at liberty to invoke its aid.

The second and third sections of the law are explicit on these points. The language used is plain and direct, and the meaning of the Congress cannot be mistaken. The public safety demanded, if the President thought proper to arrest a suspected person, that he should not be required to give the cause of his detention on return to a writ of *habeas corpus.* But it was not contemplated that such person should be detained in custody beyond a certain fixed period, unless certain judicial proceedings, known to the common law, were commenced against him. The Secretaries of State and War were directed to furnish to the judges of the courts of the United States, a list of the names of all parties, not prisoners of war, resident in their respective jurisdictions, who then were or afterwards should be held in custody by the authority of the President, and who were citizens of states in which the administration of the laws in the Federal tribunals were unimpaired. After the list was furnished, if a grand jury of the district convened and adjourned, and did not indict or present one of the persons thus named, he was entitled to his discharge; and it was the duty of the judge of the court to order him brought before him to be discharged, if he desired it. The refusal or omission to furnish the list could not operate to the injury of any one who was not indicted or presented by the grand jury; for, if twenty days had elapsed from the time of his arrest and the termination of the session of the grand jury, he was equally entitled to his discharge as if the list were furnished; and any credible person, on petition verified by affidavit, could obtain the judge's order for that purpose.

Milligan, in his application to be released from imprisonment, averred the existence of every fact necessary under the terms of this law to give the Circuit Court of Indiana jurisdiction. If he was detained in custody by the order of the President, otherwise than as a prisoner of war; if he was a citizen of Indiana and had never been in the military or naval service, and the grand jury of the district had met, after he had been arrested, for a period of twenty days, and adjourned without taking any proceedings against him, *then* the court had the right to entertain his petition and determine the lawfulness of his imprisonment. Because the word "court" is not found in the body of the second section, it was argued at the bar, that the application should have been made to a judge of the court, and not to the court itself; but this is not so, for power is expressly conferred in the last proviso of the section on the court equally with a judge of it to discharge from imprisonment. It was the manifest design of Congress to secure a certain remedy by which any one, deprived of liberty, could obtain it, if there was a judicial failure to find cause of offence against him. Courts are not, always, in session, and can adjourn on the discharge of the grand jury; and before those, who are in confinement, could take proper steps to procure their liberation. To provide for this contingency, authority was given to the judges out of court to grant relief to any party, who could show, that, under the law, he should be no longer restrained of his liberty.

It was insisted that Milligan's case was defective, because it did not state that the list was furnished to the judges; and, therefore, it was impossible to say under which section of the act it was presented.

It is not easy to see how this omission could affect the question of jurisdiction. Milligan could not know that the list was furnished, unless the judges volunteered to tell him; for the law did not require that any record should be made of it or anybody but the judges informed of it. Why aver the fact when the truth of the matter was apparent to the court without an averment? How can Milligan be harmed by the absence of the averment, when he states that he was under arrest for more than sixty days before the court and grand jury, which should have considered his case, met at Indianapolis? It is apparent, therefore, that under the *Habeas Corpus* Act of 1863 the Circuit Court of Indiana had complete jurisdiction upon this case, and, if the judges could not agree on questions vital to the progress of the cause, they had the authority (as we have shown in a previous part of this opinion), and it was their duty to certify those questions of disagreement to this court for final decision. It was argued that a final decision on the questions presented ought not to be made, because the parties who were directly concerned in the arrest and detention of Milligan, were not before the court; and their rights might be prejudiced by the answer which should be given to those questions. But this court cannot know what return will be made to the writ of *habeas corpus* when issued; and it is very clear that no one is concluded upon any question that may be raised to that return. In the sense of the law of 1802, which authorized a certificate of division, a final decision means final upon the points certified; final upon the court below, so that it is estopped from any adverse ruling in all the subsequent proceedings of the cause.

But it is said that this case is ended,

as the presumption is, that Milligan was hanged in pursuance of the order of the President.

Although we have no judicial information on the subject, yet the inference is that he is alive; for otherwise learned counsel would not appear for him and urge this court to decide his case. It can never be in this country of written constitution and laws, with a judicial department to interpret them, that any chief magistrate would be so far forgetful of his duty, as to order the execution of a man who denied the jurisdiction that tried and convinced him; *after* his case was before Federal judges with power to decide it, who, being unable to agree on the grave questions involved, had, according to known law, sent it to the Supreme Court of the United States for decision. But even the suggestion is injurious to the Executive, and we dismiss it from further consideration. There is, therefore, nothing to hinder this court from an investigation of the merits of this controversy.

The controlling question in the case is this: Upon the *facts* stated in Milligan's petition, and the exhibits filed, had the military commission mentioned in it *jurisdiction,* legally, to try and sentence him? Milligan, not a resident of one of the rebellious states, or a prisoner of war, but a citizen of Indiana for twenty years past, and never in the military or naval service, is, while at his home, arrested by the military power of the United States, imprisoned, and, on certain criminal charges preferred against him, tried, convicted, and sentenced to be hanged by a military commission, organized under the direction of the military commander of the military district of Indiana. Had this tribunal the *legal* power and authority to try and punish this man?

No graver question was ever considered by this court, nor one which more nearly concerns the rights of the whole people; for it is the birthright of every American citizen when charged with crime, to be tried and punished according to law. The power of punishment is, alone through the means which the laws have provided for that purpose, and if they are ineffectual, there is an immunity from punishment, no matter how great an offender the individual may be, or how much his crimes may have shocked the sense of justice of the country, or endangered its safety. By the protection of the law human rights are secured; withdraw that protection, and they are at the mercy of wicked rulers, or the clamor of an excited people. If there was law to justify this military trial it is not our province to interfere; if there was not, it is our duty to declare the nullity of the whole proceedings. The decision of this question does not depend on argument or judicial precedents, numerous and highly illustrative as they are. These precedents inform us of the extent of the struggle to preserve liberty and to relieve those in civil life from military trials. The founders of our government were familiar with the history of that struggle; and secured in a written constitution every right which the people had wrested from power during a contest of ages. By that Constitution and the law authorized by it this question must be determined. The provisions of that instrument on the administration of criminal justice are too plain and direct, to leave room for misconstruction or doubt of their true meaning. Those applicable to this case are found in that clause of the original Constitution which says, "That the trial of all crimes, except in case of impeachment, shall be by jury;" and in the fourth, fifth, and sixth articles of the amendments. The fourth proclaims the right to be secure in person and effects against unreasonable search and seizure; and directs that a judicial warrant shall not issue "without proof of probable cause supported by oath or affirmation." The fifth declares "that no person shall be held to answer for a capital or otherwise infamous crime unless on presentment by a grand jury, except in cases arising in the land or naval forces, or in the militia, when in actual service in time of war or public danger, nor be deprived of life, liberty, or property, without due process of law." And the sixth guarantees the right of trial by jury, in such manner and with such regulations that with upright judges, impartial juries, and an able bar, the innocent will be saved and the guilty punished. It is in these words: "In all criminal prosecutions the accused shall enjoy the right to a speedy and public trial by an impartial jury of the state and district wherein the crime shall have been committed, which district shall have been previously ascertained by law, and to be informed of the nature and cause of the accusation, to be confronted with the witnesses against him, to have compulsory process for obtaining witnesses in his favor, and to have the assistance of counsel for his defence." These securities for personal liberty thus embodied, were such as wisdom and experience had demonstrated to be necessary for the protection of those accused of crime. And so strong was the sense of the country of their importance, and so jealous were the people that these rights, highly prized, might be denied them by implication, that when the original Constitution was proposed for adoption it encountered severe opposition; and, but for the belief that it would be so amended as to embrace them, it would never have been ratified.

Time has proven the discernment of our ancestors; for even these provisions, expressed in such plain English words, that it would seem the ingenuity of man could not evade them, are *now*, after the lapse of more than seventy years, sought to be avoided. Those great and good men foresaw that troublous times would arise, when rulers and people would become restive under restraint, and seek by sharp and decisive measures to accomplish ends deemed just

and proper; and that the principles of constitutional liberty would be in peril, unless established by irrepealable law. The history of the world had taught them that what was done in the past might be attempted in the future. The Constitution of the United States is a law for rulers and people, equally in war and in peace, and covers with the shield of its protection all classes of men, at all times, and under all circumstances. No doctrine, involving more pernicious consequences, was ever invented by the wit of man than that any of its provisions can be suspended during any of the great exigencies of government. Such a doctrine leads directly to anarchy or despotism, but the theory of necessity on which it is based is false; for the government, within the Constitution, has all the powers granted to it, which are necessary to preserve its existence; as has been happily proved by the result of the great effort to throw off its just authority.

Have any of the rights guaranteed by the Constitution been violated in the case of Milligan? and if so, what are they?

Every trial involves the exercise of judicial power; and from what source did the military commission that tried him derive their authority? Certainly no part of the judicial power of the country was conferred on them; because the Constitution expressly vests it "in one supreme court and such inferior courts as the Congress may from time to time ordain and establish," and it is not pretended that the commission was a court ordained and established by Congress. They cannot justify on the mandate of the President; because he is controlled by law, and has his appropriate sphere of duty, which is to execute, not to make, the laws; and there is "no unwritten criminal code to which resort can be had as a source of jurisdiction."

But it is said that the jurisdiction is complete under the "laws and usages of war."

It can serve no useful purpose to inquire what those laws and usages are, whence they originated, where found, and on whom they operate; they can never be applied to citizens in states which have upheld the authority of the government, and where the courts are open and their process unobstructed. This court has judicial knowledge that in Indiana the Federal authority was always unopposed, and its courts always open to hear criminal accusations and redress grievances; and no usage of war could sanction a military trial there for any offence whatever of a citizen in civil life, in nowise connected with the military service. Congress could grant no such power; and to the honor of our national legislature be it said, it has never been provoked by the state of the country even to attempt its exercise. One of the plainest constitutional provisions was, therefore, infringed when Milligan was tried by a court not ordained and established by Congress, and not composed of judges appointed during good behavior.

Why was he not delivered to the Circuit Court of Indiana to be proceeded against according to law? No reason of necessity could be urged against it; because Congress had declared penalties against the offences charged, provided for their punishment, and directed that court to hear and determine them. And soon after this military tribunal was ended, the Circuit Court met, peacefully transacted its business, and adjourned. It needed no bayonets to protect it, and required no military aid to execute its judgments. It was held in a state, eminently distinguished for patriotism, by judges commissioned during the Rebellion, who were provided with juries, upright, intelligent, and selected by a marshal appointed by the President. The government had no right to conclude that Milligan, if guilty, would not receive in that court merited punishment; for its records disclose that it was constantly engaged in the trial of similar offences, and was never interrupted in its administration of criminal justice. If it was dangerous, in the distracted condition of affairs, to leave Milligan unrestrained of his liberty, because he "conspired against the government, afforded aid and comfort to rebels, and incited the people to insurrection," the *law* said arrest him, confine him closely, render him powerless to do further mischief; and then present his case to the grand jury of the district, with proofs of his guilt, and, if indicted, try him according to the course of the common law. If this had been done, the Constitution would have been vindicated, the law of 1863 enforced, and the securities for personal liberty preserved and defended.

Another guarantee of freedom was broken when Milligan was denied a trial by jury. The great minds of the country have differed on the correct interpretation to be given to various provisions of the Federal Constitution; and judicial decision has been often invoked to settle their true meaning; but until recently no one ever doubted that the right of trial by jury was fortified in the organic law against the power of attack. It is *now* assailed; but if ideas can be expressed in words, and language has any meaning, *this right*—one of the most valuable in a free country—is preserved to every one accused of crime who is not attached to the army, or navy, or militia in actual service. The sixth amendment affirms that "in all criminal prosecutions the accused shall enjoy the right to a speedy and public trial by an impartial jury," language broad enough to embrace all persons and cases; but the fifth, recognizing the necessity of an indictment, or presentment, before any one can be held to answer for high crimes, "*excepts* cases arising in the land or naval forces, or in the militia, when in actual service, in time of war or public danger;" and the framers of the Constitution, doubtless, meant to limit the right of trial by jury, in the sixth amendment, to those persons who were subject to indictment or presentment in the fifth.

The discipline necessary to the efficiency of the army and navy, required other and swifter modes of trial than are furnished by the common law courts; and, in pursuance of the power conferred by the Constitution, Congress has declared the kinds of trial, and the manner in which they shall be conducted, for offences committed while the party is in the military or naval service. Every one connected with these branches of the public service is amenable to the jurisdiction which Congress has created for their government, and, while thus serving, surrenders his right to be tried by the civil courts. *All other persons,* citizens of states where the courts are open, if charged with crime, are guaranteed the inestimable privilege of trial by jury. This privilege is a vital principle, underlying the whole administration of criminal justice; it is not held by sufferance, and cannot be frittered away on any plea of state or political necessity. When peace prevails, and the authority of the government is undisputed, there is no difficulty of preserving the safeguards of liberty; for the ordinary modes of trial are never neglected, and no one wishes it otherwise; but if society is disturbed by civil commotion—if the passions of men are aroused and the restraints of law weakened, if not disregarded—these safeguards need, and should receive, the watchful care of those intrusted with the guardianship of the Constitution and laws. In no other way can we transmit to posterity unimpaired the blessings of liberty, consecrated by the sacrifices of the Revolution.

It is claimed that martial law covers with its broad mantle the proceedings of this military commission. The proposition is this: that in a time of war the commander of an armed force (if in his opinion the exigencies of the country demand it, and of which he is to judge), has the power, within the lines of his military district, to suspend all civil rights and their remedies, and subject citizens as well as soldiers to the rule of *his will;* and in the exercise of his lawful authority cannot be restrained, except by his superior officer or the President of the United States.

If this position is sound to the extent claimed, then when war exists, foreign or domestic, and the country is subdivided into military departments for mere convenience, the commander of one of them can, if he chooses, within his limits, on the plea of necessity, with the approval of the Executive, substitute military force for and to the exclusion of the laws, and punish all persons, as he thinks right and proper, without fixed or certain rules.

The statement of this proposition shows its importance; for, if true, republican government is a failure, and there is an end of liberty regulated by law. Martial law, established on such a basis, destroys every guarantee of the Constitution, and effectually renders the "military independent of and superior to the civil power"—the attempt to do which by the King of Great Britain was deemed by our fathers such an offence, that they assigned it to the world as one of the causes which impelled them to declare their independence. Civil liberty and this kind of martial law cannot endure together; the antagonism is irreconcilable; and, in the conflict, one or the other must perish.

This nation, as experience has proved, cannot always remain at peace, and has no right to expect that it will always have wise and humane rulers, sincerely attached to the principles of the Constitution. Wicked men, ambitious of power, with hatred of liberty and contempt of law, may fill the place once occupied by Washington and Lincoln; and if this right is conceded, and the calamities of war again befall us, the dangers to human liberty are frightful to contemplate. If our fathers had failed to provide for just such a contingency, they would have been false to the trust reposed in them. They knew—the history of the world told them—the nation they were founding, be its existence short or long, would be involved in war; how often or how long continued, human foresight could not tell; and that unlimited power, wherever lodged at such a time, was especially hazardous to freemen. For this, and other equally weighty reasons, they secured the inheritance they had fought to maintain, by incorporating in a written constitution the safeguards which *time* had proved were essential to its preservation. Not one of these safeguards can the President, or Congress, or the Judiciary disturb, except the one concerning the writ of *habeas corpus*.

It is essential to the safety of every government that, in a great crisis, like the one we have just passed through, there should be a power somewhere of suspending the writ of *habeas corpus*. In every war, there are men of previously good character, wicked enough to counsel their fellow-citizens to resist the measures deemed necessary by a good government to sustain its just authority and overthrow its enemies; and their influence may lead to dangerous combinations. In the emergency of the times, an immediate public investigation according to law may not be possible; and yet, the peril to the country may be too imminent to suffer such persons to go at large. Unquestionably, there is then an exigency which demands that the government, if it should see fit in the exercise of a proper discretion to make arrests, should not be required to produce the persons arrested in answer to a writ of *habeas corpus*. The Constitution goes no further. It does not say after a writ of *habeas corpus* is denied a citizen, that he shall be tried otherwise than by the course of the common law; if it had intended this result, it was easy by the use of direct words to have accom-

plished it. The illustrious men who framed that instrument were guarding the foundations of civil liberty against the abuses of unlimited power; they were full of wisdom, and the lessons of history informed them that a trial by an established court, assisted by an impartial jury, was the only sure way of protecting the citizen against oppression and wrong. Knowing this, they limited the suspension to one great right, and left the rest to remain forever inviolable. But, it is insisted that the safety of the country in time of war demands that this broad claim for martial law shall be sustained. If this were true, it could be well said that a country, preserved at the sacrifice of all the cardinal principles of liberty, is not worth the cost of preservation. Happily, it is not so.

It will be borne in mind that this is not a question of the power to proclaim martial law, when war exists in a community and the courts and civil authorities are overthrown. Nor is it a question what rule a military commander, at the head of his army, can impose on states in rebellion to cripple their resources and quell the insurrection. The jurisdiction claimed is much more extensive. The necessities of the service, during the late Rebellion, required that the loyal states should be placed within the limits of certain military districts and commanders appointed in them; and it is urged, that this, in a military sense, constituted them the theatre of military operations; and, as in this case, Indiana had been and was again threatened with invasion by the enemy, the occasion was furnished to establish martial law. The conclusion does not follow from the premises. If armies were collected in Indiana, they were to be employed in another locality, where the laws were obstructed and the national authority disputed. On *her* soil there was no hostile foot; if once invaded, that invasion was at an end, and with it all pretext for martial law. Martial law cannot arise from a *threatened* invasion. The necessity must be actual and present; the invasion real, such as effectually closes the courts and deposes the civil administration.

It is difficult to see how the *safety* of the country required martial law in Indiana. If any of her citizens were plotting treason, the power of arrest could secure them, until the government was prepared for their trial, when the courts were open and ready to try them. It was as easy to protect witnesses before a civil as a military tribunal; and as there could be no wish to convict, except on sufficient legal evidence, surely an ordained and established court was better able to judge of this than a military tribunal composed of gentlemen not trained to the profession of the law.

It follows, from what has been said on this subject, that there are occasions when martial rule can be properly applied. If, in foreign invasion or civil war, the courts are actually closed, and it is impossible to administer criminal justice according to law, *then,* on the theatre of active military operations, where war really prevails, there is a necessity to furnish a substitute for the civil authority, thus overthrown, to preserve the safety of the army and society; and as no power is left but the military, it is allowed to govern by martial rule until the laws can have their free course. As necessity creates the rule, so it limits its duration; for, if this government is continued *after* the courts are reinstated, it is a gross usurpation of power. Martial rule can never exist where the courts are open, and in the proper and unobstructed exercise of their jurisdiction. It is also confined to the locality of actual war. Because, during the late Rebellion it could have been enforced in Virginia, where the national authority was overturned and the courts driven out, it does not follow that it should obtain in Indiana, where that authority was never disputed, and justice was always administered. And so in the case of a foreign invasion, martial rule may become a necessity in one state, when, in another, it would be "mere lawless violence."

We are not without precedents in English and American history illustrating our views of this question; but it is hardly necessary to make particular reference to them.

From the first year of the reign of Edward the Third, when the Parliament of England reversed the attainder of the Earl of Lancaster, because he could have been tried by the courts of the realm, and declared, "that in time of peace no man ought to be adjudged to death for treason or any other offence without being arraigned and held to answer; and that regularly when the king's courts are open it is a time of peace in judgment of law," down to the present day, martial law, as claimed in this case, has been condemned by all respectable English jurists as contrary to the fundamental laws of the land, and subversive of the liberty of the subject.

During the present century, an instructive debate on this question occurred in Parliament, occasioned by the trial and conviction by court-martial, at Demerara, of the Rev. John Smith, a missionary to the negroes, on the alleged ground of aiding and abetting a formidable rebellion in that colony. Those eminent statesmen, Lord Brougham and Sir James Mackintosh, participated in that debate; and denounced the trial as illegal; because it did not appear that the courts of law in Demerara could not try offences, and that "when the laws can act, every other mode of punishing supposed crimes is itself an enormous crime."

So sensitive were our Revolutionary fathers on this subject, although Boston was almost in a state of siege, when General Gage issued his proclamation of martial law, they spoke of it as an "attempt to supersede the course of the common law, and instead thereof to publish and order the use of martial law." The Virginia Assembly, also, denounced a similar measure on the part of Governor Dunmore "as an assumed power, which the king himself cannot exercise; because it annuls the law of the land and introduces the most execrable of all systems, martial law."

In some parts of the country, during the war of 1812, our officers made arbitrary arrests and, by military tribunals, tried citizens who were not in the military service. These arrests and trials, when brought to the notice of the courts, were uniformly condemned as illegal. The cases of *Smith* v. *Shaw* and *McConnell* v. *Hampden* (reported in 12 Johnson [pages 257 and 234]), are illustrations, which we cite, not only for the principles they determine, but on account of the distinguished jurists concerned in the decisions, one of whom for many years occupied a seat on this bench.

It is contended, that *Luther* v. *Borden,* decided by this court, is an authority for the claim of martial law advanced in this case. The decision is misapprehended. That case grew out of the attempt in Rhode Island to supersede the old colonial government by a revolutionary proceeding. Rhode Island, until that period, had no other form of local government than the charter granted by King Charles II, in 1663; and as that limited the right of suffrage, and did not provide for its own amendment, many citizens became dissatisfied, because the legislature would not afford the relief in their power; and without the authority of law, formed a new and independent constitution, and proceeded to assert its authority by force of arms. The old government resisted this; and as the rebellion was formidable, called out the militia to subdue it, and passed an act declaring martial law. Borden, in the military service of the *old* government, broke open the house of Luther, who supported the *new,* in order to arrest him. Luther brought suit against Borden; and the question was,

whether, under the constitution and laws of the state, Borden was justified. This court held that a state "may use its military power to put down an armed insurrection too strong to be controlled by the civil authority;" and, if the legislature of Rhode Island thought the peril so great as to require the use of its military forces and the declaration of martial law, there was no ground on which *this court* could question its authority; and as Borden acted under military orders of the charter government, which had been recognized by the political power of the country, and was upheld by the state judiciary, he was justified in breaking into and entering Luther's house. This is the extent of the decision. There was no question in issue about the power of declaring martial law under the Federal Constitution, and the court did not consider it necessary even to inquire "to what extent nor under what circumstances that power may be exercised by a state."

We do not deem it important to examine further the adjudged cases; and shall, therefore, conclude without any additional reference to authorities.

To the third question, then, on which the judges below were opposed in opinion, an answer in the negative must be returned.

It is proper to say, although Milligan's trial and conviction by a military commission was illegal, yet, if guilty of the crimes imputed to him, and his guilt had been ascertained by an established court and impartial jury, he deserved severe punishment. Open resistance to the measures deemed necessary to subdue a great rebellion, by those who enjoy the protection of government, and have not the excuse even of prejudice of section to plead in their favor, is wicked; but that resistance becomes an *enormous crime* when it assumes the form of a secret political organization, armed to oppose the laws, and seeks by stealthy means to introduce the enemies of the country into peaceful communities, there to light the torch of civil war, and thus overthrow the power of the United States. Conspiracies like these, at such a juncture, are extremely perilous; and those concerned in them are dangerous enemies to their country, and should receive the heaviest penalties of the law, as an example to deter others from similar criminal conduct. It is said the severity of the laws caused them; but Congress was obliged to enact severe laws to meet the crisis; and as our highest civil duty is to serve our country when in danger, the late war has proved that rigorous laws, when necessary, will be cheerfully obeyed by a patriotic people, struggling to preserve the rich blessings of a free government.

The two remaining questions in this case must be answered in the affirmative. The suspension of the privilege of the writ of *habeas corpus* does not suspend the writ itself. The writ issues as a matter of course; and on the return made to it the court decides whether the party applying is denied the right of proceeding any further with it.

If the military trial of Milligan was contrary to law, then he was entitled, on the facts stated in his petition, to be discharged from custody by the terms of the act of Congress of March 3d, 1863. The provision of this law having been considered in a previous part of this opinion, we will not restate the views there presented. Milligan avers he was a citizen of Indiana, not in the military or naval service, and was detained in close confinement, by order of the President, from the 5th day of October, 1864, until the 2d day of January, 1865, when the Circuit Court for the District of Indiana, with a grand jury, convened in session at Indianapolis; and afterwards, on the 27th day of the same month, adjourned without finding an indictment or presentment against him. If these averments were true (and their truth is conceded for the purposes of this case), the court was required to liberate him on taking certain oaths prescribed by law, and entering into recognizance for his good behavior.

But it is insisted that Milligan was a prisoner of war, and, therefore, excluded from the privileges of the statute. It is not easy to see how he can be treated as a prisoner of war, when he lived in Indiana for the past twenty years, was arrested there, and had not been, during the late troubles, a resident of any of the states in rebellion. If in Indiana he conspired with bad men to assist the enemy, he is punishable for it in the courts of Indiana; but, when tried for the offence, he cannot plead the rights of war; for he was not engaged in legal acts of hostility against the government, and only such persons, when captured, are prisoners of war. If he cannot enjoy the immunities attaching to the character of a prisoner of war, how can he be subject to their pains and penalties?

This case, as well as the kindred cases of Bowles and Horsey, were disposed of at the last term, and the proper orders were entered of record. There is, therefore, no additional entry required.

# Tenure of Office Act and Veto (1867)

Andrew Johnson of Tennessee, a Democrat, was the only southern senator who chose to remain in the U.S. Senate after his state seceded from the Union in 1861. Johnson's loyalty was rewarded when President Abraham Lincoln appointed him to be Tennessee's military governor after Union forces captured the state in 1862. Two years later, at Lincoln's request, the National Union party convention (the Republican nominating convention had decided to broaden its base in an effort to attract loyalist Democrats) nominated Johnson to run for vice president in the 1864 election.

On April 15, 1865, only six weeks after he took office and six days after Confederate general Robert E. Lee surrendered at Appomattox Court House, Lincoln died from an assassin's bullet, and Johnson became president. Northern Republicans in Congress regarded Johnson, a southern Jacksonian Democrat of doubtful presidential stature (his inaugural address as vice president had been a drunken harangue), with considerable suspicion.

Johnson and Congress disagreed strongly about how the reconstruction of the South should take place, with Johnson invariably the more conciliatory toward the defeated rebels and Congress the more severe. In 1865, choosing not to call Congress into special session after Lincoln died, Johnson

recognized as legitimate four new southern state governments that, in accordance with Lincoln's announced policy, were formed by conventions representing 10 percent of the prewar electorate. (See headnote to "Abraham Lincoln's Plan of Reconstruction," p. 119.) Congress responded by refusing to seat the states' elected U.S. representatives and senators. The president and Congress clashed again when Congress passed a bill to renew the Freedman's Bureau to protect and provide services for ex-slaves and a civil rights act to enforce their rights as citizens. Johnson successfully vetoed both pieces of legislation.

Johnson's political foes won a landslide in the 1866 congressional elections. Congress soon took charge of reconstruction policy making. The Reconstruction Act, passed in 1867, divided the South into five military districts, each controlled by a high-ranking army officer, and imposed severe conditions on each state for readmission to the Union. A second bill (passed as a rider to the army appropriations act) removed these districts from Johnson's supervision by requiring that all military orders be channeled through the general of the army, Ulysses S. Grant. The act also protected Grant from being replaced without the approval of the Senate.

The third major piece of reconstruc-

*tion legislation to be enacted in 1867 was the Tenure of Office Act, whose main purpose was to protect Secretary of War Edwin Stanton, a supporter of congressional reconstruction policies, from being fired by President Johnson. The act said that, without the Senate's acquiescence, the president could not fire any administration official whose appointment originally had been confirmed by the Senate. If the president declared his intent to remove someone, that person would remain in office until (or unless) the Senate confirmed the president's new nominee.*

*Johnson vetoed the Tenure of Office Act, declaring that it violated the president's constitutional power of removal. In the new, overwhelmingly Republican Congress, however, Johnson's vetoes of this and the other reconstruction bills were easily overridden.* ~

---

# Tenure of Office Act
## March 2, 1867

*Be it enacted by the Senate and House of Representatives of the United States of America in Congress assembled,* That every person holding any civil office to which he has been appointed by and with the advice and consent of the Senate, and every person who shall hereafter be appointed to any such office, and shall become duly qualified to act therein, is, and shall be entitled to hold such office until a successor shall have been in the manner appointed and duly qualified, except as herein otherwise provided: *Provided,* That the Secretaries of State, of the Treasury, of War, of the Navy, and of the Interior, the Postmaster-General, and the Attorney General, shall hold their offices respectively for and during the term of the President by whom they may have been appointed and for one month thereafter, subject to removal by

and with the advice and consent of the Senate.

SEC. 2. *And be it further enacted,* That when any officer appointed as aforesaid, excepting judges of the United States courts, shall, during a recess of the Senate, be shown, by evidence satisfactory to the President, to be guilty of misconduct in office, or crime, or for any reason shall become incapable or legally disqualified to perform its duties, in such case, and in no other, the President may suspend such officer and designate some suitable person to perform temporarily the duties of such office until the next meeting of the Senate, and until the case shall be acted upon by the Senate, and such person so designated shall take the oaths and give the bonds required by law to be taken and given by the person duly appointed to fill such office; and in such case it shall be the duty of the President, within twenty days after the first day of such next meeting of the Senate, to report to the Senate such suspension, with the evidence and reasons for his action in the case, and the name of the person so designated to perform the duties of such office. And if the Senate shall concur in such suspension and advise and consent to the removal of such officer, they shall so certify to the President, who may thereupon remove such officer, and, by and with the advice and consent of the Senate, appoint another person to such office. But if the Senate shall refuse to concur in such suspension, such officer so suspended shall forthwith resume the functions of his office, and the powers of the person so performing the duties in his stead shall cease, and the official salary and emoluments of such officer shall, during such suspension, belong to the person so performing the duties thereof, and not to the officer so suspended: *Provided, however,* That the President, in case he shall become satisfied that such suspension was made on insufficient grounds, shall be authorized, at any time before reporting such suspension to the Senate as above provided, to revoke such suspension and reinstate such officer in the performance of the duties of his office.

SEC. 3. *And be it further enacted,* That the President shall have power to fill all vacancies which may happen during the recess of the Senate by reason of death or resignation, by granting commissions which shall expire at the end of their next session thereafter. And if no appointment, by and with the advice and consent of the Senate, shall be made to such office so vacant or temporarily filled as aforesaid during such next session of the Senate, such office shall remain in abeyance, without any salary, fees, or emoluments attached thereto, until the same shall be filled by appointments thereto, by and with the advice and consent of the Senate; and during such time all the powers and duties belonging to such office shall be exercised by such other officer as may by law exercise such powers and duties in case of a vacancy in such office.

SEC. 4. *And be it further enacted,* That nothing in this act contained shall be construed to extend the term of any office the duration of which is limited by law.

SEC. 5. *And be it further enacted,* That if any person shall, contrary to the provisions of this act, accept any appointment to or employment in any office, or shall hold or exercise or attempt to hold or exercise, any such office or employment, he shall be deemed, and is hereby declared to be guilty of a high misdemeanor, and, upon trial and conviction thereof, he shall be punished therefor by a fine not exceeding ten thousand dollars, or by imprisonment not exceeding five years, or both said punishments, in the discretion of the court.

SEC. 6. *And be it further enacted,* That every removal, appointment, or employment made, had, or exercised,

contrary to the provisions of this act, and the making, signing, sealing, countersigning, or issuing of any commission or letter of authority for or in respect to any such appointment or employment, shall be deemed, and are hereby declared to be, high misdemeanors, and, upon trial and conviction thereof, every person guilty thereof shall be punished by a fine not exceeding ten thousand dollars, or by imprisonment not exceeding five years, or both said punishments, in the discretion of the court: *Provided,* That the President shall have power to make out and deliver, after the adjournment of the Senate, commissions for all officers whose appointment shall have been advised and consented to by the Senate.

SEC. 7. *And be it further enacted,* That it shall be the duty of the Secretary of the Senate, at the close of each session thereof, to deliver to the Secretary of the Treasury, and to each of his assistants, and to each of the auditors, and to each of the comptrollers of the treasury, and to the treasurer, and to the register of the treasury, a full and complete list, duly certified, of all the persons who shall have been nominated to and rejected by the Senate during such session, and a like list of all the offices to which nominations shall have been made and not confirmed and filled at such session.

SEC. 8. *And be it further enacted,* That whenever the President shall, without the advice and consent of the Senate, designate, authorize, or employ any person to perform the duties of any office, he shall forthwith notify the Secretary of the Treasury thereof; and it shall be the duty of the Secretary of the Treasury thereupon to communicate such notice to all the proper accounting and disbursing officers of his department.

SEC. 9. *And be it further enacted,* That no money shall be paid or received from the treasury, or paid or received from or retained out of any public moneys or funds of the United States, whether in the treasury or not, to or by or for the benefit of any person appointed to or authorized to action or holding or exercising the duties or functions of any officer contrary to the provisions of this act; nor shall any claim, account, voucher, order, certificate, warrant, or other instrument providing for or relating to such payment, receipt, or retention, be presented, passed, allowed, approved, certified, or paid by any officer of the United States, or by any person exercising the functions or performing the duties of any office or place of trust under the United States, for or in respect to such office, or the exercising or performing the functions or duties thereof; and every person who shall violate any of the provisions of this section shall be deemed guilty of a high misdemeanor, and, upon trial and conviction thereof, shall be punished therefor by a fine not exceeding ten thousand dollars, or by imprisonment not exceeding ten years, or both said punishments, in the discretion of the court.

SCHUYLER COLFAX,
*Speaker of the House of Representatives*
LA FAYETTE S. FOSTER,
*President of the Senate, pro tempore.*

# Veto of Tenure of Office Act

To the Senate of the United States:

I have carefully examined the bill "to regulate the tenure of certain civil offices." The material portion of the bill is contained in the 1st Section, and is of the effect following, namely:

That every person holding any civil office to which he has been appointed, by and with the advice and consent of the Senate, and every person who shall hereafter be appointed to any such office and shall become duly qualified to act therein, is and shall be entitled to hold such office until a successor shall have been appointed by the President, with the advice and consent of the Senate, and duly qualified; and that the secretaries of state, of the treasury, of war, of the Navy, and of the interior, the postmaster general, and the attorney general shall hold their offices respectively for and during the term of the President by whom they may have been appointed and for one month thereafter, subject to removal by and with the advice and consent of the Senate.

These provisions are qualified by a reservation in the 4th Section, "that nothing contained in the bill shall be construed to extend the term of any office the duration of which is limited by law." In effect, the bill provides that the President shall not remove from their places any of the civil officers whose terms of service are not limited by law without the advice and consent of the Senate of the United States. The bill in this respect conflicts, in my judgment, with the Constitution of the United States.

The question, as Congress is well aware, is by no means a new one. That the power of removal is constitutionally vested in the President of the United States is a principle which has been not more distinctly declared by judicial authority and judicial commentators than it has been uniformly practised upon by the Legislative and Executive departments of the government. The question arose in the House of Representatives so early as the 16th of June, 1789, on the bill for establishing an Executive Department, denominated "the Department of Foreign Affairs." The first clause of the bill, after recapitulating the functions of that officer and defining his duties, had these words: "To be removable from office by the President of the United States."

It was moved to strike out these words, and the motion was sustained with great ability and vigor. It was insisted that the President could not constitutionally exercise the power of removal exclusively of the Senate; that *The Federalist* so interpreted the Constitution when arguing for its adoption by the several states; that the Constitution had nowhere given the President power of removal, either expressly or by strong implication, but, on the contrary, had distinctly provided for removals from office by impeachment only. . . .

The nature of things, the great objects of society, the express objects of the Constitution itself require that this thing should be otherwise. To unite the Senate with the President in the exercise of the power, it was said, "would involve us in the most serious difficulty. Suppose a discovery of any of those events should take place when the Senate is not in session; how is the remedy to be applied? The evil could be avoided in no other way than by the Senate sitting always." In regard to the danger of the power being abused if exercised by one man, it was said "that the danger is as great with respect to the Senate, who are assembled from various parts of the continent, with different impressions and opinions"; "that such a body is more likely to misuse the power of removal than the man whom the united voice of America calls to the presidential chair. As the nature of government requires the power of removal," it was maintained, "that it should be exercised in this way by the hand capable of exerting itself with effect; and the power must be conferred on the President by the Constitution as the executive officer of the government." . . .

Under these circumstances, as a depositary of the executive authority of the nation, I do not feel at liberty to unite with Congress in reversing it by giving my approval to the bill. At the early day when this question was settled, and, indeed, at the several periods when it has subsequently been agitated, the success of the Constitution of the United

States, as a new and peculiar system of free, representative government, was held doubtful in other countries and was even a subject of patriotic apprehension among the American people themselves. A trial of nearly eighty years, through the vicissitudes of foreign conflicts and of civil war, is confidently regarded as having extinguished all such doubts and apprehensions for the future.

During that eighty years, the people of the United States have enjoyed a measure of security, peace, prosperity, and happiness never surpassed by any nation. It cannot be doubted that the triumphant success of the Constitution is due to the wonderful wisdom with which the functions of government were distributed between the three principal departments—the Legislative, the Executive, and the Judicial—and to the fidelity with which each has confined itself or been confined by the general voice of the nation within its peculiar and proper sphere. While a just, proper, and watchful jealousy of executive power constantly prevails, as it ought ever to prevail, yet it is equally true that an efficient executive, capable, in the language of the oath prescribed to the President, of executing the laws and, within the sphere of executive action, of preserving, protecting, and defending the Constitution of the United States, is an indispensable security for tranquillity at home and peace, honor, and safety abroad.

Governments have been erected in many countries upon our model. If one or many of them have thus far failed in fully securing to their people the benefits which we have derived from our system, it may be confidently asserted that their misfortune has resulted from their unfortunate failure to maintain the integrity of each of the three great departments while preserving harmony among them all.

Having at an early period accepted the Constitution in regard to the executive office in the sense in which it was interpreted with the concurrence of its founders, I have found no sufficient grounds in the arguments now opposed to that construction or in any assumed necessity of the times for changing those opinions. For these reasons I return the bill to the Senate, in which house it originated, for the further consideration of Congress which the Constitution prescribes. Insomuch as the several parts of the bill which I have not considered are matters chiefly of detail and are based altogether upon the theory of the Constitution from which I am obliged to dissent, I have not thought it necessary to examine them with a view to make them an occasion of distinct and special objections.

# Articles of Impeachment against Andrew Johnson (1868)

The Constitution stipulates that the president "shall be removed from office on Impeachment for, and Conviction of, Treason, Bribery, or other high Crimes and Misdemeanors." The House of Representatives is charged to impeach the president by majority vote; the Senate, with the chief justice of the Supreme Court presiding, then tries the president and decides whether to convict and remove. A two-thirds majority of senators is required to do so.

Andrew Johnson is the only president who has undergone the entire impeachment process. Since succeeding to the office when President Abraham Lincoln died on April 15, 1865, Johnson had been embroiled in a series of bitter controversies with Congress over Reconstruction. The secretary of war, Edwin Stanton, sided more with Congress on these issues than with the president. Congress protected Stanton from being fired by passing the Tenure of Office Act and by overriding Johnson's veto of the bill on March 2, 1867. The act barred the president from removing any Senate-approved appointee from office until the Senate confirmed the nomination of a successor.

After Congress went into recess in 1867, Johnson, taking advantage of a loophole in the Tenure of Office Act that allowed him to act temporarily when Congress was not in session, suspended Stanton as secretary of war and replaced him with Gen. Ulysses S. Grant. Reconvening in January 1868, however, the Senate disapproved Johnson's action, and Grant turned the office back to Stanton. (Johnson thought he had Grant's promise to ignore the Senate vote and thus force a confrontation with Congress and, ultimately, a decision by the Supreme Court about the constitutionality of the Tenure of Office Act, but Grant decided not to jeopardize his presidential ambitions by siding with the president and alienating congressional Republicans.) In February, acting in explicit defiance of the act, Johnson fired Stanton and appointed Gen. Lorenzo Thomas to replace him. While Thomas tried (unsuccessfully) to persuade Stanton to vacate the building, the House voted on February 21 to open an impeachment inquiry against the president.

The House took little time to act. The ardently radical Committee on Reconstruction quickly prepared an eleven-article impeachment resolution, which the House approved by a 126-47 vote on March 2 and 3, 1868, after only two days of debate. The first eight articles dealt with various aspects of Johnson's violation of the Tenure of Office Act. Article IX accused him of violating another recently enacted law *when he bypassed the general of the army to give an order to a general in the field. Articles X and XI charged that Johnson's inflammatory speeches in the 1866 congressional election campaign had sought to bring Congress into "disgrace, ridicule, hatred, contempt, and reproach."*

*Seven members of the House were appointed to present the case for removal in the Senate trial. Johnson's lawyers argued in his defense that the president was entitled to violate a law he regarded as unconstitutional in order to bring the issue before the Supreme Court. (They also argued, more narrowly, that the Tenure of Office Act did not bar Johnson from firing Stanton because Stanton had been appointed by a different president, Lincoln.) Articles IX, X, and XI were dismissed by Johnson's defenders as frivolous.*

*Thirty-six votes were needed for conviction in the fifty-four-member Senate. By most reckonings, twelve senators (nine of them Democrats) were counted as Johnson supporters and thirty as Johnson opponents. That left the decision in the hands of twelve undecided Republicans, some of whom dreaded the prospect that Senate president pro tempore and reconstruction hardliner Benjamin Wade of Ohio would (under the law that prevailed at the time) succeed to the presidency if Johnson were removed. In votes taken on May 16 and May 26, 1868, seven of the twelve voted not to convict the president. As a result, the margin in favor of conviction was 35-19, one short of the required two-thirds.*

*Johnson completed his term as president on March 4, 1869. He returned to Tennessee where, after two unsuccessful attempts to win office, he was elected by the state legislature to the U.S. Senate in 1874. On July 31, 1875, five months after taking office, Johnson died.*          ~

IN THE HOUSE OF REPRESEN-
TATIVES, UNITED STATES,
March 2, 1868

ARTICLES EXHIBITED BY THE HOUSE OF REPRESENTATIVES OF THE UNITED STATES, IN THE NAME OF THEMSELVES AND ALL THE PEOPLE OF THE UNITED STATES, AGAINST ANDREW JOHNSON, PRESIDENT OF THE UNITED STATES, IN MAINTE-NANCE AND SUPPORT OF THEIR IMPEACHMENT AGAINST HIM FOR HIGH CRIMES AND MISDE-MEANORS IN OFFICE.

## Article I

That said Andrew Johnson, President of the United States, on the 21st day of February, A.D. 1868, at Washington, in the District of Columbia, unmindful of the high duties of his office, of his oath of office, and of the requirement of the Constitution that he should take care that the laws be faithfully executed, did unlawfully and in violation of the Constitution and laws of the United States issue an order in writing for the removal of Edwin M. Stanton from the office of Secretary for the Department of War, said Edwin M. Stanton having been theretofore duly appointed and commissioned, by and with the advice and consent of the Senate of the United States, as such Secretary; and said Andrew Johnson, President of the United States, on the 12th day of August, A.D. 1867, and during the recess of said Senate, having suspended by his order Edwin M. Stanton from said office, and within twenty days after the first day of the next meeting of said Senate—that is to say, on the 12th day of December, in the year last aforesaid—having reported to said Senate such suspension, with the evidence and reasons for his action in the case and the name of the person designated to perform the duties of such office temporarily until the next meeting of the Senate; and said Senate thereafterwards, on the 13th day of January, A.D. 1868, having duly considered the evidence and reasons reported by said Andrew Johnson for said suspension, and having refused to concur in said suspension, whereby and by force of the provisions of an act entitled "An act regulating the tenure of certain civil offices," passed March 2, 1867, said Edwin M. Stanton did forthwith resume the functions of his office, whereof the said Andrew Johnson had then and there due notice; and said Edwin M. Stanton, by reason of the premises, on said 21st day of February, being lawfully entitled to hold said office of Secretary for the Department of War; which said order for the removal of said Edwin M. Stanton is in substance as follows; that is to say:

EXECUTIVE MANSION,
Washington, D.C., February 21, 1868.

HON. EDWIN M. STANTON,
  Washington, D.C.

SIR: By virtue of the power and authority vested in me as President by the Constitution and laws of the United States, you are hereby removed from office as Secretary for the Department of War, and your functions as such will terminate upon the receipt of this communication.

You will transfer to Brevet Major-General Lorenzo Thomas, Adjutant-General of the Army, who has this day been authorized and empowered to act as secretary of War ad interim, all records, books, papers, and other public property now in your custody and charge.

Respectfully, yours,

ANDREW JOHNSON

Which order was unlawfully issued with intent then and there to violate the act entitled "An act regulating the tenure

of certain civil offices," passed March 2, 1867, and with the further intent, contrary to the provisions of said act, in violation thereof, and contrary to the provisions of the Constitution of the United States, and without the advice and consent of the Senate of the United States, the said Senate then and there being in session, to remove said Edwin M. Stanton from the office of Secretary for the Department of War, the said Edwin M. Stanton being then and there Secretary for the Department of War, and being then and there in the due and unlawful execution and discharge of the duties of said office; whereby said Andrew Johnson, President of the United States, did then and there commit and was guilty of a high misdemeanor in office.

## ARTICLE II

That on said 21st day of February, A.D. 1868, at Washington, in the District of Columbia, said Andrew Johnson, President of the United States, unmindful of the high duties of his office, of his oath of office, and in violation of the Constitution of the United States, and contrary to the provisions of an act entitled "An act regulating the tenure of certain civil offices," passed March 2, 1867, without the advice and consent of the Senate of the United States, said Senate then and there being in session, and without authority of law, did with intent to violate the Constitution of the United States and the act aforesaid, issue and deliver to one Lorenzo Thomas a letter of authority in substance as follows; that is to say:

EXECUTIVE MANSION,
Washington, D.C., February 21, 1868

Brevet Major-General
LORENZO THOMAS,
  Adjutant-General United States
  Army, Washington, D.C.

SIR: The Hon. Edwin M. Stanton having been this day removed from office as Secretary for the Department of War, you are hereby authorized and empowered to act as Secretary of War ad interim, and will immediately enter upon the discharge of the duties pertaining to that office.

Mr. Stanton has been instructed to transfer to you all the records, books, papers, and other public property now in his custody and charge.

Respectfully, yours,

ANDREW JOHNSON

Then and there being no vacancy in said office of Secretary for the Department of War, whereby said Andrew Johnson, President of the United States, did then and there commit and was guilty of a high misdemeanor in office.

## ARTICLE III

That said Andrew Johnson, President of the United States, on the 21st day of February, A.D. 1868, at Washington, in the District of Columbia, did commit and was guilty of a high misdemeanor in office in this, that without authority of law, while the Senate of the United States was then and there in session, he did appoint one Lorenzo Thomas to be Secretary for the Department of War ad interim, without the advice and consent of the Senate, and with intent to violate the Constitution of the United States, no vacancy having happened in said office of Secretary for the Department of War during the recess of the Senate, and no vacancy existing in said office at the time, and which said appointment, so made by said Andrew Johnson, of said Lorenzo Thomas, is in substance as follows, that is to say:

EXECUTIVE MANSION,
Washington, D.C., February 21, 1868

Brevet Major-General
LORENZO THOMAS,
    Adjutant-General
    United States Army,
    Washington, D.C.

SIR: The Hon. Edwin M. Stanton having been this day removed from office as Secretary for the Department of War, you are hereby authorized and empowered to act as Secretary of War ad interim, and will immediately enter upon the discharge of the duties pertaining to that office.

Mr. Stanton has been instructed to transfer to you all the records, books, papers, and other public property now in his custody and charge.

Respectfully, yours,

ANDREW JOHNSON

## ARTICLE IV

That said Andrew Johnson, President of the United States, unmindful of the high duties of his office and his oath of office, in violation of the Constitution and laws of United States, on the 21st day of February, A.D. 1868, at Washington, in the District of Columbia, did unlawfully conspire with one Lorenzo Thomas, and with other persons to the House of Representatives unknown, with intent, by intimidation and threats, unlawfully to hinder and prevent Edwin M. Stanton, then and there the Secretary for the Department of War, duly appointed under the laws of the United States, from holding said office of Secretary for the Department of War, contrary to and in violation of the Constitution of the United States and of the provisions of an act entitled "An act to define and punish certain conspiracies," approved July 31, 1861; whereby said Andrew Johnson, President of the United States, did then and there commit and was guilty of a high crime in office.

## ARTICLE V

That said Andrew Johnson, President of the United States, unmindful of the high duties of his office and of his oath of office, on the 21st day of February, A.D. 1868, and on divers other days and times in said year before the 2d day of March, A.D. 1868, at Washington, in the District of Columbia, did unlawfully conspire with one Lorenzo Thomas, and with other persons to the House of Representatives unknown, to prevent and hinder the execution of an act entitled "An act regulating the tenure of certain civil offices," passed March 2, 1867, and in pursuance of said conspiracy did unlawfully attempt to prevent Edwin M. Stanton, then and there being Secretary for the Department of War, duly appointed and commissioned under the laws of the United States, from holding said office; whereby the said Andrew Johnson, President of the United States, did then and there commit and was guilty of a high misdemeanor in office.

## ARTICLE VI

That said Andrew Johnson, President of the United States, unmindful of the high duties of his office and of his oath of office, on the 21st day of February, A.D. 1868, at Washington, in the District of Columbia, did unlawfully conspire with one Lorenzo Thomas by force to seize, take, and possess the property of the United States in the Department of War, and then and there in the custody and charge of Edwin M. Stanton, Secretary for said Department, contrary to the provisions of an act entitled "An act to define and punish certain conspiracies," approved July 31, 1861, and with intent to violate and disregard an act entitled "An act regulating the tenure of certain civil offices," passed March 2, 1867; whereby said Andrew Johnson, President of the United States, did then and there commit a high crime in office.

## ARTICLE VII

That said Andrew Johnson, President of the United States, unmindful of the high duties of his office and of his oath of office, on the 21st day of February, A.D. 1868, at Washington, in the District of Columbia, did unlawfully conspire with one Lorenzo Thomas with intent unlawfully to seize, take, and possess the property of the United States in the Department of War, in the custody and charge of Edwin M. Stanton, Secretary for said Department, with intent to violate and disregard the act entitled "An act regulating the tenure of certain civil offices," passed March 2, 1867; whereby said Andrew Johnson, President of the United States, did then and there commit a high misdemeanor in office.

## ARTICLE VIII

That said Andrew Johnson, President of the United States, unmindful of the high duties of his office and of his oath of office, with intent unlawfully to control the disbursement of the moneys appropriated for the military service and for the Department of War, on the 21st day of February, A.D. 1868, at Washington, in the District of Columbia, did unlawfully, and contrary to the provisions of an act entitled "An act regulating the tenure of certain civil offices," passed March 2, 1867, and in violation of the Constitution of the United States, and without the advice and consent of the Senate of the United States, and while the Senate was then and there in session, there being no vacancy in the office of Secretary for the Department of War, and with intent to violate and disregard the act aforesaid, then and there issue and deliver to one Lorenzo Thomas a letter of authority, in writing, in substance as follows; that is to say:

EXECUTIVE MANSION
Washington, D.C., February 21, 1868

Brevet Major-General
LORENZO THOMAS,
   Adjutant-General United States
Army, Washington, D.C.

SIR: The Hon. Edwin M. Stanton having been this day removed from office as Secretary for the Department of War, you are hereby authorized and empowered to act as Secretary of War ad interim, and will immediately enter upon the discharge of the duties pertaining to that office.

Mr. Stanton has been instructed to transfer to you all the records, books, papers, and other public property now in his custody and charge.

Respectfully, yours,

ANDREW JOHNSON

whereby said Andrew Johnson, President of the United States, did then and there commit and was guilty of a high misdemeanor in office.

## ARTICLE IX

That said Andrew Johnson, President of the United States, on the 22d day of February, A.D. 1868, at Washington, in the District of Columbia, in disregard of the Constitution and the laws of the United States duly enacted, as Commander in Chief of the Army of the United States, did bring before himself then and there William H. Emory, a major-general by brevet in the Army of the United States, actually in command of the Department of Washington and the military forces thereof, and did then and there, as such Commander in Chief, declare to and instruct said Emory that part of a law of the United States, passed March 2, 1867, entitled "Act making appropriations for the support of the Army for the year ending June 30, 1868, and for other purposes," especially the second section thereof, which provides, among other things, that "all orders and instructions relating to military operations issued by the President or Secretary of War shall be issued through the General of the Army, and in case of his inability through the next in rank," was unconstitutional and in contravention of the commission of said Emory, and which said provision of law had been theretofore duly and legally promulgated by general order for the government and direction of the Army of the United States, as the said Andrew Johnson then and there well knew, with intent thereby to induce said Emory, in his official capacity as commander of the Department of Washington, to violate the provisions of said act and to take and receive, act upon, and obey such orders as he, the said Andrew Johnson, might make and give, and which should not be issued through the General of the Army of the United States, according to the provisions of said act, and with the further intent thereby to enable him, and said Andrew Johnson, to prevent the execution of the act entitled "An act regulating the tenure of certain civil offices," passed March 2, 1867, and to unlawfully prevent Edwin M. Stanton, then being Secretary for the Department of War, from holding said office and discharging the duties thereof; whereby said Andrew Johnson, President of the United States, did then and there commit and was guilty of a high misdemeanor in office.

And the House of Representatives, by protestation, saving to themselves the liberty of exhibiting at any time hereafter any further articles or other accusation or impeachment against the said Andrew Johnson, President of the United States, and also of replying to his answers which he shall make unto the articles herein preferred against him, and of offering proof to the same, and every part thereof, and to all and every other article, accusation, or impeachment which shall be exhibited by them, as the case shall require, do demand that the said Andrew Johnson may be put to answer the high crimes and misdemeanors in office here-in charged against him, and that such proceedings, examinations, trials, and judgments may be thereupon had and given as may be agreeable to law and justice.

SCHUYLER COLFAX,
Speaker of the House of
Representatives

EDWARD McPHERSON,
Clerk of the House of Representatives

Attest:

The following additional articles of impeachment were agreed to viz:

IN THE HOUSE OF REPRESENTATIVES, UNITED STATES

March 3, 1868

## ARTICLE X

That said Andrew Johnson, President of the United States, unmindful of the high duties of his office and the dignity and proprieties thereof, and of the harmony and courtesies which ought to exist and be maintained between the executive and legislative branches of the Government of the United States, designing and intending to set aside the rightful authority and powers of Congress, did attempt to bring into disgrace, ridicule, hatred, contempt, and reproach the Congress of the United States and the several branches thereof, to impair and destroy the regard and respect of all the good people of the United States for the Congress and legislative power thereof (which all officers of the Government ought inviolably to preserve and maintain) and to excite the odium and resentment of all the good people of the United States against Congress and the laws by it duly and constitutionally enacted; and, in pursuance of his said design and intent,

openly and pubicly, and before divers assemblages of the citizens of the United States, convened in divers parts thereof to meet and receive said Andrew Johnson as the Chief Magistrate of the United States, did, on the 18th day of August, A.D. 1866, and on divers other days and times, as well before as afterwards, make and deliver with a loud voice certain intemperate, inflammatory, and scandalouse harangues, and did therein utter loud threats and bitter menaces, as well against Congress as the laws of the United States, duly enacted thereby, amid the cries, jeers, and laughter of the multitudes then assembled and in hearing, which are set forth in the several specifications hereinafter written, in substance and effect, that is to say:

Specification first.—In this, that at Washington, in the District of Columbia in the Executive Mansion, to a committee of citizens who called upon the President of the United States, speaking of and concerning the Congress of the United States, said Andrew Johnson, President of the United States, heretofore, to wit, on the 18th day of August, in the year of our Lord 1866, did, in a loud voice, declare in substance and effect, among other things, that is to say:

"So far as the executive department of the Government is concerned, the effort has been made to restore the Union, to heal the breach, to pour oil into the wounds which were consequent upon the struggle, and (to speak in common phrase) to prepare, as the learned and wise physician would, a plaster healing in character and coextensive with the wound. We thought, and we think, that we had partially succeeded; but as the work progresses, as reconstruction seemed to be taking place and the country was becoming reunited, we found a disturbing and marring element opposing us. In alluding to that element, I shall go no further than your convention and the distinguished gentleman who had delivered to me the report of its proceedings. I shall make no reference to it that I do not believe the time and the occasion justify.

"We have witnessed in one department of the Government every endeavor to prevent the restoration of peace, harmony, and union. We have seen hanging upon the verge of the Government, as it were, a body called, or which assumes to be, the Congress of the United States, while in fact it is a Congress of only a part of the States. We have seen this Congress pretend to be for the Union when its every step and act tended to perpetrate disunion and make a disruption of the States inevitable. We have seen Congress gradually encroach step by step upon constitutional rights and violate, day after day and month after month, fundamental principles of the Government. We have seen a Congress that seemed to forget that there was a limit to the sphere and scope of legislation. We have seen a Congress in a minority assume to exercise power which, allowed to be consummated, would result in despotism or monarchy itself."

Specification second.—In this, that at Cleveland, in the State of Ohio, heretofore, to wit, on the 3d day of September, in the year of our Lord 1866, before a public assemblage of citizens and others, said Andrew Johnson, President of the United States, speaking of and concerning the Congress of the United States did, in a loud voice, declare in substance and effect among other things, that is to say:

"I will tell you what I did do. I called upon your Congress that is trying to break up the Government.

"In conclusion, beside that, Congress had taken much pains to poison their constituents against him. But what had a Congress done? Have they done anything to restore the Union of these States? No; on the contrary, they had done everything to prevent it; and be-

cause he stood now where he did when the rebellion commenced he had been denounced as a traitor. Who had run greater risks or made greater sacrifices than himself? But Congress, factious and domineering, had undertaken to poison the minds of the American people."

Specification third.—In this, that at St. Louis, in the State of Missouri, heretofore, to wit, on the 8th day of September, in the year of our Lord 1866, before a public assemblage of citizens and others, said Andrew Johnson, President of the United States, speaking of and concerning the Congress of the United States, did, in a loud voice, declare, in substance and effect, among other things, that is to say:

"Go on. Perhaps if you had a word or two on the subject of New Orleans, you might understand more about it than you do. And if you will go back—if you will go back and ascertain the cause of the riot at New Orleans, perhaps you will not be so prompt in calling out 'New Orleans.' If you will take up the riot at New Orleans and trace it back to its source or its immediate cause, you will find out who was responsible for the blood that was shed there. If you will take up the riot at New Orleans and trace it back to the Radical Congress, you will find that the riot at New Orleans was substantially planned. If you will take up the proceedings in their caucuses, you will understand that they there knew that a convention was to be called which was extinct by its power having expired; that it was said that the intention was that a new government was to be organized, and on the organization of that government the intention was to enfranchise one portion of the population, called the colored population, who had just been emancipated, and at the same time disenfranchise white men. When you design to talk about New Orleans you ought to understand what you are talking about. When you read the speeches that were made, and take up the facts on the Friday and Saturday before that convention sat, you will find that speeches were made incendiary in their character, exciting that portion of the population, the black population, to arm themselves and prepare for the shedding of blood. You will also find that that convention did assemble in violation of law, and the intention of that convention was to supersede the reorganized authorities in the State government of Louisiana, which had been recognized by the Government of the United States; and every man engaged in that rebellion in that convention, with the intention of superseding and upturning the civil government which had been recognized by the Government of the United States, I say that he was a traitor to the Constitution of the United States, and hence you find that another rebellion was commenced having its origin in the Radical Congress.

"So much for the New Orleans riot. And there was the cause and the origin of the blood that was shed; and every drop of blood that was shed is upon their skirts, and they are responsible for it. I could test this thing a little closer, but will not do it here tonight. But when you talk about the causes and consequences that resulted from proceedings of that kind, perhaps as I have been introduced here and you have provoked questions of this kind, though it does not provoke me, I will tell you a few wholesome things that have been done by this Radical Congress in connection with New Orleans and the extension of the elective franchise.

"I know that I have been traduced and abused. I know it has come in advance of me here, as elsewhere, that I have attempted to exercise an arbitrary power in resisting laws that were intended to be forced upon the Government; that I had abandoned the party that elected me, and that I was a traitor because I exercised the veto power in attempting and did arrest for a time a

bill that was called a 'Freedman's Bureau' bill; yes, that I was a traitor. And I have been traduced, I have been slandered, I have been maligned, I have been called Judas Iscariot, and all that. Now, my countrymen here tonight, it is very easy to indulge in epithets; it is easy to call a man a Judas and cry out traitor; but when he is called upon to give arguments and facts he is very easy to indulge in epithets; it is easy to call a man a Judas and he was one of the twelve apostles. Oh yes, the twelve apostles had a Christ. The twelve apostles had a Christ, and he never could have had a Judas unless he had had twelve apostles. If I have played the Judas, who has been my Christ that I have played the Judas with? Was it Thad. Stevens? Was it Wendell Philips? Was it Charles Sumner? These are the men that stop and compare themselves with the Saviour; and everybody that differs with them in opinion, and to try and stay and arrest the diabolical and nefarious policy, is to be denounced as a Judas.

"Well, let me say to you, if you will stand by me in this action; if you will stand by me in trying to give the people a fair chance, soldiers and citizens, to participate in these offices, God being willing, I will kick them out, I will kick them out just as fast as I can.

"Let me say to you, in concluding that what I have said I intended to say. I was not provoked into this, and I care not for their menaces, the taunts, and the jeers, I care not for threats, I do not intend to be bullied by my enemies nor overawed by my friends. But, God willing, with your help I will veto their measures whenever any of them come to me."

Which said utterances, declarations, threats, and harangues, highly censurable in any, are peculiarly indecent and unbecoming in the Chief Magistrate of the United States, by means whereof said Andrew Johnson has brought the high office of the President of the

United States into contempt, ridicule, and disgrace, to the great scandal of all good citizens, whereby said Andrew Johnson, President of the United States, did commit, and was then and there guilty of, a high misdemeanor in office.

## ARTICLE XI

That said Andrew Johnson, President of the United States, unmindful of the high duties of his office and of his oath of office, and in disregard of the Constitution and laws of the United States, did heretofore, to wit, on the 18th day of August, A.D. 1866, at the city of Washington, in the District of Columbia, by public speech, declare and affirm in substance that the Thirty-ninth Congress of the United States was not a Congress of the United States authorized by the Constitution to exercise legislative power under the same, but, on the contrary, was a Congress of only part of the States; thereby denying and intending to deny that the legislation of said Congress was valid or obligatory upon him, the said Andrew Johnson, except in so far as he saw fit to approve the same, and also thereby denying and intending to deny the power of the said Thirty-ninth Congress to propose amendments to the Constitution of the United States; and in pursuance of said declaration the said Andrew Johnson, President of the United States, afterwards, to wit, on the 21st day February, A.D. 1868, at the city of Washington, in the District of Columbia, did unlawfully, and in disregard of the require-

ment of the Constitution that he should take care that the laws be faithfully executed, attempt to prevent the execution of an act entitled "An act regulating the tenure of certain civil offices," passed March 2, 1867, by unlawfully devising and contriving, and attempting to devise and contrive, means by which he should prevent Edwin M. Stanton from forthwith resuming the functions of the office of Secretary for the Department of War, notwithstanding the refusal of the Senate to concur in the suspension theretofore made by said Andrew Johnson of said Edwin M. Stanton from said office of Secretary for the Department of War, and also by further unlawfully devising and contriving, and attempting to devise and contrive, means then and there to prevent the execution of an act entitled "An act making appropriations for the support of the Army for the fiscal year ending June 30, 1868 and for other purposes," approved March 2, 1867, and also to prevent the execution of an act entitled "An act to provide for the more efficient government of the rebel States," passed March 2, 1867, whereby the said Andrew Johnson, President of the United States, did then, to wit, on the 21st day of February, A.D. 1868, at the city of Washington, commit and was guilty of a high misdemeanor in office.

SCHUYLER COLFAX,
Speaker of the House of
Representatives

EDWARD McPHERSON,
Clerk of the House of Representatives

# The Pendleton Act (1883)

The effort to reform the federal civil service by replacing the "spoils system" (under which government employees were hired and fired at the direction of elected officials) with a "merit system" (under which personnel decisions would be made nonpolitically, according to ability) was a prominent feature of American politics after the Civil War. It culminated in the passage in 1883 of "An Act to Regulate and Improve the Civil Service of the United States." The law is better known as the Pendleton Act after its sponsor, Sen. George H. Pendleton of Ohio.

President Andrew Jackson established the spoils system. (The term was coined in 1832 by Sen. William Marcy of New York, who remarked that politicians "see nothing wrong in the rule, that to the victor belong the spoils of the enemy.") Jackson believed that government jobs, previously the preserve of a mainly upper class elite, could be learned by almost everyone and that the president, with the advice of fellow partisans in Congress, should distribute them widely among those who had supported the winning political party in the election. Later generations of victorious politicians practiced what Jackson preached. Indeed, none did so more ardently than President Abraham Lincoln.

After the Civil War, abuses of the spoils system—government jobs that were sold to the highest bidder, filled by incompetents, used to extort bribes and so on—were widely publicized in the press and by political reformers. The administration of President Ulysses S. Grant was especially notorious for its corruption. Rapidly proliferating state and national civil service reform associations traced much of the Grant administration's peculation to its reliance on the spoils system.

The death knell for spoils was sounded in 1881 when President James A. Garfield was assassinated by Charles J. Guiteau, a Republican partisan who was outraged that he had not received a prominent government job as reward for his labors on behalf of the party's ticket in the 1880 election. In the atmosphere of revulsion against spoils that followed the assassination, Congress passed the Pendleton Act in January 1883.

The Pendleton Act created a bipartisan, three-member Civil Service Commission to help the president oversee the federal personnel system and stated several purposes that were to guide the commission's labors. Partisan activity and family and personal connections as reasons for hiring, promoting, and firing government employees were to be replaced by competitive examinations and performance-based promotion and retention policies. Fi-

*nally, employees were offered protection from having to contribute money or time to political campaigns.*

*In the short term, only 10.5 percent of the federal work force (mainly clerical and technical employees) was included in the new "classified civil service." But the act empowered the president to extend the coverage to additional categories of workers. Over time, virtually the entire civil service became merit-based by virtue of presidential decisions. Ironically, these extensions of civil service coverage usually occurred for the most political of reasons: a departing president, seeking to protect his patronage appointees from being replaced by his successor, would "blanket them in" by placing their jobs under the protection of the classified civil service.* ~

*Be it enacted by the Senate and House of Representatives of the United States of America in Congress assembled,* That the President is authorized to appoint, by and with the advice and consent of the Senate, three persons, not more than two of whom shall be adherents of the same party, as Civil Service Commissioners, and said three commissioners shall constitute the United States Civil Service Commission. Said commissioners shall hold no other official place under the United States.

The President may remove any commissioner; and any vacancy in the position of commissioner shall be so filled by the President, by and with the advice and consent of the Senate, as to conform to said conditions for the first selection of commissioners.

The commissioners shall each receive a salary of three thousand five hundred dollars a year. And each of said commissioners shall be paid his necessary traveling expenses incurred in the discharge of his duty as a commissioner.

SEC. 2. That it shall be the duty of said commissioners:

FIRST. To aid the President, as he may request, in preparing suitable rules for carrying this act into effect, and when said rules shall have been promulgated it shall be the duty of all officers of the United States in the departments and offices to which any such rules may relate to aid, in all proper ways, in carrying said rules, and any modifications thereof, into effect.

SECOND. And, among other things, said rules shall provide and declare, as nearly as the conditions of good administration will warrant, as follows:

First, for open, competitive examinations for testing the fitness of applicants for the public service now classified or to be classified hereunder. Such examinations shall be practical in their character, and so far as may be shall relate to those matters which will fairly test the relative capacity and fitness of the persons examined to discharge the duties of the service into which they seek to be appointed.

Second, that all the offices, places, and employments so arranged or to be arranged in classes shall be filled by selections according to grade from among those graded highest as the results of such competitive examinations.

Third, appointments to the public service aforesaid in the department at Washington shall be apportioned among the several States and Territories and the District of Columbia upon the basis of population as ascertained at the last preceding census. Every application for an examination shall contain, among other things, a statement, under oath, setting forth his or her actual bona fide residence at the time of making the application, as well as how long he or she has been a resident of such place.

Fourth, that there shall be a period of probation before any absolute appointment or employment aforesaid.

Fifth, that no person in the public service is for that reason under any obligations to contribute to any political fund, or to render any political service, and that he will not be removed or otherwise prejudiced for refusing to do so.

Sixth, that no person in said service has any right to use his official authority or influence to coerce the political action of any person or body.

Seventh, there shall be non-competitive examinations in all proper cases before the commission, when competent persons do not compete, after notice has been given of the existence of the vacancy, under such rules as may be prescribed by the commissioners as to the manner of giving notice.

Eighth, that notice shall be given in writing by the appointing power to said commission of the persons selected for appointment or employment from among those who have been examined, of the place of residence of such persons, of the rejection of any such persons after probation, of transfers, resignations, and removals, and of the date thereof, and a record of the same shall be kept by said commission. And any necessary exceptions from said eight fundamental provisions of the rules shall be set forth in connection with such rules, and the reasons therefor shall be stated in the annual reports of the commission.

THIRD. Said commission shall, subject to the rules that may be made by the President, make regulations for, and have control of, such examinations, and, through its members or the examiners, it shall supervise and preserve the records of the same; and said commission shall keep minutes of its own proceedings.

FOURTH. Said commission may make investigations concerning the facts, and may report upon all matters touching the enforcement and effects of said rules and regulations, and concerning the action of any examiner or board of examiners hereinafter provided for, and its own subordinates, and those in the public service, in respect to the execution of this act.

FIFTH. Said commission shall make an annual report to the President for transmission to Congress, showing its own action, the rules and regulations and the exceptions thereto in force, the practical effects thereof, and any suggestions it may approve for the more effectual accomplishment of the purposes of this act.

SEC. 3. That said commission is authorized to employ a chief examiner, a part of whose duty it shall be, under its direction, to act with the examining boards, so far as practicable, whether at Washington or elsewhere, and to secure accuracy, uniformity, and justice in all their proceedings, which shall be at all times open to him. The chief examiner shall be entitled to receive a salary at the rate of three thousand dollars a year, and he shall be paid his necessary traveling expenses incurred in the discharge of his duty. The commission shall have a secretary, to be appointed by the President, who shall receive a salary of one thousand six hundred dollars per annum. It may, when necessary, employ a stenographer, and a messenger, who shall be paid, when employed, the former at the rate of one thousand six hundred dollars a year, and the latter at the rate of six hundred dollars a year. The commission shall, at Washington, and in one or more places in each State and Territory where examinations are to take place, designate and select a suitable number of persons, not less than three, in the official service of the United States, residing in said State or Territory, after consulting the head of the department or office in which such persons serve, to be members of boards of examiners, and may at any time substitute any other person in said service living in such State or Territory in the place of any one so selected. Such boards of examiners shall be so located as to make it reasonably convenient and inexpensive for applicants to attend before them; and where there are persons to be examined in any State or Territory, examinations shall be held therein at least twice in each year. It shall be the duty of the collector, postmaster, and other officers of the United States, at any place outside of the District of Columbia where examinations are directed by the President or by said board to be held, to allow the reasonable use of the public buildings for holding such examinations, and in all proper ways to facilitate the same.

SEC. 4. That it shall be the duty of the Secretary of the Interior to cause suitable and convenient rooms and accommodations to be assigned or provided, and to be furnished, heated, and lighted, at the city of Washington, for carrying on the work of said commission and said examinations, and to cause the necessary stationery and other articles to be supplied, and the necessary printing to be done for said commission.

SEC. 5. That any said commissioner, examiner, copyist, or messenger, or any person in the public service who shall willfully and corruptly, by himself or in co-operation with one or more other persons, defeat, deceive, or obstruct any person in respect of his or her right of examination according to any such rules or regulations, or who shall willfully, corruptly, and falsely mark, grade, estimate, or report upon the examination or proper standing of any person examined hereunder, or aid in so doing, or who shall willfully and corruptly make any false representations concerning the same or concerning the person examined, or who shall willfully and corruptly furnish to any person any special or secret information for the purpose of either improving or injuring the prospects or chances of any person so examined, or to be examined, being appointed, employed, or promoted, shall for each such offense be deemed guilty of a misdemeanor, and upon conviction thereof, shall be punished by a fine of not less than one hundred dollars, nor more than one thousand dollars, or by imprisonment not less than ten days,

nor more than one year, or by both such fine and imprisonment.

SEC. 6. That within sixty days after the passage of this act it shall be the duty of Secretary of the Treasury, in as near conformity as may be to the classification of certain clerks now existing under the one hundred and sixty-third section of the Revised Statutes, to arrange in classes the several clerks and persons employed by the collector, naval officer, surveyor, and appraisers, or either of them, or being in the public service, at their respective offices in each customs district where the whole number of said clerks and persons shall be all together as many as fifty. And thereafter, from time to time, on the direction of the President, said Secretary shall make the like classification or arrangement of clerks and persons so employed, in connection with any said office or offices, in any other customs district. And, upon like request, and for the purposes of this act, said Secretary shall arrange in one or more of said classes, or of existing classes, any other clerks, agents, or persons employed under his department in any said district not now classified; and every such arrangement and classification upon being made shall be reported to the President.

Second. Within said sixty days it shall be the duty of the Postmaster-General, in general conformity to said one hundred and sixty-third section, to separately arrange in classes the several clerks and persons employed, or in the public service, at each post-office, or under any postmaster of the United States, where the whole number of said clerks and persons shall together amount to as many as fifty. And thereafter, from time to time, on the direction of the President, it shall be the duty of the Postmaster-General to arrange in like classes the clerks and persons so employed in the postal service in connection with any other post-office; and every such arrangement and classification upon being made shall be reported to the President.

Third. That from time to time said Secretary, the Postmaster-General, and each of the heads of departments mentioned in the one hundred and fifty-eighth section of the Revised Statutes, and each head of an office, shall, on the direction of the President, and for facilitating the execution of this act, respectively revise any then existing classification or arrangement of those in their respective departments and offices, and shall, for the purposes of the examination herein provided for, include in one or more of such classes, so far as practicable, subordinate places, clerks, and officers in the public service pertaining to their respective departments not before classified for examination.

SEC. 7. That after the expiration of six months from the passage of this act no officer or clerk shall be appointed, and no person shall be employed to enter or be promoted in either of the said classes now existing, or that may be arranged hereunder pursuant to said rules, until he has passed an examination, or is shown to be specially exempted from such examination in conformity herewith. But nothing herein contained shall be construed to take from those honorably discharged from the military or naval service any preference conferred by the seventeen hundred and fifty-fourth section of the Revised Statutes, nor to take from the President any authority not inconsistent with this act conferred by the seventeen hundred and fifty-third section of said statutes; nor shall any officer not in the executive branch of the government, or any person merely employed as a laborer or workman, be required to be classified hereunder; nor, unless by direction of the Senate, shall any person who has been nominated for confirmation by the Senate be required to be classified or to pass an examination.

SEC. 8. That no person habitually using intoxicating beverages to excess shall be appointed to, or retained in, any office, appointment, or employment to which the provisions of this act are applicable.

SEC. 9. That whenever there are already two or more members of a family in the public service in the grades covered by this act, no other member of such family shall be eligible to appointment to any of said grades.

SEC. 10. That no recommendation of any person who shall apply for office or place under the provisions of this act which may be given by any Senator or member of the House of Representatives, except as to the character or residence of the applicant, shall be received or considered by any person concerned in making any examination or appointment under this act.

SEC. 11. That no Senator, or Representative, or Territorial Delegate of the Congress, or Senator, Representative, or Delegate elect, or any officer or employee of either of said houses, and no executive, judicial, military, or naval officer of the United States, and no clerk or employee of any department, branch or bureau of the executive, judicial, or military or naval service of the United States, shall, directly or indirectly, solicit or receive, or be in any manner concerned in soliciting or receiving, any assessment, subscription, or contribution for any political purpose whatever, from any officer, clerk, or employee of the United States, or any department, branch, or bureau thereof, or from any person receiving any salary or compensation from moneys derived from the Treasury of the United States.

SEC. 12. That no person shall, in any room or building occupied in the discharge of official duties by any officer or employee of the United States mentioned in this act, or in any navy-yard, fort, or arsenal, solicit in any manner whatever, or receive any contribution of money or any other thing of value for any political purpose whatever.

SEC. 13. No officer or employee of the United States mentioned in this act shall discharge, or promote, or degrade, or in manner change the official rank or compensation of any other officer or employee, or promise or threaten so to do, for giving or withholding or neglecting to make any contribution of money or other valuable thing for any political purpose.

SEC. 14. That no officer, clerk, or other person in the service of the United States shall, directly or indirectly, give or hand over to any other officer, clerk, or person in the service of the United States, or to any Senator or Member of the House of Representatives, or Territorial Delegate, any money or other valuable thing on account of or to be applied to the promotion of any political object whatever.

SEC. 15. That any person who shall be guilty of violating any provision of the four foregoing sections shall be deemed guilty of a misdemeanor, and shall, on conviction thereof, be punished by a fine not exceeding five thousand dollars, or by imprisonment for a term not exceeding three years, or by such fine and imprisonment both, in the discretion of the court.

Approved, January sixteenth, 1883.

# Theodore Roosevelt's First Annual Message to Congress (1901)

*Theodore Roosevelt is the youngest person ever to become president. On September 15, 1901, barely six months into his term as vice president (and six weeks shy of his forty-third birthday), Roosevelt succeeded to the presidency after President William L. McKinley succumbed to a gunshot wound. McKinley, the third president to be assassinated in a period of thirty-six years (after Abraham Lincoln in 1865 and James A. Garfield in 1881), had been shot in Buffalo, New York, on September 6 by an anarchist named Leon Czolgosz.*

*Roosevelt's vice presidency, like his presidency, was the product of an unusual set of circumstances. During his twenty-year political career as a New York state legislator, U.S. civil service commissioner, police commissioner of New York City, assistant secretary of the navy, leader of the "Rough Riders" cavalry regiment in the Spanish-American War, and governor of New York, Roosevelt had gained national popularity as a vigorous reformer. Conservative Republicans in New York disliked him, however, and to remove him from the state, party boss Thomas Platt secured Roosevelt's nomination as the Republican candidate for vice president in the 1900 election. As a young, eastern reformer, Roosevelt balanced the ticket headed by the older, conservative Ohioan McKinley. McKinley*

*and Roosevelt were elected easily.*

*Roosevelt became president at a difficult time in U.S. history. The decades since the Civil War had been marked by rapid industrialization, urbanization, and population growth. The industrial economy was shifting rapidly from small-scale manufacturing and commerce to large-scale corporations, popularly known as "trusts." The concentrations of wealth that these corporations commanded placed them in a position of extraordinary economic and political power.*

*Soon after becoming president, Roosevelt declared, "It shall be my aim to continue absolutely unbroken the policy of President McKinley for the peace, the prosperity, and the honor of our beloved country." Within weeks the new president proclaimed in his first annual message to Congress that, although he accepted the new industrial order, he wanted the federal government to take an unprecedentedly aggressive approach toward abuses of power by the trusts. Roosevelt's reputation as a "trustbuster" began with that December 3, 1901, message and continued with actions such as his early decision to sue (successfully, it turned out) to break up the Northern Securities Company under the Sherman Antitrust Act and to intervene on the miners' behalf in a 1902 coal strike.*

*In 1904 Roosevelt was nominated*

*unanimously by the Republican convention for a term as president in his own right, the first successor president in history to be given an opportunity to run. He swept every state outside the solid Democratic South to win the election.*

*During his second term, Roosevelt championed many pieces of reform legislation, including the Pure Food and Drug Act, the Meat Inspection Act, and the Hepburn Act, which empowered the government to regulate railroad rates. At the initiative of the conservationist president, 125 million acres were added to the national forest reserves, and the number of national parks was doubled. In foreign affairs, Roosevelt promoted U.S. interests aggressively.*                    ~

### White House, December 3, 1901.

To the Senate and House of Representatives:

The Congress assembles this year under the shadow of a great calamity. On the sixth of September, President McKinley was shot by an anarchist while attending the Pan-American Exposition at Buffalo, and died in that city on the fourteenth of that month.

Of the last seven elected Presidents, he is the third who has been murdered, and the bare recital of this fact is sufficient to justify grave alarm among all loyal American citizens. Moreover, the circumstances of this, the third assassination of an American President, have a peculiarly sinister significance. Both President Lincoln and President Garfield were killed by assassins of types unfortunately not uncommon in history; President Lincoln falling a victim to the terrible passions aroused by four years of civil war, and President Garfield to the revengeful vanity of a disappointed office-seeker. President McKinley was killed by an utterly depraved criminal belonging to that body of criminals who object to all

governments, good and bad alike, who are against any form of popular liberty if it is guaranteed by even the most just and liberal laws, and who are as hostile to the upright exponent of a free people's sober will as to the tyrannical and irresponsible despot. . . .

During the last five years business confidence has been restored, and the nation is to be congratulated because of its present abounding prosperity. Such prosperity can never be created by law alone, although it is easy enough to destroy it by mischievous laws. If the hand of the Lord is heavy upon any country, if flood or drought comes, human wisdom is powerless to avert the calamity. Moreover, no law can guard us against the consequences of our own folly. The men who are idle or credulous, the men who seek gains not by genuine work with head or hand but by gambling in any form, are always a source of menace not only to themselves but to others. If the business world loses its head, it loses what legislation cannot supply. Fundamentally the welfare of each citizen, and therefore the welfare of the aggregate of citizens which makes the nation, must rest upon individual thrift and energy, resolution, and intelligence. Nothing can take the place of this individual capacity; but wise legislation and honest and intelligent administration can give it the fullest scope, the largest opportunity to work to good effect.

The tremendous and highly complex industrial development which went on with ever accelerated rapidity during the latter half of the nineteenth century brings us face to face, at the beginning of the twentieth, with very serious social problems. The old laws, and the old customs which had almost the binding force of law, were once quite sufficient to regulate the accumulation and distribution of wealth. Since the industrial changes which have so enormously increased the productive power of mankind, they are no longer sufficient.

The growth of cities has gone on beyond comparison faster than the growth of the country, and the upbuilding of the great industrial centers has meant a startling increase, not merely in the aggregate of wealth, but in the number of very large individual, and especially of very large corporate, fortunes. The creation of these great corporate fortunes has not been due to the tariff nor to any other governmental action, but to natural causes in the business world, operating in other countries as they operate in our own.

The process has aroused much antagonism, a great part of which is wholly without warrant. It is not true that as the rich have grown richer the poor have grown poorer. On the contrary, never before has the average man, the wage-worker, the farmer, the small trader, been so well off as in this country and at the present time. There have been abuses connected with the accumulation of wealth; yet it remains true that a fortune accumulated in legitimate business can be accumulated by the person specially benefited only on condition of conferring immense incidental benefits upon others. Successful enterprise, of the type which benefits all mankind, can only exist if the conditions are such as to offer great prizes as the rewards of success.

The captains of industry who have driven the railway systems across this continent, who have built up our commerce, who have developed our manufactures, have on the whole done great good to our people. Without them the material development of which we are so justly proud could never have taken place. Moreover, we should recognize the immense importance of this material development of leaving as unhampered as is compatible with the public good the strong and forceful men upon whom the success of business operations inevitably rests. The slightest study of business conditions will satisfy anyone capable of forming a judgment that the personal equation is the most important factor in a business operation; that the business ability of the man at the head of any business concern, big or little, is usually the factor which fixes the gulf between striking success and hopeless failure.

An additional reason for caution in dealing with corporations is to be found in the international commercial conditions of to-day. The same business conditions which have produced the great aggregations of corporate and individual wealth have made them very potent factors in international commercial competition. Business concerns which have the largest means at their disposal and are managed by the ablest men are naturally those which take the lead in the strife for commercial supremacy among the nations of the world. America has only just begun to assume that commanding position in the international business world which we believe will more and more be hers. It is of the utmost importance that this position be not jeoparded, especially at a time when the overflowing abundance of our own natural resources and the skill, business energy, and mechanical aptitude of our people make foreign markets essential. Under such conditions it would be most unwise to cramp or to fetter the youthful strength of our Nation.

Moreover, it can not too often be pointed out that to strike with ignorant violence at the interests of one set of men almost inevitably endangers the interest of all. The fundamental rule in our national life—the rule which underlies all others—is that, on the whole, and in the long run, we shall go up or down together. There are exceptions; and in times of prosperity some will prosper far more; and in times of adversity, some will suffer far more, than others; but speaking generally, a period of good times means that all share more or less in them, and in a period of hard times all feel the stress to a greater or less degree. It surely ought not to be necessary to enter into any proof of this statement; the memory of the lean years which began in 1893 is still vivid, and we can contrast them with the conditions in this very year which is now closing. Disaster to great business enterprises can never have its effects limited to men at the top. It spreads throughout, and while it is bad for everybody, it is worst for those farthest down. The capitalist may be shorn of his luxuries; but the wage-worker may be deprived of even bare necessities.

The mechanism of modern business is so delicate that extreme care must be taken not to interfere with it in a spirit of rashness or ignorance. Many of those who have made it their vocation to denounce the great industrial combinations which are popularly, although with technical inaccuracy, known as "trusts," appeal especially to hatred and fear. These are precisely the two emotions, particularly when combined with ignorance, which unfit men for the exercise of cool and steady judgment. In facing new industrial conditions, the whole history of the world shows that legislation will generally be both unwise and ineffective unless undertaken after calm inquiry and with sober self-restraint. Much of the legislation directed at the trusts would have been exceedingly mischievous had it not also been entirely ineffective. In accordance with a well-known sociological law, the ignorant or reckless agitator has been the really effective friend of the evils which he has been nominally opposing. In dealing with business interests, for the Government to undertake by crude and ill-considered legislation to do what may turn out to be bad, would be to incur the risk of such far-reaching national disaster that it would be preferable to undertake nothing at all. The men who demand the impossible or the undesirable serve as the allies of the forces with which they are nominally at war, for they hamper those who would endeavor to find out in rational fashion

what the wrongs really are and to what extent and in what manner it is practicable to apply remedies.

All this is true; and yet it is also true that there are real and grave evils, one of the chief being over-capitalization because of its many baleful consequences; and a resolute and practical effort must be made to correct these evils.

There is a widespread conviction in the minds of the American people that the great corporations known as trusts are in certain of their features and tendencies hurtful to the general welfare. This springs from no spirit of envy or uncharitableness, nor lack of pride in the great industrial achievements that have placed this country at the head of the nations struggling for commercial supremacy. It does not rest upon a lack of intelligent appreciation of the necessity of meeting changing and changed conditions of trade with new methods, nor upon ignorance of the fact that combination of capital in the effort to accomplish great things is necessary when the world's progress demands that great things be done. It is based upon sincere conviction that combination and concentration should be, not prohibited, but supervised and within reasonable limits controlled; and in my judgment this conviction is right.

It is no limitation upon property rights or freedom of contract to require that when men receive from Government the privilege of doing business under corporate form, which frees them from individual responsibility, and enables them to call into their enterprises the capital of the public, they shall do so upon absolutely truthful representations as to the value of the property in which the capital is to be invested. Corporations engaged in interstate commerce should be regulated if they are found to exercise a license working to the public injury. It should be as much the aim of those who seek for social betterment to rid the business world of crimes of cunning as to rid the entire body politic of crimes of violence. Great corporations exist only because they are created and safeguarded by our institutions; and it is therefore our right and our duty to see that they work in harmony with these institutions.

The first essential in determining how to deal with the great industrial combinations is knowledge of the facts—publicity. In the interest of the public, the Government should have the right to inspect and examine the workings of the great corporations engaged in interstate business. Publicity is the only sure remedy which we can now invoke. What further remedies are needed in the way of governmental regulation, or taxation, can only be determined after publicity has been obtained, by process of law, and in the course of administration. The first requisite is knowledge, full and complete—knowledge which may be made public to the world.

Artificial bodies, such as corporations and joint stock or other associations, depending upon any statutory law for their existence or privileges, should be subject to proper governmental supervision, and full and accurate information as to their operations should be made public regularly at reasonable intervals.

The large corporations, commonly called trusts, though organized in one State, always do business in many States, often doing very little business in the State where they are incorporated. There is utter lack of uniformity in the State laws about them; and as no State has any exclusive interest in or power over their acts, it has in practice proved impossible to get adequate regulation through State action. Therefore, in the interest of the whole people, the Nation should, without interfering with the power of the States in the matter itself, also assume power of supervision and regulation over all corporations doing an interstate business. This is especially true where the corporation derives a portion of its wealth from the existence of some monopolistic element or tendency in its business. There would be no hardship in such supervision; banks are subject to it, and in their case it is now accepted as a simple matter of course. Indeed, it is probable that supervision of corporations by the National Government need not go so far as is now the case with the supervision exercised over them by so conservative a State as Massachusetts, in order to produce excellent results.

When the Constitution was adopted, at the end of the eighteenth century, no human wisdom could foretell the sweeping changes, alike in industrial and political conditions, which were to take place by the beginning of the twentieth century. At that time it was accepted as a matter of course that the several States were the proper authorities to regulate, so far as was then necessary, the comparatively insignificant and strictly localized corporate bodies of the day. The conditions are now wholly different and wholly different action is called for. I believe that a law can be framed which will enable the National Government to exercise control along the lines above indicated; profiting by the experience gained through the passage and administration of the Interstate-Commerce Act. If, however, the judgment of the Congress is that it lacks the constitutional power to pass such an act, then a constitutional amendment should be submitted to confer the power. . . .

THEODORE ROOSEVELT

# Theodore Roosevelt's "New Nationalism" Speech (1910)

*Theodore Roosevelt voluntarily stepped down as president at the end of his term in 1909, two years shy of his fiftieth birthday. He had announced after his election in 1904 that he would not run in 1908 because he believed in the two-term tradition for presidents and regarded the three-and-one-half years he had served after President William L. McKinley's assassination in 1901 as his first term. Still, Roosevelt took an active role in securing the 1908 Republican presidential nomination for his secretary of war and closest adviser, William Howard Taft of Ohio.*

*Taft had impressive government experience—as a judge in Cincinnati, Ohio, U.S. solicitor general, federal circuit court judge, and governor of the Philippines—before becoming secretary of war. He campaigned for president in 1908 by pledging to continue the Roosevelt record and was easily elected against the Democratic nominee, William Jennings Bryan.*

*Yet Taft was ill-suited to carry on as Roosevelt would have liked or as the voters seemed to expect. For all his experience in government, the presidency was the first truly political job that Taft had ever held. Also, in addition to being inexperienced in the tasks of public and congressional leadership, Taft believed that the president should operate with dignity and restraint. Thus, even when Taft recommended*

*Rooseveltian policies to Congress, he did not push hard to get them enacted. Taft introduced a tariff reduction plan to Congress in 1910, for example, then sat back and watched as it was crippled with hundreds of amendments. Yet in his clearly defined presidential role as chief executive, Taft actually filed twice as many antitrust suits in four years as Roosevelt had filed in seven.*

*Roosevelt grew increasingly impatient with Taft. After more than a year abroad touring Africa and Europe, Roosevelt returned home ready and eager for political combat. His "New Nationalism" speech, delivered at the August 31, 1910, dedication of the John Brown battlefield at Osawatomie, Kansas, was widely regarded as the kickoff to another presidential candidacy. In the speech, Roosevelt offered perhaps his most fully developed statement of his political philosophy. He warned of the dangers of rising concentrations of corporate and, by implication, union power. Bigness in the private sector was not intrinsically bad, Roosevelt argued, but large private organizations were prone to abuses of power that could be checked only by a large and active federal government. Within that government, the president must be "the steward of the public welfare."*

*In truth, Roosevelt did seek the Republican nomination in 1912. Although*

*he won most of the primaries he en-
tered, Taft controlled the party machinery and was chosen by the convention. Progressive Republicans then
persuaded Roosevelt to run as the
nominee of the "Bull Moose" party,
which took its name from Roosevelt's
declaration that he felt "as fit as a bull
moose." (He proved it when, after being
shot in the chest by an assailant on
October 14, 1912, he delivered a one-
hour speech and, following surgery, resumed campaigning within two weeks.)
On election day, Roosevelt ran second
to the Democratic nominee, Woodrow
Wilson, the only third-party candidate
ever to do so.*        ～

... I stand for the square deal. But
when I say that I am for the square
deal, I mean not merely that I stand for
fair play under the present rules of the
game but that I stand for having those
rules changed so as to work for a more
substantial equality of opportunity and
of reward for equally good service. One
word of warning, which, I think, is
hardly necessary in Kansas. When I say
I want a square deal for the poor man, I
do not mean that I want a square deal
for the man who remains poor because
he has not got the energy to work for
himself. If a man who has had a chance
will not make good, then he has got to
quit. And you men of the Grand Army,
you want justice for the brave man who
fought and punishment for the coward
who shirked his work. Is not that so?

Now, this means that our government, national and state, must be freed
from the sinister influence or control of
special interests. . . . We must drive the
special interests out of politics. That is
one of our tasks today. Every special
interest is entitled to justice—full, fair,
and complete—and, now, mind you, if
there were any attempt by mob violence
to plunder and work harm to the special
interest, whatever it may be, that I most
dislike, and the wealthy man, whomso-

ever he may be, for whom I have the
greatest contempt, I would fight for
him, and you would if you were worth
your salt. He should have justice. For
every special interest is entitled to justice, but not one is entitled to a vote in
Congress, to a voice on the bench, or to
representation in any public office. The
Constitution guarantees protection to
property, and we must make that promise good. But it does not give the right
of suffrage to any corporation.

The true friend of property, the true
conservative, is he who insists that
property shall be the servant and not
the master of the commonwealth; who
insists that the creature of man's making shall be the servant and not the
master of the man who made it. The
citizens of the United States must effectively control the mighty commercial
forces which they have themselves
called into being. There can be no effective control of corporations while their
political activity remains. To put an end
to it will be neither a short nor an easy
task, but it can be done.

We must have complete and effective
publicity of corporate affairs so that the
people may know beyond peradventure
whether the corporations obey the law
and whether their management entitles
them to the confidence of the public. It
is necessary that laws should be passed
to prohibit the use of corporate funds
directly or indirectly for political purposes; it is still more necessary that
such laws should be thoroughly enforced. Corporate expenditures for political purposes, and especially such expenditures by public service corporations, have supplied one of the principal
sources of corruption in our political
affairs.

It has become entirely clear that we
must have government supervision of
the capitalization, not only of public
service corporations, including, particularly, railways, but of all corporations
doing an interstate business. I do not
wish to see the nation forced into the

ownership of the railways if it can possibly be avoided, and the only alternative is thoroughgoing and effective regulation, which shall be based on a full knowledge of all the facts, including a physical valuation of property. This physical valuation is not needed, or, at least, is very rarely needed, for fixing rates; but it is needed as the basis of honest capitalization.

We have come to recognize that franchises should never be granted, except for a limited time, and never without proper provision for compensation to the public. It is my personal belief that the same kind and degree of control and supervision which should be exercised over public service corporations should be extended also to combinations which control necessaries of life, such as meat, oil, and coal, or which deal in them on an important scale. I have no doubt that the ordinary man who has control of them is much like ourselves. I have no doubt he would like to do well, but I want to have enough supervision to help him realize that desire to do well.

I believe that the officers, and, especially, the directors, of corporations should be held personally responsible when any corporation breaks the law.

Combinations in industry are the result of an imperative economic law which cannot be repealed by political legislation. The effort at prohibiting all combination has substantially failed. The way out lies, not in attempting to prevent such combinations but in completely controlling them in the interest of the public welfare. For that purpose the Federal Bureau of Corporations is an agency of first importance. Its powers, and, therefore, its efficiency, as well as that of the Interstate Commerce Commission, should be largely increased. We have a right to expect from the Bureau of Corporations and from the Interstate Commerce Commission a very high grade of public service. We should be as sure of the proper conduct of the interstate railways and the

proper management of interstate business as we are now sure of the conduct and management of the national banks, and we should have as effective supervision in one case as in the other. The Hepburn Act, and the amendment to the act in the shape in which it finally passed Congress at the last session, represent a long step in advance, and we must go yet further.

There is a widespread belief among our people that, under the methods of making tariffs which have hitherto obtained, the special interests are too influential. Probably this is true of both the big special interests and the little special interests. These methods have put a premium on selfishness, and, naturally, the selfish big interests have gotten more than their smaller, though equally selfish, brothers. The duty of Congress is to provide a method by which the interest of the whole people shall be all that receives consideration. To this end there must be an expert tariff commission, wholly removed from the possibility of political pressure or of improper business influence. Such a commission can find the real difference between cost of production, which is mainly the difference of labor cost here and abroad. As fast as its recommendations are made, I believe in revising one schedule at a time. A general revision of the tariff almost inevitably leads to logrolling and the subordination of the general public interest to local and special interests.

The absence of effective state and, especially, national restraint upon unfair money getting has tended to create a small class of enormously wealthy and economically powerful men whose chief object is to hold and increase their power. The prime need is to change the conditions which enable these men to accumulate power which it is not for the general welfare that they should hold or exercise. We grudge no man a fortune which represents his own power and sagacity when exercised with entire regard to the welfare of his fellows. . . . We should permit it to be gained only so long as the gaining represents benefit to the community. This, I know, implies a policy of a far more active governmental interference with social and economic conditions in this country than we have yet had, but I think we have got to face the fact that such an increase in governmental control is now necessary.

No man should receive a dollar unless that dollar has been fairly earned. Every dollar received should represent a dollar's worth of service rendered—not gambling in stocks but service rendered. The really big fortune, the swollen fortune, by the mere fact of its size, acquires qualities which differentiate it in kind as well as in degree from what is possessed by men of relatively small means. Therefore, I believe in a graduated income tax on big fortunes, and in another tax which is far more easily collected and far more effective—a graduated inheritance tax on big fortunes, properly safeguarded against evasion and increasing rapidly in amount with the size of the estate.

The people of the United States suffer from periodical financial panics to a degree substantially unknown among the other nations which approach us in financial strength. There is no reason why we should suffer what they escape. It is of profound importance that our financial system should be promptly investigated and so thoroughly and effectively revised as to make it certain that hereafter our currency will no longer fail at critical times to meet our needs. . . .

Nothing is more true than that excess of every kind is followed by reaction; a fact which should be pondered by reformer and reactionary alike. We are face to face with new conceptions of the relations of property to human welfare, chiefly because certain advocates of the rights of property as against the rights of men have been pushing their claims too far. The man who wrongly holds that every human right is secondary to his profit must now give way to the advocate of human welfare, who rightly maintains that every man holds his property subject to the general right of the community to regulate its use to whatever degree the public welfare may require it.

But I think we may go still further. The right to regulate the use of wealth in the public interest is universally admitted. Let us admit also the right to regulate the terms and conditions of labor, which is the chief element of wealth, directly in the interest of the common good. The fundamental thing to do for every man is to give him a chance to reach a place in which he will make the greatest possible contribution to the public welfare. Understand what I say there. Give him a chance, not push him up if he will not be pushed. Help any man who stumbles; if he lies down, it is a poor job to try to carry him; but if he is a worthy man, try your best to see that he gets a chance to show the worth that is in him.

No man can be a good citizen unless he has a wage more than sufficient to cover the bare cost of living and hours of labor short enough so that after his day's work is done he will have time and energy to bear his share in the management of the community, to help in carrying the general load. We keep countless men from being good citizens by the conditions of life with which we surround them. We need comprehensive workmen's compensation acts, both state and national laws to regulate child labor and work for women, and, especially, we need in our common schools not merely education in book learning but also practical training for daily life and work. We need to enforce better sanitary conditions for our workers and to extend the use of safety appliances for our workers in industry and commerce, both within and between the states. Also, friends, in the interest of the workingman himself we need to set our faces like flint against mob violence just as against corporate greed; against violence and injustice and lawlessness by wage workers just as much as against lawless cunning and greed and selfish arrogance of employers.

If I could ask but one thing of my fellow countrymen, my request would be that, whenever they go in for reform, they remember the two sides, and that they always exact justice from one side as much as from the other. I have small use for the public servant who can always see and denounce the corruption of the capitalist, but who cannot persuade himself, especially before election, to say a word about lawless mob violence. And I have equally small use for the man, be he a judge on the bench, or editor of a great paper, or wealthy and influential private citizen, who can see clearly enough and denounce the lawlessness of mob violence, but whose eyes are closed so that he is blind when the question is one of corruption in business on a gigantic scale. . . .

I do not ask for overcentralization; but I do ask that we work in a spirit of broad and far-reaching nationalism when we work for what concerns our people as a whole. We are all Americans. Our common interests are as broad as the continent. I speak to you here in Kansas exactly as I would speak in New York or Georgia, for the most vital problems are those which affect us all alike. The national government belongs to the whole American people, and where the whole American people are interested, that interest can be guarded effectively only by the national government. The betterment which we seek must be accomplished, I believe, mainly through the national government.

The American people are right in demanding that New Nationalism, without which we cannot hope to deal with new problems. The New National-ism puts the national need before sectional or personal advantage. It is impatient of the utter confusion that results from local legislatures attempting to treat national issues as local issues. It is still more impatient of the impotence which springs from overdivision of governmental powers, the impotence which makes it possible for local selfishness or for legal cunning, hired by wealthy special interests, to bring national activities to a deadlock. This New Nationalism regards the executive power as the steward of the public welfare. It demands of the judiciary that it shall be interested primarily in human welfare rather than in property, just as it demands that the representative body shall represent all the people rather than any one class or section of people. . . .

One of the fundamental necessities in a representative government such as ours is to make certain that the men to whom the people delegate their power shall serve the people by whom they are elected and not the special interests. I believe that every national officer, elected or appointed, should be forbidden to perform any service or receive any compensation, directly or indirectly, from interstate corporations; and a similar provision could not fail to be useful within the states.

The object of government is the welfare of the people. The material progress and prosperity of a nation are desirable chiefly so far as they lead to the moral and material welfare of all good citizens. Just in proportion as the average man and woman are honest, capable of sound judgment and high ideals, active in public affairs—but, first of all, sound in their homelife, and the father and mother of healthy children whom they bring up well—just so far, and no farther, we may count our civilization a success. We must have—I believe we have already—a genuine and permanent moral awakening, without which no wisdom of legislation or administration really means anything; and, on the other hand, we must try to secure the social and economic legislation without which any improvement due to purely mortal agitation is necessarily evanescent.

# Theodore Roosevelt's and William Howard Taft's Theories of Presidential Power (1913, 1916)

Shortly after they split the Republican party and were defeated by Democrat Woodrow Wilson in the 1912 election, former presidents Theodore Roosevelt and William Howard Taft produced a classic exchange on the proper nature of presidential power. Roosevelt's "stewardship" theory of the presidency was articulated in The Autobiography of Theodore Roosevelt, *published in 1913. Taft expounded his "literalist" theory in a 1916 book called* Our Chief Magistrate and His Powers. *The exchange is significant not just because of the light it sheds on the conflict that developed between these two former friends and close political allies, but also because it offers a striking comparison of the way most presidents regarded the presidency in the nineteenth century (Taft's view) and in the twentieth (Roosevelt's view).*

Both Roosevelt and Taft took the Constitution as their point of departure, but they differed radically on how to interpret that document. In a nutshell, Roosevelt believed that the president could do anything that the Constitution or laws did not expressly forbid, while Taft felt that the president could not do anything that the Constitution or laws did not expressly permit.

Roosevelt claimed that "I acted for the public welfare, I acted for the common well-being of all our people, whenever and in whatever manner was necessary, unless prevented by direct constitutional or legislative prohibition." He regarded the president as "a steward of the people bound actively and affirmatively to do all he could for the people, and not to content himself with the negative merit of keeping his talents undamaged in a napkin."

Taft, by contrast, believed that "the President can exercise no power which cannot be fairly and reasonably traced to some specific grant of power or justly implied and included within such express grant as proper and necessary to its exercise." He added: "There is no undefined residuum of power which he can exercise because it seems to him to be in the public interest."

Each president's philosophy of the presidency helps to explain his actions in office. Taft seldom spoke out publicly in defense of his policies, neglected the press, and, although willing to recommend legislation, stood by passively as Congress worked its will. When Congress resisted Roosevelt's legislative agenda, however, he broke precedent by making a speechmaking tour of the country, "appealing over the heads of the Senate and House leaders to the people, who were the masters of both of us." He used the press to personalize both his presi-

*dency and his agenda—Roosevelt was "TR" (the first president to be known by his initials); his programs were the "Square Deal" (which foreshadowed such labels as "New Deal," "New Frontier," and "Opportunity Society"). In foreign policy, Roosevelt was both active and, on occasion, defiant toward Congress.* ～

## Theodore Roosevelt's Stewardship Theory of the Presidency

My view was that every executive officer, and above all every executive officer in high position, was a steward of the people bound actively and affirmatively to do all he could for the people, and not to content himself with the negative merit of keeping his talents undamaged in a napkin. I declined to adopt the view that what was imperatively necessary for the nation could not be done by the President unless he could find some specific authorization to do it. My belief was that it was not only his right but his duty to do anything that the needs of the nation demanded unless such action was forbidden by the Constitution or by the laws. Under this interpretation of executive power I did and caused to be done many things not previously done by the President and the heads of the departments. I did not usurp power, but I did greatly broaden the use of executive power. In other words, I acted for the public welfare, I acted for the common well-being of all our people, whenever and in whatever manner was necessary, unless prevented by direct constitutional or legislative prohibition. . . .

The course I followed, of regarding the Executive as subject only to the people, and, under the Constitution, bound to serve the people affirmatively in cases where the Constitution does not explicitly forbid him to render the service, was substantially the course followed by both Andrew Jackson and Abraham Lincoln. Other honorable and well-meaning Presidents, such as James Buchanan, took the opposite and, as it seems to me, narrowly legalistic view that the President is the servant of Congress rather than of the people, and can do nothing, no matter how necessary it be to act, unless the Constitution explicitly commands the action. Most able lawyers who are past middle age take this view, and so do large numbers of well-meaning, respectable citizens. My successor in office took this, the Buchanan, view of the President's powers and duties.

For example, under my administration we found that one of the favorite methods adopted by the men desirous of stealing the public domain was to carry the decision of the secretary of the interior into court. By vigorously opposing such action, and only by so doing, we were able to carry out the policy of properly protecting the public domain. My successor not only took the opposite view, but recommended to Congress the passage of a bill which would have given the courts direct appellate power over the secretary of the interior in these land matters. . . . Fortunately, Congress declined to pass the bill. Its passage would have been a veritable calamity.

I acted on the theory that the President could at any time in his discretion withdraw from entry any of the public lands of the United States and reserve the same for forestry, for water-power sites, for irrigation, and other public purposes. Without such action it would have been impossible to stop the activity of the land-thieves. No one ventured to test its legality by lawsuit. My successor, however, himself questioned it, and referred the matter to Congress. Again Congress showed its wisdom by passing a law which gave the President the power which he had long exercised, and of which my successor had shorn himself.

Perhaps the sharp difference between what may be called the Lincoln-Jackson and the Buchanan-Taft schools, in their views of the power and duties of the President, may be best illustrated by comparing the attitude of my successor toward his Secretary of the Interior, Mr. Ballinger, when the latter was accused of gross misconduct in office, with my attitude toward my chiefs of department and other subordinate officers. More than once while I was President my officials were attacked by Congress, generally because these officials did their duty well and fearlessly. In every such case I stood by the official and refused to recognize the right of Congress to interfere with me excepting my impeachment or in other constitutional manner. On the other hand, wherever I found the officer unfit for his position, I promptly removed him, even although the most influential men in Congress fought for his retention. The Jackson-Lincoln view is that a President who is fit to do good work should be able to form his own judgment as to his own subordinates, and, above all, of the subordinates standing highest and in closest and most intimate touch with him. My secretaries and their subordinates were responsible to me, and I accepted the responsibility for all their deeds. As long as they were satisfactory to me I stood by them against every critic or assailant, within or without Congress; and as for getting Congress to make up my mind for me about them, the thought would have been inconceivable to me. My successor took the opposite, or Buchanan, view when he permitted and requested Congress to pass judgment on the charges made against Mr. Ballinger as an executive officer. These charges were made to the President; the President had the facts before him and could get at them at any time, and he alone had power to act if the charges were true. However, he permitted and requested Congress to investigate Mr. Ballinger. The party minority

of the committee that investigated him, and one member of the majority, declared that the charges were well-founded and that Mr. Ballinger should be removed. The other members of the majority declared the charges ill-founded. The President abode by the view of the majority. Of course believers in the Jackson-Lincoln theory of the presidency would not be content with this town meeting majority and minority method of determining by another branch of the government what it seems the especial duty of the President himself to determine for himself in dealing with his own subordinate in his own department. . . .

---

# William Howard Taft's Literalist Theory of the Presidency

While it is important to mark out the exclusive field of jurisdiction of each branch of the government, Legislative, Executive and Judicial, it should be said that in the proper working of the government there must be cooperation of all branches, and without a willingness of each branch to perform its function, there will follow a hopeless obstruction to the progress of the whole government. Neither branch can compel the other to affirmative action, and each branch can greatly hinder the other in the attainment of the object of its activities and the exercise of its discretion.

The true view of the Executive functions is, as I conceive it, that the President can exercise no power which cannot be fairly and reasonably traced to some specific grant of power or justly implied and included within such express grant as proper and necessary to its exercise. Such specific grant must be either in the Federal Constitution or in an act of Congress passed in pursuance thereof. There is no undefined residuum of power which he can exercise because it seems to him to be in the public interest, and there is nothing in the Neagle case and its definition of a law of the United States, or in other precedents, warranting such an inference. The grants of Executive power are necessarily in general terms in order not to embarrass the Executive within the field of action plainly marked for him, but his jurisdiction must be justified and vindicated by affirmative constitutional or statutory provision, or it does not exist. There have not been wanting, however, eminent men in high public office holding a different view and who have insisted upon the necessity for an undefined residuum of Executive power in the public interest. They have not been confined to the present generation. We may learn this from the complaint of a Virginia statesman, Abel P. Upshur, a strict constructionist of the old school, who succeeded Daniel Webster as Secretary of State under President Tyler. He was aroused by Story's commentaries on the Constitution to write a monograph answering and criticizing them, and in the course of this he comments as follows on the Executive power under the Constitution:

The most defective part of the Constitution beyond all question, is that which related to the Executive Department. It is impossible to read that instrument, without being struck with the loose and unguarded terms in which the powers and duties of the President are pointed out. So far as the legislature is concerned, the limitations of the Constitution, are, perhaps, as precise and strict as they could safely have been made; but in regard to the Executive, the Convention appears to have studiously selected such loose and general expressions, as would enable the President, by implication and construction either to neglect his duties or to enlarge his powers. *We have heard it gravely asserted in Congress that whatever power is neither legislative nor judiciary, is of course executive, and, as such, belongs to the President under the Constitution.* How far a majority of

that body would have sustained a doctrine so monstrous, and so utterly at war with the whole genius of our government, it is impossible to say, but this, at least, we know, that it met with no rebuke from those who supported the particular act of Executive power, in defense of which it was urged. Be this as it may, it is a reproach to the Constitution that the Executive trust is so ill-defined, as to leave any plausible pretense even to the insane zeal of party devotion, for attributing to the President of the United States the power of a despot; powers which are wholly unknown in any limited monarchy in the world.

The view that he takes as a result of the loose language defining the Executive powers seems exaggerated. But one must agree with him in his condemnation of the view of the Executive power which he says was advanced in Congress. In recent years there has been put forward a similar view by executive officials and to some extent acted on. Men who are not such strict constructionists of the Constitution as Mr. Upshur may well feel real concern if such views are to receive the general acquiescence. Mr. Garfield, when Secretary of the Interior, under Mr. Roosevelt, in his final report to Congress in reference to the power of the Executive over the public domain, said:

Full power under the Constitution was vested in the Executive Branch of the Government and the extent to which that power may be exercised is governed wholly by the discretion of the Executive unless any specific act has been prohibited either by the Constitution or by legislation.

In pursuance of this principle, Mr. Garfield, under an act for the reclamation of arid land by irrigation, which authorized him to make contracts for irrigation works and incur liability equal to the amount on deposit in the Reclamation Fund, made contracts with associations of settlers by which it was agreed that if these settlers would advance money and work, they might receive certificates from the government engineers of the labor and money furnished by them, and that such certificates might be received in the future in the discharge of their legal obligations to the government for water rent and other things under the statute. It became necessary for the succeeding administration to pass on the validity of these government certificates. They were held by Attorney-General Wickersham to be illegal, on the ground that no authority existed for their issuance. He relied on the Floyd acceptances in 7th Wallace, in which recovery was sought in the Court of Claims on commercial paper in the form of acceptances signed by Mr. Floyd when Secretary of War and delivered to certain contractors. The Court held that they were void because the Secretary of War had no statutory authority to issue them. Mr. Justice Miller, in deciding the case, said:

> The answer which at once suggests itself to one familiar with the structure of our government, in which all power is delegated, and is defined by law, constitutional or statutory, is, that to one or both of these sources we must resort

in every instance. We have no officers in this government, from the President down to the most subordinate agent, who does not hold office under the law, with prescribed duties and limited authority. And while some of these, as the President, the Legislature, and the Judiciary, exercise powers in some sense left to the more general definitions necessarily incident to fundamental law found in the Constitution, the larger portion of them are the creation of statutory law, with duties and powers prescribed and limited by that law.

My judgment is that the view of Mr. Garfield and Mr. Roosevelt, ascribing an undefined residuum of power to the President is an unsafe doctrine and that it might lead under emergencies to results of an arbitrary character, doing irremediable injustice to private right. The mainspring of such a view is that the Executive is charged with responsibility for the welfare of all the people in a general way, that he is to play the part of a Universal Providence and set all things right, and that anything that in his judgment will help the people he ought to do, unless he is expressly forbidden not to do it. The wide field of action that this would give to the Executive one can hardly limit.

# Woodrow Wilson's First State of the Union Address (1913)

Woodrow Wilson was the only professional political scientist ever to be able to implement his theories as president. Wilson, who earned his doctorate at Johns Hopkins University and later became a professor and president of Princeton University, had argued since his days as a student that the relationship between the president and Congress should be marked by cooperation rather than conflict. In his 1885 book, Congressional Government, Wilson urged that the executive departments effectively be made part of Congress so that the legislative branch could lead. By the early 1900s, however, Wilson regarded interbranch cooperation as more likely to occur if the presidency were strengthened so that the president could lead Congress.

Wilson's popularity as president of Princeton made him a prime candidate for governor of New Jersey in 1910. He was elected and, two years later, was nominated for president by the Democratic national convention on the forty-sixth ballot. The beneficiary of a split in the Republican party that prompted both President William Howard Taft and former president Theodore Roosevelt to run for president in 1912, Wilson was elected overwhelmingly.

Wilson led a newly invigorated Democratic party. Not only was he just the second Democrat to be elected president since the Civil War, but Democrats rode his coattails to gain control of both houses of Congress. Perhaps most important, Wilson committed the party to his "New Freedom" agenda, which proposed to use the power of the federal government to reduce the power of big business.

Wilson believed that the president could lead Congress by leading public opinion. To reach the people, he used oratory and written public messages effectively and created the practice of regular press conferences. Wilson's most dramatic innovation, however, was to restore the practice, which President Thomas Jefferson had abandoned in 1801 as too reminiscent of the British king's speech from the throne, of appearing personally before Congress to deliver the State of the Union address rather than sending a written message.

Standing before a joint session of the House of Representatives and the Senate on April 8, 1913, Wilson began by saying, "I am very glad indeed to have this opportunity to address the two Houses directly and to verify for myself the impression that the President of the United States is a person, not a mere department of the Government hailing Congress from some isolated island of jealous power, sending messages, not speaking naturally and with his own voice—that he is a human being trying to co-operate with other human beings in a common service."

*Wilson confined his address to a call for tariff reform, which Congress heeded by passing reductions of 15 percent and by removing tariffs entirely from some one hundred items. In an unprecedented display of legislative leadership by the president, Wilson also persuaded Congress during his first term to establish a graduated income tax; to regulate banking and unfair business competition by creating the Federal Reserve System and Federal Trade Commission, respectively; to crack down on the trusts by passing the Clayton Antitrust Act; and to aid agriculture with the Smith-Lever Act and the Federal Farm Loan Act.* ~

Gentlemen of the Congress:

I am very glad indeed to have this opportunity to address the two Houses directly and to verify for myself the impression that the President of the United States is a person, not a mere department of the Government hailing Congress from some isolated island of jealous power, sending messages, not speaking naturally and with his own voice—that he is a human being trying to co-operate with other human beings in a common service. After this pleasant experience I shall feel quite normal in all our dealings with one another.

I have called the Congress together in extraordinary session because a duty was laid upon the party now in power at the recent elections which it ought to perform promptly, in order that the burden carried by the people under existing law may be lightened as soon as possible, and in order, also, that the business interests of the country may not be kept too long in suspense as to what the fiscal changes are to be to which they will be required to adjust themselves. It is clear to the whole country that the tariff duties must be altered. They must be changed to meet the radical alteration in the conditions of our economic life which the country

has witnessed within the last generation. While the whole face and method of our industrial and commercial life were being changed beyond recognition the tariff schedules have remained what they were before the change began, or have moved in the direction they were given when no large circumstance of our industrial development was what it is to-day. Our task is to square them with the actual facts. The sooner that is done the sooner our men of business will be free to thrive by the law of nature—the nature of free business—instead of by the law of legislation and artificial arrangement.

We have seen tariff legislation wander very far afield in our day—very far indeed from the field in which our prosperity might have had a normal growth and stimulation. No one who looks the facts squarely in the face or knows anything that lies beneath the surface of action can fail to perceive the principles upon which recent tariff legislation has been based. We long ago passed beyond the modest notion of "protecting" the industries of the country and moved boldly forward to the idea that they were entitled to the direct patronage of the Government. For a long time—a time so long that the men now active in public policy hardly remember the conditions that preceded it—we have sought in our tariff schedules to give each group of manufacturers or producers what they themselves thought that they needed in order to maintain a practically exclusive market as against the rest of the world. Consciously or unconsciously, we have built up a set of privileges and exemptions from competition behind which it was easy by any, even the crudest, forms of combination to organize monopoly; until at last nothing is normal, nothing is obliged to stand the tests of efficiency and economy, in our world of big business, but everything thrives by concerted arrangement. Only new principles of action will save us from a final hard crystallization of monopoly and a complete loss of the influences that quicken enterprise and keep independent energy alive.

It is plain what those principles must be. We must abolish everything that bears even the semblance of privilege or of any kind of artificial advantage, and put our business men and producers under the stimulation of a constant necessity to be efficient, economical, and enterprising, masters of competitive supremacy, better workers and merchants than any in the world. Aside from the duties laid upon articles which we do not, and probably can not, produce, therefore, and the duties laid upon luxuries and merely for the sake of the revenues they yield, the object of the tariff duties henceforth laid must be effective competition, the whetting of American wits by contest with the wits of the rest of the world.

It would be unwise to move toward this end headlong, with reckless haste, or with strokes that cut at the very roots of what has grown up amongst us by long process and at our own invitation. It does not alter a thing to upset it and break it and deprive it of a chance to change. It destroys it. We must make changes in our fiscal laws, in our fiscal system, whose object is development, a more free and wholesome development, not revolution or upset or confusion. We must build up trade, especially foreign trade. We need the outlet and the enlarged field of energy more than we ever did before. We must build up industry as well, and must adopt freedom in the place of artificial stimulation only so far as it will build, not pull down. In dealing with the tariff the method by which this may be done will be a matter of judgment exercised item by item. To some not accustomed to the excitements and responsibilities of greater freedom our methods may in some respects and at some points seem heroic but remedies may be heroic and yet be remedies. It is our business to be sure that they are genuine remedies. Our object is clear. If our motive is above just challenge and only an occasional error of judgment is chargeable against us, we shall be fortunate.

We are called upon to render the country a great service in more matters than one. Our responsibility should be met and our methods should be thorough, as thorough as moderate and well considered, based upon the facts as they are, and not worked out as if we were beginners. We are to deal with the facts of our own day, with the facts of no other and to make laws which square with those facts. It is best, indeed it is necessary, to [begin] with the tariff. I will urge nothing upon you now at the opening of your session which can obscure that first object or divert our energies from that clearly defined duty. At a later time I may take the liberty of calling your attention to reforms which should press close upon the heels of the tariff changes, if not accompany them, of which the chief is the reform of our banking and currency laws; but just now I refrain. For the present, I put these matters on one side and think only of this one thing—of the changes in our fiscal system which may best serve to open once more the free channels of prosperity to a great people whom we would serve to the utmost and throughout both rank and file.

I sincerely thank you for your courtesy.

# Woodrow Wilson's "Fourteen Points" Speech (1918)

Woodrow Wilson was reelected narrowly in 1916 against a Republican party that, in contrast to 1912, was united behind its candidate, Supreme Court justice Charles Evans Hughes. Despite his campaign's boast that "He Kept Us Out of War," Wilson's second term was dominated by the war in Europe.

When the war began in 1914, Wilson had announced that the United States would remain neutral. But Germany was convinced that U.S. trade was sustaining its adversaries—France and, especially, Great Britain. In January 1917 Germany declared that it would attack without warning any ship that tried to pass through a wide zone in the Atlantic Ocean. On April 2, after repeated but unsuccessful protests to the German government, Wilson asked Congress to declare war on Germany. Setting an idealistic tone, Wilson said, "the right is more precious than the peace, and we shall fight for . . . a universal domination of right by such a concert of free peoples as shall bring peace and safety to all nations, and make the world at last free." Congress voted overwhelmingly for war on April 6. Wilson's stated purpose to "make the world safe for democracy" became the catchword of the U.S. effort.

Almost from the moment the United States entered World War I, Wilson wanted to issue a clear statement of U.S. objectives. He was dissuaded from doing so by the argument that any such statement could foster disagreement with the other Allied governments. In December 1917, however, the new Bolshevik government in Russia released copies of the old tsarist government's secret treaties with the Allies, charging that the documents proved that both sides in the war were fighting only in pursuit of selfish national interests. In response to Russia's action, Wilson resolved to publish a statement of U.S. war objectives that was more idealistic.

Wilson delivered the "Fourteen Points" speech (each point described a U.S. war aim) to Congress on January 8, 1918. The speech was successful in several ways. It defused the Russian charges. It infused the war-weary Allied peoples with a new sense of moral purpose. Two of the speech's points—those guaranteeing freedom of the seas and free international trade—offered assurances to Germany that made it easier for its government to surrender. Finally, in the armistice that ended the war on November 11, 1918, the Fourteen Points were accepted by the Allied governments, albeit reluctantly, as a framework for peace negotiations.

Some of the idealism of the Fourteen Points was lost in the writing of the Treaty of Versailles—for example, Allied governments insisted on steep financial reparations from Germany and *a division of German colonies among themselves. But much of Wilson's proposal—including the creation of a League of Nations that could "afford mutual guarantees of political independence and territorial integrity to great and small states alike"—was accepted.*

*Greater damage to Wilson's war goals was inflicted at home. War weariness had made many Americans reluctant to assume an ongoing postwar role in world affairs and resentful of the extraordinary power the president had gained during wartime. (Congress had voted Wilson near-total control over the economy as part of the war effort.) Wilson's unprecedented appeal on patriotic grounds for voters to give him a Democratic Congress in the 1918 midterm elections backfired, and Republicans seized control of Congress. Led by the new Senate Foreign Relations Committee chair, Sen. Henry Cabot Lodge of Massachusetts, the Senate rejected the Treaty of Versailles (including the League of Nations) on November 19, 1919.* ~

Once more, as repeatedly before, the spokesmen of the Central Empires have indicated their desire to discuss the objects of the war and the possible bases of a general peace. Parleys have been in progress at Brest-Litovsk between representatives of the Central Powers to which the attention of all the belligerents has been invited for the purpose of ascertaining whether it may be possible to extend these parleys into a general conference with regard to terms of peace and settlement. The Russian representatives presented not only a perfectly definite statement of the principles upon which they would be willing to conclude peace but also an equally definite program of the concrete application of those principles. The representatives of the Central Powers, on their part, presented an outline of settlement which, if much less definite, seemed susceptible of liberal interpretation until their specific program of practical terms was added. That program proposed no concessions at all either to the sovereignty of Russia or to the preferences of the populations with whose fortunes it dealt, but meant, in a word, that the Central Empires were to keep every foot of territory their armed forces had occupied,—every province, every city, every point of vantage,—as a permanent addition to their territories and their power. It is a reasonable conjecture that the general principles of settlement which they at first suggested originated with the more liberal statesmen of Germany and Austria, the men who have begun to feel the force of their own peoples' thought and purpose, while the concrete terms of actual settlement came from the military leaders who have no thought but to keep what they have got. The negotiations have been broken off. The Russian representatives were sincere and in earnest. They cannot entertain such proposals of conquest and domination.

The whole incident is full of significance. It is also full of perplexity. With whom are the Russian representatives dealing? For whom are the representatives of the Central Empires speaking? Are they speaking for the majorities of their respective parliaments or for the minority parties, that military and imperialistic minority which has so far dominated their whole policy and controlled the affairs of Turkey and of the Balkan states which have felt obliged to become their associates in this war? The Russian representatives have insisted, very justly, very wisely, and in the true spirit of modern democracy, that the conferences they have been holding with the Teutonic and Turkish statesmen should be held within open, not closed, doors, and all the world has been audience, as was desired. To whom have we been listening, then? To those who speak the spirit and intention of the Resolutions of the German Reichstag of the ninth of July last, the spirit and intention of the liberal leaders and parties of Germany, or to those who resist and defy that spirit and intention and insist upon conquest and subjugation? Or are we listening, in fact, to both, unreconciled and in open and hopeless contradiction? These are very serious and pregnant questions. Upon the answer to them depends the peace of the world.

But, whatever the results of the parleys at Brest-Litovsk, whatever the confusions of counsel and of purpose in the utterances of these men of the Central Empires, they have again attempted to acquaint the world with their objects in the war and have again challenged their adversaries to say what their objects are and what sort of settlement they would deem just and satisfactory. There is no good reason why that challenge should not be responded to, and responded to with the utmost candor. We did not wait for it. Not once, but again and again, we have laid our whole thought and purpose before the world, not in general terms only, but each time with sufficient definition to make it clear what sort of definitive terms of settlement must necessarily spring out of them. Within the last week Mr. Lloyd George has spoken with admirable candor and in admirable spirit for the people and Government of Great Britain. There is no confusion of counsel among the adversaries of the Central Powers, no uncertainty of principle, no vagueness of detail. The only secrecy of counsel, the only lack of fearless frankness, the only failure to make definite statement of the objects of the war, lies with Germany and her Allies. The issues of life and death hang upon these definitions. No statesman who has the least conception of his responsibility ought for a moment to permit himself to continue this tragical and appalling outpouring of blood and treasure unless he is sure beyond a peradventure that the objects of the vital sacrifice are part and parcel of the very life of Society and that the people for whom he speaks think them right and imperative as he does.

There is, moreover, a voice calling for these definitions of principle and of purpose which is, it seems to me, more thrilling and more compelling than any of the many moving voices with which the troubled air of the world is filled. It is the voice of the Russian people. They are prostrate and all but helpless, it would seem, before the grim power of Germany, which has hitherto known no relenting and no pity. Their power, apparently, is shattered. And yet their soul is not subservient. They will not yield either in principle or in action. Their conception of what is right, of what it is humane and honorable for them to accept, has been stated with a frankness, a largeness of view, a generosity of spirit, and a universal human sympathy which must challenge the admiration of every friend of mankind; and they have refused to compound their ideals or desert others that they themselves may be safe. They call to us to say what it is that we desire, in what, if in anything, our purpose and our spirit differ from theirs; and I believe that the people of the United States would wish me to respond with utter simplicity and frankness. Whether their present leaders believe it or not, it is our heartfelt desire and hope that some way may be opened whereby we may be privileged to assist the people of Russia to attain their utmost hope of liberty and ordered peace.

It will be our wish and purpose that the processes of peace, when they are begun, shall be absolutely open and that they shall involve and permit henceforth no secret understandings of any kind. The day of conquest and aggrandizement is gone by; so is also the day of secret covenants entered into in the interest of particular governments and likely at some unlooked-for moment to upset the peace of the world. It is this happy fact, now clear to the view of every public man whose thoughts do not still linger in an age that is dead and gone, which makes it possible for every nation whose purposes are consistent with justice and the pace of the world to avow now or at any other time the objects it has in view.

We entered this war because violations of right had occurred which touched us to the quick and made the life of our own people impossible unless they were corrected and the world secured once for all against their recurrence. What we demand in this war, therefore, is nothing peculiar to ourselves. It is that the world be made fit and safe to live in; and particularly that it be made safe for every peace-loving nation which, like our own, wishes to live its own life, determine its own institutions, be assured of justice and fair dealing by the other peoples of the world as against force and selfish aggression. All the peoples of the world are in effect partners in this interest, and for our own part we see very clearly that unless justice be done to others it will not be done to us. The program of the world's peace, therefore, is our program; and that program, as we see it, is this:

I. Open covenants of peace, openly arrived at, after which there shall be no private international understandings of any kind but diplomacy shall proceed always frankly and in the public view.

II. Absolute freedom of navigation upon the seas, outside territorial waters, alike in peace and in war, except as the seas may be closed in whole or in part by international action for the enforcement of international covenants.

III. The removal, so far as possible, of all economic barriers and the establishment of an equality of trade conditions among all the nations consenting to the peace and associating themselves for its maintenance.

IV. Adequate guarantees given and taken that national armaments will be reduced to the lowest point consistent with domestic safety.

V. A free, open-minded, and absolutely impartial adjustment of all colonial claims, based upon a strict observance of the principle that in determining all such questions of sovereignty the interests of the populations concerned must have equal weight with the equitable claims of the government whose title is to be determined.

VI. The evacuation of all Russian territory and such a settlement of all questions affecting Russia as will secure the best and freest cooperation of the other nations of the world in obtaining for her an unhampered and unembarrassed opportunity for the independent determination of her own political development and national policy and assure her of a sincere welcome into the society of free nations under institutions of her own choosing; and, more than a welcome, assistance also of every kind that she may need and may herself desire. The treatment accorded Russia by her sister nations in the months to come will be the acid test of their good will, of their comprehension of her needs as distinguished from their own interests, and of their intelligent and unselfish sympathy.

VII. Belgium, the whole world will agree, must be evacuated and restored, without any attempt to limit the sovereignty which she enjoys in common with all other free nations. No other single act will serve as this will serve to restore confidence among the nations in the laws which they have themselves set and determined for the government of their relations with one another. Without this healing act the whole structure and validity of internal law is forever impaired.

VIII. All French territory should be freed and the invaded portions restored, and the wrong done to France by Prussia in 1871 in the matter of Alsace-

Lorraine, which has unsettled the peace of the world for nearly fifty years, should be righted, in order that peace may once more be made secure in the interest of all.

IX. A readjustment of the frontiers of Italy should be effected along clearly recognizable lines of nationality.

X. The peoples of Austria-Hungary, whose place among the nations we wish to see safeguarded and assured, should be accorded the freest opportunity of autonomous development.

XI. Rumania, Serbia, and Montenegro should be evacuated; occupied territories restored; Serbia accorded free and secure access to the sea; and the relations of the several Balkan states to one another determined by friendly counsel along historically established lines of allegiance and nationality; and international guarantees of the political and economic independence and territorial integrity of the several Balkan states should be entered into.

XII. The Turkish portions of the present Ottoman Empire should be assured a secure sovereignty, but the other nationalities which are now under Turkish rule should be assured an undoubted security of life and an absolutely unmolested opportunity of autonomous development, and the Dardanelles should be permanently opened as a free passage to the ships and commerce of all nations under international guarantees.

XIII. An independent Polish state should be erected which should include the territories inhabited by indisputably Polish populations, which should be assured a free and secure access to the sea, and whose political and economic independence and territorial integrity should be guaranteed by international covenant.

XIV. A general association of nations must be formed under specific covenants for the purpose of affording mutual guarantees of political independence and territorial integrity to great and small states alike.

In regard to these essential rectifications of wrong and assertions of right we feel ourselves to be intimate partners of all the governments and peoples associated together against the Imperialists. We cannot be separated in interest or divided in purpose. We stand together until the end.

For such arrangements and covenants we are willing to fight and to continue to fight until they are achieved; but only because we wish the right to prevail and desire a just and stable peace such as can be secured only by removing the chief provocations to war, which this program does remove. We have no jealousy of German greatness, and there is nothing in this program that impairs it. We grudge her no achievement or distinction of learning or of pacific enterprise such as have made her record very bright and very enviable. We do not wish to injure her or to block in any way her legitimate influence or power. We do not wish to fight her either with arms or with hostile arrangements of trade if she is willing to associate herself with us and the other peace-loving nations of the world in covenants of justice and law and fair dealing. We wish her only to accept a place of equality among the peoples of the world—the new world in which we now live,—instead of a place of mastery.

Neither do we presume to suggest to her any alteration or modification of her institutions. But is it necessary, we must frankly say, and necessary as a preliminary to any intelligent dealings with her on our part, that we should know whom her spokesmen speak for when they speak to us, whether for the Reichstag majority or for the military party and the men whose creed is imperial domination.

We have spoken now, surely, in terms too concrete to admit of any further doubt or question. An evident principle runs through the whole program I have outlined. It is the principle of justice to all peoples and nationalities, and their right to live on equal terms of liberty and safety with one another, whether they be strong or weak. Unless this principle be made its foundation no part of the structure of international justice can stand. The people of the United States could act upon no other principle; and to the vindication of this principle they are ready to devote their lives, their honor, and everything that they possess. The moral climax of this the culminating and final war for human liberty has come, and they are ready to put their own strength, their own highest purpose, their own integrity and devotion to the test.

# Teapot Dome Resolution (1924)

The election of Warren G. Harding as president in 1920 marked the beginning of a lull in the long history of presidential activism and progressive politics that began with presidents Theodore Roosevelt and Woodrow Wilson and that has continued through most of the twentieth century. In May 1920, Senator Harding of Ohio had expressed the nation's weariness with change and upheaval and its desire for "normalcy" in a speech to the Home Market Club in Boston: "America's present need is not heroics, but healing; not nostrums but normalcy; not revolution but restoration, . . . not surgery but serenity." That summer the leaders of the deadlocked Republican national convention gathered in the legendary "smoke-filled room" at Chicago's Blackstone Hotel and decided to anoint Harding as the party's nominee for president. The undistinguished but appealing senator, they believed, would be a good candidate and an easily controllable president.

The Republican leaders were correct on both counts. Harding and Gov. Calvin Coolidge of Massachusetts, the party's candidate for vice president, won a landslide victory over Democratic presidential nominee James Cox, the governor of Ohio, and his running mate, former assistant navy secretary Franklin D. Roosevelt. In office, Harding took few legislative initiatives and allowed his party-picked cabinet members relatively free rein over their departments.

Harding died (probably of a heart attack) on August 2, 1923, while on a speaking tour of the West. The combination of Harding's personal popularity and the growing prominence of the presidency provoked an extraordinary outpouring of national grief. But not long after Harding's death, it became apparent that, as an inattentive president, he had unwittingly presided over one of the most corrupt administrations in history.

The most notorious scandal of the Harding administration involved the naval oil reserves at Teapot Dome, Wyoming, and Elk Hill, California. In 1921 Secretary of the Interior Albert B. Fall persuaded Secretary of the Navy Edwin Denby to transfer these oil fields to the Interior Department, with Harding's approval. Fall then leased the fields without competitive bidding—Teapot Dome to Harry F. Sinclair's Mammoth Oil Co. and Elk Hill to Edward L. Doheny's Pan-American Co.—in return for several hundred thousand dollars in bribes. In October 1923, after an eighteen-month investigation and two months after Harding's death, the Senate Committee on Public Lands and Surveys exposed the scandal in public hearings.

The Teapot Dome scandal eventu-

*ally led to the resignation of Denby, the cancellation of the oil leases, the firing of Attorney General Harry M. Daugherty, who had refused to cooperate with the Senate investigation and had ordered federal agents to spy on certain senators, and the imprisonment of Sinclair and Fall. (Incredibly, a jury acquitted Doheny.) Coolidge, who succeeded Harding as president, stayed clear of the scandal by heeding Congress's call to investigate and prosecute vigorously.* ~

*A joint resolution directing the President to institute and prosecute suits to cancel certain leases of oil lands and incidental contracts, and for other purposes.*

Whereas it appears from evidence taken by the Committee on Public Lands and Surveys of the United States Senate that certain lease of naval reserve No. 3, in the State of Wyoming, bearing date April 7, 1922, made in form by the Government of the United States, through Albert B. Fall, Secretary of the Interior, and Edwin Denby, Secretary of the Navy, as lessor, to the Mammoth Oil Co., as lessee, and that certain contract between the Government of the United States and the Pan American Petroleum & Transport Co., dated April 25, 1922, signed by Edward C. Finney, Acting Secretary of the Interior, and Edwin Denby, Secretary of the Navy, relating among other things to the construction of oil tanks at Pearl Harbor, Territory of Hawaii, and that certain lease of naval reserve No. 1, in the State of California, bearing date December 11, 1922, made in form by the Government of the United States through Albert B. Fall, Secretary of the Interior, and Edwin Denby, Secretary of the Navy, as lessor, to the Pan American Petroleum Co., as lessee, were exe-cuted under circumstances indicating fraud and corruption; and

Whereas the said leases and contract were entered into without authority on the part of the officers purporting to act in the execution of the same for the United States and in violation of the laws of Congress; and

Whereas such leases and contract were made in defiance of the settled policy of the Government adhered to through three successive administrations, to maintain in the ground a great reserve supply of oil adequate to the needs of the Navy in any emergency threatening the national security: Therefore be it

*Resolved*, etc., That the said leases and contract are against the public interest and that the lands embraced therein should be recovered and held for the purpose to which they were dedicated; and

*Resolved further,* That the President of the United States be, and he hereby is, authorized and directed immediately to cause suit to be instituted and prosecuted for the annulment and cancellation of the said leases and contract and all contracts incidental or supplemental thereto, to enjoin further extraction of oil from the said reserves under said leases or from the territory covered by the same, to secure any further appropriate incidental relief, and to prosecute such other actions or proceedings, civil and criminal, as may be warranted by the facts in relation to the making of the said leases and contract.

And the President is further authorized and directed to appoint, by and with the advice and consent of the Senate, special counsel who shall have charge and control of the prosecution of such litigation, anything in the statutes touching the powers of the Attorney General of the Department of Justice to the contrary notwithstanding.

# Myers v. United States (1926)

Article II, section 2, of the Constitution empowers the president to appoint officials to the executive branch but requires that the Senate advise and consent to each appointment in order for it to take effect. The Constitution is silent, however, as to the role of the president and the Senate in removing appointees from office.

In the first Congress to meet under the Constitution, Rep. James Madison of Virginia argued persuasively that, in passing the laws that would create the executive departments of the new government, Congress should acknowledge the president's sole power of removal. How could a president be held accountable for failing to "take Care that the Laws be faithfully executed," Madison asked, if denied control over those who work in the executive branch? But in 1867 Congress required in the Tenure of Office Act that the president obtain the consent of the Senate before removing any Senate-confirmed appointee. (See "Tenure of Office Act and Veto," p. 143.) After the provision's target, President Andrew Johnson, left office, Congress softened the Tenure of Office Act. But in 1876, Congress passed a law to give postmasters a four-year term, with Senate approval required if the president wanted to fire a postmaster before the term expired. Postmasterships were a form of political patronage that members of Con-gress valued highly and wished to protect from presidential interference.

In 1920 President Woodrow Wilson, as part of an effort to make his administration more responsive to his policies, fired Oregon postmaster Frank Myers without seeking the consent of the Senate. When Myers sued, the Justice Department asked the Supreme Court to declare the 1876 act unconstitutional. (This was the first time the executive branch had asked the Court to declare any federal law unconstitutional.) In the face of Myers's claim that Congress had created the office of postmaster and could legitimately impose conditions on how postmasters were removed, the Justice Department replied (as had Madison in 1789) that in assigning the president the executive power, the Constitution implicitly granted the removal power as well.

In a 6-3 vote, the Supreme Court affirmed the president's removal power and declared the 1876 law unconstitutional. Interestingly, the decision was written by former president (now Chief Justice) William Howard Taft. In a sweeping assertion of presidential power that resembled Theodore Roosevelt's "stewardship" theory of the presidency more than Taft's own "literalist" theory. Taft declared, "The power of removal is incident to the power of appointment, not to the power of advising and consenting to appointment, and *when the grant of the executive power is enforced by the express mandate to take care that the laws be faithfully executed, it emphasizes the necessity for including within the executive power as conferred the exclusive power of removal."* (See "Theodore Roosevelt's and William Howard Taft's Theories of Presidential Power," p. 176.)     ~

MR. CHIEF JUSTICE TAFT delivered the opinion of the Court.

This case presents the question whether under the Constitution the President has the exclusive power of removing executive officers of the United States whom he has appointed by and with the advice and consent of the Senate.

Myers, appellant's intestate, was on July 21, 1917, appointed by the President, by and with the advice and consent of the Senate, to be a postmaster of the first class at Portland, Oregon, for a term of four years. On January 20, 1920, Myers' resignation was demanded. He refused the demand. On February 2, 1920, he was removed from office by order of the Postmaster General, acting by direction of the president. February 10th, Myers sent a petition to the President and another to the Senate committee on Post Offices, asking to be heard, if any charges were filed. He protested to the Department against his removal, and continued to do so until the end of his term. He pursued no other occupation and drew compensation for no other service during the interval. On April 21, 1921, he brought this suit in the Court of Claims for his salary from the date of his removal, which, as claimed by supplemental petition filed after July 21, 1921, the end of his term, amounted to $8,838.71. In August, 1920, the President made a recess appointment of one Jones, who took office September 19, 1920.

The Court of Claims gave judgment against Myers, and this is an appeal

from that judgment. The Court held that he had lost his right of action because of his delay in suing, citing *Arant* v. *Lane,* 249 U.S. 367; *Nicholas* v. *United States,* 257 U.S. 71, and *Norris* v. *United States,* 257 U.S. 77. These cases show that when a United States officer is dismissed, whether in disregard of the law or from mistake as to the facts of his case, he must promptly take effective action to assert his rights. But we do not find that Myers failed in this regard. He was constant in his efforts at reinstatement. A hearing before the Senate Committee could not be had till the notice of his removal was sent to the Senate or his successor was nominated. From the time of his removal until the end of his term, there were three sessions of the Senate without such notice or nomination. He put off bringing his suit until the expiration of the Sixty-sixth Congress, March 4, 1921. After that, and three months before his term expired, he filed his petition. Under these circumstances, we think his suit was not too late. Indeed the Solicitor General, while not formally confessing error in this respect, conceded at the bar that no laches had been shown.

By the 6th section of the Act of Congress of July 12, 1876, 19 Stat. 80, 81, c. 179, under which Myers was appointed with the advice and consent of the Senate as a first-class postmaster, it is provided that

"Postmasters of the first, second and third classes shall be appointed and may be removed by the President by and with the advice and consent of the Senate and shall hold their offices for four years unless sooner removed or suspended according to law."

The Senate did not consent to the President's removal of Myers during his term. If this statute, in its requirement that his term should be four years unless sooner removed by the President by and with the consent of the Senate, is valid, the appellant, Myers' administratrix, is entitled to recover his unpaid salary for his full term, and the judgment of the Court of Claims must be reversed. The Government maintains that the requirement is invalid, for the reason that under Article II of the Constitution the President's power of removal of executive officers appointed by him with the advice and consent of the Senate is full and complete without consent of the Senate. If this view is sound, the removal of Myers by the President without the Senate's consent was legal and the judgment of the Court of Claims against the appellant was correct and must be affirmed, though for a different reason from that given by that court. We are therefore confronted by the constitutional question and can not avoid it.

The relevant parts of Article II of the Constitution are as follows:

"Section 1. The executive Power shall be vested in a President of the United States of America. . . .

"Section 2. The President shall be commander in chief of the Army and Navy of the United States, and of the Militia of the several States, when called into the actual Service of the United States; he may require the Opinion, in writing, of the principal Officer in each of the executive Departments, upon any subject relating to the duties of their respective Offices, and he shall have Power to grant Reprieves and Pardons for Offences against the United States, except in Cases of Impeachment.

"He shall have Power, by and with the Advice and Consent of the Senate, to make Treaties, provided two thirds of the Senators present concur; and he shall nominate, and by and with the Advice and Consent of the Senate, shall appoint Ambassadors, other public Ministers and Consuls, Judges of the Supreme Court, and all other Officers of the United States whose Appointments are not herein otherwise provided for, and which shall be estab-lished by Law: but the Congress may by Law vest the Appointment of such inferior Officers, as they think proper, in the President alone, in the Courts of Law, or in the Heads of Departments.

"The President shall have Power to fill up all Vacancies that may happen during the Recess of the Senate, by granting Commissions which shall expire at the End of their next Session.

"Section 3. He shall from time to time give to the Congress information of the State of the Union and recommend to their consideration such measures as he shall judge necessary and expedient; he may, on extraordinary occasions, convene both Houses or either of them, and in case of disagreement between them with respect to the time of adjournment, he may adjourn them to such time as he shall think proper; he shall receive Ambassadors and other public Ministers; he shall take Care that the Laws be faithfully executed, and shall Commission all the Officers of the United States.

"Section 4. The President, Vice President and all civil Officers of the United States, shall be removed from Office on Impeachment for, and Conviction of, Treason, Bribery, or other High Crimes and Misdemeanors."

Section 1 of Article III, provides:

"The judicial power of the United States shall be vested in one supreme court and in such inferior courts as the Congress may from time to time ordain and establish. The judges, both of the Supreme and inferior Courts, shall hold their offices during good behavior. . . ."

The question where the power of removal of executive officers appointed by the President by and with the advice and consent of the Senate was vested, was presented early in the first session of the First Congress. There is no express provision respecting removals in the Constitution, except as Section 4 of Article II, above quoted, provides for removal from office by impeachment. The subject was not discussed in the

Constitutional Convention. Under the Articles of Confederation, Congress was given the power of appointing certain executive officers of the Confederation, and during the Revolution and while the Articles were given effect, Congress exercised the power of removal. May, 1776, 4 Journals of the Continental Congress, Library of Congress Ed., 361; August 1, 1777, 8 Journals, 596; January 7, 1779, 13 Journals, 32-33; June 1779, 14 Journals, 542, 712, 714; November 23, 1780, 18 Journals, 1085; December 1, 1780, 18 Journals, 1115.

Consideration for the executive power was initiated in the Constitutional Convention by the seventh resolution in the Virginia Plan, introduced by Edmund Randolph. 1 Farrand, Records of the Federal Convention, 21. It gave to the Executive "all the executive powers of the Congress under the Confederation," which would seem therefore to have intended to include the power of removal which had been exercised by that body as incident to the power of appointment. As modified by the Committee of the Whole this resolution declared for a national executive of one person, to be elected by the legislature, with power to carry into execution the national laws and to appoint to offices in cases not otherwise provided for. It was referred to the Committee on Detail, 1 Farrand, 230, which recommended that the executive power should be vested in a single person, to be styled the President of the United States; that he should take care that the laws of the United States be duly and faithfully executed, and that he should commission all the officers of the United States and appoint officers in all cases not otherwise provided by the Constitution. 2 Farrand, 185. The committee further recommended that the Senate be given power to make treaties, and to appoint ambassadors and judges of the Supreme Court.

After the great compromises of the Convention—the one giving the States equality of representation in the Senate, and the other placing the election of the President, not in Congress as once voted, but in an electoral college, in which the influence of larger States in the selection would be more nearly in proportion to their population—the smaller States, led by Roger Sherman, fearing that under the second compromise the President would constantly be chosen from one of the larger States, secured a change by which the appointment of all officers, which theretofore had been left to the President without restriction, was made subject to the Senate's advice and consent, and the making of treaties and the appointments of ambassadors, public ministers, consuls and judges of the Supreme Court were transferred to the President, but made subject to the advice and consent of the Senate. This third compromise was effected in special committee, in which Gouverneur Morris of Pennsylvania represented the larger States and Roger Sherman the smaller States. Although adopted finally without objection by any State in the last days of the Convention, members from the larger States, like Wilson and others, criticized this limitation of the President's power of appointment of executive officers and the resulting increase of the power of the Senate. 2 Farrand, 537, 538, 539.

In the House of Representatives of the First Congress, on Tuesday, May 18, 1789, Mr. Madison moved in the Committee of the Whole that there should be established three executive departments—one of Foreign Affairs, another of the Treasury, and a third of War—at the head of each of which there should be a Secretary, to be appointed by the President by and with the advice and consent of the Senate, and to be removable by the President. The committee agreed to the establishment of a Department of Foreign Affairs, but a discussion ensued as to making the Secretary removable by the

President. 1 Annals of Congress, 370, 371. "The question was now taken and carried, by a considerable majority, in favor of declaring the power of removal to be in the President." 1 Annals of Congress, 383.

On June 16, 1789, the House resolved itself into a Committee of the Whole on a bill proposed by Mr. Madison for establishing an executive department to be denominated the Department of Foreign Affairs, in which the first clause, after stating the title of the officer and describing his duties, had these words: "to be removable from office by the President of the United States." 1 Annals of Congress, 455. After a very full discussion the question was put: shall the words "to be removable by the President" be struck out? It was determined in the negative—yeas 20, nays 34. 1 Annals of Congress, 576.

On June 22, in the renewal of the discussion, "Mr. Benson moved to amend the bill, by altering the second clause, so as to imply the power of removal to be in the President alone. The clause enacted that there should be a chief clerk, to be appointed by the Secretary of Foreign Affairs, and employed as he thought proper, and who, in case of vacancy, should have the charge and custody of all records, books, and papers appertaining to the department. The amendment proposed that the chief clerk, 'whenever the said principal officer shall be removed from office by the President of the United States, or in any other case of vacancy,' should during such vacancy, have the charge and custody of all records, books, and papers appertaining to the department." 1 Annals of Congress, 578.

"Mr. Benson stated that his objection to the clause 'to be removable by the President' arose from an idea that the power of removal by the President hereafter might appear to be exercised by virtue of a legislative grant only, and consequently be subjected to legislative instability, when he was well satisfied in

his own mind that it was fixed by a fair legislative construction of the Constitution." 1 Annals of Congress, 579.

"Mr. Benson declared, if he succeeded in this amendment, he would move to strike out the words in the first clause, 'to be removable by the President' which appeared somewhat like a grant. Now, the mode he took would evade that point and establish a legislative construction of the Constitution. He also hoped his amendment would succeed in reconciling both sides of the House to the decision, and quieting the minds of gentlemen." 1 Annals of Congress, 578.

Mr. Madison admitted the objection made by the gentleman near him (Mr. Benson) to the words in the bill. He said: "They certainly may be construed to imply a legislative grant of the power. He wished everything like ambiguity expunged, and the sense of the House explicitly declared, and therefore seconded the motion. Gentlemen have all proceeded on the idea that the Constitution vests the power in the President; and what arguments were brought forward respecting the convenience or inconvenience of such disposition of the power, were intended only to throw light upon what was meant by the compilers of the Constitution. Now, as the words proposed by the gentleman from New York expressed to his mind the meaning of the Constitution, he should be in favor of them, and would agree to strike out those agreed to in the committee." 1 Annals of Congress, 578, 579.

Mr. Benson's first amendment to alter the second clause by the insertion of the italicized words, made that clause to read as follows:

"That there shall be in the State Department an inferior officer to be appointed by the said principal officer, and to be employed therein as he shall deem proper, to be called the Chief Clerk in the Department of Foreign Affairs, *and who, whenever the principal officer shall be removed from office by the President of the United States,* or in any other case of vacancy, shall, during such vacancy, have charge and custody of all records, books and papers appertaining to said department."

The first amendment was then approved by a vote of thirty to eighteen. 1 Annals of Congress, 580. Mr. Benson then moved to strike out in the first clause the words "to be removable by the President," in pursuance of the purpose he had already declared, and this second motion of his was carried by a vote of thirty-one to nineteen. 1 Annals of Congress, 585.

The bill as amended was ordered to be engrossed, and read the third time the next day, June 24, 1789, and was then passed by a vote of twenty-nine to twenty-two, and the Clerk was directed to carry the bill to the Senate and desire their concurrence. 1 Annals of Congress, 591.

It is very clear from this history that the exact question which the House voted upon was whether it should recognize and declare the power of the President under the Constitution to remove the Secretary of Foreign Affairs without the advice and consent of the Senate. That was what the vote was taken for. Some effort has been made to question whether the decision carries the result claimed for it, but there is not the slightest doubt, after an examination of the record, that the vote was, and was intended to be, a legislative declaration that the power to remove officers appointed by the President and the Senate vested in the President alone, and until the Johnson Impeachment trial in 1868, its meaning was not doubted even by those who questioned its soundness.

The discussion was a very full one. Fourteen out of the twenty-nine who voted for the passage of the bill, and eleven of the twenty-two who voted against the bill took part in the discussion. Of the members of the House, eight had been in the Constitutional

Convention, and of these, six voted with the majority, and two, Roger Sherman and Eldridge Gerry, the latter of whom had refused to sign the Constitution, voted in the minority. After the bill as amended had passed the House, it was sent to the Senate, where it was discussed in secret session, without report. The critical vote there was upon the striking out of the clause recognizing and affirming the unrestricted power of the President to remove. The Senate divided by ten to ten, requiring the deciding vote of the Vice-President, John Adams, who voted against striking out, and in favor of the passage of the bill as it had left the House.[1] Ten of the Senators had been in the Constitutional Convention, and of them six voted that the power of removal was in the President alone. The bill having passed as it came from the House was signed by President Washington and became a law. Act of July 27, 1789, 1 Stat. 28, c. 4.

The bill was discussed in the House at length and with great ability. The report of it in the Annals of Congress is extended. James Madison was then a leader in the House, as he had been in the Convention. His arguments in support of the President's constitutional power of removal independently of Congressional provision, and without the consent of the Senate, were masterly, and he carried the House.

It is convenient in the course of our discussion of this case to review the reasons advanced by Mr. Madison and his associates for their conclusion, supplementing them, so far as may be, by additional considerations which lead this Court to concur therein.

First. Mr. Madison insisted that Article II by vesting the executive power in the President was intended to grant to him the power of appointment and removal of executive officers except as thereafter expressly provided in that Article. He pointed out that none of the chief purposes of the Convention was to separate the legislative from the executive functions. He said:

"If there is a principle in our Constitution, indeed in any free Constitution, more sacred than another, it is that which separates the Legislative, Executive and Judicial powers. If there is any point in which the separation of the Legislative and Executive powers ought to be maintained with great caution, it is that which relates to officers and offices." 1 Annals of Congress, 581.

Their union under the Confederation had not worked well; as the members of the convention knew. Montesquieu's view that the maintenance of independence as between the legislative, the executive and the judicial branches was a security for the people had their full approval. Madison in the Convention, 2 Farrand, Records of the Federal Convention, 56. *Kendall* v. *United States,* 12 Peters 524, 610. Accordingly, the Constitution was so framed as to vest in the Congress all legislative powers therein granted, to vest in the President the executive power, and to vest in one Supreme Court and such courts as Congress might establish, the judicial power. From this division on principle, the reasonable construction of the Constitution must be that the branches should be kept separate in all cases in which they were not expressly blended, and the Constitution should be expounded to blend them no more than it affirmatively requires. Madison, 1 Annals of Congress, 497. This rule of construction has been confirmed by this Court in *Meriwether* v. *Garrett,* 102 U.S. 472, 515; *Kilbourn* v. *Thompson,* 103 U.S. 168, 190; *Mugler* v. *Kansas,* 123 U.S. 623, 662.

The debates in the Constitutional Convention indicated an intention to create a strong Executive, and after a controversial discussion the executive power of the Government was vested in one person and many of his important functions were specified so as to avoid the humiliating weakness of the Congress during the Revolution and under the Articles of Confederation. 1 Farrand, 66-97.

Mr. Madison and his associates in the discussion in the House dwelt at length upon the necessity there was for construing Article II to give the President the sole power of removal in his responsibility for the conduct of the executive branch, and enforced this by emphasizing his duty expressly declared in the third section of the Article to "take care that the laws be faithfully executed." Madison, 1 Annals of Congress, 496, 497.

The vesting of the executive power in the President was essentially a grant of the power to execute the laws. But the President alone and unaided could not execute the laws. He must execute them by the assistance of subordinates. This view has since been repeatedly affirmed by this Court. *Wilcox* v. *Jackson,* 13 Peters 498, 513; *United States* v. *Eliason,* 16 Peters 291, 302; *Wilson* v. *United States,* 1 How. 290, 297; *Cunningham* v. *Neagle,* 135 U.S. 1, 63; *Russell Co.* v. *United States,* 261 U.S. 514, 523. As he is charged specifically to take care that they be faithfully executed, the reasonable implication, even in the absence of express words, was that as part of his executive power he should select those who were to act for him under his direction in the execution of the laws. The further implication must be, in the absence of any express limitation respecting removals, that as his selection of administrative officers is essential to the execution of the laws by him, so must be his power of removing those for whom he can not continue to be responsible. Fisher Ames, 1 Annals of Congress, 474. It was urged that the natural meaning of the term "executive power" granted the President included the appointment and removal of executive subordinates. If such appointments and removals were not an exercise of the executive power, what were they? They certainly were not the exercise of legislative or judicial power in government as usually understood.

It is quite true that, in state and colonial governments at the time of the Constitutional Convention, power to make appointments and removals had sometimes been lodged in the legislatures or in the courts, but such a disposition of it was really vesting part of the executive power in another branch of the Government. In the British system, the Crown, which was the executive, had the power of appointment and removal of executive officers, and it was natural, therefore, for those who framed our Constitution to regard the words "executive power" as including both. *Ex Parte Grossman,* 267 U.S. 87, 110. Unlike the power of conquest of the British Crown, considered and rejected as a precedent for us in *Fleming* v. *Page,* 9 How. 603, 618, the association of removal with appointment of executive officers is not incompatible with our republican form of Government.

The requirement of the second section of Article II that the Senate should advise and consent to the Presidential appointments, was to be strictly construed. The words of section 2, following the general grant of executive power under section 1, were either an enumeration and emphasis of specific functions of the Executive, not all inclusive, or were limitations upon the general grant of the executive power, and as such, being limitations, should not be enlarged beyond the words used. Madison, 1 Annals, 462, 463, 464. The executive power was given in general terms, strengthened by specific terms where emphasis was regarded as appropriate, and was limited by direct expressions where limitation was needed, and the fact that no express limit was placed on the power of removal by the Executive was convincing indication that none was intended. This is the same construction of Article II as that of Alexander Hamilton quoted *infra.*

Second. The view of Mr. Madison and his associates was that not only did the grant of executive power to the President in the first section of Article II carry with it the power of removal, but the express recognition of the power of appointment in the second section enforced this view on the well approved principle of constitutional and statutory construction that the power of removal of executive officers was incident to the power of appointment. It was agreed by the opponents of the bill, with only one or two exceptions, that as a constitutional principle the power of appointment carried with it the power of removal. Roger Sherman, 1 Annals of Congress, 491. This principle as a rule of constitutional and statutory construction, then generally conceded, has been recognized ever since. *Ex Parte Hennen,* 13 Peters 230, 259; *Reagan* v. *United States,* 182 U.S. 419; *Shurtleff* v. *United States,* 189 U.S. 311, 315. The reason for the principle is that those in charge of and responsible for administering functions of government who select their executive subordinates need in meeting their responsibility to have the power to remove those whom they appoint.

Under section 2 of Article II, however, the power of appointment by the Executive is restricted in its exercise by the provision that the Senate, a part of the legislative branch of the Government, may check the action of the Executive by rejecting the officers he selects. Does this make the Senate part of the removing power? And this, after the whole discussion in House is read attentively, is the real point which was considered and decided in the negative by the vote already given.

The history of the clause by which the Senate was given a check upon the President's power of appointment makes it clear that it was not prompted by any desire to limit removals. As already pointed out, the important purpose of those who brought about the restriction was to lodge in the Senate, where the small States had equal representation with the larger States, power to prevent the President from making too many appointments from the larger States. Roger Sherman and Oliver Ellsworth, delegates from Connecticut, reported to its Governor: "The equal representation of the States in the Senate and the voice of that branch in the appointment to offices will secure the rights of the lesser as well as of the greater States." 3 Farrand, 99. The formidable opposition to the Senate's veto on the President's power of appointment indicated that, in construing its effect, it should not be extended beyond its express application to the matter of appointments. This was made apparent by remarks of Abraham Baldwin, of Georgia, in the debate in the First Congress. He had been a member of the Constitutional Convention. In opposing the construction which would extend the Senate's power to check appointments to removals from office, he said:

"I am well authorized to say that the mingling of the powers of the President and Senate was strongly opposed in Convention which had the honor to submit to the consideration of the United States and the different States the present system for the government of the Union. Some gentlemen opposed it to the last, and finally it was the principal ground on which they refused to give it their signature and assent. One gentleman called it a monstrous and unnatural connexion and did not hesitate to affirm it would bring on convulsions in the government. This objection was not confined to the walls of the Convention; it has been subject of newspaper declamation and perhaps justly so. Ought we not, therefore, to be careful not to extend this unchaste connexion any further?" 1 Annals of Congress, 557.

Madison said:

"Perhaps there was no argument urged with more success or more plausibly grounded against the Constitution under which we are now deliberating than that founded on the mingling of the executive and legislative branches of the Government in one body. It has been objected that the Senate have too much of the executive power even, by having control over the President in the appointment to office. Now shall we extend this connexion between the legislative and executive departments which will strengthen the objection and diminish the responsibility we have in the head of the Executive?" 1 Annals of Congress, 380.

It was pointed out in this great debate that the power of removal, though equally essential to the executive power, is different in its nature from that of appointment. Madison, 1 Annals of Congress, 497, *et seq.;* Clymer, 1 Annals, 489; Sedgwick, 1 Annals, 522; Ames, 1 Annals, 541, 542; Hartley, 1 Annals, 481. A veto by the Senate—a part of the legislative branch of the Government—upon removals is a much greater limitation upon the executive branch and a much more serious blending of the legislative with the executive than a rejection of a proposed appointment. It is not to be implied. The rejection of a nominee of the President for a particular office does not greatly embarrass him in the conscientious discharge of his high duties in the selection of those who are to aid him, because the President usually has an ample field from which to select for office, according to his preference, competent and capable men. The Senate has full power to reject newly proposed appointees whenever the President shall remove the incumbents. Such a check enables the Senate to prevent the filling of offices with bad or incompetent men or with those against whom there is tenable objection.

The power to prevent the removal of an officer who has served under the President is different from the authority to consent to or reject his appointment. When a nomination is made, it may be presumed that the Senate is, or may become, as well advised as to the fitness of the nominee as the President, but in the nature of things the defects in ability or intelligence or loyalty in the administration of the laws of one who has served as an officer under the President, are facts as to which the President, or his trusted subordinates, must be better informed than the Senate, and the power to remove him may, therefore, be regarded as confined, for very sound and practical reasons, to the governmental authority which has administrative control. The power of removal is incident to the power of appointment, not to the power of advising and consenting to appointment, and when the grant of the executive power is enforced by the express mandate to take care that the laws be faithfully executed, it emphasizes the necessity for including within the executive power as conferred the exclusive power of removal.

Oliver Ellsworth was a member of the Senate of the First Congress, and was active in securing the imposition of the Senate restriction upon appointments by the President. He was the author of the Judiciary Act in that Congress, and subsequently Chief Justice of the United States. His view as to the meaning of this article of the Constitution, upon the point as to whether the advice of the Senate was necessary to removal, like that of Madison, formed and expressed almost in the very atmosphere of the Convention, was entitled to great weight. What he said in the discussion in the Senate was reported by Senator William Patterson, 2 Bancroft, History of the Constitution of the United States, 192, as follows:

"The three distinct powers, legislative, judicial and executive should be placed in different hands. 'He shall take care that the laws be faithfully executed' are sweeping words. The officers should be attentive to the President to whom the Senate is not a council. To turn a man out of office is an exercise neither of legislative nor of judicial power; it is like a tree growing upon land that has been granted. The advice of the Senate does not make the appointment. The President appoints. There are certain restrictions in certain cases, but the restriction is as to the appointment and not as to the removal."

In the discussion in the first Congress fear was expressed that such a constitutional rule of construction as was involved in the passage of the bill would expose the country to tyranny through the abuse of the exercise of the power of removal by the President. Underlying such fears was the fundamental misconception that the President's attitude in his exercise of power is one of opposition to the people, while the Congress is their only defender in the Government, and such a misconception may be noted in the discussion had before this Court. This view was properly contested by Mr. Madison in the discussion (1 Annals of Congress, 461), by Mr. Hartley (1 Annals, 481), by Mr. Lawrence (1 Annals, 485), and by Mr. Scott (1 Annals, 533). The President is a representative of the people just as the members of the Senate and of the House are, and it may be, at some times, on some subjects, that the President elected by all the people is rather more representative of them all than are the members of either body of the Legislature whose constituencies are local and not countrywide; and, as the President is elected for four years, with the mandate of the people to exercise his executive power under the Constitution, there would seem to be no reason for construing that instrument in such a way as to limit and hamper that power beyond the limitations of it, expressed or fairly implied.

Another argument advanced in the First Congress against implying the power of removal in the President alone from its necessity in the proper administration of the executive power, was that all embarrassment in this respect could be avoided by the President's power of suspension of officers, disloyal or incompetent, until the Senate could act. To this, Mr. Benson, said:

"Gentlemen ask, will not the power of suspending an officer be sufficient to prevent mal-conduct? Here is some inconsistency in their arguments. They declare that Congress have no right to construe the Constitution in favor of the President, with respect to removal; yet they propose to give a construction in favor of the power of suspension being exercised by him. Surely gentlemen do not pretend that the President has the power of suspension granted expressly by the Constitution; if they do, they have been more successful in their researches into that instrument than I have been. If they are willing to allow a power of suspending, it must be because they construe some part of the Constitution in favor of such a grant. The construction in this case must be equally unwarrantable. But admitting it proper to grant this power, what then? When an officer is suspended, does the place become vacant? May the President proceed to fill it up? Or must the public business be likewise suspended? When we say an officer is suspended, it implies that the place is not vacant; but the parties may be heard, and, after the officer is freed from the objections that have been taken to his conduct, he may proceed to execute the duties attached to him. What would be the consequence of this? If the Senate, upon its meeting, were to acquit the officer, and replace him in his station, the President would then have a man forced on him whom he considered as unfaithful; and could not, consistent with duty, and a proper regard to the general welfare, go so far as to entrust him with full communications relative to the business of his department. Without a confidence in the Executive department, its operations would be subject to perpetual discord, and the administration of the

Government become impracticable." 1 Annals of Congress, 506.

Mr. Vining said:

"The Departments of Foreign Affairs and War are peculiarly within the powers of the President, and he must be responsible for them; but take away his controlling power, and upon what principle do you require his responsibility?

"The gentlemen say the President may suspend. They were asked if the Constitution gave him this power any more than the other? Do they contend the one to be a more inherent power than the other? If they do not, why shall it be objected to us that we are making a Legislative construction of the Constitution, when they are contending for the same thing?" 1 Annals of Congress, 512.

In the case before us, the same suggestion has been made for the same purpose, and we think it is well answered in the foregoing. The implication of removal by the President alone is no more a strained construction of the Constitution than that of suspension by him alone, and the broader power is much needed and more strongly to be implied.

Third. Another argument urged against the constitutional power of the President alone to remove executive officers appointed by him with the consent of the Senate is that, in the absence of an express power of removal granted to the President, power to make provision for removal of all such officers is vested in the Congress by section 8 of Article I.

Mr. Madison, mistakenly thinking that an argument like this was advanced by Roger Sherman, took it up and answered it as follows:

"He seems to think (if I understand him rightly) that the power of displacing from office is subject to Legislative discretion; because, having a right to create, it may limit or modify as it thinks proper. I shall not say but at first view this doctrine may seem to have some plausibility. But when I consider that the Constitution clearly intended to maintain a marked distinction between the Legislative, Executive and Judicial powers of Government; and when I consider that if the Legislature has a power, such as is contended for, they may subject and transfer at discretion powers from one department of our Government to another; they may, on that principle, exclude the President altogether from exercising any authority in the removal of officers; they may give [it] to the Senate alone, or the President and Senate combined; they may vest it in the whole Congress; or they may reserve it to be exercised by this house. When I consider the consequences of this doctrine, and compare them with the true principles of the Constitution, I own that I can not subscribe to it. . . ." 1 Annals of Congress, 495, 496.

Of the eleven members of the House who spoke from amongst the twenty-two opposing the bill, two insisted that there was no power of removing officers after they had been appointed, except by impeachment, and that the failure of the Constitution expressly to provide another method of removal involved this conclusion. Eight of them argued that the power of removal was in the President and the Senate—that the House had nothing to do with it; and most of these were very insistent upon this view in establishing their contention that it was improper for the House to express in legislation any opinion on the constitutional question whether the President could remove without the Senate's consent.

The constitutional construction that excludes Congress from legislative power to provide for the removal of superior officers finds support in the second section of Article II. By it the appointment of all officers, whether superior or inferior, by the President is declared to be subject to the advice and consent of the Senate. In the absence of any specific provision to the contrary, the power of appointment to executive office carries with it, as a necessary incident, the power of removal. Whether the Senate must concur in the removal is aside from the point we are now considering. That point is, that by the specific constitutional provision for appointment of executive officers with its necessary incident of removal, the power of appointment and removal is clearly provided for by the Constitution, and the legislative power of Congress in respect to both is excluded save by the specific exception as to inferior offices in the clause that follows, *viz*, "but the Congress may by law vest the appointment of such inferior officers, as they think proper, in the President alone, in the Courts of Law, or in the Heads of Departments." These words, it has been held by this Court, give to Congress the power to limit and regulate removal of such inferior officers by heads of departments when it exercises its constitutional power to lodge the power of appointment with them. *United States* v. *Perkins,* 116 U.S. 483, 485. Here, then, is an express provision, introduced in words of exception, for the exercise by Congress of legislative power in the matter of appointments and removals in the case of inferior executive officers. The phrase "But Congress may by law vest" is equivalent to "excepting that Congress may by law vest." By the plainest implication it excludes Congressional dealing with appointments or removals of executive officers not falling within the exception, and leaves unaffected the executive power of the President to appoint and remove them.

A reference of the whole power of removal to general legislation by Congress is quite out of keeping with the plan of government devised by the framers of the Constitution. It could never have been intended to leave to Congress unlimited discretion to vary fundamentally the operation of the great independent executive branch of government and thus most seriously to weaken it. It would be a delegation by the Convention to Congress of the function of defining the primary boundaries of another of the three great divisions of government. The inclusion of removals of executive officers in the executive power vested in the President by Article II, according to its usual definition, and the implication of his power of removal of such officers from the provision of section 2 expressly recognizing in him the power of their appointment, are a much more natural and appropriate source of the removing power.

It is reasonable to suppose also that, had it been intended to give to Congress power to regulate or control removals in the manner suggested, it would have been included among the specifically enumerated legislative powers in Article I, or in the specified limitations on the executive power in Article II. The difference between the grant of legislative power under Article I to Congress, which is limited to powers therein enumerated, and the more general grant of the executive power to the President under Article II, is significant. The fact that the executive power is given in general terms strengthened by specific terms where emphasis is appropriate, and limited by direct expressions where limitation is needed and that no express limit is placed on the power of removal by the executive, is a convincing indication that none was intended.

It is argued that the denial of the legislative power to regulate removals in some way involves the denial of power to prescribe qualifications for office, or reasonable classification for promotion, and yet that has been often exercised. We see no conflict between the latter power and that of appointment and removal, provided of course that the qualifications do not so limit selection and so trench upon executive choice as to be in effect legislative designation. As Mr. Madison said in the First Congress:

"The powers relative to offices are partly Legislative and partly Executive. The Legislature creates the office, defines the powers, limits its duration and annexes a compensation. This done, the Legislative power ceases. They ought to have nothing to do with designating the man to fill the office. That I conceive to be of an Executive nature. Although it be qualified in the Constitution, I would not extend or strain that qualification beyond the limits precisely fixed for it. We ought always to consider the Constitution with an eye to the principles upon which it was founded. In this point of view, we shall readily conclude that if the Legislature determines the powers, the honors, and emoluments of an office, we should be insecure if they were to designate the officer also. The nature of things restrains and confines the Legislative and Executive authorities in this respect; and hence it is that the Constitution stipulates for the independence of each branch of the Government." 1 Annals of Congress, 581, 582.

The legislative power here referred to by Mr. Madison is the legislative power of Congress under the Constitution, not legislative power independently of it. Article II expressly and by implication withholds from Congress power to determine who shall appoint and who shall remove except as to inferior offices. To Congress under its legislative power is given the establishment of offices, the determination of their functions and jurisdiction, the prescribing of reasonable and relevant qualifications and rules of eligibility of appointees, and the fixing of the term for which they are to be appointed, and their compensation—all except as otherwise provided by the Constitution.

An argument in favor of full Congressional power to make or withhold provision for removals of all appointed by the President is sought to be found in an asserted analogy between such a power in Congress and its power in the establishment of inferior federal courts.

By Article III the judicial power of the United States is vested in one Supreme Court and in such inferior courts as the Congress may from time to time establish. By section 8 of Article I, also, Congress is given power to constitute tribunals inferior to the Supreme Court. By the second section the judicial power is extended to all cases in law and equity under this Constitution and to a substantial number of other classes of cases. Under the accepted construction the cases mentioned in this section are treated as a description and reservoir of the judicial power of the United States and a boundary of that federal power as between the United States and the States, and the field of jurisdiction within the limits of which Congress may vest particular jurisdiction in any one inferior federal court which it may constitute. It is clear that the mere establishment of a federal inferior court does not vest that court with all the judicial power of the United States as conferred in the second section of Article III, but only that conferred by Congress specifically on the particular court. It must be limited territorially and in the classes of cases to be heard; and the mere creation of the court does not confer jurisdiction except as it is conferred in the law of its creation or its amendments. It is said that, similarly, in the case of the executive power which is "vested in the President," the power of appointment and removal can not arise until Congress creates the office and its duties and powers, and must accordingly be exercised and limited only as Congress shall in the creation of the office prescribe.

We think there is little or no analogy between the two legislative functions of Congress in the cases suggested. The judicial power described in the second section of Article III is vested in the courts collectively, but is manifestly to be distributed to different courts and conferred or withheld as Congress shall in its discretion provide their respective jurisdictions, and is not all to be vested in one particular court. Any other construction would be impracticable. The duty of Congress, therefore, to make provision for the vesting of the whole federal judicial power in federal courts, were it held to exist, would be one of imperfect obligation and unenforceable. On the other hand, the moment an office and its powers and duties are created, the power of appointment and removal, as limited by the Constitution, vests in the Executive. The functions of distributing jurisdiction to courts, and the exercise of it when distributed and vested, are not at all parallel to the creation of an office, and the mere right of appointment to, and of removal from, the office, which at once attaches to the Executive by virtue of the Constitution.

Fourth. Mr. Madison and his associates pointed out with great force the unreasonable character of the view that the Convention intended, without express provision, to give to Congress or the Senate, in case of political or other differences, the means of thwarting the Executive in the exercise of his great powers and in the bearing of his great responsibility, by fastening upon him, as subordinate executive officers, men who by their inefficient service under him, by their lack of loyalty to the service, or by their different views of policy, might make his taking care that the laws be faithfully executed most difficult or impossible.

As Mr. Madison said in the debate in the First Congress:

"Vest this power in the Senate jointly with the President, and you abolish at once that great principle of unity and responsibility in the Executive department, which was intended for the security of liberty and the public good. If the President should possess alone the power of removal from office, those who are employed in the execution of the law will be in their proper situation, and the chain of dependence be preserved; the lowest officers, the middle grade, and the highest, will depend, as they ought, on the President, and the President on the community." 1 Annals of Congress, 499.

Mr. Boudinot of New Jersey said upon the same point:

"The supreme Executive officer against his assistant; and the Senate are to sit as judges to determine whether sufficient cause of removal exists. Does not this set the Senate over the head of the President? But suppose they shall decide in favor of the officer, what a situation is the President then in, surrounded by officers with whom, by his situation, he is compelled to act, but in whom he can have no confidence, reversing the privilege given him by the Constitution, to prevent his having officers imposed upon him who do not meet his approbation?" 1 Annals of Congress, 468.

Mr. Sedgwick of Massachusetts asked the question:

"Shall a man under these circumstances be saddled upon the President, who has been appointed for no other purpose but to aid the President in performing certain duties? Shall he be continued, I ask again, against the will of the President? If he is, where is the responsibility? Are you to look for it in the President, who has no control over the officer, no power to remove him if he acts unfeelingly or unfaithfully? Without you make him responsible, you weaken and destroy the strength and beauty of your system." 1 Annals of Congress, 522.

Made responsible under the Constitution for the effective enforcement of the law, the President needs as an indispensable aid to meet it the disciplinary influence upon those who act under him of a reserve power of removal. But it is contended that executive officers appointed by the President with the consent of the Senate are bound by the statutory law and are not his servants to do his will, and that his obligation to care for the faithful execution of the laws does not authorize him to treat them as such. The degree of guidance in the discharge of their duties that the President may exercise over executive officers varies with the character of their service as prescribed in the law under which they act. The highest and most important duties which his subordinates perform are those in which they act for him. In such cases they are exercising not their own but his discretion. This field is a very large one. It is sometimes described as political. *Kendall* v. *United States,* 12 Peters, 524 at p. 610. Each head of a department is and must be the President's *alter ego* in the matters of that department where the President is required by law to exercise authority.

The extent of the political responsibility thrust upon the President is brought out by Mr. Justice Miller, speaking for the Court in *Cunningham* v. *Neagle,* 135 U.S. 1 at p. 63:

"The Constitution, section 3, Article 2, declares that the President 'shall take care that the laws be faithfully executed,' and he is provided with the means of fulfilling this obligation by his authority to commission all the officers of the United States, and by and with the advice and consent of the Senate to appoint the most important of them to fill vacancies. He is declared to be commander-in-chief of the army and navy of the United States. The duties which are thus imposed upon him he is further enabled to perform by the recognition in the Constitution, and the creation by Acts of Congress, of executive departments, which have varied in number from four or five to seven or eight, the heads of which are familiarly called cabinet ministers. These aid him in the performance of the great duties of his office and represent him in a thousand acts to which it can hardly be supposed his personal attention is called, and thus he is enabled to fulfill the duty of his great department, expressed in the phrase that 'he shall take care that the laws be faithfully executed.' "

He instances executive dealings with foreign governments, as in the case of Martin Koszta, and he might have added the Jonathan Robbins case as argued by John Marshall in Congress, 5 Wheat. Appendix 1, and approved by this Court in *Fong Yue Ting* v. *United States,* 149 U.S. 698, 714. He notes the President's duty as to the protection of the mails, as to which the case of *In re Debs,* 158 U.S. 564, 582-584 affords an illustration. He instances executive obligation in protection of the public domain, as in *United States* v. *San Jacinto Tin Co.,* 125 U.S. 273, and *United States* v. *Hughes,* 11 How. 552. The possible extent of the field of the President's political executive power may be judged by the fact that the quasi-civil governments of Cuba, Porto Rico and the Philippines, in the silence of Congress, had to be carried on for several years solely under his direction as commander in chief.

In all such cases, the discretion to be exercised is that of the President in determining the national public interest and in directing the action to be taken by his executive subordinates to protect it. In this field his cabinet officers must do his will. He must place in each member of his official family, and his chief executive subordinates, implicit faith. The moment that he loses confidence in the intelligence, ability, judgment or loyalty of any one of them, he must have the power to remove him without delay. To require him to file charges and submit them to the consideration of the Senate might make impossible that unity and co-ordination in executive administration essential to effective action.

The duties of the heads of departments and bureaus in which the discretion of the President is exercised and which we have described, are the most important in the whole field of executive action of the government. There is nothing in the Constitution which permits a distinction between the removal of the head of a department or a bureau, when he discharges a political duty of the President or exercises his discretion, and the removal of executive officers engaged in the discharge of their other normal duties. The imperative reasons requiring an unrestricted power to remove the most important of his subordinates in their most important duties must, therefore, control the interpretation of the Constitution as to all appointed by him.

But this is not to say that there are not strong reasons why the President should have a like power to remove his appointees charged with the other duties than those above described. The ordinary duties of officers prescribed by statute come under the general administrative control of the President by virtue of the general grant to him of the executive power, and he may properly supervise and guide their construction of the statutes under which they act in order to secure that unitary and uniform execution of the laws which Article II of the Constitution evidently contemplated in vesting general executive power in the President alone. Laws are often passed with specific provision for the adoption of regulations by a department or bureau head to make the law workable and effective. The ability and judgment manifested by the official thus empowered, as well as his energy and stimulation of his subordinates, are subjects which the President must consider and supervise in his administrative control. Finding such officers to be negligent and inefficient, the President should have the power to remove them. Of course there may be duties so peculiarly and specifically committed to the discretion of a particular officer as to raise a question whether the President may overrule or revise the officer's interpretation of his statutory duty in a particular instance. Then there may be duties of a quasi-judicial character imposed on executive officers and members of executive tribunals whose decisions after hearing affect interests of individuals, the discharge of which the President can not in a particular case properly influence or control. But even in such a case he may consider the decision after its rendition as a reason for removing the officer, on the ground that the discretion regularly entrusted to that officer by statute has not been on the whole intelligently or wisely exercised. Otherwise he does not discharge his own constitutional duty of seeing that the laws be faithfully executed.

We have devoted much space to this discussion and decision of the question of the Presidential power of removal in the First Congress, not because a Congressional conclusion on a constitutional issue is conclusive, but, first, because of our agreement with the reasons upon which it was avowedly based; second, because this was the decision of the First Congress, on a question of primary importance in the organization of the Government, made within two years after the Constitutional Convention and within a much shorter time after its ratification; and, third, because that Congress numbered among its leaders those who had been members of the Convention. It must necessarily constitute a precedent upon which many future laws supplying the machinery of the new Government would be based, and, if erroneous, it would be likely to evoke dissent and departure in future Congresses. It would come at once before the executive branch of the Government for compliance, and might well be brought before the judicial branch for a test of its validity. As, we shall see, it was soon accepted as a final decision of the question by all branches of the Government.

It was of course to be expected that the decision would be received by lawyers and jurists with something of the same division of opinion as that manifested in Congress, and doubts were often expressed as to its correctness.

But the acquiescence which was promptly accorded it after a few years was universally recognized.

A typical case of such acquiescence was that of Alexander Hamilton. In discussion in the House of Representatives in 1789, Mr. White and others cited the opinion of Mr. Hamilton in respect of the necessity for the consent of the Senate to removals by the President, before they should be effective. (1 Annals, First Congress, 456.) It was expressed in No. 77 of the Federalist, as follows:

"It has been mentioned as one of the advantages to be expected from the co-operation of the Senate in the business of appointments, that it would contribute to the stability of the Administration. The consent of that body would be necessary to displace as well as to appoint. A change of the Chief Magistrate, therefore, would not occasion so violent or so general a revolution in the officers of the Government as might be expected if he were the sole disposer of offices."

Hamilton changed his view of this matter during his incumbency as Secretary of the Treasury in Washington's Cabinet, as is shown by his view of Washington's first proclamation of neutrality in the war between France and Great Britain. That proclamation was at first criticized as an abuse of executive authority. It has now come to be regarded as one of the greatest and most valuable acts of the first President's Administration, had has been often followed by succeeding Presidents. Hamilton's argument was that the Constitution, by vesting the executive power in the President, gave him the right, as the organ of intercourse between the Nation and foreign nations, to interpret national treaties and to declare neutrality. He deduced this from Article II of the Constitution on the executive power, and followed exactly the reasoning of Madison and his associates as to the executive power upon which the legislative decision of the First Congress as to Presidential removals depends, and he cites it as authority. He said:

"The second article of the Constitution of the United States, section first, establishes this general proposition, that 'the Executive Power shall be vested in a President of the United States of America.'

"The same article, in a succeeding section, proceeds to delineate particular cases of executive power. It declares, among other things, that the President shall be commander in chief of the army and navy of the United States, and of the militia of the several states, when called into the actual service of the United States; that he shall have power, by and with the advice and consent of the Senate, to make treaties; that it shall be his duty to receive ambassadors and other public ministers, *and to take care that the laws be faithfully executed.*

"It would not consist with the rules of sound construction, to consider this enumeration of particular authorities as derogating from the more comprehensive grant in the general clause, further than as it may be coupled with express restrictions or limitations; as in regard to the co-operation of the Senate in the appointment of officers and the making of treaties; which are plainly qualifications of the general executive powers of appointing officers and making treaties. The difficulty of a complete enumeration of all the cases of executive authority, would naturally dictate the use of general terms, and would render it improbable that a specification of certain particulars was designed as a substitute for those terms, when antecedently used. The different mode of expression employed in the Constitution, in regard to the two powers, the legislative and the executive, serves to confirm this inference. In the article which gives the legislative powers of the government, the expressions are 'All legislative pow-

ers herein granted shall be vested in a congress of the United States.' In that which grants the executive power, the expressions are *'The executive power* shall be vested in a President of the United States.'

"The enumeration ought therefore to be considered, as intended merely to specify the principal articles implied in the definition of executive power; leaving the rest to flow from the general grant of that power, interpreted in conformity with other parts of the Constitution, and with the principles of free government.

"The general doctrine of our Constitution then is, that the executive power of the nation is vested in the President; subject only to the exceptions and qualifications, which are expressed in the instrument.

"Two of these have already been noticed; the participation of the Senate in the appointment of officers, and in the making of treaties. A third remains to be mentioned; the right of the legislature to 'declare war and grant letters of marque and reprisal.'

"With these exceptions, the executive power of the United States is completely lodged in the President. This mode of construing the Constitution has indeed been recognized by Congress in formal acts upon full consideration and debate; of which the power of removal from office is an important instance. It will follow that if a proclamation of neutrality is merely an executive act, as it is believed, has been shown, the step which has been taken by the President is liable to no just exception on the score of authority." 7 J. C. Hamilton's "Works of Hamilton," 80-81.

The words of a second great constitutional authority, quoted as in conflict with the Congressional decision, are those of Chief Justice Marshall. They were used by him in his opinion in *Marbury* v. *Madison,* 1 Cranch, 137 (1803). The judgment in that case is one of the great landmarks in the history of the construction of the Constitution of the United States, and is of supreme authority, first, in respect of the power and duty of the Supreme Court and other courts to consider and pass upon the validity of acts of Congress enacted in violation of the limitations of the Constitution, when properly brought before them in cases in which the rights of the litigating parties require such consideration and decision, and, second, in respect of the lack of power of Congress to vest in the Supreme Court original jurisdiction to grant the remedy of mandamus in cases in which by the Constitution it is given only appellate jurisdiction. But it is not to be regarded as such authority in respect of the power of the President to remove officials appointed by the advice and consent of the Senate, for that question was not before the Court.

The case was heard upon a rule served upon James Madison, Secretary of State, to show cause why writ of mandamus should not issue directing the defendant, Madison, to deliver to William Marbury his commission as a justice of the peace for the County of Washington in the District of Columbia. The rule was discharged by the Supreme Court for the reason that the Court had no jurisdiction in such a case to issue a writ for mandamus.

The Court had, therefore, nothing before it calling for a judgment upon the merits of the question of issuing the mandamus. Notwithstanding this, the opinion considered preliminarily, first, whether the relator had the right to the delivery of the commission, and, second, whether it was the duty of the Secretary of State to deliver it to him, and a duty which could be enforced in a court of competent jurisdiction at common law by a writ of mandamus. The facts disclosed by affidavits filed were, that President Adams had nominated Marbury to be a justice of the peace in the District of Columbia, under a law of Congress providing for such appoint-

ment, by and with the advice and consent of the Senate, for the term of five years, and that the Senate had consented to such an appointment; that the President had signed the commission as provided by the Constitution, and had transmitted it to the Secretary of State, who, as provided by statute, had impressed the seal of the United States thereon. The opinion of the Chief Justice on these questions was, that the commission was only evidence of the appointment; that, upon delivery of the signed commission by the President to the Secretary of State, the office was filled and the occupant was thereafter entitled to the evidence of his appointment in the form of the commission; that the duty of the Secretary in delivering the commission to the officer entitled was merely ministerial and could be enforced by mandamus; that the function of the Secretary in this regard was entirely to be distinguished from his duty as a subordinate to the President in the discharge of the President's political duties which could not be controlled.

It would seem that this conclusion applied, under the reasoning of the opinion, whether the officer was removable by the President or not, if in fact the President had not removed him. But the opinion assumed that, in the case of a removable office, the writ would fail, on the presumption that there was in such a case discretion of the appointing power to withhold the commission. And so the Chief Justice proceeded to express an opinion on the question whether the appointee was removable by the President. He said: "As the law creating the office, gave the officer a right to hold it for five years, independent of the executive, the appointment was not revocable, but vested in the officer legal rights which are protected by the laws of his country."

There was no answer by Madison to the rule issued in the case. The case went by default. It did not appear, even by avowed opposition to the issue of the writ, that the President had intervened in the matter at all. It would seem to have been quite consistent with the case as shown that this was merely an arbitrary refusal by the Secretary to perform his ministerial function, and, therefore, that the expression of opinion that the officer was not removable by the President was unnecessary, even to the conclusion that a writ in a proper case could issue. However this may be, the whole statement was certainly *obiter dictum* with reference to the judgment actually reached. The question whether the officer was removable was not argued to the Court by any counsel contending for that view. Counsel for the relator, who made the only argument, contended that the officer was not removable by the President, because he held a judicial office and under the Constitution could not be deprived of his office for the five years of his term by Presidential action. The opinion contains no wider discussion of the question than that quoted above.

While everything that the great Chief Justice said, whether *obiter dictum* or not, challenges the highest and most respectful consideration, it is clear that the mere statement of the conclusion made by him, without any examination of the discussion which went on in the First Congress, and without reference to the elaborate arguments there advanced to maintain the decision of 1789, can not be regarded as authority in considering the weight to be attached to that decision—a decision, which as we shall see, he subsequently recognized as a well-established rule of constitutional construction.

In such a case we may well recur to the Chief Justice's own language in *Cohens* v. *Virginia,* 6 Wheat. 264, 399, in which, in declining to yield to the force of his previous language in *Marbury* v. *Madison,* which was unnecessary to the judgment in that case and was *obiter dictum,* he said:

"It is a maxim, not to be disregarded, that general expressions, in every opinion, are to be taken in connection with the case in which those expressions are used. If they go beyond the case, they may be respected, but ought not to control the judgment in a subsequent suit when the very point is presented for decision. The reason of this maxim is obvious. The question actually before the court is investigated with care and considered in its full extent. Other principles which may serve to illustrate it, are considered in their relation to the case decided, but their possible bearing on all other cases is seldom completely investigated."

The weight of this dictum of the Chief Justice as to a Presidential removal, in *Marbury* v. *Madison,* was considered by this Court in *Parsons* v. *United States,* 167 U.S. 324. It was a suit by Parsons against the United States for the payment of the balance due for his salary and fees as United States District Attorney for Alabama. He had been commissioned as such, under the statute, for the term of four years from the date of the commission, subject to the conditions prescribed by law. There was no express power of removal provided. Before the end of the four years he was removed by the President. He was denied recovery.

The language of the Court in *Marbury* v. *Madison,* already referred to, was pressed upon this Court to show that Parsons was entitled, against the Presidential action of removal, to continue in office. If it was authoritative and stated the law as to an executive office, it ended the case; but this Court did not recognize it as such, for the reason that the Chief Justice's language relied on was not germane to the point decided in *Marbury* v. *Madison.* If his language was more than a dictum, and was a decision, then the *Parson's* case overrules it.

Another distinction, suggested by Mr. Justice Peckham in *Parson's* case was that the remarks of the Chief Justice were in reference to an office in the District of Columbia, over which, by Art. I, sec. 8, subd. 17, Congress had exclusive jurisdiction in all cases, and might not apply to offices outside the District in respect to which the constant practice and the Congressional decision had been the other way (p. 335). How much weight should be given to this distinction, which might accord to the special exclusive jurisdiction conferred on Congress over the District power to ignore the usual constitutional separation between the executive and legislative branches of the Government, we need not consider.

If the Chief Justice, in *Marbury* v. *Madison,* intended to express an opinion for the Court inconsistent with the legislative decision of 1789, it is enough to observe that he changed his mind; for otherwise it is inconceivable that he should have written and printed his full account of the discussion and decision in the First Congress and his acquiescence in it, to be found in his Life of Washington (Vol. V, pages 192-200).

He concluded his account as follows:

"After an ardent discussion which consumed several days, the committee divided; and the amendment [i.e. to strike out from the original bill the words 'to be removable by the President'] was negatived by a majority of thirty-four to twenty. The opinion thus expressed by the house of representatives did not explicitly convey their sense of the Constitution. Indeed the express grant of the power to the president, rather implied a right in the legislature to give or withhold it at their discretion. To obviate any misunderstanding of the principle on which the question had been decided, Mr. Benson [later] moved in the house, when the report of the committee of the whole was taken up, to amend the second clause in the bill so as clearly to imply the power of removal to be solely in the president. He gave notice that if he should succeed in this, he would move to strike out the words which had been the subject of debate. If those words continued, he said the power of removal by the president might hereafter appear to be exercised by virtue of a legislative grant only and consequently be subjected to legislative instability; when he was well satisfied in his own mind, that it was by fair construction, fixed in the constitution. The motion was seconded by Mr. Madison, and both amendments were adopted. As the bill passed into a law, it has ever been considered as a full expression of the sense of the legislature on this important part of the American constitution."

This language was first published in 1807, four years after the judgment in *Marbury* v. *Madison,* and the edition was revised by the Chief Justice in 1832. 3 Beveridge, Life of Marshall, 248, 252, 272, 273.

Congress, in a number of acts, followed and enforced the legislative decision of 1789 for seventy-four years. In the act of the First Congress, which adapted to the Constitution the ordinance of 1787 for the government of the Northwest Territory, which had provided for the appointment and removal of executive territorial officers by the Congress under the Articles of Confederation, it was said "in all cases where the United States in Congress assembled, might, by the said ordinance revoke any commission or remove from any office, the President is hereby declared to have the same powers of revocation and removal." 1 Stat. 53, c. 8. This was approved eleven days after the act establishing the Department of Foreign Affairs, and was evidently in form a declaration in accord with the legislative constitutional construction of the latter act. In the provision for the Treasury and War Departments, the same formula was used as occurred in the act creating the Department of Foreign Affairs; but it was omitted from other creative acts only because the decision was thought to be settled constitutional construction. *In re Hennen*, 13 Peters 230, 259.

Occasionally we find that Congress thought it wiser to make express what would have been understood. Thus, in the Judiciary Act of 1789, we find it provided in § 27, 1 Stat. 87, c. 20, "that marshal shall be appointed in and for each district for the term of four years, but shall be removable at pleasure, whose duty it shall be to attend the District and Circuit Court." That act became a law on September 24th, a month after the Congressional debate on removals. It was formulated by a Senate committee, of which Oliver Ellsworth was chairman, and which presumably was engaged in drafting it during the time of that debate. Section 35 of the same act provided for the appointment of an attorney for the United States to prosecute crimes and conduct civil actions on behalf of the United States, but nothing was said as to his term of office or as to his removal. The difference in the two cases was evidently to avoid any inference from the fixing of the term that a conflict with the legislative decision of 1789 was intended.

In the Act of May 15, 1820, 3 Stat. 582, c. 102, Congress provided that thereafter all district attorneys, collectors of customs, naval officer, surveyors of the customs, navy agents, receivers of public moneys for land, registers of the land office, paymasters in the army, the apothecary general, the assistant apothecaries general, and the commissary general of purchases, to be appointed under the laws of the United States, should be appointed for the term of four years, but should be removable from office at pleasure.

It is argued that these express provisions for removal at pleasure indicate that, without them, no such power would exist in the President. We can not accede to this view. Indeed, the conclusion that they were adopted to show conformity to the legislative decision of 1789 is authoritatively settled by a specific decision of this Court.

In the *Parsons* case, 167 U.S. 324, already referred to, the exact question which the Court had to decide was whether under § 769 of the Revised Statutes, providing that district attorneys should be appointed for a term of four years and their commissions should cease and expire at the expiration of four years from their respective dates, the appellant, having been removed by the President from his office as district attorney before the end of his term, could recover his salary for the remainder of the term. If the President had no power of removal, then he could recover. The Court held that under that section the President did have the power of removal, because of the derivation of the section from the Act of 1820, above quoted. In § 769 the specific provision of the Act of 1820 that the officers should be removable from office at pleasure was omitted. This Court held that the section should be construed as having been passed in the light of the acquiescence of Congress in the decision of 1789, and therefore included the power of removal by the President, even though the clause for removal was omitted. This reasoning was essential to the conclusion reached and makes the construction by this Court of the Act of 1820 authoritative. The Court used, in respect of the Act of 1820, this language (167 U.S. 324, 339):

"The provision for a removal from office at pleasure was not necessary for the exercise of that power by the President, because of the fact that he was then regarded as being clothed with such power in any event. Considering the construction of the Constitution in this regard as given by the Congress of 1789, and having in mind the constant and uniform practice of the Government in harmony with such construction, we must construe this act as providing absolutely for the expiration of the term of office at the end of four years, and not as giving a term that shall last, at all events, for that time, and we think the provision that the officials were removable from office at pleasure was but a recognition of the construction thus almost universally adhered to and acquiesced in as to the power of the President to remove."

In the Act of July 17, 1862, 12 Stat. 596, c. 200, Congress actually requested the President to make removals in the following language:

"the President of the United States be, and hereby is, authorized and requested to dismiss and discharge from the military service, either in the army, navy, marine corps, or volunteer force, any officer for any cause which, in his judgment, either renders such officer unsuitable for, or whose dismissal would promote, the public service."

Attorney General Devens (15 Op. A. G. 421) said of this act that, so far as it gave authority to the President, it was simply declaratory of the long-established law; that the force of the act was to be found in the word "requested," by which it was intended to re-enforce strongly this power in the hands of the President at a great crisis of the state—a comment by the Attorney General which was expressly approved by this Court in *Blake* v. *United States,* 103 U.S. 227, 234.

The acquiescence in the legislative decision of 1789 for nearly three-quarters of a century by all branches of the government has been affirmed by this Court in unmistakable terms. In *Parsons* v. *United States,* already cited, in which the matter of the power of removal was reviewed at length in connection with that legislative decision, this Court, speaking by Mr. Justice Peckham, said (page 330):

"Many distinguished lawyers originally had very different opinions in regard to this power from the one arrived at by this Congress, but when the question was alluded to in after years they recognized that the decision of Congress in 1789 and the universal practice of the Government under it, had settled the question beyond any power of alteration."

We find this confirmed by Chancellor Kent's and Mr. Justice Story's comments. Chancellor Kent, in writing to Mr. Webster in January, 1830, concerning the decision of 1789, said:

"I heard the question debated in the summer of 1789, and Madison, Benson, Ames, Lawrence, etc. were in favor of the right of removal by the President, and such has been the opinion ever since and the practice. I thought they were right because I then thought this side uniformly right."

Then, expressing subsequent pause and doubt upon this construction as an original question because of Hamilton's original opinion in The Federalist, already referred to, he continued:

"On the other hand, it is too late to call the President's power in question after a declaratory act of Congress and an acquiescence of half a century. We should hurt the reputation of our government with the world, and we are accused already of the Republican tendency of reducing all executive power into the legislative, and making Congress a national convention. That the President grossly abuses the power of removal is manifest, but it is the evil genius of Democracy to be the sport of factions." 1 Private Correspondence of Daniel Webster, Fletcher Webster ed., 486; 1903 National ed., Little Brown Co.

In his Commentaries, referring to this question, the Chancellor said:

"This question has never been made the subject of judicial discussion; and the construction given to the Constitution in 1789 has continued to rest on this loose, incidental, declaratory opinion of Congress, and the sense and practice of government since that time. It may now be considered as firmly and definitely settled, and there is good sense and practical utility in the construction." 1 Kent Commentaries, Lecture 14, p. 310, Subject, Marshals.

Mr. Justice Story, after a very full discussion of the decision of 1789, in which he intimates that as an original question he would favor the view of the minority, says:

"That the final decision of this question so made was greatly influenced by the exalted character of the President then in office, was asserted at the time, and has always been believed. Yet the doctrine was opposed, as well as supported, by the highest talents and patriotism of the country. The public, however, acquiesced in this decision; and it constitutes, perhaps, the most extraordinary case in the history of the government of a power, conferred by implication on the executive by the assent of a bare majority of Congress, which has not been questioned on many other occasions. Even the most jealous advocates of state rights seem to have slumbered over this vast reach of authority; and have left it untouched, as the neutral ground of controversy, in which they desired to reap no harvest, and from which they retired, without leaving any protestations of title or contest. Nor is this general acquiescence and silence without a satisfactory explanation." 2 Story, Constitution, § 1543.

He finds that, until a then very recent period, namely the Administration of President Jackson, the power of unrestricted removal had been exercised by all the Presidents, but that moderation and forbearance had been shown, that under President Jackson, however, an opposite course had been pursued extensively and brought again the executive power of removal to a severe scrutiny. The learned author then says:

"If there has been any aberration from the true constitutional exposition of the power of removal (which the reader must decide for himself), it will be difficult, and perhaps impracticable, after forty years' experience, to recall the practice to correct theory. But, at all events, it will be a consolation to those who love the Union, and honor a devotion to the patriotic discharge of duty, that in regard to 'inferior officers' (which appellation probably includes ninety-nine out of a hundred of the lucrative offices in the government), the remedy for any permanent abuse is still within the power of Congress, by the simple expedient of requiring the consent of the Senate to removals in such cases." 2 Story Constitution, § 1544.

In an article by Mr. Fish contained in the American Historical Association Reports, 1899, p. 67, removals from office, not including Presidential removals in the Army and the Navy, in the administrations from Washington to Johnson, are stated to have been as follows: Washington 17; Adams 19; Jefferson 62; Madison 24; Jackson 180; Van Buren 43; Harrison and Tyler 389; Polk 228; Taylor 491; Fillmore 73; Pierce 771; Buchanan 253; Lincoln 1400; Johnson 726. These, we may infer, were all made in conformity to the legislative decision of 1789.

Mr. Webster is cited as opposed to the decision of the First Congress. His views were evoked by the controversy between the Senate and President Jackson. The alleged general use of patronage for political purposes by the President, and his dismissal of Duane, Secretary of the Treasury, without reference to the Senate, upon Duane's refusal to remove government deposits from the United States Bank, awakened bitter criticism in the Senate, and led to an extended discussion of the power of removal by the President. In a speech, May 7, 1834, on the President's protest, Mr. Webster asserted that the power of removal, without the consent of the Senate, was in the President alone, according to the established construction of the Constitution, and that Duane's dismissal could not be justly said to be a usurpation. 4 Webster, Works, 103-105.

A year later, in February, 1835, Mr. Webster seems to have changed his views somewhat, and in support of a bill requiring the President in making his removals from office to send to the Senate his reasons therefor, made an extended argument against the correctness of the decision of 1789. He closed his speech thus: "But I think the decision of 1789 has been established by practice, and recognized by subsequent laws, as the settled construction of the Constitution, and that it is our duty to act upon the case accordingly for the present; without admitting that Congress may not, hereafter, if necessity shall require it, reverse the decision of 1789." 4 Webster, 179, 198. Mr. Webster denied that the vesting of the executive power in the President was a grant of power. It amounted, he said, to no more than merely naming the department. Such a construction, although having the support of as great an expounder of the Constitution as Mr. Webster, is not in accord with the usual canon of interpretation of that instrument, which requires that real effect should be given to all the words it uses. *Prout* v. *Starr,* 188 U.S. 537, 544; *Hurtado* v. *California,* 110 U.S. 516, 534; *Prigg* v. *Pennsylvania,* 16 Pet. 539, 612; *Holmes* v. *Jennison,* 14 Pet. 540, 570-571; *Cohens* v. *Virginia,* 6 Wheat. 264, 398; *Marbury* v. *Madison, supra,* at p. 174. Nor can we concur in Mr. Webster's apparent view that when Congress, after full consideration and with the acquiescence and long practice of all the branches of the Government, has established the construction of the Constitution, it may by its mere subsequent legislation reverse such construction. It is not give power by itself thus to amend the Constitution. It is not unjust to note that Mr. Webster's final conclusion on this head was reached after pronounced political controversy with General Jackson, which he concedes may have affected his judgment and attitude on the subject.

Mr. Clay and Mr. Calhoun, acting upon a like impulse, also vigorously attacked the decision; but no legislation of any kind was adopted in that period to reverse the established constitutional construction, while its correctness was vigorously asserted and acted on by the Executive. On February 10, 1835, President Jackson declined to comply with the Senate resolution, regarding the charge which caused the removal of officials from office, saying:

"The President in cases of this nature possesses the exclusive power of removal from office, and, under the sanctions of his official oath and of his liability to impeachment, he is bound to exercise it whenever the public welfare shall require. If, on the other hand, from corrupt motives he abuses this power, he is exposed to the same responsibilities. On no principle known to our institutions can he be required to account for the manner in which he discharges this portion of his public duties, save only in the mode and under the forms prescribed by the Constitution." 3 Messages of the Presidents, 1352.

In *Ex parte Hennen,* 13 Peters 230, decided by this Court in 1839, the prevailing effect of the legislative decision of 1789 was fully recognized. The question there was of the legality of the removal from office by a United States District Court of its clerk, appointed by it under § 7 of the Judiciary Act, 1 Stat. 76, c. 20. The case was ably argued and the effect of the legislative decision of the First Congress was much discussed. The Court said (pp. 258-259):

"The Constitution is silent with respect to the power of removal from office, where the tenure is not fixed. It provides that the judges, both of the supreme and inferior courts, shall hold their offices during good behavior. But no tenure is fixed for the office of clerks. . . . It can not, for a moment, be admitted that it was the intention of the Constitution that those offices which are denominated inferior offices should be held during life. And if removable at pleasure, by whom is such removal to be made? In the absence of all constitutional provision or statutory regulation, it would seem to be a sound and necessary rule to consider the power of removal as incident to the power of appointment. This power of removal from office was a subject much disputed, and upon which a great diversity of opinion was entertained in the early history of his government. This related, however, to the power of the President to remove officers appointed with the concurrence of the Senate; and the great question was whether the removal was to be by the President alone, or with the concurrence of the Senate, both constituting the appointed power. No one denied the power of the President and the Senate, jointly to remove, where the tenure of the office was not fixed by the Constitution, which was a full recognition of the principle that the power of removal was incident to the power of appointment. But it was very early adopted as the practical construction of the Constitution that this power was vested in the President alone. And such would appear to have been the legislative construction of the Constitution. For in the organization of the three great departments of State, War and Treasury, in the year 1789, provision is made for the appointment of a subordinate officer by the head of the department, who should have the charge and custody of the records, books, and papers appertaining to the office, when the head of the department should be removed from the office by the President of the United States. (1 Story, 5, 31, 47.) When the Navy Department was established in the year 1798 (1 Story, 498), provision is made for the charge and custody of the books, records, and documents of the department, in case of vacancy in the office of secretary, by removal or otherwise. It is not here said, by removal by the Presi-

dent, as is done with respect to the heads of the other departments; and yet there can be no doubt that he holds his office by the same tenure as the other secretaries, and is removable by the President. The change of phraseology arose, probably, from its having become the settled and well understood construction of the Constitution that the power of removal was vested in the President alone, in such cases, although the appointment of the officer was by the President and Senate."

The legislative decision of 1789 and this Court's recognition of it were followed, in 1842, by Attorney General Legare, in the Administration of President Tyler (4 Op. A. G. 1); in 1847, by Attorney General Clifford, in the Administration of President Polk (4 Op. A. G. 603); by Attorney General Crittenden, in the Administration of President Fillmore (5 Op. A. G. 288, 290); by Attorney General Cushing, in the Administration of President Buchanan (6 Op. A. G. 4); all of whom delivered opinions of a similar tenor.

It has been sought to make an argument, refuting our conclusion as to the President's power of removal of executive officers, by reference to the statutes passed and practice prevailing from 1789 until recent years in respect of the removal of judges, whose tenure is not fixed by Article III of the Constitution, and who are not strictly United States Judges under that article. The argument is that, as there is no express constitutional restriction as to the removal of such judges, they come within the same class as executive officers, and that statutes and practice in respect of them may properly be used to refute the authority of the legislative decision of 1789 and acquiescence therein.

The fact seems to be that judicial removals were not considered in the discussion in the First Congress, and that the First Congress, August 7, 1789, 1 Stat. 50-53, c. 8, and succeeding Congresses until 1804, assimilated the judges appointed for the territories to those appointed under Article III, and provided life tenure for them, while other officers of those territories were appointed for a term of years unless sooner removed. See as to such legislation dissenting opinion of Mr. Justice McLean in *United States* v. *Guthrie,* 17 How. 284, 308. In *American Insurance Company* v. *Canter,* 1 Peters 511 (1828), it was held that the territorial courts were not constitutional courts in which the judicial power conferred by the Constitution on the general government could be deposited. After some ten or fifteen years, the judges in some territories were appointed for a term of years, and the Governor and other officers were appointed for a term of years unless sooner removed. In Missouri and Arkansas only were the judges appointed for four years if not sooner removed.

After 1804, removals were made by the President of territorial judges appointed for terms of years, before the ends of their terms. They were sometimes suspended and sometimes removed. Between 1804 and 1867, there were ten removals of such judges in Minnesota, Utah, Washington, Oregon and Nebraska. The executive department seemed then to consider that territorial judges were subject to removal just as if they had been executive officers, under the legislative decision of 1789. Such was the opinion of Attorney General Crittenden on the question of the removal of the Chief Justice of Minnesota Territory (5 Op. A.G. 288) in 1851. Since 1867, territorial judges have been removed by the President, seven in Arizona, one in Hawaii, one in Indian Territory, two in Idaho, three in New Mexico, two in Utah, one in Wyoming.

The question of the President's power to remove such a judge, as viewed by Mr. Crittenden, came before this Court in *United States* v. *Guthrie,* 17 How. 284. The relator Goodrich, who had been removed by the President

form his office as a territorial judge, sought by mandamus to compel the Secretary of the treasury to draw his warrant for the relator's salary for the remainder of his term after removal, and contested the Attorney General's opinion that the President's removal in such a case was valid. This Court did not decide this issue, but held that it had no power to issue a writ of mandamus in such a case. Mr. Justice McLean delivered a dissenting opinion (at page 308). He differed form the Court in its holding that mandamus would not issue. He expressed a doubt as to the correctness of the legislative decision of the First Congress as to the power of removal by the President along of executive officers appointed by him with the consent of the Senate, but admitted that the decision as to them had been so acquiesced in, and the practice had so conformed to it, that it could not be set advise. But he insisted that the statutes and practice which had governed the appointment and removal of territorial judges did not come within the scope and effect of the legislative decision of 1789. He pointed out that the argument upon which the decision rested was based on the necessity for Presidential removals in the discharge by the President of his executive duties and his taking care that the laws be faithfully executed, and that such an argument could not apply to the judges over whose judicial duties he could not properly exercise any supervision or control after their appointment and confirmation.

In the case of *McAllister* v. *United States,* 141 U.S. 174, a judge of the District Court of Alaska, it was held, could be deprived of a right to salary as such by his suspension under Revised Statutes 1768. That section gave the President in his descretion authority to suspend any civil officer appointed by and with the advice and consent of the Senate, except judges of the courts of the United States, until the end of the next session of the Senate, and to designate some suitable person, subject to be removed in his discretion by the designation of another, to perform the duties of such suspended officer. It was held that the words "except judges of the courts of the United States" applied to judges appointed under Article III and did not apply to territorial judges, and that the President under § 1768 had power to suspend a territorial judge during a recess of the Senate, and no recovery could be had for salary during that suspended period. Mr. Justice Field, with Justices Gray and Brown, dissented on the ground that in England by the act of 13th William III, it had become established law that judges should hold their offices independent of executive removal, and that our Constitution expressly makes such limitation as to the only judges specifically mentioned in it and should be construed to carry such limitation as to other judges appointed under its provisions.

Referring in *Parsons* v. *United States,* 167 U.S. 324, at p. 337, to the *McAllister* case, this Court said:

"The case contains nothing in opposition to the contention as to the practical construction that had been given to the Constitution by Congress in 1789, and by the government generally since that time and up to the Act of 1867."

The questions whether a judge appointed by the president with the consent of the Senate under an act of Congress, not under authority of Article III of the Constitution, can be removed by the President alone without the consent of the Senate, second, whether the legislative decision of 1789 covers such a case, and third, whether Congress may provide for his removal in some other way, present considerations different from those which apply in the removal of executive officers, and therefore we do not decide them.

We come now to consider an argument advanced and strongly pressed on behalf of the complainant, that this case concerns only the removal of a postmaster; that a postmaster is an inferior officer; that such an office was not included within the legislative decision of 1789, which related only to superior officers to be appointed by the President by and with the advice and consent of the Senate. This, it is said, is the distinction which Chief Justice Marshall had in mind in *Marbury* v. *Madison,* in the language already discussed in respect of the President's power to remove a District of Columbia justice of the peace appointed and confirmed for a term of years. We find nothing in *Marbury* v. *Madison* to indicate any such distinction. It can not be certainly affirmed whether the conclusion there stated was based on a dissent from the legislative decision of 1789, or on the fact that the office was created under the special power of Congress exclusively to legislate for the District of Columbia, or on the fact that the office was a judicial one or on the circumstance that it was an inferior office. In view of the doubt as to what was really the basis of the remarks relied on, and their *obiter dictum* character, they can certainly not be used to give weight to the argument that the 1789 decision only related to superior officers.

The very heated discussions during General Jackson's Administration, except as to the removal of Secretary Duane, related to the distribution of offices which were, most of them, inferior offices, and it was the operation of the legislative decision of 1789 upon the power of of incumbents of such offices that led the General to refuse to comply with the request of the Senate that he give his reasons for the removals therefrom. It was to such inferior officers that Chancellor Kent's letter to Mr. Webster, already quoted, was chiefly directed; and the language cited from his Commentaries on the decision of 1789 was used with reference to the removal of United States marshals. It was such inferior offices that Mr. Justice Story conceded to be covered by the legislative decision, in his Treatise on the Constitution, already cited, when he suggested a method by which the abuse of patronage in such offices might be avoided. It was with reference to removals from such inferior offices that the already cited opinions of the Attorneys General, in which the legislative decision of 1789 was referred to as controlling authority, were delivered. That of Attorney General Legare (4 Op. A. G. 1) affected the removal of a surgeon in the Navy. The opinion of Attorney General Clifford (4 Op. A. G. 603, 612) involved an officer of the same rank. The opinion of Attorney General Cushing (6 Op. A. G. 4) covered the office of military storekeeper. Finally, *Parson's* case, where it was the point in judgment, conclusively establishes for this Court that the legislative decision of 1789 applied to a United States attorney, an inferior officer.

It is further pressed on us that, even though the legislative decision of 1789 included inferior officers, yet under the legislative power given Congress with respect to such officers, it might directly legislate as to the method of their removal without changing their method of appointment by the President with the consent of the Senate. We do not think the language of the Constitution justifies such a contention.

Section 2 of Article II, after providing that the President shall nominate and with the consent of the Senate appoint ambassadors, other public ministers, consuls, judges of the Supreme Court and all other officers of the United States whose appointments are not herein otherwise provided for, and which shall be established by law, contains the proviso "but the Congress may by law vest the appointment of such inferior officers as they think proper in the President alone, in the courts of law or in the heads of departments." In *United States* v. *Perkins,* 116 U.S. 483,

a cadet engineer, a graduate of the Naval Academy, brought suit to recover his salary for the period after his removal by the Secretary of the Navy. It was decided that his right was established by Revised Statutes 1229, providing that no officer in the military or naval service should in time of peace be dismissed from service, except in pursuance of a sentence of court-martial. The section was claimed to be an infringement upon the constitutional prerogative of the Executive. The Court of Claims refused to yield to this argument and said:

"Whether or not Congress can restrict the power of removal incident to the power of appointment to those officers who are appointed by the President by and with the advice and consent of the Senate under the authority of the Constitution, Article 2, Section 2, does not arise in this case, and need not be considered. We have no doubt that when Congress by law vests the appointment of inferior officers in the heads of departments, it may limit and restrict the power of removal as it deems best for the public interest. The constitutional authority in Congress to thus vest the appointment implies authority to limit, restrict, and regulate the removal by such laws as Congress may enact in relation to the officers so appointed. The head of a department has no constitutional prerogative of appointment to offices independently of the legislation of Congress, and by such legislation he must be governed, not only in making appointments but in all that is incident thereto."

This language of the Court of Claims was approved by this Court and the judgment was affirmed.

The power to remove inferior executive officers, like that to remove superior executive officers, is an incident of the power to appoint them, and is in its nature an executive power. The authority of Congress given by the excepting clause to vest the appointment of such inferior officers in the heads of departments carries with it authority incidentally to invest the heads of departments with power to remove. It has been the practice of Congress to do so and this Court has recognized this power. The Court also has recognized in the *Perkins* case that Congress, in committing the appointment of such inferior officers to the heads of departments, may prescribe incidental regulations controlling and restricting the latter in the exercise of the power of removal. But the Court never has held, nor reasonably could hold, although it is argued to the contrary on behalf of the appellant, that the excepting clause enables Congress to draw to itself, or to either branch of it, the power to remove or the right to participate in the exercise of that power. To do this would be to go beyond the words and implications of that clause and to infringe the constitutional principle of the separation of governmental powers.

Assuming then the power of Congress to regulate removals as incidental to the exercise of its constitutional power to vest appointments of inferior officers in the heads of departments, certainly so long as Congress does not exercise that power, the power of removal must remain where the Constitution places it, with the President, as part of the executive power, in accordance with the legislative decision of 1789 which we have been considering.

Whether the action of Congress in removing the necessity for the advice and consent of the Senate, and putting the power of appointment in the President alone, would make his power of removal in such case any more subject to Congressional legislation than before is a question this Court did not decide in the *Perkins* case. Under the reasoning upon which the legislative decision of 1789 was put, it might be difficult to avoid a negative answer, but it is not before us and we do not decide it.

The *Perkins* case is limited to the vesting by Congress of the appointment of an inferior officer in the head of a department. The condition upon which the power of Congress to provide for the removal of inferior officers rests is that it shall vest the appointment in some one other than the President with the consent of the Senate. Congress may not obtain the power and provide for the removal of such officer except on that condition. If it does not choose to entrust the appointment of such inferior officers to less authority than the President with the consent of the Senate, it has no power of providing for their removal. That is the reason why the suggestion of Mr. Justice Story, relied upon in this discussion, can not be supported, if it is to have the construction which is contended for. He says that, in regard to inferior officers under the legislative decision of 1789, "the remedy for any permanent abuse (i.e. of executive patronage) is still within the power of Congress by the simple expedient of requiring the consent of the Senate to removals in such cases." It is true that the remedy for the evil of political executive removals of inferior offices is with Congress by a simple expedient, but it includes a change of the power of appointment from the President with the consent of the Senate. Congress must determine first that the office is inferior, and second that it is willing that the office shall be filled by appointment by some other authority than the President with the consent of the Senate. That the latter may be an important consideration is manifest, and is the subject of comment by this Court in its opinion in the case of *Shurtleff* v. *United States,* 189 U.S. 311, 315, where this Court said:

"To take away this power of removal in relation to an inferior office created by statute, although that statute provided for an appointment thereto by the President and confirmation by the Senate, would require very clear and explicit language. It should not be held to be taken away by mere inference or implication. Congress has regarded the office as of sufficient importance to make it proper to fill it by appointment to be made by the President and confirmed by the Senate. It has thereby classed it as appropriately coming under the direct supervision of the President and to be administered by officers appointed by him (and confirmed by the Senate) with reference to his constitutional responsibility to see that the laws are faithfully executed. Art. 2, sec. 3.''

It is said that, for forty years or more, postmasters were all by law appointed by the Postmaster General. This was because Congress under the excepting clause so provided. But thereafter Congress required certain classes of them to be, as they are now, appointed by the President with the consent of the Senate. This is an indication that Congress deemed appointments by the President with the consent of the Senate essential to the public welfare, and, until it is willing to vest their appointment in the head of the Department, they will be subject to removal by the President alone, and any legislation to the contrary must fall as in conflict with the Constitution.

Summing up, then, the facts as to acquiescence by all branches of the Government in the legislative decision of 1789, as to executive officers, whether superior or inferior, we find that from 1789 until 1863, a period of 74 years, there was no act of Congress, no executive act, and no decision of this Court at variance with the declaration of the First Congress, but there was, as we have seen, clear, affirmative recognition of it by each branch of the Government.

Our conclusion on the merits, sustained by the arguments before stated, is that Article II grants to the President the executive power of the Government, i.e., the general administrative control of those executing the laws, including the power of appointment and removal of executive officers—a conclusion confirmed by his obligation to take care that the laws be faithfully executed; that Article II excludes the exercise of legislative power by Congress to provide for appointments and removals, except only as granted therein to Congress in the matter of inferior offices; that Congress is only given power to provide for appointments and removals of inferior officers after it has vested, and on condition that it does vest, their appointment in other authority than the President with the Senate's consent; that the provisions of the second section of Article II, which blend action by the legislative branch, or by part of it, in the work of the executive, are limitations to be strictly construed and not to be extended by implication; that the President's power of removal is further established as an incident to his specifically enumerated function of appointment by and with the advice of the Senate, but that such incident does not by implication extend to removals the Senate's power of checking appointments; and finally that to hold otherwise would make it impossible for the President, in case of political or other differences with the Senate or Congress, to take care that the laws be faithfully executed.

We come now to a period in the history of the Government when both Houses of Congress attempted to reverse this constitutional construction and to subject the power of removing executive officers appointed by the President and confirmed by the Senate to the control of the Senate—indeed, finally, to the assumed power in Congress to place the removal of such officers anywhere in the Government.

This reversal grew out of the serious political difference between the two Houses of Congress and President Johnson. There was a two-thirds majority of the Republican party in control of each House of Congress, which resented what it feared would be Mr. Johnson's obstructive course in the enforcement of the reconstruction measures, in respect of the States whose people had lately been at war against the National Government. This led the two Houses to enact legislation to curtail the then acknowledged powers of the President. It is true that, during the latter part of Mr. Lincoln's term, two important, voluminous acts were passed, each containing a section which seemed inconsistent with the legislative decision of 1789, (Act of February 25, 1863, 12 Stat. 665, c. 58, § 1, Act of March 3, 1865, 13 Stat. 489, c. 79, § 12); but they were adopted without discussion of the inconsistency and were not tested by executive or judicial inquiry. The real challenge to the decision of 1789 was begun by the Act of July 13, 1866, 14 Stat. 92, c. 176, forbidding dismissals of Army and Navy officers in time of peace without a sentence by court-martial, which this Court, in *Blake* v. *United States,* 103 U.S. 227, at p. 235, attributed to the growing differences between President Johnson and Congress.

Another measure having the same origin and purpose was a rider on an army appropriation act of March 2, 1867, 14 Stat. 487, c. 170, § 2, which fixed the headquarters of the General of the Army of the United States at Washington, directed that all orders relating to military operations by the President or Secretary of War should be issued through the General of the Army, who should not be removed, suspended, or relieved from command, or assigned to duty elsewhere, except at his own request, without the previous approval of the Senate; and that any orders or instructions relating to military operations issued contrary to this should be void; and that any officer of the Army who should issue, knowingly transmit, or obey any orders issued contrary to the provisions of this section, should be liable to imprisonment for years. By the

Act of March 27, 1868, 15 Stat. 44, c. 34, § 2, the next Congress repealed a statutory provision as to appeals in *habeas corpus* cases, with the design, as was avowed by Mr. Schenck, chairman of the House Committee on Ways and Means, of preventing this Court from passing on the validity of reconstruction legislation. 81 Congressional Globe, pages 1881, 1883; *Ex parte McArdle,* 7 Wall. 506.

But the chief legislation in support of the reconstruction policy of Congress was the Tenure of Office Act, of March 2, 1867, 14 Stat. 430, c. 154, providing that all officers appointed by and with the consent of the Senate should hold their offices until their successors should have in like manner been appointed and qualified, and that certain heads of departments, including the Secretary of War, should hold their offices during the term of the President by whom appointed and one month thereafter subject to removal by consent of the Senate. The Tenure of Office Act was vetoed, but it was passed over the veto. The House of Representatives preferred articles of impeachment against President Johnson for refusal to comply with, and for conspiracy to defeat, the legislation above referred to, but he was acquitted for lack of a two-thirds vote for conviction in the Senate.

In *Parsons* v. *United States, supra,* the Court thus refers to the passage of the Tenure of Office Act (p. 340):

"The President, as is well known, vetoed the tenure of office act, because he said it was unconstitutional in that it assumed to take away the power of removal constitutionally vested in the President of the United States—a power which had been uniformly exercised by the Executive Department of the Government from its foundation. Upon the return of the bill to Congress it was passed over the President's veto by both houses and became a law. The continued an uninterrupted practice of the Government from 1789 was thus broken in upon and changed by the passage of this act, so that, if constitutional, thereafter all executive officers whose appointments had been made with the advice and consent of the Senate could not be removed by the President without the concurrence of the Senate in such order of removal.

"Mr. Blaine, who was in Congress at the time, in afterwards speaking of this bill, said: 'It was an extreme proposition—a new departure from the long-established usage of the Federal Government—and for that reason, if for no other, personally degrading to the incumbent of the Presidential chair. It could only have grown out of abnormal excitement created by dissensions between the two great departments of the Government. ... The measure was resorted to as one of self-defense against the alleged aggressions and unrestrained power of the executive department.' Twenty Years of Congress, vol. 2, 273, 274."

The extreme provisions of all this legislation were a full justification for the considerations so strongly advanced by Mr. Madison and his associates in the First Congress for insisting that the power of removal of executive officers by the President alone was essential in the division of powers between the executive and the legislative bodies. It exhibited in a clear degree the paralysis to which a partisan Senate and Congress could subject the executive arm and destroy the principle of executive responsibility and separation of the powers, sought for by the framers of our Government, if the President had no power of removal save by consent of the Senate. It was an attempt to re-distribute the powers and minimize those of the President.

After President Johnson's term ended, the injury and invalidity of the Tenure of Office Act in its radical innovation were immediately recognized by the Executive and objected to. General Grant, succeeding Mr. Johnson in the Presidency, earnestly recommended in his first message the total repeal of the act, saying:

"It may be well to mention here the embarrassment possible to arise from leaving on the statute books the so-called 'tenure-of-office acts,' and to earnestly recommend their total repeal. It could not have been the intention of the framers of the Constitution, when providing that appointments made by the President should receive the consent of the Senate, that the latter should have the power to retain in office persons placed there by Federal appointment, against the will of the President. The law is inconsistent with a faithful and efficient administration of the Government. What faith can an Executive put in officials forced upon him, and those, too, whom he has suspended for reason? How will such officials be likely to serve an Administration which they know does not trust them?" 9 Messages and papers of the Presidents, 3992.

While in response to this, a bill for repeal of that act passed the House, it failed in the Senate, and, though the law was changed, it still limited the Presidential power of removal. The feeling growing out of the controversy with President Johnson retained the act on the statute book until 1887, when it was repealed. 24 Stat. 500, c. 353. During this interval, on June 8, 1872, Congress passed an act reorganizing and consolidating the Post Office Department, and provided that the Postmaster General and his three assistants should be appointed by the President by and with the advice and consent of the Senate and might be removed in the same manner. 17 Stat. 284, c. 335 § 2. In 1876 the act here under discussion was passed, making the consent of the Senate necessary both to the appointment and removal of first, second and third class postmasters. 19 Stat. 80, c. 179, § 6.

In the same interval, in March, 1886,

President Cleveland, in discussing the requests which the Senate had made for his reasons for removing officials, and the assumption that the Senate had the right to pass upon those removals and thus to limit the power of the President, said:

"I believe the power to remove or suspend such officials is vested in the President alone by the Constitution, which in express terms provides that 'the executive power shall be vested in a President of the United States of America,' and that 'he shall take care that the laws be faithfully executed.'

"The Senate belongs to the executive branch of the Government. When the Constitution by express provision super-added to its legislative duties the right to advise and consent to appointments to office and to sit as a court of impeachment, it conferred upon that body all the control and regulation of Executive action supposed to be necessary for the safety of the people; and this express and special grant of such extraordinary powers, not in any way related to or growing out of general Senatorial duties, and in itself a departure from the general plan of our Government, should be held, under a familiar maxim of construction, to exclude every other right of interference with Executive functions." 11 Messages and Papers of the Presidents, 4964.

The attitude of the Presidents on this subject has been unchanged and uniform to the present day whenever an issue has clearly been raised. In a message withholding his approval of an act which he thought infringed upon the executive power of removal, President Wilson said:

"It has, I think, always been the accepted construction of the Constitution that the power to appoint officers of this kind carries with it, as an incident, the power to remove. I am convinced that the Congress is without constitutional power to limit the appointing power and its incident, the power of

removal, derived from the Constitution." 59 Congressional Record (June 4, 1920), 8609.

And President Coolidge, in a message to Congress, in response to a resolution of the Senate that it was the sense of that body that the President should immediately request the resignation of the then Secretary of the Navy, replied:

"No official recognition can be given to the passage of the Senate resolution relative to their opinion concerning members of the Cabinet or other officers under executive control.

". . . The dismissal of an officer of the Government, such as is involved in this case, other than by impeachment, is exclusively an executive function. I regard this as a vital principle of our Government." 65 Congressional Record (Feb. 13, 1924), 2335.

In spite of the foregoing Presidential declarations, it is contended that, since the passage of the Tenure of Office Act, there has been general acquiescence by the Executive in the power of Congress to forbid the President alone to remove executive officers—an acquiescence which has changed any formerly accepted constitutional construction to the contrary. Instances are cited of the signed approval by President Grant and other Presidents of legislation in derogation of such construction. We think these are all to be explained, not by acquiescence therein, but by reason of the otherwise valuable effect of the legislation approved. Such is doubtless the explanation of the executive approval of the Act of 1876, which we are considering, for it was an appropriation act on which the section here in question was imposed as a rider.

In the use of Congressional legislation to support or change a particular construction of the Constitution by acquiescence, its weight for the purpose must depend not upon the nature of the question, but also upon the attitude of the executive and judicial branches of the Government, as well as upon the number of instances in the execution of the law in which opportunity for objection in the courts or elsewhere is afforded. When instances which actually involve the question are rare, or have not in fact occurred, the weight of the mere presence of acts on the statute book for a considerable time, as showing general acquiescence in the legislative assertion of a questioned power, is minimized. No instance is cited to us where any question has arisen respecting a removal of a Postmaster General or one of his assistants. The President's request for resignations of such officers is generally complied with. The same thing is true of the postmasters. There have been many executive removals of them and but few protests or objections. Even when there has been a refusal by a postmaster to resign, removal by the President has been followed by a nomination of a successor, and the Senate's confirmation has made unimportant the inquiry as to the necessity for the Senate's consent to the removal.

Other acts of Congress are referred to which contain provisions said to be inconsistent with the 1789 decision. Since the provision for an Interstate Commerce Commission, in 1887, many administrative boards have been created whose members are appointed by the President, by and with the advice and consent of the Senate, and in the statutes creating them have been provisions for the removal of the members for specified causes. Such provisions are claimed to be inconsistent with the independent power of removal by the President. This, however, is shown to be unfounded by the case of *Shurtleff* v. *United States,* 189 U.S. 311 (1903). That concerned an act creating a board of general appraisers, 26 Stat. 131, 136, c. 407, § 12, and providing for their removal for inefficiency, neglect of duty or malfeasance in office. The President removed an appraiser without notice or hearing. It was forcibly contended that the affirmative language of the statute

implied the negative of the power to remove, except for cause and after a hearing. This would have been the usual rule of construction, but the Court declined to apply it. Assuming for the purpose of that case only, but without deciding, that Congress might limit the President's power to remove, the Court held that, in the absence of constitutional or statutory provision otherwise, the President could by virtue of his general power of appointment remove an officer, though appointed by and with the advice and consent of the Senate, and notwithstanding specific provisions for his removal for cause, on the ground that the power of removal inhered in the power to appoint. This is an indication that many of the statutes cited are to be reconciled to the unrestricted power of the President to remove, if he chooses to exercise his power.

There are other later acts pointed out in which, doubtless, the inconsistency with the independent power of the President to remove is clearer, but these can not be said really to have received the acquiescence of the executive branch of the government. Whenever there has been a real issue in respect of the question of Presidential removals, the attitude of the Executive in Congressional message has been clear and positive against the validity of such legislation. The language of Mr. Cleveland in 1886, twenty years after the Tenure of Office Act, in his controversy with the Senate in respect of his independence of that body in the matter of removing inferior officers appointed by him and confirmed by the Senate, was quite as pronounced as that of General Jackson in a similar controversy in 1835. Mr. Wilson in 1920 and Mr. Coolidge in 1924 were quite as all-embracing in their views of the power of removal as General Grant in 1869, and as Mr. Madison and Mr. John Adams in 1789.

The fact seems to be that all departments of the Government have constantly had in mind, since the passage of the Tenure of Office Act, that the question of power of removal by the President of officers appointed by him with the Senate's consent, has not been settled adversely to the legislative action of 1789 but, in spite of Congressional action, has remained open until the conflict should be subjected to judicial investigation and decision.

The action of this Court can not be said to constitute assent to a departure from the legislative decision of 1789, when the *Parsons* and *Shurtleff* cases, one decided in 1897, and the other in 1903, are considered; for they certainly leave the question open. *Wallace* v. *United States,* 257 U.S. 541. Those cases indicate no tendency to depart from the view of the First Congress. This Court has, since the Tenure of Office Act, manifested an earnest desire to avoid a final settlement of the question until it should be inevitably presented, as it is here.

An argument *ab inconvenienti* has been made against our conclusion in favor of the executive power of removal by the President, without the consent of the Senate—that it will open the door to a reintroduction of the spoils system. The evil of the spoils system aimed at in the civil service law and its amendments is in respect of inferior offices. It has never been attempted to extend that law beyond them. Indeed, Congress forbids its extension to appointments confirmed by the Senate, except with the consent of the Senate. Act of January 16, 1883, 22 Stat. 403, 406, c. 27, sec. 7. Reform in the federal civil service was begun by the Civil Service Act of 1883. It has been developed from that time, so that the classified service now includes a vast majority of all the civil officers. It may still be enlarged by further legislation. The independent power of removal by the President alone, under present conditions, works no practical interference with the merit system. Political appointments of inferior officers are still maintained in one important class, that of the first, second and third class postmasters, collectors of internal revenue, marshals, collectors of customs and other officers of that kind, distributed through the country. They are appointed by the President with the consent of the Senate. It is the intervention of the Senate in their appointment, and not in their removal, which prevents their classification into the merit system. If such appointments were vested in the heads of departments to which they belong, they could be entirely removed from politics, and that is what a number of Presidents have recommended. President Hayes, whose devotion to the promotion of the merit system and the abolition of the spoils system was unquestioned, said, in his 4th Annual Message, of December 6, 1880, that the first step to improvement in the civil service must be a complete divorce between Congress and the executive on the matter of appointments, and he recommended the repeal of the Tenure of Office Act of 1867 for this purpose. 10 & 11 Messages and Papers of the Presidents, 4555-4557. The extension of the merit system rests with Congress.

What, then, are the elements that enter into our decision of this case? We have first a construction of the Constitution made by a Congress which was to provide by legislation for the organization of the Government in accord with the Constitution which had just then been adopted, and in which there were, as representatives and senators, a considerable number of those who had been members of the Convention that framed the Constitution and presented it for ratification. It was the Congress that launched the Government. It was the Congress that rounded out the Constitution itself by the proposing of the first ten amendments which had in effect been promised to the people as a consideration for the ratification. It was the Congress in which Mr. Madison, one of the first in the framing of the Constitution, led also in the organization of the government under it. It was a Congress whose constitutional decisions have always been regarded, as they should be regarded, as of the greatest weight in the interpretation of that fundamental instrument. This construction was followed by the legislative department and the executive department continuously for seventy-three years, and this although the matter, in the heat of political differences between the Executive and the Senate in President Jackson's time, was the subject of bitter controversy, as we have seen. This Court has repeatedly laid down the principle that a contemporaneous legislative exposition of the Constitution when the founders of our Government and framers of our Constitution were actively participating in public affairs, acquiesced in for a long term of years, fixes the construction to be given its provisions. *Stuart* v. *Laird,* 1 Cranch 299, 309; *Martin* v. *Hunter's Lessee,* 1 Wheat. 304, 351; *Cohens* v. *Virginia,* 6 Wheat. 264, 420; *Prigg* v. *Pennsylvania,* 16 Pet. 544, 621; *Cooley* v. *Board of Wardens, etc.,* 12 How. 299, 315; *Burroughs-Giles Lithographing Company* v. *Sarony,* 111 U.S. 53, 57; *Ames* v. *Kansas,* 111 U.S. 449, 463-469; *The Laura,* 114 U.S. 411, 416; *Wisconsin* v. *Pelican Ins. Co.,* 127 U.S. 265, 297; *McPherson* v. *Blacker,* 146 U.S. 1, 28, 33, 35; *Knowlton* v. *Moore,* 178 U.S. 41, 56; *Fairbank* v. *United States,* 181 U.S. 283, 308; *Ex parte Grossman* 267 U.S. 87, 118.

We are now asked to set aside this construction, thus buttressed, and adopt an adverse view, because the Congress of the United States did so during a heated political difference of opinion between the then President and the majority leaders of Congress over the reconstruction measures adopted as a means of restoring to their proper status the States which attempted to withdraw from the Union at the time of the Civil War. The extremes to which the majority in both Houses carried legislative measures in that matter are now recognized by all who calmly review the history of that episode in our Government, leading to articles of impeachment against President Johnson, and his acquittal. Without animadverting on the character of the measures taken, we are certainly justified in saying that they should not be given the weight affecting proper constitutional construction to be accorded to that reached by the First Congress of the United States during a political calm and acquiesced in by the whole Government for three-quarters of a century, especially when the new construction contended for has never been acquiesced in by either the executive or the judicial departments. While this Court has studiously avoided deciding the issue until it was presented in such a way that it could not be avoided, in the references it has made to the history of the question, and in the presumptions it has indulged in favor of a statutory construction not inconsistent with the legislative decision of 1789, it has indicated a trend of view that we should not and can not ignore. When, on the merits, we find our conclusion strongly favoring the view which prevailed in the first Congress, we have no hesitation in holding that conclusion to be correct; and it therefore follows that the Tenure of Office Act of 1867, in so far as it attempted to prevent the President from removing executive officers who had been appointed by him and by and with the advice and consent of the Senate, was invalid, and that subsequent legislation of the same effect was equally so.

For the reasons given, we must therefore hold that the provision of the law of 1876, by which the unrestricted power of removal of first class postmasters is denied to the President, is in violation of the Constitution, and invalid. This leads to an affirmance of the judgment of the Court of Claims.

Before closing this opinion, we wish to express the obligation of the Court to Mr. Pepper for his able brief and argument as a friend of the Court. Undertaken at our request, our obligation is none the less if we find ourselves obliged to take a view adverse to his. The strong presentation of arguments against the conclusion of the Court is of the utmost value in enabling the Court to satisfy itself that it has fully considered all that can be said.

*Judgment affirmed.*

## Note

1. Maclay shows the vote ten to ten. Journal of William Maclay, 116. John Adams' Diary shows nine to nine. 3 C. F. Adams, Works of John Adams, 412. Ellsworth's name appears in Maclay's list as voting against striking out, but not in that of Adams—evidently an inadvertence.

# Herbert C. Hoover's "Rugged Individualism" Speech (1928)

Herbert C. Hoover was one of the best-loved and most-admired men in the United States at the time he was elected president in 1928. He was one of the most-hated when he was voted out of office four years later.

Hoover, a small-town boy from Iowa who worked his way through college at Stanford University, was a highly successful international mining engineer before coming to public prominence during and after World War I for his work in U.S. food production and food distribution among the starving people of Europe. His public reputation grew during eight successful years as secretary of commerce in the Harding and Coolidge administrations. In 1928 Hoover was easily nominated for president by the Republican party.

Hoover's opponent in the election was Gov. Al Smith of New York. Smith was a Catholic (the first Catholic ever to be nominated for president), a cigar-smoking machine politician, and a thoroughgoing New Yorker. He also was an unabashed liberal who proposed that the federal government provide the country with public works, farm relief programs, stronger protection of workers, and regulation of banking and industry.

Hoover, both as the heir to and as a participant in eight years of general prosperity under Republican rule, articulated a very different, mainly probusiness philosophy of government. In an October 22, 1928, speech to an audience in New York, Hoover argued that the government of the United States, in contrast to European governments, had wisely pursued a course of "rugged individualism" since the end of the world war. "When the Republican Party came into full power" in 1920, Hoover proclaimed, "it went at once resolutely back to our fundamental conception of the state and the rights and responsibilities of the individual. Thereby it restored confidence and hope in the American people, it freed and stimulated enterprise, it restored the government to its position as an umpire instead of a player in the economic game."

Hoover defeated Smith overwhelmingly in the election. Barely six months into his term, however, the stock market crashed on October 29, 1929. Hoover tried to reassure the country that the economy was fundamentally sound and would recover on its own, even as it sank into the greatest depression in U.S. history. Twenty-five percent of the work force lost their jobs.

In the face of catastrophic and ever-worsening economic conditions, Hoover clung to his philosophy that the federal government should play a minimal role in providing help to those in need. In the 1930 midterm elections he lost control of Congress, and in 1932 he was *defeated for reelection by Smith's successor as governor of New York, Franklin D. Roosevelt.*  ~

When the war closed, the most vital of all issues both in our own country and throughout the world was whether the governments should continue their wartime ownership and operation of many instrumentalities of production and distribution. We were challenged with a peacetime choice between the American system of rugged individualism and a European philosophy of diametrically opposed doctrines—doctrines of paternalism and state socialism. The acceptance of these ideas would have meant the destruction of self-government through centralization of government. It would have meant the undermining of the individual initiative and enterprise through which our people have grown to unparalleled greatness.

The Republican Party from the beginning resolutely turned its face away from these ideas and these war practices. A Republican Congress cooperated with the Democratic administration to demobilize many of our war activities. At that time the two parties were in accord upon that point. When the Republican Party came into full power, it went at once resolutely back to our fundamental conception of the state and the rights and responsibilities of the individual. Thereby it restored confidence and hope in the American people, it freed and stimulated enterprise, it restored the government to its position as an umpire instead of a player in the economic game. For these reasons the American people have gone forward in progress while the rest of the world has halted, and some countries have even gone backward. If anyone will study the causes of retarded recuperation in Europe, he will find much of it due to stifling of private initiative, on one hand, and

overloading of the government with business, on the other.

There has been revived in this campaign, however, a series of proposals which, if adopted, would be a long step toward the abandonment of our American system and a surrender to the destructive operation of governmental conduct of commercial business. Because the country is faced with difficulty and doubt over certain national problems—that is, Prohibition, farm relief, and electrical power—our opponents propose that we must thrust government a long way into the businesses which give rise to these problems. In effect, they abandon the tenets of their own party and turn to state socialism as a solution for the difficulties presented by all three. It is proposed that we shall change from Prohibition to the state purchase and sale of liquor. If their agricultural relief program means anything, it means that the government shall directly or indirectly buy and sell and fix prices of agricultural products. And we are to go into the hydroelectric power business. In other words, we are confronted with a huge program of government in business.

There is, therefore, submitted to the American people a question of fundamental principle. That is: Shall we depart from the principles of our American political and economic system, upon which we have advanced beyond all the rest of the world, in order to adopt methods based on principles destructive of its very foundations? And I wish to emphasize the seriousness of these proposals. I wish to make my position clear; for this goes to the very roots of American life and progress.

I should like to state to you the effect that this projection of government in business would have upon our system of self-government and our economic system. That effect would reach to the daily life of every man and woman. It would impair the very basis of liberty and freedom, not only for those left outside the fold of expanded bureaucracy but for those embraced within it.

Let us first see the effect upon self-government. When the federal government undertakes to go into commercial business it must at once set up the organization and administration of that business, and it immediately finds itself in a labyrinth, every alley of which leads to the destruction of self-government. Commercial business requires a concentration of responsibility. Self-government requires decentralization and many checks and balances to safeguard liberty. Our government to succeed in business would need become in effect a despotism. There at once begins the destruction of self-government.

The first problem of the government about to adventure in commercial business is to determine a method of administration. It must secure leadership and direction. Shall this leadership be chosen by political agencies or shall we make it elective? The hard, practical fact is that leadership in business must come through the sheer rise in ability and character. That rise can only take place in the free atmosphere of competition. Competition is closed by bureaucracy. Political agencies are feeble channels through which to select able leaders to conduct commercial business.

Government, in order to avoid the possible incompetence, corruption, and tyranny of too great authority in individuals entrusted with commercial business, inevitably turns to boards and commissions. To make sure that there are checks and balances, each member of such boards and commissions must have equal authority. Each has his separate responsibility to the public, and at once we have the conflict of ideas and the lack of decision which would ruin any commercial business. It has contributed greatly to the demoralization of our shipping business. Moreover, these commissions must be representative of different sections and different political parties, so that at once we have

an entire blight upon coordinated action within their ranks which destroys any possibility of effective administration.

Moreover, our legislative bodies cannot in fact delegate their full authority to commissions or to individuals for the conduct of matters vital to the American people; for if we would preserve government by the people we must preserve the authority of our legislators in the activities of our government.

Thus, every time the federal government goes into a commercial business, 531 senators and congressmen become the actual board of directors of that business. Every time a state government goes into business, 100 or 200 state senators and legislators become the actual directors of that business. Even if they were supermen and if there were no politics in the United States, no body of such members could competently direct commercial activities; for that requires initiative, instant decision, and action. It took Congress six years of constant discussion to even decide what the method of administration of Muscle Shoals should be.

When the federal government undertakes to go into business, the state governments are at once deprived of control and taxation of that business; when a state government undertakes to go into business, it at once deprives the municipalities of taxation and control of that business. Municipalities, being local and close to the people, can, at times, succeed in business where federal and state governments must fail. We have trouble enough with logrolling in legislative bodies today. It originates naturally from desires of citizens to advance their particular section or to secure some necessary service. It would be multiplied a thousandfold were the federal and state governments in these businesses.

The effect upon our economic progress would be even worse. Business progressiveness is dependent on competition. New methods and new ideas are the outgrowth of the spirit of adventure, of individual initiative, and of individual enterprise. Without adventure there is no progress. No government administration can rightly take chances with taxpayers' money.

There is no better example of the practical incompetence of government to conduct business than the history of our railways. During the war the government found it necessary to operate the railways. That operation continued until after the war. In the year before being freed from government operation, they were not able to meet the demands for transportation. Eight years later we find them under private enterprise transporting 15 percent more goods and meeting every demand for service. Rates have been reduced by 15 percent and net earnings increased from less than 1 percent on their valuation to about 5 percent. Wages of employees have improved by 13 percent. The wages of railway employees are today 121 percent above prewar, while the wages of government employees are today only 65 percent above prewar. That should be a sufficient commentary upon the efficiency of government operation. . . .

Bureaucracy is ever desirous of spreading its influence and its power. You cannot extend the mastery of the government over the daily working life of a people without at the same time making it the master of the people's souls and thoughts. Every expansion of government in business means that government in order to protect itself from the political consequences of its errors and wrongs is driven irresistibly without peace to greater and greater control of the nation's press and platform. Free speech does not live many hours after free industry and free commerce die.

It is a false liberalism that interprets itself into the government operation of commercial business. Every step of bureaucratizing of the business of our country poisons the very roots of liberalism—that is, political equality, free speech, free assembly, free press, and equality of opportunity. It is the road not to more liberty, but to less liberty. Liberalism should be found not striving to spread bureaucracy but striving to set bounds to it. True liberalism seeks all legitimate freedom first in the confident belief that without such freedom the pursuit of all other blessings and benefits is vain. That belief is the foundation of all American progress, political as well as economic.

Liberalism is a force truly of the spirit, a force proceeding from the deep realization that economic freedom cannot be sacrificed if political freedom is to be preserved. Even if governmental conduct of business could give us more efficiency instead of less efficiency, the fundamental objection to it would remain unaltered and unabated. It would destroy political equality. It would increase rather than decrease abuse and corruption. It would stifle initiative and invention. It would undermine the development of leadership. It would cramp and cripple the mental and spiritual energies of our people. It would extinguish equality and opportunity. It would dry up the spirit of liberty and progress. For these reasons primarily it must be resisted. For 150 years liberalism has found its true spirit in the American system, not in the European systems.

I do not wish to be misunderstood in this statement. I am defining a general policy. It does not mean that our government is to part with one iota of its national resources without complete protection to the public interest. I have already stated that where the government is engaged in public works for purposes of flood control, of navigation, of irrigation, of scientific research or national defense, or in pioneering a new art, it will at times necessarily produce power or commodities as a by-product. But they must be a by-product of the major purpose, not the major purpose itself.

Nor do I wish to be misinterpreted as believing that the United States is a free-for-all and devil-take-the-hindmost. The very essence of equality of opportunity and of American individualism is that there shall be no domination by any group or combination in this republic, whether it be business or political. On the contrary, it demands economic justice as well as political and social justice. It is no system of laissez faire.

I feel deeply on this subject because during the war I had some practical experience with governmental operation and control. I have witnessed not only at home but abroad the many failures of government in business. I have seen its tyrannies, its injustices, its destructions of self-government, its undermining of the very instincts which carry our people forward to progress. I have witnessed the lack of advance, the lowered standards of living, the depressed spirits of people working under such a system. My objection is based not upon theory or upon a failure to recognize wrong or abuse, but I know the adoption of such methods would strike at the very roots of American life and would destroy the very basis of American progress.

Our people have the right to know whether we can continue to solve our great problems without abandonment of our American system. I know we can. We have demonstrated that our system is responsive enough to meet any new and intricate development in our economic and business life. We have demonstrated that we can meet any economic problem and still maintain our democracy as master in its own house, and that we can at the same time preserve equality of opportunity and individual freedom.

In the last fifty years we have discovered that mass production will produce articles for us at half the cost they required previously. We have seen the resultant growth of large units of production and distribution. This is big business. Many businesses must be bigger, for our tools are bigger, our country is bigger. We now build a single dynamo of 100,000 horsepower. Even fifteen years ago that would have been a big business all by itself. Yet today advance in production requires that we set ten of these units together in a row.

The American people from bitter experience have a rightful fear that great business units might be used to dominate our industrial life and by illegal and unethical practices destroy equality of opportunity.

Years ago the Republican administration established the principle that such evils could be corrected by regulation. It developed methods by which abuses could be prevented while the full value of industrial progress could be retained for the public. It insisted upon the principle that when great public utilities were clothed with the security of partial monopoly, whether it be railways, power plants, telephones, or what not, then there must be the fullest and most complete control of rates, services, and finances by government or local agencies. It declared that these businesses must be conducted with glass pockets.

As to our great manufacturing and distributing industries, the Republican Party insisted upon the enactment of laws that not only would maintain competition but would destroy conspiracies to destroy the smaller units or dominate and limit the equality of opportunity among our people.

One of the great problems of government is to determine to what extent the government shall regulate and control commerce and industry and how much it shall leave it alone. No system is perfect. We have had many abuses in the private conduct of business. That every good citizen resents. It is just as important that business keep out of government as that government keep out of business.

Nor am I setting up the contention that our institutions are perfect. No human ideal is ever perfectly attained, since humanity itself is not perfect.

The wisdom of our forefathers in their conception that progress can only be attained as the sum of the accomplishment of free individuals has been reinforced by all of the great leaders of the country since that day. Jackson, Lincoln, Cleveland, McKinley, Roosevelt, Wilson, and Coolidge have stood unalterably for these principles.

And what have been the results of our American system? Our country has become the land of opportunity to those born without inheritance, not merely because of the wealth of its resources and industry but because of this free-dom of initiative and enterprise. Russia has natural resources equal to ours. Her people are equally industrious, but she has not had the blessings of 150 years of our form of government and of our social system.

By adherence to the principles of decentralized self-government, ordered liberty, equal opportunity, and freedom to the individual, our American experiment in human welfare has yielded a degree of well-being unparalleled in all the world. It has come nearer to the abolition of poverty, to the abolition of fear of want than humanity has ever reached before. Progress of the past seven years is the proof of it. This alone furnishes the answer to our opponents, who ask us to introduce destructive elements into the system by which this has been accomplished.

# Franklin D. Roosevelt's
# First Inaugural Address (1933)

Franklin D. Roosevelt was the last president to be inaugurated on March 4; the Twentieth Amendment (1933) advanced the start of the president's term to January 20. During the long winter between Roosevelt's election against President Herbert C. Hoover in November 1932 (the most overwhelming victory against an incumbent president in history) and his inauguration in March, the Great Depression that had sunk the nation into economic inactivity worsened. Factories to produce goods and land to grow crops were abundant, but they had fallen into disuse. On February 14 Roosevelt himself was the target of an assassination attempt in Miami by an unemployed bricklayer, the only president-elect ever to be almost killed.

Roosevelt saw one of his main challenges in office as trying to restore the people's confidence in government and raise their personal morale. It was a challenge to which he was well suited, despite his privileged upbringing on a family estate in Hyde Park, New York. Always self-confident and infectiously optimistic, Roosevelt nonetheless had developed empathy with suffering from his bout with polio during the early 1920s. (The disease left him crippled for the rest of his life.) In the best-remembered line of his inaugural address, Roosevelt proclaimed that "the only thing we have to fear is fear it-self—nameless, unreasoning, unjustified terror which paralyzes needed efforts to convert retreat into advance."

Roosevelt also used his address to make clear his contempt for the probusiness policies of the Harding, Coolidge, and Hoover administrations. "The money changers have fled from their high seats in the temple of our civilization," he said. "We may now restore that temple to the ancient truths. The measure of that restoration lies in the extent to which we apply social values more noble than mere monetary profit."

Finally, Roosevelt pledged in general terms to pursue active and helpful government policies to combat the depression, using and perhaps extending the full powers of the presidency to do so. "It is to be hoped," Roosevelt said, "that the normal balance of executive and legislative authority may be wholly adequate to meet the unprecedented task before us. . . . But in the event that . . . the national emergency is still critical . . . I shall ask the Congress for the one remaining instrument to meet the crisis—broad executive power to wage a war against the emergency as great as the power that would be given me if we were in fact invaded by a foreign foe."

Roosevelt's cousin, former president Theodore Roosevelt, was the first to describe the presidency as a "bully *pulpit" for moral leadership. Franklin Roosevelt made full use of the pulpit in 1933 and afterward. In response to his inaugural address, one half million people wrote to express their thanks and support, an unprecedented out-pouring of mail. A week later, on March 13, Roosevelt delivered the first of twenty-seven informal radio ad-dresses, called "fireside chats," which marked a revolutionary advance in presidential communications with the American people.*

*In his acceptance speech at the 1932 Democratic convention, Roosevelt had pledged "a new deal for the American people." The vague phrase became the catchword for his presidency. More than anything else, "New Deal" came to mean presidentially sponsored fed-eral government programs to support both the general goal of economic pros-perity and the particular needs of peo-ple who were economically dis-tressed.* ~

President Hoover, Mr. Chief Justice, my friends:

This is a day of national consecration, and I am certain that my fellow-Americans expect that on my induction into the Presidency I will address them with a candor and a decision which the present situation of our nation impels.

This is pre-eminently the time to speak the truth, the whole truth, frankly and boldly. Nor need we shrink from honestly facing conditions in our country today. This great nation will endure as it has endured, will revive and will prosper.

So first of all let me assert my firm belief that the only thing we have to fear is fear itself—nameless, unreasoning, unjustified terror which paralyzes needed efforts to convert retreat into advance.

In every dark hour of our national life a leadership of frankness and vigor has met with that understanding and sup-port of the people themselves which is essential to victory. I am convinced that you will again give that support to lead-ership in these critical days.

In such a spirit on my part and on yours we face our common difficulties. They concern, thank God, only material things. Values have shrunken to fantas-tic levels; taxes have risen; our ability to pay has fallen, government of all kinds is faced by serious curtailment of in-come; the means of exchange are frozen in the currents of trade; the withered leaves of industrial enterprise lie on every side; farmers find no markets for their produce; the savings of many years in thousands of families are gone.

More important, a host of unem-ployed citizens face the grim problem of existence, and an equally great number toil with little return. Only a foolish optimist can deny the dark realities of the moment.

Yet our distress comes from no fail-ure of substance. We are stricken by no plague of locusts. Compared with the perils which our forefathers conquered because they believed and were not afraid, we have still much to be thank-ful for. Nature still offers her bounty and human efforts have multiplied it. Plenty is at our doorstep, but a gener-ous use of it languishes in the very sight of the supply.

Primarily, this is because the rulers of the exchange of mankind's goods have failed through their own stubbornness and their own incompetence, have ad-mitted their failure and abdicated. Practices of the unscrupulous money changers stand indicted in the court of public opinion, rejected by the hearts and minds of men. True, they have tried, but their efforts have been cast in the pattern of an outworn tradition. Faced by failure of credit, they have proposed only the lending of more money.

Stripped of the lure of profit by which to induce our people to follow their false leadership, they have resorted to exhortations, pleading tearfully for restored confidence. They know only the rules of a generation of self-seekers.

They have no vision, and when there is no vision the people perish.

The money changers have fled from their high seats in the temple of our civilization. We may now restore that temple to the ancient truths.

The measure of the restoration lies in the extent to which we apply social values more noble than mere monetary profit.

Happiness lies not in the mere possession of money; it lies in the joy of achievement, in the thrill of creative effort.

The joy and moral stimulation of work no longer must be forgotten in the mad chase of evanescent profits. These dark days will be worth all they cost us if they teach us that our true destiny is not to be ministered unto but to minister to ourselves and to our fellow-men.

Recognition of the falsity of material wealth as the standard of success goes hand in hand with the abandonment of the false belief that public office and high political position are to be valued only by the standards of pride of place and personal profit; and there must be an end to a conduct in banking and in business which too often has given to a sacred trust the likeness of callous and selfish wrongdoing.

Small wonder that confidence languishes, for it thrives only on honesty, on honor, on the sacredness of obligations, on faithful protection, on unselfish performance. Without them it cannot live.

Restoration calls, however, not for changes in ethics alone. This nation asks for action, and action now.

Our greatest primary task is to put people to work. This is no unsolvable problem if we face it wisely and courageously.

It can be accomplished in part by direct recruiting by the government itself, treating the task as we would treat the emergency of a war, but at the same time, through this employment accomplishing greatly needed projects to stimulate and reorganize the use of our natural resources.

Hand in hand with this, we must frankly recognize the overbalance of population in our industrial centers and, by engaging on a national scale in the redistribution, endeavor to provide a better use of the land for those best fitted for the land.

The task can be helped by definite efforts to raise the values of agricultural products and with this the power to purchase the output of our cities.

It can be helped by preventing realistically the tragedy of the growing loss, through foreclosure, of our small homes and our farms.

It can be helped by insistence that the Federal, State and local governments act forthwith on the demand that their cost be drastically reduced.

It can be helped by the unifying of relief activities which today are often scattered, uneconomical and unequal. It can be helped by national planning for and supervision of all forms of transportation and of communications and other utilities which have a definitely public character.

There are many ways in which it can be helped, but it can never be helped merely by talking about it. We must act, and act quickly.

Finally, in our progress toward a resumption of work we require two safeguards against a return of the evils of the old order; there must be a strict supervision of all banking and credits and investments; there must be an end to speculation with other people's money, and there must be provision for an adequate but sound currency.

These are the lines of attack. I shall presently urge upon a new Congress in special session detailed measures for their fulfillment, and I shall seek the immediate assistance of the several States.

Through this program of action we address ourselves to putting our own national house in order and making income balance outgo.

Our international trade relations, though vastly important, are, in point of time and necessity, secondary to the establishment of a sound national economy.

I favor as a practical policy the putting of first things first. I shall spare no effort to restore world trade by international economic readjustment, but the emergency at home cannot wait on that accomplishment.

The basic thought that guides these specific means of national recovery is not narrowly nationalistic.

It is the insistence, as a first consideration, upon the interdependence of the various elements in, and parts of, the United States—a recognition of the old and permanently important manifestation of the American spirit of the pioneer.

It is the way to recovery. It is the immediate way. It is the strongest assurance that the recovery will endure.

In the field of world policy I would dedicate this nation to the policy of the good neighbor—the neighbor who resolutely respects himself and, because he does so, respects the rights of others—the neighbor who respects his obligations and respects the sanctity of his agreements in and with a world of neighbors.

If I read the temper of our people correctly, we now realize as we have never before, our interdependence on each other; that we cannot merely take, but we must give as well; that if we are to go forward we must move as a trained and loyal army willing to sacrifice for the good of a common discipline, because, without such discipline, no progress is made, no leadership becomes effective.

We are, I know, ready and willing to submit our lives and property to such discipline because it makes possible a leadership which aims at a larger good.

This I propose to offer, pledging that the larger purposes will bind upon us all as a sacred obligation with a unity of duty hitherto evoked only in time of armed strife.

With this pledge taken, I assume unhesitatingly the leadership of this great army of our people, dedicated to a disciplined attack upon our common problems.

Action in this image and to this end is feasible under the form of government which we have inherited from our ancestors.

Our Constitution is so simple and practical that it is possible always to meet extraordinary needs by changes in emphasis and arrangement without loss of essential form.

That is why our constitutional system has proved itself the most superbly enduring political mechanism the modern world has produced. It has met every stress of vast expansion of territory, of foreign wars, of bitter internal strife, of world relations.

It is to be hoped that the normal balance of executive and legislative authority may be wholly adequate to meet the unprecedented task before us. But it may be that an unprecedented demand and need for undelayed action may call for temporary departure from that normal balance of public procedure.

I am prepared under my constitutional duty to recommend the measures that a stricken nation in the midst of a stricken world may require.

These measures, or such other measures as the Congress may build out of its experience and wisdom, I shall seek, within my constitutional authority, to bring to speedy adoption.

But in the event that the Congress shall fail to take one of these two courses, and in the event that the national emergency is still critical, I shall not evade the clear course of duty that will then confront me.

I shall ask the Congress for the one remaining instrument to meet the crisis—broad executive power to wage a war against the emergency as great as the power that would be given me if we were in fact invaded by a foreign foe.

For the trust reposed in me I will return the courage and the devotion that befit the time. I can do no less.

We face the arduous days that lie before us in the warm courage of national unity; with the clear consciousness of seeking old and precious moral values; with the clean satisfaction that comes from the stern performance of duty by old and young alike.

We aim at the assurance of a rounded and permanent national life.

We do not distrust the future of essential democracy. The people of the United States have not failed. In their need they have registered a mandate that they want direct, vigorous action.

They have asked for discipline and direction under leadership. They have made me the present instrument of their wishes. In the spirit of the gift I take it.

In this dedication of a nation we humbly ask the blessing of God. May He protect each and every one of us! May He guide me in the days to come!

# Humphrey's Executor v. United States (1935)

*Chief Justice William Howard Taft's opinion in the case of* Myers v. United States *(1926) was so sweeping in its defense of the president's constitutional power of removal as to suggest that no government official was immune from a presidential firing for any reason. (See "Myers v. United States," p. 192) By implication, members of independent regulatory agencies such as the Interstate Commerce Commission, the Food and Drug Administration, and the Federal Trade Commission served at the president's sufferance, even though Congress had assigned to these members terms of fixed duration that, by law, could be abridged only for "inefficiency, neglect of duty, or malfeasance in office."*

*In 1933 President Franklin D. Roosevelt wrote a series of letters to William E. Humphrey, an outspoken administration critic who had been appointed to a seven-year term on the Federal Trade Commission by President Herbert C. Hoover in 1931. The president's first letter asked Humphrey to resign as commissioner so that "the aims and purposes of the Administration with respect to the work of the Commission can be carried out most effectively with personnel of my own choosing." When Humphrey refused to resign, Roosevelt notified him on October 7 that he was fired.*

*Humphrey died in early 1934, never* *having accepted the propriety of his removal. But the executor of his estate sued the government for the salary Humphrey was not paid after being forced from office. The executor argued that Roosevelt had fired Humphrey for avowedly political, and thus legally impermissible, reasons.*

*The case reached the Supreme Court, which sided with Humphrey's executor by a unanimous 9-0 vote. Writing for the court, Justice George Sutherland argued that the* Myers *ruling did not apply to Humphrey's situation. Because Frank Myers, a postmaster, had been an employee of a federal agency that clearly was "an arm or an eye of the Executive," the president's constitutional responsibility as chief executive included the power to remove him, unfettered by Congress. But the Federal Trade Commission, like other independent regulatory agencies, was "an administrative body created by Congress to carry into effect legislative policies." Thus, Congress had the constitutional right to legislate its own guidelines for removing Humphrey or any other employee.*

*The Supreme Court's decision in* Humphrey's Executor *was announced on May 27, 1935. It was one of a historically unprecedented series of decisions in 1935 and 1936 (and hardly the most consequential of them) that overturned presidential actions and ad-*

*ministration-supported laws. Yet the ruling in* Humphrey's Executor *reportedly infuriated Roosevelt more than any other—he took it as a personal insult by the justices—and, in the opinion of some of his aides, provoked the president to try to "pack" the Court.* (See "Franklin D. Roosevelt's 'Court-packing' Address," p. 270.) ~

MR. JUSTICE SUTHERLAND delivered the opinion of the Court.

Plaintiff brought suit in the Court of Claims against the United States to recover a sum of money alleged to be due the deceased for salary as a Federal Trade Commissioner from October 8, 1933, when the President undertook to remove him from office, to the time of his death on February 14, 1934. The court below has certified to this court two questions (Act of February 13, 1925, § 3 (a), c. 229, 43 Stat. 936, 939; 28 U.S.C. § 288), in respect of the power of the President to make the removal. The material facts which give rise to the questions are as follows:

William E. Humphrey, the decedent, on December 10, 1931, was nominated by President Hoover to succeed himself as a member of the Federal Trade Commission, and was confirmed by the United States Senate. He was duly commissioned for a term of seven years expiring September 25, 1938; and, after taking the required oath of office, entered upon his duties. On July 25, 1933, President Roosevelt addressed a letter to the commissioner asking for his resignation, on the ground "that the aims and purposes of the Administration with respect to the work of the Commission can be carried out most effectively with personnel of my own selection," but disclaiming any reflection upon the commissioner personally or upon his services. The commissioner replied, asking time to consult his friends. After some further correspondence upon the subject, the President on August 31, 1933, wrote the commissioner expressing the hope that the resignation would be forthcoming and saying:

"You will, I know, realize that I do not feel that your mind and my mind go along together on either the policies or the administering of the Federal Trade Commission, and, frankly, I think it is best for the people of this country that I should have a full confidence."

The commissioner declined to resign; and on October 7, 1933, the President wrote him:

"Effective as of this date you are hereby removed from the office of Commissioner of the Federal Trade Commission."

Humphrey never acquiesced in this action, but continued thereafter to insist that he was still a member of the commission, entitled to perform its duties and receive the compensation provided by law at the rate of $10,000 per annum. Upon these and other facts set forth in the certificate, which we deem it unnecessary to recite, the following questions are certified:

"1. Do the provisions of section 1 of the Federal Trade Commission Act, stating that 'any commissioner may be removed by the President for inefficiency, neglect of duty, or malfeasance in office,' restrict or limit the power of the President to remove a commissioner except upon one or more of the causes named?

"If the foregoing question is answered in the affirmative, then—

"2. If the power of the President to remove a commissioner is restricted or limited as shown by the foregoing interrogatory and the answer made thereto, is such a restriction or limitation valid under the Constitution of the United States? "

The Federal Trade Commission Act, c. 311, 38 Stat. 717; 15 U.S.C. § § 41, 42, creates a commission of five members to be appointed by the President by and with the advice and consent of the Senate, and § 1 provides:

"Not more than three of the commissioners shall be members of the same political party. The first commissioners appointed shall continue in office for terms of three, four, five, six, and seven years, respectively, from the date of the taking effect of this Act, the term of each to be designated by the President, but their successors shall be appointed for terms of seven years, except that any person chosen to fill a vacancy shall be appointed only for the unexpired term of the commissioner whom he shall succeed. The commission shall choose a chairman from its own membership. No commissioner shall engage in any other business, vocation, or employment. Any commissioner may be removed by the President for inefficiency, neglect of duty, or malfeasance in office...."

Section 5 of the act in part provides:

"That unfair methods of competition in commerce are hereby declared unlawful.

The commission is hereby empowered and directed to prevent persons, partnerships, or corporations, except banks, and common carriers subject to the Acts to regulate commerce, from using unfair methods of competition in commerce."

In exercising this power, the commission must issue a complaint stating its charges and giving notice of hearing upon a day to be fixed. A person, partnership, or corporation proceeded against is given the right to appear at the time and place fixed and show cause why an order to cease and desist should not be issued. There is provision for intervention by others interested. If the commission finds the method of competition is one prohibited by the act, it is directed to make a report in writing stating its findings as to the facts, and to issue and cause to be served a cease and desist order. If the order is disobeyed, the commission may apply to the appropriate circuit court of appeals for its enforcement. The party subject to the order may seek and obtain a review in the circuit court of appeals in a manner provided by the act.

Section 6, among other things, gives the commission wide powers of investigation in respect of certain corporations subject to the act, and in respect of other matters, upon which it must report to Congress with recommendations. Many such investigations have been made, and some have served as the basis of congressional legislation.

Section 7 provides:

"That in any suit in equity brought by or under the direction of the Attorney General as provided in the antitrust Acts, the court may, upon the conclusion of the testimony therein, if it shall be then of opinion that the complainant is entitled to relief, refer said suit to the commission, as a master in chancery, to ascertain and report an appropriate form of decree therein. The commission shall proceed upon such notice to the parties and under such rules of procedure as the court may prescribe, and upon the coming in of such report such exceptions may be filed and such proceedings had in relation thereto as upon the report of a master in other equity causes, but the court may adopt or reject such report, in whole or in part, and enter such decree as the nature of the case may in its judgment require."

*First.* The question first to be considered is whether, by the provisions of § 1 of the Federal Trade Commission Act already quoted, the President's power is limited to removal for the specific causes enumerated therein. The negative contention of the government is based principally upon the decision of this court in *Shurtleff v. United States,* 189 U.S. 311. That case involved the power of the President to remove a general appraiser of merchandise appointed under the Act of June 10, 1890, 26 Stat. 131. Section 12 of the act provided for the appointment by the President, by and with the advice and consent of the Senate, of nine general appraisers of merchandise who "may be removed from office at any time by the President for inefficiency, neglect of duty, or malfeasance in office." The President removed Shurtleff without assigning any course therefor. The Court of Claims dismissed plaintiff's petition to recover salary, upholding the President's power to remove for causes other than those stated. In this court Shurtleff relied upon the maxim *expressio unius est exclusio alterius;* but this court held that while the rule expressed in the maxim was a very proper one and founded upon justifiable reasoning in many instances, it "should not be accorded controlling weight when to do so would involve the alteration of the universal practice of the government for over a century and the consequent curtailment of the powers of the executive in such an unusual manner." What the court meant by this expression appears from a reading of the opinion. That opinion—after saying that no term of office was fixed by the act and that, with the exception of judicial officers provided for by the Constitution, no civil officer has ever held office by life tenure since the foundation of the government—points out that to construe the statute as contended for by Shurtleff would give the appraiser the right to hold office during his life or until found guilty of some act specified in the statute the result of which would be a complete revolution in respect of the general tenure of office, effected by implication with regard to that particular office only.

"We think it quite inadmissible," the court said (pp. 316, 318), "to attribute an intention on the part of Congress to make such an extraordinary change in the usual rule governing the tenure of office, and one which is to be applied to this particular office only, without stating such intention in plain and explicit language, instead of leaving it to be implied from doubtful inferences.... We cannot bring ourselves to the belief that Congress ever intended this result while omitting to use language which would put that intention beyond doubt."

These circumstances, which led the court to reject the maxim as inapplicable, are exceptional. In the face of the unbroken precedent against life tenure, except in the case of the judiciary, the conclusion that Congress intended that, from among all other civil officers, appraisers alone should be selected to hold office for life was so extreme as to forbid, in the opinion of the court, any ruling which would produce that result if it reasonably could be avoided. The situation here presented is plainly and wholly different. The statute fixes a term of office, in accordance with many precedents. The first commissioners appointed are to continue in office for terms of three, four, five, six, and seven years, respectively; and their successors are to be appointed for terms of seven years—any commissioner being subject to removal by the President for inefficiency, neglect of duty, or malfeasance in office. The words of the act are definite and unambiguous.

The government says the phrase "continue in office" is of no legal significance and, moreover, applies only to the first commissioners. We think it has significance. It may be that, literally, its application is restricted as suggested; but it, nevertheless, lends support to a view contrary to that of the government as to the meaning of the entire requirement in respect of tenure; for it is not easy to suppose that Congress intended to secure the first commissioners against removal except for the causes specified and deny like security to their successors. Putting this phrase aside, however, the fixing of a definite term subject to removal for cause, unless there be some countervailing provision or circumstance indicating the contrary, which here we are unable to find, is enough to establish the legislative intent that the term is not to be curtailed in the absence of such cause. But if the intention of Congress that no removal should be made during the specified term except for one or more of the enumerated causes were not clear upon the face of the statute, as we think it is, it would be made clear by a consideration of the character of the commission and the legislative history which accompanied and preceded the passage of the act.

The commission is to be non-partisan; and it must, from the very nature of its duties, act with entire impartiality. It is charged with the enforcement of no policy except the policy of the law. Its duties are neither political nor executive, but predominantly quasi-judicial and quasi-legislative. Like the Interstate Commerce Commission, its members are called upon to exercise the trained judgment of a body of experts "appointed by law and informed by experience." *Illinois Central R. Co.* v. *Interstate Commerce Comm'n,* 206 U.S. 441, 454; *Standard Oil Co.* v. *United States,* 283 U.S. 235, 238-239.

The legislative reports in both houses of Congress clearly reflect the view that a fixed term was necessary to the effective and fair administration of the law. In the report to the Senate (No. 597, 63d Cong., 2d Sess., pp. 10-11) the Senate Committee on Interstate Commerce, in support of the bill which afterwards became the act in question, after referring to the provision fixing the term of office at seven years, so arranged that the membership would not be subject to complete change at any one time, said:

"The work of this commission will be of a most exacting and difficult character, demanding persons who have experience in the problems to be met— that is, a proper knowledge of both the public requirements and the practical affairs of industry. It is manifestly desirable that the terms of the commissioners shall be long enough to give them an opportunity to acquire the expertness in dealing with these special questions concerning industry that comes from experience."

The report declares that one advantage which the commission possessed over the Bureau of Corporations (an executive subdivision in the Department of Commerce which was abolished by the act) lay in the fact of its independence, and that it was essential that the commission should not be open to the suspicion of partisan direction. The report quotes (p. 22) a statement to the committee by Senator Newlands, who reported the bill, that the tribunal should be of high character and "independent of any department of the government ... a board or commission of dignity, permanence, and ability, independent of executive authority, except in its selection, and independent in character."

The debates in both houses demonstrate that the prevailing view was that the commission was not to be "subject to anybody in the government by ... only to the people of the United States"; free from "political domination or control" or the "probability or possibility of such a thing"; to be "separate and apart from any existing department of the government—not subject to the orders of the President."

More to the same effect appears in the debates, which were long and thorough and contain nothing to the contrary. While the general rule precludes the use of these debates to explain the meaning of the words of the statute, they may be considered as reflecting light upon its general purposes and the evils which it sought to remedy. *Federal Trade Comm'n* v. *Raladam Co.,* 283 U.S. 643, 650.

Thus, the language of the act, the legislative reports, and the general purposes of the legislation as reflected by the debates, all combine to demonstrate the Congressional intent to create a body of experts who shall gain experience by length of service—a body which shall be independent of executive authority, *except in its selection,* and free to exercise its judgment without the leave or hindrance of any other official or any department of the government. To the accomplishment of these purposes, it is clear that Congress was of opinion that length and certainty of tenure would vitally contribute. And to hold that, nevertheless, the members of the commission continue in office at the mere will of the President, might be to thwart, in large measure, the very ends which Congress sought to realize by definitely fixing the term of office.

We conclude that the intent of the act is to limit the executive power of removal to the causes enumerated, the existence of none of which is claimed here; and we pass to the second question.

*Second.* To support its contention that the removal provision of § 1, as we have just construed it, is an unconstitutional interference with the executive power of the President, the government's chief reliance is *Myers* v. *United States,* 272 U.S. 52. That case has been so recently decided, and the prevailing and dissenting opinions so fully review the general subject of the power of executive removal, that further discussion would add little of value to the wealth of material there collected. These opinions examine at length the historical, legislative and judicial data bearing upon the question, beginning with what is called "the decision of 1789" in the first Congress and coming down almost to the day when the opinions were delivered. They occupy 243 pages of the volume in which they are printed. Nevertheless, the narrow point actually decided was only that the President had power to remove a postmaster of the first class, without the advice and consent of the Senate as required by act of Congress. In the course of the opinion of the court, expressions occur which tend to sustain the government's contention, but these are beyond the

point involved and, therefore, do not come within the rule of *stare decisis.* In so far as they are out of harmony with the views here set forth, these expressions are disapproved. A like situation was presented in the case of *Cohens* v. *Virginia,* 6 Wheat. 264, 399, in respect of certain general expressions in the opinion in *Marbury* v. *Madison,* 1 Cranch 137. Chief Justice Marshall, who delivered the opinion in the *Marbury* case, speaking again for the court in the *Cohens* case, said:

"It is a maxim, not to be disregarded, that general expressions, in every opinion, are to be taken in connection with the case in which those expressions are used. If they go beyond the case, they may be respected, but ought not to control the judgment in a subsequent suit, when the very point is presented for decision. The reason of this maxim is obvious. The question actually before the Court is investigated with care, and considered in its full extent. Other principles which may serve to illustrate it, are considered in their relation to the case decided, but their possible bearing on all other cases is seldom completely investigated."

And he added that these general expressions in the case of *Marbury* v. *Madison* were to be understood with the limitations put upon them by the opinion in the *Cohens* case. See, also, *Carroll* v. *Lessee of Carroll,* 16 How. 275, 286-287; *O'Donoghue* v. *United States,* 289 U.S. 516, 550.

The office of a postmaster is so essentially unlike the office now involved that the decision in the *Myers* case cannot be accepted as controlling our decision here. A postmaster is an executive officer restricted to the performance of executive functions. He is charged with no duty at all related to either the legislative or judicial power. The actual decision in the *Myers* case finds support in the theory that such an officer is merely one of the units in the executive department and, hence, inherently subject to the exclusive and illimitable power of removal by the Chief Executive, whose subordinate and aid he is. Putting aside *dicta,* which may be followed if sufficiently persuasive but which are not controlling, the necessary reach of the decision goes far enough to include all purely executive officers. It goes no farther;—much less does it include an officer who occupies no place in the executive department and who exercises no part of the executive power vested by the Constitution in the President.

The Federal Trade Commission is an administrative body created by Congress to carry into effect legislative policies embodied in the statute in accordance with the legislative standard therein prescribed, and to perform other specified duties as a legislative or as a judicial aid. Such a body cannot in any proper sense be characterized as an arm or an eye of the executive. Its duties are performed without executive leave and, in the contemplation of the statute, must be free from executive control. In administering the provisions of the statute in respect of "unfair methods of competition"—that is to say in filling in and administering the details embodied by that general standard—the commission acts in part quasi-legislatively and in part quasi-judicially. In making investigations and reports thereon for the information of Congress under § 6, in aid of the legislative power, it acts as a legislative agency. Under § 7, which authorizes the commission to act as a master in chancery under rules prescribed by the court, it acts as an agency of the judiciary. To the extent that it exercises any executive function—as distinguished from executive power in the constitutional sense—it does so in the discharge and effectuation of its quasi-legislative or quasi-judicial powers, or as an agency of the legislative or judicial departments of the government.[1]

If Congress is without authority to prescribe causes for removal of members of the trade commission and limit executive power of removal accordingly, that power at once becomes practically all-inclusive in respect of civil officers with the exception of the judiciary provided for by the Constitution. The Solicitor General, at the bar, apparently recognizing this to be true, with commendable candor, agreed that his view in respect of the removability of members of the Federal Trade Commission necessitated a like view in respect of the Interstate Commerce Commission and the Court of Claims. We are thus confronted with the serious question whether not only the members of these quasi-legislative and quasi-judicial bodies, but the judges of the legislative Court of Claims, exercising judicial power (*Williams* v. *United States,* 289 U.S. 553, 565-567), continue in office only at the pleasure of the President.

We think it plain under the Constitution that illimitable power of removal is not possessed by the President in respect of officers of the character of those just named. The authority of Congress, in creating quasi-legislative or quasi-judicial agencies, to require them to act in discharge of their duties independently of executive control cannot well be doubted; and that authority includes, as an appropriate incident, power to fix the period during which they shall continue in office, and to forbid their removal except for cause in the meantime. For it is quite evident that one who holds his office only during the pleasure of another, cannot be depended upon to maintain an attitude of independence against the latter's will.

The fundamental necessity of maintaining each of the three general departments of government entirely free from the control or coercive influence, direct or indirect, of either of the others, has often been stressed and is hardly open to serious question. So much is implied in the very fact of the separation of the powers of these departments by the Constitution; and in the rule which recognizes their essential co-equality. The sound application of a principle that makes one master in his own house precludes him from imposing his control in the house of another who is master there. James Wilson, one of the framers of the Constitution and a former justice of this court, said that the independence of each department required that its proceedings "should be free from the remotest influence, direct or indirect, of either of the other two powers." Andrews, The Works of James Wilson (1896), vol. 1, p. 367. And Mr. Justice Story in the first volume of his work on the Constitution, 4th ed., § 530, citing No. 48 of the Federalist, said that neither of the departments in reference to each other "ought to possess, directly or indirectly, an overruling influence in the administration of their respective powers." And see *O'Donoghue* v. *United States, supra,* at pp. 530-531.

The power of removal here claimed for the President falls within this principle, since its coercive influence threatens the independence of a commission, which is not only wholly disconnected from the executive department, but which, as already fully appears, was created by Congress as a means of carrying into operation legislative and judicial powers, and as an agency of the legislative and judicial departments.

In the light of the question now under consideration, we have reëxamined the precedents referred to in the *Myers* case, and find nothing in them to justify a conclusion contrary to that which we have reached. The so-called "decision of 1789" had relation to a bill proposed by Mr. Madison to establish an executive Department of Foreign Affairs. The bill provided that the principal officer was "to be removable from office by the President of the United States." This clause was changed to read "whenever the principal officer shall be removed from office by the President of the United States" certain things should follow, thereby, in connection with the debates, recognizing and confirming, as the court thought in the *Myers* case, the sole power of the President in the matter. We shall not discuss the subject further, since it is so fully covered by the opinions in the *Myers* case, except to say that the office under consideration by Congress was not only purely executive, but the officer one who was responsible to the President, and to him alone, in a very definite sense. A reading of the debates shows that the President's illimitable power of removal was not considered in respect of other than executive officers. And it is pertinent to observe that when, at a later time, the tenure of office for the Controller of the Treasury was under consideration, Mr. Madison quite evidently thought that, since the duties of the office were not purely of an executive nature but partook of the judiciary quality as well, a different rule in respect of executive removal might well apply. 1 Annals of Congress, cols. 611-612.

In *Marbury* v. *Madison, supra,* pp. 162, 165-166, it is made clear that Chief Justice Marshall was of opinion that a justice of the peace for the District of Columbia was not removable at the will of the President; and that there was a distinction between such an officer and officers appointed to aid the President in the performance of his constitutional duties. In the latter case, the distinction he saw was that "their acts are his acts" and his will, therefore, controls; and, by way of illustration, he adverted to the act establishing the Department of Foreign Affairs, which was the subject of the "decision of 1789."

The result of what we now have said is this: Whether the power of the President to remove an officer shall prevail over the authority of Congress to condition the power by fixing a definite term and precluding a removal except for cause, will depend upon the character of the office; the *Myers* decision, affirming the power of the President alone to make the removal is confined to purely executive officers; and as to officers of the kind here under consideration, we hold that no removal can be made during the prescribed term for which the officer is appointed, except for one or more of the causes named in the applicable statute.

To the extent that, between the decision in the *Myers* case, which sustains the unrestrictable power of the President to remove purely executive officers, and our present decision that such power does not extend to an office such as that here involved, there shall remain a field of doubt, we leave such cases as may fall within it for future consideration and determination as they may arise.

In accordance with the foregoing, the questions submitted are answered.

> *Question No. 1, Yes.*
> *Question No. 2, Yes.*

MR. JUSTICE McREYNOLDS agrees that both questions should be answered in the affirmative. A separate opinion in *Myers* v. *United States,* 272 U.S. 178, states his views concerning the power of the President to remove appointees.

## Note

1. The provision of § 6 (d) of the act which authorizes the President to direct an investigation and report by the commission in relation to alleged violations of the anti-trust acts, is so obviously collateral to the main design of the act as not to detract from the force of this general statement as to the character of that body.

# United States v. Curtiss-Wright Export Corporation (1936)

United States v. Curtiss-Wright *is perhaps the most important Supreme Court decision in history concerning the president's constitutional powers in foreign affairs. The expansive view of presidential power that the decision endorsed is all the more remarkable because in 1935 and 1936 the Court had been unusually hostile to the New Deal domestic policies of President Franklin D. Roosevelt. (See "Humphrey's Executor v. United States," p. 241, and "Franklin D. Roosevelt's 'Court-packing' Address," p. 270.) Indeed, the author of the Court's opinion in the case, Justice George Sutherland, was one of the most ardent judicial foes of the New Deal. Yet, in* United States v. Curtiss-Wright, *Sutherland and all but one of his fellow justices promulgated a constitutional theory that regarded "the President as the sole organ of the federal government in the field of international relations," even though the Constitution had not explicitly conferred such a role.*

*The case was triggered by the government's effort to limit the so-called Chaco War between Bolivia and Paraguay, which had taken 100,000 lives and jeopardized the peace of all of South America. On May 28, 1934, Congress passed a law that granted the president the power to prohibit, at his discretion, the sale of any or all U.S.-made arms to the two nations. Later*

*that day, Roosevelt issued an order that banned all such sales.*

*In 1936 the Curtiss-Wright Export Corporation was indicted for conspiring to sell machine guns to Bolivia, a violation of the president's order. The corporation and its officers replied in federal court by challenging the constitutionality of the law under which the president acted. They claimed that Congress had made an unconstitutional delegation of power to the president.*

*In favoring the president's position in the case, the Court could simply have decided that Congress's delegation of power to the president was constitutional. But in several recent rulings that had overturned Roosevelt's New Deal domestic programs, Sutherland and his conservative colleagues had accused Congress of delegating power to the president indiscriminately. Thus, a new constitutional theory was needed if the Court were to justify the position of the president and Congress in the* Curtiss-Wright *case.*

*Sutherland found his theory in the concept of sovereignty. The United States had been formed as a nation by previously separate states. These states had domestic powers at the time they united, Sutherland argued, and in writing the Constitution they had described which of these powers would be granted to the national government. But because the states had never had power to deal in international relations, the national government that was formed by the Constitution did not have to rely for its foreign affairs powers on any explicit constitutional authorization. Instead, as the plan of government for a nation, the Constitution implicitly granted the national government all the traditional sovereign powers that any nation wields, except as specifically limited by the document itself.*

*The sovereign powers of the United States in international affairs, Sutherland continued, obviously reside in the president: "he, not Congress, has the better opportunity of knowing the conditions which prevail in foreign countries, and especially is this true in time of war. He has his confidential sources of information. He has his agents in the form of diplomatic, consular, and other officials." Indeed, Sutherland and the Court suggested that Roosevelt may not even have needed Congress's permission to ban the sale of arms to Bolivia and Paraguay.* ~

MR. JUSTICE SUTHERLAND delivered the opinion of the Court.

On January 27, 1936, an indictment was returned in the court below, the first count of which charges that appellees, beginning with the 29th day of May, 1934, conspired to sell in the United States certain arms of war, namely fifteen machine guns, to Bolivia, a country then engaged in armed conflict in the Chaco, a violation of the Joint Resolution of Congress approved May 28, 1934, and the provisions of a proclamation issued on the same day by the President of the United States pursuant to authority conferred by § 1 of the resolution. In pursuance of the conspiracy, the commission of certain overt acts was alleged, details of which need not be stated. The Joint Resolution (c.

365, 48 Stat. 811) follows:

"*Resolved by the Senate and House of Representatives of the United States of America in Congress assembled,* That if the President finds that the prohibition of the sale of arms and munitions of war in the United States to those countries now engaged in armed conflict in the Chaco may contribute to the reestablishment of peace between those countries, and if after consultation with the governments of other American Republics and with their cooperation, as well as that of such other governments as he may deem necessary, he makes proclamation to that effect, it shall be unlawful to sell, except under such limitations and exceptions as the President prescribes, any arms or munitions of war in any place in the United States to the countries now engaged in that armed conflict, or to any person, company, or association acting in the interest of either country, until otherwise ordered by the President or by Congress.

"Sec. 2. Whoever sells any arms or munitions of war in violation of section 1 shall, on conviction, be punished by a fine not exceeding $10,000 or by imprisonment not exceeding two years, or both."

The President's proclamation (48 Stat. 1744), after reciting the terms of the Joint Resolution, declares:

"Now, therefore, I, Franklin D. Roosevelt, President of the United States of America, acting under and by virtue of the authority conferred in me by the said joint resolution of Congress, do hereby declare and proclaim that I have found that the prohibition of the sale of arms and munitions of war in the United States to those countries now engaged in armed conflict in the Chaco may contribute to the reestablishment of peace between those countries, and that I have consulted with the governments of other American Republics and have been assured of the cooperation of such governments as I have deemed necessary as contemplated by the said joint resolution; and I do hereby admonish all citizens of the United States and every person to abstain from every violation of the provisions of the joint resolution above set forth, hereby made applicable to Bolivia and Paraguay, and I do hereby warn them that all violations of such provisions will be rigorously prosecuted.

"And I do hereby enjoin upon all officers of the United States charged with the execution of the laws thereof, the utmost diligence in preventing violations of the said joint resolution and this my proclamation issued thereunder, and in bringing to trial and punishment any offenders against the same.

"And I do hereby delegate to the Secretary of State the power of prescribing exceptions and limitations to the application of the said joint resolution of May 28, 1934, as made effective by this my proclamation issued thereunder."

On November 14, 1935, this proclamation was revoked (49 Stat. 3480), in the following terms:

"Now, therefore, I, Franklin D. Roosevelt, President of the United States of America, do hereby declare and proclaim that I have found that the prohibition of the sale of arms and munitions of war in the United States to Bolivia or Paraguay will no longer be necessary as a contribution to the reestablishment of peace between those countries, and the above-mentioned Proclamation of May 28, 1934, is hereby revoked as to the sale of arms and munitions of war to Bolivia or Paraguay from and after November 29, 1935, provided, however, that this action shall not have the effect of releasing or extinguishing any penalty, forfeiture or liability incurred under the aforesaid Proclamation of May 28, 1934, or the Joint Resolution of Congress approved by the President on the same date; and that the said Proclamation and Joint Resolution shall be treated as remaining in force for the purpose of sustaining any proper action or prosecution for the enforcement of such penalty, forfeiture or liability."

Appellees severally demurred to the first count of the indictment on the grounds (1) that it did not charge facts sufficient to show the commission by appellees of any offense against any law of the United States; (2) that this count of the indictment charges a conspiracy to violate the joint resolution and the Presidential proclamation, both of which had expired according to the terms of the joint resolution by reason of the revocation contained in the Presidential proclamation of November 14, 1935, and were not in force at the time when the indictment was found. The points urged in support of the demurrers were, first, that the joint resolution effects an invalid delegation of legislation power to the executive; second, that the joint resolution never became effective because of the failure of the President to find essential jurisdictional facts; and third, that the second proclamation operated to put an end to the alleged liability under the joint resolution.

The court below sustained the demurrers upon the first point, but overruled them on the second and third points. 14 F. Supp. 230. The government appealed to this court under the provisions of the Criminal Appeals Act of March 2, 1907, 34 Stat. 1246, as amended, U.S.C. Title 18, § 682. That act authorizes the United States to appeal from a district court direct to this court in criminal cases where, among other things, the decision sustaining a demurrer to the indictment or any count thereof is based upon the invalidity or construction of the statute upon which the indictment is founded.

*First.* It is contended that by the Joint Resolution, the going into effect and continued operation of the resolution was conditioned (a) upon the President's judgment as to its beneficial effect upon the reestablishment of peace between the countries engaged in armed conflict in the Chaco; (b) upon the making of a proclamation, which was left to his unfettered discretion, thus constituting an attempted substitution of the President's will for that of Congress; (c) upon the making of a proclamation putting an end to the operation of the resolution, which again was left to the President's unfettered discretion; and (d) further, that the extent of its operation in particular cases was subject to limitation and exception by the President, controlled by no standard. In each of these particulars, appellees urge that Congress abdicated its essential functions and delegated them to the Executive.

Whether, if the Joint Resolution had related solely to internal affairs it would be open to the challenge that it constituted an unlawful delegation of legislative power to the Executive, we find it unnecessary to determine. The whole aim of the resolution is to affect a situation entirely external to the United States, and falling within the category of foreign affairs. The determination which we are called to make, therefore, is whether the Joint Resolution, as applied to that situation, is vulnerable to attack under the rule that forbids a delegation of the law-making power. In other words, assuming (but not deciding) that the challenged delegation, if it were confined to internal affairs, would be invalid, may it nevertheless be sustained on the ground that its exclusive aim is to afford a remedy for a hurtful condition within foreign territory?

It will contribute to the elucidation of the question if we first consider the differences between the powers of the federal government in respect of foreign or external affairs and those in respect of domestic or internal affairs. That there are differences between them, and that these differences are fundamental, may not be doubted.

The two classes of powers are different, both in respect of their origin and their nature. The broad statement that the federal government can exercise no powers except those specifically enumerated in the Constitution, and such implied powers as are necessary and proper to carry into effect the enumerated powers, is categorically true only in respect of our internal affairs. In that field, the primary purpose of the Constitution was to carve from the general mass of legislative powers *then possessed by the states* such portions as it was thought desirable to vest in the federal government, leaving those not included in the enumeration still in the states. *Carter* v. *Carter Coal Co.,* 298 U.S. 238, 294. That this doctrine applies only to powers which the states had, is self evident. And since the states severally never possessed international powers, such powers could not have been carved from the mass of state powers but obviously were transmitted to the United States from some other source. During the colonial period, those powers were possessed exclusively by and were entirely under the control of the Crown. By the Declaration of Independence, "the Representatives of the United States of America" declared the United [not the several] Colonies to be free and independent states, and as such to have "full Power to levy War, conclude Peace, contract Alliances, establish Commerce and to do all other Acts and Things which Independent States may of right do."

As a result of the separation from Great Britain by the colonies acting as a unit, the powers of external sovereignty passed from the Crown not to the colonies severally, but to the colonies in their collective and corporate capacity as the United States of America. Even before the declaration, the colonies were a unit in foreign affairs, acting through a common agency—namely the Continental Congress, composed of delegates from the thirteen colonies. That agency exercised the powers of war and peace, raised an army, created a navy, and finally adopted the Declaration of Independence. Rulers come and go; governments end and forms of government change; but sovereignty survives. A political society cannot endure without a supreme will somewhere. Sovereignty is never held in suspense. When, therefore, the external sovereignty of Great Britain in respect of the colonies ceased, it immediately passed to the Union. *See Penhallow* v. *Doane,* 3 Dall. 54, 80-81. That fact was given practical application almost at once. The treaty of peace, made on September 23, 1783, was concluded between his Brittanic Majesty and the "United States of America." 8 Stat.—European Treaties—80.

The Union existed before the Constitution, which was ordained and established among other things to form "a more perfect Union." Prior to that event, it is clear that the Union, declared by the Articles of Confederation to be "perpetual," was the sole possessor of external sovereignty and in the Union it remained without change save in so far as the Constitution in express terms qualified its exercise. The Framers' Convention was called and exerted its powers upon the irrefutable postulate that though the states were several their people in respect of foreign affairs were one. Compare *The Chinese Exclusion Case,* 130 U.S. 581, 604, 606. In that convention, the entire absence of state power to deal with those affairs was thus forcefully stated by Rufus King:

"The states were not 'sovereigns' in the sense contended for by some. They did not possess the peculiar features of sovereignty,—they could not make war, nor peace, nor alliances, nor treaties. Considering them as political beings, they were dumb, for they could not speak to any foreign sovereign whatever. They were deaf, for they would not hear any propositions from such sovereign. They had not even the organs or faculties of defence or offence, for they could not of themselves raise troops, or equip vessels, for war." 5 Elliott's Debates 212.[1]

It results that the investment of the federal government with the powers of external sovereignity did not depend upon the affirmative grants of the Constitution. The powers to declare and wage war, to conclude peace, to make treaties, to maintain diplomatic relations with other sovereignities, if they had never been mentioned in the Constitution, would have vested in the federal government as necessary concomitants of nationality. Neither the Constitution nor the laws passed in pursuance of it have any force in foreign territory unless in respect of our own citizens (see *American Banana Co.* v. *United Fruit Co.,* 213 U.S. 347, 356); and operations of the nation in such territory must be governed by treaties, international understandings and compacts, and the principles of international law. As a member of the family of nations, the right and power of the United States in that field are equal to the right and power of the other members of the international family. Otherwise, the United States is not completely sovereign. The power to acquire territory by discovery and occupation (*Jones* v. *United States,* 137 U.S. 202, 212), the power to expel undesirable aliens (*Fong Yue Ting* v. *United States,* 149 U.S. 698, 705 *et seq.*), the power to make such international agreements as do not constitute treaties in the constitutional sense (*Altman & Co.* v. *United States,* 224 U.S. 583, 600-601; Crandall, Treaties, Their Making and Enforcement, 2d ed., p. 102 and note 1), none of which is expressly affirmed by the Constitution, nevertheless exist as inherently inseparable from the conception of nationality. This the court recognized, and in each of the cases cited found the warrant for its conclusions not in the provisions of the Constitution, but in the law of nations.

In *Burnet* v. *Brooks,* 288 U.S. 378, 396, we said, "As a nation with all the attributes of sovereignty, the United States is vested with all the powers of government necessary to maintain an effective control of international relations." Cf. *Carter* v. *Carter Coal Co., supra,* p. 295.

Not only, as we have shown, is the federal power over external affairs in origin and essential character different from that over internal affairs, but participation in the exercise of the power is significantly limited. In this vast external realm, with its important, complicated, delicate and manifold problems, the President alone has the power to speak or listen as a representative of the nation. He *makes* treaties with the advice and consent of the Senate; but he alone negotiates. Into the field of negotiation the Senate cannot intrude; and Congress itself is powerless to invade it. As Marshall said in his great argument of March 7, 1800, in the House of Representatives, "The President is the sole organ of the nation in its external relations, and its sole representative with foreign nations." Annals, 6th Cong., col. 613. The Senate Committee on Foreign Relations at a very early day in our history (February 15, 1816), reported to the Senate, among other things, as follows:

"The President is the constitutional representative of the United States with regard to foreign nations. He manages our concerns with foreign nations and must necessarily be most competent to determine when, how, and upon what subjects negotiation may be urged with the greatest prospect of success. For his conduct he is responsible to the Constitution. The committee consider this responsibility the surest pledge for the faithful discharge of his duty. They think the interference of the Senate in the direction of foreign negotiations calculated to diminish that responsibility and thereby to impair the best security for the national safety. The nature of transactions with foreign nations, moreover, requires caution and unity of de-sign, and their success frequently depends on secrecy and dispatch." U.S. Senate, Reports, Committee on Foreign Relations, vol. 8, p. 24.

It is important to bear in mind that we are here dealing not alone with an authority vested in the President by an exertion of legislative power, but with such an authority plus the very delicate, plenary and exclusive power of the President as the sole organ of the federal government in the field of international relations—a power which does not require as a basis for its exercise an act of Congress, but which, of course, like every other governmental power, must be exercised in subordination to the applicable provisions of the Constitution. It is quite apparent that it, in the maintenance of our international relations, embarrassment—perhaps serious embarrassment—is to be avoided and success for our aims achieved, congressional legislation which is to be made effective through negotiation and inquiry within the international field must often accord to the President a degree of discretion and freedom from statutory restriction which would not be admissible were domestic affairs alone involved. Moreover, he, not Congress, has the better opportunity of knowing the conditions which prevail in foreign countries, and especially is this true in time of war. He has his confidential sources of information. He has his agents in the form of diplomatic, consular and other officials. Secrecy in respect of information gathered by them may be highly necessary, and the premature disclosure of it productive by harmful results. Indeed, so clearly is this true that the first President refused to accede to a request to lay before the House of Representatives the instructions, correspondence and documents relating to the negotiation of the Jay Treaty—a refusal the wisdom of which was recognized by the House itself and has never since been doubted. In his reply to the request, President Washington said:

"The nature of foreign negotiations requires caution, and their success must often depend on secrecy; and even when brought to a conclusion a full disclosure of all the measures, demands, or eventual concessions which may have been proposed or contemplated would be extremely impolitic; for this might have a pernicious influence on future negotiations, or produce immediate inconveniences, perhaps danger and mischief, in relation to other powers. The necessity of such caution and secrecy was one cogent reason for vesting the power of making treaties in the President, with the advice and consent of the Senate, the principle on which that body was formed confining it to a small number of members. To admit, then, a right in the House of Representatives to demand and to have as a matter of course all the papers respecting a negotiation with a foreign power would be to establish a dangerous precedent." 1 Messages and Papers of the Presidents, p. 194.

The marked difference between foreign affairs and domestic affairs in this respect is recognized by both houses of Congress in the very form of their requisitions for information from the executive departments. In the case of every department except the Department of State, the resolution *directs* the official to furnish the information. In the case of the State Department, dealing with foreign affairs, the President is *requested* to furnish the information "if not incompatible with the public interest." A statement that to furnish the information is not compatible with the public interest rarely, if ever, is questioned.

When the President is to be authorized by legislation to act in respect of a matter intended to affect a situation in foreign territory, the legislator properly bears in mind the important consideration that the form of the President's action—or, indeed, whether he shall act at all—may well depend, among other things, upon the nature of the confiden-

tial information which he has or may thereafter receive, or upon the effect which his action may have upon our foreign relations. This consideration, in connection with what we have already said on the subject, discloses the unwisdom of requiring Congress in this field of governmental power to lay down narrowly definite standards by which the President is to be governed. As this court said in *Mackenzie* v. *Hare,* 239 U.S. 299, 311, "As a government, the United States is invested with all the attributes of sovereignty. As it has the character of nationality it has the powers of nationality, especially those which concern its relations and intercourse with other countries. *We should hesitate long before limiting or embarrassing such powers."* (Italics supplied.)

In the light of the foregoing observations, it is evident that this court should not be in haste to apply a general rule which will have the effect of condemning legislation like that under review as constituting an unlawful delegation of legislative power. The principles which justify such legislation find overwhelming support in the unbroken legislative practice which has prevailed almost from the inception of the national government to the present day.

Let us examine, in chronological order, the acts of legislation which warrant this conclusion:

The Act of June 4, 1794, authorized the President to lay, regulate and revoke embargoes. He was "authorized" "whenever, in his opinion, the public safety shall so require" to lay the embargo upon all ships and vessels in the ports of the United States, including those of foreign nations "under such regulations as the circumstances of the case may require, and to continue or revoke the same, whenever he shall think proper." C. 41, 1 Stat. 372. A prior joint resolution of May 7, 1794 (1 Stat. 401), had conferred *unqualified* power on the President to grant clearances, notwithstanding an existing embargo, to ships or vessels belonging to citizens of the United States bound to any port beyond the Cape of Good Hope.

The Act of March 3, 1795 (c. 53, 1 Stat. 444), gave the President authority to permit the exportation of arms, cannon and military stores, the law prohibiting such exports to the contrary notwithstanding, the only prescribed guide for his action being that such exports should be in "cases connected with the security of the commercial interest of the United States, and for public purposes only."

By the Act of June 13, 1798 (c. 53, § 5, 1 Stat. 566), it was provided that if the government of France "shall clearly disavow, and shall be found to refrain from the aggressions, depredations and hostilities" theretofore maintained against vessels and property of the citizens of the United States, "in violation of the faith of treaties, and the laws of nations, and shall thereby acknowledge the just claims of the United States to be considered as in all respects neutral, . . . it shall be lawful for the President of the United States, being well ascertained of the premises, to remit and discontinue the prohibitions and restraints hereby enacted and declared; and he shall be, and is hereby authorized to make proclamation thereof accordingly."

By § 4 of the Act of February 9, 1799 (c. 2, 1 Stat. 615), it was made "lawful" for the President, "if he shall deem it expedient and consistent with the interest of the United States," by order to remit certain restraints and prohibitions imposed by the act with respect to the French Republic, and also to revoke any such order "whenever, in his opinion, the interest of the United States shall require."

Similar authority, qualified in the same way, was conferred by § 6 of the Act of February 7, 1800, c. 10, 2 Stat. 9.

Section 5 of the Act of March 3, 1805 (c. 41, 2 Stat. 341), made it lawful for the President, whenever an armed vessel entering the harbors or waters within the jurisdiction of the United States and required to depart therefrom should fail to do so, not only to employ the land and naval forces to compel obedience, but "if he shall think it proper, it shall be lawful for him to forbid, by proclamation, all intercourse with such vessel, and with every armed vessel of the same nation, and the officers and crew thereof; to prohibit all supplies and aid from being furnished them" and to do various other things connected therewith. Violation of the President's proclamation was penalized.

On February 28, 1806, an act was passed (c. 9, 2 Stat. 351) to suspend commercial intercourse between the United States and certain parts of the Island of St. Domingo. A penalty was prescribed for its violation. Notwithstanding the positive provisions of the act, it was by § 5 made "lawful" for the President to remit and discontinue the restraints and prohibitions imposed by the act at any time "if he shall deem it expedient and consistent with the interests of the United States" to do so. Likewise in respect of the Non-intercourse Act of March 1, 1809 (c. 24, 2 Stat. 528), the President was "authorized" (§ 11, p. 530), in case either of the countries affected should so revoke or modify her edicts "as that they shall cease to violate the neutral commerce of the United States," to proclaim the fact, after which the suspended trade might be renewed with the nation so doing.

Practically every volume of the United States Statutes contains one or more acts or joint resolutions of Congress authorizing action by the President in respect of subjects affecting foreign relations, which either leave the exercise of the power to his unrestricted judgment, or provide a standard far more general than that which has always been considered requisite with regard to domestic affairs. Many, though not all, of these acts are designated in the footnote.[2]

It well may be assumed that these legislative precedents were in mind when Congress passed the joint resolutions of April 22, 1898, 30 Stat. 739; March 14, 1912, 37 Stat. 630; and January 31, 1922, 42 Stat. 361, to prohibit the export of coal or other war material. The resolution of 1898 authorized the President "in his discretion, and with such limitations and exceptions as shall seem to him expedient" to prohibit such exportations. The striking identity of language found in the second resolution mentioned above and in the one now under review will be seen upon comparison. The resolution of March 14, 1912, provides:

"That whenever the President shall find that in any American country conditions of domestic violence exist which are promoted by the use of arms or munitions of war procured from the United States, and shall make proclamation thereof, it shall be unlawful to export except under such limitations and exceptions as the President shall prescribe any arms or munitions of war from any place in the United States to such country until otherwise ordered by the President or by Congress.

"Sec. 2. That any shipment of material hereby declared unlawful after such a proclamation shall be punishable by fine not exceeding ten thousand dollars, or imprisonment not exceeding two years, or both."

The third resolution is in substantially the same terms, but extends to any country in which the United States exercises extraterritorial jurisdiction, and provides for the President's action not only when conditions of domestic violence exist which *are* promoted, but also when such conditions *may be* promoted, by the use of such arms or munitions of war.

We had occasion to review these embargo and kindred acts in connection with an exhaustive discussion of the general subject of delegation of legislative power in a recent case, *Panama*

*Refining Co.* v. *Ryan,* 293 U.S. 388, 421-422, and in justifying such acts, pointed out that they confided to the President "an authority which was cognate to the conduct by him of the foreign relations of the government."

The result of holding that the joint resolution here under attack is void and unenforceable as constituting an unlawful delegation of legislative power would be to stamp this multitude of comparable acts and resolutions as likewise invalid. And while this court may not, and should not, hesitate to declare acts of Congress, however many times repeated, to be unconstitutional if beyond all rational doubt it finds them to be so, an impressive array of legislation such as we have just set forth, enacted by nearly every Congress from the beginning of our national existence to the present day, must be given unusual weight in the process of reaching a correct determination of the problem. A legislative practice such as we have here, evidenced not by only occasional instances, but marked by the movement of a steady stream for a century and a half of time, goes a long way in the direction of providing the presence of unassailable ground for the constitutionality of the practice, to be found in the origin and history of the power involved, or in its nature, or in both combined.

In *The Laura,* 114 U.S. 411, 416, this court answered a challenge to the constitutionality of a statute authorizing the Secretary of the Treasury to remit or mitigate fines and penalties in certain cases, by repeating the language of a very early case (*Stuarta* v. *Laird,* 1 Cranch 299, 309) that the long practice and acquiescence under the statute was a "practical exposition ... too strong and obstinate to be shaken or controlled. Of course, the question is at rest, and ought not now to be disturbed." In *Burrow-Giles Lithographic Co.* v. *Sarony,* 111 U.S. 53, 57, the constitutionality of R.S. § 4952, conferring upon the author, inventor, designer or proprietor of a photograph certain rights, was involved. Mr. Justice Miller, speaking for the court, disposed of the point by saying: "The construction placed upon the Constitution by the first act of 1790, and the act of 1802, by the men who were contemporary with its formation, many of whom were members of the convention which framed it, is of itself entitled to very great weight, and when it is remembered that the rights thus established have not been disputed during a period of nearly a century, it is almost conclusive."

In *Field* v. *Clark,* 143 U.S. 649, 691, this court declared that ". . . the practical construction of the Constitution, as given by so many acts of Congress, and embracing almost the entire period of our national existence, should not be overruled, unless upon a conviction that such legislation was clearly incompatible with the supreme law of the land." The rule is one which has been stated and applied many times by this court. As examples, see *Ames* v. *Kansas,* 111 U.S. 449, 469; *McCulloch* v. *Maryland,* 4 Wheat. 316, 401; *Downes* v. *Bidwell,* 182 U.S. 244, 286.

The uniform, long-continued and undisputed legislative practice just disclosed rests upon an admissible view of the Constitution which, even if the practice found far less support in principle than we think it does, we should not feel at liberty at this late day to disturb.

We deem it unnecessary to consider, *seriatim,* the several clauses which are said to evidence the unconstitutionality of the Joint Resolution as involving an unlawful delegation of legislative power. It is enough to summarize by saying that, both upon principle and in accordance with precedent, we conclude there is sufficient warrant for the broad discretion vested in the President to determine whether the enforcement of the statute will have a beneficial effect

upon the reestablishment of peace in the affected countries; whether he shall make proclamation to bring the resolution into operation; whether and when the resolution shall cease to operate and to make proclamation accordingly; and to prescribe limitations and exceptions to which the enforcement of the resolution shall be subject.

*Second.* The second point raised by the demurrer was that the Joint Resolution never became effective because the President failed to find essential jurisdictional facts; and the third point was that the second proclamation of the President operated to put an end to the alleged liability of appellees under the Joint Resolution. In respect of both points, the court below overruled the demurrer, and thus far sustained the government.

The government contends that upon an appeal by the United States under the Criminal Appeals Act from a decision holding an indictment bad, the jurisdiction of the court does not extend to questions decided in favor of the United States, but that such questions may only be reviewed in the usual way after conviction. We find nothing in the words of the statute or in its purposes which justifies this conclusion. The demurrer in the present case challenges the validity of the statute upon three separate and distinct grounds. If the court below had sustained the demurrer without more, an appeal by the government necessarily would have brought here for our determination all of these grounds, since in that case the record would not have disclosed whether the court considered the statute invalid upon one particular ground or upon all of the grounds alleged. The judgment of the lower court is that the statute is invalid. Having held that this judgment cannot be sustained upon the particular ground which that court assigned, it is now open to this court to inquire whether or not the judgment can be sustained upon the rejected grounds which also challenge the validity of the statute and, therefore, constitute a proper subject of review by this court under the Criminal Appeals Act. *United States* v. *Hastings, 296* U.S. 188, 192.

In *Langnes* v. *Green,* 282 U.S. 531, where the decree of a district court had been assailed upon two grounds and the circuit court of appeals had sustained the attack upon one of such grounds only, we held that a respondent in certiorari might nevertheless urge in this court in support of the decree the ground which the intermediate appellate court had rejected. That principle is applicable here.

We proceed, then, to a consideration of the second and third grounds of the demurrers which, as we have said, the court below rejected.

1. The Executive proclamation recites, "I have found that the prohibition of the sale of arms and munitions of war in the United States to those countries now engaged in armed conflict in the Chaco may contribute to the reestablishment of peace between those countries, and that I have consulted with the governments of other American Republics *and have been assured of the cooperation of such governments as I have deemed necessary as contemplated by the said joint resolution.*" This finding satisfies every requirement of the Joint Resolution. There is no suggestion that the resolution is fatally uncertain or indefinite; and a finding which follows its language, as this finding does, cannot well be challenged as insufficient.

But appellees, referring to the words which we have italicized above, contend that the finding is insufficient because the President does not declare that the cooperation of such governments as he deemed necessary included any American republic and, therefore, the recital contains no affirmative showing of compliance in this respect with the Joint Resolution. The criticism seems to us wholly wanting in substance. The President recites that he has consulted with the governments of other American republics, and that he has been assured of the cooperation of such governments as he deemed necessary *as contemplated by the joint resolution.* These recitals, construed together, fairly include within their meaning American republics.

2. The second proclamation of the President, revoking the first proclamation, it is urged, and the effect of putting an end to the Joint Resolution, and in accordance with a well-settled rule, no penalty could be enforced or punishment inflicted thereafter for an offense committed during the life of the Joint Resolution in the absence of a provision in the resolution to that effect. There is no doubt as to the general rule or as to the absence of a saving clause in the Joint Resolution. But is the case presented one which makes the rule applicable?

It was not within the power of the President to repeal the Joint Resolution; and his second proclamation did not purport to do so. It "revoked" the first proclamation; and the question is, did the revocation of the proclamation have the effect of abrogating the resolution or of precluding its enforcement in so far as that involved the prosecution and punishment of offenses committed during the life of the first proclamation? We are of opinion that it did not.

Prior to the first proclamation, the Joint Resolution was an existing law, but dormant, awaiting the creation of a particular situation to render it active. No action or lack of action on the part of the President could destroy its potentiality. Congress alone could do that. The happening of the designated events—namely, the finding of certain conditions and the proclamation by the President—did not call the law into being. It created the occasion for it to function. The second proclamation did not put an end to the law or affect what had been done in violation of the law. The effect of the proclamation was simply to remove for the future, a condition of affairs which admitted of its exercise.

We should have had a different case if the Joint Resolution had expired by its own terms upon the issue of the second proclamation. Its operative force, it is true, was limited to the period of time covered by the first proclamation. And when the second proclamation was issued, the resolution ceased to be a rule for the future. It did not cease to be the law for the antecedent period of time. The distinction is clearly pointed out by the Superior Court of Judicature of New Hampshire in *Stevens* v. *Diamond,* 6 N.H. 330, 332, 333. There, a town by-law provided that if certain animals should be found going at large between the first day of April and the last day of October, etc., the owners would incur a prescribed penalty. The trial court directed the jury that the by-law, being in force for a year only, had expired so that the defendant could not be called upon to answer for a violation which occurred during the designated period. The state appellate court reversed, saying that when laws "expire by their own limitation, or are repealed, they cease to be the law in relation to the past, as well as the future, and can no longer be enforced in any case. No case is, however, to be found in which it was ever held before that they thus ceased to be law, unless they expired by express limitation in themselves, or were repealed. It has never been decided that they cease to be law, merely because the time they were intended to regulate had expired. . . . A very little consideration of the subject will convince any one that a limitation of the time to which a statute is to apply, is a very different thing from the limitation of the time a statute is to continue in force."

The first proclamation of the President was in force from the 28th day of May, 1934, to the 14th day of November, 1935. If the Joint Resolution had in no way depended upon Presidential action, but had provided explicitly that, at any time between May 28, 1934, and November 14, 1935, it should be unlawful to sell arms or munitions of war to the countries engaged in armed conflict in the Chaco, it certainly could not be successfully contended that the law would expire with the passing of the time fixed in respect of offenses committed during the period.

The judgment of the court below must be reversed and the cause remanded for further proceedings in accordance with the foregoing opinion.

*Reversed.*

MR. JUSTICE McREYNOLDS does not agree. He is of opinion that the court below reached the right conclusion and its judgment ought to be affirmed.

MR. JUSTICE STONE took no part in the consideration or decision of this case.

## Notes

1. In general confirmation of the foregoing views, see 1 Story on the Constitution, 4th ed., § § 198-217, and especially § § 210, 211, 213, 214, 215 (p. 153), 216.
2. Thus, the President has been broadly "authorized" to suspend embargo acts passed by Congress, "if in his judgment the public interest should require it" (Act of December 19, 1806, c. 1, § 3, 2 Stat. 411), or if, "in the judgment of the President," there has been such suspension of hostilities abroad as may render commerce of the United States sufficiently safe. Act of April 22, 1808, c. 52, 2 Stat. 490. See, also, Act of March 3, 1817, c. 39, § 2, 3 Stat. 361. Compare, but as to reviving an embargo act, the Act of May 1, 1810, c. 39, § 4, 2 Stat. 605.

   Likewise, Congress has passed numerous acts laying tonnage and other duties on foreign ships, in retaliation for duties enforced on United States vessels, but providing that if the President should be satisfied that the countervailing duties were repealed or abolished, then he might by proclamation suspend the duties as to vessels of the nation so acting. Thus, the President has been "authorized" to proclaim the suspension. Act of January 7, 1824, c. 4, § 4, 4 Stat. 3; Act of May 24, 1828, c. 111, 4 Stat. 308; Act of July 24, 1897, c. 13, 30 Stat. 214. Or it has been provided that the suspension should take effect whenever the President "shall be satisfied" that the discrimination duties have been abolished. Act of March 3, 1815, c. 77, 3 Stat. 224; Act of May 31, 1830, c. 219, § 2, 4 Stat. 425. Or that the President "may direct" that the tonnage duty shall cease to be levied in such circumstances. Act of July 13, 1832, c. 207, § 3, 4 Stat. 578. And compare Act of June 26, 1884, c. 121, § 14, 23 Stat. 53, 57.

Other acts, for retaliation against discriminations as to United States commerce, have placed broad powers in the hands of the President, "authorizing" even the total exclusion of vessels of any foreign country so offending (Act of June 19, 1886, c. 421, § 17, 24 Stat. 79, 83), or the increase of duties on its goods or their total exclusion from the United States (Act of June 17, 1930, c. 497, § 388, 46 Stat. 590, 704), or the exclusion of its goods or the detention, in certain circumstances, of its vessels, or the exclusion of its vessels or nationals from privileges similar to those which it has denied to citizens of the United States (Act of September 8, 1916, c. 463, § § 804-806, 39 Stat. 756, 799-800). As to discriminations by particular countries, it has been made lawful for the President, by proclamation, which he "may in his discretion, apply . . . to any part or all" of the subjects named, to exclude certain goods of the offending country, or its vessels. Act of March 3, 1887, c. 339, 24 Stat. 475. And compare Act of July 26, 1892, c. 248, 27 Stat. 267. Com-

pare, also, authority given the Postmaster General to reduce or enlarge rates of foreign postage, among other things, for the purpose of counteracting any adverse measures affecting our postal intercourse with foreign countries. Act of March 3, 1851, c. 20, § 2, 9 Stat. 587, 589.

The President has been "authorized" to suspend an act providing for the exercise of judicial functions by ministers, consuls and other officers of the United States in the Ottoman dominions and Egypt whenever he "shall receive satisfactory information" that the governments concerned have organized tribunals likely to secure to United States citizens the same impartial justice enjoyed under the judicial functions exercised by the United States officials. Act of March 23, 1874, c. 62, 18 Stat. 23.

Congress has also passed acts for the enforcement of treaties or conventions, to be effective only upon proclamation of the President. Some of them may be noted which "authorize" the President to make proclamation when he shall be "satisfied" or shall receive "satisfactory evidence" that the other nation has complied: Act of August 5, 1854, c. 269, § § 1, 2, 10 Stat. 587; Act of March 1, 1873, c. 213, § § 1, 2, 17 Stat. 482; Act of August 15, 1876, c. 290, 19 Stat. 200; Act of December 17, 1903, c. 1, 33 Stat. 3. *Cf.* Act of June 11, 1864, c. 116, § 1, 13 Stat. 121; Act of February 21, 1893, c. 150, 27 Stat. 472.

Where appropriate, Congress has provided that violation of the President's proclamations authorized by the foregoing acts shall be penalized. See, *e. g.,* Act of June 19, 1886; Act of March 3, 1887; Act of September 8, 1916; Act of June 17, 1930—all *supra.*

# Report of the Brownlow Commission (1937)

The inauguration of President Franklin D. Roosevelt on March 4, 1933, was followed by an explosion of legislative activity aimed at combating the depression. During Roosevelt's fabled "first hundred days," Congress passed more than a dozen pieces of major administration-sponsored legislation, including the Agricultural Adjustment Act, the Tennessee Valley Authority Act, the National Industrial Recovery Act, and the Glass-Steagall Banking Act. After the 1934 midterm elections, in which the president's party (the Democrats) broke historical precedent by gaining seats in Congress, Congress passed the National Labor Relations Act and the Social Security Act, among others. Cumulatively, these laws created a large and active role for the federal government in the nation's economy.

Because Roosevelt doubted the loyalty and ability of most of the existing departments and agencies, which had been created in less active times and were staffed mainly by Republican presidents, he persuaded Congress to authorize new agencies to carry out his new programs. By adding so many components to the executive branch, however, Roosevelt created an administrative nightmare. He was frustrated by his inability to get the information he needed from the bureaucracy or to communicate effectively his desires for action.

On March 20, 1936, Roosevelt appointed the Committee on Administrative Management, better known as the Brownlow Commission after its chair, Louis D. Brownlow. (The two other members were the political scientists Charles E. Merriam and Luther Gulick.) The commission's charge was to design and recommend an overhaul of the executive branch that would make it more efficient and responsive to the president. On January 8, 1937, Brownlow and his colleagues issued their report, whose contents Roosevelt had influenced and with which he agreed entirely.

Arguing that "the president needs help," the Brownlow Commission recommended that the president be authorized to hire a personal staff consisting of six assistants "possessed of high competence, great physical vigor, and a passion for anonymity." The purpose of these assistants would be to help the president "in obtaining quickly and without delay all pertinent information possessed by any of the executive departments so as to guide him in making his responsible decisions; and then when decisions have been made, to assist him in seeing to it that every administrative department and agency affected is promptly informed."

In addition to these new personal staff positions for each president, the

*Brownlow Commission recommended
that the Executive Office of the President (EOP) be created to serve the
long-term interests of the presidency.
The main components of the EOP were
to be the Bureau of the Budget, then
housed in the Treasury Department,
and the Civil Service Commission, an
independent agency.*

*After receiving the Brownlow Commission's report, Roosevelt immediately asked Congress for authorization
to implement its recommendations.
Angry over the president's effort to
"pack" the Supreme Court, however
(see "Franklin D. Roosevelt's 'Court-
packing' Address," p. 270), Congress
did not approve the president's request
until April 1939. (Even then, the Civil
Service Commission was left independent.) On September 8, 1939, Roosevelt
issued Executive Order 8248, and the
Brownlow Commission's major proposals took effect.*    ~

The need for action in realizing democracy was as great in 1789 as it is
today. It was thus not by accident but
by deliberate design that founding fathers set the American Executive in the
Constitution on a solid foundation. Sad
experience under the Articles of Confederation, with an almost headless
Government and committee management, had brought the American Republic to the edge of ruin. Our forefathers had broken away from hereditary
government and pinned their faith on
democratic rule, but they had not found
a way to equip the new democracy for
action. Consequently, there was grim
purpose in resolutely providing for a
Presidency which was to be a national
office. The President is indeed the one
and only national officer representative
of the entire Nation. There was hesitation on the part of some timid souls in
providing the President with an election independent of the Congress; with
a longer term than most governors of

that day; with the duty of informing the
Congress as to the state of the Union
and of recommending to its consideration "such Measures as he shall judge
necessary and expedient"; with a two-
thirds veto; with a wide power of appointment; and with military and diplomatic authority. But this reluctance was
overcome in the face of need and a
democratic executive established.

Equipped with these broad constitutional powers, reenforced by statute, by
custom, by general consent, the American Executive must be regarded as one
of the very greatest contributions made
by our Nation to the development of a
modern democracy—a unique institution the value of which is as evident in
times of stress and strain as in periods
of quiet.

As an instrument for carrying out the
judgment and will of the people of a
nation, the American Executive occupies an enviable position among the
executives of the states of the world,
combining as it does the elements of
popular control and the means for vigorous action and leadership—uniting
stability and flexibility. The American
Executive as an institution stands
across the path of those who mistakenly
assert that democracy must fail because
it can neither decide promptly nor act
vigorously.

Our Presidency unites at least three
important functions. From one point of
view the President is a political leader—
leader of a party, leader of the Congress,
leader of a people. From another point
of view he is head of the Nation in the
ceremonial sense of the term, the symbol
of our American national solidarity.
From still another point of view the
President is the Chief Executive and
administrator within the Federal system
and service. In many types of government these duties are divided or only in
part combined, but in the United States
they have always been united in one and
the same person whose duty it is to
perform all of these tasks.

Your Committee on Administrative Management has been asked to investigate and report particularly upon the last function; namely, that of administrative management—the organization for the performance of the duties imposed upon the President in exercising the executive power vested in him by the Constitution of the United States.

## Improving the Machinery of Government

Throughout our history we have paused now and then to see how well the spirit and purpose of the Nation is working out in the machinery of everyday government with a view to making such modifications and improvements as prudence and the spirit of progress might suggest. Our Government was the first to set up in its formal Constitution a method of amendment, and the spirit of America has been from the beginning of our history the spirit of progressive changes to meet conditions shifting perhaps more rapidly here than elsewhere in the world.

Since the Civil War, as the tasks and responsibilities of our Government have grown with the growth of the Nation in sweep and power, some notable attempts have been made to keep our administrative system abreast of the new times. The assassination of President Garfield by a disappointed office seeker aroused the Nation against the spoils system and led to the enactment of the civil-service law of 1883. We have struggled to make the principle of this law effective for half a century. The confusion in fiscal management led to the establishment of the Bureau of the Budget and the budgetary system in 1921. We still strive to realize the goal set for the Nation at that time. And, indeed, many other important forward steps have been taken.

Now we face again the problem of governmental readjustment, in part as the result of the activities of the Nation during the desperate years of the industrial depression, in part because of the very growth of the Nation, and in part because of the vexing social problems of our times. There is room for vast increase in our national productivity and there is much bitter wrong to set right in neglected ways of human life. There is need for improvement of our governmental machinery to meet new conditions and to make us ready for the problems just ahead.

Facing one of the most troubled periods in all the troubled history of mankind, we wish to set our affairs in the very best possible order to make the best use of all of our national resources and to make good our democratic claims. If America fails, the hopes and dreams of democracy over all the world go down. We shall not fail in our task and our responsibility, but we cannot live upon our laurels alone.

We seek modern types of management in National Government best fitted for the stern situations we are bound to meet, both at home and elsewhere. As to ways and means of improvement, there are naturally sincere differences of judgment and opinion, but only a treasonable design could oppose careful attention to the best and soundest practices of government available for the American Nation in the conduct of its heavy responsibilities.

## The Foundations of Governmental Efficiency

The efficiency of government rests upon two factors: the consent of the governed and good management. In a democracy consent may be achieved readily, though not without some effort, as it is the cornerstone of the Constitution. Efficient management in a democracy is a factor of peculiar significance.

Administrative efficiency is not merely a matter of paper clips, time clocks, and standardized economies of motion. These are but minor gadgets.

Real efficiency goes much deeper down. It must be built into the structure of a government just as it is built into a piece of machinery.

Fortunately the foundations of effective management in public affairs, no less than in private, are well known. They have emerged universally wherever men have worked together for some common purpose, whether through the state, the church, the private association, or the commercial enterprise. They have been written into constitutions, charters, and articles of incorporation, and exist as habits of work in the daily life of all organized peoples. Stated in simple terms these canons of efficiency require the establishment of a responsible and effective chief executive as the center of energy, direction, and administrative management; the systematic organization of all activities in the hands of qualified personnel under the direction of the chief executive; and to aid him in this, the establishment of appropriate managerial and staff agencies. There must also be provision for planning, a complete fiscal system, and means for holding the Executive accountable for his program.

Taken together, these principles, drawn from the experience of mankind in carrying on large-scale enterprises, may be considered as the first requirement of good management. They comprehend the subject matter of administrative management as it is dealt with in this report. Administrative management concerns itself in a democracy with the executive and his duties, with managerial and staff aides, with organization, with personnel, and with the fiscal system because these are the indispensable means of making good the popular will in a people's government.

## Modernizing our Governmental Management

In the light of these canons of efficiency, what must be said of the Government of the United States today? Speaking in the broadest terms at this point, and in detail later on, we find in the American Government at the present time that the effectiveness of the Chief Executive is limited and restricted, in spite of the clear intent of the Constitution to the contrary; that the work of the Executive Branch is badly organized; that the managerial agencies are weak and out of date; that the public service does not include its share of men and women of outstanding capacity and character; and that the fiscal and auditing systems are inadequate. These weaknesses are found at the center of our Government and involve the office of the Chief Executive itself.

While in general principle our organization of the Presidency challenges the admiration of the world, yet in equipment for administrative management our Executive Office is not fully abreast of the trend of our American times, either in business or in government. Where, for example, can there be found an executive in any way comparable upon whom so much petty work is thrown? Or who is forced to see so many persons on unrelated matters and to make so many decisions on the basis of what may be, because of the very press of work, incomplete information? How is it humanly possible to know fully the affairs and problems of over 100 separate major agencies, to say nothing of being responsible for their general direction and coordination?

These facts have been known for many years and are so well appreciated that it is not necessary for us to prove again that the President's administrative equipment is far less developed than his responsibilities, and that a major task before the American Government is to remedy this dangerous situation. What we need is not a new principle, but a modernizing of our managerial equipment.

This is not a difficult problem in

itself. In fact, we have already dealt with it successfully in State governments, in city governments, and in large-scale private industry. Gov. Frank O. Lowden in Illinois, Gov. Alfred E. Smith in New York, Gov. Harry F. Byrd in Virginia, and Gov. William Tudor Gardiner in Maine, among others, have all shown how similar problems can be dealt with in large governmental units. The Federal Government is more extensive and more complicated, but the principles of reorganization are the same. On the basis of experience and our examination of the Executive Branch we conclude that the following steps should now be taken:

1. To deal with the greatly increased duties of executive management falling upon the President the White House staff should be expanded.

2. The managerial agencies of the Government, particularly those dealing with the budget, efficiency research, personnel, and planning, should be greatly strengthened and developed as arms of the Chief Executive.

3. The merit system should be extended upward, outward, and downward to cover all non-policy-determining posts, and the civil service system should be reorganized and opportunities established for a career system attractive to the talent of the Nation.

4. The whole Executive Branch of Government should be overhauled and the present 100 agencies reorganized under a few large departments in which every executive activity would find its place.

5. The fiscal system should be extensively revised in the light of the best governmental and private practice, particularly with reference to financial records, audit, and accountability of the Executive to the Congress. . . .

## The Purpose of Reorganization

In proceeding to the reorganization of the Government it is important to keep prominently before us the ends of reorganization. Too close a view of machinery must not cut off from sight the true purpose of efficient management. Economy is not the only objective, though reorganization is the first step to savings; the elimination of duplication and contradictory policies is not the only objective, though this will follow; a simple and symmetrical organization is not the only objective, though the new organization will be simple and symmetrical; higher salaries and better jobs are not the only objectives, though these are necessary; better business methods and fiscal controls are not the only objectives, though these too are demanded. There is but one grand purpose, namely, to make democracy work today in our National Government; that is, to make our Government an up-to-date, efficient, and effective instrument for carrying out the will of the Nation. It is for this purpose that the Government needs thoroughly modern tools of management.

As a people we congratulate ourselves justly on our skill as managers—in the home, on the farm, in business big and little—and we properly expect that management in government shall be of the best American model. We do not always get these results, and we must modestly say "we count not ourselves to have attained," but there is a steady purpose in America to press forward until the practices of our governmental administration are as high as the purpose and standards of our people. We know that bad management may spoil good purposes, and that without good management democracy itself cannot achieve its highest goals.

### I. The White House Staff

In this broad program of administrative reorganization the White House itself is involved. The President needs help. His immediate staff assistance is entirely inadequate. He should be given a small number of executive assistants who would be his direct aides in dealing with the managerial agencies and administrative departments of the Government. These assistants, probably not exceeding six in number, would be in addition to his present secretaries, who deal with the public, with the Congress, and with the press and the radio. These aides would have no power to make decisions or issue instructions in their own right. They would not be interposed between the President and the heads of his departments. They would not be assistant presidents in any sense. Their function would be, when any matter was presented to the President for action affecting any part of the administrative work of the Government, to assist him in obtaining quickly and without delay all pertinent information possessed by any of the executive departments so as to guide him in making his responsible decisions; and then when decisions have been made, to assist him in seeing to it that every administrative department and agency affected is promptly informed. Their effectiveness in assisting the President will, we think, be directly proportional to their ability to discharge their functions with restraint. They would remain in the background, issue no orders, make no decisions, emit no public statements. Men for these positions should be carefully chosen by the President from within and without the Government. They should be men in whom the President has personal confidence and whose character and attitude is such that they would not attempt to exercise power on their own account. They should be possessed of high competence, great physical vigor, and a passion for anonymity. They should be installed in the White House itself, directly accessible to the President. In the selection of these aides the President should be free to call on departments from time to time for the assignment of persons who, after a tour of duty as his

aides, might be restored to their old positions.

This recommendation arises from the growing complexity and magnitude of the work of the President's office. Special assistance is needed to insure that all matters coming to the attention of the President have been examined from the over-all managerial point of view, as well as from all standpoints that would bear on policy and operation. It also would facilitate the flow upward to the President of information upon which he is to base his decisions and the flow downward from the President of the decisions once taken for execution by the department or departments affected. Thus such a staff would not only aid the President but would also be of great assistance to the several executive departments and to the managerial agencies in simplifying executive contacts, clearance, and guidance.

The President should also have at his command a contingent fund to enable him to bring in from time to time particular persons possessed of particular competency for a particular purpose and whose services he might usefully employ for short periods of time.

The President in his regular office staff should be given a greater number of positions so that he will not be compelled, as he has been compelled in the past, to use for his own necessary work persons carried on the payrolls of other departments.

If the President be thus equipped he will have but the ordinary assistance that any executive of a large establishment is afforded as a matter of course.

In addition to this assistance in his own office the President must be given direct control over and be charged with immediate responsibility for the great managerial functions of the Government which affect all of the administrative departments.... These functions are personnel management, fiscal and organizational management, and planning management. Within these three groups may be comprehended all of the essential elements of business management.

The development of administrative management in the Federal Government requires the improvement of the administration of these managerial activities, not only by the central agencies in charge, but also by the departments and bureaus. The central agencies need to be strengthened and developed as managerial arms of the Chief Executive, better equipped to perform their central responsibilities and to provide the necessary leadership in bringing about improved practices throughout the Government.

The three managerial agencies, the Civil Service Administration, the Bureau of the Budget, and the national Resources Board should be a part and parcel of the Executive Office. Thus the President would have reporting to him directly the three managerial institutions whose work and activities would affect all of the administrative departments.

The budgets for the managerial agencies should be submitted to the Congress by the President as a part of the budget for the Executive Office. This would distinguish these agencies from the operating administrative departments of the Government, which should report to the President through the heads of departments who collectively compose his Cabinet. Such an arrangement would materially aid the President in his work of supervising the administrative agencies and would enable the Congress and the people to hold him to strict accountability for their conduct. . . .

# Franklin D. Roosevelt's "Court-packing" Address (1937)

On February 5, 1937, President Franklin D. Roosevelt, reacting to a long string of Supreme Court decisions that were hostile to the New Deal, asked Congress to add as many as six new positions to the Court, one for every sitting justice seventy years or older. The proposal was highly controversial from the start, and whatever small chance for passage it may have had was lost that spring when the Court abandoned its anti-New Deal posture in a series of cases that was instantly dubbed "the switch in time that saved nine." A watered-down version of the Court-packing plan was tabled into oblivion on July 22, 1937, by a Senate vote of 70-20.

Roosevelt's frustration with the Supreme Court was longstanding. When he became president in 1933, the Court was dominated by conservatives. (The four most conservative justices—George Sutherland, Willis Van Devanter, James C. McReynolds, and Pierce Butler—were known as the "Four Horsemen.") In 1935 and 1936, the Court overturned an unprecedented number of important federal laws that Roosevelt and Congress had enacted to combat the depression, including the National Industrial Recovery Act, the Agricultural Adjustment Act, and the Railway Pension Act. Other important New Deal legislation, such as the Social Security Act and the National Labor Relations Act, seemed doomed to a similar fate.

Privately, Roosevelt raged against the Court; publicly, he was relatively quiet, fearing public reaction to any political assault he might launch against the judicial branch. In 1936 Roosevelt ran a cautious campaign for reelection and was returned to office by the largest electoral vote plurality in history (523-8). Scarcely two weeks after his inauguration in 1937, however, the president revealed to a startled cabinet, Congress, and nation his proposal to expand the number of Supreme Court justices from nine to fifteen, which would enable him to appoint six New Deal sympathizers to the Court immediately.

In a severe political miscalculation, Roosevelt initially defended the Court-packing plan as an effort to relieve the workload of the justices, six of whom (including the Four Horsemen) were in their seventies. Not only was this rationale inaccurate—Chief Justice Charles Evans Hughes was able to demonstrate easily to Congress that the Court had never been more efficient in handling its caseload—but it was wildly implausible. Critics accurately attacked the president for disguising his real intention, which was to dilute the conservatives' influence on the Court.

On March 9, in a radio-broadcast fireside chat to the nation, Roosevelt *changed tactics and spoke frankly of his concern that "the Court has been acting not as a judicial body, but as a policy-making body." He conceded his intention of " 'packing the Court' . . . if by that phrase [is meant] . . . that I would appoint Justices who will not undertake to override the judgment of the Congress on legislative policy."*

*Politically, Roosevelt's speech was too little, too late: the Court-packing plan was dead. But in a series of decisions beginning later in March, Justice Owen Roberts, a previous ally of the Court's conservatives, began voting to uphold New Deal laws. Several other justices retired within a few years, and Roosevelt eventually appointed nine justices. Although his later claim that he had lost the Court-packing battle but won the war was too sweeping (the battle was a major defeat in its own right, and it marked the birth of the conservative coalition of Republicans and southern Democrats that dominated Congress for decades), Roosevelt never encountered another problem with the Supreme Court.*   ~

Tonight, sitting at my desk in the White House, I make my first radio report to the people in my second term of office.

I am reminded of that evening in March, four years ago, when I made my first radio report to you. We were then in the midst of the great banking crisis.

Soon after, with the authority of the Congress, we asked the Nation to turn over all of its privately held gold, dollar for dollar, to the Government of the United States.

Today's recovery proves how right that policy was.

But when, almost two years later, it came before the Supreme Court its constitutionality was upheld only by a five-to-four vote. The change of one vote would have thrown all the affairs of this great Nation back into hopeless chaos.

In effect, four Justices ruled that the right under a private contract to exact a pound of flesh was more sacred than the main objectives of the Constitution to establish an enduring Nation.

In 1933 you and I knew that we must never let our economic system get completely out of joint again—that we could not afford to take the risk of another great depression.

We also became convinced that the only way to avoid a repetition of those dark days was to have a government with power to prevent and to cure the abuses and the inequalities which had thrown that system out of joint.

We then began a program of remedying those abuses and inequalities—to give balance and stability to our economic system—to make it bombproof against the causes of 1929.

Today we are only part-way through that program—and recovery is speeding up to a point where the dangers of 1929 are again becoming possible, not this week or month perhaps, but within a year or two.

National laws are needed to complete that program. Individual or local or state effort alone cannot protect us in 1937 any better than ten years ago.

It will take time—and plenty of time—to work out our remedies administratively even after legislation is passed. To complete our program of protection in time, therefore, we cannot delay one moment in making certain that our National Government has power to carry through.

Four years ago action did not come until the eleventh hour. It was almost too late.

If we learned anything from the depression we will not allow ourselves to run around in new circles of futile discussion and debate, always postponing the day of decision.

The American people have learned from the depression. For in the last three national elections an overwhelming majority of them voted a mandate that the Congress and the President begin the task of providing that protection—not after long years of debate, but now.

The Courts, however, have cast doubts on the ability of the elected Congress to protect us against catastrophe by meeting squarely our modern social and economic conditions.

We are at a crisis in our ability to proceed with that protection. It is a quiet crisis. There are no lines of depositors outside closed banks. But to the far-sighted it is far-reaching in its possibilities of injury to America.

I want to talk with you very simply about the need for present action in this crisis—the need to meet the unanswered challenge of one-third of a Nation ill-nourished, ill-clad, ill-housed.

Last Thursday I described the American form of Government as a three horse team provided by the Constitution to the American people so that their field might be plowed. The three horses are, of course, the three branches of government—the Congress, the Executive and the Courts. Two of the horses are pulling in unison today; the third is not. Those who have intimated that the President of the United States is trying to drive that team, overlook the simple fact that the President, as Chief Executive, is himself one of the three horses.

It is the American people themselves who are in the driver's seat.

It is the American people themselves who want the furrow plowed.

It is the American people themselves who expect the third horse to pull in unison with the other two.

I hope that you have re-read the Constitution of the United States in these past few weeks. Like the Bible, it ought to be read again and again.

It is an easy document to understand when you remember that it was called into being because the Articles of Confederation under which the original thirteen States tried to operate after the Revolution showed the need of a National Government with power enough to handle national problems. In its Preamble, the Constitution states that it was intended to form a more perfect Union and promote the general welfare; and the powers given to the Congress to carry out those purposes can be best described by saying that they were all the powers needed to meet each and every problem which then had a national character and which could not be met by merely local action.

But the framers went further. Having in mind that in succeeding generations many other problems then undreamed of would become national problems, they gave to the Congress the ample broad powers "to levy taxes ... and provide for the common defense and general welfare of the United States."

That, my friends, is what I honestly believe to have been the clear and underlying purpose of the patriots who wrote a Federal Constitution to create a National Government with national power, intended as they said, "to form a more perfect union ... for ourselves and our posterity."

For nearly twenty years there was no conflict between the Congress and the Court. Then Congress passed a statute which, in 1803, the Court said violated an express provision of the Constitution. The Court claimed the power to declare it unconstitutional and did so declare it. But a little later the Court itself admitted that it was an extraordinary power to exercise and through Mr. Justice Washington laid down this limitation upon it: "It is but a decent respect due to the wisdom, the integrity and the patriotism of the legislative body, by which any law is passed, to presume in favor of its validity until its violation of the Constitution is proved beyond all reasonable doubt."

But since the rise of the modern movement for social and economic progress through legislation, the Court has more and more often and more and more boldly asserted a power to veto laws passed by the Congress and State Legislatures in complete disregard of this original limitation.

In the last four years the sound rule of giving statutes the benefit of all reasonable doubt has been cast aside. The Court has been acting not as a judicial body, but as a policy-making body.

When the Congress has sought to stabilize national agriculture, to improve the conditions of labor, to safeguard business against unfair competition, to protect our national resources, and in many other ways, to serve our clearly national needs, the majority of the Court has been assuming the power to pass on the wisdom of these Acts of the Congress—and to approve or disapprove the public policy written into these laws.

That is not only my accusation. It is the accusation of most distinguished Justices of the present Supreme Court. I have not the time to quote to you the language used by dissenting Justices in many of these cases. But in the case holding the Railroad Retirement Act unconstitutional, for instance, Chief Justice Hughes said in a dissenting opinion that the majority opinion was a "departure from sound principles," and placed "an unwarranted limitation upon the commerce clause." And three other Justices agreed with him.

In the case holding the A.A.A. unconstitutional, Justice Stone said of the majority opinion that it was a "tortured construction of the Constitution." And two other Justices agreed with him.

In the case holding the New York Minimum Wage Law unconstitutional, Justice Stone said that the majority were actually reading into the Constitution their own "personal economic predilections," and that if the legislative power is not left free to choose the methods of solving the problems of poverty, subsistence and health of large numbers in the community, then "government is to be rendered impotent."

And two other Justices agreed with him.

In the face of these dissenting opinions, there is no basis for the claim made by some members of the Court that something in the Constitution has compelled them regretfully to thwart the will of the people.

In the face of such dissenting opinions, it is perfectly clear, that as Chief Justice Hughes has said: "We are under a Constitution, but the Constitution is what the Judges say it is."

The Court in addition to the proper use of its judicial functions has improperly set itself up as a third House of the Congress—a super-legislature, as one of the justices has called it—reading into the Constitution words and implications which are not there, and which were never intended to be there.

We have, therefore, reached the point as a Nation where we must take action to save the Constitution from the Court and the Court from itself. We must find a way to take an appeal from the Supreme Court to the Constitution itself. We want a Supreme Court which will do justice under the Constitution—not over it. In our Courts we want a government of laws and not of men.

I want—as all Americans want—an independent judiciary as proposed by the framers of the Constitution. That means a Supreme Court that will enforce the Constitution as written—that will refuse to amend the Constitution by the arbitrary exercise of judicial power—amendment by judicial say-so. It does not mean a judiciary so independent that it can deny the existence of facts universally recognized.

How then could we proceed to perform the mandate given us? It was said in last year's Democratic platform, "If these problems cannot be effectively solved within the Constitution, we shall seek such clarifying amendment as will assure the power to enact those laws, adequately to regulate commerce, protect public health and safety, and safeguard economic security." In other words, we said we would seek an amendment only if every other possible means by legislation were to fail.

When I commenced to review the situation with the problem squarely before me, I came by a process of elimination to the conclusion that, short of amendments, the only method which was clearly constitutional, and would at the same time carry out other much needed reforms, was to infuse new blood into all our Courts. We must have men worthy and equipped to carry out impartial justice. But, at the same time, we must have Judges who will bring to the Courts a present-day sense of the Constitution—Judges who will retain in the Courts the judicial functions of a court, and reject the legislative powers which the courts have today assumed.

In forty-five out of the forty-eight States of the Union, Judges are chosen not for life but for a period of years. In many States Judges must retire at the age of seventy. Congress has provided financial security by offering life pensions at full pay for Federal Judges on all Courts who are willing to retire at seventy. In the case of Supreme Court Justices, that pension is $20,000 a year. But all Federal Judges, once appointed, can, if they choose, hold office for life, no matter how old they may get to be.

What is my proposal? It is simply this: whenever a Judge or Justice of any Federal Court has reached the age of seventy and does not avail himself of the opportunity to retire on a pension, a new member shall be appointed by the President then in office, with the approval, as required by the Constitution, of the Senate of the United States.

The plan has two chief purposes. By bringing into the judicial system a steady and continuing stream of new and younger blood, I hope, first, to make the administration of all Federal justice speedier and, therefore, less costly; secondly, to bring to the decision of social and economic problems younger men who have had personal experience and contact with modern facts and circumstances under which average men have to live and work. This plan will save our national Constitution from hardening of the judicial arteries.

The number of Judges to be appointed would depend wholly on the decision of present Judges now over seventy, or those who would subsequently reach the age of seventy.

If, for instance, any one of the six Justices of the Supreme Court now over the age of seventy should retire as provided under the plan, no additional place would be created. Consequently, although there never can be more than fifteen, there may be only fourteen, or thirteen, or twelve. And there may be only nine.

There is nothing novel or radical about this idea. It seeks to maintain the Federal bench in full vigor. It has been discussed and approved by many persons of high authority ever since a similar proposal passed the House of Representatives in 1869.

Why was the age fixed at seventy? Because the laws of many States, the practice of the Civil Service, the regulations of the Army and Navy, and the rules of many of our Universities and of almost every great private business enterprise, commonly fix the retirement age at seventy years or less.

The statute would apply to all the courts in the Federal system. There is general approval so far as the lower Federal courts are concerned. The plan has met opposition only so far as the Supreme Court of the United States itself is concerned. If such a plan is good for the lower courts it certainly ought to be equally good for the highest Court from which there is no appeal.

Those opposing this plan have sought to arouse prejudice and fear by crying that I am seeking to "pack" the Supreme Court and that a baneful precedent will be established.

What do they mean by the words "packing the Court"?

Let me answer this question with a bluntness that will end all *honest* misunderstanding of my purposes.

If by that phrase "packing the Court" it is charged that I wish to place on the bench spineless puppets who would disregard the law and would decide specific cases as I wished them to be decided, I make this answer: that no President fit for his office would appoint, and no Senate of honorable men fit for their office would confirm, that kind of appointees to the Supreme Court.

But if by that phrase the charge is made that I would appoint and the Senate would confirm Justices worthy to sit beside present members of the Court who understand those modern conditions, that I will appoint Justices who will not undertake to override the judgment of the Congress on legislative policy, that I will appoint Justices who will act as Justices and not as legislators—if the appointment of such Justices can be called "packing the Courts," then I say that I and with me the vast majority of the American people favor doing just that thing—now.

Is it a dangerous precedent for the Congress to change the number of the Justices? The Congress has always had, and will have, that power. The number of Justices has been changed several times before, in the Administrations of John Adams and Thomas Jefferson— both signers of the Declaration of Independence—Andrew Jackson, Abraham Lincoln and Ulysses S. Grant.

I suggest only the addition of Justices to the bench in accordance with a clearly defined principle relating to a clearly defined age limit. Fundamentally, if in the future, America cannot trust the Congress it elects to refrain from abuse of our Constitutional usages, democracy will have failed far beyond the importance to it of any kind of precedent concerning the Judiciary.

We think it so much in the public interest to maintain a vigorous judiciary that we encourage the retirement of elderly Judges by offering them a life pension at full salary. Why then should we leave the fulfillment of this public policy to chance or make it dependent upon the desire or prejudice of any individual Justice?

It is the clear intention of our public policy to provide for a constant flow of new and younger blood into the Judiciary. Normally every President appoints a large number of District and Circuit Judges and a few members of the Supreme Court. Until my first term practically every President of the United States had appointed at least one member of the Supreme Court. President Taft appointed five members and named a Chief Justice; President Wilson, three; President Harding, four, including a Chief Justice.

Such a succession of appointments should have provided a Court well-balanced as to age. But chance and the disinclination of individuals to leave the Supreme bench have now given us a Court in which five Justices will be over seventy-five years of age before next June and one over seventy. Thus a sound public policy has been defeated.

I now propose that we establish by law an assurance against any such ill-balanced Court in the future. I propose that hereafter, when a Judge reaches the age of seventy, a new and younger Judge shall be added to the Court automatically. In this way I propose to enforce a sound public policy by law instead of leaving the composition of our Federal Courts, including the highest, to be determined by chance or the personal decision of individuals.

If such a law as I propose is regarded as establishing a new precedent, is it not a most desirable precedent?

Like all lawyers, like all Americans, I regret the necessity of this controversy. But the welfare of the United States, and indeed of the Constitution itself, is what we all must think about first. Our difficulty with the Court today rises not from the Court as an institution but from human beings within it. But we cannot yield our constitutional destiny to the personal judgment of a few men who, being fearful of the future, would deny us the necessary means of dealing with the present.

This plan of mine is no attack on the Court; it seeks to restore the Court to its rightful and historic place in our system of Constitutional Government and to have it resume its high task of building anew on the Constitution "a system of living law." The Court itself can best undo what the Court has done.

I have thus explained to you the reasons that lie behind our efforts to secure results by legislation within the Constitution. I hope that thereby the difficult process of constitutional amendment may be rendered unnecessary. But let us examine that process.

There are many types of amendment proposed. Each one is radically different from the other. There is no substantial group within the Congress or outside it who are agreed on any single amendment.

It would take months or years to get substantial agreement upon the type and language of an amendment. It would take months and years thereafter to get a two-thirds majority in favor of that amendment in *both* Houses of the Congress.

Then would come the long course of ratification by three-fourths of all the States. No amendment which any powerful economic interests or the leaders of any powerful political party have had reason to oppose has ever been ratified within anything like a reasonable time. And thirteen States which contain only five percent of the voting population can block ratification even though the thirty-five States with ninety-five percent of the population are in favor of it.

A very large percentage of newspaper publishers, Chambers of Commerce, Bar Associations, Manufacturers' Association, who are trying to give the impression that they really do want a constitutional amendment would be the first to exclaim as soon as an amendment was proposed, "Oh! I was for an amendment all right, but this amendment that you have proposed is not the kind of an amendment that I was thinking about. I am, therefore, going to spend my time, my efforts and my money to block that amendment, although I would be awfully glad to help get some other kind of amendment ratified."

Two groups oppose my plan on the ground that they favor a constitutional amendment. The first includes those who fundamentally object to social and economic legislation along modern lines. This is the same group who during the campaign last Fall tried to block the mandate of the people.

Now they are making a last stand. And the strategy of that last stand is to suggest the time-consuming process of amendment in order to kill off by delay the legislation demanded by the mandate.

To them I say: I do not think you will be able long to fool the American people as to your purposes.

The other group is composed of those who honestly believe the amendment process is the best and who would be willing to support a reasonable amendment if they could agree on one.

To them I say: we cannot rely on an amendment as the immediate or only answer to our present difficulties. When the time comes for action, you will find that many of those who pretend to support you will sabotage any constructive amendment which is proposed. Look at these strange bedfellows of yours. When before have you found them really at your side in your fights for progress?

And remember one thing more. Even if an amendment were passed, and even if in the years to come it were to be ratified, its meaning would depend upon the kind of Justices who would be sitting on the Supreme Court bench. An amendment, like the rest of the Constitution, is what the Justices say it is rather than what its framers or you might hope it is.

This proposal of mine will not infringe in the slightest upon the civil or religious liberties so dear to every American.

My record as Governor and as President proves my devotion to those liberties. You who know me can have no fear that I would tolerate the destruction by any branch of government of any part of our heritage of freedom.

The present attempt by those opposed to progress to play upon the fears of danger to personal liberty brings again to mind that crude and cruel strategy tried by the same opposition to frighten the workers of America in a pay-envelope propaganda against the Social Security Law. The workers were not fooled by that propaganda then. The people of America will not be fooled by such propaganda now.

I am in favor of action through legislation:

First, because I believe that it can be passed at this session of the Congress.

Second, because it will provide a reinvigorated, liberal-minded Judiciary necessary to furnish quicker and cheaper justice from bottom to top.

Third, because it will provide a series of Federal Courts willing to enforce the Constitution as written, and unwilling to assert legislative powers by writing into it their own political and economic policies.

During the past half century the balance of power between the three great branches of the Federal Government, has been tipped out of balance by the Courts in direct contradiction of the high purposes of the framers of the Constitution. It is my purpose to restore that balance. You who know me will accept my solemn assurance that in a world in which democracy is under attack, I seek to make American democracy succeed. You and I will do our part.

# Franklin D. Roosevelt's "Four Freedoms" Speech (1941)

After World War I, the United States sank into a mood of isolationism in foreign policy that was embodied by the slogan "America first!" In early 1935, at the height of President Franklin D. Roosevelt's political popularity, Congress yielded to an outpouring of public protest and rejected his modest proposal that the United States join the World Court. In October 1937, responding to the rise of militant fascism in Germany (under Adolph Hitler) and in Italy (under Benito Mussolini) and to Japanese aggression in Asia, Roosevelt tried to alert the nation to the "solidarity and interdependence about the modern world, . . . which makes it impossible for any nation completely to isolate itself from political and economic upheavals in the rest of the world." But public reaction was tepid to his call to "quarantine" aggressor nations for the sake of the national self-interest. Indeed, Congress passed neutrality acts in 1935 and 1937 that prohibited the sale of U.S. arms or ammunition to any belligerent nation.

Hitler's September 1939 invasion of Poland, which brought Great Britain and France into the war with Germany and Italy, prompted Roosevelt to denounce the neutrality acts and, in September 1940, to violate them by asserting inherent powers as commander in chief and agreeing to send fifty allegedly "overage" naval destroyers to Britain in return for the right to lease certain British territories in the western Atlantic for U.S. military bases. In the face of the longstanding two-term tradition for presidents, Roosevelt's unprecedented election to a third term in November 1940 (his slogan against Republican Wendell Willkie was "Don't change horses in midstream," a reference to the need for trusted leadership in uncertain international conditions) constituted a strong endorsement of his policies. But the president still had to maneuver carefully to steer the country toward further active support of Britain and the other Allies, whose survival he believed was vital to U.S. security.

In 1941 Roosevelt took a new tack in his effort to promote U.S. aid to nations that were at war with the Axis powers of Germany, Italy, and Japan. In his January 1941 State of the Union address, Roosevelt appealed to American idealism by citing "four essential human freedoms" to which all people were entitled. The first two—freedom of speech and expression and freedom of religion—derived from the Bill of Rights to the Constitution. The third—freedom from want—extended the New Deal view of government-promoted economic sufficiency for all people to the international arena. The fourth was freedom from fear, which, according to Roosevelt, ultimately meant widespread disarmament.

*The "Four Freedoms" speech roused public support for Roosevelt's proposed Lend-Lease program of military aid to Britain and the Soviet Union. The act, which was passed narrowly by Congress on March 11, 1941, gave the president virtually unlimited power to order the manufacture of any defense article and to "sell, transfer title to, exchange, lease, lend or otherwise dispose of" these articles to the "government of any country whose defense the President deems vital to the defense of the United States." In August 1941, the four freedoms were incorporated into the Atlantic Charter, which stated Allied war aims.* ~

Mr. Speaker, members of the 77th Congress:

I address you, the members of this new Congress, at a moment unprecedented in the history of the union. I use the word "unprecedented" because at no previous time has American security been as seriously threatened from without as it is today.

Since the permanent formation of our government under the Constitution in 1789, most of the periods of crisis in our history have related to our domestic affairs. And, fortunately, only one of these—the four-year war between the States—ever threatened our national unity. Today, thank God, 130,000,000 Americans in forty-eight States have forgotten points of the compass in our national unity.

It is true that prior to 1914 the United States often has been disturbed by events in other continents. We have been engaged in two wars with European nations and in a number of undeclared wars in the West Indies, in the Mediterranean and in the Pacific, for the maintenance of American rights and for the principles of peaceful commerce. But in no case had a serious threat been raised against our national safety or our continued independence.

What I seek to convey is the historic truth that the United States as a nation has at all times maintained opposition—clear, definite opposition—to any attempt to lock us in behind an ancient Chinese wall while the procession of civilization went past. Today, thinking of our children and of their children, we oppose enforced isolation for ourselves or for any other part of the Americas.

That determination of ours, extending over all these years, was proved, for example, in the early days during the quarter century of wars following the French Revolution.

While the Napoleonic struggle did threaten interests of the United States because of the French foothold in the West Indies and in Louisiana, and while we engaged in the War of 1812 to vindicate our right to peaceful trade, it is nevertheless clear that neither France nor Great Britain nor any other nation was aiming at domination of the whole world.

And in like fashion, from 1815 to 1914—ninety-nine years—no single war in Europe or in Asia constituted a real threat against our future or against the future of any other American nation.

Except in the Maximilian interlude in Mexico, no foreign power sought to establish itself in this hemisphere. And the strength of the British fleet in the Atlantic has been a friendly strength; it is still a friendly strength.

Even when the World War broke out in 1914 it seemed to contain only a small threat of danger to our own American future. But as time went on, as we remember, the American people began to visualize what the downfall of democratic nations might mean to our own democracy.

We need not overemphasize imperfections in the peace of Versailles. We need not harp on failure of the democracies to deal with problems of world reconstruction. We should remember that the peace of 1919 was far less unjust than the kind of pacification which began even before Munich, and which is being carried on under the new order of tyranny that seeks to spread over every continent today.

The American people have unalterably set their faces against that tyranny.

I suppose that every realist knows that the democratic way of life is at this moment being directly assailed in every part of the world—assailed either by arms or by secret spreading of poisonous propaganda by those who seek to destroy unity and promote discords in nations that are still at peace.

During sixteen long months this assault has blotted out the whole pattern of democratic life in an appalling number of independent nations, great and small. And the assailants are still on the march, threatening other nations, great and small.

Therefore, as your President, performing my constitutional duty to "give to the Congress information of the state of the union," I find it unhappily necessary to report that the future and the safety of our country and of our democracy are overwhelmingly involved in events far beyond our borders.

Armed defense of democratic existence is now being gallantly waged in four continents. If that defense fails, all the population and all the resources of Europe and Asia, Africa and Australia will be dominated by conquerors. And let us remember that the total of those populations in those four continents, the total of those populations and their resources greatly exceeds the sum total of the population and the resources of the whole of the Western Hemisphere—yes, many times over.

In times like these it is immature—and, incidentally, untrue—for anybody to brag that an unprepared America, single-handed and with one hand tied behind its back, can hold off the whole world.

No realistic American can expect from a dictator's peace international generosity, or return to true independence, or world disarmament, or freedom of expression, or freedom of religion—or even good business. Such a peace would bring no security for us or for our neighbors. Those who would give up essential liberty to purchase a little temporary safety deserve neither liberty nor safety.

As a nation we may take pride in the fact that we are soft-hearted; but we cannot afford to be soft-headed. We must always be wary of those who with sounding brass and a tinkling cymbal preach the ism of appeasement. We must especially beware of that small group of selfish men who would clip the wings of the American eagle to feather their own nests.

I have recently pointed out how quickly the tempo of modern warfare could bring into our very midst the physical attack which we must eventually expect if the dictator nations win this war.

There is much loose talk of our immunity from immediate and direct invasion from across the seas. Obviously, as long as the British Navy retains its power, no such danger exists. Even if there were no British Navy it is not probable that any enemy would be stupid enough to attack us by landing troops in the United States from across thousands of miles of ocean, until it had acquired strategic bases from which to operate.

But we learn much from the lessons of the past years in Europe—particularly the lesson of Norway, whose essential seaports were captured by treachery and surprise built up over a series of years.

The first phase of the invasion of this hemisphere would not be the landing of regular troops. The necessary strategic points would be occupied by secret agents and by their dupes—and great numbers of them are already here and in Latin America.

As long as the aggressor nations

maintain the offensive they, not we, will choose the time and the place, and the method of their attack.

And that is why the future of all the American Republics is today in serious danger. That is why this annual message to the Congress is unique in our history. That is why every member of the executive branch of the government and every member of the Congress face great responsibility—great accountability.

The need of the moment is that our actions and our policy should be devoted primarily—almost exclusively—to meeting this foreign peril. For all our domestic problems are now a part of the great emergency.

Just as our national policy in internal affairs has been based upon a decent respect for the rights and the dignity of all of our fellow men within our gates, so our national policy in foreign affairs has been based on a decent respect for the rights and the dignity of all nations, large and small. And the justice of morality must and will win in the end.

Our national policy is this:

First, by an impressive expression of the public will and without regard to partisanship, we are committed to all-inclusive national defense.

Second, by an impressive expression of the public will and without regard to partisanship, we are committed to full support of all those resolute people everywhere who are resisting aggression and are thereby keeping war away from our hemisphere. By this support we express our determination that the democratic cause shall prevail, and we strengthen the defense and the security of our own nation.

Third, by an impressive expression of the public will and without regard to partisanship, we are committed to the proposition that principles of morality and considerations for our own security will never permit us to acquiesce in a peace dictated by aggressors and sponsored by appeasers. We know that enduring peace cannot be bought at the cost of other people's freedom.

In the recent national election there was no substantial difference between the two great parties in respect to that national policy. No issue was fought out on this line before the American electorate. And today it is abundantly evident that American citizens everywhere are demanding and supporting speedy and complete action in recognition of obvious danger.

Therefore, the immediate need is a swift and driving increase in our armament production. Leaders of industry and labor have responded to our summons. Goals of speed have been set. In some cases these goals are being reached ahead of time. In some cases we are on schedule; in other cases there are slight but not serious delays. And in some cases—and, I am sorry to say, very important cases—we are still concerned by the slowness of the accomplishment of our plans.

The Army and Navy, however, have made substantial progress during the past year. Actual experience is improving and speeding up our methods of production with every passing day. And today's best is not good enough for tomorrow.

I am not satisfied with the progress thus far made. The men in charge of the program represent the best in training, in ability and in patriotism. They are not satisfied with the progress thus far made. None of us will be satisfied until the job is done.

No matter whether the original goal was set too high or too low, our objective is quicker and better results.

To give you two illustrations:

We are behind schedule in turning out finished airplanes. We are working day and night to solve the innumerable problems and to catch up.

We are ahead of schedule in building warships, but we are working to get even further ahead of that schedule.

To change a whole nation from a

basis of peacetime production of implements of peace to a basis of wartime production of implements of war is no small task. The greatest difficulty comes at the beginning of the program, when new tools, new plant facilities, new assembly lines, new shipways must first be constructed before the actual material begins to flow steadily and speedily from them.

The Congress, of course, must rightly keep itself informed at all times of the progress of the program. However, there is certain information, as the Congress itself will readily recognize, which, in the interests of our own security and those of the nations that we are supporting, must of needs be kept in confidence.

New circumstances are constantly begetting new needs for our safety. I shall ask this Congress for greatly increased new appropriations and authorizations to carry on what we have begun.

I also ask this Congress for authority and for funds sufficient to manufacture additional munitions and war supplies of many kinds, to be turned over to those nations which are now in actual war with aggressor nations. Our most useful and immediate role is to act as an arsenal for them as well as for ourselves. They do not need manpower, but they do need billions of dollars' worth of the weapons of defense.

The time is near when they will not be able to pay for them all in ready cash. We cannot, and we will not, tell them that they must surrender merely because of present inability to pay for the weapons which we know they must have.

I do not recommend that we make them a loan of dollars with which to pay for these weapons—a loan to be repaid in dollars. I recommend that we make it possible for those nations to continue to obtain war materials in the United States, fitting their orders into our own program. And nearly all of their material would, if the time ever came, be useful in our own defense.

For what we send abroad we shall be repaid, repaid with a reasonable time following the close of hostilities, repaid in similar materials, or at our option in other goods of many kinds which they can produce and which we need.

Let us say to the democracies:

We Americans are vitally concerned in your defense of freedom. We are putting forth our energies, our resources and our organizing powers to give you the strength to regain and maintain a free world. We shall send you in ever-increasing numbers, ships, planes, tanks, guns. That is our purpose and our pledge.

In fulfillment of this purpose we will not be intimidated by the threats of dictators that they will regard as a breach of international law or as an act of war our aid to the democracies which dare to resist their aggression. Such aid is not an act of war, even if a dictator should unilaterally proclaim it so to be.

And when the dictators—if the dictators—are ready to make war upon us, they will not wait for an act of war on our part.

They did not wait for Norway or Belgium or the Netherlands to commit an act of war. Their only interest is in a new one-way international law which lacks mutuality in its observances and therefore becomes an instrument of oppression. The happiness of future generations of Americans may well depend on how effective and how immediate we can make our aid felt. No one can tell the exact character of the emergency situations that we may be called upon to meet. The nation's hands must not be tied when the nation's life is in danger.

Yes, and we must prepare, all of us prepare, to make the sacrifices that the emergency—almost as serious as war itself—demands. Whatever stands in the way of speed and efficiency in defense, in defense preparations at any time, must give way to the national need.

A free nation has the right to expect full cooperation from all groups. A free nation has the right to look to the leaders of business, of labor and of agriculture to take the lead in stimulating effort, not among other groups but within their own groups.

The best way of dealing with the few slackers or troublemakers in our midst is, first, to shame them by patriotic example, and if that fails, to use the sovereignty of government to save government.

As men do not live by bread alone, they do not fight by armament alone. Those who man our defenses and those behind them who build our defenses must have the stamina and the courage which come from unshakable belief in the manner of life which they are defending. The mighty action that we are calling for cannot be based on a disregard for all the things worth fighting for.

The nation takes great satisfaction and much strength from the things which have been done to make its people conscious of their individual stakes in the preservation of democratic life in America. Those things have toughened the fiber of our people, have renewed their faith and strengthened their devotion to the institutions we make ready to protect.

Certainly this is no time for any of us to stop thinking about the social and economic problems which are the root cause of the social revolution which is today a supreme factor in the world. For there is nothing mysterious about the foundations of a healthy and strong democracy.

The basic things expected by our people of their political and economic systems are simple. They are:

Equality of opportunity for youth and for others.

Jobs for those who can work.

Security for those who need it.

The ending of special privilege for the few.

The preservation of civil liberties for all.

The employment of the fruits of scientific progress in a wider and constantly rising standard of living.

These are the simple, the basic things that must never be lost sight of in the turmoil and unbelievable complexity of our modern world. The inner and abiding strength of our economic and political systems is dependent upon the degree to which they fulfill these expectations.

Many subjects connected with our social economy call for immediate improvement. As examples:

We should bring more citizens under the coverage of old-age pension and unemployment insurance.

We should widen the opportunities for adequate medical care.

We should plan a better system by which persons deserving or needing gainful employment may obtain it.

I have called for personal sacrifice, and I am assured of the willingness of almost all Americans to respond to that call. A part of the sacrifice means the payment of more money in taxes. In my budget message I will recommend that a greater portion of this great defense program be paid for from taxation than we are paying for today. No person should try, or be allowed to get rich out of the program, and the principle of tax payments in accordance with ability to pay should be constantly before our eyes to guide our legislation.

If the Congress maintains these principles the voters, putting patriotism ahead of pocketbooks, will give you their applause.

In the future days which we seek to make secure, we look forward to a world founded upon four essential human freedoms.

The first is freedom of speech and expression—everywhere in the world.

The second is freedom of every person to worship God in his own way—everywhere in the world.

The third is freedom from want, which, translated into world terms, means economic understanding which will secure to every nation a healthy peacetime life for its inhabitants—everywhere in the world.

The fourth is freedom from fear, which, translated into world terms means a world-wide reduction of armaments to such a point and in such a thorough fashion that no nation will be in a position to commit an act of physical aggression against any neighbor—anywhere in the world.

That is no vision of a distant millenium. It is a definite basis for a kind of world attainable in our own time and generation. That kind of world is the very antithesis of the so-called "new order" of tyranny which the dictators seek to create with the crash of a bomb.

To that new order we oppose the greater conception—the moral order. A good society is able to face schemes of world domination and foreign revolutions alike without fear.

Since the beginning of our American history we have been engaged in change, in a perpetual, peaceful revolution, a revolution which goes on steadily, quietly, adjusting itself to changing conditions without the concentration camp or the quicklime in the ditch. The world order which we seek is the cooperation of free countries, working together in a friendly, civilized society.

This nation has placed its destiny in the hands, heads and hearts of its millions of free men and women, and its faith in freedom under the guidance of God. Freedom means the supremacy of human rights everywhere. Our support goes to those who struggle to gain those rights and keep them. Our strength is our unity of purpose.

To that high concept there can be no end save victory.

# Franklin D. Roosevelt's War Message (1941)

U.S. concern with the menace of Adolph Hitler's Germany left Japan free to pursue its imperialistic aims in Asia and the Pacific. During the 1930s Japan successfully invaded Manchuria, then all of China. In 1940, after France and the Netherlands fell to Germany, President Franklin D. Roosevelt initially tried to conciliate the nonmilitaristic elements in Japan in order to restrain their government from seizing the Dutch East Indies and French Indochina. When that policy failed, Roosevelt imposed a ban on the unlicensed export of U.S. petroleum and metal to Japan, which desperately needed these materials for its war machine. In September 1940 Japan cast its lot with the Axis powers: it signed a treaty with Germany and Italy in which all three nations agreed to declare war on a country that attacked any one of them.

Negotiations between the United States and Japan proved fruitless but continued throughout 1941. On December 7, 1941, however, Japan launched a crippling surprise air attack against the fleet anchored at the U.S. naval base in Hawaii's Pearl Harbor. Japan's main purpose—which was fulfilled only in the short term—was to eliminate the one military force that could obstruct its territorial ambitions.

On December 8 Roosevelt appeared before a joint session of Congress to ask for a declaration of war. He began his speech, which was nationally broadcast on radio, by saying, "Yesterday, December 7, 1941—a date which will live in infamy—the United States of America was suddenly and deliberately attacked by naval and air forces of the Empire of Japan." Roosevelt conceded that Japan had caused "severe damage to American naval and military forces."

Congress responded to the president's call by voting unanimously to declare war on Japan. On December 11, Germany and Italy responded by declaring war on the United States. World War II was fully under way.

As during World War I, Congress delegated vast powers to the president to prosecute the war as he saw fit. But Roosevelt appropriated additional powers on his own by invoking the president's constitutional authority as commander in chief and by citing earlier emergency proclamations. He unilaterally created executive agencies that, cumulatively, controlled every activity of the economy that was remotely related to the war effort. In an extreme case, Roosevelt told Congress on September 7, 1942, that if it did not repeal certain provisions of the Emergency Price Control Act, "I shall accept the responsibility, and I shall act.... The President has the power, under the Constitution and under Congres-

*sional acts, to take measures necessary to avert a disaster which would interfere with the winning of the war.... When the war is won, the powers under which I act automatically revert to the people—to whom they belong."*

*Roosevelt's assertion of presidential power was unprecedented—not even Abraham Lincoln during the Civil War had claimed the right to repeal a specific congressional statute. But in the heat of the war effort, the public supported the president, and Congress did as Roosevelt asked.*

*Roosevelt was elected to a fourth term in November 1944. It was apparent, by then, that the United States and its allies soon would defeat the Axis powers in both Europe and Asia. But Roosevelt, who died of natural causes on April 12, 1945, did not live to see that day.*     ~

Yesterday, December 7, 1941—a date which will live in infamy—the United States of America was suddenly and deliberately attacked by naval and air forces of the Empire of Japan.

The United States was at peace with that nation and, at the solicitation of Japan, was still in conversation with its Government and its Emperor looking toward the maintenance of peace in the Pacific. Indeed, one hour after Japanese air squadrons had commenced bombing in Oahu, the Japanese Ambassador to the United States and his colleague delivered to the Secretary of State a formal reply to a recent American message. While this reply stated that it seemed useless to continue the existing diplomatic negotiations, it contained no threat or hint of war or armed attack.

It will be recorded that the distance of Hawaii from Japan makes it obvious that the attack was deliberately planned many days or even weeks ago. During the intervening time the Japanese Government has deliberately sought to deceive the United States by false statements and expressions of hope for continued peace.

The attack yesterday on the Hawaiian Islands has caused severe damage to American naval and military forces. Very many American lives have been lost. In addition American ships have been reported torpedoed on the high seas between San Francisco and Honolulu.

Yesterday the Japanese Government also launched an attack againt Malaya. Last night Japanese forces attacked Hong Kong. Last night Japanese forces attacked Guam. Last night Japanese forces attacked the Philippine Islands. Last night the Japanese attacked Wake Island. This morning the Japanese attacked Midway Island.

Japan has, therefore, undertaken a surprise offensive extending throughout the Pacific area. The facts of yesterday speak for themselves. The people of the United States have already formed their opinions and well understand the implications to the very life and safety of our nation.

As Commander-in-Chief of the Army and Navy, I have directed that all measures be taken for our defense.

Always will we remember the character of the onslaught against us.

No matter how long it may take us to overcome this premeditated invasion, the American people in their righteous might will win through to absolute victory.

I believe I interpret the will of the Congress and of the people when I assert that we will not only defend ourselves to the uttermost but will make very certain that this form of treachery shall never endanger us again.

Hostilities exist. There is no blinking at the fact that our people, our territory and our interests are in grave danger.

With confidence in our armed forces—with the unbonded determination of our people—we will gain the inevitable triumph—so help us God.

I ask that the Congress declare that since the unprovoked and dastardly attack by Japan on Sunday, December seventh, a state of war has existed between the United States and the Japanese Empire.

# The Truman Doctrine (1947)

Harry S Truman succeeded to the presidency when President Franklin D. Roosevelt died on April 12, 1945. Truman, a Missouri politician who had been vice president for just eighty-two days, became president as World War II was drawing to a close. On May 7, 1945, Germany surrendered. Japan succumbed on September 2, less than a month after U.S. warplanes, acting at Truman's instruction, dropped atomic bombs on the Japanese cities of Hiroshima and Nagasaki.

The United States and the Soviet Union were allies during the war, but severe tensions developed afterward when the Soviets imposed Communist puppet governments on the East European nations they had taken from the Germans. The Soviets justified the effort to surround themselves with friendly "satellites" as a precaution against future foreign invasions; but to the United States, the takeover of Poland, Czechoslovakia, Romania, and other countries looked like the first steps in a Soviet effort to attain worldwide domination.

U.S.-Soviet tensions came to a head in Greece in February 1947. After years of German occupation, Greece was torn by a civil war between the British-backed monarchy and Communist-led revolutionaries. Already overburdened by the demands of its own postwar reconstruction, Great Britain notified the United States on February 21 that it could no longer afford to support Greece and would have to cut off aid after March 31. The likely consequence of the British withdrawal, nearly all agreed, would be a Communist victory in Greece and, soon after, the extension of Soviet domination to Turkey and all the nations of the eastern Mediterranean.

Truman's response to the British announcement was swift and certain. On March 12, 1947, the president appeared before a joint session of Congress to proclaim the doctrine that soon after bore his name. "I believe," Truman said, "that it must be the policy of the United States to support free peoples who are resisting attempted subjugation by armed minorities or by outside pressures." Despite the opposition of conservative isolationists who did not want the United States to become the world's police officer and of certain liberals who dreaded confrontation with the Soviet Union, the Republican-dominated Congress in May approved Truman's request for $400 million in aid to Greece and Turkey by margins of nearly three to one in both the House of Representatives and the Senate.

Aid to Greece and Turkey was the first manifestation of the Truman Doctrine and of the "containment" theory that underlay it. The Marshall Plan of *massive economic aid to Europe (1947), the airlift of food and other supplies to Soviet-beleaguered West Berlin (1948), and the formation of the North Atlantic Treaty Organization (1949) to defend Western Europe and North America against possible Soviet attack were others. The containment theory, which received its most famous articulation in an unsigned 1947* Foreign Affairs *article by foreign service officer George F. Kennan, provided the basis for U.S. foreign policy in the "cold war" with the Soviet Union. Kennan had urged "the adroit and vigilant application of counter-force at a series of constantly shifting geographical points, corresponding to the shifts and maneuvers of Soviet policy."*

*The Truman Doctrine, like the Monroe Doctrine (see "The Monroe Doctrine," p. 63) and other presidential doctrines, was an individual president's statement of long-term foreign policy goals, not a law or an irreversible course of action. As a matter of political reality, however, although no president can impose such a doctrine on an unwilling nation, only a president's declarations of foreign policy have any chance of being accepted as national goals.* ~

Mr. President, Mr. Speaker, Members of the Congress of the United States:

The gravity of the situation which confronts the world today necessitates my appearance before a joint session of the Congress.

The foreign policy and the national security of this country are involved.

One aspect of the present situation, which I present to you at this time for your consideration and decision, concerns Greece and Turkey.

The United States has received from the Greek Government an urgent appeal for financial and economic assistance. Preliminary reports from the American Economic Mission now in Greece and reports from the American Ambassador in Greece corroborate the statement of the Greek Government that assistance is imperative if Greece is to survive as a free nation.

I do not believe that the American people and the Congress wish to turn a deaf ear to the appeal of the Greek Government.

Greece is not a rich country. Lack of sufficient natural resources has always forced the Greek people to work hard to make both ends meet. Since 1940, this industrious, peace loving country has suffered invasion, four years of cruel enemy occupation, and bitter internal strife.

When forces of liberation entered Greece they found that the retreating Germans had destroyed virtually all the railways, roads, port facilities, communications, and merchant marine. More than a thousand villages had been burned. Eighty-five percent of the children were tubercular. Livestock, poultry, and draft animals had almost disappeared. Inflation had wiped out practically all savings.

As a result of these tragic conditions, a militant minority, exploiting human want and misery, was able to create political chaos which, until now, has made economic recovery impossible.

Greece is today without funds to finance the importation of those goods which are essential to bare subsistence. Under these circumstances the people of Greece cannot make progress in solving their problems of reconstruction. Greece is in desperate need of financial and economic assistance to enable it to resume purchases of food, clothing, fuel, and seeds. These are indispensable for the subsistence of its people and are obtainable only from abroad. Greece must have help to import the goods necessary to restore internal order and security so essential for economic and political recovery.

The Greek Government has also asked for the assistance of experienced

American administrators, economists and technicians to insure that the financial and other aid given to Greece shall be used effectively in creating a stable and self-sustaining economy and in improving its public administration.

The very existence of the Greek state is today threatened by the terrorist activities of several thousand armed men, led by Communists, who defy the government's authority at a number of points, particularly along the northern boundaries. A Commission appointed by the United Nations Security Council is at present investigating disturbed conditions in northern Greece and alleged border violations along the frontier between Greece on the one hand and Albania, Bulgaria, and Yugoslavia on the other.

Meanwhile, the Greek Government is unable to cope with the situation. The Greek army is small and poorly equipped. It needs supplies and equipment if it is to restore authority to the government throughout Greek territory.

Greece must have assistance if it is to become a self-supporting and self-respecting democracy.

The United States must supply this assistance. We have already extended to Greece certain types of relief and economic aid but these are inadequate.

There is no other country to which democratic Greece can turn.

No other nation is willing and able to provide the necessary support for a democratic Greek government.

The British Government, which has been helping Greece, can give no further financial or economic aid after March 31. Great Britain finds itself under the necessity of reducing or liquidating its commitments in several parts of the world, including Greece.

We have considered how the United Nations might assist in this crisis. But the situation is an urgent one requiring immediate action, and the United Nations and its related organizations are not in a position to extend help of the kind that is required.

It is important to note that the Greek Government has asked for our aid in utilizing effectively the financial and other assistance we may give to Greece, and in improving its public administration. It is of the utmost importance that we supervise the use of any funds made available to Greece, in such a manner that each dollar spent will count toward making Greece self-supporting, and will help to build an economy in which a healthy democracy can flourish.

No government is perfect. One of the chief virtues of a democracy, however, is that its defects are always visible and under democratic processes can be pointed out and corrected. The government of Greece is not perfect. Nevertheless it represents 85 percent of the members of the Greek Parliament who were chosen in an election last year. Foreign observers, including 692 Americans, considered this election to be a fair expression of the views of the Greek people.

The Greek Government has been operating in an atmosphere of chaos and extremism. It has made mistakes. The extension of aid by this country does not mean that the United States condones everything that the Greek Government has done or will do. We have condemned in the past, and we condemn now, extremist measures of the right or the left. We have in the past advised tolerance, and we advise tolerance now.

Greece's neighbor, Turkey, also deserves our attention.

The future of Turkey as an independent and economically sound state is clearly no less important to the freedom-loving peoples of the world than the future of Greece. The circumstances in which Turkey finds itself today are considerably different from those of Greece. Turkey has been spared the disasters that have beset Greece. And during the war, the United States and Great Britain furnished Turkey with material aid.

Nevertheless, Turkey now needs our support.

Since the war Turkey has sought additional financial assistance from Great Britain and the United States for the purpose of effecting that modernization necessary for the maintenance of its national integrity.

That integrity is essential to the preservation of order in the Middle East.

The British Government has informed us that, owing to its own difficulties, it can no longer extend financial or economic aid to Turkey.

As in the case of Greece, if Turkey is to have the assistance it needs, the United States must supply it. We are the only country able to provide that help.

I am fully aware of the broad implications involved if the United States extends assistance to Greece and Turkey, and I shall discuss these implications with you at this time.

One of the primary objectives of the foreign policy of the United States is the creation of conditions in which we and other nations will be able to work out a way of life free from coercion. This was a fundamental issue in the war with Germany and Japan. Our victory was won over countries which sought to impose their will, and their way of life, upon other nations.

To ensure the peaceful development of nations, free from coercion, the United States has taken a leading part in establishing the United Nations. The United Nations is designed to make possible lasting freedom and independence for all its members. We shall not realize our objectives, however, unless we are willing to help free peoples to maintain their free institutions and their national integrity against aggressive movements that seek to impose upon them totalitarian regimes. This is no more than a frank recognition that totalitarian regimes imposed upon free peoples, by direct or indirect aggression, undermine the foundations of international peace and hence the security of the United States.

The peoples of a number of countries of the world have recently had totalitarian regimes forced upon them against their will. The Government of the United States has made frequent protests against coercion and intimidation, in violation of the Yalta agreement, in Poland, Rumania, and Bulgaria. I must also state that in a number of other countries there have been similar developments.

At the present moment in world history nearly every nation must choose between alternative ways of life. The choice is too often not a free one.

One way of life is based upon the will of the majority, and is distinguished by free institutions, representative government, free elections, guarantees of individual liberty, freedom of speech and religion, and freedom from political oppression.

The second way of life is based upon the will of a minority forcibly imposed upon the majority. It relies upon terror and oppression, a controlled press and radio, fixed elections, and the suppression of personal freedoms.

I believe that it must be the policy of the United States to support free peoples who are resisting attempted subjugation by armed minorities or by outside pressures.

I believe that we must assist free peoples to work out their own destinies in their own way.

I believe that our help should be primarily through economic and financial aid which is essential to economic stability and orderly political processes.

The world is not static, and the *status quo* is not sacred. But we cannot allow changes in the *status quo* in violation of the Charter of the United Nations by such methods as coercion, or by such subterfuges as political infiltration. In helping free and independent nations to maintain their freedom, the United States will be giving effect to the principles of the Charter of the United Nations.

It is necessary only to glance at a map to realize that the survival and integrity of the Greek nation are of grave importance in a much wider situation. If Greece should fall under the control of an armed minority, the effect upon its neighbor, Turkey, would be immediate and serious. Confusion and disorder might well spread throughout the entire Middle East.

Moreover, the disappearance of Greece as an independent state would have a profound effect upon those countries in Europe whose peoples are struggling against great difficulties to maintain their freedoms and their independence while they repair the damages of war.

It would be an unspeakable tragedy if these countries, which have struggled so long against overwhelming odds, should lose that victory for which they sacrificed so much. Collapse of free institutions and loss of independence would be disastrous not only for them but for the world. Discouragement and possibly failure would quickly be the lot of neighboring peoples striving to maintain their freedom and independence.

Should we fail to aid Greece and Turkey in this fateful hour, the effect will be far reaching to the West as well as to the East.

We must take immediate and resolute action.

I therefore ask the Congress to provide authority for assistance to Greece and Turkey in the amount of $400,000,000 for the period ending June 30, 1948. In requesting these funds, I have taken into consideration the maximum amount of relief assistance which would be furnished to Greece out of the $350,000,000 which I recently requested that the Congress authorize for the prevention of starvation and suffering in countries devastated by the war.

In addition to funds, I ask the Con-

gress to authorize the detail of American civilian and military personnel to Greece and Turkey, at the request of those countries, to assist in the tasks of reconstruction, and for the purpose of supervising the use of such financial and material assistance as may be furnished. I recommend that authority also be provided for the instruction and training of selected Greek and Turkish personnel.

Finally, I ask that the Congress provide authority which will permit the speediest and most effective use, in terms of needed commodities, supplies, and equipment, of such funds as may be authorized.

If further funds, or further authority, should be needed for the purposes indicated in this message, I shall not hesitate to bring the situation before the Congress. On this subject the Executive and Legislative branches of the Government must work together.

This is a serious course upon which we embark.

I would not recommend it except that the alternative is much more serious.

The United States contributed $341,000,000,000 toward winning World War II. This is an investment in world freedom and world peace.

The assistance that I am recommending for Greece and Turkey amounts to little more than 1/10 of 1 percent of this investment. It is only common sense that we should safeguard this investment and make sure that it was not in vain.

The seeds of totalitarian regimes are nurtured by misery and want. They spread and grow in the evil soil of poverty and strife. They reach their full growth when the hope of a people for a better life has died.

We must keep that hope alive.

The free peoples of the world look to us for support in maintaining their freedoms.

If we falter in our leadership, we may

endanger the peace of the world—and we shall surely endanger the welfare of this Nation.

Great responsibilities have been placed upon us by the swift movement of events.

I am confident that the Congress will face these responsibilities squarely.

# Harry S Truman's Point Four Message to Congress (1949)

In 1948 Harry S Truman ran for a term as president in his own right. His chances of winning seemed small. The voters had elected a Republican Congress in 1946, the first in almost two decades. The various wings of the Democratic party nominated three candidates for president: Truman, the official nominee; former vice president Henry A. Wallace, who opposed the Truman Doctrine and the president's other actions to contain Soviet expansionism (see "The Truman Doctrine," p. 288); and South Carolina governor J. Strom Thurmond, who disliked Truman's liberal policies on civil rights for blacks. Finally, Truman was not personally popular. He had accepted Franklin D. Roosevelt's view of the modern presidency as a powerful leadership office but lacked many of Roosevelt's public leadership skills, especially inspiration and oratory.

Truman's surprise election victory over his Democratic rivals and Gov. Thomas E. Dewey, the Republican nominee (Truman won 303 electoral votes to 189 for Dewey, 39 for Thurmond, and 0 for Wallace), was the political upset of the century. But it won him little support in Congress for his domestic politics. Few items from the president's "Fair Deal" agenda were enacted. Among those defeated were national health insurance, repeal of the Taft-Hartley Act (see "Youngs-town Sheet and Tube Co. v. Sawyer," p. 307), and civil rights legislation.

Foreign policy was an entirely different matter. With bipartisan support in Congress, Truman fulfilled Roosevelt's hope that the United States, for the first time in its history, would assume the ongoing responsibilities of international leadership rather than retreat into postwar isolation.

In his January 20, 1949, inaugural address, Truman proposed that, in addition to rebuilding Europe and resisting Soviet aggression, the United States should create a program to assist the developing nations of Asia, Africa, and Latin America. In the address, which was organized around four main points, the president especially emphasized Point Four—"a bold new program for making the benefits of our scientific advances and industrial progress available for the improvement and growth of underdeveloped areas."

Part of Truman's motive in proposing Point Four was altruistic: the underdeveloped nations were suffering economically. Part of his motive was political: the United States had been laboring to halt the spread of communism in Europe and wanted to do the same elsewhere. Also, to the extent that impoverished nations became prosperous, they would provide markets for U.S. goods.

Point Four was spelled out in detail

*in a special message that Truman sent to Congress on June 24, 1949. In 1950 Congress passed the Act for International Development and appropriated money for the technical assistance program of the United Nations. Within a few years, trainees from several dozen countries had been brought to the United States to receive technical guidance, and U.S. "technical missionaries" were at work abroad to promote agriculture, public health, literacy, and other programs of economic assistance.* ~

To the Congress of the United States:

In order to enable the United States, in cooperation with other countries, to assist the peoples of economically under-developed areas to raise their standards of living, I recommend the enactment of legislation to authorize an expanded program of technical assistance for such areas, and an experimental program for encouraging the outflow of private investment beneficial to their economic development. These measures are the essential first steps in an undertaking which will call upon private enterprise and voluntary organizations in the United States, as well as the Government, to take part in a constantly growing effort to improve economic conditions in the less developed regions of the world.

The grinding poverty and the lack of economic opportunity for many millions of people in the economically under-developed parts of Africa, the Near and Far East, and certain regions of Central and South America, constitute one of the greatest challenges of the world today. In spite of their age-old economic and social handicaps, the peoples in these areas have in recent decades been stirred and awakened. The spread of industrial civilization, the growing understanding of modern concepts of government, and the impact of two world wars have changed their lives and their outlook. They are eager to play a greater part in the community of nations.

All these areas have a common problem. They must create a firm economic base for the democratic aspirations of their citizens. Without such an economic base, they will be unable to meet the expectations which the modern world has aroused in their peoples. If they are frustrated and disappointed, they may turn to false doctrines which hold that the way of progress lies through tyranny.

For the United States the great awakening of these peoples holds tremendous promise. It is not only a promise that new and stronger nations will be associated with us in the cause of human freedom, it is also a promise of new economic strength and growth for ourselves.

With many of the economically under-developed areas of the world, we have long had ties of trade and commerce. In many instances today we greatly needed the products of their labor and their resources. If the productivity and the purchasing power of these countries are expanded, our own industry and agriculture will benefit. Our experience shows that the volume of our foreign trade is far greater with highly developed countries than it is with countries having a low standard of living and inadequate industry. To increase the output and the national income of the less developed regions is to increase our own economic stability.

In addition, the development of these areas is of utmost importance to our efforts to restore the economies of the free European nations. As the economies of the under-developed areas expand, they will provide needed products for Europe and will offer a better market for European goods. Such expansion is an essential part of the growing system of world trade which is necessary for European recovery.

Furthermore, the development of

these areas will strengthen the United Nations and the fabric of world peace. The preamble to the Charter of the United Nations states that the economic and social advancement of all people is an essential bulwark of peace. Under Article 56 of the charter, we have promised to take separate action and to act jointly with other nations for "higher standards of living, full employment, and conditions of economic and social progress and development."

For these reasons, assistance in the development of the economically under-developed areas has become one of the major elements of our foreign policy. In my inaugural address, I outlined a program to help the peoples of these areas to attain greater production as a way of prosperity and peace.

The major effort in such a program must be local in character; it must be made by the people of the under-developed areas themselves. It is essential, however, to the success of their effort that there be help from abroad. In some cases, the peoples of these areas will be unable to begin their part of this great enterprise without initial aid from other countries.

The aid that is needed falls roughly into two categories. The first is the technical, scientific and managerial knowledge necessary to economic development. This category includes not only medical and educational knowledge and assistance and advice in such basic fields as sanitation, communications, road building and governmental services, but also, and perhaps most important, assistance in the survey of resources and in planning for long-range economic development.

The second category is production goods—machinery and equipment—and financial assistance in the creation of productive enterprises. The underdeveloped areas need capital for port and harbor development, roads and communications, irrigation and drainage projects, as well as for public utili-ties and the whole range of extractive, processing and manufacturing industries. Much of the capital required can be provided by these areas themselves, in spite of their low standards of living. But much must come from abroad.

The two categories of aid are closely related. Technical assistance is necessary to lay the groundwork for productive investment. Investment, in turn, brings with it technical assistance. In general, however, technical surveys of resources and of the possibilities of economic development must precede substantial capital investment. Furthermore, in many of the areas concerned, technical assistance in improving sanitation, communications or education is required to create conditions in which capital investment can be fruitful.

This country, in recent years, has conducted relatively modest programs of technical cooperation with other countries. In the field of education, channels of exchange and communication have been opened between our citizens and those of other countries. To some extent, the expert assistance of a number of Federal agencies, such as the Public Health Service and the Department of Agriculture, has been made available to other countries. We have also participated in the activities of the United Nations, its specialized agencies, and other international organizations to disseminate useful techniques among nations.

Through these various activities, we have gained considerable experience in rendering technical assistance to other countries. What is needed now is to expand and integrate these activities and to concentrate them particularly on the economic development of underdeveloped areas.

Much of the aid that is needed can be provided most effectively through the United Nations. Shortly after my inaugural address, this government asked the Economic and Social Council of the United Nations to consider what the

United Nations and the specialized international agencies could do in this program.

The Secretary General of the United Nations thereupon asked the United Nations secretariat and the secretariats of the specialized international agencies to draw up cooperative plans for technical assistance to under-developed areas. As a result, a survey was made of technical projects suitable for agencies in such fields as industry, labor, agriculture, scientific research with respect to natural resources, and fiscal management. The total cost of the program submitted as a result of this survey was estimated to be about 35 million dollars for the first year. It is expected that the United Nations and the specialized international agencies will shortly adopt programs for carrying out projects of the type included in this survey.

In addition to our participation in this work of the United Nations, much of the technical assistance required can be provided directly by the United States to countries needing it. A careful examination of the existing information concerning the under-developed countries shows particular need for technicians and experts with United States training in plant and animal diseases, malaria and typhus control, water supply and sewer systems, metallurgy and mining, and nearly all phases of industry.

It has already been shown that experts in these fields can bring about tremendous improvements. For example, the health of the people of many foreign communities has been greatly improved by the work of United States sanitary engineers in setting up modern water supply systems. The food supply of many areas has been increased as the result of the advice of United States agricultural experts in the control of animal diseases and the improvement of crops. These are only examples of the wide range of benefits resulting from the careful application of modern techniques to local problems. The benefits which a comprehensive program of expert assistance will make possible can only be revealed by studies and surveys undertaken as a part of the program itself.

To inaugurate the program, I recommend a first year appropriation of not to exceed 45 million dollars. This includes 10 million dollars already requested in the 1950 Budget for activities of this character. The sum recommended will cover both our participation in the programs of the international agencies and the assistance to be provided directly by the United States.

In every case, whether the operation is conducted through the United Nations, the other international agencies, or directly by the United States, the country receiving the benefit of the aid will be required to bear a substantial portion of the expense.

The activities necessary to carry out our program of technical aid will be diverse in character and will have to be performed by a number of different government agencies and private instrumentalities. It will be necessary to utilize not only the resources of international agencies and the United States Government, but also the facilities and the experience of the private business and nonprofit organizations that have long been active in this work.

Since a number of Federal agencies will be involved in the program, I recommend that the administration of the program be vested in the President, with authority to delegate to the Secretary of State and to other government officers, as may be appropriate. With such administrative flexibility, it will be possible to modify the management of the program as it expands and to meet the practical problems that will arise in its administration in the future.

The second category of outside aid needed by the under-developed areas is the provision of capital for the creation of productive enterprise. The International Bank for Reconstruction and Development and the Export-Import Bank have provided some capital for under-developed areas, and, as the economic growth of these areas progresses, should be expected to provide a great deal more. In addition, private sources of funds must be encouraged to provide a major part of the capital required.

In view of the present troubled condition of the world—the distortion of world trade, the shortage of dollars, and the aftereffects of the war—the problem of substantially increasing the flow of American capital abroad presents serious difficulties. In all probability novel devices will have to be employed if the investment from this country is to reach proportions sufficient to carry out the objectives of our program.

All countries concerned with the program should work together to bring about conditions favorable to the flow of private capital. To this end we are negotiating agreements with other countries to protect the American investor from unwarranted or discriminatory treatment under the laws of the country in which he made his investment.

In negotiating such treaties we do not, of course, ask privileges for American capital greater than those granted to other investors in under-developed countries or greater than we ourselves grant in this country. We believe that American enterprise should not waste local resources, should provide adequate wages and working conditions for local labor, and should bear an equitable share of the burden of local taxes. At the same time, we believe that investors will send their capital abroad on an increasing scale only if they are given assurance against risk of loss through expropriation without compensation, unfair or discriminatory treatment, destruction through war or rebellion, or the inability to convert their earnings into dollars.

Although our investment treaties will be directed at mitigating such risks, they cannot eliminate them entirely. With the best will in the world a foreign country, particularly an under-developed country, may not be able to obtain the dollar exchange necessary for the prompt remittance of earnings on dollar capital. Damage or loss resulting from internal and international violence may be beyond the power of our treaty signatories to control.

Many of these conditions of instability in under-developed areas which deter foreign investment are themselves a consequence of the lack of economic development which only foreign investment can cure. Therefore, to wait until stable conditions are assured before encouraging the outflow of capital to under-developed areas would defer the attainment of our objectives indefinitely. It is necessary to take vigorous action now to break out of this vicious circle.

Since the development of under-developed economic areas is of major importance in our foreign policy, it is appropriate to use the resources of the government to accelerate private efforts toward that end. I recommend, therefore, that the Export-Import Bank be authorized to guarantee United States private capital, invested in productive enterprises abroad which contribute to economic development in under-developed areas, against the risks peculiar to those investments.

This guarantee activity will at the outset be largely experimental. Some investments may require only a guarantee against the danger of inconvertibility, others may need protection against the danger of expropriation and other dangers as well. It is impossible at this time to write a standard guarantee. The Bank will, of course, be able to require the payment of premiums for such protection, but there is no way now to determine what premium rates will be most appropriate in the long run. Only experience can provide answers to these questions.

The Bank has sufficient resources at the present time to begin the guarantee program and to carry on its lending activities as well without any increase in its authorized funds. If the demand for guarantees should prove large, and lending activities continue on the scale expected, it will be necessary to request the Congress at a later date to increase the authorized funds of the Bank.

The enactment of these two legislative proposals, the first pertaining to technical assistance and the second to the encouragement of foreign investment, will constitute a national endorsement of a program of major importance in our efforts for world peace and economic stability. Nevertheless, these measures are only the first steps. We are here embarking on a venture that extends far into the future. We are at the beginning of a rising curve of activity, private, governmental and international, that will continue for many years to come. It is all the more important, therefore, that we start promptly.

In the economically under-developed areas of the world today there are new creative energies. We look forward to the time when these countries will be stronger and more independent than they are now, and yet more closely bound to us and to other nations by ties of friendship and commerce, and by kindred ideals. On the other hand, unless we aid the newly awakened spirit in these peoples to find the course of fruitful development, they may fall under the control of those whose philosophy is hostile to human freedom, thereby prolonging the unsettled state of the world and postponing the achievement of permanent peace.

Before the peoples of these areas we hold out the promise of a better future through the democratic way of life. It is vital that we move quickly to bring the meaning of that promise home to them in their daily lives.

# Harry S Truman's
# Korean War Address (1950)

Harry S Truman's final term as president was dominated by the Korean War. At the end of World War II, previously Japanese-occupied Korea had been divided along the thirty-eighth parallel into a Soviet-dominated north and a U.S.-dominated south. On June 25, 1950, troops from Communist North Korea swept across the border in a massive invasion of South Korea, which had been left unprotected by U.S. troops since June 1949. To conform with both his containment policy and the Truman Doctrine (see "The Truman Doctrine," p. 288), Truman felt that he had no choice but to help South Korea repel the Communist aggressor, although Gen. Douglas MacArthur and Secretary of State Dean Acheson advised him that South Korea was outside the perimeter of vital U.S. defense interests.

On the day of North Korea's invasion, Truman called for an emergency meeting of the Security Council of the recently formed United Nations (UN). Because the Soviet UN representative was boycotting the council to protest its exclusion of the new Communist government in China, the United States was able to push through a resolution condemning the invasion and asking UN member nations to "render every assistance" to South Korea. That evening, relying on the resolution and on his constitutional authority as commander in chief, Truman authorized MacArthur to transport supplies to South Korea and to bomb military targets. Five days later, Truman committed U.S. soldiers to combat.

Not until June 27 did the president meet with congressional leaders. Although most of them—in the bipartisan spirit of foreign policy making that prevailed at the time—supported his actions and would willingly have secured a congressional resolution of support, Truman believed there was ample precedent for the president to undertake limited military actions unilaterally and did not want to foster the impression that he was relying on Congress for his authority. In addition, he cited the Senate's overwhelming ratification of the UN charter in 1945 and congressional passage of the United Nations Participation Act, which subjected the United States to certain kinds of UN decisions.

On July 19 in a broadcast speech to the nation, Truman stressed the cooperative nature of the UN effort, claiming that fifty-two of the body's fifty-nine members "have given their support" and noting that MacArthur's forces would fight under the UN flag. But the president did not minimize the magnitude of the U.S. effort that would be required: a substantial increase in the size of the armed forces, *including use of the draft; an estimated $10 billion in spending; higher taxes; and the diversion of industries from peacetime to wartime production.*

*Despite Truman's claim, the defense of South Korea turned out to be almost entirely a U.S. affair, eventually involving a million soldiers and $15 billion in spending. The fighting went well for a time: MacArthur's ingenious landing at Inchon, behind enemy lines, drove North Korean forces back across the border by October. Although this victory accomplished the original UN goal of restoring South Korea's security, Truman followed MacArthur's advice to invade North Korea. The results of this decision were disastrous: in late November, China entered the war in force, driving MacArthur's army into retreat. The addition of more U.S. troops accomplished only a military stalemate, which lasted for the duration of the Truman presidency. Along the way, Truman lost control of MacArthur. Eventually, claiming the deference due him as commander in chief, the president fired the general in 1951.*

*The longer the Korean War lasted, the more unpopular it became. But as an assertion of presidential power in war making, the Korean war was unprecedented. As the historian Arthur M. Schlesinger, Jr., later wrote in his 1973 book,* The Imperial Presidency, *"By bringing the nation into war without congressional authorization and by then successfully defending his exercise of independent presidential initiative, Truman enormously expanded assumptions of presidential prerogative."*    ~

My fellow citizens:

At noon today I sent a message to the Congress about the situation in Korea. I want to talk to you tonight about that situation and about what it means to the security of the United States and to our hopes for peace in the world.

Korea is a small country, thousands of miles away, but what is happening there is important to every American.

On Sunday, June 25th, Communist forces attacked the Republic of Korea.

This attack has made it clear, beyond all doubt, that the international Communist movement is willing to use armed invasion to conquer independent nations. An act of aggression such as this creates a very real danger to the security of all free nations.

The attack upon Korea was an outright breach of the peace and a violation of the Charter of the United Nations. By their actions in Korea, Communist leaders have demonstrated their contempt for the basic moral principles on which the United Nations is founded. This is a direct challenge to the efforts of the free nations to build the kind of world in which men can live in freedom and peace.

This challenge has been presented squarely. We must meet it squarely.

It is important for all of us to understand the essential facts as to how the situation in Korea came about.

Before and during World War II, Korea was subject to Japanese rule. When the fighting stopped, it was agreed that troops of the Soviet Union would accept the surrender of the Japanese soldiers in the northern part of Korea, and that American forces would accept the surrender of the Japanese in the southern part. For this purpose, the 38th parallel was used as the dividing line.

Later, the United Nations sought to establish Korea as a free and independent nation. A commission was sent out to supervise a free election in the whole of Korea. However, this election was held only in the southern part of the country, because the Soviet Union refused to permit an election for this purpose to be held in the northern part. Indeed, the Soviet authorities even refused to permit the United Nations Commission to visit northern Korea.

Nevertheless, the United Nations decided to go ahead where it could. In August 1948 the Republic of Korea was established as a free and independent nation in that part of Korea south of the 38th parallel.

In December 1948, the Soviet Union stated that it had withdrawn its troops from northern Korea and that a local government had been established there. However, the Communist authorities never have permitted the United Nations observers to visit northern Korea to see what was going on behind that part of the Iron Curtain.

It was from that area, where the Communist authorities have been unwilling to let the outside world see what was going on, that the attack was launched against the Republic of Korea on June 25th. That attack came without provocation and without warning. It was an act of raw aggression, without a shadow of justification.

I repeat that it was an act of raw aggression. It had no justification whatever.

The Communist invasion was launched in great force, with planes, tanks, and artillery. The size of the attack, and the speed with which it was followed up, make it perfectly plain that it had been plotted long in advance.

As soon as word of the attack was received, Secretary of State Acheson called me at Independence, Mo., and informed me that, with my approval, he would ask for an immediate meeting of the United Nations Security Council. The Security Council met just 24 hours after the Communist invasion began.

One of the main reasons the Security Council was set up was to act in such cases as this—to stop outbreaks of aggression in a hurry before they develop into general conflicts. In this case the Council passed a resolution which called for the invaders of Korea to stop fighting, and to withdraw. The Council called on all members of the United Nations to help carry out this resolution. The Communist invaders ignored the action of the Security Council and kept right on with their attack.

The Security Council then met again. It recommended that members of the United Nations help the Republic of Korea repel the attack and help restore peace and security in that area.

Fifty-two of the 59 countries which are members of the United Nations have given their support to the action taken by the Security Council to restore peace in Korea.

These actions by the United Nations and its members are of great importance. The free nations have now made it clear that lawless aggression will be met with force. The free nations have learned the fateful lesson of the 1930's. That lesson is that aggression must be met firmly. Appeasement leads only to further aggression and ultimately to war.

The principal effort to help the Koreans preserve their independence, and to help the United Nations restore peace, has been made by the United States. We have sent land, sea, and air forces to assist in these operations. We have done this because we know that what is at stake here is nothing less than our own national security and the peace of the world.

So far, two other nations—Australia and Great Britain—have sent planes to Korea; and six other nations—Australia, Canada, France, Great Britain, the Netherlands, and New Zealand—have made naval forces available.

Under the flag of the United Nations a unified command has been established for all forces of the members of the United Nations fighting in Korea. Gen. Douglas MacArthur is the commander of this combined force.

The prompt action of the United Nations to put down lawless aggression, and the prompt response to this action by free peoples all over the world, will stand as a landmark in mankind's long search for a rule of law among nations.

Only a few countries have failed to endorse the efforts of the United Nations to stop the fighting in Korea. The most important of these is the Soviet Union. The Soviet Union has boycotted the meetings of the United Nations Security Council. It has refused to support the actions of the United Nations with respect to Korea.

The United States requested the Soviet Government, 2 days after the fighting started, to use its influence with the North Koreans to have them withdraw. The Soviet Government refused.

The Soviet Government has said many times that it wants peace in the world, but its attitude toward this act of aggression against the Republic of Korea is in direct contradiction of its statements.

For our part, we shall continue to support the United Nations action to restore peace in the world.

We know that it will take a hard, tough fight to halt the invasion, and to drive the Communists back. The invaders have been provided with enough equipment and supplies for a long campaign. They overwhelmed the lightly armed defense forces of the Korean Republic in the first few days and drove southward.

Now, however, the Korean defenders have reorganized and are making a brave fight for their liberty, and an increasing number of American troops have joined them. Our forces have fought a skillful, rearguard delaying action, pending the arrival of reinforcements. Some of these reinforcements are now arriving; others are on the way from the United States.

I should like to read you a part of a report I have received from General Collins, Chief of Staff of the United States Army. General Collins and General Vandenberg, Chief of Staff of the Air Force, have just returned from an inspection trip to Korea and Japan.

This is what General Collins had to say: "The United States Armed Forces in Korea are giving a splendid account of themselves.

"Our Far Eastern forces were organized and equipped primarily to perform peaceful occupation duties in Japan. However, under General MacArthur's magnificent leadership, they have quickly adapted themselves to meet the deliberately planned attack of the North Korean Communist forces, which are well-equipped, well-led, and battle-trained, and which have at times outnumbered our troops by as much as 20 to 1.

"Our Army troops, ably supported by tactical aircraft of the United States Air Force and Navy and our Australian friends, flying under the most adverse conditions of weather, have already distinguished themselves in the most difficult of military operations—a delaying action. The fact that they are preventing the Communists from overrunning Korea—which this calculated attack had been designed to accomplish—is a splendid tribute to the ability of our Armed Forces to convert quickly from the peaceful duties of occupation to the grim duties of war.

"The task that confronts us is not an easy one, but I am confident of the outcome."

I shall also read to you part of a report that I received from General MacArthur within the last few hours.

General MacArthur says:

"It is, of course, impossible to predict with any degree of accuracy the future incidents of a military campaign. Over a broad front involving continuous local struggles, there are bound to be ups and downs, losses as well as successes. . . . But the issue of battle is now fully joined and will proceed along lines of action in which we will not be without choice. Our hold upon the southern part of Korea represents a secure base. Our casualties, despite overwhelming odds, have been relatively light. Our strength will continually increase while that of the enemy will relatively decrease. His supply line is insecure. He has had his great chance and failed to exploit it. We are now in Korea in force, and with God's help we are there to stay until the constitutional authority of the Republic of Korea is fully restored."

These and other reports I have received show that our Armed Forces are acting with close teamwork and efficiency to meet the problems facing us in Korea.

These reports are reassuring, but they also show that the job ahead of us in Korea is long and difficult.

Furthermore, the fact that Communist forces have invaded Korea is a warning that there may be similar acts of aggression in other parts of the world. The free nations must be on their guard, more than ever before, against this kind of sneak attack.

It is obvious that we must increase our military strength and preparedness immediately. There are three things we need to do.

First, we need to send more men, equipment, and supplies to General MacArthur.

Second, in view of the world situation, we need to build up our own Army, Navy, and Air Force over and above what is needed in Korea.

Third, we need to speed up our work with other countries in strengthening our common defenses.

To help meet these needs, I have already authorized increases in the size of our Armed Forces. These increases will come in part from volunteers, in part from Selective Service, and in part from the National Guard and the Reserves. I have also ordered that military supplies and equipment be obtained at a faster rate.

The necessary increases in the size of our Armed Forces, and the additional equipment they must have, will cost about $10 billion, and I am asking the Congress to appropriate the amount required.

These funds will be used to train men and equip them with tanks, planes, guns, and ships, in order to build the strength we need to help assure peace in the world.

When we have worked out with other free countries an increased program for our common defense, I shall recommend to the Congress that additional funds be provided for this purpose. This is of great importance. The free nations face a worldwide threat. It must be met with a worldwide defense. The United States and other free nations can multiply their strength by joining with one another in a common effort to provide this defense. This is our best hope for peace.

The things we need to do to build up our military defense will require considerable adjustment in our domestic economy. We have a tremendously rich and productive economy, and it is expanding every year.

Our job now is to divert to defense purposes more of that tremendous productive capacity—more steel, more aluminum, more of a good many things.

Some of the additional production for military purposes can come from making fuller use of plants which are not operating at capacity. But many of our industries are already going full tilt, and until we can add new capacity, some of the resources we need for the national defense will have to be taken from civilian uses.

This requires us to take certain steps to make sure that we obtain the things we need for national defense, and at the same time guard against inflationary price rises.

The steps that are needed now must be taken promptly.

In the message which I sent to the Congress today, I described the economic measures which are required at this time.

First, we need laws which will insure prompt and adequate supplies for military and essential civilian use. I have therefore recommended that the Congress give the Government power to guide the flow of materials into essential uses, to restrict their use for nonessential purposes, and to prevent the accumulation of unnecessary inventories.

Second, we must adopt measures to prevent inflation and to keep our Government in a sound financial condition. One of the major causes of inflation is the excessive use of credit. I have recommended that the Congress authorize the Government to set limits on installment buying and to curb speculation in agricultural commodities. In the housing field, where Government credit is an important factor, I have already directed that credit restraints be applied, and I have recommended that the Congress authorize further controls.

As an additional safeguard against inflation, and to help finance our defense needs, it will be necessary to make substantial increases in taxes. This is a contribution to our national security that every one of us should stand ready to make. As soon as a balanced and fair program can be worked out, I shall lay it before the Congress. This tax program will have as a major aim the elimination of profiteering.

Third, we should increase the production of goods needed for national defense. We must plan to enlarge our defense production, not just for the immediate future, but for the next several years. This will be primarily a task for our businessmen and workers. However, to help obtain the necessary increases, the Government should be authorized to provide certain types of financial assistance to private industry to increase defense production.

Our military needs are large, and to meet them will require hard work and steady effort. I know that we can produce what we need if each of us does his part—each man, each woman, each soldier, each civilian. This is a time for all of us to pitch in and work together.

I have been sorry to hear that some people have fallen victim to rumors in the last week or two, and have been buying up various things they have heard would be scarce. That is foolish— I say that is foolish, and it is selfish, very selfish, because hoarding results in entirely unnecessary local shortages.

Hoarding food is especially foolish. There is plenty of food in this country. I have read that there have been runs on sugar in some cities. That is perfectly ridiculous. We now have more sugar available than ever before. There are ample supplies of our other basic foods also.

Now, I sincerely hope that every American housewife will keep this in mind when she does her daily shopping.

If I had thought that we were actually threatened by shortages of essential consumer goods, I should have recommended that price control and rationing be immediately instituted. But there is no such threat. We have to fear only those shortages which we ourselves artificially create.

Every businessman who is trying to profiteer in time of national danger— and every person who is selfishly trying to get more than his neighbor—is doing just exactly the thing that any enemy of this country would want him to do.

If prices should rise unduly because of excessive buying or speculation, I know our people will want the Government to take action, and I will not hesitate to recommend rationing and price control.

We have the resources to meet our needs. Far more important, the American people are unified in their belief in democratic freedom. We are united in detesting Communist slavery.

We know that the cost of freedom is high. But we are determined to preserve our freedom—no matter what the cost.

I know that our people are willing to do their part to support our soldiers and sailors and airmen who are fighting in Korea. I know that our fighting men can count on each and every one of you.

Our country stands before the world as an example of how free men, under God, can build a community of neighbors, working together for the good of all.

That is the goal we seek not only for ourselves, but for all people. We believe that freedom and peace are essential if men are to live as our Creator intended us to live. It is this faith that has guided us in the past, and it is this faith that will fortify us in the stern days ahead.

# Youngstown Sheet and Tube Co. v. Sawyer (1952)

On April 8, 1952, President Harry S Truman ordered Secretary of Commerce Charles Sawyer "to take possession of and operate the plants and facilities of certain steel companies," including the Youngstown Sheet and Tube Co. Truman acted partly out of the fear that an impending strike for higher wages (a goal he supported) by the steelworkers' unions would jeopardize the ability of the United States to maintain both its military effort in the Korean War and its commitments to supply arms to Europe. He was not alone in this belief; Robert Lovett, the secretary of defense, and Dean Acheson, the secretary of state, agreed.

Truman had the authority under the Labor-Management Relations Act of 1947 (better known as the Taft-Hartley Act) to impose a court-ordered, sixty-day "cooling off" period on both labor and management whenever the nation's health or safety was imperiled. But for political reasons—Truman opposed the act and had sought its repeal—he was unwilling to do so. Instead, he grounded his authority to seize the mills in the existence of a wartime emergency and in his authority "as President of the United States and Commander in Chief of the Armed Forces." Truman was aware that previous presidents, including Abraham Lincoln and Franklin D. Roosevelt, had seized private property without prior congressional authorization. He also knew that only once—and never to a sitting president—had the Supreme Court declared a presidential action unconstitutional during a war. (See "Ex Parte Milligan," p. 128.)

Truman conceded in an April 9, 1952, report that Congress had the power to countermand his steel seizure order, confident that it would not. In this assessment he was correct. Although certain that the steel companies would sue to have the Supreme Court declare the order unconstitutional, Truman was confident of its support as well, not just because of the Court's history of deference to the president in foreign and military matters but also because he had appointed three of the nine justices and believed that three others were either pro-union or pro-presidential prerogative. In this assessment Truman was wrong.

On June 2, 1952, ruling in the case of Youngstown Sheet and Tube Co. v. Sawyer (also known as the Steel Seizure Case), the Supreme Court declared President Truman's order to Secretary Sawyer unconstitutional by a 6-3 vote. Because seven of the nine justices (including all six in the majority) wrote separate opinions and only three endorsed Justice Hugo L. Black's opinion of the Court in its entirety, the full implications of this ruling for presidential power were (and remain) *unclear. About the only thing that a majority of justices could agree on was that Congress had foreclosed the president from seizing industries during national emergencies by rejecting a proposed amendment to the Taft-Hartley Act that would have conferred such authority.*

*Although Truman lost the case, his constitutional claim that the president has an inherent, unstated constitutional power to act in cases of national emergency was accepted, to one degree or another, by a majority of the justices. Black rejected this argument, as did Justice William O. Douglas. But the three dissenting justices (Chief Justice Fred M. Vinson and Justices Sherman Minton and Stanley F. Reed) and at least two of the justices who voted with Black (Robert H. Jackson, in a celebrated opinion, and Tom C. Clark) endorsed it to one degree or another.*   ∼

MR. JUSTICE BLACK delivered the opinion of the Court.

We are asked to decide whether the President was acting within his constitutional power when he issued an order directing the Secretary of Commerce to take possession of and operate most of the Nation's steel mills. The mill owners argue that the President's order amounts to lawmaking, a legislative function which the Constitution has expressly confided to the Congress and not to the President. The Government's position is that the order was made on findings of the President that his action was necessary to avert a national catastrophe which would inevitably result from a stoppage of steel production, and that in meeting this grave emergency the President was acting within the aggregate of his constitutional powers as the Nation's Chief Executive and the Commander in Chief of the Armed Forces of the United States. The issue emerges here from the following series of events:

In the latter part of 1951, a dispute arose between the steel companies and their employees over terms and conditions that should be included in new collective bargaining agreements. Long-continued conferences failed to resolve the dispute. On December 18, 1951, the employees' representative, United Steelworkers of America, C.I.O., gave notice of an intention to strike when the existing bargaining agreements expired on December 31. The Federal Mediation and Conciliation Service then intervened in an effort to get labor and management to agree. This failing, the President on December 22, 1951, referred the dispute to the Federal Wage Stabilization Board[1] to investigate and make recommendations for fair and equitable terms of settlement. This Board's report resulted in no settlement. On April 4, 1952, the Union gave notice of a nation-wide strike called to begin at 12:01 a.m. April 9. The indispensability of steel as a component of substantially all weapons and other war materials led the President to believe that the proposed work stoppage would immediately jeopardize our national defense and that governmental seizure of the steel mills was necessary in order to assure the continued availability of steel. Reciting these considerations for his action, the President, a few hours before the strike was to begin, issued Executive Order 10340, a copy of which is attached as an appendix, *post,* p. 589. The order directed the Secretary of Commerce to take possession of most of the steel mills and keep them running. The Secretary immediately issued his own possessory orders, calling upon the presidents of the various seized companies to serve as operating managers for the United States. They were directed to carry on their activities in accordance with regulations and directions of the Secretary. The next morning the President sent a message to Congress reporting his action. Cong.

Rec., April 9, 1952, p. 3962. Twelve days later he sent a second message. Cong. Rec., April 21, 1952, p. 4192. Congress has taken no action.

Obeying the Secretary's orders under protest, the companies brought proceedings against him in the District Court. Their complaints charged that the seizure was not authorized by an act of Congress or by any constitutional provisions. The District Court was asked to declare the orders of the President and the Secretary invalid and to issue preliminary and permanent injunctions restraining their enforcement. Opposing the motion for preliminary injunction, the United States asserted that a strike disrupting steel production for even a brief period would so endanger the well-being and safety of the Nation that the President had "inherent power" to do what he had done— power "supported by the Constitution, by historical precedent, and by court decisions." The Government also contended that in any event no preliminary injunction should be issued because the companies had made no showing that their available legal remedies were inadequate or that their injuries from seizure would be irreparable. Holding against the Government on all points, the District Court on April 30 issued a preliminary injunction restraining the Secretary from "continuing the seizure and possession of the plants ... and from acting under the purported authority of Executive Order No. 10340." 103 F. Supp. 569. On the same day the Court of Appeals stayed the District Court's injunction. 90 U.S. App. D.C. —, 197 F. 2d 582. Deeming it best that the issues raised be promptly decided by this Court, we granted certiorari on May 3 and set the cause for argument on May 12. 343 U.S. 937.

The President's power, if any, to issue the order must stem either from an act of Congress or from the Constitution itself. There is no statute that expressly authorizes the President to take posses-

sion of property as he did here. Nor is there any act of Congress to which our attention has been directed from which such a power can fairly be implied. Indeed, we do not understand the Government to rely on statutory authorization for this seizure. There are two statutes which do authorize the President to take both personal and real property under certain conditions.[2] However, the Government admits that these conditions were not met and that the President's order was not rooted in either of the statutes. The Government refers to the seizure provisions of one of these statutes (§ 201 (b) of the Defense Production Act) as "much too cumbersome, involved, and time-consuming for the crisis which was at hand."

Moreover, the use of the seizure technique to solve labor disputes in order to prevent work stoppages was not only unauthorized by any congressional enactment; prior to this controversy, Congress had refused to adopt that method of settling labor disputes. When the Taft-Hartley Act was under consideration in 1947, Congress rejected an amendment which would have authorized such governmental seizures in cases of emergency.[3] Apparently it was thought that the technique of seizure, like that of compulsory arbitration, would interfere with the process of collective bargaining.[4] Consequently, the plan Congress adopted in that Act did not provide for seizure under any circumstances. Instead, the plan sought to bring about settlements by use of the customary devices of mediation, conciliation, investigation by boards of inquiry, and public reports. In some instances temporary injunctions were authorized to provide cooling-off periods. All this failing, unions were left free to strike after a secret vote by employees as to whether they wished to accept their employers' final settlement offer.[5]

It is clear that if the President had authority to issue the order he did, it must be found in some provision of the Constitution. And it is not claimed that express constitutional language grants this power to the President. The contention is that presidential power should be implied from the aggregate of his powers under the Constitution. Particular reliance is placed on provisions in Article II which says that "The executive Power shall be vested in a President . . ."; that "he shall take Care that the Laws be faithfully executed"; and that he "shall be Commander in Chief of the Army and Navy of the United States."

The order cannot properly be sustained as an exercise of the President's military power as Commander in Chief of the Armed Forces. The Government attempts to do so by citing a number of cases upholding broad powers in military commanders engaged in day-to-day fighting in a theater of war. Such cases need not concern us here. Even though "theater of war" be an expanding concept, we cannot with faithfulness to our constitutional system hold that the Commander in Chief of the Armed Forces has the ultimate power as such to take possession of private property in order to keep labor disputes from stopping production. This is a job for the Nation's lawmakers, not for its military authorities.

Nor can the seizure order be sustained because of the several constitutional provisions that grant executive power to the President. In the framework of our Constitution, the President's power to see that the laws are faithfully executed refutes the idea that he is to be a lawmaker. The Constitution limits his functions in the lawmaking process to the recommending of laws he thinks wise and the vetoing of laws he thinks bad. And the Constitution is neither silent nor equivocal about who shall make laws which the President is to execute. The first section of the first article says that "All legislative Powers herein granted shall

be vested in a Congress of the United States. . . ." After granting many powers to the Congress, Article I goes on to provide that Congress may "make all Laws which shall be necessary and proper for carrying into Execution the foregoing Powers, and all other Powers vested by this Constitution in the Government of the United States, or in any Department or Officer thereof."

The President's order does not direct that a congressional policy be executed in a manner prescribed by Congress—it directs that a presidential policy be executed in a manner prescribed by the President. The preamble of the order itself, like that of many statutes, sets out reasons why the President believes certain policies should be adopted, proclaims these policies as rules of conduct to be followed, and again, like a statute, authorizes a government official to promulgate additional rules and regulations consistent with the policy proclaimed and needed to carry that policy into execution. The power of Congress to adopt such public policies as those proclaimed by the order is beyond question. It can authorize the taking of private property for public use. It can make laws regulating the relationships between employers and employees, prescribing rules designed to settle labor disputes, and fixing wages and working conditions in certain fields of our economy. The Constitution does not subject this lawmaking power of Congress to presidential or military supervision or control.

Is is said that other Presidents without congressional authority have taken possession of private business enterprises in order to settle labor disputes. But even if this be true, Congress has not thereby lost its exclusive constitutional authority to make laws necessary and proper to carry out the powers vested by the Constitution "in the Government of the United States, or any Department or Officer thereof."

The Founders of this Nation entrusted the lawmaking power to the Congress alone in both good and bad times. It would do no good to recall the historical events, the fears of power and the hopes for freedom that lay behind their choice. Such a review would but confirm our holding that this seizure order cannot stand.

The judgment of the District Court is Affirmed.

MR. JUSTICE JACKSON, concurring in the judgment and opinion of the Court.

That comprehensive and undefined presidential powers hold both practical advantages and grave dangers for the country will impress anyone who has served as legal adviser to a President in time of transition and public anxiety. While an interval of detached reflection may temper teachings of that experience, they probably are a more realistic influence on my views than the conventional materials of judicial decision which seem unduly to accentuate doctrine and legal fiction. But as we approach the question of presidential power, we half overcome mental hazards by recognizing them. The opinions of judges, no less than executives and publicists, often suffer the infirmity of confusing the issue of a power's validity with the cause it is invoked to promote, of confounding the permanent executive office with its temporary occupant. The tendency is strong to emphasize transient results upon policies—such as wages or stabilization—and lose sight of enduring consequences upon the balanced power structure of our Republic.

A judge, like an executive adviser, may be surprised at the poverty of really useful and unambiguous authority applicable to concrete problems of executive power as they actually present themselves. Just what our forefathers did envision, or would have envisioned had they foreseen modern conditions, must be divined from materials almost as enigmatic as the dreams Joseph was called upon to interpret for Pharaoh. A century and a half of partisan debate and scholarly speculation yields no net result but only supplies more or less apt quotations from respected sources on each side of any question. They largely cancel each other.[1] And court decisions are indecisive because of the judicial practice of dealing with the largest questions in the most narrow way.

The actual art of governing under our Constitution does not and cannot conform to judicial definitions of the power of any of its branches based on isolated clauses or even single Articles torn from context. While the Constitution diffuses power the better to secure liberty, it also contemplates that practice will integrate the dispersed powers into a workable government. It enjoins upon its branches separateness but interdependence, autonomy but reciprocity. Presidential powers are not fixed but fluctuate, depending upon their disjunction or conjunction with those of Congress. We may well begin by a somewhat over-simplified grouping of practical situations in which a President may doubt, or others may challenge, his powers, and by distinguishing roughly the legal consequences of this factor of relativity.

1. When the President acts pursuant to an express or implied authorization of Congress, his authority is at its maximum, for it includes all that he possesses in his own right plus all that Congress can delegate.[2] In these circumstances, and in these only, may he be said (for what it may be worth) to personify federal sovereignty. If his act is held unconstitutional under these circumstances, it usually means that the Federal Government as an undivided whole lacks power. A seizure executed by the President pursuant to an Act of Congress would be supported by the strongest of presumptions and the widest latitude of judicial interpretation, and the burden of persuasion would rest

heavily upon any who might attack it.

2. When the President acts in absence of either a congressional grant or denial of authority, he can only rely upon his own independent powers, but there is a zone of twilight in which he and Congress may have concurrent authority, or in which its distribution is uncertain. Therefore, congressional inertia, indifference or quiescence may sometimes, at least as a practical matter, enable, if not invite, measures on independent presidential responsibility. In this area, any actual test of power is likely to depend on the imperatives of events and contemporary imponderables rather than on abstract theories of law.[3]

3. When the President takes measures incompatible with the expressed or implied will of Congress, his power is at its lowest ebb, for then he can rely only upon his own constitutional powers minus any constitutional powers of Congress over the matter. Courts can sustain exclusive presidential control in such a case only by disabling the Congress from acting upon the subject.[4] Presidential claim to a power at once so conclusive and preclusive must be scrutinized with caution, for what is at stake is the equilibrium established by our constitutional system.

Into which of these classifications does this executive seizure of the steel industry fit? It is eliminated from the first by admission, for it is conceded that no congressional authorization exists for this seizure. That takes away also the support of the many precedents and declarations which were made in relation, and must be confined, to this category.[5]

Can it then be defended under flexible tests available to the second category? It seems clearly eliminated from that class because Congress has not left seizure of private property an open field but has covered it by three statutory policies inconsistent with this seizure.

In cases where the purpose is to supply needs of the Government itself, two courses are provided: one, seizure of a plant which fails to comply with obligatory orders placed by the Government;[6] another, condemnation of facilities, including temporary use under the power of eminent domain.[7] The third is applicable where it is the general economy of the country that is to be protected rather than exclusive governmental interests.[8] None of these were invoked. In choosing a different and inconsistent way of his own, the President cannot claim that it is necessitated or invited by failure of Congress to legislate upon the occasions, grounds and methods for seizure of industrial properties.

This leaves the current seizure to be justified only by the severe tests under the third grouping, where it can be supported only by any reminder of executive power after subtraction of such powers as Congress may have over the subject. In short, we can sustain the President only by holding that seizure of such strike-bound industries is within his domain and beyond control by Congress. Thus, this Court's first review of such seizures occurs under circumstances which leave presidential power most vulnerable to attack and in the least favorable of possible constitutional postures.

I did not suppose, and I am not persuaded, that history leaves it open to question, at least in the courts, that the executive branch, like the Federal Government as a whole, possesses only delegated powers. The purpose of the Constitution was not only to grant power, but to keep it from getting out of hand. However, because the President does not enjoy unmentioned powers does not mean that the mentioned ones should be narrowed by niggardly construction. Some clauses could be made almost unworkable, as well as immutable, by refusal to indulge some latitude of interpretation for changing times. I have heretofore, and do now, give to the enumerated powers the scope and elasticity afforded by what seem to be reasonable, practical implications instead of the rigidity dictated by a doctrinaire textualism.

The Solicitor General seeks the power of seizure in three clauses of the Executive Article, the first reading, "The executive Power shall be vested in a President of the United States of America." Lest I be thought to exaggerate, I quote the interpretation which his brief puts upon it: "In our view, this clause constitutes a grant of all the executive powers of which the Government is capable." If that be true, it is difficult to see why the forefathers bothered to add several specific items, including some trifling ones.[9]

The example of such unlimited executive power that must have most impressed the forefathers was the prerogative exercised by George III, and the description of its evils in the Declaration of Independence leads me to doubt that they were creating their new Executive in his image. Continental European examples were no more appealing. And if we seek instruction from our own times, we can match it only from the executive powers in those governments we disparagingly describe as totalitarian. I cannot accept the view that this clause is a grant in bulk of all conceivable executive power but regard it as an allocation to the presidential office of the generic powers thereafter stated.

The clause on which the Government next relies is that "The President shall be Commander in Chief of the Army and Navy of the United States. . . ." These cryptic words have given rise to some of the most persistent controversies in our constitutional history. Of course, they imply something more than an empty title. But just what authority goes with the name has plagued presidential advisers who would not waive or narrow it by nonassertion yet cannot say where it begins or ends. It undoubtedly puts the Nation's armed forces under presidential command. Hence, this loose appellation is sometimes advanced as support for any presidential action, internal or external, involving use of force, the idea being that it vests power to do anything, anywhere, that can be done with an army or navy.

That seems to be the logic of an argument tendered at our bar—that the President having, on his own responsibility, sent American troops abroad derives from that act "affirmative power" to seize the means of producing a supply of steel for them. To quote, "Perhaps the most forceful illustration of the scope of Presidential power in this connection is the fact that American troops in Korea, whose safety and effectiveness are so directly involved here, were sent to the field by an exercise of the President's constitutional powers." Thus, it is said, he has invested himself with "war powers."

I cannot foresee all that it might entail if the Court should indorse this argument. Nothing in our Constitution is plainer than that declaration of a war is entrusted only to Congress. Of course, a state of war may in fact exist without a formal declaration. But no doctrine that the Court could promulgate would seem to me more sinister and alarming than that a President whose conduct of foreign affairs is so largely uncontrolled, and often even is unknown, can vastly enlarge his mastery over the internal affairs of the country by his own commitment of the Nation's armed forces to some foreign venture.[10] I do not, however, find it necessary or appropriate to consider the legal status of the Korean enterprise to discountenance argument based on it.

Assuming that we are in a war *de facto*, whether it is or is not a war *de jure*, does that empower the Commander in Chief to seize industries he thinks necessary to supply our army? The Constitution expressly places in Congress power "to raise and *support* Armies" and "to *provide* and *maintain* a Navy." (Emphasis supplied.) This certainly lays upon Congress primary responsibility for supplying the armed forces. Congress alone controls the raising of revenues and their appropriation and may determine in what manner and by what means they shall be spent for military and naval procurement. I suppose no one would doubt that Congress can take over war supply as a Government enterprise. On the other hand, if Congress sees fit to rely on free private enterprise collectively bargaining with free labor for support and maintenance of our armed forces, can the Executive, because of lawful disagreements incidental to that process, seize the facility for operation upon Government-imposed terms?

There are indications that the Constitution did not contemplate that the title Commander in Chief *of the Army and Navy* will constitute him also Commander in Chief of the country, its industries and its inhabitants. He has no monopoly of "war powers," whatever they are. While Congress cannot deprive the President of the command of the army and navy, only Congress can provide him an army or navy to command. It is also empowered to make rules for the "Government and Regulation of land and naval Forces," by which it may to some unknown extent impinge upon even command functions.

That military powers of the Commander in Chief were not to supersede representative government of internal affairs seems obvious from the Constitution and from elementary American history. Time out of mind, and even now in many parts of the world, a military commander can seize private housing to shelter his troops. Not so, however, in the United States, for the Third Amendment says, "No Soldier shall, in time of peace be quartered in any house, without the consent of the Owner, nor in time of war, but in a manner to be prescribed by law." Thus, even in war time, his seizure of needed military housing must be authorized by Congress. It also was expressly left to Congress to "provide for calling forth the Militia to execute the Laws of the Union, suppress Insurrections and repel Invasions...." [11] Such a limitation on the command power, written at a time when the militia rather than a standing army was contemplated as the military weapon of the Republic, underscores the Constitution's policy that Congress, not the Executive, should control utilization of the war power as an instrument of domestic policy. Congress, fulfilling that function, has authorized the President to use the army to enforce certain civil rights. [12] On the other hand, Congress has forbidden him to use the army for the purpose of executing general laws except when *expressly* authorized by the Constitution or by Act of Congress. [13]

While broad claims under this rubric often have been made, advice to the President in specific matters usually has carried overtones that powers, even under this head, are measured by the command functions usual to the topmost officer of the army and navy. Even then, heed has been taken of any efforts of Congress to negative his authority. [14]

We should not use this occasion to circumscribe, much less to contract, the lawful role of the President as Commander in Chief. I should indulge the widest latitude of interpretation to sustain his exclusive function to command the instruments of national force, at least when turned against the outside world for the security of our society. But, when it is turned inward, not because of rebellion but because of a lawful economic struggle between industry and labor, it should have no such indulgence. His command power is not such an absolute as might be implied from that office in militaristic system but is subject to limitations consistent with a constitutional Republic whose law and policy-making branch is a representative Congress. The purpose of lodging dual titles in one man was to insure that the civilian would control the military, not to enable the military to subordinate the presidential office. No penance would ever expiate the sin against free government of holding that a President can escape control of executive powers by law through assuming his military role. What the power of command may include I do not try to envision, but I think it is not a military prerogative, without support of law, to seize persons or property because they are important or even essential for the military and naval establishment.

The third clause in which the Solicitor General finds seizure powers is that "he shall take Care that the Laws be faithfully executed...." [15] That authority must be matched against words of the Fifth Amendment that "No person shall be ... deprived of life, liberty or property, without due process of law...." One gives a governmental authority that reaches so far as there is law, the other gives a private right that authority shall go no farther. These signify about all there is of the principle that ours is a government of laws, not of men, and that we submit ourselves to rulers only if under rules.

The Solicitor General lastly grounds support of the seizure upon nebulous, inherent powers never expressly granted but said to have accrued to the office from the customs and claims of preceding administrations. The plea is for a resulting power to deal with a crisis or an emergency according to the necessities of the case, the unarticulated assumption being that necessity knows no law.

Loose and irresponsible use of adjectives colors all nonlegal and much legal discussion of presidential powers. "Inherent" powers, "implied" powers, "incidental" powers, "plenary" powers, "war" powers and "emergency" powers are used, often interchangeably and without fixed or ascertainable meanings.

The vagueness and generality of the clauses that set forth presidential powers afford a plausible basis for pressures within and without an administration for presidential action beyond that supported by those whose responsibility it is to defend his actions in court. The claim of inherent and unrestricted presidential powers has long been a persuasive dialectical weapon in political controversy. While it is not surprising that counsel should grasp support from such unadjudicated claims of power, a judge cannot accept self-serving press statements of the attorney for one of the interested parties as authority in answering a constitutional question, even if the advocate was himself. But prudence has counseled that actual reliance on such nebulous claims stop short of provoking a judicial test. [16]

The Solicitor General, acknowledging that Congress has never authorized the seizure here, says practice of prior Presidents has authorized it. He seeks color of legality from claimed executive precedents, chief of which is President Roosevelt's seizure on June 9, 1941, of the California plant of the North American Aviation Company. Its superficial similarities with the present case, upon analysis, yield to distinctions so decisive that it cannot be regarded as even a precedent, much less an authority for the present seizure. [17]

The appeal, however, that we declare the existence of inherent powers *ex necessitate* to meet an emergency asks us to do what many think would be wise, although it is something the forefathers omitted. They knew what emergencies were, knew the pressures they engender for authoritative action, knew, too, how they afford a ready pretext for usurpation. We may also suspect that they suspected that emergency powers would tend to kindle emergencies. Aside from suspension of the privilege of the writ of habeas corpus in time of rebellion or invasion, when the public safety may require it, [18] they made no express provision for exercise of extraordinary authority because of a crisis.[19] I do not think we rightfully may so amend their work, and, if we could, I am not convinced it would be wise to do so, although many modern nations have forthrightly recognized that war and economic crises may upset the normal balance between liberty and authority. Their experience with emergency powers may not be irrelevant to the argument here that we should say that the Executive, of his own volition, can invest himself with undefined emergency powers.

Germany, after the First World War, framed the Weimar Constitution, designed to secure her liberties in the Western tradition. However, the President of the Republic, without concurrence of the Reichstag, was empowered temporarily to suspend any or all individual rights if public safety and order were seriously disturbed or endangered. This proved a temptation to every government, whatever its shade of opinion, and in 13 years suspension of rights was invoked on more than 250 occasions. Finally, Hitler persuaded President Von Hindenberg to suspend all such rights, and they were never restored.[20]

The French Republic provided for a very different kind of emergency government known as the "state of siege." It differed from the German emergency dictatorship, particularly in that emergency powers could not be assumed at will by the Executive but could only be granted as a parliamentary measure. And it did not, as in Germany, result in a suspension or abrogation of law but was a legal institution governed by special legal rules and terminable by parliamentary authority.[21]

Great Britain also has fought both World Wars under a sort of temporary dictatorship created by legislation.[22] As Parliament is not bound by written constitutional limitations, it established a crisis government simply by delegation to its Ministers of a larger measure than usual of its own unlimited power, which is exercised under its supervision by Ministers whom it may dismiss. This has been called the "high-water mark in the voluntary surrender of liberty," but, as Churchill put it, "Parliament stands custodian of these surrendered liberties, and its most sacred duty will be to restore them in their fullness when victory has crowned our exertions and our perseverance."[23] Thus, parliamentary control made emergency powers compatible with freedom.

This contemporary foreign experience may be inconclusive as to the wisdom of lodging emergency powers somewhere in a modern government. But it suggests that emergency powers are consistent with free government only when their control is lodged elsewhere than in the Executive who exercises them. That is the safeguard that would be nullified by our adoption of the "inherent powers" formula. Nothing in my experience convinced me that such risks are warranted by any real necessity, although such powers would, of course, be an executive convenience.

In the practical working of our Government we already have evolved a technique within the framework of the Constitution by which normal executive powers may be considerably expanded to meet an emergency. Congress may and has granted extraordinary authorities which lie dormant in normal times but may be called into play by the Executive in war or upon proclamation of a national emergency. In 1939, upon congressional request, the Attorney General listed ninety-nine such separate statutory grants by Congress of emergency or wartime executive powers.[24] They were invoked from time to time as need appeared. Under this procedure we retain Government by law— special, temporary law, perhaps, but law nonetheless. The public may know the extent and limitations of the powers that can be asserted, and persons affected may be informed from the statute of their rights and duties.

In view of the ease, expedition and safety with which Congress can grant and has granted large emergency powers, certainly ample to embrace this crisis, I am quite unimpressed with the argument that we should affirm possession of them without statute. Such power either has no beginning or it has no end. If it exists, it need submit to no legal restraint. I am not alarmed that it would plunge us straightway into dictatorship, but it is at least a step in that wrong direction.

As to whether there is imperative necessity for such powers, it is relevant to note the gap that exists between the President's paper powers and his real powers. The Constitution does not disclose the measure of the actual controls wielded by the modern presidential office. That instrument must be understood as an Eighteenth-Century sketch of a government hoped for, not as a blueprint of the Government that is. Vast accretions of federal power, eroded from that reserved by the States, have magnified the scope of presidential activity. Subtle shifts take place in the centers of real power that do not show on the face of the Constitution.

Executive power has the advantage of concentration in a single head in whose choice the whole Nation has a part, making him the focus of public hopes and expectations. In drama, magnitude and finality his decisions so far overshadow any others that almost alone he fills the public eye and ear. No other personality in public life can begin to compete with him in access to the public mind through modern methods of communications. By his prestige as head of state and his influence upon public opinion he exerts a leverage upon those who are supposed to check and balance his power which often cancels their effectiveness.

Moreover, rise of the party system has made a significant extra-constitutional supplement to real exec-utive power. No appraisal of his necessities is realistic which overlooks that he heads a political system as well as a legal system. Party loyalties and interests, sometimes more binding than law, extend his effective control into branches of government other than his own and he often may win, as a political leader, what he cannot command under the Constitution. Indeed, Woodrow Wilson, commenting on the President as leader both of his party and of the Nation, observed, "If he rightly interpret the national thought and boldly insist upon it, he is irresistible.... His office is anything he has the sagacity and force to make it." [25] I cannot be brought to believe that this country will suffer if the Court refuses further to aggrandize the presidential office, already so potent and so relatively immune from judicial review,[26] at the expense of Congress.

But I have no illusion that any decision by this Court can keep power in the hands of Congress if it is not wise and timely in meeting its problems. A crisis that challenges the President equally, or perhaps primarily, challenges Congress. If not good law, there was worldly wisdom in the maxim attributed to Napoleon that "The tools belong to the man who can use them." We may say that power to legislate for emergencies belongs in the hands of Congress, but only Congress itself can prevent power from slipping through its fingers.

The essence of our free Government is "leave to live by no man's leave, underneath the law"—to be governed by those impersonal forces which we call law. Our Government is fashioned to fulfill this concept so far as humanly possible. The Executive, except for recommendation and veto, has no legislative power. The executive action we have here originates in the individual will of the President and represents an exercise of authority without law. No one, perhaps not even the President, knows the limits of the power he may seek to exert in this instance and the parties affected cannot learn the limit of their rights. We do not know today what powers over labor or property would be claimed to flow from Government possession if we should legalize it, what rights to compensation would be claimed or recognized, or on what contingency it would end. With all its defects, delays and inconveniences, men have discovered no technique for long preserving free government except that the Executive be under the law, and that the law be made by parliamentary deliberations.

Such institutions may be destined to pass away. But it is the duty of the Court to be last, not first, to give them up.[27]

MR. CHIEF JUSTICE VINSON, with whom MR. JUSTICE REED and MR. JUSTICE MINTON join, dissenting.

... We are not called upon today to expand the Constitution to meet a new situation. For, in this case, we need only look to history and time-honored principles of constitutional law—principles that have been applied consistently by all branches of the Government throughout our history. It is those who assert the invalidity of the Executive Order who seek to amend the Constitution in this case.

### III.

A review of executive action demonstrates that our Presidents have on many occasions exhibited the leadership contemplated by the Framers when they made the President Commander in Chief, and imposed upon him the trust to "take Care that the Laws be faithfully executed." With or without explicit statutory authorization, Presidents have at such times dealt with national emergencies by acting promptly and resolutely to enforce legislative programs, at least to save

those programs until Congress could act. Congress and the courts have responded to such executive initiative with consistent approval.

Our first President displayed at once the leadership contemplated by the Framers. When the national revenue laws were openly flouted in some sections of Pennsylvania, President Washington, without waiting for a call from the state government, summoned the militia and took decisive steps to secure the faithful execution of the laws.[30] When international disputes engendered by the French revolution threatened to involve this country in war, and while congressional policy remained uncertain, Washington issued his Proclamation of Neutrality. Hamilton, whose defense of the Proclamation has endured the test of time, invoked the argument that the Executive has the duty to do that which will preserve peace until Congress acts and, in addition, pointed to the need for keeping the Nation informed of the requirements of existing laws and treaties as part of the faithful execution of the laws.[31]

President John Adams issued a warrant for the arrest of Jonathan Robbins in order to execute the extradition provisions of a treaty. This action was challenged in Congress on the ground that no specific statute prescribed the method to be used in executing the treaty. John Marshall, then a member of the House of Representatives, made the following argument in support of the President's action:

"The treaty, which is a law, enjoins the performance of a particular object. The person who is to perform this object is marked out by the Constitution, since the person is named who conducts the foreign intercourse, and is to take care that the laws be faithfully executed. The means by which it is to be performed, the force of the nation, are in the hands of this person. Ought not this person to perform the object, although the particular mode of using the means has not been prescribed? Congress, unquestionably, may prescribe the mode, and Congress may devolve on others the whole execution of the contract; but, till this be done, it seems the duty of the Executive department to execute the contract by any means it possesses." [32]

Efforts in Congress to discredit the President for his action failed.[33] Almost a century later, this Court had occasion to give its express approval to "the masterly and conclusive argument of John Marshall." [34]

Jefferson's initiative in the Louisiana Purchase, the Monroe Doctrine, and Jackson's removal of Government deposits from the Bank of the United States further serve to demonstrate by deed what the Framers described by word when they vested the whole of the executive power in the President.

Without declaration of war, President Lincoln took energetic action with the outbreak of the War Between the States. He summoned troops and paid them out of the Treasury without appropriation therefor. He proclaimed a naval blockade of the Confederacy and seized ships violating that blockade. Congress, far from denying the validity of these acts, gave them express approval. The most striking action of President Lincoln was the Emancipation Proclamation, issued in aid of the successful prosecution of the War Between the States, but wholly without statutory authority.[35]

In an action furnishing a most apt precedent for this case, President Lincoln without statutory authority directed the seizure of rail and telegraph lines leading to Washington.[36] Many months later, Congress recognized and confirmed the power of the President to seize railroads and telegraph lines and provided criminal penalties for interference with Government operation.[37] This Act did not confer on the President any additional powers of seizure. Congress plainly rejected the view that the President's act had been without legal sanction until ratified by the legislature.

Sponsors of the bill declared that its purpose was only to confirm the power which the President already possessed.[38] Opponents insisted a statute authorizing seizure was unnecessary and might even be construed as limiting existing Presidential powers.[39]

Other seizures of private property occurred during the War Between the States, just as they had occurred during previous wars.[40] In *United States* v. *Russell*, 13 Wall. 623 (1872), three river steamers were seized by Army Quartermasters on the ground of "imperative military necessity." This Court affirmed an award of compensation, stating:

"Extraordinary and unforeseen occasions arise, however, beyond all doubt, in cases of extreme necessity in time of war or of immediate and impending public danger, in which private property may be impressed into the public service, or may be seized and appropriated to the public use, or may even be destroyed without the consent of the owner.

"Exigencies of the kind do arise in time of war or impending public danger, but it is the emergency, as was said by a great magistrate, that gives the right, and it is clear that the emergency must be shown to exist before the taking can be justified. Such a justification may be shown, and when shown the rule is well settled that the officer taking private property for such a purpose, if the emergency is fully proved, is not a trespasser, and that the government is bound to make full compensation to the owner." [41]

In *In re Neagle,* 135 U.S. 1 (1890), this Court held that a federal officer had acted in line of duty when he was guarding a Justice of this Court riding circuit. It was conceded that there was no specific statute authorizing the President to assign such a guard. In holding that such a statute was not necessary, the Court broadly stated the question as follows:

"[The President] is enabled to fulfil the duty of his great department, expressed in the phrase that 'he shall take care that the laws be faithfully executed.'

"Is this duty limited to the enforcement of acts of Congress or of treaties of the United States according to their *express terms,* or does it include the rights, duties and obligations growing out of the Constitution itself, our international relations, and all the protection implied by the nature of the government under the Constitution?" [42]

The latter approach was emphatically adopted by the Court.

President Hayes authorized the widespread use of federal troops during the Railroad Strike of 1877.[43] President Cleveland also used the troops in the Pullman Strike of 1895 and his action is of special significance. No statute authorized this action. No call for help had issued from the Governor of Illinois; indeed Governor Altgeld disclaimed the need for supplemental forces. But the President's concern was that federal laws relating to the free flow of interstate commerce and the mails be continuously and faithfully executed without interruption.[44] To further this aim his agents sought and obtained the injunction upheld by this Court in *In re Debs,* 158 U.S. 564 (1895). The Court scrutinized each of the steps taken by the President to insure execution of the "mass of legislation" dealing with commerce and the mails and gave his conduct full approval. Congress likewise took note of this use of Presidential power to forestall apparent obstacles to the faithful execution of the laws. By separate resolutions, both the Senate and the House commended the Executive's action.[45]

President Theodore Roosevelt seriously contemplated seizure of Pennsylvania coal mines if a coal shortage necessitated such action.[46] In his autobiography, President Roosevelt expounded the "Stewardship Theory" of Presidential power, stating that "the executive as subject only to the people, and, under the Constitution, bound to serve the people affirmatively in cases where the Constitution does not explic-

itly forbid him to render the service." [47] Because the contemplated seizure of the coal mines was based on this theory, then ex-President Taft criticized President Roosevelt in a passage in his book relied upon by the District Court in this case. Taft, Our Chief Magistrate and His Powers (1916), 139-147. In the same book, however, President Taft agreed that such powers of the President as the duty to "take Care that the Laws be faithfully executed" could not be confined to "express Congressional statutes." *Id.,* at 88. *In re Neagle, supra,* and *In re Debs, supra,* were cited as conforming with Taft's concept of the office, *id.,* at pp. 88-94, as they were later to be cited with approval in his opinion as Chief Justice in *Myers* v. *United States,* 272 U.S. 52, 133 (1926).[48]

In 1909, President Taft was informed that government-owned oil lands were being patented by private parties at such a rate that public oil lands would be depleted in a matter of months. Although Congress had explicitly provided that these lands were open to purchase by United States citizens, 29 Stat. 526 (1897), the President nevertheless ordered the lands withdrawn from sale "[i]n aid of proposed legislation." In *United States* v. *Midwest Oil Co.,* 236 U.S. 459 (1915), the President's action was sustained as consistent with executive practice throughout our history. An excellent brief was filed in the case by the Solicitor General, Mr. John W. Davis, together with Assistant Attorney General Knaebel, later Reporter for this Court. In this brief, the situation confronting President Taft was described as "an emergency; there was no time to wait for the action of Congress." The brief then discusses the powers of the President under the Constitution in such a case:

"Ours is a self-sufficient Government within its sphere. (*Ex parte Siebold,* 100 U.S., 371, 395; *in re Debs,* 158 U.S., 564, 578.) 'Its means are adequate to its ends (*McCulloch* v. *Maryland,* 4

Wheat, 316, 424), and it is rational to assume that its active forces will be found equal in most things to the emergencies that confront it. While perfect flexibility is not to be expected in a Government of divided powers, and while division of power is one of the principal features of the Constitution, it is the plain duty of those who are called upon to draw the dividing lines to ascertain the essential, recognize the practical, and avoid a slavish formalism which can only serve to ossify the Government and reduce its efficiency without any compensating good. The function of making laws is peculiar to Congress, and the Executive can not exercise that function to any degree. But this is not to say that all of the *subjects* concerning which laws might be made are perforce removed from the possibility of Executive influence. The Executive may act upon things and upon men in many relations which have not, though they might have, been actually regulated by Congress. In other words, just as there are fields which are peculiar to Congress and fields which are peculiar to the Executive, so there are fields which are common to both, in the sense that the Executive may move within them until they shall have been occupied by legislative action. These are not the fields of legislative prerogative, but fields within which the lawmaking power may enter and dominate whenever it chooses. This situation results from the fact that the President is the active agent, not of Congress, but of the Nation. As such he performs the duties which the Constitution lays upon him immediately, and as such, also, he executes the laws and regulations adopted by Congress. He is the agent of the people of the United States, deriving all his powers from them and responsible directly to them. In no sense is he the agent of Congress. He obeys and executes the laws of Congress, not because Congress is enthroned in authority over him, but because the Constitution directs him to do so.

"Therefore it follows that in ways short of making laws or disobeying them, the Executive may be under a grave constitutional duty to act for the national protection in situations not covered by the acts of Congress, and in which, even, it may not be said that his action is the direct expression of any particular one of the independent powers which are granted to him specifically by the Constitution. Instances wherein the President has felt and fulfilled such a duty have not been rare in our history, though, being for the public benefit and approved by all, his acts have seldom been challenged in the courts. We are able, however, to present a number of apposite cases which were subjected to judicial inquiry."

The brief then quotes from such cases as *In re Debs, supra,* and *In re Neagle, supra,* and continues:

"As we understand the doctrine of the *Neagle case,* and the cases therein cited, it is clearly this: The Executive is authorized to exert *the power of the United States* when he finds this necessary for the protection of the agencies, the instrumentalities, or the property of the Government. This does not mean an authority to disregard the wishes of Congress on the subject, when that subject lies within its control and when those wishes have been expressed, and it certainly does not involve the slightest semblance of a power to legislate, much less to suspend legislation already passed by Congress. It involves the performance of specific acts, not of a legislative but purely of an executive character—acts which are not in themselves laws, but which presuppose a law authorizing him to perform them. This law is not expressed, either in the Constitution or in the enactments of Congress, but reason and necessity compel that it be implied from the exigencies of the situation.

"In none of the cases which we have mentioned, nor in the cases cited in the extracts taken from the *Neagle case,* was it possible to say that the action of the President was directed, expressly or impliedly, by Congress. The situations dealt with had never been covered by any act of Congress, and there was no ground whatever for a contention that the possibility of their occurrence had ever been specifically considered by the legislative mind. In none of those cases did the action of the President amount merely to the execution of some specific law.

"Neither does any of them stand apart in principle from the case at bar, as involving the exercise of specific constitutional powers of the President in a degree in which this case does not involve them. Taken collectively, the provisions of the Constitution which designate the President as the official who must represent us in foreign relations, in commanding the Army and Navy, in keeping Congress informed of the state of the Union, in insuring the faithful execution of the laws and in recommending new ones, considered in connection with the sweeping declaration that the executive power shall be vested in him, completely demonstrate that his is the watchful eye, the active hand, the overseeing dynamic force of the United States." [49]

This brief is valuable not alone because of the caliber of its authors but because it lays bare in succinct reasoning the basis of the executive practice which this Court approved in the *Midwest Oil* case.

During World War I, President Wilson established a War Labor Board without awaiting specific direction by Congress.[50] With William Howard Taft and Frank P. Walsh as co-chairmen, the Board had as its purpose the prevention of strikes and lockouts interfering with the production of goods needed to meet the emergency. Effectiveness of War Labor Board decision was accomplished by Presidential action, including seizure of industrial plants.[51] Seizure of the Nation's railroads was also ordered by President Wilson.[52]

Beginning with the Bank Holiday Proclamation[53] and continuing through World War II, executive leadership and initiative were characteristic of President Franklin D. Roosevelt's administration. In 1939, upon the outbreak of war in Europe, the President proclaimed a limited national emergency for the purpose of strengthening our national defense.[54] In May of 1941, the danger from the Axis belligerents having become clear, the President proclaimed "an unlimited national emergency" calling for mobilization of the Nation's defenses to repel aggression.[55] The President took the initiative in strengthening our defenses by acquiring rights from the British Government to establish air bases in exchange for over-age destroyers.[56]

In 1941, President Roosevelt acted to protect Iceland from attack by Axis powers, when British forces were withdrawn, by sending our forces to occupy Iceland. Congress was informed of this action on the same day that our forces reached Iceland.[57] The occupation of Iceland was but one of "at least 125 incidents" in our history in which Presidents, "without congressional authorization, and in the absence of a declaration of war, [have] ordered the Armed Forces to take action or maintain positions abroad." [58]

Some six months before Pearl Harbor, a dispute at a single aviation plant at Inglewood, California, interrupted a segment of the production of military aircraft. In spite of the comparative insignificance of this work stoppage to total defense production as contrasted with the complete paralysis now threatened by a shutdown of the entire basic steel industry, and even though our armed forces were not then engaged in combat, President Roosevelt ordered the seizure of the plant "pursuant to the powers vested in [him] by the Constitution and laws of the United States, as President of the United States of America and Commander in Chief of the Army and Navy of the United States." [59] The Attorney General (Jackson) vigorously proclaimed that the President had the moral duty to keep this Nation's defense effort a "going concern." His ringing moral justification was coupled with a legal justification equally well stated:

"The Presidential proclamation rests upon the aggregate of the Presidential powers derived from the Constitution itself and from statutes enacted by the Congress.

"The Constitution lays upon the President the duty to take care that the laws be faithfully executed. Among the laws which he is required to find means to execute are those which direct him to equip an enlarged army, to provide for a strengthened navy, to protect Government property, to protect those who are engaged in carrying out the business of the Government, and to carry out the provisions of the Lend-Lease Act. For the faithful execution of such laws the President has back of him not only each general law-enforcement power conferred by the various acts of Congress but the aggregate of all such laws plus that wide discretion as to method vested in him by the Constitution for the purpose of executing the laws.

"The Constitution also places on the President the responsibility and vests in him the powers of Commander in Chief of the Army and of the Navy. These weapons for the protection of the continued existence of the Nation are placed in his sole command and the implication is clear that he should not allow them to become paralyzed by failure to obtain supplies for which Congress has appropriated the money and which it has directed the President to obtain." [60]

At this time, Senator Connally proposed amending the Selective Training and Service Act to authorize the President to seize any plant where an interruption of production would unduly impede the defense effort.[61] Proponents of the measure in no way implied that the legislation would add to the powers already possessed by the President[62] and the amendment was opposed as unnecessary since the President already had the power.[63] The amendment relating to plant seizures was not approved at that session of Congress.[64]

Meanwhile, and also prior to Pearl Harbor, the President ordered the seizure of a shipbuilding company and an aircraft parts plant.[65] Following the declaration of war, but prior to the Smith-Connally Act of 1943, five additional industrial concerns were seized to avert interruption of needed production.[66] During the same period, the President directed seizure of the Nation's coal mines to remove an obstruction to the effective prosecution of the war.[67]

The procedures adopted by President Roosevelt closely resembled the methods employed by President Wilson. A National War Labor Board, like its predecessor of World War I, was created by Executive Order to deal effectively and fairly with disputes affecting defense production.[68] Seizures were considered necessary, upon disobedience of War Labor Board orders, to assure that the mobilization effort remained a "going concern," and to enforce the economic stabilization program.

At the time of the seizure of the coal mines, Senator Connally's bill to provide a statutory basis for seizures and for the War Labor Board was again before Congress. As stated by its sponsor, the purpose of the bill was not to augment Presidential power, but to "let the country know that the Congress is squarely behind the President." [69] As in the case of the legislative recognition of President Lincoln's power to seize, Congress again recognized that the President already had the necessary power, for there was no intention to "ratify" past actions of doubtful validity. Indeed, when Senator Tydings offered an amendment to the Connally bill expressly to confirm and validate the seizure of the coal mines, sponsors of the bill opposed the amendment as casting doubt on the legality of the seizure and the amendment was defeated.[70] When the Connally bill, S. 796, came before the House, all parts after the enacting clause were stricken and a bill introduced by Representative Smith of Virginia was substituted and passed. This action in the House is significant because the Smith bill did not contain the provisions authorizing seizure by the President but did contain provisions controlling and regulating activities in respect to properties seized by the Government under statute "or otherwise." [71] After a conference, the seizure provisions of the Connally bill, enacted as the Smith-Connally or War Labor Disputes Act of 1943, 57 Stat. 163, were agreed to by the House.

Following passage of the Smith-Connally Act, seizures to assure continued production on the basis of terms recommended by the War Labor Board were based upon that Act as well as upon the President's power under the Constitution and the laws generally. A question did arise as to whether the statutory language relating to "any plant, mine, or facility equipped for the manufacture, production, or mining of any articles or materials" [72] authorized the seizure of properties of Montgomery Ward & Co., a retail department store and mail-order concern. The Attorney General (Biddle) issued an opinion that the President possessed the power to seize Montgomery Ward properties to prevent a work stoppage whether or not the terms of the Smith-Connally Act authorized such a seizure. [73] This opinion was in line with the views on Presidential powers maintained by the Attorney General's predecessors (Murphy[74] and Jackson[75]) and his successor (Clark[76]). Accordingly, the President ordered seizure of the Chicago properties of Montgomery Ward in April, 1944, when that company refused to obey a War Labor Board order concerning the bargaining representative of its employees in Chicago. [77] In Congress, a Select Committee to Investigate Seizure of the Property of Montgomery Ward & Co., assuming that the terms of the Smith-Connally Act did not cover this seizure, concluded that the seizure "was not only within the constitutional power but was the plain duty of the President." [78] Thereafter, an election determined the bargaining representative for the Chicago employees and the properties were returned to Montgomery Ward & Co. In December, 1944, after continued defiance of a series of War Labor Board orders, President Roosevelt ordered the seizure of Montgomery Ward properties throughout the country. [79] The Court of Appeals for the Seventh Circuit upheld this seizure on statutory grounds and also indicated its disapproval of a lower court's denial of

seizure power apart from express statute. [80]

More recently, President Truman acted to repel aggression by employing our armed forces in Korea. [81] Upon the intervention of the Chinese Communists, the President proclaimed the existence of an unlimited national emergency requiring the speedy build-up of our defense establishment. [82] Congress responded by providing for increased manpower and weapons for our own armed forces, by increasing military aid under the Mutual Security Program and by enacting economic stabilization measures, as previously described.

This is but a cursory summary of executive leadership. But it amply demonstrates that Presidents have taken prompt action to enforce the laws and protect the country whether or not Congress happened to provide in advance for the particular method of execution. At the minimum, the executive actions reviewed herein sustain the action of the President in this case. And many of the cited examples of Presidential practice go far beyond the extent of power necessary to sustain the President's order to seize the steel mills. The fact that temporary executive seizures of industrial plants to meet an emergency have not been directly tested in this Court furnishes not the slightest suggestion that such actions have been illegal. Rather, the fact that Congress and the courts have consistently recognized and given their support to such executive action indicates that such a power of seizure has been accepted throughout our history.

History bears out the genius of the Founding Fathers, who created a Government subject to law but not left subject to inertia when vigor and initiative are required.

## IV.

Focusing now on the situation confronting the President on the night of

April 8, 1952, we cannot but conclude that the President was performing his duty under the Constitution to "take Care that the Laws be faithfully executed"—a duty described by President Benjamin Harrison as "the central idea of the office."[83]

The President reported to Congress the morning after the seizure that he acted because a work stoppage in steel production would immediately imperil the safety of the Nation by preventing execution of the legislative programs for procurement of military equipment. And, while a shutdown could be averted by granting the price concessions requested by plaintiffs, granting such concessions would disrupt the price stabilization program also enacted by Congress. Rather than fail to execute either legislative program, the President acted to execute both.

Much of the argument in this case has been directed at straw men. We do not now have before us the case of a President acting solely on the basis of his own notions of the public welfare. Nor is there any question of unlimited executive power in this case. The President himself closed the door to any such claim when he sent his Message to Congress stating his purpose to abide by any action of Congress, whether approving or disapproving his seizure action. Here, the President immediately made sure that Congress was fully informed of the temporary action he had taken only to preserve the legislative programs from destruction until Congress could act.

The absence of a specific statute authorizing seizure of the steel mills as a mode of executing the laws—both the military procurement program and the anti-inflation program—has not until today been thought to prevent the President from executing the laws. Unlike an administrative commission confined to the enforcement of the statute under which it was created, or the head of a department when administering a particular statute, the President is a constitutional officer charged with taking care that a "mass of legislation" be executed. Flexibility as to mode of execution to meet critical situations is a matter of practical necessity. This practical construction of the "Take Care" clause, advocated by John Marshall, was adopted by this Court in *In re Neagle, In re Debs* and other cases cited *supra*. See also *Ex parte Quirin*, 317 U.S. 1, 26 (1942). Although more restrictive views of executive power, advocated in dissenting opinions of Justices Holmes, McReynolds and Brandeis, were emphatically rejected by this Court in *Myers* v. *United States, supra,* members of today's majority treat these dissenting views as authoritative.

There is no statute prohibiting seizure as a method of enforcing legislative programs. Congress has in no wise indicated that its legislation is not to be executed by the taking of private property (subject of course to the payment of just compensation) if its legislation cannot otherwise be executed. Indeed, the Universal Military Training and Service Act authorizes the seizure of *any* plant that fails to fill a Government contract[84] or the properties of *any* steel producer that fails to allocate steel as directed for defense production.[85] And the Defense Production Act authorizes the President to requisition equipment and condemn real property needed without delay in the defense effort.[86] Where Congress authorizes seizure in instances not necessarily crucial to the defense program, it can hardly be said to have disclosed an intention to prohibit seizures where essential to the execution of that legislative program.

Whatever the extent of Presidential power on more tranquil occasions, and whatever the right of the President to execute legislative programs as he sees fit without reporting the mode of execution to Congress, the single Presidential purpose disclosed on this record is to faithfully execute the laws by acting in an emergency to maintain the status quo, thereby preventing collapse of the legislative programs until Congress could act. The President's action served the same purposes as a judicial stay entered to maintain the status quo in order to preserve the jurisdiction of a court. In his Message to Congress immediately following the seizure, the President explained the necessity of his action in executing the military procurement and anti-inflation legislative programs and expressed his desire to cooperate with any legislative proposals approving, regulating or rejecting the seizure of the steel mills. Consequently, there is no evidence whatever of any Presidential purpose to defy Congress or act in any way inconsistent with the legislative will.

In *United States* v. *Midwest Oil Co., supra,* this Court approved executive action where, as here, the President acted to preserve an important matter until Congress could act—even though his action in that case was contrary to an express statute. In this case, there is no statute prohibiting the action taken by the President in a matter not merely important but threatening the very safety of the Nation. Executive inaction in such a situation, courting national disaster, is foreign to the concept of energy and initiative in the Executive as created by the Founding Fathers. . . .

# Notes

### Mr. Justice Black

1. This Board was established under Executive Order 10233, 16 Fed. Reg. 3503.
2. The Selective Service Act of 1948, 62 Stat. 604, 625-627, 50 U. S. C. App. (Supp. IV) § 468; the Defense Production Act of 1950, Tit. II, 64 Stat. 798, as amended, 65 Stat. 132.
3. 93 Cong. Rec. 3637-3645.
4. 93 Cong. Rec. 3835-3836.
5. Labor Management Relations Act, 1947, 61 Stat. 136, 152-156, 29 U. S. C (Supp. IV) §§ 141, 171-180.

### Mr. Justice Jackson

1. A Hamilton may be matched against a Madison. 7 The Works of Alexander Hamilton, 76-117; 1 Madison, Letters and Other Writings, 611-654. Professor Taft is counterbalanced by Theodore Roosevelt. Taft, Our Chief Magistrate and His Powers, 139-140; Theodore Roosevelt, Autobiography, 388-389. It even seems that President Taft cancels out Professor Taft. Compare his "Temporary Petroleum Withdrawal No. 5" of September 27, 1909, *United States* v. *Midwest Oil Co.,* 236 U. S. 459, 467, 468, with his appraisal of executive power in "Our Chief Magistrate and His Powers" 139-140.
2. It is in this class of cases that we find the broadest recent statements of presidential power, including those relied on here. *United States* v. *Curtiss-Wright Corp.,* 299 U. S. 304, involved, not the question of the President's power to act without congressional authority, but the question of his right to act under and in accord with an Act of Congress. The constitutionality of the Act under which the President had proceeded was assailed on the ground that it delegated legislative powers to the President. Much of the Court's opinion is *dictum,* but the *ratio decidendi* is contained in the following language:

   "When the President is to be authorized by legislation to act in respect of a matter intended to affect a situation in foreign territory, the legislator properly bears in mind the important consideration that the form of the President's action—or, indeed, whether he shall act at all—may well depend, among other things, upon the nature of the confidential information which he has or may thereafter receive, or upon the effect which his action may have upon our foreign relations. This consideration, in connection with what we have already said on the subject, discloses the unwisdom of requiring Congress in this field of governmental power to lay down narrowly definite standards by which the President is to be governed. As this court said in *Mackenzie* v. *Hare,* 239 U. S. 299, 311, 'As a government, the United States is invested with all the attributes of sovereignty. As it has the character of nationality it has the powers of nationality, especially those which concern its relations and intercourse with other countries. *We should hesi-*

*tate long before limiting or embarrassing such powers.' (Italics supplied.)" Id.,* at 321-322.

That case does not solve the present controversy. It recognized internal and external affairs as being in separate categories, and held that the strict limitation upon congressional delegations of power to the President over internal affairs does not apply with respect to delegations of power in external affairs. It was intimated that the President might act in external affairs without congressional authority, but not that he might act contrary to an Act of Congress.

Other examples of wide definition of presidential powers under statutory authorization are *Chicago & Southern Air Lines, Inc.* v. *Waterman Steamship Corp.,* 333 U. S. 103, and *Hirabayashi* v. *United States,* 320 U. S. 81. But see, *Jecker* v. *Montgomery,* 13 How. 498, 515; *United States* v. *Western Union Telegraph Co.,* 272 F. 311; aff'd, 272 F. 893; rev'd on consent of the parties, 260 U. S. 754; *United States Harness Co.* v. *Graham,* 288 F. 929.

3. Since the Constitution implies that the writ of habeas corpus may be suspended in certain circumstances but does not say by whom, President Lincoln asserted and maintained it as an executive function in the face of judicial challenge and doubt. *Ex parte Merryman,* 17 Fed. Cas. 144; *Ex parte Milligan,* 4 Wall. 2, 125; see *Ex parte Bollman,* 4 Cranch 75, 101. Congress eventually ratified his action. Habeas Corpus Act of March 3, 1863, 12 Stat. 755. See Hall, Free Speech in War Time, 21 Col. L. Rev. 526. Compare *Myers* v. *United States,* 272 U. S. 52, with *Humphrey's Executor* v. *United States,* 295 U. S. 602; and *Hirabayashi* v. *United States,* 320 U. S. 81, with the case at bar. Also compare *Ex parte Vallandigham,* 1 Wall. 243, with *Ex parte Milligan, supra.*

4. President Roosevelt's effort to remove a Federal Trade Commissioner was found to be contrary to the policy of Congress and impinging upon an area of congressional control, and so his removal power was cut down accordingly. *Humphrey's Executor* v. *United States,* 295 U. S. 602. However, his exclusive power of removal in executive agencies, affirmed in *Myers* v. *United States,* 272 U. S. 52, continued to be asserted and maintained. *Morgan* v. *Tennessee Valley Authority,* 115 F. 2d 990, cert. denied,

312 U. S. 701; *In re Power to Remove Members of the Tennessee Valley Authority,* 39 Op. Atty. Gen. 145; President Roosevelt's Message to Congress of March 23, 1938, The Public Papers and Addresses of Franklin D. Roosevelt, 1938 (Rosenman), 151.

5. The oft-cited Louisiana Purchase had nothing to do with the separation of powers as between the President and Congress, but only with state and federal power. The Louisiana Purchase was subject to rather academic criticism, not upon the ground that Mr. Jefferson acted without authority from Congress, but that neither had express authority to expand the boundaries of the United States by purchase or annexation. Mr. Jefferson himself had strongly opposed the doctrine that the States' delegation of powers to the Federal Government could be enlarged by resort to implied powers. Afterwards in a letter to John Breckenridge, dated August 12, 1803, he declared:

"The Constitution has made no provision for our holding foreign territory, still less for incorporating foreign nations into our Union. The executive in seizing the fugitive occurrence which so much advances the good of their country, have done an act beyond the Constitution. The Legislature in casting behind them metaphysical subtleties, and risking themselves like faithful servants, must ratify and pay for it, and throw themselves on their country for doing for them unauthorized, what we know they would have done for themselves had they been in a situation to do it." 10 The Writings of Thomas Jefferson 407, 411.

6. Selective Service Act of 1948, § 18, 62 Stat. 625, 50 U. S. C. App. (Supp. IV) § 468 (c).

7. Defense Production Act of 1950, § 201, 64 Stat. 799, amended, 65 Stat. 132, 50 U. S. C. App. (Supp. IV) § 2081. For the latitude of the condemnation power which underlies this Act, see *United States* v. *Westinghouse Co.,* 339 U. S. 261, and cases therein cited.

8. Labor Management Relations Act, 1947, §§ 206-210, 61 Stat. 136, 155, 156, 29 U. S. C. (Supp. IV) §§ 141, 176-180. The analysis, history and application of this Act are fully covered by the opinion of the Court, supplemented by that of MR. JUSTICE FRANKFURTER and of MR. JUSTICE BURTON, in which I concur.

9. "... he may require the Opinion, in writing, of the principal Officer in each of the executive Departments, upon any Subject relating to the Duties of their respective Offices...." U. S. Const., Art. II, § 2. He "... shall Commission all the Officers of the United States." U. S. Const., Art. II, § 3. Matters such as those would seem to be inherent in the Executive if anything is.

10. How widely this doctrine espoused by the President's counsel departs from the early view of presidential power is shown by a comparison. President Jefferson, without authority from Congress, sent the American fleet into the Mediterranean, where it engaged in a naval battle with the Tripolitan fleet. He sent a message to Congress on December 8, 1801, in which he said:

"Tripoli, the least considerable of the Barbary States, had come forward with demands unfounded either in right or in compact, and had permitted itself to denounce war on our failure to comply before a given day. The style of the demand admitted but one answer. I sent a small squadron of frigates into the Mediterranean ... with orders to protect our commerce against the threatened attack.... Our commerce in the Mediterranean was blockaded and that of the Atlantic in peril.... One of the Tripolitan cruisers having fallen in with and engaged the small schooner *Enterprise*, ... was captured, after a heavy slaughter of her men.... Unauthorized by the Constitution, without the sanction of Congress, to go beyond the line of defense, the vessel, being disabled from committing further hostilities, was liberated with its crew. The Legislature will doubtless consider whether, by authorizing measures of offense also, they will place our force on an equal footing with that of its adversaries. I communicate all material information on this subject, that in the exercise of this important function confided by the Constitution to the Legislature exclusively their judgment may form itself on a knowledge and consideration of every circumstance of weight." I Richardson, Messages and Papers of the Presidents, 314.

U. S. Const., Art. I, § 8, cl. 15.

14 Stat. 29, 16 Stat. 143, 8 U. S. C. § 55.

20 Stat. 152, 10 U. S. C. § 15.

In 1940, President Roosevelt proposed to transfer to Great Britain certain over-age destroyers and small patrol boats then under construction. He did not presume to rely upon any claim of constitutional power as Commander in Chief. On the contrary, he was advised that such destroyers—if certified not to be essential to the defense of the United States—could be "transferred, exchanged, sold, or otherwise disposed of," because Congress had so authorized him. Accordingly, the destroyers were exchanged for air bases. In the same opinion, he was advised that Congress had prohibited the release or transfer of the so-called "mosquito boats" then under construction, so those boats were not transferred. *Acquisition of Naval and Air Bases in Exchange for Over-age Destroyers,* 39 Op. Atty. Gen. 484. See also *Training of British Flying Students in the United States,* 40 Op. Atty. Gen. 58.

15. U. S. Const., Art. II, § 3.

16. President Wilson, just before our entrance into World War I, went before the Congress and asked its approval of his decision to authorize merchant ships to carry defensive weapons. He said:

"No doubt I already possess that authority without special warrant of law, by the plain implication of my constitutional duties and powers; but I prefer, in the present circumstances, not to act upon general implication. I wish to feel that the authority and the power of the Congress are behind me in whatever it may become necessary for me to do. We are jointly the servants of the people and must act together and in their spirit, so far as we can divine and interpret it." XVII Richardson, *op. cit.,* 8211.

When our Government was itself in need of shipping whilst ships flying the flags of nations overrun by Hitler, as well as belligerent merchantmen, were immobilized in American harbors where they had taken refuge, President Roosevelt did not assume that it was in his power to seize such foreign vessels to make up our own deficit. He informed Congress: "I am satisfied, after consultation with the heads of the interested departments and agencies of the Government, that we should have statutory authority to take over any such vessels as our needs may require ...." 87 Cong. Rec. 3072 (77th Cong., 1st Sess.); The Public Papers and Addresses of Franklin D. Roosevelt, 1941 (Rosenman), 94. The necessary statutory authority was shortly forthcoming. 55 Stat. 242.

In his first inaugural address President

Roosevelt pointed out two courses to obtain legislative remedies, one being to enact measures he was prepared to recommend, the other to enact measures "the Congress may build out of its experience and wisdom." He continued, "But in the event that the Congress shall fail to take one of these two courses, and in the event that the national emergency is still critical, I shall not evade the clear course of duty that will then confront me. *I shall ask the Congress for the one remaining instrument to meet the crisis*—broad Executive power to wage a war against the emergency, as great as the power that would be given to me if we were in fact invaded by a foreign foe." (Emphasis supplied.) The Public Papers and Addresses of Franklin D. Roosevelt, 1933 (Rosenman), 15.

On March 6, 1933, President Roosevelt proclaimed the Bank Holiday. The Proclamation did not invoke constitutional powers of the Executive but expressly and solely relied upon the Act of Congress of October 6, 1917, 40 Stat. 411, § 5 (b), as amended. He relied steadily on legislation to empower him to deal with economic emergency. The Public Papers and Addresses of Franklin D. Roosevelt, 1933 (Rosenman), 24.

It is interesting to note Holdsworth's comment on the powers of legislation by proclamation when in the hands of the Tudors. "The extent to which they could be legally used was never finally settled in this century, because the Tudors made so tactful a use of their powers that no demand for the settlement of this question was raised." 4 Holdsworth, History of English Law, 104.

17. The North American Aviation Company was under direct and binding contracts to supply defense items to the Government. No such contracts are claimed to exist here. Seizure of plants which refused to comply with Government orders had been expressly authorized by Congress in § 9 of the Selective Service Act of 1940, 54 Stat. 885, 892, so that the seizure of the North American plant was entirely consistent with congressional policy. The company might have objected on technical grounds to the seizure, but it was taken over with acquiescence, amounting to all but consent, of the owners who had admitted that the situation was beyond their control. The strike involved in the North American

case was in violation of the union's collective agreement and the national labor leaders approved the seizure to end the strike. It was described as in the nature of an insurrection, a Communist-led political strike against the Government's lend-lease policy. Here we have only a loyal, lawful, but regrettable economic disagreement between management and labor. The North American plant contained government-owned machinery, material and goods in the process of production to which workmen were forcibly denied access by picketing strikers. Here no Government property is protected by the seizure. See New York Times of June 10, 1941, pp. 1, 14 and 16, for substantially accurate account of the proceedings and the conditions of violence at the North American plant.

The North American seizure was regarded as an execution of congressional policy. I do not regard it as a precedent for this, but, even if I did, I should not bind present judicial judgment by earlier partisan advocacy.

Statements from a letter by the Attorney General to the Chairman of the Senate Committee on Labor and Public Welfare, dated February 2, 1949, with reference to pending labor legislation, while not cited by any of the parties here, are sometimes quoted as being in support of the "inherent" powers of the President. The proposed bill contained a mandatory provision that during certain investigations the disputants in a labor dispute should continue operations under the terms and conditions of employment existing prior to the beginning of the dispute. It made no provision as to how continuance should be enforced and specified no penalty for disobedience. The Attorney General advised that in appropriate circumstances the United States would have access to the courts to protect the national health, safety and welfare. This was the rule laid down by this Court in *Texas & N. O. R. Co.* v. *Brotherhood of Railway Clerks,* 281 U. S. 548. The Attorney General observed:

"However, with regard to the question of the power of the Government under Title III, I might point out that the inherent power of the President to deal with emergencies that affect the health, safety and welfare of the entire Nation is exceedingly great. See Opinion of Attorney General Murphy of October 4, 1939 (39 Op. A. G. 344, 347); *United*

*States* v. *United Mine Workers of America,* 330 U. S. 258 (1947)." See Hearings before the Senate Committee on Labor and Public Welfare on S. 249, 81st Cong., 1st Sess. 263.

Regardless of the general reference to "inherent powers," the citations were instances of congressional authorization. I do not suppose it is open to doubt that power to see that the laws are faithfully executed was ample basis for the specific advice given by the Attorney General in this letter.

18. U. S. Const., Art. I, § 9, cl. 2.
19. I exclude, as in a very limited category by itself, the establishment of martial law. Cf. *Ex parte Milligan,* 4 Wall. 2; *Duncan* v. *Kahanamoku,* 327 U. S. 304.
20. 1 Nazi Conspiracy and Aggression 126-127; Rossiter, Constitutional Dictatorship, 33-61; Brecht, Prelude to Silence, 138.
21. Rossiter, Constitutional Dictatorship, 117-129.
22. Defence of the Realm Act, 1914, 4 & 5 Geo. V, c. 29, as amended, c. 63; Emergency Powers (Defence) Act, 1939, 2 & 3 Geo. VI, c. 62; Rossiter, Constitutional Dictatorship, 135-184.
23. Churchill, The Unrelenting Struggle, 13. See also *id.,* at 279-281.
24. 39 Op. Atty. Gen. 348.
25. Wilson, Constitutional Government in the United States, 68-69.
26. Rossiter, The Supreme Court and the Commander in Chief, 126-132.
27. We follow the judicial tradition instituted on a memorable Sunday in 1612, when King James took offense at the independence of his judges and, in rage, declared: "Then I am to be *under* the law—which it is treason to affirm." Chief Justice Coke replied to his King: "Thus wrote Bracton, 'The King ought not to be under any man, but he is under God and the Law.'" 12 Coke 65 (as to its verity, 18 Eng. Hist. Rev. 664-675); 1 Campbell, Lives of the Chief Justices (1849), 272.

## Mr. Chief Justice Vinson

30. 4 Annals of Congress 1411, 1413 (1794).
31. IV Works of Hamilton (Lodge ed. 1904) 432-444.
32. 10 Annals of Congress 596, 613-614 (1800); also printed in 5 Wheat., App. pp. 3, 27 (1820).
33. 10 Annals of Congress 619 (1800).
34. *Fong Yue Ting* v. *United States,* 149 U. S. 698, 714 (1893).
35. See *Prize Cases,* 2 Black 635 (1863);

Randall, Constitutional Problems Under Lincoln (1926); Corwin, The President: Office and Powers (1948 ed.), 277-281.
36. War of the Rebellion, Official Records of the Union and Confederate Armies, Series I, Vol. II (1880), pp. 603-604.
37. 12 Stat. 334 (1862).
38. Senator Wade, Cong. Globe, 37th Cong., 2d Sess. 509 (1862); Rep. Blair, *id.,* at 548.
39. Senators Browning, Fessenden, Cowan, Grimes, *id.,* at 510, 512, 516, 520.
40. In 1818, the House Committee on Military Affairs recommended payment of compensation for vessels seized by the Army during the War of 1812. American State Papers, Claims (1834), 649. *Mitchell* v. *Harmony,* 13 How. 115, 134 (1852), involving seizure of a wagon train by an Army officer during the Mexican War, noted that such executive seizure was proper in case of emergency, but affirmed a personal judgment against the officer on the ground that no emergency had been found to exist. The judgment was paid by the United States pursuant to Act of Congress. 10 Stat. 727 (1852).
41. 13 Wall., at 627-628. Such a compensable taking was soon distinguished from the noncompensable taking and destruction of property during the extreme exigencies of a military campaign. *United States* v. *Pacific R. Co.,* 120 U. S. 227 (1887).
42. 135 U. S., at 64.
43. Rich, The Presidents and Civil Disorder (1941), 72-86.
44. Cleveland, The Government in the Chicago Strike of 1894 (1913).
45. 26 Cong. Rec. 7281-7284, 7544-7546 (1894).
46. Theodore Roosevelt, Autobiography (1916 ed.), 479-491.
47. *Id.,* at 378.
48. *Humphrey's Executor* v. *United States,* 295 U. S. 602, 626 (1935), disapproved expressions in the *Myers* opinion only to the extent that they related to the President's power to remove members of quasi-legislative and quasi-judicial commissions as contrasted with executive employees.
49. Brief for the United States, No. 278, October Term, 1914, pp. 11, 75-77, 88-90.
50. National War Labor Board. Bureau of Labor Statistics, Bull. 287 (1921).
51. *Id.,* at 24-25, 32-34. See also, 2 Official U. S. Bull. (1918), No. 412; 8 Baker, Woodrow Wilson, Life & Letters (1939),

400-402; Berman, Labor Disputes and the President (1924), 125-153; Pringle, The Life and Times of William Howard Taft (1939), 915-925.

52. 39 Stat. 619, 645 (1916), provides that the President may take possession of any system of transportation in time of war. Following seizure of the railroads by President Wilson, Congress enacted detailed legislation regulating the mode of federal control. 40 Stat. 451 (1918).

When Congress was considering the statute authorizing the President to seize communications systems whenever he deemed such action necessary during the war, 40 Stat. 904 (1918), Senator (later President) Harding opposed on the ground that there was no need for such stand-by powers because, in event of a present necessity, the Chief Executive "ought to" seize communications lines, "else he would be unfaithful to his duties as such Chief Executive." 56 Cong. Rec. 9064 (1918).

53. 48 Stat. 1689 (1933).

54. 54 Stat. 2643 (1939).

55. 55 Stat. 1647 (1941).

56. 86 Cong. Rec. 11354 (1940) (Message of the President). See 39 Op. Atty. Gen. 484 (1940). Attorney General Jackson's opinion did not extend to the transfer of "mosquito boats," solely because an express statutory prohibition on transfer was applicable.

57. 87 Cong. Rec. 5868 (1941) (Message of the President).

58. Powers of the President to Send the Armed Forces Outside the United States, Report prepared by executive department for use of joint committee of Senate Committees on Foreign Relations and Armed Services, 82d Cong., 1st Sess., Committee Print, 2 (1951).

59. Exec. Order 8773, 6 Fed. Reg. 2777 (1941).

60. See 89 Cong. Rec. 3992 (1943). The Attorney General also noted that the dispute at North American Aviation was Communist inspired and more nearly resembled an insurrection than a labor strike. The relative size of North American Aviation and the impact of an interruption in production upon our defense effort were not described.

61. 87 Cong. Rec. 4932 (1941). See also S. 1600 and S. 2054, 77th Cong., 1st Sess. (1941).

62. Reps. May, Whittington; 87 Cong. Rec. 5895, 5972 (1941).

63. Reps. Dworshak, Feddis, Harter, Dirksen, Hook; 87 Cong. Rec. 5901, 5910,

5974, 5975 (1941).

64. The plant seizure amendment passed the Senate, but was rejected in the House after a Conference Committee adopted the amendment. 87 Cong. Rec. 6424 (1941).

65. Exec. Order 8868, 6 Fed. Reg. 4349 (1941); Exec. Order 8928, 6 Fed. Reg. 5559 (1941).

66. Exec. Order 9141, 7 Fed. Reg. 2961 (1942); Exec. Order 9220, 7 Fed. Reg. 6413 (1942); Exec. Order 9225, 7 Fed. Reg. 6627 (1942); Exec. Order 9254, 7 Fed. Reg. 8333 (1942); Exec. Order 9351, 8 Fed. Reg. 8097 (1943).

67. Exec. Order 9340, 8 Fed. Reg. 5695 (1943).

68. Exec. Order 9017, 7 Fed. Reg. 237 (1942); 1 Termination report of the National War Labor Board 5-11.

69. 89 Cong. Rec. 3807 (1943). Similar views of the President's existing power were expressed by Senators Lucas, Wheeler, Austin and Barkley. Id., at 3885-3887, 3896, 3992.

70. 89 Cong. Rec. 3989-3992 (1943).

71. S. 796, 78th Cong., 1st Sess., §§ 12, 13 (1943), as passed by the House.

72. 57 Stat. 163, 164 (1943).

73. 40 Op. Atty. Gen. 312 (1944). See also Hearings before House Select Committee to Investigate Seizure of Montgomery Ward & Co., 78th Cong., 2d Sess. 117-132 (1944).

74. 39 Op. Atty. Gen. 343, 347 (1939).

75. Note 60, supra.

76. Letter introduced in Hearings before Senate Committee on Labor and Public Welfare on S. 249, 81st Cong., 1st Sess. 232 (1949) pointing to the "exceedingly great" powers of the President to deal with emergencies even before the Korean crisis.

77. Exec. Order 9438, 9 Fed. Reg. 4459 (1944).

78. H. R. Rep. No. 1904, 78th Cong., 2d Sess. 25 (1944) (the Committee divided along party lines).

79. Exec. Order 9508, 9 Fed. Reg. 15079 (1944).

80. United States v. Montgomery Ward & Co., 150 F. 2d 369 (C. A. 7th Cir. 1945), reversing 58 F. Supp. 408 (N. D. Ill. 1945). See also Ken-Rad Tube & Lamp Corp. v. Badeau, 55 F. Supp. 193, 197-199 (W. D. Ky. 1944), where the court held that a seizure was proper with or without express statutory authorization.

81. United States Policy in the Korean Crisis (1950), Dept. of State Pub. 3922.

82. 15 Fed. Reg. 9029 (1950).

83. Harrison, This Country of Ours (1897), 98.

84. 62 Stat. 604, 626 (1948), 50 U. S. C. App. (Supp. IV) § 468 (c).

85. 62 Stat. 604, 627 (1948), 50 U. S. C. App. (Supp. IV) § 468 (h) (1).

86. Tit. II, 64 Stat. 798, 799 (1950), as amended, 65 Stat. 138 (1951).

# Richard Nixon's "Checkers" Speech (1952)

Following the advice of party leaders, Republican presidential nominee Dwight D. Eisenhower selected Sen. Richard Nixon of California, whom he did not know, as his vice-presidential running mate in 1952. Nixon, who was thirty-nine years old and a staunch Republican partisan, helped to balance the ticket, headed as it was by a sixty-one-year-old former general who had not even decided which party he belonged to until shortly before running for president. Nixon also was known as an effective, tireless political campaigner and an ardent anti-Communist. In a celebrated case, he had exposed Alger Hiss, a high State Department official during the 1940s, as a Communist.

On September 18, 1952, the New York Post printed a story that accused Nixon of using a secret $18,000 fund created by sixty-six California business interests to pay for his personal expenses. The headline—"SECRET NIXON FUND!—Secret Rich Men's Trust Fund Keeps Nixon in Style Far Beyond His Salary"—was more sensational than the story, and the story was more sensational than the reality. In truth, Nixon used the fund only to pay his political expenses and had a very modest lifestyle. Nonetheless, the charge instantly became the major issue of the campaign. Part of the reason for the prominence of the story was its underlying charge of hypocrisy, since Nixon's vice-presidential campaign had concentrated on the corruption that allegedly infested the Democratic administration of President Harry S Truman.

Just as important, however, was the rapidly growing public perception of the importance of the vice presidency and, consequently, of the need to assess the presidential caliber of the candidates who were nominated for vice president. In 1945 when President Franklin D. Roosevelt died, Vice President Truman had succeeded to the presidency unaware of the existence of the atomic bomb or of the diplomatic plans that had been laid for the post-World War II era. Soon after, the development of intercontinental ballistic missiles armed with nuclear warheads raised the specter of virtually instant total war. In such a world, many voters realized, the nation could not afford the luxury of having an uninformed, incapable vice president succeed to the presidency.

When the charges against Nixon were made public, several of Eisenhower's advisers urged him to ask his running mate to resign from the ticket. But on September 21 Eisenhower encouraged Nixon "to go on a nationwide television program and tell them everything there is to tell." The Republican National Committee bought a half-hour of television time on the evening *of September 23. Nixon's political fate hung in the balance.*

*Speaking to fifty-five million people—up to that time, the largest audience ever to watch a television broadcast—Nixon defended his fund as a device "to pay for political expenses that I did not think should be charged to the taxpayers of the United States." He described his modest lifestyle, noting even that his wife, Pat, "doesn't have a mink coat. But she does have a respectable Republican cloth coat." The most memorable line from Nixon's speech came in defense of a personal gift he had received that he vowed never to return. "You know what it was. It was a little cocker spaniel dog in a crate that [a supporter] sent all the way from Texas. Black and white spotted. And our little girl—Trisha, the 6-year-old—named it Checkers."*

*At the end of his speech, Nixon called upon viewers to let the Republican National Committee know whether or not they thought he should resign as the party's vice-presidential nominee. The response was overwhelmingly in Nixon's favor. Nixon remained on the ticket, and on election day he and Eisenhower were elected in a landslide.* ~

My Fellow Americans:

I come before you tonight as a candidate for the Vice Presidency and as a man whose honesty and integrity have been questioned.

The usual political thing to do when charges are made against you is to either ignore them or to deny them without giving details.

I believe we've had enough of that in the United States, particularly with the present Administration in Washington, D.C. To me the office of the Vice Presidency of the United States is a great office, and I feel that the people have got to have confidence in the integrity of the men who run for that office and

who might obtain it.

I have a theory, too, that the best and only answer to a smear or to an honest misunderstanding of the facts is to tell the truth. And that's why I'm here tonight. I want to tell you my side of the case.

I am sure that you have read the charge and you've heard that I, Senator Nixon, took $18,000 from a group of my supporters.

Now, what was wrong? And let me say that it was wrong—I'm saying, incidentally, that it was wrong and not just illegal. Because it isn't a question of whether it was legal or illegal, that isn't enough. The question is, was it morally wrong?

I say that it was morally wrong if any of that $18,000 went to Senator Nixon for my personal use. I say that it was morally wrong if it was secretly given and secretly handled. And I say that it was morally wrong if any of the contributors got special favors for the contributions that they made.

And now to answer those questions let me say this:

Not one cent of the $18,000 or any other money of that type ever went to me for my personal use. Every penny of it was used to pay for political expenses that I did not think should be charged to the taxpayers of the United States.

It was not a secret fund. As a matter of fact, when I was on "Meet the Press," some of you may have seen it last Sunday—Peter Edson came up to me after the program and he said, "Dick, what about this fund we hear about?" And I said, Well, there's no secret about it. Go out and see Dana Smith, who was the administrator of the fund. And I gave him his address, and I said that you will find that the purpose of the fund simply was to defray political expenses that I did not feel should be charged to the Government.

And third, let me point out, and I want to make this particularly clear, that no contributor to this fund, no contributor to any of my campaigns, has ever received any consideration that he would not have received as an ordinary constituent.

I just don't believe in that and I can say that never, while I have been in the Senate of the United States, as far as the people that contributed to this fund are concerned, have I made a telephone call for them to an agency, or have I gone down to an agency in their behalf. And the record will show that, the records which are in the hands of the Administration.

But then some of you will say and rightly, "Well, what did you use the fund for, Senator? Why did you have to have it?"

Let me tell you in just a word how a Senate office operates. First of all, a Senator gets $15,000 a year in salary. He gets enough money to pay for one trip a year, a round trip that is, for himself and his family between his home and Washington, D.C.

And then he gets an allowance to handle the people that work in his office, to handle his mail. And the allowance for my State of California is enough to hire thirteen people.

And let me say, incidentally, that that allowance is not paid to the Senator—it's paid directly to the individuals that the Senator puts on his payroll, that all of these people and all of these allowances are for strictly official business. Business, for example, when a constituent writes in and wants you to go down to the Veterans Administration and get some information about his GI policy. Items of that type for example.

But there are other expenses which are not covered by the Government. And I think I can best discuss those expenses by asking you some questions. Do you think that when I or any other Senator makes a political speech, has it printed, should charge the printing of that speech and the mailing of that speech to the taxpayers?

Do you think, for example, when I or any other Senator makes a trip to his home state to make a purely political speech that the cost of that trip should be charged to the taxpayers?

Do you think when a Senator makes political broadcasts or political television broadcasts, radio or television, that the expense of those broadcasts should be charged to the taxpayers?

Well, I know what your answer is. The same answer that audiences give me whenever I discuss this particular problem. The answer is, "no." The taxpayers shouldn't be required to finance items which are not official business but which are primarily political business.

But then the question arises, you say, "Well, how do you pay for these and how can you do it legally?"

And there are several ways that it can be done, incidentally, and that it is done legally in the United States Senate and in the Congress.

The first way is to be a rich man. I don't happen to be a rich man so I couldn't use that.

Another way that is used is to put your wife on the payroll. Let me say, incidentally, my opponent, my opposite number for the Vice Presidency on the Democratic ticket, does have his wife on the payroll. And has had her on his payroll for the ten years—the past ten years.

Now just let me say this. That's his business and I'm not critical of him for doing that. You will have to pass judgment on that particular point. But I have never done that for this reason. I have found that there are so many deserving stenographers and secretaries in Washington that needed the work that I just didn't feel it was right to put my wife on the payroll.

My wife's sitting over here. She's a wonderful stenographer. She used to teach stenography and she used to teach shorthand in high school. That was when I met her. And I can tell you folks that she's worked many hours at night and many hours on Saturdays and

Sundays in my office and she's done a fine job. And I'm proud to say tonight that in the six years I've been in the House and the Senate of the United States, Pat Nixon has never been on the Government payroll.

There are other ways that these finances can be taken care of. Some who are lawyers, and I happen to be a lawyer, continue to practice law. But I haven't been able to do that. I'm so far away from California that I've been so busy with my Senatorial work that I have not engaged in any legal practice.

And also as far as law practice is concerned, it seemed to me that the relationship between an attorney and the client was so personal that you couldn't possibly represent a man as an attorney and then have an unbiased view when he presented his case to you in the event that he had one before the Government.

And so I felt that the best way to handle these necessary political expenses of getting my message to the American people and the speeches I made, the speeches that I had printed, for the most part, concerned this one message—of exposing this Administration, the communism in it, the corruption in it—the only way that I could do that was to accept the aid which people in my home state of California who contributed to my campaign and who continued to make these contributions after I was elected were glad to make.

And let me say I am proud of the fact that not one of them has ever asked me for a special favor. I'm proud of the fact that not one of them has ever asked me to vote on a bill other than as my own conscience would dictate. And I am proud of the fact that the taxpayers by subterfuge or otherwise have never paid one dime for expenses which I thought were political and shouldn't be charged to the taxpayers.

Let me say, incidentally, that some of you may say, "Well, that's all right, Senator; that's your explanation, but have you got any proof?"

And I'd like to tell you this evening that just about an hour ago we received an independent audit of this entire fund.

I suggested to Gov. Sherman Adams, who is the chief of staff of the Dwight Eisenhower campaign, that an independent audit and legal report be obtained. And I have that audit here in my hand.

It's an audit made by the Price, Waterhouse & Co. firm, and the legal opinion by Gibson, Dunn & Crutcher, lawyers in Los Angeles, the biggest law firm and incidentally one of the best ones in Los Angeles.

I'm proud to be able to report to you tonight that this audit and this legal opinion is being forwarded to General Eisenhower. And I'd like to read to you the opinion that was prepared by Gibson, Dunn & Crutcher and based on all the pertinent laws and statutes, together with the audit report prepared by the certified public accountants.

"It is our conclusion that Senator Nixon did not obtain any financial gain from the collection and disbursement of the fund by Dana Smith; that Senator Nixon did not violate any Federal or state law by reason of the operation of the fund, and that neither the portion of the fund paid by Dana Smith directly to reimburse him for designated office expenses constituted income to the Senator which was either reportable or taxable as income under applicable tax laws. (signed) Gibson, Dunn & Crutcher by Alma H. Conway."

Now that, my friends, is not Nixon speaking, but that's an independent audit which was requested because I want the American people to know all the facts and I'm not afraid of having independent people go in and check the facts, and that is exactly what they did.

But then I realize that there are still some who may say, and rightly so, and let me say that I recognize that some will continue to smear regardless of what the truth may be, but that there has been understandably some honest misunderstanding on this matter, and there's some that will say:

"Well, maybe you were able, Senator, to fake this thing. How can we believe what you say? After all, is there a possibility that maybe you got some sums in cash? Is there a possibility that you may have feathered your own nest?"

And so now what I am going to do—and incidentally this is unprecedented in the history of American politics—I am going at this time to give to this television and radio audience a complete financial history; everything I've earned; everything I've spent; everything I owe. And I want you to know the facts. I'll have to start early.

I was born in 1913. Our family was one of modest circumstances and most of my early life was spent in a store out in East Whittier. It was a grocery store—one of those family enterprises. The only reason we were able to make it go was because my mother and dad had five boys and we all worked in the store.

I worked my way through college and to a great extent through law school. And then, in 1940, probably the best thing that ever happened to me happened, I married Pat—sitting over here. We had a rather difficult time after we were married, like so many of the young couples who may be listening to us. I practiced law; she continued to teach school. I went into the service.

Let me say that my service record was not a particularly unusual one. I went to the South Pacific. I guess I'm entitled to a couple of battle stars. I got a couple of letters of commendation but I was just there when the bombs were falling and then I returned. I returned to the United States and in 1946 I ran for the Congress.

When we came out of the war, Pat and I—Pat during the war had worked as a stenographer and in a bank and as an economist for a Government agency—and when we came out the

total of our savings from both my law practice, her teaching and all the time that I was in the war—the total for that entire period was just a little less than $10,000. Every of cent of that, incidentally, was in Government bonds.

Well, that's where we start when I go into politics. Now what have I earned since I went into politics? Well, here it is—I jotted it down, let me read the notes. First of all I've had my salary as a Congressman and as a Senator. Second, I have received a total in this past six years of $1,600 from estates which were in my law firm at the time that I severed my connection with it.

And, incidentally, as I said before, I have not engaged in any legal practice and have not accepted any fees from business that came into the firm after I went into politics. I have made an average of approximately $1,500 a year from nonpolitical speaking engagements and lectures. And then, fortunately, we've inherited a little money. Pat sold her interest in her father's estate for $3,000 and I inherited $1,500 from my grandfather.

We live rather modestly. For four years we lived in an apartment in Park Fairfax, in Alexandria, Va. The rent was $80 a month. And we saved for the time that we could buy a house.

Now, that was what we took in. What did we do with this money? What do we have today to show for it? This will surprise you, because it is so little, I suppose, as standards generally go, of people in public life. First of all, we've got a house in Washington which cost $41,000 and on which we owe $20,000.

We have a house in Whittier, Calif., which cost $13,000 and on which we owe $10,000. My folks are living there at the present time.

I have just $4,000 in life insurance, plus my G.I. policy which I've never been able to convert and which will run out in two years. I have no life insurance whatever on Pat. I have no life insurance on our two youngsters, Patricia and Julie. I own a 1950 Oldsmobile car. We have our furniture. We have no stocks and bonds of any type. We have no interest of any kind, direct or indirect, in any business.

Now, that's what we have. What do we owe? Well, in addition to the mortgage, the $20,000 mortgage on the house in Washington, the $10,000 one on the house in Whittier, I owe $4,500 to the Riggs Bank in Washington, D.C. with interest 4½ per cent.

I owe $3,000 to my parents and the interest on that loan which I pay regularly, because it's the part of the savings they made through the years they were working so hard, I pay regularly 4 per cent interest. And then I have a $500 loan which I have on my life insurance.

Well, that's about it. That's what we have and that's what we owe. It isn't very much but Pat and I have the satisfaction that every dime that we've got is honestly ours. I should say this— that Pat doesn't have a mink coat. But she does have a respectable Republican cloth coat. And I always tell her that she'd look good in anything.

One other thing I probably should tell you because if I don't they'll probably be saying this about me too, we did get something—a gift—after the election. A man down in Texas heard Pat on the radio mention the fact that our two youngsters would like to have a dog. And, believe it or not, the day before we left on this campaign trip we got a message from Union Station in Baltimore saying they had a package for us. We went down to get it. You know what it was.

It was a little cocker spaniel dog in a crate that he sent all the way from Texas. Black and white spotted. And our little girl—Trisha, the 6-year-old—named it Checkers. And you know, the kids love the dog and I just want to say this right now, that regardless of what they say about it, we're gonna keep it.

It isn't easy to come before a nationwide audience and air your life as I've done. But I want to say some things before I conclude that I think most of you will agree on. Mr. Mitchell, the chairman of the Democratic National Committee, made the statement that if a man couldn't afford to be in the United States Senate he shouldn't run for the Senate.

And I just want to make my position clear. I don't agree with Mr. Mitchell when he says that only a rich man should serve his Government in the United States Senate or in the Congress.

I don't believe that represents the thinking of the Democratic party, and I know that it doesn't represent the thinking of the Republican Party.

I believe that it's fine that a man like Governor Stevenson who inherited a fortune from his father can run for President. But I also feel that it's essential in this country of ours that a man of modest means can also run for President. Because, you know, remember Abraham Lincoln, you remember what he said: "God must have loved the common people—he made so many of them."

And now I'm going to suggest some courses of conduct.

First of all, you have read in the papers about other funds now. Mr. Stevenson, apparently, had a couple. One of them in which a group of business people paid and helped to supplement the salaries of state employees. Here is where the money went directly into their pockets.

And I think that what Mr. Stevenson should do should be to come before the American people as I have, give the names of the people that have contributed to that fund; give the names of the people who put this money into their pockets at the same time that they were receiving money from their state government, and see what favors, if any, they gave out for that.

I don't condemn Mr. Stevenson for what he did. But until the facts are in there is a doubt that will be raised.

And as far as Mr. Sparkman is concerned, I would suggest the same thing. He's had his wife on the payroll. I don't condemn him for that. But I think that he should come before the American people and indicate what outside sources of income he has had.

I would suggest that under the circumstances both Mr. Sparkman and Mr. Stevenson should come before the American people as I have and make a complete financial statement as to their financial history. And if they don't it will be an admission that they have something to hide. And I think that you will agree with me.

Because, folks, remember, a man that's to be President of the United States, a man that's to be Vice President of the United States must have the confidence of the people. And that's why I'm doing what I'm doing, and that's why I suggest that Mr. Stevenson and Mr. Sparkman since they are under attack should do what I am doing.

Now, let me say this: I know that this is not the last of the smears. In spite of my explanation tonight other smears will be made; others have been made in the past. And the purpose of the smears, I know, is this—to silence me, to make me let up.

Well, they just don't know who they're dealing with. I'm going to tell you this: I remember in the dark days of the Hiss case some of the same columnists, some of these same radio commentators who are attacking me now and misrepresenting my position were violently opposing me at the time I was after Alger Hiss.

But I continued to fight because I knew I was right. And I can say to this great television and radio audience that I have no apologies to the American people for my part in putting Alger Hiss where he is today.

And as far as this is concerned, I intend to continue to fight.

Why do I feel so deeply? Why do I feel that in spite of the smears, the misunderstandings, the necessities for a man to come up here and bare his soul as I have? Why is it necessary for me to continue this fight?

And I want to tell you why. Because, you see, I love my country. And I think my country is in danger. And I think that the only man that can save America at this time is the man that's running for President on my ticket— Dwight Eisenhower.

You say, "Why do I think it's in danger?" and I say look at the record. Seven years of the Truman-Acheson Administration and what's happened? Six hundred million people lost to the Communists, and a war in Korea in which we have lost 117,000 American casualties.

And I say to all of you that a policy that results in a loss of 600,000,000 to the Communists and a war which costs us 117,000 American casualties isn't good enough for America.

And I say that those in the State Department that made the mistakes which caused that war and which resulted in those losses should be kicked out of the State Department just as fast as we can get 'em out of there.

And let me say that I know Mr. Stevenson won't do that. Because he defends the Truman policy and I know that Dwight Eisenhower will do that, and that he will give America the leadership that it needs.

Take the problem of corruption. You've read about the mess in Washington. Mr. Stevenson can't clean it up because he was picked by the man, Truman, under whose Administration the mess was made. You wouldn't trust a man who made the mess to clean it up—that's Truman. And by the same token you can't trust the man who was picked by the man that made the mess to clean it up—and that's Stevenson.

And so I say, Eisenhower, who owes nothing to Truman, nothing to the big city bosses, he is the man that can clean up the mess in Washington.

Take Communism. I say that as far as that subject is concerned, the danger is great to America. In the Hiss case they got the secrets which enabled them to break the secret State Department code. They got secrets in the atomic bomb case which enabled 'em to get the secret of the atomic bomb, five years before they would have gotten it by their own devices.

And I say that any man who called the Alger Hiss case a "red herring" isn't fit to be President of the United States. I say that a man who like Mr. Stevenson had pooh-poohed and ridiculed the Communist threat in the United States—he said that they are phantoms among ourselves; he's accused us that have attempted to expose the Communists of looking for Communists in the Bureau of Fisheries and Wildlife—I say that a man who says that isn't qualified to be President of the United States.

And I say that the only man who can lead us in this fight to rid the Government of both those who are Communists and those who have corrupted this Government is Eisenhower, because Eisenhower, you can be sure recognizes the problem and he knows how to deal with it.

Now let me say that, finally, this evening I want to read to you just briefly excerpts from a letter which I received, a letter which, after all this is over, no one can take away from me. It reads as follows:

"Dear Senator Nixon,

"Since I'm only 19 years of age I can't vote in this Presidential election but believe me if I could you and General Eisenhower would certainly get my vote. My husband is in the Fleet Marines in Korea. He's a corpsman on the front lines and we have a two-month-old son he's never seen. And I feel confident that with great Americans like you and General Eisenhower in the White House, lonely Americans like

myself will be united with their loved ones now in Korea.

"I only pray to God that you won't be too late. Enclosed is a small check to help you in your campaign. Living on $85 a month it is all I can afford at present. But let me know what else I can do."

Folks, it's a check for $10, and it's one that I will never cash.

And just let me say this. We hear a lot about prosperity these days but I say, why can't we have prosperity built on peace rather than prosperity built on war? Why can't we have prosperity and an honest government in Washington, D.C., at the same time. Believe, me, we can. And Eisenhower is the man that can lead this crusade to bring us that kind of prosperity.

And, now, finally, I know that you wonder whether or not I am going to stay on the Republican ticket or resign.

Let me say this: I don't believe that I ought to quit because I'm not a quitter. And, incidentally, Pat's not a quitter. After all, her name was Patricia Ryan and she was born on St. Patrick's Day, and you know the Irish never quit.

But the decision, my friends, is not mine. I would do nothing that would harm the possibilities of Dwight Eisenhower to become President of the United States. And for that reason I am submitting to the Republican National Committee tonight through this television broadcast the decision which is theirs to make.

Let them decide whether my position on the ticket will help or hurt. And I am going to ask you to help them decide. Wire and write the Republican National Committee whether you think I should stay on or whether I should get off. And whatever their decision is, I will abide by it.

But just let me say this last word. Regardless of what happens I'm going to continue this fight. I'm going to campaign up and down America until we drive the crooks and the Communists and those that defend them out of Washington. And remember, folks, Eisenhower is a great man. Believe me. He's a great man. And a vote for Eisenhower is a vote for what's good for America.

# Dwight D. Eisenhower's Presidential Disability Letter (1958)

*The original Constitution was hopelessly vague on the subject of what would happen if the president became disabled. Article II, section 1, paragraph 6, said only: "In case of the ... Inability [of the President] to discharge the Powers and Duties of the said Office, the Same shall devolve on the Vice President ... until the Disability be removed, or a President shall be elected." John Dickinson of Delaware asked his fellow delegates to the Constitutional Convention, "What is the extent of the term 'disability,' and who is to be the judge of it?" No one answered him.*

*Lack of a definition for disability or a procedure for temporarily removing a disabled president left the nation without a leader for parts of nine presidencies before 1952, including the final seventeen months of Woodrow Wilson's second administration. President Dwight D. Eisenhower's ailments—a heart attack in 1955, an ileitis attack and operation in 1956, and a stroke in 1957—finally brought matters to a head. Eisenhower lamented that while he was in surgery, "the country was without a Chief Executive, the armed forces without a Commander in Chief."*

*On March 3, 1958, Eisenhower wrote an open letter to Vice President Richard Nixon stating that if the president ever were disabled again, he would instruct the vice president to serve as acting president until the disability passed. If Eisenhower were unable to communicate for some reason, Nixon could make the decision to become acting president on his own authority. In either event, Eisenhower would decide when it was time for him to resume the powers and duties of the presidency.*

*The Eisenhower letter made no provision for mental illness or any other presidential disability that the president might refuse to acknowledge. Nor did the letter have the force of law, which may have left any veto, appointment, military command, or other official action by a vice president serving as acting president open to legal challenge.*

*Despite these limitations, when John F. Kennedy became president in 1961, he sent a similar letter to Vice President Lyndon B. Johnson. When Johnson became president after Kennedy was assassinated on November 22, 1963, he sent a letter to Speaker of the House John McCormack, who was next in the line of succession in the absence of a vice president. (Johnson transferred the arrangement to Vice President Hubert H. Humphrey after the 1964 election.) Eventually, in 1967, presidential disabilities were covered by the Twenty-fifth Amendment to the Constitution. (See "Transfer of Power from President Ronald Reagan to Vice President George Bush," p. 472.)* ~

The President and the Vice President have agreed that the following procedures are in accord with the purposes and provisions of Article 2, Section 1, of the Constitution, dealing with Presidential disability. They believe that these procedures, which are intended to apply to themselves only, are in no sense outside or contrary to the Constitution but are consistent with its present provisions and implement its clear intent.

1. In the event of inability the President would—if possible—so inform the Vice President, and the Vice President would serve as Acting President, exercising the powers and duties of the office until the inability had ended.

2. In the event of an inability which would prevent the President from so communicating with the Vice President, the Vice President, after such consultation as seems to him appropriate under the circumstances, would decide upon the devolution of the powers and duties of the Office and would serve as Acting President until the inability had ended.

3. The President, in either event, would determine when the inability had ended and at that time would resume the full exercise of the powers and duties of the Office.

# The Kennedy-Nixon Debates (1960)

Until 1960 presidential candidates never debated each other. (The famous debates between Abraham Lincoln and Stephen Douglas took place during the Illinois Senate campaign of 1858.) Even with the coming of television in the 1950s, debates were effectively forestalled by a federal law that required stations to give all minor as well as major party candidates equal time on the air.

In 1960, however, the Democratically-controlled Congress voted to suspend the equal-time provision in order to force Vice President Richard Nixon, the Republican presidential nominee, to debate the lesser-known Democratic candidate, Sen. John F. Kennedy of Massachusetts. Nixon, confident both of his debating skills and, after the "Checkers" speech, of his television ability, readily agreed to debate Kennedy four times during late September and October. (See "Richard Nixon's 'Checkers' Speech," p. 333.)

The first Kennedy-Nixon debate, held in a television studio in Chicago on September 26, turned out to be politically crucial. Eighty million people watched, setting a new record for the largest television audience in history. The format was less that of a classic debate than of a joint press conference—a panel of reporters asked each candidate questions.

Nixon and Kennedy differed little from each other on substantive issues. As a result, the political outcome of the debate turned on matters of appearance and style. Kennedy won handily on both counts. He was tanned, rested, and dressed in a dark blue suit that stood out well against the grey studio set. (Television still showed only black-and-white pictures.) Nixon, who had been ill, eschewed professional makeup and wore a light grey suit that faded into the background. He looked pale-skinned, hollow-eyed, and dark-bearded.

As to style, Kennedy spoke directly into the television camera and, regardless of the questions, gave answers that sounded the themes he wanted to emphasize. (His opening statement in this debate, which was supposed to be devoted to domestic policy, began by stressing the decline of U.S. prestige in the world.) In contrast, Nixon responded to Kennedy's points, often disagreeing but sometimes agreeing. Nixon's first words of the evening were, "The things that Senator Kennedy has said, many of us can agree with."

The first debate gave the Kennedy campaign a boost in enthusiasm and public support that carried it to a narrow victory on election day.

The lesson many political leaders learned from the Kennedy-Nixon experience was that the better-known candidate in a presidential election *has more to lose in debates and should avoid them. Thus, the next round of presidential debates did not take place until 1976, when President Gerald R. Ford, trailing badly in the polls, felt he had no choice but to face his opponent, former Georgia governor Jimmy Carter. In 1980 President Carter had similar political reasons to debate Ronald Reagan, the ex-governor of California.*

*In contrast to 1960, the Ford-Carter and Carter-Reagan debates set a precedent that subsequent presidential candidates have been loath to ignore for fear of alienating voters. Thus, debates also occurred in 1984 and 1988.* ~

**Kennedy.** In the election of 1860 Abraham Lincoln said the question was whether this nation could exist half slave or half free. In the election of 1960, and with the world around us, the question is whether the world will exist half slave or half free, whether it will move in the direction of freedom, in the direction of the road that we are taking, or whether it will move in the direction of slavery.

I think it will depend in great measure upon what we do here in the United States, on the kind of society that we build, on the kind of strength that we maintain.

We discuss tonight domestic issues, but I would not want any implication to be given that this does not involve directly our struggle with Mr. Khrushchev for survival. Mr. Khrushchev is in New York, and he maintains the Communist offensive throughout the world because of the productive power of the Soviet Union itself.

The Chinese Communists have always had a large population, but they are important and dangerous now because they are mounting a major effort within their own country; the kind of country we have here, the kind of society we have, the kind of strength we build in the United States will be the defense of freedom.

If we do well here, if we meet our obligations, if we are moving ahead, then I think freedom will be secure around the world. If we fail, then freedom fails.

Therefore, I think the question before the American people is, Are we doing as much as we can do? Are we as strong as we should be? Are we as strong as we must be if we are going to maintain our independence, and if we're going to maintain and hold out the hand of friendship to those who look to us for assistance, to those who look to us for survival? I should make it very clear that I do not think we're doing enough, that I am not satisfied as an American with the progress that we are making.

This is a great country, but I think it could be a greater country, and this is a powerful country, but I think it could be a more powerful country.

I'm not satisfied to have 50 percent of our steel mill capacity unused. I'm not satisfied when the United States had last year the lowest rate of economic growth of any major industrialized society in the world—because economic growth means strength and vitality. It means we're able to sustain our defense. It means we're able to meet our commitments abroad.

I'm not satisfied when we have over $19 billion worth of food, some of it rotting even though there is a hungry world and even though 4 million Americans wait every month for a food package from the government, which averages 5 cents a day per individual. I saw cases in West Virginia, here in the United States, where children took home part of their school lunch in order to feed their families, because I don't think we are meeting our obligations toward these Americans.

I'm not satisfied when the Soviet Union is turning out twice as many scientists and engineers as we are.

I'm not satisfied when many of our teachers are inadequately paid or when our children go to school in part-time shifts. I think we should have an educational system second to none.

I'm not satisfied when I see men like Jimmy Hoffa, in charge of the largest union in the United States, still free.

I'm not satisfied when we are failing to develop the natural resources of the United States to the fullest. Here in the United States, which developed the Tennessee Valley and which built the Grand Coulee and the other dams in the northwest United States, at the present rate of hydropower production—and that is the hallmark of an industrialized society—the Soviet Union by 1975 will be producing more power than we are.

These are all the things I think in this country that can make our society strong or can mean that it stands still.

I'm not satisfied until every American enjoys his full constitutional rights. If a Negro baby is born, and this is true also of Puerto Ricans and Mexicans in some of our cities, he has about one-half as much chance to get through high school as a white baby. He has one-third as much chance to get through college as a white student. He has about a third as much chance to be a professional man, and about half as much chance to own a house. He has about four times as much chance that he'll be out of work in his life as the white baby. I think we can do better. I don't want the talents of any American to go to waste.

I know that there are those who say that we want to turn everything over to the government. I don't at all. I want the individuals to meet their responsibilities and I want the states to meet their responsibilities. But I think there is also a national responsibility.

The argument has been used against every piece of social legislation in the last twenty-five years. The people of the United States individually could not have developed the Tennessee Valley. Collectively, they could have.

A cotton farmer in Georgia or a peanut farmer or a dairy farmer in Wisconsin or Minnesota—he cannot protect himself against the forces of supply and demand in the marketplace, but working together in effective governmental programs, he can do so.

Seventeen million Americans who live over sixty-five on an average social security check of about $78 a month—they're not able to sustain themselves individually, but they can sustain themselves through the social security system.

I don't believe in big government, but I believe in effective governmental action, and I think that's the only way that the United States is going to maintain its freedom; it's the only way that we're going to move ahead. I think we can do a better job. I think we're going to have to do a better job if we are going to meet the responsibilities which time and events have placed upon us.

We cannot turn the job over to anyone else. If the United States fails, then the whole cause of freedom fails, and I think it depends in great measure on what we do here in this country.

The reason Franklin Roosevelt was a good neighbor in Latin America was because he was a good neighbor in the United States, because they felt that the American society was moving again. I want us to recapture that image. I want people in Latin America and Africa and Asia to start to look to America to see how we're doing things, to wonder what the president of the United States is doing, and not to look at Khrushchev or look at the Chinese Communists. That is the obligation upon our generation.

In 1933 Franklin Roosevelt said in his inaugural that this generation of Americans has a "rendezvous with destiny." I think our generation of Americans has the same rendezvous. The question now is, Can freedom be maintained under the most severe attack it has ever known? I think it can be, and I think in the final analysis it depends upon what we do here. I think it's time America started moving again.

**Nixon.** The things that Senator Kennedy has said, many of us can agree with. There is no question but that we cannot discuss our internal affairs in the United States without recognizing that they have a tremendous bearing on our international position. There is no question but that this nation cannot stand still, because we are in a deadly competition, a competition not only with the men in the Kremlin but the men in Peking. We're ahead in this competition, as Senator Kennedy, I think, has implied. But when you're in a race, the only way to stay ahead is to move ahead, and I subscribe completely to the spirit that Senator Kennedy has expressed tonight, the spirit that the United States should move ahead.

Where then do we disagree?

I think we disagree on the implication of his remarks tonight and on the statements that he has made on many occasions during his campaign to the effect that the United States has been standing still. We heard tonight, for example, the statement made that our growth and national product last year was the lowest of any industrial nation in the world.

Now, last year, of course, was 1958. That happened to be a recession year, but when we look at the growth of GNP this year—a year of recovery—we find that it is 6.9 percent and one of the highest in the world today. More about that later.

Looking then to this problem of how the United States should move ahead and where the United States is moving, I think it is well that we take the advice of a very famous campaigner, "Let's look at the record."

Is the United States standing still?

Is it true that this administration, as Senator Kennedy has charged, has been an administration of retreat, of defeat, of stagnation?

Is it true that as far as this country is concerned in the field of electric power, and all of the fields that he has mentioned, we have not been moving ahead?

Well, we have a comparison that we can make. We have the record of the Truman administration of seven and one-half years, and the seven and one-half years of the Eisenhower administration.

When we compare these two records in the areas that Senator Kennedy has discussed tonight, I think we find that America has been moving ahead.

Let's take schools. We have built more schools in these last seven and one-half years than we built in the previous seven and one-half, for that matter in the previous twenty years.

Let's take hydroelectric power. We have developed more hydroelectric power in these seven and one-half years than we developed in any previous administration in history.

Let us take hospitals. We find that more have been built in this administration than in the previous administration. The same is true of highways.

Let's put it in terms that all of us can understand.

We often hear gross national product discussed, and in this respect may I say that when we compare the growth in this administration with that of the previous administration, that there was a total growth of 11 percent over seven years; in this administration there has been a total growth of 19 percent over seven years.

That shows that there has been more growth in this administration than in its predecessor. But let's not put it there; let's put it in terms of the average family.

What has happened to you?

We find that your wages have gone up five times as much in the Eisenhower administration as they did in the Truman administration.

What about the prices you pay?

We find that the prices you pay went up five times as much in the Truman administration as they did in the Eisenhower administration.

What's the net result of this?

This means that the average family income went up 15 percent in the Eisenhower years as against 2 percent in the Truman years.

Now, this is not standing still, but good as this record is, may I emphasize it isn't enough. A record is never something to stand on, it's something to build on, and in building on this record I believe that we have the secret for progress. We know the way to progress and I think first of all our own record proves that we know the way.

Senator Kennedy has suggested that he believes he knows the way.

I respect the sincerity with which he makes that suggestion, but on the other hand, when we look at the various programs that he offers, they do not seem to be new. They seem to be simply retreads of the programs of the Truman administration which preceded him, and I would suggest that during the course of the evening he might indicate those areas in which his programs are new, where they will mean more progress than we had then.

What kind of programs are we for?

We are for programs that will expand educational opportunities, that will give to all Americans their equal chance for education, for all of the things which are necessary and dear to the hearts of our people.

We are for programs in addition which will see that our medical care for the aged is much better handled than it is at the present time.

Here again may I indicate that Senator Kennedy and I are not in disagreement as to the aim. We both want to help the old people. We want to see that they do have adequate medical care. The question is the means.

I think that the means that I advocate will reach that goal better than the means that he advocates.

I could give better examples but for whatever it is, whether it's in the field of housing or health or medical care or schools or the development of electric power, we have programs which we believe will move America, move her forward and build on the wonderful record that we have made over these past seven and one-half years.

Now, when we look at these programs, might I suggest that in evaluating them we often have a tendency to say that the test of a program is how much you are spending. I will concede that in all of the areas to which I have referred, Senator Kennedy would have the federal government spend more than I would have it spend.

I costed out the cost of the Democratic platform. It runs a minimum of $13.2 billion a year more than we are presently spending to a maximum of $18 billion a year more than we are presently spending.

Now, the Republican platform will cost more, too. It will cost a minimum of $4 billion a year more, a maximum of $4.9 billion a year more than we are presently spending.

Now, does this mean that his program is better than ours?

Not at all, because it isn't a question of how much the federal government spends. It isn't a question of which government does the most. It's a question of which administration does the right things, and in our case I do believe that our programs will stimulate the creative energies of 180 million free Americans.

I believe the programs that Senator Kennedy advocates will have a tendency to stifle those creative energies.

I believe, in other words, that his programs will lead to the stagnation of the motive power that we need in this country to get progress.

The final point that I would like to make is this: Senator Kennedy has suggested in his speeches that we lack compassion for the poor, for the old, and for others that are unfortunate.

Let us understand throughout this campaign that his motives and mine are sincere. I know what it means to be poor. I know what it means to see people who are unemployed.

# Dwight D. Eisenhower's Farewell Address (1961)

Dwight D. Eisenhower was elected president in 1952 and was reelected in 1956, both times in landslide victories against Gov. Adlai Stevenson of Illinois. Although he was the first Republican president since Herbert C. Hoover, Eisenhower was not a partisan figure. His prepresidential career had been spent in the military, most prominently as Supreme Allied Commander during World War II and Supreme Commander of the North Atlantic Treaty Organization (NATO) from 1950 until he resigned to run for president. Eisenhower did not cast his first vote until 1948 and was wooed by both parties to be their nominee in 1952. He finally declared himself a Republican but generally accepted the New Deal domestic policies of President Franklin D. Roosevelt and the internationalist foreign policy of President Harry S Truman, both of whom were Democrats.

Eisenhower's subdued partisanship was an important element of his politically shrewd leadership style. It helped him to work cooperatively with Congress, which was controlled by the Democrats during six of his eight years as president. It also enabled him to conduct what the political scientist Fred Greenstein has called a "hidden-hand presidency," in which Eisenhower exerted power behind the scenes while presenting to the public the image of a chief of state who was detached from petty political conflicts.

Eisenhower left office in 1961 with his popularity intact. Although at seventy he was then the oldest person ever to have served as president, Eisenhower would have liked a third term. But he was barred from running by the Twenty-second Amendment, enacted in 1951, which limits each president to no more than two terms. Ironically, the first president to be restricted by the amendment—which had been passed by the Republican Eightieth Congress as a posthumous rebuke to four-term Democratic president Franklin Roosevelt—was a Republican. (So was the second, Ronald Reagan.)

Eisenhower was the first president to deliver a televised farewell address, three days before the end of his presidency on January 17, 1961. Eisenhower's farewell address is the best-remembered such address since George Washington's in 1796. (See "George Washington's Farewell Address," p. 48.)

The farewell address abounded in surprises. Eisenhower was not renowned as an orator, yet his speech was both thoughtful and moving. He was best known as a general, yet his speech warned the nation to keep a close watch on the "military-industrial complex" (a term he coined), which consisted of professional military leaders and corporate defense contractors.

*Eisenhower also cautioned against the excesses of technology and warned the nation not to overreact to crises foreign and domestic.*

*Eisenhower's farewell address was not as well suited to the mood of the country as President John F. Kennedy's bold and challenging inaugural address, which was delivered three days later, on January 20. (See "John F. Kennedy's Inaugural Address," p. 355.) As time went by, however, the wisdom of the farewell address became better appreciated.*  ~

My fellow Americans:

Three days from now, after half a century in the service of our country, I shall lay down the responsibilities of office as, in traditional and solemn ceremony, the authority of the Presidency is vested in my successor.

This evening I come to you with a message of leave-taking and farewell, and to share a few final thoughts with you, my countrymen.

Like every other citizen, I wish the new President, and all who will labor with him, Godspeed. I pray that the coming years will be blessed with peace and prosperity for all.

Our people expect their President and the Congress to find essential agreement on issues of great moment, the wise resolution of which will better shape the future of the Nation.

My own relations with the Congress, which began on a remote and tenuous basis when, long ago, a member of the Senate appointed me to West Point, have since ranged to the intimate during the war and immediate post-war period, and, finally, to the mutually interdependent during these past eight years.

In this final relationship, the Congress and the Administration have, on most vital issues, cooperated well, to serve the national good rather than mere partisanship, and so have assured that the business of the Nation should go forward. So, my official relationship with the Congress ends in a feeling, on my part, of gratitude that we have been able to do so much together.

We now stand ten years past the midpoint of a century that has witnessed four major wars among great nations. Three of these involved our own country. Despite these holocausts America is today the strongest, the most influential and most productive nation in the world. Understandably proud of this preeminence, we yet realize that America's leadership and prestige depend, not merely upon our unmatched material progress, riches and military strength, but on how we use our power in the interests of world peace and human betterment.

Throughout America's adventure in free government, our basic purposes have been to keep the peace; to foster progress in human achievement, and to enhance liberty, dignity and integrity among people and among nations. To strive for less would be unworthy of a free and religious people. Any failure traceable to arrogance, or our lack of comprehension or readiness to sacrifice would inflict upon us grievous hurt both at home and abroad.

Progress toward these noble goals is persistently threatened by the conflict now engulfing the world. It commands our whole attention, absorbs our very beings. We face a hostile ideology—global in scope, atheistic in character, ruthless in purpose, and insidious in method. Unhappily the danger it poses promises to be of indefinite duration. To meet it successfully, there is called for, not so much the emotional and transitory sacrifices of crisis, but rather those which enable us to carry forward steadily, surely, and without complaint the burdens of a prolonged and complex struggle—with liberty the stake. Only thus shall we remain, despite every provocation, on our charted course toward permanent peace and human betterment.

Crises there will continue to be. In meeting them, whether foreign or domestic, great or small, there is a recurring temptation to feel that some spectacular and costly action could become the miraculous solution to all current difficulties. A huge increase in newer elements of our defense; development of unrealistic programs to cure every ill in agriculture; a dramatic expansion in basic and applied research—these and many other possibilities, each possibly promising in itself, may be suggested as the only way to the road we wish to travel.

But each proposal must be weighed in the light of a broader consideration: the need to maintain balance in and among national programs—balance between the private and the public economy, balance between cost and hoped for advantage—balance between the clearly necessary and the comfortably desirable; balance between our essential requirements as a nation and the duties imposed by the nation upon the individual; balance between actions of the moment and the national welfare of the future. Good judgment seeks balance and progress; lack of it eventually finds imbalance and frustration.

The record of many decades stands as proof that our people and their government have, in the main, understood these truths and have responded to them well, in the face of stress and threat. But threats, new in kind or degree, constantly arise. I mention two only.

A vital element in keeping the peace is our military establishment. Our arms must be mighty, ready for instant action, so that no potential aggressor may be tempted to risk his own destruction.

Our military organization today bears little relation to that known by any of my predecessors in peacetime, or indeed by the fighting men of World War II or Korea.

Until the latest of our world conflicts, the United States had no armaments industry. American makers of plowshares could, with time and as required, make swords as well. But now we can no longer risk emergency improvisation of national defense; we have been compelled to create a permanent armaments industry of vast proportions. Added to this, three and a half million men and women are directly engaged in the defense establishment. We annually spend on military security more than the net income of all United States corporations.

This conjunction of an immense military establishment and a large arms industry is new in the American experience. The total influence—economic, political, even spiritual—is felt in every city, every State house, every office of the Federal government. We recognize the imperative need for this development. Yet we must not fail to comprehend its grave implications. Our toil, resources and livelihood are all involved; so is the very structure of our society.

In the councils of government, we must guard against the acquisition of unwarranted influence, whether sought or unsought, by the military-industrial complex. The potential for the disastrous rise of misplaced power exists and will persist.

We must never let the weight of this combination endanger our liberties or democratic processes. We should take nothing for granted. Only an alert and knowledgeable citizenry can compel the proper meshing of the huge industrial and military machinery of defense with our peaceful methods and goals, so that security and liberty may prosper together.

Akin to, and largely responsible for the sweeping changes in our industrial-military posture, has been the technological revolution during recent decades.

In this revolution, research has become central; it also becomes more formalized, complex, and costly. A steadily increasing share is conducted for, by, or by the direction of, the Federal government.

Today, the solitary inventor, tinkering in his shop, has been overshadowed by task forces of scientists in laboratories and testing fields. In the same fashion, the free university, historically the fountainhead of free ideas and scientific discovery, has experienced a revolution in the conduct of research. Partly because of the huge costs involved, a government contract becomes virtually a substitute for intellectual curiosity. For every old blackboard there are now hundreds of new electronic computers.

The prospect of domination of the nation's scholars by Federal employment, project allocations, and the power of money is ever present—and is gravely to be regarded.

Yet, in holding scientific research and discovery in respect, as we should, we must also be alert to the equal and opposite danger that public policy could itself become the captive of a scientific-technological elite.

It is the task of statesmanship to mold, to balance, and to integrate these and other forces, new and old, within the principle of our democratic system—ever aiming toward the supreme goals of our free society.

Another factor in maintaining balance involves the element of time. As we peer into society's future, we—you and I, and our government—must avoid the impulse to live only for today, plundering, for our own ease and convenience, the precious resources of tomorrow. We cannot mortgage the material assets of our grandchildren without risking the loss also of their political and spiritual heritage. We want democracy to survive for all generations to come, not to become the insolvent phantom of tomorrow.

Down the long lane of the history yet to be written America knows that this world of ours, ever growing smaller, must avoid becoming a community of dreadful fear and hate, and be, instead, a proud confederation of mutual trust and respect.

Such a confederation must be one of equals. The weakest must come to the conference table with the same confidence as do we, protected as we are by our moral, economic, and military strength. That table, though scarred by many past frustrations, cannot be abandoned for the certain agony of the battlefield.

Disarmament, with mutual honor and confidence, is a continuing imperative. Together, we must learn how to compose differences, not with arms, but with intellect and decent purpose. Because this need is so sharp and apparent I confess that I lay down my official responsibilities in this field with a definite sense of disappointment. As one who has witnessed the horror and the lingering sadness of war—as one who knows that another war could utterly destroy this civilization which has been so slowly and painfully built over thousands of years—I wish I could say tonight that a lasting peace is in sight.

Happily, I can say that war has been avoided. Steady progress toward our ultimate goal has been made. But, so much remains to be done. As a private citizen, I shall never cease to do what little I can to help the world advance along that road.

So—this is my last good night to you as your President—I thank you for the many opportunities you have given me for public service in war and peace. I trust that in that service you find things worthy; as for the rest of it, I know you will find ways to improve performance in the future.

You and I—my fellow citizens—need to be strong in our faith that all nature under God, will reach the goal of peace with justice. May we be ever unswerving in devotion to principle, confident but humble with power, diligent in pursuit of the Nation's great goals.

To all the peoples of the world, I once more give expression to America's prayerful and continuing aspiration:

We pray that peoples of all faiths, all races, all nations, may have their great human needs satisfied; that those now denied opportunity shall come to enjoy it to the full; that all who yearn for freedom may experience its spiritual blessings; that those who have freedom will understand, also, its heavy responsibilities; that all who are insensitive to the needs of others will learn charity; that the scourges of poverty, disease and ignorance will be made to disappear from the earth, and that, in the goodness of time, all peoples will come to live together in a peace guaranteed by the binding force of mutual respect and love.

# John F. Kennedy's Inaugural Address (1961)

John F. Kennedy was elected president in 1960, at the end of Dwight D. Eisenhower's second term. The contrasts between the two presidents were dramatic and visible: the youngest man ever to be elected president (Kennedy was forty-three) was replacing the oldest man ever to leave the office; a Democrat was replacing a Republican; a celebrated World War II combat hero was replacing a celebrated World War II commander; and a professional politician who had served three terms in the House of Representatives and two terms as the junior senator from Massachusetts was replacing a career military leader whose first elective office was the presidency. Most important, perhaps, Kennedy's election replaced a defender of caution, prudence, and restraint with an advocate of change and energy.

Kennedy's inaugural address, delivered outdoors from the East Front of the Capitol on a bright but bitterly cold day, accentuated most of these contrasts. He emphasized his youth by noting that "the torch has been passed to a new generation of Americans— born in this century." He reached out to the Soviet Union: "Let us never negotiate out of fear. But let us never fear to negotiate." But he also pledged that "we shall pay any price, bear any burden, meet any hardship, support any friend, oppose any foe to assure the survival and the success of liberty." Finally, in the best-remembered phrase of his presidency, Kennedy summoned the idealism of the American people: "ask not what your country can do for you—ask what you can do for your country."

Kennedy had come to office in the closest presidential election in history: he led Vice President Richard Nixon by just 120,000 popular votes out of almost 69 million cast, and his party lost seats to the Republicans in Congress. As a result, Kennedy was frustrated in his efforts to persuade Congress to pass his major domestic policy initiatives—medical care for the aged, civil rights, federal aid to education, and a tax cut. He was more successful in creating new foreign policy programs, including the Peace Corps, the Alliance for Progress (with Latin America), and a treaty with the Soviet Union to ban the testing of nuclear weapons in the atmosphere.

During the fall of 1963, Kennedy made several trips around the country to build support for his 1964 reelection bid, which he hoped would be so successful that Congress would enact his domestic agenda. While riding through Dallas, Texas, in an open car on November 22, Kennedy was shot in the head and neck. Shortly afterwards, he died at a nearby hospital without regaining consciousness. Although police *quickly apprehended his alleged assassin, ex-Marine and Communist sympathizer Lee Harvey Oswald, Oswald's own murder while in police custody by Dallas nightclub owner Jack Ruby fostered speculation that the Kennedy assassination may have been the product of a conspiracy. Nonetheless, a special presidential commission headed by Chief Justice Earl Warren concluded in 1964 that Oswald had acted alone.*

*The combination of Kennedy's youth and glamour and his sudden, violent death has given the late president a special place in the memories of the American people. Public opinion polls often find that the public regards Kennedy as the greatest president in history, a verdict not shared even by admiring historians.*   ~

We observe today not a victory of party but a celebration of freedom—symbolizing an end as well as a beginning—signifying renewal as well as change. For I have sworn before you and Almighty God the same solemn oath our forebears prescribed nearly a century and three quarters ago.

The world is very different now. For man holds in his mortal hands the power to abolish all forms of human poverty and all forms of human life. And yet the same revolutionary beliefs for which our forebears fought are still at issue around the globe—the belief that the rights of man come not from the generosity of the state but from the hand of God.

We dare not forget today that we are the heirs of that first revolution. Let the word go forth from this time and place, to friend and foe alike, that the torch has been passed to a new generation of Americans—born in this century, tempered by war, disciplined by a hard and bitter peace, proud of our ancient heritage—and unwilling to witness or permit the slow undoing of those human rights to which this nation has always

been committed, and to which we are committed today at home and around the world.

Let every nation know, whether it wishes us well or ill, that we shall pay any price, bear any burden, meet any hardship, support any friend, oppose any foe to assure the survival and the success of liberty.

This much we pledge—and more.

To those old allies whose cultural and spiritual origins we share, we pledge the loyalty of faithful friends. United, there is little we cannot do in a host of cooperative ventures. Divided, there is little we can do—for we dare not meet a powerful challenge at odds and split asunder.

To those new states whom we welcome to the ranks of the free, we pledge our word that one form of colonial control shall not have passed away merely to be replaced by a far more iron tyranny. We shall not always expect to find them supporting our view. But we shall always hope to find them strongly supporting their own freedom—and to remember that, in the past, those who foolishly sought power by riding the back of the tiger ended up inside.

To those peoples in the huts and villages of half the globe struggling to break the bonds of mass misery, we pledge our best efforts to help them help themselves, for whatever period is required—not because the communists may be doing it, not because we seek their votes, but because it is right. If a free society cannot help the many who are poor, it cannot save the few who are rich.

To our sister republics south of our border, we offer a special pledge—to convert our good words into good deeds—in a new alliance for progress—to assist free men and free governments in casting off the chains of poverty. But this peaceful revolution of hope cannot become the prey of hostile powers. Let all our neighbors know that we shall join with them to oppose aggression or subversion anywhere in the Americas. And let every other power know that this Hemisphere intends to remain the master of its own house.

To that world assembly of sovereign states, the United Nations, our last best hope in an age where the instruments of war have far outpaced the instruments of peace, we renew our pledge of support—to prevent it from becoming merely a forum for invective—to strengthen its shield of the new and the weak—and to enlarge the area in which its writ may run.

Finally, to those nations who would make themselves our adversary, we offer not a pledge but a request: that both sides begin anew the quest for peace, before the dark powers of destruction unleashed by science engulf all humanity in planned or accidental self-destruction.

We dare not tempt them with weakness. For only when our arms are sufficient beyond doubt can we be certain beyond doubt that they will never be employed.

But neither can two great and powerful groups of nations take comfort from our present course—both sides overburdened by the cost of modern weapons, both rightly alarmed by the steady spread of the deadly atom, yet both racing to alter that uncertain balance of terror that stays the hand of mankind's final war.

So let us begin anew—remembering on both sides that civility is not a sign of weakness, and sincerity is always subject to proof. Let us never negotiate out of fear. But let us never fear to negotiate.

Let both sides explore what problems unite us instead of belaboring those problems which divide us.

Let both sides, for the first time, formulate serious and precise proposals for the inspection and control of arms—and bring the absolute power to destroy other nations under the absolute control of all nations.

Let both sides seek to invoke the wonders of science instead of its terrors. Together let us explore the stars, conquer the deserts, eradicate disease, tap the ocean depths and encourage the arts and commerce.

Let both sides unite to heed in all corners of the earth the command of Isaiah—to "undo the heavy burdens . . . (and) let the oppressed go free."

And if a beach-head of cooperation may push back the jungle of suspicion, let both sides join in creating a new endeavor, not a new balance of power, but a new world of law, where the strong are just and the weak secure and the peace preserved.

All this will not be finished in the first one hundred days. Nor will it be finished in the first one thousand days, nor in the life of this Administration, nor even perhaps in our lifetime on this planet. But let us begin.

In your hands, my fellow citizens, more than mine, will rest the final success or failure of our course. Since this country was founded, each generation of Americans has been summoned to give testimony to its national loyalty. The graves of young Americans who answered the call to service surround the globe.

Now the trumpet summons us again—not as a call to bear arms, though arms we need—not as a call to battle, though embattled we are—but a call to bear the burden of a long twilight struggle, year in and year out, "rejoicing in hope, patient in tribulation"—a struggle against the common enemies of man: tyranny, poverty, disease and war itself.

Can we forge against these enemies a grand and global alliance, North and South, East and West, that can assure a more fruitful life for all mankind? Will you join in that historic effort?

In the long history of the world, only a few generations have been granted the role of defending freedom in its hours of maximum danger. I do not shrink from this responsibility—I welcome it. I do not believe that any of us would exchange places with any other people or any other generation. The energy, the faith, the devotion which we bring to this endeavor will light our country and all who serve it—and the glow from that fire can truly light the world.

And so, my fellow Americans: ask not what your country can do for you—ask what you can do for your country.

My fellow citizens of the world: ask not what America will do for you, but what together we can do for the freedom of man.

Finally, whether you are citizens of America or citizens of the world, ask of us here the same high standards of strength and sacrifice which we ask of you. With a good conscience our only sure reward, with history the final judge of our deeds, let us go forth to lead the land we love, asking His blessing and His help, but knowing that here on earth God's work must truly be our own.

# The Cuban Missile Crisis: President John F. Kennedy's Letter to Soviet Premier Nikita Khrushchev (1962)

Soon after becoming president in 1961, President John F. Kennedy endorsed a plan developed by the Central Intelligence Agency (CIA) during the Eisenhower administration to arm, train, and land fourteen hundred Cuban exiles in Cuba in an attempt to overthrow the Communist government of Fidel Castro. The April 17, 1961, operation, which came to be known as the Bay of Pigs invasion after the location in Cuba where the exile forces landed, was a complete failure. All but two hundred of the invading Cubans were captured, and the United States was embarrassed before the world. Speaking at a press conference, Kennedy accepted full blame for the failure.

Both Castro and his patron, Soviet leader Nikita Khrushchev, were convinced that the United States would launch a subsequent full-scale invasion of Cuba. For this reason, and also so that the Soviet Union would have a much greater number of nuclear missiles aimed directly at the United States than the twenty it previously had, Khrushchev secretly placed sixty-six intermediate-range missiles in Cuba.

On October 15, 1962, Kennedy received photographic evidence of the Soviet nuclear presence in Cuba. Kennedy quietly formed an "executive committee" (ExCom) of high administration officials to prepare a U.S. response. (ExCom included Secretary of State Dean Rusk, Secretary of Defense Robert S. McNamara, Attorney General Robert F. Kennedy, CIA director John McCone, a number of military leaders, and others.) Publicly, the president carried on business as usual, even appearing at a campaign rally in Chicago.

ExCom's initial judgment was that the United States should launch an air strike against the missile sites in Cuba. Taking a more cautious and less overtly aggressive approach, Kennedy imposed a naval blockade around Cuba to prevent Soviet ships from bringing in supplies. Through diplomatic channels and in a televised address to the nation on October 22 (the first public report of what had been happening), Kennedy then demanded that the Soviet missiles be withdrawn. Nuclear war between the United States and the Soviet Union seemed more likely than at any other time in history.

Soviet reaction to the U.S. blockade and the president's demand was hard to ascertain. A conciliatory message from Khrushchev was received on October 26; a harsh one followed on October 27. Kennedy decided to ignore the latter and reply to the former. Kennedy's October 27 letter to Khrushchev laid out part of the basis for the agreement that ended the crisis: the Soviet missiles would be removed in return for a

*U.S. pledge not to invade Cuba. In 1989, at a conference of officials who had participated in their respective nations' decision making during the Cuban missile crisis, it was revealed that Kennedy also promised to remove obsolete U.S. nuclear missiles from Turkey.*          ~

Dear Mr. Chairman:

I have read your letter of October 26th with great care and welcomed the statement of your desire to seek a prompt solution to the problem. The first thing that needs to be done, however, is for work to cease on offensive missile bases in Cuba and for all weapons systems in Cuba capable of offensive use to be rendered inoperable, under effective United Nations arrangements.

Assuming this is done promptly, I have given my representatives in New York instructions that will permit them to work out this weekend—in cooperation with the Acting Secretary General and your representative—an arrangement for a permanent solution to the Cuban problem along the lines suggested in your letter of October 26th. As I read your letter, the key elements of your proposals—which seem generally acceptable as I understand   em—are as follows:

1) You would agree to remove these weapons systems from Cuba under appropriate United Nations observation and supervision; and undertake, with suitable safeguards, to halt the further introduction of such weapons systems into Cuba.

2) We, on our part, would agree—upon the establishment of adequate ar-

rangements through the United Nations to ensure the carrying out and continuation of these commitments—(a) to remove promptly the quarantine measures now in effect and (b) to give assurances against an invasion of Cuba. I am confident that other nations of the Western Hemisphere would be prepared to do likewise.

If you will give your representative similar instructions, there is no reason why we should not be able to complete these arrangements and announce them to the world within a couple of days. The effect of such a settlement on easing world tensions would enable us to work toward a more general arrangement regarding "other armaments," as proposed in your second letter which you made public. I would like to say again that the United States is very much interested in reducing tensions and halting the arms race; and if your letter signifies that you are prepared to discuss a detente affecting NATO and the Warsaw Pact, we are quite prepared to consider with our allies any useful proposals.

But the first ingredient, let me emphasize, is the cessation of work on missile sites in Cuba and measures to render such weapons inoperable, under effective international guarantees. The continuation of this threat, or a prolonging of this discussion concerning Cuba by linking these problems to the broader questions of European and world security, would surely lead to an intensification of the Cuban crisis and a grave risk to the peace of the world. For this reason I hope we can quickly agree along the lines outlined in this letter and in your letter of October 26th.

# Lyndon B. Johnson's "Great Society" Speech (1964)

*Vice President Lyndon B. Johnson succeeded to the presidency when President John F. Kennedy was assassinated on November 22, 1963. Arriving that evening in Washington from Dallas, Texas, Johnson pledged to a national television audience that the phrase "Let us continue" would be the watchword of his administration. Capitalizing on the new public disposition to support virtually anything the posthumously beloved, slain president had proposed, Johnson persuaded Congress to enact most of the unfinished business of Kennedy's "New Frontier" agenda in 1964, including the most sweeping civil rights act in history and a large reduction in income taxes.*

*Johnson, who had served as Senate majority leader during the 1950s and challenged Kennedy for the 1960 Democratic presidential nomination, also wanted to make his own mark on history. Within a few months, he chose the phrase "Great Society" as the theme for his administration. In a May 22, 1964, commencement address at the University of Michigan, Johnson developed the Great Society theme in detail.*

*According to Johnson, the United States already had become "the rich society and the powerful society" and now was challenged to reach "upward." The effort to build a Great Society would have two main goals. The first*

*was "an end to poverty and racial injustice." The other was "to advance the quality of our American civilization." As Johnson described it, "the Great Society is a place where every child can find knowledge to enrich his mind and to enlarge his talents. It is a place where leisure is a welcome chance to build and reflect, not a feared cause of boredom and restlessness. It is a place where the city of man serves not only the needs of the body and the demands of commerce, but the desire for beauty and the hunger for community."*

*Johnson ran for president in 1964 against Republican senator Barry Goldwater of Arizona, an arch-conservative who was viewed by many voters as a dangerous extremist. In addition to winning a personal landslide victory, Johnson brought in on his coattails a Congress that was two-thirds Democratic. In 1965 and 1966, the 89th Congress passed a long list of Great Society initiatives: the Voting Rights Act, the Older Americans Act, the Freedom of Information Act, and legislation to establish Medicare and Medicaid, the National Endowment of the Arts and Humanities, the Department of Transportation, the Department of Housing and Urban Development, highway beautification, and urban mass transit, among others.*

*Yet, these accomplishments, al-*

*though substantial, did not fulfill
Johnson's vision of the Great Society.
Problems developed in the implementation of many of the programs, and
poverty proved to be more intractable
than had been envisioned. Moreover,
the war in Vietnam diverted attention
and funding from the president's domestic agenda.*          ~

. . . The purpose of protecting the life of
our Nation and preserving the liberty of
our citizens is to pursue the happiness
of our people. Our success in that pursuit is the test of our success as a
nation. For a century we labored to
settle and to subdue a continent. For
half a century, we called upon un-
bounded invention and untiring industry to create an order of plenty for all of
our people. The challenge of the next
half century is whether we have the
wisdom to use that wealth to enrich and
elevate our national life, and to advance
the quality of our American civilization.

Your imagination, your initiative and
your indignation will determine
whether we build a society where
progress is the servant of our needs, or a
society where old values and new vi-
sions are buried under unbridled
growth.

For in your time we have the opportunity to move not only toward the rich
society and the powerful society, but
upward to the Great Society. The Great
Society rests on abundance and liberty
for all. It demands an end to poverty
and racial injustice, to which we are
totally committed in our time. But that
is just the beginning.

The Great Society is a place where
every child can find knowledge to enrich his mind and to enlarge his talents.
It is a place where leisure is a welcome
chance to build and reflect, not a feared
cause of boredom and restlessness. It is
a place where the city of man serves not
only the needs of the body and the
demands of commerce, but the desire

for beauty and the hunger for community.

It is a place where man can renew
contact with nature. It is a place which
honors creation for its own sake and for
what it adds to the understanding of
the race. It is a place where men are
more concerned with the quality of
their goals than the quantity of their
goods. But most of all, the great society
is not a safe harbor, a resting place, a
final objective, a finished work. It is a
challenge constantly renewed, beckon-
ing us toward a destiny where the
meaning of our lives matches the mar-
velous products of our labor.

So I want to talk to you today about
three places where we begin to build the
Great Society—in our cities, in our
countryside, and in our classrooms. . . .

Aristotle said, "Men come together in
cities in order to live, but they remain
together in order to live the good life."

It is harder and harder to live the
good life in American cities today. The
catalogue of ills is long: There is the
decay of the centers and the despoiling
of the suburbs. There is not enough
housing for our people or transportation
for our traffic. Open land is vanishing
and old landmarks are violated. Worst
of all, expansion is eroding the precious
and time-honored values of community
with neighbors and communion with
nature. The loss of these values breeds
loneliness and boredom and indifference. Our society will never be great
until our cities are great. Today the
frontier of imagination and innovation
is inside those cities, and not beyond
their borders. . . .

A second place where we begin to
build the Great Society is in our countryside. We have always prided ourselves on being not only America the
strong and America the free, but America the beautiful. Today that beauty is
in danger. The water we drink, the food
we eat, the very air that we breathe, are
threatened with pollution. Our parks
are overcrowded. Our seashores over-

burdened. Green fields and dense forests are disappearing.

A few years ago we were greatly concerned about the Ugly American. Today we must act to prevent an Ugly America.

For once the battle is lost, once our natural splendor is destroyed, it can never be recaptured. And once man can no longer walk with beauty or wonder at nature, his spirit will wither and his sustenance be wasted.

A third place to build the Great Society is in the classrooms of America. There your children's lives will be shaped. Our society will not be great until every young mind is set free to scan the farthest reaches of thought and imagination. We are still far from that goal. . . . In many places, classrooms are overcrowded and curricula are outdated. Most of our qualified teachers are underpaid, and many of our paid teachers are unqualified.

So we must give every child a place to sit and a teacher to learn from. Poverty must not be a bar to learning, and learning must offer an escape from poverty.

But more classrooms and more teachers are not enough. We must seek an educational system which grows in excellence as it grows in size. This means better training for our teachers. It means preparing youth to enjoy their hours of leisure as well as their hours of labor. It means exploring new techniques of teaching, to find new ways to stimulate the love of learning and the capacity for creation.

These are three of the central issues of the Great Society. While our government has many programs directed at those issues, I do not pretend that we have the full answer to those problems. But I do promise this: We are going to assemble the best thought and the broadest knowledge from all over the world to find those answers for America. . . .

There are those timid souls who say this battle cannot be won, that we are condemned to a soulless wealth. I do not agree. We have the power to shape the civilization that we want. But we need your will, your labor, your hearts, if we are to build that kind of society.

Those who came to this land sought to build more than just a new country. They sought a free world.

So I have come here today to your campus to say that you can make their vision our reality. Let us from this moment begin our work so that in the future men will look back and say: It was then, after a long and weary way, that man turned the exploits of his genius to the full enrichment of his life.

Thank you. Goodbye.

# Lyndon B. Johnson's Gulf of Tonkin Message (1964)

Two themes dominated the five-and-one-half-year presidency of Lyndon B. Johnson: the Great Society (see "Lyndon B. Johnson's 'Great Society' Speech," p. 361) and the war in Vietnam. Much to Johnson's distress, the latter gradually overshadowed the former.

Since winning its independence from France on the battlefield in 1954, Vietnam had been divided into two halves that were ruled by separate governments, Communist North Vietnam (headed by the hero of the revolution, Ho Chi Minh) and anti-Communist South Vietnam. Unsatisfied with this arrangement, North Vietnam and Vietcong guerrillas in South Vietnam had been fighting the South Vietnamese government in an effort to reunify the country under Communist rule. President Dwight D. Eisenhower had sent weapons and economic aid to South Vietnam during the 1950s. His successor, President John F. Kennedy, added 16,500 U.S. military advisers to the war effort.

In early 1964 aides to President Johnson privately drafted a congressional resolution that would give the president a virtual blank check to conduct the Vietnam War as he saw fit. Johnson feared that such a proposal would generate too much controversy. But on August 2 and 4, 1964, reports reached Washington that two U.S. naval destroyers, the Maddox and the C.

Turner Joy, had been attacked by North Vietnamese patrol boats in the Gulf of Tonkin near North Vietnam. The attack was described as unprovoked: in truth, the Maddox was gathering sensitive intelligence information and the South Vietnamese navy was assaulting North Vietnam at the time of the attack, but these facts became public knowledge only when the Senate Foreign Relations Committee uncovered them in 1968.

On August 5, 1964, Johnson sent what became known as the "Gulf of Tonkin message" to Congress, urging it to pass a resolution of support for his leadership. The resolution stated that "Congress approves and supports the determination of the President, as Commander-in-Chief, to take all necessary measures to repel any armed attack against the forces of the United States and to prevent further aggression." It also declared that the United States was "prepared, as the President determines, to take all necessary steps, including the use of armed force, to assist any member or protocol state of the Southeast Asia Collective Defense Treaty requesting assistance in defense of its freedom."

On August 7, the Gulf of Tonkin Resolution passed unanimously in the House of Representatives and with only two dissenting votes in the Senate.

*In later years, as the U.S. military commitment became much larger and more controversial, Johnson claimed that the Gulf of Tonkin Resolution provided ample authority for his administration's policies, which included assigning more than one half million U.S. soldiers to active combat in Vietnam. Publicly, Under Secretary of State Nicholas Katzenbach told Congress in 1967 that the resolution, in conjunction with U.S. treaty obligations, was the "functional equivalent" of a declaration of war. Privately, Johnson compared it to "grandma's nightshirt—it covered everything."*

*Despite the U.S. military effort, the Vietcong and North Vietnamese continued their assault on the government of South Vietnam. The war became increasingly unpopular in the United States, first on the college campuses, then nationwide. In a largely symbolic act, Congress repealed the Gulf of Tonkin Resolution on December 31, 1970.* ~

To the Congress of the United States:

Last night I announced to the American people that the North Vietnamese regime had conducted further deliberate attacks against U.S. naval vessels operating in international waters, and that I had therefore directed air action against gun boats and supporting facilities used in these hostile operations. This air action has now been carried out with substantial damage to the boats and facilities. Two U.S. aircraft were lost in the action.

After consultation with the leaders of both parties in the Congress, I further announced a decision to ask the Congress for a Resolution expressing the unity and determination of the United States in supporting freedom and in protecting peace in Southeast Asia.

These latest actions of the North Vietnamese regime have given a new and grave turn to the already serious situation in Southeast Asia. Our commitments in that area are well known to the Congress. They were first made in 1954 by President Eisenhower. They were further defined in the Southeast Asia Collective Defense Treaty approved by the Senate in February 1955.

This Treaty with its accompanying protocol obligates the United States and other members to act in accordance with their Constitutional processes to meet Communist aggression against any of the parties or protocol states.

Our policy in Southeast Asia has been consistent and unchanged since 1954. I summarized it on June 2 in four simple propositions:

1. *America keeps her word.* Here as elsewhere, we must and shall honor our commitments.

2. *The issue is the future of Southeast Asia as a whole.* A threat to any nation in that region is a threat to all, and a threat to us.

3. *Our purpose is peace.* We have no military, political or territorial ambitions in the area.

4. *This is not just a jungle war, but a struggle for freedom on every front of human activity.* Our military and economic assistance to South Vietnam and Laos in particular has the purpose of helping these countries to repel aggression and strengthen their independence.

The threat to the free nations of Southeast Asia has long been clear. The North Vietnamese regime has constantly sought to take over South Vietnam and Laos. This Communist regime has violated the Geneva Accords for Vietnam. It has systematically conducted a campaign of subversion, which includes the direction, training, and supply of personnel and arms for the conduct of guerrilla warfare in South Vietnamese territory. In Laos, the North Vietnamese regime has maintained military forces, used Laotian territory for infiltration into South Vietnam, and most recently carried out combat operations—all in direct violation of the Geneva Agreements of 1962.

In recent months, the actions of the North Vietnamese regime have become steadily more threatening. In May, following new acts of Communist aggression in Laos, the United States undertook reconnaissance flights over Laotian territory, at the request of the Government of Laos. These flights had the essential mission of determining the situation in territory where Communist forces were preventing inspection by the International Control Commission. When the Communists attacked these aircraft, I responded by furnishing escort fighters with instructions to fire when fired upon. Thus, these latest North Vietnamese attacks on our naval vessels are not the first direct attack on armed forces of the United States.

As President of the United States I have concluded that I should now ask the Congress, on its part, to join in affirming the national determination that all such attacks will be met, and that the U.S. will continue in its basic policy of assisting the free nations of the area to defend their freedom.

As I have repeatedly made clear, the United States intends no rashness, and seeks no wider war. We must make it clear to all that the United States is united in its determination to bring about the end of Communist subversion and aggression in the area. We seek the full and effective restoration of the international agreements signed in Geneva in 1954, with respect to South Vietnam, and again in Geneva in 1962, with respect to Laos.

I recommend a Resolution expressing the support of the Congress for all necessary action to protect our armed forces and to assist nations covered by the SEATO Treaty. At the same time, I assure the Congress that we shall continue readily to explore any avenues of political solution that will effectively guarantee the removal of Communist subversion and the preservation of the independence of the nations of the area.

The Resolution could well be based upon similar resolutions enacted by the Congress in the past—to meet the threat to Formosa in 1955, to meet the threat to the Middle East in 1957, and to meet the threat in Cuba in 1962. It could state in the simplest terms the resolve and support of the Congress for action to deal appropriately with attacks against our armed forces and to defend freedom and preserve peace in southeast Asia in accordance with the obligations of the United States under the Southeast Asia Treaty. I urge the Congress to enact such a Resolution promptly and thus to give convincing evidence to the aggressive Communist nations, and to the world as a whole, that our policy in Southeast Asia will be carried forward—and that the peace and security of the area will be preserved.

The events of this week would in any event have made the passage of a Congressional Resolution essential. But there is an additional reason for doing so at a time when we are entering on three months of political campaigning. Hostile nations must understand that in such a period the United States will continue to protect its national interests, and that in these matters there is no division among us.

# Richard Nixon's "Silent Majority" Address on Vietnam (1969)

Richard Nixon's election as president in 1968 marked one of the greatest political comebacks in U.S. history. After losing the 1960 presidential election to John F. Kennedy, Nixon was defeated two years later in a bid to become governor of California. The day after his defeat, Nixon angrily declared his retirement from politics. "You won't have Nixon to kick around anymore," he told a stunned audience of reporters, "because, gentlemen, this is my last press conference." In 1968 Nixon won the Republican nomination in a series of primary victories that convinced party leaders he still could appeal to voters.

Nixon faced a Democratic party torn in three directions by the New Frontier and Great Society programs of Presidents John F. Kennedy and Lyndon B. Johnson and, especially, by the unpopular war in Vietnam. Democratic governor George C. Wallace of Alabama ran as an independent candidate who opposed the party's domestic policies. Antiwar Democratic senators Eugene J. McCarthy of Minnesota and, later, Robert F. Kennedy of New York effectively challenged Johnson's bid for renomination, causing the president to withdraw from the race at the conclusion of a March 31 television address in which he announced a partial halt to U.S. air attacks against North Vietnam. Kennedy was killed by assassin

Sirhan Sirhan, a Palestinian nationalist, after winning the June 4 California primary. In the end the Democrats nominated Vice President Hubert H. Humphrey to oppose Nixon.

The 1968 election was overshadowed by Vietnam. Nixon, hoping to benefit from Democratic discord, said only that he had a "secret plan" to end the war, which, for reasons of diplomatic strategy, he would not reveal. Humphrey felt bound to support the policies of the Johnson administration, even as he hinted that he would be a more conciliatory negotiator as president. On election day Nixon eked out a victory over Humphrey that was almost as narrow as his own defeat by Kennedy eight years earlier.

On November 3, 1969, President Nixon announced his plan to obtain "peace with honor" in Vietnam in a televised address to the nation. The plan had two components. First, in accordance with the new Nixon Doctrine that the United States would help Asian nations militarily with materiel but not manpower, the war would be "Vietnamized"—that is, U.S. troops would be withdrawn gradually from Vietnam while the South Vietnamese army received supplies and training that would enable it to defeat the North Vietnamese and Vietcong by itself. (In the meantime, U.S. bombing raids on North Vietnam would be in-

*creased.) Second, the president would try to negotiate a withdrawal of North Vietnamese soldiers from South Vietnam.*

*Politically, Nixon's speech was an effort to undercut antiwar demonstrators, who had flooded Washington on October 15 and were planning another massive protest in mid-November. He appealed to "the great silent majority of my fellow Americans," who, in contrast to the protestors, presumably supported his policies.*

*Nixon's "silent majority" appeal evoked a tremendous response—mail, telephone calls, telegrams, and petitions. But it did nothing to satisfy the war's critics. Some of his controversial military operations during the subsequent Vietnamization process, such as the U.S. incursion into Cambodia in 1970 and the "Christmas bombing" of North Vietnam in 1972, widened fears that the U.S. war effort would be renewed.*

*In 1973 the Nixon administration concluded an agreement with North Vietnam that ended direct U.S. participation in the war in exchange for the return of U.S. prisoners. Nixon secretly promised South Vietnamese president Nguyen Van Thieu that the United States would not allow his government to be overthrown by the Communists. But Nixon resigned as president in 1974, and when South Vietnam was unable to defend itself against a North Vietnamese offensive in 1975, Congress refused to allow President Gerald R. Ford to reinvolve the United States in the fighting.* ~

Good evening, my fellow Americans:

Tonight I want to talk to you on a subject of deep concern to all Americans and to many people in all parts of the world—the war in Vietnam.

I believe that one of the reasons for the deep division about Vietnam is that many Americans have lost confidence in what their Government has told them about our policy. The American people cannot and should not be asked to support a policy which involves the overriding issues of war and peace unless they know the truth about that policy.

Tonight, therefore, I would like to answer some of the questions that I know are on the minds of many of you listening to me.

How and why did America get involved in Vietnam in the first place?

How has this administration changed the policy of the previous administration?

What has really happened in the negotiations in Paris and on the battlefront in Vietnam?

What choices do we have if we are to end the war?

What are the prospects for peace?

Now, let me begin by describing the situation I found when I was inaugurated on January 20.

~ The war had been going on for 4 years.

~ 31,000 Americans had been killed in action.

~ The training program for the South Vietnamese was behind schedule.

~ 540,000 Americans were in Vietnam with no plans to reduce the number.

~ No progress had been made at the negotiations in Paris and the United States had not put forth a comprehensive peace proposal.

~ The war was causing deep division at home and criticism from many of our friends as well as our enemies abroad.

In view of these circumstances there were some who urged that I end the war at once by ordering the immediate withdrawal of all American forces.

From a political standpoint this would have been a popular and easy course to follow. After all, we became involved in the war while my predecessor was in office. I could blame the defeat which would be the result of my action on him and come out as the peacemaker. Some put it to me quite bluntly: This was the only way to avoid allowing Johnson's war to become Nixon's war.

But I had a greater obligation than to think only of the years of my administration and of the next election. I had to think of the effect of my decision on the next generation and on the future of peace and freedom in America and in the world.

Let us all understand that the question before us is not whether some Americans are for peace and some Americans are against peace. The question at issue is not whether Johnson's war becomes Nixon's war.

The great question is: How can we win America's peace?

Well, let us turn now to the fundamental issue. Why and how did the United States become involved in Vietnam in the first place?

Fifteen years ago North Vietnam, with the logistical support of Communist China and the Soviet Union, launched a campaign to impose a Communist government on South Vietnam by instigating and supporting a revolution.

In response to the request of the Government of South Vietnam, President Eisenhower sent economic aid and military equipment to assist the people of South Vietnam in their efforts to prevent a communist takeover. Seven years ago, President Kennedy sent 16,000 military personnel to Vietnam as combat advisers. Four years ago, President Johnson sent American combat forces to South Vietnam.

Now, many believe that President Johnson's decision to send American combat forces to South Vietnam was wrong. And many others—I among them—have been strongly critical of the way the war has been conducted.

But the question facing us today is: Now that we are in the war, what is the best way to end it?

In January I could only conclude that the precipitate withdrawal of American forces from Vietnam would be a disaster not only for South Vietnam but for the United States and for the cause of peace.

For the South Vietnamese, our precipitate withdrawal would inevitably allow the Communists to repeat the massacres which followed their takeover in the North 15 years before.

~ They then murdered more than 50,000 people and hundreds of thousands more died in slave labor camps.

~ We saw a prelude of what would happen in South Vietnam when the Communists entered the city of Hue last year. During their brief rule there, there was a bloody reign of terror in which 3,000 civilians were clubbed, shot to death, and buried in mass graves.

~ With the sudden collapse of our support, these atrocities of Hue would become the nightmare of the entire nation—and particularly for the million and a half Catholic refugees who fled to South Vietnam when the Communists took over in the North.

For the United States, this first defeat in our Nation's history would result in a collapse of confidence in American leadership, not only in Asia but throughout the world.

Three American Presidents have recognized the great stakes involved in Vietnam and understood what had to be done.

In 1963, President Kennedy, with his characteristic eloquence and clarity, said: ". . . we want to see a stable government there, carrying on a struggle to maintain its national independence.

"We believe strongly in that. We are not going to withdraw from that effort. In my opinion, for us to withdraw from that effort would mean a collapse not only of South Viet-Nam, but Southeast Asia. So we are going to stay there."

President Eisenhower and President Johnson expressed the same conclusion during their terms of office.

For the future of peace, precipitate withdrawal would thus be a disaster of immense magnitude.

~ A nation cannot remain great if it betrays its allies and lets down its friends.

~ Our defeat and humiliation in South Vietnam without question would promote recklessness in the councils of those great powers who have not yet abandoned their goals of world conquest.

~ This would spark violence wherever our commitments help maintain the peace—in the Middle East, in Berlin, eventually even in the Western Hemisphere.

Ultimately, this would cost more lives.

It would not bring peace; it would bring more war.

For these reasons, I rejected the recommendation that I should end the war by immediately withdrawing all of our forces. I chose instead to change American policy on both the negotiating front and battlefront.

In order to end a war fought on many fronts, I initiated a pursuit for peace on many fronts.

In a television speech on May 14, in a speech before the United Nations, and on a number of other occasions I set forth our peace proposals in great detail.

~ We have offered the complete withdrawal of all outside forces within 1 year.

~ We have proposed a cease-fire under international supervision.

~ We have offered free elections under international supervision with the Communists participating in the organization and conduct of the elections as an organized political force. And the Saigon Government has pledged to accept the result of the elections.

We have not put forth our proposals on a take-it-or-leave-it basis. We have indicated that we are willing to discuss the proposals that have been put forth by the other side. We have declared that anything is negotiable except the right of the people of South Vietnam to determine their own future. At the Paris peace conference, Ambassador Lodge has demonstrated our flexibility and good faith in 40 public meetings.

Hanoi has refused even to discuss our proposals. They demand our unconditional acceptance of their terms, which are that we withdraw all American forces immediately and unconditionally and that we overthrow the Government of South Vietnam as we leave.

We have not limited our peace initiatives to public forums and public statements. I recognized, in January, that a long and bitter war like this usually cannot be settled in a public forum. That is why in addition to the public statements and negotiations I have explored every possible private avenue that might lead to a settlement.

Tonight I am taking the unprecedented step of disclosing to you some of our other initiatives for peace—initiatives we undertook privately and secretly because we thought we thereby might open a door which publicly would be closed.

I did not wait for my inauguration to begin my quest for peace.

~ Soon after my election, through an individual who is directly in contact on a personal basis with the leaders of North Vietnam, I made two private offers for a rapid, comprehensive settlement. Hanoi's replies called in effect for our surrender before negotiations.

~ Since the Soviet Union furnishes most of the military equipment for North Vietnam, Secretary of State Rogers, my Assistant for National Security Affairs, Dr. Kissinger, Ambassador Lodge, and I, personally, have met on a number of occasions with representatives of the Soviet Government to enlist their assistance in getting meaningful negotiations started. In addition, we have had extended discussions directed toward that same end with representatives of other governments which have diplomatic relations with North Vietnam. None of these initiatives have to date produced results.

~ In mid-July, I became convinced that it was necessary to make a major move to break the deadlock in the Paris talks. I spoke directly in this office, where I am now sitting, with an individual who had known Ho Chi Minh on a personal basis for 25 years. Through him I sent a letter to Ho Chi Minh.

I did this outside of the usual diplomatic channels with the hope that with the necessity of making statements for propaganda removed, there might be constructive progress toward bringing the war to an end. Let me read from that letter to you now.

Dear Mr. President:
I realize that it is difficult to communicate meaningfully across the gulf of four years of war. But precisely because of this gulf, I wanted to take this opportunity to reaffirm in all solemnity my desire to work for a just peace. I deeply believe that the war in Vietnam has gone on too long and delay in bringing it to an end can benefit no one—least of all the people of Vietnam. . . .
The time has come to move forward at the conference table toward an early resolution of this tragic war. You will find us forthcoming and open-minded in a common effort to bring the blessings of peace to the brave people of Vietnam. Let history record that at this critical juncture, both sides turned their face toward peace rather than toward conflict and war.

I received Ho Chi Minh's reply on August 30, 3 days before his death. It simply reiterated the public position North Vietnam had taken at Paris and flatly rejected my initiative.

The full text of both letters is being released to the press.

~ In addition to the public meetings that I have referred to, Ambassador Lodge has met with Vietnam's chief negotiator in Paris in 11 private sessions.

~ We have taken other significant initiatives which must remain secret to keep open some channels of communication which may still prove to be productive.

But the effect of all the public, private, and secret negotiations which have been undertaken since the bombing halt a year ago and since this administration came into office on January 20, can be summed up in one sentence: No progress whatever has been made except agreement on the shape of the bargaining table.

Well now, who is at fault?

It has become clear that the obstacle in negotiating an end to the war is not the President of the United States. It is not the South Vietnamese Government.

The obstacle is the other side's absolute refusal to show the least willingness to join us in seeking a just peace. And it will not do so while it is convinced that all it has to do is to wait for our next concession, and our next concession after that one, until it gets everything it wants.

There can now be no longer any question that progress in negotiation depends only on Hanoi's deciding to negotiate, to negotiate seriously.

I realize that this report on our efforts on the diplomatic front is discouraging to the American people, but the American people are entitled to know the truth—the bad news as well as the good news—where the lives of our young men are involved.

Now let me turn, however, to a more encouraging report on another front.

At the time we launched our search for peace I recognized we might not succeed in bringing an end to the war through negotiation. I, therefore, put into effect another plan to bring peace—a plan which will bring the war to an end regardless of what happens on the negotiating front.

It is in line with a major shift in U.S. foreign policy which I described in my press conference at Guam on July 25. Let me briefly explain what has been described as the Nixon Doctrine—a policy which not only will help end the war in Vietnam, but which is an essential element of our program to prevent future Vietnams.

We Americans are a do-it-yourself people. We are an impatient people. Instead of teaching someone else to do a job, we like to do it ourselves. And this trait has been carried over into our foreign policy.

In Korea and again in Vietnam, the United States furnished most of the money, most of the arms, and most of the men to help the people of those countries defend their freedom against Communist aggression.

Before any American troops were committed to Vietnam, a leader of another Asian country expressed this opinion to me when I was traveling in Asia as a private citizen. He said: "When you are trying to assist another nation defend its freedom, U.S. policy should be to help them fight the war but not to fight the war for them."

Well, in accordance with this wise counsel, I laid down in Guam three principles as guidelines for future American policy toward Asia:

~ First, the United States will keep all of its treaty commitments.

~ Second, we shall provide a shield if a nuclear power threatens the freedom of a nation allied with us or of a nation whose survival we consider vital to our security.

~ Third, in cases involving other types of aggression, we shall furnish military and economic assistance when requested in accordance with our treaty commitments. But we shall look to the nation directly threatened to assume the primary responsibility of providing the manpower for its defense.

After I announced this policy, I found that the leaders of the Philippines, Thailand, Vietnam, South Korea, and other nations which might be threatened by Communist aggression, welcomed this new direction in American foreign policy.

The defense of freedom is everybody's business—not just America's business. And it is particularly the responsibility of the people whose freedom is threatened. In the previous administration, we Americanized the war in Vietnam. In this administration, we are Vietnamizing the search for peace.

The policy of the previous administration not only resulted in our assuming the primary responsibility for fighting the war, but even more significantly did not adequately stress the goal of strengthening the South Vietnamese so that they could defend themselves when we left.

The Vietnamization plan was launched following Secretary Laird's visit to Vietnam in March. Under the plan, I ordered first a substantial increase in the training and equipment of South Vietnamese forces.

In July, on my visit to Vietnam, I changed General Abrams' orders so that they were consistent with the objectives of our new policies. Under the new orders, the primary mission of our troops is to enable the South Vietnamese forces to assume the full responsibility for the security of South Vietnam.

Our air operations have been reduced by over 20 percent.

And now we have begun to see the results of this long overdue change in American policy in Vietnam.

~ After 5 years of Americans going into Vietnam, we are finally bringing American men home. By December 15, over 60,000 men will have been withdrawn from South Vietnam—including 20 percent of all of our combat forces.

~ The South Vietnamese have continued to gain in strength. As a result they have been able to take over combat responsibilities from our American troops.

Two other significant developments have occurred since this administration took office.

~ Enemy infiltration, infiltration which is essential if they are to launch a major attack, over the last 3 months is less than 20 percent of what it was over the same period last year.

~ Most important—United States casualties have declined during the last 2 months to the lowest point in 3 years.

Let me now turn to our program for the future.

We have adopted a plan which we have worked out in cooperation with the South Vietnamese for the complete withdrawal of all U.S. combat ground forces, and their replacement by South Vietnamese forces on an orderly scheduled timetable. This withdrawal will be made from strength and not from weakness. As South Vietnamese forces become stronger, the rate of American withdrawal can become greater.

I have not and do not intend to announce the timetable for our program. And there are obvious reasons for this decision which I am sure you will understand. As I have indicated on several occasions, the rate of withdrawal will depend on developments on three fronts.

One of these is the progress which can be or might be made in the Paris talks. An announcement of a fixed timetable for our withdrawal would completely remove any incentive for the enemy to negotiate an agreement. They would simply wait until our forces had withdrawn and then move in.

The other two factors on which we will base our withdrawal decisions are the level of enemy activity and the progress of the training programs of the South Vietnamese forces. And I am glad to be able to report tonight progress on both of these fronts has been greater than we anticipated when we started the pro-

gram in June for withdrawal. As a result, our timetable for withdrawal is more optimistic now than when we made our first estimates in June. Now, this clearly demonstrates why it is not wise to be frozen in on a fixed timetable.

We must retain the flexibility to base each withdrawal decision on the situation as it is at that time rather than on estimates that are no longer valid.

Along with this optimistic estimate, I must—in all candor—leave one note of caution.

If the level of enemy activity significantly increases we might have to adjust our timetable accordingly.

However, I want the record to be completely clear on one point.

At the time of the bombing halt just a year ago, there was some confusion as to whether there was an understanding on the part of the enemy that if we stopped the bombing of North Vietnam they would stop the shelling of cities in South Vietnam. I want to be sure that there is no misunderstanding on the part of the enemy with regard to our withdrawal program.

We have noted the reduced level of infiltration, the reduction of our casualties, and are basing our withdrawal decisions partially on those factors.

If the level of infiltration or our casualties increase while we are trying to scale down the fighting, it will be the result of a conscious decision by the enemy.

Hanoi could make no greater mistake than to assume that an increase in violence will be to its advantage. If I conclude that increased enemy action jeopardizes our remaining forces in Vietnam, I shall not hesitate to take strong and effective measures to deal with that situation.

This is not a threat. This is a statement of policy, which as Commander in Chief of our Armed Forces, I am making in meeting my responsibility for the protection of American fighting men wherever they may be.

My fellow Americans, I am sure you can recognize from what I have said that we really only have two choices open to us if we want to end this war.

~ I can order an immediate, precipitate withdrawal of all Americans from Vietnam without regard to the effects of that action.

~ Or we can persist in our search for a just peace through a negotiated settlement if possible, or through continued implementation of our plan for Vietnamization if necessary—a plan in which we will withdraw all of our forces from Vietnam on a schedule in accordance with our program, as the South Vietnamese become strong enough to defend their own freedom.

I have chosen this second course.
It is not the easy way.
It is the right way.

It is a plan which will end the war and serve the cause of peace—not just in Vietnam but in the Pacific and in the world.

In speaking of the consequences of a precipitate withdrawal, I mentioned that our allies would lose confidence in America.

Far more dangerous, we would lose confidence in ourselves. Oh, the immediate reaction would be a sense of relief that our men were coming home. But as we saw the consequences of what we had done, inevitable remorse and divisive recrimination would scar our spirit as a people.

We have faced other crises in our history and have become stronger by rejecting the easy way out and taking the right way in meeting our challenges. Our greatness as a nation has been our capacity to do what had to be done when we knew our course was right.

I recognize that some of my fellow citizens disagree with the plan for peace I have chosen. Honest and patriotic Americans have reached different conclusions as to how peace should be achieved.

In San Francisco a few weeks ago, I saw demonstrators carrying signs reading: "Lose in Vietnam, bring the boys home."

Well, one of the strengths of our free society is that any American has a right to reach that conclusion and to advocate that point of view. But as President of the United States, I would be untrue to my oath of office if I allowed the policy of this Nation to be dictated by the minority who hold that point of view and who try to impose it on the Nation by mounting demonstrations in the street.

For almost 200 years, the policy of this Nation has been made under our Constitution by those leaders in the Congress and the White House elected by all of the people. If a vocal minority, however fervent its cause, prevails over reason and the will of the majority, this Nation has no future as a free society.

And now I would like to address a word, if I may, to the young people of this Nation who are particularly concerned, and I understand why they are concerned, about this war.

I respect your idealism.
I share your concern for peace.
I want peace as much as you do.

There are powerful personal reasons I want to end this war. This week I will have to sign 83 letters to mothers, fathers, wives, and loved ones of men who have given their lives for America in Vietnam. It is very little satisfaction to me that this is only one-third as many letters as I signed the first week in office. There is nothing I want more than to see the day come when I do not have to write any of those letters.

~ I want to end the war to save the lives of those brave young men in Vietnam.

~ But I want to end it in a way which will increase the chance that their younger brothers and their sons will not have to fight in some future Vietnam someplace in the world.

~ And I want to end the war for another reason. I want to end it so that the energy and dedication of you, our young people, now too often directed into bitter hatred against those responsible for the war, can be turned to the great challenges of peace, a better life for all Americans, a better life for all people on this earth.

I have chosen a plan for peace. I believe it will succeed.

If it does succeed, what the critics say now won't matter. If it does not succeed, anything I say then won't matter.

I know it may not be fashionable to speak of patriotism or national destiny these days. But I feel it is appropriate to do so on this occasion.

Two hundred years ago this Nation was weak and poor. But even then, America was the hope of millions in the world. Today we have become the strongest and richest nation in the world. And the wheel of destiny has turned so that any hope the world has for the survival of peace and freedom will be determined by whether the American people have the moral stamina and the courage to meet the challenge of free world leadership.

Let historians not record that when America was the most powerful nation in the world we passed on the other side of the road and allowed the last hopes for peace and freedom of millions of people to be suffocated by the forces of totalitarianism.

And so tonight—to you, the great silent majority of my fellow Americans—I ask for your support.

I pledged in my campaign for the Presidency to end the war in a way that we could win the peace. I have initiated a plan of action which will enable me to keep that pledge.

The more support I can have from the American people, the sooner that pledge can be redeemed; for the more divided we are at home, the less likely the enemy is to negotiate at Paris.

Let us be united for peace. Let us also be united against defeat. Because let us understand: North Vietnam cannot defeat or humiliate the United States. Only Americans can do that.

Fifty years ago, in this room and at this very desk, President Woodrow Wilson spoke words which caught the imagination of a war-weary world. He said: "This is the war to end war." His dream for peace after World War I was shattered on the hard realities of great power politics and Woodrow Wilson died a broken man.

Tonight I do not tell you that the war in Vietnam is the war to end wars. But I do say this: I have initiated a plan which will end this war in a way that will bring us closer to that great goal to which Woodrow Wilson and every American President in our history has been dedicated—the goal of a just and lasting peace.

As President I hold the responsibility for choosing the best path to that goal and then leading the Nation along it.

I pledge to you tonight that I shall meet this responsibility with all of the strength and wisdom I can command in accordance with your hopes, mindful of your concerns, sustained by your prayers.

Thank you and good night.

# Spiro T. Agnew's Media Speech (1969)

Spiro T. Agnew was the generally unknown, eighteen-month governor of Maryland when Republican presidential nominee Richard Nixon surprised the nation by tapping him as his vice-presidential running mate in the 1968 election. Agnew's relative anonymity, which Nixon had calculated would render him politically neutral in the election, instead made him an object of controversy and derision. "Spiro Who?" bumper stickers sprouted up around the country; a Democratic television commercial displayed the words "Agnew for Vice President?" over a soundtrack of laughter, then ended with a voice solemnly intoning, "This would be funny if it weren't so serious."

After his inauguration as vice president, Agnew became controversial in a different way. Nixon assigned Agnew the role that President Dwight D. Eisenhower had assigned Nixon when he was vice president: to launch the fiercely partisan attacks on the administration's political adversaries that the president, out of concern for the dignity of his office, did not want to make personally. Agnew assumed this role with relish, variously attacking antiwar demonstrators, "radic-libs" in Congress (so-called radical-liberals including certain Republicans) and a host of alliterative targets, including "nattering nabobs of negativism," "pusillanimous pussyfooters," "vicars of vacillation," and a new "4-H Club— the 'hopeless, hysterical hypochondriacs of history.' "

Agnew's most effective charges, however, were fired against the television news media in a nationally televised speech (rare coverage for a vice president) in Des Moines, Iowa, on November 13, 1969. The particular occasion for the attack was the critical "instant analysis" that "a small band of network commentators and self-appointed analysts" had provided for viewers directly after a television address on Vietnam that President Nixon had delivered the week before. (See "Richard Nixon's 'Silent Majority' Address on Vietnam," p. 367.) But Agnew ranged widely in his assault. He charged a "small group of men, numbering perhaps no more than a dozen anchormen, commentators and executive producers," with being an elite, closed community that imposed its narrow East Coast view of the news on an unsuspecting nation, which derived most of its knowledge of government and politics from television news programs.

As vice president, Agnew earned Nixon's appreciation for a difficult assignment well done, but never his respect. Yet Agnew became so popular within the Republican party that Nixon had no choice but to keep him on the ticket for the 1972 presidential election. By January 1973, Agnew was *the early front-runner for the 1976 Republican presidential nomination. In October 1973, however, revelations of financial scandal forced the vice president to resign in disgrace. (See "Resignation of Vice President Spiro T. Agnew," p. 384.)* ~

Tonight I want to discuss the importance of the television news medium to the American people. No nation depends more on the intelligent judgment of its citizens. No medium has a more profound influence over public opinion. Nowhere in our system are there fewer checks on vast power. So, nowhere should there be more conscientious responsibility exercised than by the news media. The question is, Are we demanding enough of our television news presentations? And are the men of this medium demanding enough of themselves?

Monday night a week ago, President Nixon delivered the most important address of his Administration, one of the most important of our decade. His subject was Vietnam. His hope was to rally the American people to see the conflict through to a lasting and just peace in the Pacific. For 32 minutes, he reasoned with a nation that has suffered almost a third of a million casualties in the longest war in its history.

When the President completed his address—an address, incidentally, that he spent weeks in the preparation of—his words and policies were subjected to instant analysis and querulous criticism. The audience of 70 million Americans gathered to hear the President of the United States was inherited by a small band of network commentators and self-appointed analysts, the majority of whom expressed in one way or another their hostility to what he had to say.

It was obvious that their minds were made up in advance. Those who recall the fumbling and groping that followed

President Johnson's dramatic disclosure of his intention not to seek another term have seen these men in cogenuine state of unpreparedness. This was not it.

One commentator twice contradicted the President's statement about the exchange of correspondence with Ho Chi Minh. Another challenged the President's abilities as a politician. A third asserted that the President was following a Pentagon line. Others, by the expression on their faces, the tone of their questions and the sarcasm of their responses, made clear their sharp disapproval. . . .

Now every American has a right to disagree with the President of the United States and to express publicly that disagreement. But the President of the United States has a right to communicate directly with the people who elected him, and the people of this country have the right to make up their own minds and form their own opinions about a Presidential address without having a President's words and thoughts characterized through the prejudices of hostile critics before they can even be digested.

When Winston Churchill rallied public opinion to stay the course against Hitler's Germany, he didn't have to contend with a gaggle of commentators raising doubts about whether he was reading public opinion right, or whether Britain had the stamina to see the war through.

When President Kennedy rallied the nation in the Cuban missile crisis, his address to the people was not chewed over by a roundtable of critics who disparaged the course of action he'd asked America to follow.

The purpose of my remarks tonight is to focus your attention on this little group of men who not only enjoy a right of instant rebuttal to every Presidential address, but, more importantly, wield a free hand in selecting, presenting and interpreting the great issues in our nation. . . .

According to studies, for millions of Americans the networks are the sole source of national and world news. In Will Rogers' observation, what you knew was what you read in the newspaper. Today for millions of Americans, it's what they see and hear on their television sets.

Now how is this network news determined? A small group of men, numbering perhaps no more than a dozen anchormen, commentators and executive producers ... decide what 40 to 50 million Americans will learn of the day's events in the nation and the world.

We cannot measure this power and influence by the traditional democratic standards, for these men can create national issues overnight.

They can make or break by their coverage and commentary a moratorium on the war.

They can elevate men from obscurity to national prominence within a week. They can reward some politicians with national exposure and ignore others.

For millions of Americans the network reporter who covers a continuing issue—like the ABM or civil rights—becomes, in effect, the presiding judge in a national trial by jury.

It must be recognized that the networks have made important contributions to the national knowledge—for news, documentaries and specials. They have often used their power constructively and creatively to awaken the public conscience to critical problems. The networks made hunger and black lung disease national issues overnight. The TV networks have done what no other medium could have done in terms of dramatizing the horrors of war. The networks have tackled our most difficult social problems with a directness and an immediacy that's the gift of their medium. They focus the nation's attention on its environmental abuses—on pollution in the Great Lakes and the threatened ecology of the Everglades. . . .

Nor is their power confined to the substantive. A raised eyebrow, an inflection of the voice, a caustic remark dropped in the middle of a broadcast can raise doubts in a million minds about the veracity of a public official or the wisdom of a Government policy.

One Federal Communications Commissioner considers the powers of the networks equal to that of local, state and Federal Governments all combined. Certainly it represents a concentration of power over American public opinion unknown in history.

Now what do Americans know of the men who wield this power? Of the men who produce and direct the network news, the nation knows practically nothing. Of the commentators, most Americans know little other than that they reflect an urbane and assured presence seemingly well-informed on every important matter.

We do know that to a man these commentators and producers live and work in the geographical and intellectual confines of Washington, D.C., or New York City, the latter of which James Reston terms the most unrepresentative community in the entire United States.

Both communities bask in their own provincialism, their own parochialism.

We can deduce that these men read the same newspapers. They draw their political and social views from the same sources. Worse, they talk constantly to one another, thereby providing artifical reinforcement to their shared viewpoints.

Do they allow their biases to influence the selection and presentation of the news? David Brinkley states objectivity is impossible to normal human behavior. Rather, he says, we should strive for fairness.

Another anchorman on a network news show contends, and I quote: "You can't expunge all our private convictions just because you sit in a seat like this and a camera starts to stare at you.

I think your program has to reflect what your basic feelings are. I'll plead guilty to that." . . .

The American people would rightly not tolerate this concentration of power in the Government.

Is it not fair and relevant to question its concentration in the hands of a tiny, enclosed fraternity of privileged men elected by no one and enjoying a monopoly sanctioned and licensed by Government?

The views of the majority of this fraternity do not—and I repeat, not—represent the views of America.

That is why such a great gulf existed between how the nation received the President's address and how the networks reviewed it. . . .

As with other American institutions, perhaps it is time that the networks were made more responsive to the views of the nation and more responsible to the people they serve.

Now I want to make myself perfectly clear. I'm not asking for Government censorship or any other kind of censorship. I'm asking whether a form of censorship already exists when the news that 40 million Americans receive each night is determined by a handful of men responsible only to their corporate employers and is filtered through a handful of commentators who admit to their own set of biases.

The questions I'm raising here tonight should have been raised by others long ago. They should have been raised by those Americans who have traditionally considered the preservation of freedom of speech and freedom of the press their special provinces of responsibility.

They should have been raised by those Americans who share the view of the late Justice Learned Hand that right conclusions are more likely to be gathered out of a multitude of tongues than through any kind of authoritative selection.

Advocates for the networks have claimed a First Amendment right to the same unlimited freedoms held by the great newspapers of America.

But the situations are not identical. Where the New York Times reaches 800,000 people, N.B.C. reaches 20 times that number on its evening news. Nor can the tremendous impact of seeing television film and hearing commentary be compared with reading the printed page.

A decade ago, before the network news acquired such dominance over public opinion, Walter Lippmann spoke to the issue. He said there's an essential and radical difference between television and printing. The three or four competing television stations control virtually all that can be received over the air by ordinary television sets. But besides the mass circulation dailies, there are weeklies, monthlies, out-of-town newspapers and books. If a man doesn't like his newspaper, he can read another from out of town or wait for a weekly news magazine. It's not ideal, but it's infinitely better than the situation in television.

There if a man doesn't like what the networks are showing, all he can do is turn them off and listen to a phonograph.

Now a virtual monopoly of a whole medium of communication is not something that democratic people should blindly ignore. And we are not going to cut off our television sets and listen to the phonograph just because the airways belong to the networks. They don't. They belong to the people. . . . And in the networks' endless pursuit of controversy, we should ask: What is the end value—to enlighten or to profit? What is the end result—to inform or to confuse? How does the ongoing exploration for more action, more excitement, more drama serve our national search for internal peace and stability?

Gresham's Law seems to be operating in the network news. Bad news drives out good news. The irrational is more controversial than the rational. Concurrence can no longer compete with dissent. . . .

The labor crisis settled at the negotiating table is nothing compared to the confrontation that results in a strike— or better yet, violence along the picket lines.

Normality has become the nemesis of the network news. Now the upshot of all this controversy is that a narrow and distorted picture of America often emerges from the televised news.

A single, dramatic piece of the mosaic becomes in the minds of millions the entire picture. And the American who relies upon television for his news might conclude that the majority of American students are embittered radicals. That the majority of black Americans feel no regard for their country. That violence and lawlessness are the rule rather than the exception on the American campus.

We know that none of these conclusions is true.

Perhaps the place to start looking for a credibility gap is not in the offices of the Government in Washington but in the studios of the networks in New York.

Television may have destroyed the old stereotypes, but has it not created new ones in their places?

What has this passionate pursuit of controversy done to the politics of progress through local compromise essential to the functioning of a democratic society?

The members of Congress or the Senate who follow their principles and philosophy quietly in a spirit of compromise are unknown to many Americans, while the loudest and most extreme dissenters on every issue are known to every man in the street.

How many marches and demonstrations would we have if the marchers did not know that the ever-faithful TV cameras would be there to record their antics for the next news show?

We've heard demands that Senators and Congressmen and judges make known all their financial connections so that the public will know who and what influences their decisions and their votes. Strong arguments can be made for that view.

But when a single commentator or producer, night after night, determines for millions of people how much of each side of a great issue they are going to see and hear, should he not first disclose his personal views on the issue as well?

In this search for excitement and controversy, has more than equal time gone to the minority of Americans who specialize in attacking the United States—its institutions and its citizens?

Tonight I've raised questions. I've made no attempt to suggest the answers. The answers must come from the media men. They are challenged to turn their critical powers on themselves, to direct their energy, their talent and their conviction toward improving the quality and objectivity of news presentation.

They are challenged to structure their own civic ethics to relate their great responsibilities they hold.

And the people of America are challenged, too, challenged to press for responsible news presentations. The people can let the networks know that they want their news straight and objective. The people can register their complaints on bias through mail to the networks and phone calls to local stations. This is one case where the people must defend themselves; where the citizen, not the Government, must be the reformer; where the consumer can be the most effective crusader.

By way of conclusion, let me say that every elected leader in the United States depends on these men of the media. Whether what I've said to you tonight will be heard or seen at all by the nation is not my decision, it's not your decision, it's their decision.

In tomorrow's edition of the Des Moines Register, you'll be able to read a news story detailing what I've said tonight. Editorial comment will be reserved for the editorial page, where it belongs.

Should not the same wall of separation exist between news and comment on the nation's networks?

Now, my friends, we'd never trust such power, as I've described, over public opinion in the hands of an elected Government. It's time we questioned it in the hands of a small and unelected elite.

The great networks have dominated America's airwaves for decades. The people are entitled to a full accounting of their stewardship.

# Richard Nixon's China Trip Announcement (1971)

The political career of Richard Nixon was constructed on a foundation of anticommunism. In his first election to the House of Representatives in 1946, Nixon charged incumbent Democrat Jerry Voorhis of being a socialist. Four years later, running for the Senate, Nixon labeled his opponent, Sen. Helen Gahagan Douglas, as the "pink lady." In 1952 Nixon ran for vice president by accusing the Democrats of being not just corrupt (see "Richard Nixon's 'Checkers' Speech," p. 333) but also soft on communism. Most notably, Nixon gained national fame when, after becoming chair of a subcommittee of the House Un-American Activities Committee in 1948, he uncovered evidence that Alger Hiss, a former high-ranking official of the State Department, was a Communist.

Nixon's rise to political prominence on the basis of anticommunism reflected (and contributed to) the tenor of the times. In the late 1940s the United States and the Soviet Union had ended their World War II alliance by entering into the "cold war." (See "The Truman Doctrine," p. 288.) A longstanding friendship between the United States and China also came to an end when, in 1949, a Communist revolution led by Mao Zedong overthrew the government of Chiang Kai-shek. Even after Chiang and his supporters fled to the offshore island of

Formosa, the United States continued to recognize his government as the legitimate government of China. Relations between the U.S. government and the Maoist government of mainland China were nonexistent; the rhetoric of the two nations was mutually hostile.

Politically, few Democrats or liberal Republicans during the 1950s and 1960s dared broach the subject of better relations with Communist China, for fear of bringing down the wrath of conservatives. All the more surprising, then, that on July 15, 1971, President Nixon appeared on national television to read a three-and-one-half minute announcement that he would be traveling to China sometime in early 1972 at the invitation of the Communist government. The purpose of the visit, Nixon announced, would be "to seek the normalization of relations" between the United States and China. The president also revealed that the trip had been arranged at his direction through a series of secret visits to China by his national security adviser, Henry Kissinger, during the preceding two years. Nixon made the China trip, which was politically and diplomatically successful, in February 1972.

Many analysts believe that only a staunch anti-Communist like Nixon could have ended hostility to the most populous nation in the world without provoking widespread political opposi-

*tion. Part of his motive seems to have been to take advantage of the developing hostility between China and the Soviet Union by forging a relationship between the United States and China. Playing one Communist nation off against the other, Nixon also was welcomed to the Soviet Union by Leonid Brezhnev in May 1972, where he signed a strategic arms limitation treaty.*

*Nixon's trips to both China and the Soviet Union were the first by a U.S. president. "Summit" meetings (Winston Churchill coined the term in 1953) between the president and the leader of one or more other nations were rare until World War II but have become commonplace since then.*   ~

Good evening.

I have requested this television time tonight to announce a major development in our efforts to build a lasting peace in the world.

As I have pointed out on a number of occasions over the past three years, there can be no stable and enduring peace without the participation of the Peoples Republic of China and its 750 million people. That is why I have undertaken initiatives in several areas to open the door for more normal relations between our two countries.

In pursuance of that goal, I sent Dr. Kissinger, my Assistant for National Security Affairs, to Peking during his recent world tour for the purpose of having talks with Premier Chou En-lai. The announcement I shall now read is being issued simultaneously in Peking and in the United States.

Premier Chou En-lai and Dr. Henry Kissinger, President Nixon's Assistant for National Security Affairs, held talks in Peking from July 9 to 11, 1971. Knowing of President Nixon's expressed desire to visit the Peoples Republic of China, Premier Chou En-lai, on behalf of the Government of the Peoples Republic of China, has extended an invitation to President Nixon to visit China at an appropriate date before May 1972. President Nixon has accepted the invitation with pleasure.

The meeting between the leaders of China and the United States is to seek the normalization of relations between the two countries and also to exchange views on questions of concern to the two sides. In anticipation of the inevitable speculation which will follow this announcement, I want to put our policy in the clearest possible context.

Our action in seeking a new relationship with the Peoples Republic of China will not be at the expense of our old friends. It is not directed against any other nation. We seek friendly relations with all nations. Any nation can be our friend without being any other nation's enemy.

I have taken this action because of my profound conviction that all nations will gain from a reduction of tensions and a better relationship between the United States and the Peoples Republic of China.

It is in that spirit that I will undertake what I deeply hope will become a journey for peace, peace not just for our generation, but for future generations on this earth we share together.

Thank you and good night.

# Resignation of Vice President Spiro T. Agnew (1973)

Vice President Spiro T. Agnew was the second vice president in history to resign from office. The first, John C. Calhoun, had a falling out with President Andrew Jackson and, near the end of his term in 1832, resigned to accept South Carolina's election to the Senate. Agnew, in contrast, had reasonably good relations with President Richard Nixon and resigned in 1973 as part of a plea bargain with the Justice Department.

On August 1, 1973, U.S. Attorney for Maryland George Beall, a Republican, privately informed Agnew's attorney that the vice president was being investigated for allegedly having accepted payoffs from private architectural and engineering firms that did business with the government while he was serving as county executive of Baltimore County, governor of Maryland, and vice president. (The charges also included not paying income taxes on the bribes.) Seven days later Agnew revealed at a press conference that the investigation was taking place and proclaimed his innocence. His request to Speaker of the House Carl Albert that the House of Representatives begin an impeachment inquiry into his activities was widely regarded as an effort to preempt the criminal investigation. (Albert quickly rejected the request.) Closing the net even more tightly, the Justice Department issued an opinion stating that a vice president, unlike a president, can be indicted while in office because the vice president's functions are not "indispensable to the orderly operation of government."

On September 27 Beall began presenting evidence of Agnew's wrongdoing to a Baltimore grand jury. Agnew continued his public defense, vowing to an audience of Republican women on September 29 that "I will not resign if indicted." Privately, however, his lawyers negotiated a plea bargain with the Justice Department.

On October 10, with the negotiations complete, Agnew sent a one-sentence letter of resignation to Secretary of State Henry Kissinger, following Calhoun's precedent. In return for his resignation as vice president and, later that day, his plea of nolo contendere (no contest) to one count of income tax evasion, the Justice Department did not seek Agnew's indictment on other charges. It did, however, submit a forty-page document to the federal grand jury in Baltimore that described all of the payoffs that Agnew had accepted. Agnew was sentenced to a fine of $10,000 and three years of unsupervised probation.

Agnew's resignation left the vice presidency vacant. All sixteen previous vacancies in the office had been left unfilled. But under the Twenty-fifth Amendment (1967), President

*Nixon was charged to appoint, with the approval of both houses of Congress, a new vice president. On October 12 Nixon nominated House Republican leader Gerald R. Ford. Ford's appointment was confirmed on December 6.*    ~

# Excerpts from Justice Department Document Submitting Evidence against Agnew to the Grand Jury

## I. The Relationship of Mr. Agnew, I. H. Hammerman II and Jerome B. Wolff.

In the spring of 1967, shortly after Mr. Agnew had taken office as Governor of Maryland, he advised Hammerman that it was customary for engineers to make substantial cash payments in return for engineering contracts with the state of Maryland. Mr. Agnew instructed Hammerman to contact Wolff, then the new chairman-director of the Maryland State Roads Commission, to arrange for the establishment of an understanding pursuant to which Wolff would notify Hammerman as to which engineering firms were in line for state contracts so that Hammerman could solicit and obtain from those engineering firms cash payments in consideration therefor.

Hammerman, as instructed, discussed the matter with Wolff, who was receptive but who requested that the cash payments to be elicited from the engineers be split in three equal shares among Agnew, Hammerman and Wolff. Hammerman informed Mr. Agnew of Wolff's attitude; Mr. Agnew informed Hammerman that the split of the cash monies would be 50 percent for Mr. Agnew, 25 per cent for Hammerman and 25 per cent for Wolff. Hammerman carried that message to Wolff, who

agreed to that split.

The scheme outlined above was then put into operation. Over the course of the approximately 18 months of Mr. Agnew's remaining tenure as Governor of Maryland, Hammerman made contact with approximately eight engineering firms. Informed periodically by Wolff as to which engineering firms were in line to receive state contracts, Hammerman successfully elicited from seven engineering firms substantial cash payments pursuant to understandings between Hammerman and the various engineers to whom he was talking that the substantial cash payments were in return for the state work being awarded to those engineering firms. The monies collected in that manner by Hammerman were split (among Hammerman, Agnew and Wolff) in accordance with the understanding earlier reached. . . .

Wolff, as chairman-director of the Maryland State Roads Commission, made inititial tentative decisions with regard to which engineering firms should be awarded which state contracts. These tentative decisions would then be discussed by Wolff with Governor Agnew. Although Governor Agnew accorded Wolff's tentative decisions great weight, the Governor always exercised the final decision-making authority. . . .

Hammerman also successfully solicited, at Governor Agnew's instruction, a substantial cash payment from a financial institution in return for that institution's being awarded a major role in the financing of a large issue of state bonds.

## II. The Relationship between Mr. Agnew and Allen Green.

Shortly after Mr. Agnew's election in November 1966 as governor of Maryland, he complained to Allen Green, principal of a large engineering firm, about the financial burdens to be imposed upon Mr. Agnew by his role as Governor. Green responded by saying that his company had benefited from state work and had been able to generate some cash funds from which he would be willing to provide Mr. Agnew with some financial assistance. Mr. Agnew indicated that he would be grateful for such assistance.

Beginning shortly thereafter, Green delivered to Mr. Agnew six to nine times a year an envelope containing between $2,000 and $3,000 in cash. Green's purpose was to elicit from the Agnew administration as much state work for his engineering firm as possible. That purpose was clearly understood by Governor Agnew. . . .

Green continued to make cash payments to Vice President Agnew three or four times a year up to and including December 1972. These payments were usually about $2,000 each. The payments were made both in Mr. Agnew's vice presidential office and at his residence in the Sheraton-Park Hotel, Washington, D.C. The payments were not discontinued until after the initiation of the Baltimore County investigation by the United States Attorney for the District of Maryland in January 1973.

## III. The Relationship between Mr. Agnew and Lester Matz.

Lester Matz, a principal in another large engineering firm, began making corrupt payments while Mr. Agnew was County Executive of Baltimore County in the early 1960s. In those days, Matz paid 5 per cent of his fees from Baltimore County contracts in cash to Mr. Agnew through one of Mr. Agnew's close associates.

After Mr. Agnew became Governor of Maryland, Matz decided to make his payments directly to Governor Agnew. He made no payments until that summer of 1968 when he and his partner calculated that they owed Mr. Agnew

approximately $20,000 in consideration for work which their firm had already received from the Governor's administration. The $20,000 in cash was generated in an illegal manner and was given by Matz to Governor Agnew in a manila envelope in Governor Agnew's office on or about July 16, 1968. . . .

Matz made no further corrupt payments to Mr. Agnew until shortly after Mr. Agnew became Vice President, at which time Matz calculated that he owed Mr. Agnew approximately $10,000 more from jobs and fees which the Matz firm had received from Governor Agnew's administration since July 1968. After generating $10,000 in cash in an illegal manner, Matz met with Mr. Agnew in the Vice President's office and gave him approximately $10,000 in cash in an envelope. . . .

In or around April 1971, Matz made a cash payment to Vice President Agnew of $2,500 in return for the awarding by the General Services Administration of a contract to a small engineering firm in which Matz had a financial ownership interest. An intermediary was instrumental in the arrangement for that particular corrupt payment.

---

## Agnew's Letter of Resignation, Addressed to Secretary of State Kissinger

October 10, 1973

The Honorable Henry A. Kissinger
The Secretary of State
Washington, D.C. 20520
Dear Mr. Secretary:
 I hereby resign the Office of Vice President of the United States, effective immediately.

Sincerely,

/s/Spiro T. Agnew

# The War Powers Resolution (1973)

The U.S. failure in the Vietnam War belied the widely accepted post-World War II belief that the executive branch, with its superior sources of information, its unity of command, and its ability to act with dispatch, should be responsible to determine when and how the nation should go to war. In 1973 Congress passed the War Powers Resolution and, after President Richard Nixon vetoed the act, overrode his veto on November 7 by a margin of 284-135 in the House of Representatives and 75-18 in the Senate.

The War Powers Resolution states that before committing U.S. armed forces to hostile or dangerous situations, the president should consult with Congress "in every possible instance." After committing the armed forces, the president should report the actions in writing to congressional leaders. Within sixty (or, by special presidential request, ninety) days, the U.S. forces must be withdrawn unless Congress votes to authorize their continued involvement. Even within that period, Congress can vote to withdraw the forces.

Despite the act's overwhelming support in Congress, both conservative and liberal opponents proved to be prescient in their criticisms. Conservatives echoed Nixon, who vetoed the act as being "both unconstitutional and dangerous to the best interest of the na-

tion." A few liberals, led by Democratic senator Thomas F. Eagleton of Missouri, noted that the act effectively sanctions virtually any presidential use of force for ninety days. Although Congress has the legal power to force a withdrawal, charged Frank Church, a Democratic senator from Idaho, "I cannot imagine a situation where a President would take us into a foreign war of major proportions under circumstances that would not cause both the public and Congress to rally around the flag, at least for sixty days."

Since 1973, every president has questioned the constitutionality of the War Powers Resolution. A number of military operations have been undertaken by presidents Gerald R. Ford (the Vietnam evacuation and Mayaguez rescue), Jimmy Carter (the attempted Iranian hostage rescue), and Ronald Reagan (the Lebanon mission, Grenada invasion, bombing of Libya, and naval escort to oil tankers in the Persian Gulf). In few instances has the president complied with the letter, much less the spirit, of the act. Prior consultation with Congress (usually a few congressional leaders) has been perfunctory or nonexistent. Written reports often have not been filed. Congress never has voted to force the end of a mission.

To be sure, a future president would find it more difficult to involve the

*United States in a Vietnam-style war because of the War Powers Resolution. But the main lesson of nearly two decades of experience under the act is that no law can substitute for political will if Congress intends to curb the president's role in war making.*   ~

## Short Title

**Section 1.** This joint resolution may be cited as the "War Powers Resolution."

## Purpose and Policy

**Section 2.** (a) It is the purpose of this joint resolution to fulfill the intent of the framers of the Constitution of the United States and insure that the collective judgment of both the Congress and the president will apply to the introduction of United States armed forces into hostilities, or into situations where imminent involvement in hostilities is clearly indicated by the circumstances, and to the continued use of such forces in hostilities or in such situations.

(b) Under article 1, section 8, of the Constitution, it is specifically provided that the Congress shall have the power to make all laws necessary and proper for carrying into execution, not only its own powers but also all other powers vested by the Constitution in the government of the United States, or in any department or officer thereof.

(c) The constitutional powers of the president as commander-in-chief to introduce United States armed forces into hostilities, or into situations where imminent involvement in hostilities is clearly indicated by the circumstances, are exercised only pursuant to (1) a declaration of war, (2) specific statutory authorization, or (3) a national emergency created by attack upon the United States, its territories or possessions, or its armed forces.

## Consultation

**Section 3.** The president in every possible instance shall consult with Congress before introducing United States armed forces into hostilities or into situations where imminent involvement in hostilities is clearly indicated by the circumstances, and after every such introduction shall consult regularly with the Congress until United States armed forces are no longer engaged in hostilities or have been removed from such situations.

## Reporting

**Section 4.** (a) In the absence of a declaration of war, in any case in which United States armed forces are introduced—

(1) into hostilities or into situations where imminent involvement in hostilities is clearly indicated by the circumstances;

(2) into the territory, airspace, or waters of a foreign nation, while equipped for combat, except for deployments which relate solely to supply, replacement, repair, or training of such forces; or

(3) in numbers which substantially enlarge United States armed forces equipped for combat already located in a foreign nation;

the President shall submit within 48 hours to the Speaker of the House of Representatives and to the president pro tempore of the Senate a report, in writing, setting forth—

(A) the circumstances necessitating the introduction of United States armed forces;

(B) the constitutional and legislative authority under which such introduction took place; and

(C) the estimated scope and duration of the hostilities or involvement.

(b) The president shall provide such

other information as the Congress may request in the fulfillment of its constitutional responsibilities with respect to committing the nation to war and to the use of United States armed forces abroad.

(c) Whenever United States armed forces are introduced into hostilities or into any situation described in subsection (a) of this section, the president shall, so long as such armed forces continue to be engaged in such hostilities or situation, report to the Congress periodically on the status of such hostilities or situation as well as on the scope and duration of such hostilities or situation, but in no event shall he report to the Congress less often than once every six months.

## Congressional Action

**Section 5.** (a) Each report submitted pursuant to section 4(a) (1) shall be transmitted to the Speaker of the House of Representatives and to the president pro tempore of the Senate on the same calendar day. Each report so transmitted shall be referred to the Committee on Foreign Affairs of the House of Representatives and to the Committee on Foreign Relations of the Senate for appropriate action. If, when the report is transmitted, the Congress has adjourned sine die or has adjourned for any period in excess of three calendar days, the Speaker of the House of Representatives and the president pro tempore of the Senate, if they seem it advisable (or if petitioned by at least 30 percent of the membership of their respective houses) shall jointly request the president to convene Congress in order that it may consider the report and take appropriate action pursuant to this section.

(b) Within sixty calendar days after a report is submitted or is required to be submitted pursuant to section 4(a) (1), whichever is earlier, the president shall terminate any use of United States

armed forces with respect to which such report was submitted (or required to be submitted), unless the Congress (1) has declared war or has enacted a specific authorization for such use of United States armed forces, (2) has extended by law such sixty-day period, or (3) is physically unable to meet as a result of an armed attack upon the United States. Such sixty-day period shall be extended for not more than an additional thirty days if the president determines and certifies to the Congress in writing that unavoidable military necessity respecting the safety of the United States armed forces requires the continued use of such armed forces in the course of bringing about a prompt removal of such forces.

(c) Notwithstanding subsection (b), at any time that United States armed forces are engaged in hostilities outside the territory of the United States, its possessions and territories without a declaration of war or specific statutory authorization, such forces shall be removed by the president if the Congress so directs by concurrent resolution.

## Congressional Priority Procedures for Joint Resolution or Bill

**Section 6.** (a) Any joint resolution or bill introduced pursuant to section 5(b) at least thirty calendar days before the expiration of the sixty-day period specified in such section shall be referred to the Committee on Foreign Affairs of the House of Representatives or the Committee on Foreign Relations of the Senate, as the case may be, and such committee shall report one such joint resolution or bill, together with its recommendations, not later than twenty-four calendar days before the expiration of the sixty-day period specified in such section, unless such house shall otherwise determine by the yeas and nays.

(b) Any joint resolution or bill so reported shall become the pending business of the house in question (in the case of the Senate the time for debate shall be equally divided between the proponents and the opponents), and shall be voted on within three calendar days thereafter, unless such house shall otherwise determine by yeas and nays.

(c) Such a joint resolution or bill passed by one house shall be referred to the committee of the other house named in subsection (a) and shall be reported out not later than fourteen calendar days before the expiration of the sixty-day period specified in section 5(b). The joint resolution or bill so reported shall become the pending business of the house in question and shall be voted on within three calendar days after it has been reported, unless such house shall otherwise determine by yeas and nays.

(d) In the case of any disagreement between the two houses of Congress with respect to a joint resolution or bill passed by both houses, conferees shall be promptly appointed and the committee of conference shall make and file a report with respect to such resolution or bill not later than four calendar days before the expiration of the sixty-day period specified in section 5(b). In the event the conferees are unable to agree within forty-eight hours, they shall report back to their respective houses in disagreement. Notwithstanding any rule in either house concerning the printing of conference reports in the Record or concerning any delay in the consideration of such reports, such report shall be acted on by both houses not later than the expiration of such sixty-day period.

## Congressional Priority Procedures for Concurrent Resolution

**Section 7.** (a) Any concurrent resolution introduced pursuant to section 5(c) shall be referred to the Committee on Foreign Affairs of the House of Representatives or the Committee on Foreign Relations of the Senate, as the case may be, and one such concurrent resolution shall be reported out by such committee together with its recommendations within fifteen calendar days, unless such house shall otherwise determine by the yeas and nays.

(b) Any concurrent resolution so reported shall become the pending business of the house in question (in the case of the Senate the time for debate shall be equally divided between the proponents and the opponents) and shall be voted on within three calendar days thereafter, unless such house shall otherwise determine by yeas and nays.

(c) Such a concurrent resolution passed by one house shall be referred to the committee of the other house named in subsection (a) and shall be reported out by such committee together with its recommendations within fifteen calendar days and shall thereupon become the pending business of such house and shall be voted upon within three calendar days, unless such house shall otherwise determine by yeas and nays.

(d) In the case of any disagreement between the two houses of Congress with respect to a concurrent resolution passed by both houses, conferees shall be promptly appointed and the committee of conference shall make and file a report with respect to such concurrent resolution within six calendar days after the legislation is referred to the committee of conference. Notwithstanding any rule in either house concerning the printing of conference reports in the Record or concerning any delay in the consideration of such reports, such report shall be acted on by both houses not later than six calendar days after the conference report is filed. In the event the conferees are unable to agree within forty-eight hours, they shall report back to their respective houses in disagreement.

## Interpretation of Joint Resolution

**Section 8.** (a) Authority to introduce United States armed forces into hostilities or into situations wherein involvement in hostilities is clearly indicated by the circumstances shall not be inferred—

(1) from any provision of law (whether or not in effect before the date of the enactment of this joint resolution), including any provision contained in any appropriation act, unless such provision specifically authorizes the introduction of United States armed forces into hostilities or into such situations and states that it is intended to constitute specific statutory authorization within the meaning of this joint resolution; or

(2) from any treaty heretofore or henceafter ratified unless such treaty is implemented by legislation specifically authorizing the introduction of United States armed forces into hostilities or into such situations and stating that it is intended to constitute specific statutory authorization within the meaning of this joint resolution.

(b) Nothing in this joint resolution shall be construed to require any further specific statutory authorization to permit members of United States armed forces to participate jointly with members of the armed forces of one or more foreign countries in the headquarters operations of high-level military commands which were established prior to the date of enactment of this joint resolution and pursuant to the United Nations Charter or any treaty ratified by the United States prior to such date.

(c) For purposes of this joint resolution, the term "introduction of United States armed forces" includes the assignment of members of such armed forces to command, coordinate, participate in the movement of, or accompany the regular or irregular military forces of any foreign country or government when such military forces are engaged, or there exists an imminent threat that such forces will become engaged, in hostilities.

(d) Nothing in this joint resolution—

(1) is intended to alter the constitutional authority of the Congress or of the president, or the provisions of existing treaties; or

(2) shall be construed as granting any authority to the president with respect to the introduction of United States armed forces into hostilities or into situations wherein involvement in hostilities is clearly indicated by the circumstances which authority he would not have had in the absence of this joint resolution.

## Separability Clause

**Section 9.** If any provision of this joint resolution or the application thereof to any person or circumstance is held invalid, the remainder of the joint resolution and the application of such provision to any other person or circumstance shall not be affected thereby.

## Effective Date

**Section 10.** This joint resolution shall take effect on the date of its enactment.

Passed over presidential veto Nov. 7, 1973.

# Proposed Articles of Impeachment against Richard Nixon (1974)

On July 17, 1972, five burglars who were secretly employed by the Committee to Re-elect the President (better known by its acronym, CREEP) were caught breaking into the offices of the Democratic National Committee in Washington's Watergate hotel. The chain of command that had authorized the break-in, as well as a host of other illegal and unethical campaign activities, reached high into the administration of President Richard Nixon. In an effort to avoid embarrassing revelations, Nixon and some of his closest aides in the White House responded to news of the burglary by trying to obstruct official investigations into what had happened.

A combination of activities brought evidence to light of Nixon's involvement in the Watergate coverup, including: diligent investigations by reporters Bob Woodward and Carl Bernstein of the Washington Post in late 1972 and 1973; hearings by a special bipartisan Senate committee chaired by Democratic senator Sam Ervin of North Carolina during the summer of 1973; testimony before the Ervin committee by White House counsel John Dean and other participants in the Watergate affair regarding their own, each other's, and (in Dean's case) the president's culpability; and the release of secret White House tape recordings.

In February 1974 the House Judi-ciary Committee began to consider impeaching the president for "high Crimes and Misdemeanors," only the second serious presidential impeachment inquiry in U.S. history. (See "Articles of Impeachment against Andrew Johnson," p. 149.) By late July the committee was ready to vote. Between July 27 and 29, it decided to recommend three articles of impeachment to the full House of Representatives.

Article I, approved by a bipartisan 27-11 vote, charged President Nixon with violating both his oath to preserve, protect, and defend the Constitution and his constitutional charge to take care that the laws be faithfully executed by taking actions that obstructed the administration of justice in the Watergate case. These actions included: withholding evidence, condoning perjury, approving the payment of "hush money," interfering with lawful investigations, and making false and misleading statements.

Article II, approved 28-10, contended that the president had misused and abused both his executive authority and the resources of various executive agencies, including the Federal Bureau of Investigation, the Central Intelligence Agency, the Internal Revenue Service, and the Criminal Division and the Office of Watergate Special Prosecution Force of the Justice Department. This article involved not *only the Watergate coverup, but other misdeeds as well, such as a covert break-in, sponsored by White House operatives, into the office of Dr. Lewis Fielding, who was psychiatrist to former Defense Department employee Daniel Ellsberg.*

*Article III, approved 21-17, charged Nixon with contempt of Congress for not cooperating with the House Judiciary Committee's investigation.*

*Because the committee's unstated working standard for an impeachable offense was that it be an indictable crime "to the manifest injury of the people of the United States," it voted down two other proposed articles of impeachment. The first, which faulted the president for the secret bombing of Cambodia, was judged not to be criminal. The second, Nixon's evasion of income taxes, was found to be a personal but not a political crime.*    ～

## Resolution

Impeaching Richard M. Nixon, President of the United States, of high crimes and misdemeanors.

*Resolved,* That Richard M. Nixon, President of the United States, is impeached for high crimes and misdemeanors, and that the following articles of impeachment be exhibited to the Senate:

Articles of impeachment exhibited by the House of Representatives of the United States of America in the name of itself and of all of the people of the United States of America, against Richard M. Nixon, President of the United States of America, in maintenance and support of its impeachment against him for high crimes and misdemeanors.

## Article I

In his conduct of the office of President of the United States, Richard M. Nixon, in violation of his constitutional oath faithfully to execute the office of President of the United States and, to the best of his ability, preserve, protect, and defend the Constitution of the United States, and in violation of his constitutional duty to take care that the laws be faithfully executed, has prevented, obstructed, and impeded the administration of justice, in that:

On June 17, 1972, and prior thereto, agents of the Committee for the Re-election of the President committed unlawful entry of the headquarters of the Democratic National Committee in Washington, District of Columbia, for the purpose of securing political intelligence. Subsequent thereto, Richard M. Nixon, using the powers of his high office, engaged personally and through his subordinates and agents, in a course of conduct or plan designed to delay, impede, and obstruct the investigation of such unlawful entry; to cover up, conceal and protect those responsible; and to conceal the existence and scope of other unlawful covert activities.

The means used to implement this course of conduct or plan included one or more of the following:

(1) making or causing to be made false or misleading statements to lawfully authorized investigative officers and employees of the United States;

(2) withholding relevant and material evidence or information from lawfully authorized investigative officers and employees of the United States.

(3) approving, condoning, acquiescing in, and counseling witnesses with respect to the giving of false or misleading statements to lawfully authorized investigative officers and employees of the United States and false or misleading testimony in duly instituted judicial and congressional proceedings;

(4) interfering or endeavoring to interfere with the conduct of investigations by the Department of Justice of the United States, the Federal Bureau of Investigation, the Office of Watergate Special Prosecution Force, and

Congressional Committees;

(5) approving, condoning, and acquiescing in, the surreptitious payment of substantial sums of money for the purpose of obtaining the silence or influencing the testimony of witnesses, potential witnesses or individuals who participated in such unlawful entry and other illegal activities;

(6) endeavoring to misuse the Central Intelligence Agency, an agency of the United States;

(7) disseminating information received from officers of the Department of Justice of the United States to subjects of investigations conducted by lawfully authorized investigative officers and employees of the United States, for the purpose of aiding and assisting such subjects in their attempts to avoid criminal liability;

(8) making false or misleading public statements for the purpose of deceiving the people of the United States into believing that a thorough and complete investigation had been conducted with respect to allegations of misconduct on the part of personnel of the executive branch of the United States and personnel of the Committee for Re-election of the President, and that there was no involvement of such personnel in such misconduct; or

(9) endeavoring to cause prospective defendants, and individuals duly tried and convicted, to expect favored treatment and consideration in return for their silence or false testimony, or rewarding individuals for their silence or false testimony.

In all of this, Richard M. Nixon has acted in a manner contrary to his trust as President and subversive of constitutional government, to the great prejudice of the cause of law and justice and to the manifest injury of the people of the United States.

Wherefore Richard M. Nixon, by such conduct, warrants impeachment and trial, and removal from office.

## Article II

Using the powers of the office of President of the United States, Richard M. Nixon, in violation of his constitutional oath faithfully to execute the office of President of the United States and, to the best of his ability, preserve, protect, and defend the Constitution of the United States, and in disregard of his constitutional duty to take care that the laws be faithfully executed, has repeatedly engaged in conduct violating the constitutional rights of citizens, impairing the due and proper administration of justice and the conduct of lawful inquiries, or contravening the laws governing agencies of the executive branch and the purposes of these agencies.

This conduct has included one or more of the following:

(1) He has, acting personally and through his subordinates and agents, endeavored to obtain from the Internal Revenue Service, in violation of the constitutional rights of citizens, confidential information contained in income tax returns for purposes not authorized by law, and to cause, in violation of the constitutional rights of citizens, income tax audits or other income tax investigations to be initiated or conducted in a discriminatory manner.

(2) He misused the Federal Bureau of Investigation, the Secret Service, and other executive personnel, in violation or disregard of the constitutional rights of citizens, by directing or authorizing such agencies or personnel to conduct or continue electronic surveillance or other investigations for purposes unrelated to national security, the enforcement of laws, or any other lawful function of his office; he did direct, authorize, or permit the use of information obtained thereby for purposes unrelated to national security, the enforcement of laws, or any other lawful function of his office; and he did direct the concealment of certain records

made by the Federal Bureau of Investigation of electronic surveillance.

(3) He has, acting personally and through his subordinates and agents, in violation or disregard of the constitutional rights of citizens, authorized and permitted to be maintained a secret investigative unit within the office of the President, financed in part with money derived from campaign contributions, which unlawfully utilized the resources of the Central Intelligence Agency, engaged in covert and unlawful activities, and attempted to prejudice the constitutional right of an accused to a fair trial.

(4) He has failed to take care that the laws were faithfully executed by failing to act when he knew or had reason to know that his close subordinates endeavored to impede and frustrate lawful inquiries by duly constituted executive, judicial, and legislative entities concerning the unlawful entry into the headquarters of the Democratic National Committee, and the cover-up thereof, and concerning other unlawful activities, including those relating to the confirmation of Richard Kleindienst as Attorney General of the United States, the electronic surveillance of private citizens, the break-in into the offices of Dr. Lewis Fielding, and the campaign financing practices of the Committee to Re-elect the President.

(5) In disregard of the rule of law, he knowingly misused the executive power by interfering with agencies of the executive branch, including the Federal Bureau of Investigation, the Criminal Division, and the Office of Watergate Special Prosecution Force, of the Department of Justice, and the Central Intelligence Agency, in violation of his duty to take care that the laws be faithfully executed.

In all of this, Richard M. Nixon has acted in a manner contrary to his trust as President and subversive of constitutional government, to the great prejudice of the cause of law and justice and to the manifest injury of the people of the United States.

Wherefore Richard M. Nixon, by such conduct, warrants impeachment and trial, and removal from office.

**Article III**

In his conduct of the office of President of the United States, Richard M. Nixon, contrary to his oath faithfully to execute the office of President of the United States and, to the best of his ability, preserve, protect, and defend the Constitution of the United States, and in violation of his constitutional duty to take care that the laws be faithfully executed, has failed without lawful cause or excuse to produce papers and things as directed by duly authorized subpoenas issued by the Committee on the Judiciary of the House of Representatives on April 11, 1974, May 15, 1974, May 30, 1974, and June 24, 1974, and willfully disobeyed such subpoenas. The subpoenaed papers and things were deemed necessary by the Committee in order to resolve by direct evidence fundamental, factual questions relating to Presidential direction, knowledge, or approval of actions demonstrated by other evidence to be substantial grounds for impeachment of the President. In refusing to produce these papers and things, Richard M. Nixon, substituting his judgment as to what materials were necessary for the inquiry, interposed the powers of the Presidency against the lawful subpoenas of the House of Representatives, thereby assuming to himself functions and judgments necessary to the exercise of the sole power of impeachment vested by the Constitution in the House of Representatives.

In all of this, Richard M. Nixon has acted in a manner contrary to his trust as President and subversive of constitutional government, to the great prejudice of the cause of law and justice, and to the manifest injury of the people of the United States.

Wherefore Richard M. Nixon, by such conduct, warrants impeachment and trial, and removal from office.

# United States v. Nixon (1974)

In June 1973 the special Senate Watergate committee, chaired by Sen. Sam Ervin of North Carolina, learned in testimony from former White House aide Alexander P. Butterfield that President Richard Nixon had installed a secret, voice-activated audiotaping system in the Oval Office of the White House and in other presidential offices. The revelation, which seemed to indicate that conclusive evidence existed regarding the truth or falsehood of the president's and other administration officials' versions of the Watergate affair, marked a turning point in the investigation. It also touched off a lengthy political and legal battle for control of the tapes.

Several investigating bodies, including the Senate committee, the House Judiciary Committee, and the Watergate special prosecutor, subpoenaed lists of tapes in late 1973 and early 1974. At various times, bending to overwhelming political pressure, Nixon released transcripts of various taped discussions. But he continued to claim that the president's right of executive privilege justified his decision not to comply with any of the subpoenas. Eventually, the request of Special Watergate Prosecutor Leon Jaworski, who stated that he needed sixty-four tapes as evidence in the criminal trial of several former Nixon aides, came before the Supreme Court for review.

On July 24, 1974, a unanimous Court ruled that Nixon must turn over the tapes to Judge John J. Sirica, the judge in the Watergate trial. Chief Justice Warren E. Burger, writing for all of his colleagues, conceded the existence of a limited executive privilege under the Constitution, a doctrine the Court had never before declared. Burger wrote that under the separation of powers a "President and those who assist him must be free to explore alternatives in the process of shaping policies and making decisions and to do so in a way many would be unwilling to express except privately." But, he continued, this privilege does not outweigh the explicit constitutional right that defendants have to a fair trial and to due process. Thus, "absent a claim of need to protect military, diplomatic or sensitive national security secrets," executive privilege must give way. Since the president had made no such claims in this case, the Court ordered Nixon to comply with Jaworski's subpoena and turn over the tapes.

Nixon had considered defying the Supreme Court decision if the vote were close. (Four of the justices were Nixon appointees.) But in the face of a unanimous ruling, he agreed to turn over the tapes. ~

MR. CHIEF JUSTICE BURGER delivered the opinion of the court.

These cases present for review the denial of a motion, filed on behalf of the President of the United States, in the case of *United States v. Mitchell et al.* to quash a third-party subpoena *duces tecum* issued by the United States District Court for the District of Columbia, pursuant to Fed. Rule Crim. Proc. 17 (c). The subpoena directed the President to produce certain tape recordings and documents relating to his conversations with aides and advisers. The court rejected the President's claims of absolute executive privilege, of lack of jurisdiction, and of failure to satisfy the requirements of Rule 17 (c). The President appealed to the Court of Appeals. We granted the United States' petition for certiorari before judgment, and also the President's responsive cross-petition for certiorari before judgment, because of the public importance of the issues presented and the need for their prompt resolution.

On March 1, 1974, a grand jury of the United States District Court for the District of Columbia returned an indictment charging seven named individuals with various offenses, including conspiracy to defraud the United States and to obstruct justice. Although he was not designated as such in the indictment, the grand jury named the President, among others, as an unindicted coconspirator. On April 18, 1974, upon motion of the Special Prosecutor, a subpoena *duces tecum* was issued pursuant to Rule 17 (c) to the President by the United States District Court and made returnable on May 2, 1974. This subpoena required the production, in advance of the September 9 trial date, of certain tapes, memoranda, papers, transcripts, or other writings relating to certain precisely identified meetings between the President and others. The Special Prosecutor was able to fix the time, place and persons present at these discussions because the White House daily logs and appointment records had been delivered to him. On April 30, the

President publicly released edited transcripts of 43 conversations: portions of 20 conversations subject to subpoena in the present case were included. On May 1, 1974, the President's counsel filed a "special appearance" and a motion to quash the subpoena, under Rule 17 (c). This motion was accompanied by a formal claim of privilege. At a subsequent hearing, further motions to expunge the grand jury's action naming the President as an unindicted coconspirator and for protective orders against the disclosure of that information were filed or raised orally by counsel for the President.

On May 20, 1974, the District Court denied the motion to quash and the motions to expunge and for protective orders. It further ordered "the President or any subordinate officer, official or employee with custody or control of the documents or objects subpoenaed," to deliver to the District Court, on or before May 31, 1974, the originals of all subpoenaed items, as well as an index and analysis of those items, together with tape copies of those portions of the subpoenaed recordings for which transcripts had been released to the public by the President on April 30. The District Court rejected jurisdictional challenges based on a contention that the dispute was nonjusticiable because it was between the special prosecutor and the Chief Executive and hence "intra-executive" in character; it also rejected the contention that the judiciary was without authority to review an assertion of executive privilege by the President. The court's rejection of the first challenge was based on the authority and powers vested in the Special Prosecutor by the regulation promulgated by the Attorney General; the court concluded that a justiciable controversy was presented. The second challenge was held to be foreclosed by the decision in *Nixon v. Sirica,* (1973).

The District Court held that the judiciary, not the President, was the final arbiter of a claim of executive privilege. The court concluded that, under the circumstances of this case, the presumptive privilege was overcome by the Special Prosecutor's prima facie "demonstration of need sufficiently compelling to warrant judicial examination in chambers. . . ." The court held, finally, that the Special Prosecutor has satisfied the requirements of Rule 17 (c). The District Court stayed its order pending appellate review on condition that review was sought before 4 p.m., May 24. The court further provided that matters filed under seal remain under seal when transmitted as part of the record.

On May 24, 1974, the President filed a timely notice of appeal from the District Court order, and the certified record from the District Court was docketed in the United States Court of Appeals for the District of Columbia Circuit. On the same day, the President also filed a petition for writ of mandamus in the Court of Appeals seeking review of the District Court order.

Later on May 24, the Special Prosecutor also filed, in this Court, a petition for a writ of certiorari before judgment. On May 31, the petition was granted with an expedited briefing schedule. On June 6, the President filed, under seal, a cross-petition for writ of certiorari before judgment. This cross-petition was granted June 15, 1974, and the case was set for argument on July 8, 1974.

# I
# Jurisdiction

The threshold question presented is whether the May 20, 1974, order of the District Court was an appealable order and whether this case was properly "in," 28 U.S.C. § 1254, the United States Court of Appeals when the petition for certiorari was filed in this court. Court of Appeals jurisdiction under 28 U.S.C. § 1291 encompasses only "final

decisions of the district courts." Since the appeal was timely filed and all other procedural requirements were met, the petition is properly before this Court for consideration if the District Court order was final.

The finality requirement of 28 U.S.C. § 1291 embodies a strong congressional policy against piecemeal reviews, and against obstructing or impeding an ongoing judicial proceeding by interlocutory appeals. See, e.g., *Cobbledick* v. *United States,* (1940). This requirement ordinarily promotes judicial efficiency and hastens the ultimate termination of litigation. In applying this principle to an order denying a motion to quash and requiring the production of evidence pursuant to a subpoena *duces tecum,* it has been repeatedly held that the order is not final and hence not applicable. This court has

"consistently held that the necessity for expedition in the administration of the criminal law justifies putting one who seeks to resist the production of desired information to a choice between compliance with a trial court's order to produce prior to any review of that order, and resistance to that order with the concomitant possibility of an adjudication of contempt if his claims are rejected on appeal."

The requirement of submitting to contempt, however, is not without exception and in some instances the purposes underlying the finality rule require a different result. For example, in *Perlman* v. *United States,* (1918), a subpoena had been directed to a third party requesting certain exhibits; the appellant, who owned the exhibits, sought to raise a claim of privilege. The Court held an order compelling production was appealable because it was unlikely that the third party would risk a contempt citation in order to allow immediate review of the appellant's claim of privilege. That case fell within the "limited class of cases where denial of immediate review would render impossible any review of an individual's claims," *United States* v. *Ryan.*

Here too the traditional contempt avenue to immediate appeal is peculiarly inappropriate due to the unique setting in which the question arises. To require a President of the United States to place himself in the posture of disobeying an order of the court merely to trigger the procedural mechanism for review of the ruling would be unseemly, and present an unnecessary occasion for constitutional confrontation between two branches of the Government. Similarly, a federal judge should not be placed in the posture of issuing a citation to a President simply in order to invoke a review. The issue whether a President can be cited for contempt could itself engender protracted litigation, and would further delay both review on the merits of his claim of privilege and the ultimate termination of the underlying criminal action for which his evidence is sought. These considerations lead us to conclude that the order of the District Court was an appealable order. The appeal from that order was therefore properly "in" the Court of Appeals, and the case is now properly before this Court on the writ of certiorari before judgment.

## II
## Justiciability

In the District Court, the President's counsel argued that the court lacked jurisdiction to issue the subpoena because the matter was an intra-branch dispute between a subordinate and superior officer of the Executive Branch and hence not subject to judicial resolution. That argument has been renewed in this Court with emphasis on the contention that the dispute does not present a "case" or "controversy" which can be adjudicated in the federal courts. The President's counsel argues that the federal courts should not intrude into areas committed to the other branches of Government. He views the present dispute as essentially a "jurisdictional" dispute within the Executive Branch which he analogizes to a dispute between two congressional committees. Since the Executive Branch has exclusive authority and absolute discretion to decide whether to prosecute a case, *Confiscation Cases,* (1869), *United States* v. *Cox,* (1965), it is contended that a President's decision is final in determining what evidence is to be used in a given criminal case. Although his counsel concedes the President has delegated certain specific powers to the Special Prosecutor, he has not "waived nor delegated to the Special Prosecutor the President's duty to claim privilege as to all materials ... which fall within the President's inherent authority to refuse to disclose to any executive officer." Brief for the President 47. The Special Prosecutor's demand for the items therefore presents, in the view of the President's counsel, a political question under *Baker* v. *Carr,* (1962), since it involves a "textually demonstrable" grant of power under Art. II.

The mere assertion of a claim of an "intra-branch dispute," without more, has never operated to defeat federal jurisdiction; justiciability does not depend on such surface inquiry. In *United States* v. *ICC,* (1949), the Court observed, "courts must look behind names that symbolize the parties to determine whether a justiciable case of controversy is presented."

Our starting point is the nature of the proceeding for which the evidence is sought—here a pending criminal prosecution. It is a judicial proceeding in a federal court alleging violation of federal laws and is brought in the name of the United States as sovereign. *Berger* v. *United States* (1935). Under the authority of Art. II § 2, Congress has vested in the Attorney General the power to conduct the criminal litigation of the United States Government. It has also vested in him the power to appoint subordinate officers to assist him in the discharge of his duties. Acting pursuant to those statutes, the Attorney General has delegated the authority to represent the United States in these particular matters to a Special Prosecutor with unique authority and tenure. The regulation gives the Special Prosecutor explicit power to contest the invocation of executive privilege in the process of seeking evidence deemed relevant to the performance of these specially designated duties.

So long as this regulation is extant it has the force of law. In *Accardi* v. *Shaughnessy,* (1953), regulations of the Attorney General delegated certain of his discretionary powers to the Board of Immigration Appeals and required that Board to exercise its own discretion on appeals in deportation cases. The Court held that so long as the Attorney General's regulations remained operative, he denied himself the authority to exercise the discretion delegated to the Board even though the original authority was his and he could reassert it by amending the regulations. *Service* v. *Dulles,* (1957), and *Vitarelli* v. *Seaton,* (1959), reaffirmed the basic holding of *Accardi.*

Here, as in *Accardi,* it is theoretically possible for the Attorney General to amend or revoke the regulation defining the Special Prosecutor's authority. But he has not done so. So long as this regulation remains in force the Executive Branch is bound by it, and indeed the United States as the sovereign composed of the three branches is bound to respect and to enforce it. Moreover, the delegation of authority to the Special Prosecutor was not to be removed without the "consensus" of eight designated leaders of Congress.

The demands of and the resistance to the subpoena present an obvious controversy in the ordinary sense, but that alone is not sufficient to meet constitutional standards. In the constitutional sense, controversy means more than disagreement and conflict; rather it means the kind of controversy courts traditionally resolve. Here at issue is the production or nonproduction of specified evidence deemed by the Special Prosecutor to be relevant and admissible in a pending criminal case. It is sought by one official of the Government within the scope of his express authority; it is resisted by the Chief Executive on the ground of his duty to preserve the confidentiality of the communications of the President. Whatever the correct answer on the merits, these issues are "of a type which are traditionally justiciable." *United States* v. *ICC.* The independent Special Prosecutor with his asserted need for the subpoenaed materials in the underlying criminal prosecution is opposed by the President with his steadfast assertion of privilege against disclosure of the material. This setting assures there is "that concrete adverseness which sharpens the presentation of issues upon which the court so largely depends for illumination of difficult constitutional questions." *Baker* v. *Carr.* Moreover, since the matter is one arising in the regular course of a federal criminal prosecution, it is within the traditional scope of Art. III power.

In the light of the uniqueness of the setting in which the conflict arises, the fact that both parties are officers of the Executive Branch cannot be viewed as a barrier to justiciability. It would be inconsistent with the applicable law and regulation, and the unique facts of this case to conclude other than that the Special Prosecutor has standing to bring this action and that a justiciable controversy is presented for decision.

## III
## Rule 17 (c)

The subpoena *duces tecum* is challenged on the ground that the Special Prosecutor failed to satisfy the requirements of Fed. Rule Crim. Proc. 17 (c), which governs the issuance of subpoenas *duces tecum* in federal criminal proceedings. If we sustained this challenge, there would be no occasion to reach the claim of privilege asserted with respect to the subpoenaed material. Thus we turn to the question whether the requirements of Rule 17 (c) have been satisfied. See *Arkansas-Louisiana Gas Co.* v. *Dept. of Public Utilities,* (1938); *Ashwander* v. *Tennessee Valley Authority,* (1936). (Brandeis, J., concurring.)

Rule 17 (c) provides:

> "A subpoena may also command the person to whom it is directed to produce the books, papers, documents or other objects designated therein. The court on motion made promptly may quash or modify the subpoena if compliance would be unreasonable or oppressive. The court may direct that books, papers, documents or objects designated in the subpoena be produced before the court at a time prior to the trial or prior to the time when they are to be offered in evidence and may upon their production permit the books, papers, documents or objects or portions thereof to be inspected by the parties and their attorneys."

A subpoena for documents may be quashed if their production would be "unreasonable or oppressive," but not otherwise. The leading case in this Court interpreting this standard is *Bowman Dairy Co.* v. *United States,* (1950). This case recognized certain fundamental characteristics of the subpoena *duces tecum* in criminal cases: (1) it was not intended to provide a means of discovery for criminal cases. (2) its chief innovation was to expedite the trial by providing a time and place *before* trial for the inspection of subpoenaed materials. As both parties agree, cases decided in the wake of *Bowman* have generally followed Judge Weinfeld's formulation in *United States* v. *Iozia,* (SDNY 1952), as to the required showing. Under this test, in order to require production prior to trial, the moving party must show: (1)

that the documents are evidentiary and relevant; (2) that they are not otherwise procurable reasonably in advance of trial by exercise of due diligence; (3) that the party cannot properly prepare for trial without such production and inspection in advance of trial and that the failure to obtain such inspection may tend unreasonably to delay the trial; (4) that the application is made in good faith and is not intended as a general "fishing expedition."

Against this background, the Special Prosecutor, in order to carry his burden, must clear three hurdles: (1) relevancy; (2) admissibility; (3) specificity. Our own review of the record necessarily affords a less comprehensive view of the total situation than was available to the trial judge and we are unwilling to conclude that the District Court erred in the evaluation of the Special Prosecutor's showing under Rule 17 (c). Our conclusion is based on the record before us, much of which is under seal. Of course, the contents of the subpoenaed tapes could not at that stage be described fully by the Special Prosecutor, but there was a sufficient likelihood that each of the tapes contains conversations relevant to the offenses charged in the indictment. *United States* v. *Gross,* (SDNY 1959). With respect to many of the tapes, the Special Prosecutor offered the sworn testimony or statements of one or more of the participants in the conversations as to what was said at the time. As for the remainder of the tapes, the identity of the participants and the time and place of the conversations, taken in their total context, permit a rational inference that at least part of the conversations relate to the offenses charged in the indictment.

We also conclude there was a sufficient preliminary showing that each of the subpoenaed tapes contains evidence admissible with respect to the offenses charged in the indictment. The most cogent objection to the admissibility of the taped conversations here at issue is that they are a collection of out-of-court statements by declarants who will not be subject to cross-examination and that the statements are therefore inadmissible hearsay. Here, however, most of the tapes apparently contain conversations to which one or more of the defendants named in the indictment were party. The hearsay rule does not automatically bar all out-of-court statements by a defendant in a criminal case. Declarations by one defendant may also be admissible against other defendants upon a sufficient showing, by independent evidence, of a conspiracy among one or more other defendants and the declarant and if the declarations at issue were in furtherance of that conspiracy. The same is true of declarations of coconspirators who are not defendants in the case on trial. *Dutton* v. *Evans,* (1970). Recorded conversations may also be admissible for the limited purpose of impeaching the credibility of any defendant who testifies or any other coconspirator who testifies. Generally, the need for evidence to impeach witnesses is insufficient to require its production in advance of trial. See, *e.g.* *United States* v. *Carter,* (D.D.C. 1954). Here, however, there are other valid potential evidentiary uses for the same material and the analysis and possible transcription of the tapes may take a significant period of time. Accordingly, we cannot say that the District Court erred in authorizing the issuance of the subpoena *duces tecum.*

Enforcement of a pretrial subpoena *duces tecum* must necessarily be committed to the sound discretion of the trial court since the necessity for the subpoena most often turns upon a determination of arbitrariness or that the trial court finding was without record support, an appellate court will not ordinarily disturb a finding that the applicant for a subpoena complied with Rule 17 (c). See, *e.g.* *Sue* v. *Chicago Transit Authority,* (CA7 1960); *Shotkin*

v. *Nelson,* (CA10 1944).

In a case such as this, however, where a subpoena is directed to a President of the United States, appellate review, in deference to a coordinate branch of government, should be particularly meticulous to ensure that the standards of Rule 17 (c) have been correctly applied. *United States* v. *Burr,* (1807). From our examination of the materials submitted by the Special Prosecutor to the District Court in support of his motion for the subpoena, we are persuaded that the District Court's denial of the President's motion to quash the subpoena was consistent with Rule 17 (c). We also conclude that the Special Prosecutor has made a sufficient showing to justify a subpoena for production *before* trial. The subpoenaed materials are not available from any other source, and their examination and processing should not await trial in the circumstances shown.

## IV
## The Claim of Privilege
### A

Having determined that the requirements of Rule 17 (c) were satisfied, we turn to the claim that the subpoena should be quashed because it demands "confidential conversations between a President and his close advisors that it would be inconsistent with the public interest to produce." App. 48a. The first contention is a broad claim that the separation of powers doctrine precludes judicial review of a President's claim of privilege. The second contention is that if he does not prevail on the claim of absolute privilege, the court should hold as a matter of constitutional law that privilege prevails over the subpoena *duces tecum.*

In the performance of assigned constitutional duties each branch of the Government must initially interpret the Constitution, and the interpretation of its powers by any branch is due great respect from the others. The President's counsel, as we have noted, reads the Constitution as providing the absolute privilege of confidentiality for all presidential communications. Many decisions of this court, however, have unequivocally reaffirmed the holding of *Marbury* v. *Madison,* (1803), that "it is emphatically the province and duty of the judicial department to say what the law is."

No holding of the Court has defined the scope of judicial power specifically relating to the enforcement of a subpoena for confidential presidential communications for use in a criminal prosecution, but other exercises of powers by the Executive Branch and the Legislative Branch have been found invalid as in conflict with the Constitution. *Powell* v. *McCormack, Youngstown.* In a series of cases, the Court interpreted the explicit immunity conferred by express provisions of the Constitution on Members of the House and Senate by the Speech or Debate Clause, U.S. Const. Art. I, § 6. *Doe* v. *McMillan,* (1973); *Gravel* v. *United States,* (1973); *United States* v. *Brewster,* (1972); *United States* v. *Johnson,* (1966). Since this Court has consistently exercised the power to construe and delineate claims arising under express powers, it must follow that the court has authority to interpret claims with respect to powers alleged to derive from enumerated powers.

Our system of government "requires that federal courts on occasion interpret the Constitution in a manner at variance with the construction given the document by another branch." *Powell* v. *McCormack.* And in *Baker* v. *Carr,* 369 U.S., at 211, the Court stated:

> "[d]eciding whether a matter has in any measure been committed by the Constitution to another branch of government, or whether the action of that branch exceeds whatever authority has been committed, is itself a delicate exercise in constitutional interpretation,

and is a responsibility of this Court as ultimate interpreter of the Constitution."

Notwithstanding the deference each branch must accord the others, the "judicial power of the United States" vested in the federal courts by Art. III, § 1 of the Constitution can no more be shared with the Executive Branch than the Chief Executive, for example, can share with the Judiciary the veto power, or the Congress share with the Judiciary the power to override a presidential veto. Any other conclusion would be contrary to the basic concept of separation of powers and the checks and balances that flow from the scheme of a tripartite government. The Federalist, No. 47. We therefore reaffirm that it is "emphatically the province and the duty" of this Court "to say what the law is" with respect to the claim of privilege presented in this case. *Marbury* v. *Madison.*

### B

In support of his claim of absolute privilege, the President's counsel urges two grounds one of which is common to all governments and one of which is peculiar to our system of separation of powers. The first ground is the valid need for protection of communications between high government officials and those who advise and assist them in the performance of their manifold duties; the importance of this confidentiality is too plain to require further discussion. Human experience teaches that those who expect public dissemination of their remarks may well temper candor with a concern for appearances and for their own interests to the detriment of the decisionmaking process. Whatever the nature of the privilege of confidentiality of presidential communications in the exercise of Art. II powers the privilege can be said to derive from the supremacy of each branch within its own assigned area of constitutional duties. Certain powers and privileges flow from the nature of enumerated powers; the protection of the confidentiality of presidential communications has similar constitutional underpinnings.

The second ground asserted by the President's counsel in support of the claim of absolute privilege rests on the doctrine of separation of powers. Here it is argued that the independence of the Executive Branch within its own sphere, *Humphrey's Executor* v. *United States, Kilbourn* v. *Thompson,* (1880), insulates a president from a judicial subpoena in an ongoing criminal prosecution, and thereby protects confidential presidential communications.

However, neither the doctrine of separation of powers, nor the need for confidentiality of high level communications, without more, can sustain an absolute, unqualified presidential privilege of immunity from judicial process under all circumstances. The President's need for complete candor and objectivity from advisers calls for great deference from the courts. However, when the privilege depends solely on the broad undifferentiated claim of public interest in the confidentiality of such conversations, a confrontation with other values arises. Absent a claim of need to protect military, diplomatic or sensitive national security secrets, we find it difficult to accept the argument that even the very important interest in confidentiality of presidential communications is significantly diminished by production of such material for *in camera* inspection with all the protection that a district court will be obliged to provide.

The impediment that an absolute, unqualified privilege would place in the way of the primary constitutional duty of the Judicial Branch to do justice in criminal prosecutions would plainly conflict with the function of the courts under Art. III. In designing the structure of our Government and di-

viding and allocating the sovereign power among three coequal branches, the Framers of the Constitution sought to provide a comprehensive system, but the separate powers were not intended to operate with absolute independence.

"While the Constitution diffuses power the better to secure liberty, it also contemplates that practice will integrate the dispersed powers into a workable government. It enjoins upon its branches separateness but interdependence, autonomy but reciprocity." *Youngstown Sheet & Tube Co.* v. *Sawyer,* (1952) (Jackson, J., concurring).

To read Art. II powers of the President as providing an absolute privilege as against a subpoena essential to enforcement of criminal statutes on no more than a generalized claim of the public interest in confidentiality of nonmilitary and nondiplomatic discussions would upset the constitutional balance of "a workable government" and gravely impair the role of the courts under Art. III.

## C

Since we conclude that the legitimate needs of the judicial process may outweigh presidential privilege, it is necessary to resolve those competing interests in a manner that preserves the essential functions of each branch. The right and indeed the duty to resolve that question does not free the judiciary from according high respect to the representations made on behalf of the President. *United States* v. *Burr,* (1807).

The expectation of a President to the confidentiality of his conversations and correspondence, like the claim of confidentiality of judicial deliberations, for example, has all the values to which we accord deference for the privacy of all citizens and added to those values the necessity for protection of the public interest in candid, objective, and even blunt or harsh opinions in presidential decisionmaking. A President and those who assist him must be free to explore alternatives in the process of shaping policies and making decisions and to do so in a way many would be unwilling to express except privately. These are the considerations justifying a presumptive privilege for presidential communications. The privilege is fundamental to the operation of government and inextricably rooted in the separation of powers under the Constitution. In *Nixon* v. *Sirica,* (1973), the Court of Appeals held that such presidential communications are "presumptively privileged," and this position is accepted by both parties in the present litigation. We agree with Mr. Chief Justice Marshall's observation, therefore, that "in no case of this kind would a court be required to proceed against the President as against an ordinary individual." *United States* v. *Burr,* (CCD Va. 1807).

But this presumptive privilege must be considered in light of our historic commitment to the rule of law. This is nowhere more profoundly manifest than in our view that "the twofold aim [of criminal justice] is that guilt shall not escape or innocence suffer." *Berger* v. *United States,* (1935). We have elected to employ an adversary system of criminal justice in which the parties contest all issues before a court of law. The need to develop all relevant facts in the adversary system is both fundamental and comprehensive. The ends of criminal justice would be defeated if judgments were to be founded on a partial or speculative presentation of the facts. The very integrity of the judicial system and public confidence in the system depend on full disclosure of all the facts, within the framework of the rules of evidence. To ensure that justice is done, it is imperative to the function of courts that compulsory process be available for the production of evidence needed either by the prosecution or by the defense.

Only recently the Court restated the ancient proposition of law, albeit in the context of a grand jury inquiry rather than a trial,

> "'that the public ... has a right to every man's evidence' except for those persons protected by a constitutional, common law, or statutory privilege." *United States* v. *Bryan,* (1949); *Blackmer* v. *United States, Branzburg* v. *United States,* (1973).

The privileges referred to by the Court are designed to protect weighty and legitimate competing interests. Thus, the Fifth Amendment to the Constitution provides that no man "shall be compelled in any criminal case to be a witness against himself." And, generally, an attorney or a priest may not be required to disclose what has been revealed in professional confidence. These and other interests are recognized in law by privileges against forced disclosure, established in the Constitution, by statute, or at common law. Whatever their origins, these exceptions to the demand for every man's evidence are not lightly created or expansively construed, for they are in derogation of the search for truth.

In this case the President challenges a subpoena served on him as a third party requiring the production of materials for use in a criminal prosecution on the claim that he has a privilege against disclosure of confidential communications. He does not place his claim of privilege on the ground they are military or diplomatic secrets. As to these areas of Art. II duties the courts have traditionally shown the utmost deference to presidential responsibilities. In *C. & S. Air Lines* v. *Waterman Steamship Corp.,* (1948), dealing with presidential authority involving foreign policy considerations, the Court said:

> "The President, both as Commander-in-Chief and as the Nation's organ for foreign affairs, has available intelligence services whose reports are not and ought not to be published to the world.

It would be intolerable that courts, without the relevant information, should review and perhaps nullify actions of the Executive taken on information properly held secret."

In *United States* v. *Reynolds,* (1952), dealing with a claimant's demand for evidence in a damage case against the Government the Court said:

"It may be possible to satisfy the court, from all the circumstances of the case, that there is a reasonable danger that compulsion of the evidence will expose military matters which, in the interest of national security, should not be divulged. When this is the case, the occasion for the privilege is appropriate, and the court should not jeopardize the security which the privilege is meant to protect by insisting upon an examination of the evidence, even by the judge alone, in chambers."

No case of the Court, however, has extended this high degree of deference to a President's generalized interest in confidentiality. Nowhere in the Constitution, as we have noted earlier, is there any explicit reference to a privilege of confidentiality, yet to the extent this interest relates to the effective discharge of a President's powers, it is constitutionally based.

The right to the production of all evidence at a criminal trial similarly has constitutional dimensions. The Sixth Amendment explicitly confers upon every defendant in a criminal trial the right "to be confronted with the witnesses against him" and "to have compulsory process for obtaining witnesses in his favor." Moreover, the Fifth Amendment also guarantees that no person shall be deprived of liberty without due process of law. It is the manifest duty of the courts to vindicate those guarantees and to accomplish that it is essential that all relevant and admissible evidence be produced.

In this case we must weigh the importance of the general privilege of confidentiality of presidential communications in performance of his

responsibilities against the inroads of such a privilege on the fair administration of criminal justice. The interest in preserving confidentiality is weighty indeed and entitled to great respect. However we cannot conclude that advisers will be moved to temper the candor of their remarks by the infrequent occasions of disclosure because of the possibility that such conversations will be called for in the context of criminal prosecution.

On the other hand, the allowance of the privilege to withhold evidence that is demonstrably relevant in a criminal trial would cut deeply into the guarantee of due process of law and gravely impair the basic function of the courts. A President's acknowledged need for confidentiality in the communications of his office is general in nature whereas the constitutional need for production of relevant evidence in a criminal proceeding is specific and central to the fair adjudication of a particular criminal case in the administration of justice. Without access to specific facts a criminal prosecution may be totally frustrated. The President's broad interest in confidentiality of communications will not be vitiated by disclosure of a limited number of conversations preliminarily shown to have some bearing on the pending criminal cases.

We conclude that when the ground for asserting privilege as to subpoenaed materials sought for use in a criminal trial is based only on the generalized interest in confidentiality, it cannot prevail over the fundamental demands of due process of law in the fair administration of criminal justice. The generalized assertion of privilege must yield to the demonstrated, specific need for evidence in a pending criminal trial.

## D

We have earlier determined that the District Court did not err in authorizing the issuance of the subpoena. If a president concludes that compliance with a subpoena would be injurious to the public interest he may properly, as was done here, invoke a claim of privilege on the return of the subpoena. Upon receiving a claim of privilege from the Chief Executive, it became the further duty of the District Court to treat the subpoenaed material as presumptively privileged and to require the Special Prosecutor to demonstrate that the presidential material was "essential to the justice of the [pending criminal] case." *United States* v. *Burr*. Here the District Court treated the material as presumptively privileged, proceeded to find that the Special Prosecutor had made a sufficient showing to rebut the presumption and ordered an *in camera* examination of the subpoenaed material. On the basis of our examination of the record we are unable to conclude that the District Court erred in ordering the inspection. Accordingly we affirm the order of the District Court that subpoenaed materials be transmitted to that court. We now turn to the important question of the District Court's responsibilities in conducting the *in camera* examination of presidential materials or communications delivered under the compulsion of the subpoena *duces tecum*.

### E

Enforcement of the subpoena *duces tecum* was stayed pending this Court's resolution of the issues raised by the petitions for certiorari. Those issues now having been disposed of, the matter of implementation will rest with the District Court. "[T]he guard, furnished to [President] to protect him from being harassed by vexatious and unnecessary subpoenas, is to be looked for in the conduct of the [district] court after the subpoenas have issued; not in any circumstances which is to precede their being issued." *United States* v. *Burr*. Statements that meet the test of admis-

sibility and relevance must be isolated; all other material must be excised. At this stage the District Court is not limited to representations of the Special Prosecutor as to the evidence sought by the subpoena; the material will be available to the District Court. It is elementary that *in camera* inspection of evidence is always a procedure calling for scrupulous protection against any release or publication of material not found by the court, at that stage, probably admissible in evidence and relevant to the issues of the trial for which it is sought. That being true of an ordinary situation, it is obvious that the District Court has a very heavy responsibility to see to it that presidential conversations, which are either not relevant or not admissible, are accorded that high degree of respect due the President of the United States. Mr. Chief Justice Marshall sitting as a trial judge in the *Burr* case, was extraordinarily careful to point out that:

> "[I]n no case of this kind would a Court be required to proceed against the President as against an ordinary individual." *United States* v. *Burr*, (No. 14,694).

Marshall's statement cannot be read to mean in any sense that a President is above the law, but relates to the singularly unique role under Art. II of a President's communications and activities, related to the performance of duties under that Article. Moreover, a President's communications and activities encompass a vastly wider range of sensitive material than would be true of any "ordinary individual." It is therefore necessary in the public interest to afford presidential confidentiality the greatest protection consistent with the fair administration of justice. The need for confidentiality even as to idle conversations with associates in which casual reference might be made concerning political leaders within the country or foreign statesmen is too obvious to call for further treatment. We have no doubt that the District Judge will at all times accord to presidential records that high degree of deference suggested in *United States* v. *Burr,* and will discharge his responsibility to see to it that until released to the Special Prosecutor no *in camera* material is revealed to anyone. This burden applies with even greater force to excised material; once the decision is made to excise, the material is restored to its privileged status and should be returned under seal to its lawful custodian.

Since this matter came before the Court during the pendency of a criminal prosecution, and on representations that time is of the essence, the mandate shall issue forthwith.

*Affirmed*

MR. JUSTICE REHNQUIST took no part in the consideration or decision of these cases.

# Richard Nixon's "Smoking Gun" Tapes (1974)

On August 2, 1974, responding to the order of the Supreme Court in the case of United States v. Nixon *nine days earlier* (see "United States v. Nixon," p. 397), *President Richard Nixon turned over a number of Watergate-related tape recordings to Judge John J. Sirica. On August 5 he publicly released transcripts of three of those tapes.*

*The transcripts, which included three conversations between Nixon and White House chief of staff H. R. Haldeman on June 23, 1972, destroyed any hope Nixon may have had to avoid impeachment by the House of Representatives and conviction and removal by a two-thirds vote of the Senate. In those conversations Nixon approved a plan suggested by Haldeman to have top officials at the Central Intelligence Agency (CIA) tell L. Patrick Gray III, the acting director of the Federal Bureau of Investigation (FBI), not to conduct a serious investigation of the June 17 Watergate burglary on national security grounds. Nixon also reacted to Haldeman's subsequent report on his conversation with CIA director Richard C. Helms and deputy director Vernon A. Walters.*

*Nixon accompanied the release of the transcripts with a statement that admitted his political motive in trying to halt the Watergate investigation. "I recognize that this additional material I am now furnishing may further dam-* age my case," he conceded.

*The release of the June 23 tape transcripts was the "smoking gun" in the Watergate investigation—that is, the first piece of evidence that indisputably demonstrated Nixon's active role in the coverup. Vice President Gerald R. Ford announced that he no longer would proclaim his belief in the president's innocence. Republicans in Congress, including the ten members of the House Judiciary Committee who had voted against every proposed article of impeachment, publicly denounced Nixon, all but guaranteeing that the House would vote to impeach the president and that the Senate would vote to convict. (See "Proposed Articles of Impeachment against Richard Nixon," p. 392.)*

*Rep. Charles E. Wiggins of California, Nixon's most articulate defender on the Judiciary Committee, spoke tearfully for almost all the president's supporters: "I am now possessed of information which establishes beyond a reasonable doubt that on June 23, 1972, the President personally agreed to certain actions, the purpose and intent of which were to interfere with the FBI investigation of the Watergate break-in.... [If he does not,] I am prepared to conclude that the magnificent career of public service of Richard Nixon must be terminated involuntarily and shall support those portions*

410

*of Article I [of the impeachment reso-lutions] which are sustained by the evidence."*    ~

## Meeting: The President and Haldeman, Oval Office, June 23, 1972 (10:04 – 11:39 a.m.)

**H. [Haldeman]** Now, on the investigation, you know the Democratic break-in thing, we're back in the problem area because the FBI is not under control, because Gray doesn't exactly know how to control it and they have—their investigation is now leading into some productive areas—because they've been able to trace the money—not through the money itself—but through the bank sources—the banker. And, and it goes in some directions we don't want it to go. Ah, also there have been some things—like an informant came in off the street to the FBI in Miami who was a photographer or has a friend who is a photographer who developed some films through this guy Barker and the films had pictures of Democratic National Committee letterhead documents and things. So it's things like that that are filtering in. Mitchell came up with yesterday, and John Dean analyzed very carefully last night and concludes, concurs now with Mitchell's recommendation that the only way to solve this, and we're set up beautifully to do it, ah, in that and that—the only network that paid any attention to it last night was NBC—they did a massive story on the Cuban thing.

**P. [President Nixon]** That's right.

**H.** That the way to handle this now is for us to have Walters call Pat Gray and just say, "Stay to hell out of this—this is ah, business here we don't want you to go any further on it." That's not an unusual development, and ah, that would take care of it.

**P.** What about Pat Gray—you mean Pat Gray doesn't want to?

**H.** Pat does want to. He doesn't know how to, and he doesn't have, he doesn't have any basis for doing it. Given this, he will then have the basis. He'll call Mark Felt in and the two of them—and Mark Felt wants to cooperate because he's ambitious—

**P.** Yeah.

**H.** He'll call him in and say, "We've got the signal from across the river to put the hold on this." And that will fit rather well because the FBI agents who are working the case, at this point, feel that's what it is.

**P.** This is CIA? They've traced the money? Who'd they trace it to?

**H.** Well they've traced it to a name, but they haven't gotten to the guy yet.

**P.** Would it be somebody here?

**H.** Ken Dahlberg.

**P.** Who the hell is Ken Dahlberg?

**H.** He gave $25,000 in Minnesota and, ah, the check went directly to this guy Barker.

**P.** It isn't from the Committee, though, from Stans?

**H.** Yeah. It is. It's directly traceable and there's some more through some Texas people that went to the Mexican bank which can also be traced to the Mexican bank—they'll get their names today.

**H.** —And (pause)

**P.** Well, I mean, there's no way—I'm just thinking if they don't cooperate, what do they say? That they were approached by the Cubans. That's what Dahlberg has to say, the Texans too, that they—

**H.** Well, if they will. But then we're relying on more and more people all the time. That's the problem and they'll stop if we could take this other route.

**P.** All right.

**H.** And you seem to think the thing to do is get them to stop?

**P.** Right, fine.

**H.** They say the only way to do that is from White House instructions. And it's got to be to Helms and to—ah, what's his name. . . . ? Walters.

**P.** Walters.

**H.** And the proposal would be that Ehrlichman and I call them in, and say, ah—

**P.** All right, fine. How do you call him in—I mean you just—well, we protected Helms from one hell of a lot of things.

**H.** That's what Ehrlichman says.

**P.** Of course, this Hunt, that will uncover a lot of things. You open that scab there's a hell of a lot of things and we just feel that it would be very detrimental to have this thing go any further. This involves these Cubans, Hunt, and a lot of hanky-panky that we have nothing to do with ourselves. Well what the hell, did Mitchell know about this?

**H.** I think so. I don't think he knew the details, but I think he knew.

**P.** He didn't know how it was going to be handled though—with Dahlberg and the Texans and so forth? Well who was the asshole that did? Is it Liddy? Is that the fellow? He must be a little nuts!

**H.** He is.

**P.** I mean he just isn't well screwed on is he? Is that the problem?

**H.** No, but he was under pressure, apparently, to get more information, and as he got more pressure, he pushed the people harder to move harder—

**P.** Pressure from Mitchell?

**H.** Apparently.

**P.** Oh, Mitchell. Mitchell was at the point (unintelligible).

**H.** Yeah.

**P.** All right, fine, I understand it all. We won't second-guess Mitchell and the rest. Thank God it wasn't Colson.

**H.** The FBI interviewed Colson yesterday. They determined that would be a good thing to do. To have him take an interrogation, which he did, and that—the FBI guys working the case concluded that there were one or two possibilities—one, that this was a White House—they don't think that there is anything at the Election Committee—they think it was either a

White House operation and they had some obscure reasons for it—non-political, or it was a—Cuban and the CIA. And after their interrogation of Colson yesterday, they concluded it was not the White House, but are now convinced it is a CIA thing, so the CIA turnoff would—

**P.** Well, not sure of their analysis, I'm not going to get that involved. I'm (unintelligible).

**H.** No, sir, we don't want you to.

**P.** You call them in.

**H.** Good deal.

**P.** Play it tough. That's the way they play it and that's the way we are going to play it.

**H.** O.K.

**P.** When I saw that news summary, I questioned whether it's a bunch of crap, but I thought, er, well it's good to have them off us awhile, because when they start bugging us, which they have, our little boys will not know how to handle it. I hope they will though.

**H.** You never know.

**P.** Good.

(Other matters are discussed. Then the conversation returns to the break-in coverup strategy.)

**P.** When you get in—when you get in (unintelligible) people, say, "Look the problem is that this will open the whole, the whole Bay of Pigs thing, and the President just feels that ah, without going into the details—don't, don't lie to them to the extent to say there is no involvement, but just say this is a comedy of errors, without getting into it, the President believes that it is going to open the whole Bay of Pigs thing up again. And, ah, because these people are plugging for (unintelligible) and that they should call the FBI in and (unintelligible) don't go any further into this case period!

**P.** (inaudible) our cause—

**H.** Get more done for our cause by the opposition than by us.

**P.** Well, can you get it done?

**H.** I think so.

## Meeting: The President and Haldeman, Oval Office, June 23, 1972 (1:04 – 1:13 p.m.)

**P.** O.K., just postpone (scratching noises) (unintelligible). Just say (unintelligible) very bad to have this fellow Hunt, ah, he knows too damned much, if he was involved—you happen to know that? If it gets out that this is all involved, the Cuba thing it would be a fiasco. It would make the CIA look bad, it's going to make Hunt look bad, and it is likely to blow the whole Bay of Pigs thing which we think would be very unfortunate—both for CIA, and for the country, at this time, and for American foreign policy. Just tell him to lay off. Don't you?

**H.** Yep. That's the basis to do it on. Just leave it at that.

**P.** I don't know if he'll get any ideas for doing it because our concern political (unintelligible). Helms is not one to (unintelligible)—I would just say, lookit, because of the Hunt involvement, whole cover basically this.

**H.** Yep. Good move.

**P.** Well, they've got some pretty good ideas on this Meany thing. Shultz did a good paper. I read it all (voices fade).

## Meeting: The President and Haldeman, Executive Office Building, June 23, 1972 (2:20 – 2:45 p.m.)

**H.** No problem

**P.** (unintelligible)

**H.** Well, it was kind of interesting. Walters made the point and I didn't mention Hunt, I just said that the thing was leading into directions that were going to create potential problems because they were exploring leads that led back into areas that would be harmful to the CIA and harmful to the government (unintelligible) didn't have any-

thing to do (unintelligible).
(Telephone)

**P.** Chuck? I wonder if you would give John Connally a call he's on his trip—I don't want him to read it in the paper before Monday about this quota thing and say—look, we're going to do this, but that I checked, I asked you about the situation (unintelligible) had an understanding it was only temporary and ah (unintelligible) O.K.? I just don't want him to read it in the papers. Good. Fine.

**H.** (unintelligible) I think Helms did to (unintelligible) said, I've had no—

**P.** God (unintelligible).

**H.** Gray called and said, yesterday, and said that he thought—

**P.** Who did? Gray?

**H.** Gray called Helms and said I think we've run right into the middle of a CIA covert operation.

**P.** Gray said that?

**H.** Yeah. And (unintelligible) said nothing we've done at this point and ah (unintelligible) says well it sure looks to me like it is (unintelligible) and ah, that was the end of that conversation (unintelligible) the problem is it tracks back to the Bay of Pigs and it tracks back to some other the leads run out to people who had no involvement in this, except by contacts and connection, but it gets to areas that are liable to be raised? The whole problem (unintelligible) Hunt. So at that point he kind of got the picture. He said, he said we'll be very happy to be helpful (unintelligible) handle anything you want. I would like to know the reason for being helpful, and I made it clear to him he wasn't going to get explicit (unintelligible) generality, and he said fine. And Walters (unintelligible). Walters is going to make a call to Gray. That's the way we put it and that's the way it was left.

**P.** How does that work though, how, they've got to (unintelligible) somebody from the Miami bank.

**H.** (unintelligible). The point John makes—the Bureau is going on on this because they don't know what they are uncovering (unintelligible) continue to pursue it. They don't need to because they already have their case as far as the charges against these men (unintelligible) and ah, as they pursue it (unintelligible) exactly, but we didn't in any way say we (unintelligible). One thing Helms did raise. He said, Gray— he asked Gray why they thought they had run into a CIA thing and Gray said because of the characters involved and the amount of money involved, a lot of dough. (unintelligible) and ah, (unintelligible)

**P.** (unintelligible)

**H.** Well, I think they will.

**P.** If it runs (unintelligible) what the hell who knows (unintelligible) contributed CIA.

**H.** Yeah, it's money CIA gets money (unintelligible) I mean their money

moves in a lot of different ways, too.

**P.** Yeah. How are (unintelligible)—a lot of good—

**H.** (unintelligible)

**P.** Well you remember what the SOB did on my book? When I brought out the fact, you know—

**H.** Yeah.

**P.** that he knew all bout Dulles? (Expletive deleted) Dulles knew. Dulles told me. I know, I mean (unintelligible) had the telephone call. Remember, I had a call put in—Dulles just blandly said and knew why.

**H.** Yeah.

**P.** Now, what the hell! Who told him to do it? The President? (unintelligible)

**H.** Dulles was no more Kennedy's man than (unintelligible) was your man (unintelligible)

**P.** (unintelligible) covert operation— do anything else (unintelligible).

# Richard Nixon's Resignation Speech as President (1974)

After protesting many times that he would defend his presidency until the end, President Richard Nixon announced in a televised address on August 8, 1974, that he would resign the office effective noon the next day. In the aftermath of the House Judiciary Committee's bipartisan vote to recommend impeachment, the Supreme Court's decision in United States v. Nixon, and the release of the incriminating "smoking gun" tapes, impeachment and conviction were certain. At an August 7 meeting, the House Republican leader, John J. Rhodes of Arizona, and Senate Republican leader Hugh Scott of Pennsylvania had told Nixon that there were only around ten votes for him in each house of Congress. For Nixon to fight on not only would be pointless but would cost him the extensive benefits that former presidents receive and would increase the likelihood that he would be prosecuted in federal court for his role in the Watergate coverup.

In his speech, Nixon admitted only to having made mistaken judgments, claiming that even "they were made in what I believed at the time to be the best interest of the Nation." He also suggested that but for the political hopelessness of his position, and the paralysis that a long impeachment process would cause in the government, the right thing for him to do would be to continue the fight for vindication.

On the morning of August 9, Nixon wrote a terse letter of resignation to Secretary of State Henry Kissinger and bade an emotional farewell to the White House staff before boarding Air Force One to his home in California.

Richard Nixon is the only president ever to resign from office. His resignation spared him from being the first president ever to be impeached and removed from office.          ~

Good evening.

This is the 37th time I have spoken to you from this office, where so many decisions have been made that shaped the history of this Nation. Each time I have done so to discuss with you some matter that I believe affected the national interest.

In all the decisions I have made in my public life, I have always tried to do what was best for the Nation. Throughout the long and difficult period of Watergate, I have felt it was my duty to persevere, to make every possible effort to complete the term of office to which you elected me.

In the past few days, however, it has become evident to me that I no longer have a strong enough political base in the Congress to justify continuing that effort. As long as there was such a base, I felt strongly that it was necessary to see the constitutional process through to its conclusion, that to do otherwise would be unfaithful to the spirit of that deliberately difficult process and a dangerously destabilizing precedent for the future.

But with the disappearance of that base, I now believe that the constitutional purpose has been served, and there is no longer a need for the process to be prolonged.

I would have preferred to carry through to the finish whatever the personal agony it would have involved, and my family unanimously urged me to do so. But the interest of the Nation must always come before any personal considerations.

From the discussions I have had with Congressional and other leaders, I have concluded that because of the Watergate matter I might not have the support of the Congress that I would consider necessary to back the very difficult decisions and carry out the duties of this office in the way the interests of the Nation would require.

I have never been a quitter. To leave office before my term is completed is abhorrent to every instinct in my body. But as President, I must put the interest of America first. America needs a full-time President and a full-time Congress, particularly at this time with problems we face at home and abroad.

To continue to fight through the months ahead for my personal vindication would almost totally absorb the time and attention of both the President and the Congress in a period when our entire focus should be on the great issues of peace abroad and prosperity without inflation at home.

Therefore, I shall resign the Presidency effective at noon tomorrow. Vice President Ford will be sworn in as President at that hour in this office.

As I recall the high hopes for America with which we began this second term, I feel a great sadness that I will not be here in this office working on your be-

half to achieve those hopes in the next 2½ years. But in turning over direction of the Government to Vice President Ford, I know, as I told the Nation when I nominated him for that office 10 months ago, that the leadership of America will be in good hands.

In passing this office to the Vice President, I also do so with the profound sense of the weight of responsibility that will fall on his shoulders tomorrow and, therefore, of the understanding, the patience, the cooperation he will need from all Americans.

As he assumes that responsibility, he will deserve the help and the support of all of us. As we look to the future, the first essential is to begin healing the wounds of this Nation, to put the bitterness and divisions of the recent past behind us, and to rediscover those shared ideals that lie at the heart of our strength and unity as a great and as a free people.

By taking this action, I hope that I will have hastened the start of that process of healing which is so desperately needed in America.

I regret deeply any injuries that may have been done in the course of the events that led to this decision. I would say only that if some of my judgments were wrong, and some were wrong, they were made in what I believed at the time to be the best interest of the Nation.

To those who have stood with me during these past difficult months, to my family, my friends, to many others who joined in supporting my cause because they believed it was right, I will be eternally grateful for your support.

And to those who have not felt able to give me your support, let me say I leave with no bitterness toward those who have opposed me, because all of us, in the final analysis, have been concerned with the good of the country, however our judgments might differ.

So, let us all now join together in affirming that common commitment and in helping our new President succeed for the benefit of all Americans.

I shall leave this office with regret at not completing my term, but with gratitude for the privilege of serving as your President for the past 5½ years. These years have been a momentous time in the history of our Nation and the world. They have been a time of achievement in which we can all be proud, achievements that represent the shared efforts of the Administration, the Congress, and the people.

But the challenges ahead are equally great, and they, too, will require the support and the efforts of the Congress and the people working in cooperation with the new Administration.

We have ended America's longest war, but in the work of securing a lasting peace in the world, the goals ahead are even more far-reaching and more difficult. We must complete a structure of peace so that it will be said of this generation, our generation of Americans, by the people of all nations, not only that we ended one war but that we prevented future wars.

We have unlocked the doors that for a quarter of a century stood between the United States and the People's Republic of China.

We must now ensure that the one quarter of the world's people who live in the People's Republic of China will be and remain not our enemies but our friends.

In the Middle East, 100 million people in the Arab countries, many of whom have considered us their enemy for nearly 20 years, now look on us as their friends. We must continue to build on that friendship so that peace can settle at last over the Middle East and so that the cradle of civilization will not become its grave.

Together with the Soviet Union we have made the crucial breakthroughs that have begun the process of limiting nuclear arms. But we must set as our goal not just limiting but reducing and finally destroying these terrible weapons so that they cannot destroy civilization and so that the threat of nuclear war will no longer hang over the world and the people.

We have opened the new relation with the Soviet Union. We must continue to develop and expand that new relationship so that the two strongest nations of the world will live together in cooperation rather than confrontation.

Around the world, in Asia, in Africa, in Latin America, in the Middle East, there are millions of people who live in terrible poverty, even starvation. We must keep as our goal turning away from production for war and expanding production for peace so that people everywhere on this earth can at last look forward in their children's time, if not in our own time, to having the necessities for a decent life.

Here in America, we are fortunate that most of our people have not only the blessings of liberty but also the means to live full and good and, by the world's standards, even abundant lives. We must press on, however, toward a goal of not only more and better jobs but of full opportunity for every American and of what we are striving so hard right now to achieve, prosperity without inflation.

For more than a quarter of a century in public life I have shared in the turbulent history of this era. I have fought for what I believed in. I have tried to the best of my ability to discharge those duties and meet those responsibilities that were entrusted to me.

Sometimes I have succeeded and sometimes I have failed, but always I have taken heart from what Theodore Roosevelt once said about the man in the arena, "whose face is marred by dust and sweat and blood, who strives valiantly, who errs and comes short again and again because there is not effort without error and shortcoming, but who does actually strive to do the deed, who knows the great enthusiasms, the great devotions, who spends himself in a worthy cause, who at the best knows in the end the triumphs of high achievements and who at the worst, if he fails, at least fails while daring greatly."

I pledge to you tonight that as long as I have a breath of life in my body, I shall continue in that spirit. I shall continue to work for the great causes to which I have been dedicated throughout my years as a Congressman, a Senator, a Vice President, and President, the cause of peace not just for America but among all nations, prosperity, justice, and opportunity for all of our people.

There is one cause above all to which I have been devoted and to which I shall always be devoted for as long as I live.

When I first took the oath of office as President 5½ years ago, I made this sacred commitment, to "consecrate my office, my energies, and all the wisdom I can summon to the cause of peace among nations."

I have done my very best in all the days since to be true to that pledge. As a result of these efforts, I am confident that the world is a safer place today, not only for the people of America but for the people of all nations, and that all of our children have a better chance than before of living in peace rather than dying in war.

This, more than anything, is what I hoped to achieve when I sought the Presidency. This, more than anything, is what I hope will be my legacy to you, to our country, as I leave the Presidency.

To have served in this office is to have felt a very personal sense of kinship with each and every American. In leaving it, I do so with this prayer: May God's grace be with you in all the days ahead.

# Remarks by President Gerald R. Ford after His Swearing-in (1974)

Since the enactment of the Twenty-fifth Amendment in 1967, the president has been charged to fill a vacancy in the vice presidency by nominating a new vice president, subject to the approval of a majority of both houses of Congress, voting separately. When Vice President Spiro T. Agnew resigned in October 1973, President Richard Nixon nominated House Minority Leader Gerald R. Ford of Michigan to be vice president. Congress confirmed the nomination overwhelmingly in December.

Ford was a twenty-five-year veteran of the House at the time of his appointment. Elected thirteen times by his Grand Rapids, Michigan, congressional district, Ford was chosen by House Republicans to be their leader in 1965. After a time, he grew frustrated by the Republicans' failure to become the majority party in the House—and thus to elect him as Speaker. Indeed, Ford planned to retire from politics when his term expired in 1975.

Ford never had presidential ambitions. Nor had he ever been regarded by others in politics as "presidential timber." Yet from the moment of his appointment as vice president, Ford was aware that he might be called upon to serve as president if Nixon either resigned or was impeached and removed from office. When Nixon's resignation took effect at noon on August 9, 1974, Ford was sworn in as president in the East Room of the White House by Chief Justice Warren E. Burger.

Like other vice presidents who had succeeded to the presidency, Ford delivered no formal inaugural address. In view of the unprecedented circumstances of his succession, however, he did make some brief televised remarks, which he characterized as "just a little straight talk among friends." With relief, Ford proclaimed that "our long national nightmare is over. Our Constitution works; our great Republic is a Government of laws and not of men." Aware that he was the first unelected vice president to become president, Ford said: "I am acutely aware that you have not elected me as your President by your ballots, and so I ask you to confirm me as your President with your prayers."

Ford's solid, unpretentious, even ordinary style struck a responsive chord among the American people, whose faith in government had been severely tested during the preceding decade by assassinations, the war in Vietnam, and Watergate. In the first Gallup poll to be conducted after the new president took office, Ford was approved by a margin of 71 percent to 3 percent. ~

Mr. Chief Justice, my dear friends, my fellow Americans:

The oath that I have taken is the same oath that was taken by George Washington and by every President under the Constitution. But I assume the Presidency under extraordinary circumstances, never before experienced by Americans. This is an hour of history that troubles our minds and hurts our hearts.

Therefore, I feel it is my first duty to make an unprecedented compact with my countrymen. Not an inaugural address, not a fireside chat, not a campaign speech—just a little straight talk among friends. And I intend it to be the first of many.

I am acutely aware that you have not elected me as your President by your ballots, and so I ask you to confirm me as your President with your prayers. And I hope that such prayers will be the first of many.

If you have not chosen me by secret ballot, neither have I gained office by any secret promises. I have not campaigned either for the Presidency or the Vice Presidency. I have not subscribed to any partisan platform. I am indebted to no man, and only to one woman—my dear wife—as I begin this very difficult job.

I have not sought this enormous responsibility, but I will not shirk it. Those who nominated and confirmed me as Vice President were my friends and are my friends. They were of both parties, elected by all the people and acting under the Constitution in their name. It is only fitting then that I should pledge to them and to you that I will be the President of all the people.

Thomas Jefferson said the people are the only sure reliance for the preservation of our liberty. And down the years, Abraham Lincoln renewed this American article of faith saying, "Is there any better way or equal hope in the world?"

I intend, on Monday next, to request of the Speaker of the House of Representatives and the President pro tempore of the Senate the privilege of appearing before the Congress to share with my former colleagues and with you, the American people, my views on the priority business of the Nation and to solicit your views and their views. And may I say to the Speaker and the others, if I could meet with you right after these remarks, I would appreciate it.

Even though this is late in an election year, there is no way we can go forward except together and no way anybody can win except by serving the people's urgent needs. We cannot stand still or slip backwards. We must go forward now together.

To the peoples and the governments of all friendly nations, and I hope that could encompass the whole world, I pledge an uninterrupted and sincere search for peace. America will remain strong and united, but its strength will remain dedicated to the safety and sanity of the entire family of man, as well as to our own precious freedom.

I believe that truth is the glue that holds government together, not only our Government, but civilization itself. That bond, though strained, is unbroken at home and abroad.

In all my public and private acts as your President, I expect to follow my instincts of openness and candor with full confidence that honesty is always the best policy in the end.

My fellow Americans, our long national nightmare is over. Our Constitution works; our great Republic is a Government of laws and not of men. Here the people rule. But there is a higher power, by whatever name we honor Him, who ordains not only righteousness but love, not only justice but mercy.

As we bind up the internal wounds of Watergate, more painful and more poisonous than those of foreign wars, let us restore the golden rule to our political process, and let brotherly love purge our hearts of suspicion and of hate.

In the beginning, I asked you to pray

for me. Before closing, I ask again your prayers, for Richard Nixon and for his family. May our former President, who brought peace to millions, find it for himself. May God bless and comfort his wonderful wife and daughters, whose love and loyalty will forever be a shining legacy to all who bear the lonely burdens of the White House.

I can only guess at those burdens, although I have witnessed at close hand the tragedies that befell three Presidents and the lesser trials of others.

With all the strength and all the good sense I have gained from life, with all the confidence my family, my friends, and my dedicated staff impart to me, and with the good will of countless Americans I have encountered in recent visits to 40 states, I now solemnly reaffirm my promise I made to you last December 6: to uphold the Constitution, to do what is right as God gives me to see the right, and to do the very best I can for America.

God helping me, I will not let you down.

Thank you.

# The Nixon Pardon (1974)

President Richard Nixon's resignation left him subject to indictment, trial, and possible conviction for obstructing justice in the Watergate investigation. On Sunday morning, September 8, 1974, President Gerald R. Ford announced to a national television audience that he was using the pardon power of his office to grant Nixon a *"full, free and absolute pardon . . . for all offenses against the United States which he . . . has committed or may have committed"* as president. Ford's exercise of the pardon power—the only constitutional power of the presidency that may not be checked by Congress or the Supreme Court—effectively freed Nixon from prosecution for any federal crime.

In announcing the pardon, Ford noted several reasons for his decision, including the former president's health and mental anguish and the difficulty of securing a fair trial. More than anything else, though, Ford argued that *"someone must write 'The End' "* to the Watergate affair, lest *"ugly passions . . . again be aroused."*

Nixon received the pardon with a statement conceding only *"mistakes and misjudgments"* in his handling of the Watergate affair. Responding to critics who complained that Ford should have insisted on a greater expression of contrition from Nixon as a condition for granting the pardon, ad-

ministration officials said that the very act of accepting the pardon was, in effect, a confession of guilt by the former president.

Ford paid a severe political price for the Nixon pardon. He was roundly criticized in Congress and the media, and his public approval rating instantly dropped twenty percentage points in the polls. When the House Judiciary Committee conducted hearings to investigate why the pardon was granted, Ford appeared personally before the committee—the first time in history that a president had testified to a congressional committee under oath—to deny that he and Nixon had made any secret arrangement to exchange the promise of a pardon for Nixon's agreement to resign.

Ford's loss of public support enfeebled his presidency in the face of severe foreign and domestic problems. At home, inflation and unemployment rose steadily higher, producing an unprecedented economic *"stagflation"* that standard economic remedies did not address. Abroad, South Vietnam fell to the Communists, and the Soviet Union, taking advantage of weakened U.S. resolve, successfully aided revolutions throughout the third world. Congressional Republicans suffered severe losses in the 1974 elections. Ford himself was the victim of two assassination attempts in September 1975. In addi-

*tion, he nearly lost the 1976 Republican presidential nomination to Ronald Reagan, the former governor of California. In the course of beating back the challenge from the conservative Reagan, Ford dropped his own appointed vice president, the liberal former New York governor Nelson A. Rockefeller, from the ticket.*

*Ford waged a hard and generally effective campaign against the Democratic presidential nominee, former Georgia governor Jimmy Carter, in the 1976 election. But he was defeated narrowly, bringing his two-and-one-half year presidency to an end.* ~

Ladies and gentlemen, I have come to a decision which I felt I should tell you, and all of my fellow American citizens, as soon as I was certain in my own mind and in my own conscience that it was the right thing to do.

I have learned already in this office that the difficult decisions always come to this desk. I must admit that many of them do not look at all the same as the hypothetical questions that I have answered freely and perhaps too fast on previous occasions. My customary policy is to try and get all the facts and to consider the opinions of my countrymen and to take counsel with my most valued friends. But these seldom agree, and in the end the decision is mine.

To procrastinate, to agonize and to wait for a more favorable turn of events that may never come, or more compelling external pressures that may as well be wrong as right, is itself a decision of sorts and a weak course for a President to follow.

I have promised to uphold the Constitution, to do what is right as God gives me to see the right, and to do the very best that I can for America. I have asked your help and your prayers not only when I became President, but many times since.

The Constitution is the supreme law of our land and it governs our actions as citizens. Only the laws of God, which govern our consciences, are superior to it. As we are a nation under God, so I am sworn to uphold our laws with the help of God. And I have sought such guidance and searched my own conscience with special diligence to determine the right thing for me to do with respect to my predecessor in this place, Richard Nixon, and his loyal wife and family.

Theirs is an American tragedy in which we all have played a part. It could go on and on and on, or someone must write "The End" to it.

I have concluded that only I can do that. And if I can, I must.

There are no historic or legal precedents to which I can turn in this matter, none that precisely fit the circumstances of a private citizen who has resigned the presidency of the United States. But it is common knowledge that serious allegations and accusations hang like a sword over our former President's head, threatening his health, as he tries to reshape his life, a great part of which was spent in the service of this country and by the mandate of its people.

After years of bitter controversy and divisive national debate, I have been advised and I am compelled to conclude that many months and perhaps more years will have to pass before Richard Nixon could obtain a fair trial by jury in any jurisdiction of the United States under governing decisions of the Supreme Court.

I deeply believe in equal justice for all Americans, whatever their station or former station. The law, whether human or divine, is no respecter of persons but the law is a respecter of reality. The facts as I see them are that a former President of the United States, instead of enjoying equal treatment with any other citizen accused of violating the law, would be cruelly and excessively penalized either in preserving the presumption of his innocence or in obtaining a speedy determination of his guilt in order to repay a legal debt to society.

During this long period of delay and potential litigation, ugly passions would again be aroused, and our people would again be polarized in their opinions, and the credibility of our free institutions of government would again be challenged at home and abroad. In the end, the courts might well hold that Richard Nixon had been denied due process and the verdict of history would even more be inconclusive with respect to those charges arising out of the period of his presidency of which I am presently aware.

But it is not the ultimate fate of Richard Nixon that most concerns me—though surely it deeply troubles every decent and every compassionate person. My concern is the immediate future of this great country. In this I dare not depend upon my personal sympathy as a longtime friend of the former President nor my professional judgment as a lawyer. And I do not.

As President, my primary concern must always be the greatest good of all the people of the United States, whose servant I am.

As a man, my first consideration is to be true to my own convictions and my own conscience.

My conscience tells me clearly and certainly that I cannot prolong the bad dreams that continue to reopen a chapter that is closed. My conscience tells me that only I, as President, have the constitutional power to firmly shut and seal this book. My conscience says it is my duty, not merely to proclaim domestic tranquility, but to use every means that I have to ensure it.

I do believe that the buck stops here, that I cannot rely upon public opinion polls to tell me what is right. I do believe that right makes might, and that if I am wrong 10 angels swearing I was right would make no difference. I do believe with all my heart and mind and spirit that I, not as President, but as a humble servant of God, will receive justice without mercy if I fail to show mercy.

Finally, I feel that Richard Nixon and his loved ones have suffered enough, and will continue to suffer no matter what I do, no matter what we as a great and good nation can do together to make his goal of peace come true.

Now, therefore, I, Gerald R. Ford, President of the United States, pursuant to the pardon power conferred upon me by Article II, Section 2, of the Constitution, have granted and by these presents do grant a full, free, and absolute pardon unto Richard Nixon for all offenses against the United States which he, Richard Nixon, has committed or may have committed or taken part in during the period from January 20, 1969, through August 9, 1974.

In witness whereof, I have hereunto set my hand this 8th day of September in the year of our Lord Nineteen Hundred Seventy Four, and of the independence of the United States of America the 199th.

# Remarks Announcing the Camp David Accords (1978)

*Jimmy Carter, the former governor of Georgia, narrowly defeated President Gerald R. Ford in the 1976 election—the first time a challenger had unseated an incumbent president since Franklin D. Roosevelt defeated Herbert C. Hoover in 1932. Carter stressed domestic issues in his presidential campaign and entered office with no experience in world affairs. Yet the greatest success of his presidency came in the area of foreign policy. Even more remarkable, it came in the part of the world—the Middle East—where international tensions were thought to be at their highest.*

*Carter seized the opportunity that was created when, in November 1977, Egyptian president Anwar Sadat of Egypt visited Israel, the Jewish homeland, and, one month later, Prime Minister Menachem Begin of Israel visited Egypt, a leading Arab nation. The two leaders were seeking to defuse tensions between their countries, which had fought wars in 1967 and 1973.*

*When negotiations between Egypt and Israel slowed to a standstill during the summer of 1978, Carter invited Sadat and Begin to join him at the presidential retreat at Camp David, Maryland, for an extended round of negotiations. The sessions began on September 4 and, despite numerous moments of frustration and seeming*

*failure, concluded successfully thirteen days later.*

*On September 17, 1978, Carter, Begin, and Sadat returned to Washington to announce triumphantly that two agreements had been signed. Taken together, the two agreements—called "A Framework for Peace in the Middle East Agreed to at Camp David" and "A Framework for the Conclusion of a Peace Treaty between Egypt and Israel"—provided an outline for peace in the Middle East. The first attempted (unsuccessfully, it later turned out) to provide a diplomatic structure to determine the future of the West Bank, which Israel had seized from the Arab nation of Jordan in the June 1967 war. The second, which proved to be more successful, provided in part for the return to Egypt of Israeli-occupied territory in the Sinai desert in exchange for a treaty of peace between the two nations.*

*The agreements were announced jointly by Carter, Begin, and Sadat at a televised White House signing ceremony on the evening of September 17. Both foreign leaders praised Carter effusively for keeping the negotiations going and bringing them to a successful conclusion. Begin began his remarks by saying, "The Camp David conference should be renamed. It was the Jimmy Carter Conference. . . . [T]he President of the United States won the day."* ~

## President Carter's Remarks

When we first arrived at Camp David, the first thing upon which we agreed was to ask the people of the world to pray that our negotiations would be successful. Those prayers have been answered far beyond any expectations. We are privileged to witness tonight a significant achievement in the cause of peace, an achievement none thought possible a year ago, or even a month ago, an achievement that reflects the courage and wisdom of these two leaders.

Through 13 long days at Camp David, we have seen them display determination and vision and flexibility which was needed to make this agreement come to pass. All of us owe them our gratitude and respect. They know that they will always have my personal admiration.

There are still great difficulties that remain and many hard issues to be settled. The questions that have brought warfare and bitterness to the Middle East for the last 30 years will not be settled overnight. But we should all recognize the substantial achievements that have been made.

One of the agreements that President Sadat and Prime Minister Begin are signing tonight is entitled, "A Framework For Peace in the Middle East."

This framework concerns the principles and some specifics in the most substantive way which will govern a comprehensive peace settlement. It deals specifically with the future of the West Bank and Gaza, and the need to resolve the Palestinian problem in all its aspects. The framework document proposes a five-year transitional period in the West Bank and Gaza during which the Israeli military government will be withdrawn and a self-governing authority will be elected with full autonomy.

It also provides for Israeli forces to remain in specified locations during this period to protect Israel's security.

The Palestinians will have the right to participate in the determination of their own future, in negotiations which will resolve the final status of the West Bank and Gaza, and then to produce an Israeli-Jordanian peace treaty.

These negotiations will be based on all the provisions and all the principles of the United Nations Security Council Resolution 242. And it provides that Israel may live in peace within secure and recognized borders.

This great aspiration of Israel has been certified without constraint with the greatest degree of enthusiasm by President Sadat, the leader of one of the greatest nations on earth. The other document is entitled, "Framework For the Conclusion of a Peace Treaty," between Egypt and Israel.

It provides for the full exercise of Egyptian sovereignty over the Sinai. It calls for the full withdrawal of Israeli forces from the Sinai; and after an interim withdrawal which will be accomplished very quickly, the establishment of normal, peaceful relations between the two countries, including diplomatic relations.

Together with accompanying letters, which we will make public tomorrow, these two Camp David agreements provide the basis for progress and peace throughout the Middle East.

There is one issue on which agreement has not been reached. Egypt states that the agreement to remove Israeli settlements from Egyptian territory is a prerequisite to a peace treaty. Israel states that the issue of Israeli settlements should be resolved during the peace negotiations. That is a substantial difference.

Within the next two weeks, the Knesset will decide on the issue of these settlements.

Tomorrow night, I will go before the Congress to explain these agreements more fully, and to talk about their implications for the United States, and for the world. For the moment, and in closing, I want to speak more personally about my admiration for all of those who have taken part in this process, and my hope that the promise of this moment will be fulfilled.

During the last two weeks the members of all three delegations have spent endless hours, day and night, talking, negotiating, grappling with problems that have divided their people for 30 years. Whenever there was a danger that human energy would fail, or patience would be exhausted, or good will would run out—and there were such moments—these two leaders and the able advisers in all delegations found the resources within them to keep the chances for peace alive.

Well, the long days at Camp David are over. But many months of difficult negotiations still lie ahead.

I hope that the foresight and the wisdom that have made this session a success will guide these leaders and the leaders of all nations as they continue the process toward peace.

Thank you very much.

## President Sadat's Remarks

Dear President Carter, in this historic moment, I would like to express to you my heartfelt congratulations and appreciation. For long days and nights, you devoted your time and energy to the pursuit of peace. You have been most courageous when you took the gigantic step of convening this meeting. The challenge was great, and the risks were high, but so was your determination.

You made a commitment to be a full partner in the peace process. I am happy to say that you have honored your commitment.

The signing of the framework for the comprehensive peace settlement has a significance far beyond the event. It signals the emergence of a new peace initiative with the American nation in the heart of the entire process.

In the weeks ahead, important decisions have to be made if we are to proceed on the road to peace. We have to reaffirm the faith of the Palestinian people in the ideal of peace.

The continuation of your active role is indispensable. We need your help and the support of the American people. Let me seize this opportunity to thank each and every American for his genuine interest in the cause of people in the Middle East.

Dear friend, we came to Camp David with all the good will and faith we possessed, and we left Camp David a few minutes ago with a renewed sense of hope and inspiration. We are looking forward to the days ahead with an added determination to pursue the noble goal of peace.

Your able assistants spared no effort to bring out this happy conclusion. We appreciate the spirit and dedication. Our hosts at Camp David and the State of Maryland were most generous and hospitable. To each one of them and to all those who are watching this great event, I say thank you.

Let us join in a prayer to God Almighty to guide our path. Let us pledge to make the spirit of Camp David a new chapter in the history of our nation.

Thank you, Mr. President.

## Prime Minister Begin's Remarks

Mr. President of the United States, Mr. President of the Arab Republic of Egypt, ladies and gentlemen: The Camp David conference should be renamed. It was the Jimmy Carter Conference.

The President took an initiative most imaginative in our time and brought President Sadat and myself and our colleagues and friends and advisers together under one roof. In itself it was a great achievement.

The President took a great risk on himself and did it with great civil courage, and it was a famous French field commander who said that it is much more difficult to show civil courage than military courage.

And the President worked. As far as my historic experience is concerned, I think that he worked harder than our forefathers did in Egypt, building the pyramids. (Laughter, applause)

Yes, indeed, he worked day and night, and so did we —

**The President:** Amen.

**Prime Minister Begin:** Day and night. We used to go to bed at Camp David between 3:00 and 4:00 o'clock in the morning, arise, as we are used to since our boyhood, at 5:00 or 6:00, and continue working.

The President showed interest in every section, every paragraph, every sentence, every word, every letter of the framework agreements.

We had some difficult moments, as usually, there are some crises in negotiations; as usually, somebody gives a hint that perhaps he would like to pick up and go home. It is all usual. But ultimately, ladies and gentlemen, the President of the United States won the day. And peace now celebrates victory for the nations of Egypt and Israel and for all mankind.

Mr. President, we, the Israelis, thank you from the bottom of our hearts for all you have done for the sake of peace, for which we prayed and yearned more than 30 years. The Jewish people suffered much, too much. And therefore, peace to us is a striving, coming innermost from our heart and soul.

Now when I came here to the Camp David conference, I said perhaps as a result of our work, one day people will, in every corner of the world, be able to say "Habemus pacem" in the spirit of these days. Can we say so tonight? Not yet. We still have to go the road until my friend President Sadat and I sign the peace treaties.

We promised each other that we shall do so within three months.

Mr. President, tonight, at this celebration of the great historic event, let us

promise each other that we shall do it earlier than within three months.

Mr. President, you inscribed your name forever in the history of two ancient civilized peoples, the people of Egypt and the people of Israel.

Thank you, Mr. President.

**The President:** Thank you very much.

**Prime Minister Begin:** I would like to say a few words about my friend, President Sadat. We met for the first time in our lives last November in Jerusalem. He came to us as a guest, a former enemy, and during our first meeting, we became friends.

In the Jewish teachings, there is a tradition that the greatest achievement of a human being is to turn his enemy into a friend, and this we do in reciprocity. Since then, we had some difficult days. I am not going now to tell you the saga of those days. Everything belongs to the past. Today, I visited President Sadat in his cabin because in Camp David you don't have houses, you only have cabins. He then came to visit me. We shook hands. And, thank God, we again could have said to each other, "You are my friend."

And, indeed, we shall go on working and understanding, and with friendship and with good will. We will still have problems to solve. Camp David proved that any problem can be solved, if there is good will and understanding and some wisdom.

May I thank my own colleagues and friends, the Foreign Minister, the Finance Minister; Professor Barak who was the Attorney General. Now he is going to be His Honor, the Justice of the Supreme Court, the Israeli Brandeis and Dr. Rosenntz and our wonderful Ambassador to the United States, Mr. Simcha Dinitz, and all our friends, because without them, that achievement wouldn't have been possible.

I express my thanks to all the members of the American delegation, headed by the Secretary of State, a man whom we love and respect. So I express my thanks to all the members of the Egyptian delegation who worked so hard together with us, headed by Deputy Prime Minister, Mr. Touhamy, for all they have done to achieve this moment. It is a great moment in the history of our nations and indeed of mankind.

I looked for a precedent; I didn't find it. It was a unique conference, perhaps one of the most important since the Vienna Conference in the 19th century; perhaps.

Now, ladies and gentlemen, allow me to turn to my own people from the White House in my native tongue.

(Brief remarks in Hebrew)

Thank you, ladies and gentlemen.

## Signing the Accords: President Carter's Remarks

The first document that we will sign is entitled, "A Framework For Peace in the Middle East Agreed at Camp David," and the text of these two documents will be released tomorrow. The documents will be signed by President Sadat and Prime Minister Begin. It will be witnessed by me.

We have to exchange three documents, so we'll all sign three times for this one.

I might say that the first document is quite comprehensive in nature, encompassing a framework by which Israel can later negotiate peace treaties between herself and Lebanon, Syria, Jordan, as well as the outline of this document that we will now sign.

As you will later see, in studying the documents, it also provides for the realization of the hopes and dreams of the people who live in the West Bank and Gaza Strip and will assure Israel peace in the generations ahead.

This second document is the one relating to a framework for a peace treaty between Egypt and Israel. This is the document that calls for the completion of the peace treaty negotiations within three months. I have noticed the challenge extended by these two gentlemen to each other. They will complete within three months—I might say that this document encompasses almost all of the issues between the two countries and resolves those issues. A few lines remain to be drawn on maps and the question of the settlements is to be resolved. Other than that, most of the major issues are resolved already in this document.

We will now sign this document as well.

(Signing of document)

**The President:** Thank you very much.

# Jimmy Carter's "Crisis of Confidence" Speech (1979)

The summer of 1979 was a time of gasoline shortages, raging inflation and interest rates, and widespread dissatisfaction with the leadership of President Jimmy Carter. Indeed, with some exceptions, Carter had grown steadily less effective "inside the beltway" (that is, with Congress, the national press corps, and the rest of the Washington political community) and steadily less popular with the American people ever since the first months of his presidency.

On July 5 Carter began an unprecedented effort to revive his presidency. Convinced that people would not watch, the president canceled a televised address on energy that was scheduled for that evening. The next day, he retreated to Camp David to reflect on the underlying causes of the energy crisis and the nation's other problems. During the course of the following week, Carter met there with more than one hundred invited visitors, including political, business, labor, and religious leaders, to discuss politics, public policy, and philosophy. He also made some unannounced helicopter visits to speak with average families in their homes. On the evening of July 15 Carter gave a televised speech from the Oval Office of the White House that, while dealing with energy (he proposed a ten-year, $142 billion program to obtain energy independence), dwelt on the "crisis of confidence" that he believed was enfeebling the American spirit.

Carter's speech began with an extended mea culpa, quoting criticisms of his leadership from some of the people with whom he had spoken during his Camp David retreat. (He reported, for example, that a southern governor had told him, "Mr. President, you are not leading this Nation—you're just managing the Government.") Carter then described his perception of "a fundamental threat to American democracy," namely, a "crisis of the American spirit" that was marked by loss of faith in the country and confidence in the future. "Restoring that faith and that confidence to America is now the most important task we face," the president concluded.

Although Carter never spoke the word, his address soon became known as the "malaise" speech. Critics charged that the president was blaming the American people for his own failure to solve soluble problems. The broader public reaction was initially more positive, but Carter quickly dissipated whatever political gains he had made by firing five cabinet members during the week following the speech. To a nation unused to having its president take soul-searching retreats, the firings reinforced doubts about the stability and competence of President Carter's leadership. ∼

Good evening.

This is a special night for me. Exactly three years ago on July 15, 1976, I accepted the nomination of my party to run for President of the United States. I promised you a President who is not isolated from the people, who feels your pain and who shares your dreams and who draws his strength and his wisdom from you.

During the past 3 years I have spoken to you on many occasions about national concerns, the energy crisis, reorganizing the Government, our Nation's economy and issues of war and especially peace. But over those years the subjects of the speeches, the talks and the press conferences have become increasingly narrow, focused more and more on what the isolated world of Washington thinks is important. Gradually you have heard more and more about what the Government thinks or what the Government should be doing and less and less about our Nation's hopes, our dreams and our vision of the future.

Ten days ago I had planned to speak to you again about a very important subject—energy. For the fifth time I would have described the urgency of the problem and laid out a series of legislative recommendations to the Congress. But as I was preparing to speak, I began to ask myself the same question that I now know has been troubling many of you. Why have we not been able to get together as a nation to resolve our serious energy problem?

It's clear that the true problems of our Nation are much deeper—deeper than gasoline lines or energy shortages, deeper even than inflation or recession. And I realize more than ever that as President I need your help. So, I decided to reach out and to listen to the voices of America.

I invited to Camp David people from almost every segment of our society—business and labor, teachers and preachers, Governors, mayors and private citizens. And then I left Camp David to listen to other Americans, men and women like you. It has been an extraordinary 10 days, and I want to share with you what I've heard.

First of all, I got a lot of personal advice. Let me quote a few of the typical comments that I wrote down.

This from a Southern governor: "Mr. President, you are not leading this Nation—you're just managing the Government."

"You don't see the people enough any more."

"Some of your Cabinet members don't seem loyal. There is not enough discipline among your disciples."

"Don't talk to us about politics or the mechanics of government, but about an understanding of our common good."

"Mr. President, we're in trouble. Talk to us about blood and sweat and tears."

"If you lead, Mr. President, we will follow."

Many people talked about themselves and about the condition of our Nation. This from a young woman in Pennsylvania: "I feel so far from government. I feel like ordinary people are excluded from political power."

And this from a young Chicano: "Some of us have suffered from recession all our lives."

"Some people have wasted energy, but others haven't had anything to waste."

And this from a religious leader: "No material shortage can touch the important things like God's love for us or our love for one another."

And I like this one particularly from a black woman who happens to be the mayor of a small Mississippi town: "The big shots are not the only ones who are important. Remember, you can't sell anything on Wall Street unless someone digs it up somewhere else first."

This kind of summarized a lot of other statements: "Mr. President, we are confronted with a moral and a spiritual crisis."

Several of our discussions were on energy and I have a notebook full of comments and advice. I'll read just a few.

"We can't go on consuming 40 percent more energy than we produce. When we import oil we are also importing inflation plus unemployment."

"We've got to use what we have. The Middle East has only 5 percent of the world's energy, but the United States has 24 percent."

And this is one of the most vivid statements: "Our neck is stretched over the fence and OPEC has the knife."

"There will be other cartels and other shortages. American wisdom and courage right now can set a path to follow in the future."

This was a good one: "Be bold, Mr. President. We may make mistakes, but we are ready to experiment."

And this one from a labor leader got to the heart of it: "The real issue is freedom. We must deal with the energy problem on a war footing."

And the last that I'll read: "When we enter the moral equivalent of war, Mr. President, don't issue us BB guns."

These 10 days confirmed my belief in the decency and the strength and the wisdom of the American people, but it also bore out some of my longstanding concerns about our Nation's underlying problems.

I know, of course, being President, that government actions and legislation can be very important. That is why I've worked hard to put my campaign promises into law—and I have to admit, with just mixed success. But after listening to the American people I have been reminded again that all the legislation in the world can't fix what's wrong with America. So, I want to speak to you first tonight about a subject even more serious than energy or inflation. I want to talk to you right now about a fundamental threat to American democracy.

I do not mean our political and civil liberties. They will endure. And I do not refer to the outward strength of America, a nation that is at peace tonight everywhere in the world, with unmatched economic power and military might.

The threat is nearly invisible in ordinary ways. It is a crisis of confidence. It is a crisis that strikes at the very heart and soul and spirit of our national will. We can see this crisis in the growing doubt about the meaning of our own lives and in the loss of a unity of purpose for our Nation.

The erosion of our confidence in the future is threatening to destroy the social and the political fabric of America.

The confidence that we have always had as a people is not simply some romantic dream or a proverb in a dusty book that we read just on the Fourth of July. It is the idea we founded our Nation on and has guided our development as a people. Confidence in the future has supported everything else— public institutions and private enterprise, our own families, and the very Constitution of the United States. Confidence has defined our course and has served as a link between generations. We've always believed in something called progress. We've always had a faith that the days of our children would be better than our own.

Our people are losing that faith, not only in government itself, but in the ability as citizens to serve as the ultimate rulers and shapers of our democracy. As a people we know our past and we are proud of it. Our progress has been part of the living history of America, even the world. We always believed that we were part of a great movement of humanity itself called democracy, involved in the search for freedom and that belief has always strengthened us in our purpose. But just as we are losing our confidence in the future, we are also beginning to close the door on our past.

In a Nation that was proud of hard work, strong families, close knit communities, and our faith in God, too many of us now tend to worship self-indulgence and consumption. Human identity is no longer defined by what one does, but by what one owns. But we've discovered that owning things and consuming things does not satisfy our longing for meaning. We've learned that piling up material goods cannot fill the emptiness of lives which have no confidence or purpose.

The symptoms of this crisis of the American spirit are all around us. For the first time in the history of our country the majority of our people believe that the next 5 years will be worse than the past 5 years. Two-thirds of our people do not even vote. The productivity of American workers is actually dropping and the willingness of Americans to save for the future has fallen below that of all other people in the Western world.

As you know, there is a growing disrespect for government and for churches and for schools, the news media, and other institutions. This is not a message of happiness or reassurance, but it is the truth and it is a warning.

These changes did not happen overnight. They've come upon us gradually over the last generation, years that were filled with shocks and tragedy.

We were sure that ours was a nation of the ballet, not the bullet, until the murders of John Kennedy and Robert Kennedy and Martin Luther King Jr. We were taught that our armies were always invincible and our causes were always just, only to suffer the agony of Vietnam. We respected the Presidency as a place of honor until the shock of Watergate.

We remember when the phrase "sound as a dollar" was an expression of absolute dependability, until 10 years of inflation began to shrink our dollars and our savings. We believed that our Nation's resources were limitless until 1973 when we had to face a growing dependence on foreign oil.

These wounds are still very deep. They have never been healed.

Looking for a way out of this crisis, our people have turned to the Federal Government and found it isolated from the mainstream of our Nation's life. Washington, D.C., has become an island. The gap between our citizens and our government has never been so wide. The people are looking for honest answers, not easy answers; clear leadership, not false claims and evasiveness and politics as usual.

What you see too often in Washington and elsewhere around the country is a system of government that seems incapable of action. You see a Congress twisted and pulled in every direction by hundreds of well-financed and powerful special interests.

You see every extreme position defended to the last vote, almost to the last breath by one unyielding group or another. You often see a balanced and a fair approach that demands sacrifice, a little sacrifice from everyone, abandoned like an orphan without support and without friends.

Often you see paralysis and stagnation and drift. You don't like it, and neither do I. What can we do?

First of all, we must face the truth and then we can change our course. We simply must have faith in each other, faith in our ability to govern ourselves and faith in the future of this Nation.

Restoring that faith and that confidence to America is now the most important task we face. It is a true challenge of this generation of Americans.

One of the visitors to Camp David last week put it this way: "We've got to stop crying and start sweating, stop talking and start walking, stop cursing and start praying. The strength we need will not come from the White House, but from every house in America."

We know the strength of America. We are strong. We can regain our unity. We can regain our confidence. We are the heirs of generations who survived threats much more powerful and awesome than those that challenge us now. Our fathers and mothers were strong men and women who shaped a new society during the Great Depression, who fought world wars and who carved out a new charter of peace for the world.

We ourselves are the same Americans who just 10 years ago put a man on the moon. We are the generation that dedicated our society to the pursuit of human rights and equality. And we are the generation that will win the war on the energy problem and in that process rebuild the unity and confidence of America.

We are at a turning point in our history. There are two paths to choose. One is a path I warned about tonight, the path that leads to fragmentation and self-interest. Down that road lies a mistaken idea of freedom, the right to grasp for ourselves some advantage over others. That path would be one of constant conflict between narrow interests ending in chaos and immobility. It is a certain route to failure.

All the traditions of our past, all the lessons of our heritage, all the promises of our future point to another path, the path of common purpose and the restoration of American values. That path leads to true freedom for our Nation and ourselves. We can take the first steps down that path as we begin to solve our energy problem.

Energy will be the immediate test of our ability to unite this Nation and it can also be the standard around which we rally. On the battlefield of energy we can win for our Nation a new confidence, and we can seize control again of our common destiny.

In little more than two decades we've gone from a position of energy independence to one in which almost half the oil we use comes from foreign countries, at prices that are going through the roof. Our excessive dependence on OPEC has already taken a tremendous toll on our economy and our people. This is the direct cause of the long lines which have made millions of you spend aggravating hours waiting for gasoline. It's a cause of the increased inflation and unemployment that we now face. This intolerable dependence on foreign oil threatens our economic independence and the very security of our Nation.

The energy crisis is real. It is worldwide. It is a clear and present danger to our Nation. These are facts and we simply must face them.

What I have to say to you now about energy is simple and vitally important.

Point one: I am tonight setting a clear goal for the energy policy of the United States. Beginning this moment, this Nation will never use more foreign oil than we did in 1977—never. From now on, every new addition to our demand for energy will be met from our own production and our own conservation. The generation-long growth in our dependence on foreign oil will be stopped dead in its tracks right now and then reversed as we move through the 1980s, for I am tonight setting the further goal of cutting our dependence on foreign oil by one-half by the end of the next decade—a saving of over 4½ million barrels of imported oil per day.

Point two: To ensure that we meet these targets, I will use my Presidential authority to set import quotas. I am announcing tonight that for 1979 and 1980, I will forbid the entry into this country of one drop of foreign oil more than these goals allow. These quotas will ensure a reduction in imports even below the ambitious levels we set at the recent Tokyo summit.

Point three: To give us energy security, I am asking for the most massive peacetime commitment of funds and resources in our Nation's history to develop America's own alternative sources of fuel—from coal, from oil shale, from plant products for gasohol, from unconventional gas, from the Sun.

I propose the creation of an energy security corporation to lead this effort to replace 2½ million barrels of imported oil per day by 1990. The corporation will issue up to $5 billion in energy bonds, and I especially want them to be in small denominations so that average Americans can invest directly in America's energy security.

Just as a similar synthetic rubber corporation helped us win World War II, so will we mobilize American determination and ability to win the energy war. Moreover, I will soon submit legislation to Congress calling for the creation of this Nation's first solar bank which will help us achieve the crucial goal of 20 percent of our energy coming from solar power by the year 2000.

These efforts will cost money, a lot of money, and that is why Congress must enact the windfall profits tax without delay. It will be money well spent. Unlike the billions of dollars that we ship to foreign countries to pay for foreign oil, these funds will be paid by Americans to Americans. These funds will go to fight, not to increase, inflation and unemployment.

Point four: I'm asking Congress to mandate, to require as a matter of law, that our Nation's utility companies cut their massive use of oil by 50 percent within the next decade and switch to other fuels, especially coal, our most abundant energy source.

Point five: To make absolutely certain that nothing stands in the way of achieving these goals, I will urge Congress to create an Energy Mobilization Board which, like the War Production Board in World War II, will have the responsibility and authority to cut through the redtape, the delays, and the endless roadblocks to completing key energy projects.

We will protect our environment. But when this Nation critically needs a refinery or a pipeline, we will build it.

Point six: I am proposing a bold conservation program to involve every State, county and city and every average American in our energy battle. This effort will permit you to build conserva-

tion into your home and your lives at a cost you can afford.

I ask Congress to give me authority for mandatory conservation and for standby gasoline rationing. To further conserve energy, I'm proposing tonight an extra $10 billion over the next decade to strengthen our public transportation systems. And I'm asking you for your good and for your Nation's security to take no unnecessary trips, to use car pools or public transportation whenever you can, to park your car one extra day per week, to obey the speed limit and to set your thermostats to save fuel. Every act of energy conservation like this is more than just common sense—I tell you it is an act of patriotism.

Our Nation must be fair to the poorest among us, so we will increase aid to needy Americans to cope with rising energy prices. We often think of conservation only in terms of sacrifice. In fact, it is the most painless and immediate way of rebuilding our Nation's strength. Every gallon of oil each one of us saves is a new form of production. It gives us more freedom, more confidence, that much more control over our own lives.

So the solution of our energy crisis can also help us to conquer the crisis of the spirit in our country. It can rekindle our sense of unity, our confidence in the future and give our Nation and all of us individually a new sense of purpose.

You know we can do it. We have the natural resources. We have more oil in our shale alone than several Saudi Arabias. We have more coal than any Nation on earth. We have the world's highest level of technology. We have the most skilled work force, with innovative genius, and I firmly believe that we have the national will to win this war.

I do not promise you that this struggle for freedom will be easy. I do not promise a quick way out of our Nation's problems, when the truth is that the only way out is an all out effort.

What I do promise you is that I will lead our fight and I will enforce fairness in our struggle and I will ensure honesty. And above all, I will act.

We can manage the short-term shortages more effectively and we will, but there are no short-term solutions to our long-range problems. There is simply no way to avoid sacrifice.

Twelve hours from now I will speak again in Kansas City, to expand and to explain further our energy program. Just as the search for solutions to our energy shortages has now led us to a new awareness of our Nation's deeper problems, so our willingness to work for those new solutions in energy can strengthen us to attack those deeper problems.

I will continue to travel this country, to hear the people of America. You can help me to develop a national agenda for the 1980s. I will listen and I will act. We will act together. These were the promises I made three years ago and I intend to keep them.

Little by little we can and we must rebuild our confidence. We can spend until we empty our treasuries, and we may summon all the wonders of science. But we can succeed only if we tap our greatest resources—America's people, America's values, and America's confidence.

I have seen the strength of America in the inexhaustible resources of our people. In the days to come, let us renew that strength in the struggle for an energy-secure nation.

In closing, let me say this: I will do my best, but I will not do it alone. Let your voice be heard. Whenever you have a chance, say something good about our country. With God's help and for the sake of our Nation, it is time for us to join hands in America. Let us commit ourselves together to a rebirth of the American spirit. Working together with our common faith we cannot fail.

Thank you and good night.

# Ronald Reagan's First Inaugural Address (1981)

Ronald Reagan was a professional movie and television actor and a New Deal Democrat for most of his life. In 1966, four years after changing his party registration from Democrat to Republican, Reagan entered elective politics by running for governor of California as a conservative Republican. He won and, after a brief and unsuccessful late bid for the Republican presidential nomination against Richard Nixon in 1968, was reelected as governor in 1970. After leaving the governorship in 1975, Reagan challenged President Gerald R. Ford for the party's 1976 presidential nomination. He was defeated, but came very close to winning. Reagan's strong conservative credentials and exceptional ability as a television orator, which had been honed throughout his career in show business, made him a formidable candidate in any election he entered.

In 1980 Reagan swept easily to the Republican presidential nomination. (His main rival was former United Nations ambassador George Bush, whom Reagan tapped at the convention as his vice-presidential running mate.) Capitalizing on severe economic conditions at home and, abroad, on the year-long seizure of more than fifty American hostages by militant revolutionaries in Iran, Reagan surpassed Franklin D. Roosevelt's 1932 record and defeated President Jimmy Carter by the largest electoral vote majority in history against an incumbent president (489 votes for Reagan to 49 for Carter).

Reagan's inauguration as president also was unprecedented in some ways. Two weeks shy of his seventieth birthday, Reagan was the oldest person ever to be inaugurated as president. (Previously, William Henry Harrison had been.) He was inaugurated on the West Front of the Capitol, not the traditional East Front. And he coordinated part of his speech with television cameras, which showed viewers the Washington Monument, the Jefferson and Lincoln memorials, and Arlington National Cemetery, even as Reagan spoke of them.

Reagan's first inaugural address advanced the two main themes of his political career, of his 1980 campaign, and, subsequently, of his presidency: the failings of big government and a fervent optimism that national problems could be overcome. "The economic ills we suffer . . . will go away," Reagan proclaimed. "They will go away because we as Americans have the capacity now, as we've had it in the past, to do whatever needs to be done to preserve this last and greatest bastion of freedom. . . . In this present crisis, government is not the solution to our problem; government is the problem."

Moments after Reagan's inauguration was completed, Iran freed the

*American hostages. The new president asked Carter, who had negotiated their release, to go to West Germany to greet them on the first leg of their trip home.*    ～

To a few of us here today this is a solemn and most momentous occasion. And, yet, in the history of our Nation it is a commonplace occurrence. The orderly transfer of authority as called for in the Constitution routinely takes place, as it has for almost two centuries, and few of us stop to think how unique we really are. In the eyes of many in the world, this every-4-year ceremony we accept as normal is nothing less than a miracle.

Mr. President, I want our fellow citizens to know how much you did to carry on this tradition. By your gracious cooperation in the transition process you have shown a watching world that we are a united people pledged to maintaining a political system which guarantees individual liberty to a greater degree than any other, and I thank you and your people for all your help in maintaining the continuity which is the hallmark of our Republic.

The business of our Nation goes forward. These United States are confronted with an economic affliction of great proportions. We suffer from the longest and one of the worst sustained inflations in our national history. It distorts our economic decisions, penalizes thrift and crushes the struggling young and the fixed-income elderly alike. It threatens to shatter the lives of millions of our people.

Idle industries have cast workers into unemployment, human misery, and personal indignity. Those who do work are denied a fair return for their labor by a tax system which penalizes successful achievement and keeps us from maintaining full productivity.

But great as our tax burden is, it has not kept pace with public spending. For decades we have piled deficit upon deficit, mortgaging our future and our children's future for the temporary convenience of the present. To continue this long trend is to guarantee tremendous social, cultural, political, and economic upheavals.

You and I, as individuals, can, by borrowing, live beyond our means, but for only a limited period of time. Why, then, should we think that collectively, as a nation, we're not bound by that same limitation? We must act today in order to preserve tomorrow. And let there be no misunderstanding—we are going to begin to act, beginning today.

The economic ills we suffer have come upon us over several decades. They will not go away in days, weeks, or months, but they will go away. They will go away because we as Americans have the capacity now, as we've had in the past, to do whatever needs to be done to preserve this last and greatest bastion of freedom.

In this present crisis, government is not the solution to our problem; government is the problem. From time to time we've been tempted to believe that society has become too complex to be managed by self-rule, that government by an elite group is superior to government for, by, and of the people. Well, if no one among us is capable of governing himself, then who among us has the capacity to govern someone else? All of us together—in and out of government—must bear the burden. The solutions we seek must be equitable with no one group singled out to pay a higher price.

We hear much of special interest groups. Well, our concern must be for a special interest group that has been too long neglected. It knows no sectional boundaries or ethnic and racial divisions, and it crosses political party lines. It is made up of men and women who raise our food, patrol our streets, man our mines and factories, teach our children, keep our homes, and heal us when we're sick—professionals, industrialists, shopkeepers, clerks, cabbies, and truck drivers. They are, in short, "We the people," this breed called Americans.

Well, this administration's objective will be a healthy, vigorous, growing economy that provides equal opportunities for all Americans with no barriers born of bigotry or discrimination. Putting America back to work means putting all Americans back to work. Ending inflation means freeing all Americans from the terror of runaway living costs. All must share in the productive work of this "new beginning," and all must share in the bounty of a revived economy. With the idealism and fair play which are the core of our system and our strength, we can have a strong and prosperous America at peace with itself and the world.

So, as we begin, let us take inventory. We are a nation that has a government—not the other way around. And this makes us special among the nations of the Earth. Our government has no power except that granted it by the people. It is time to check and reverse the growth of government which shows signs of having grown beyond the consent of the governed.

It is my intention to curb the size and influence of the Federal establishment and to demand recognition of the distinction between the powers granted to the Federal Government and those reserved to the States or to the people. All of us need to be reminded that the Federal Government did not create the States; the States created the Federal Government.

Now so there will be no misunderstanding, it's not my intention to do away with government. It is rather to make it work—work with us, not over us; to stand by our side, not ride on our back. Government can and must provide opportunity, not smother it; foster productivity, not stifle it.

If we look to the answer as to why for so many years we achieved so much,

prospered as no other people on Earth, it was because here in this land we unleashed the energy and individual genius of man to a greater extent than has ever been done before. Freedom and the dignity of the individual have been more available and assured here than in any other place on Earth. The price for this freedom at times has been high. But we have never been unwilling to pay that price.

It is no coincidence that our present troubles parallel and are proportionate to the intervention and intrusion in our lives that result from unnecessary and excessive growth of government. It is time for us to realize that we're too great a nation to limit ourselves to small dreams. We're not, as some would have us believe, doomed to an inevitable decline. I do not believe in a fate that will fall on us no matter what we do. I do believe in a fate that will fall on us if we do nothing. So, with all the creative energy at our command, let us begin an era of national renewal. Let us renew our determination, our courage, and our strength. And let us renew our faith and our hope.

We have every right to dream heroic dreams. Those who say we're in a time when there are no heroes, they just don't know where to look. You can see heroes every day going in and out of factory gates. Others, a handful in number, produce food enough to feed all of us and much of the world beyond. You meet heroes across a counter. And they're on both sides of that counter. There are entrepreneurs with faith in themselves and faith in an idea who create new jobs, new wealth and opportunity. They're individuals and families whose taxes support the government and whose voluntary gifts support church, charity, culture, art, and education. Their patriotism is quiet but deep. Their values sustain our national life.

Now, I have used the words "they" and "their" in speaking of these heroes. I could say "you" and "your," because

I'm addressing the heroes of whom I speak—you, the citizens of this blessed land. Your dreams, your hopes, your goals are going to be the dreams, the hopes, and the goals of this administration, so help me God.

We shall reflect the compassion that is so much a part of your makeup. How can we love our country and not love our countrymen; and loving them, reach out a hand when they fall, heal them when they're sick, and provide opportunity to make them self-sufficient so they will be equal in fact and not just in theory?

Can we solve the problems confronting us? Well, the answer is an unequivocal and emphatic "yes." To paraphrase Winston Churchill, I do not take the oath I've just taken with the intention of presiding over the dissolution of the world's strongest economy.

In the days ahead I will propose removing the roadblocks that have slowed our economy and reduced productivity. Steps will be taken aimed at restoring the balance between the various levels of government. Progress may be slow, measured in inches and feet, not miles, but we will progress. It is time to reawaken this industrial giant, to get government back within its means, and to lighten our punitive tax burden. And these will be our first priorities, and on these principles, there will be no compromise.

On the eve of our struggle for independence a man who might have been one of the greatest among the Founding Fathers, Dr. Joseph Warren, president of the Massachusetts Congress, said to his fellow Americans, "Our country is in danger, but not to be despaired of. . . . On you depend the fortunes of America. You are to decide the important question on which rests the happiness and liberty of millions yet unborn. Act worthy of yourselves."

Well, I believe we, the Americans of today, are ready to act worthy of ourselves, ready to do what must be done to ensure happiness and liberty for ourselves, our children, and our children's children. And as we renew ourselves here in our own land, we will be seen as having greater strength throughout the world. We will again be the exemplar of freedom and a beacon of hope for those who do not now have freedom.

To those neighbors and allies who share our ideal of freedom, we will strengthen our historic ties and assure them of our support and firm commitment. We will match loyalty with loyalty. We will strive for mutually beneficial relations. We will not use our friendship to impose on their sovereignty, for our own sovereignty is not for sale.

As for the enemies of freedom, those who are potential adversaries, they will be reminded that peace is the highest aspiration of the American people. We will negotiate for it, sacrifice for it; we will not surrender for it now or ever.

Our forbearance should never be misunderstood. Our reluctance for conflict should not be misjudged as a failure of will. When action is required to preserve our national security, we will act. We will maintain sufficient strength to prevail if need be, knowing that if we do so we have the best chance of never having to use that strength.

Above all we must realize that no arsenal or no weapon in the arsenals of the world is so formidable as the will and moral courage of free men and women. It is a weapon our adversaries in today's world do not have. It is a weapon that we as Americans do have. Let that be understood by those who practice terrorism and prey upon their neighbors.

I'm told that tens of thousands of prayer meetings are being held on this day, and for that I'm deeply grateful. We are a nation under God, and I believe God intended for us to be free. It would be fitting and good, I think, if each Inaugural Day in future years it should be declared a day of prayer.

This is the first time in our history that this ceremony has been held, as you've been told, on this West Front of the Capitol. Standing here, one faces a magnificent vista, opening up on this city's special beauty and history. At the end of this open mall are those shrines to the giants on whose shoulders we stand.

Directly in front of me, the monument to a monumental man. George Washington, father of our country. A man of humility who came to greatness reluctantly. He led America out of revolutionary victory into infant nationhood. Off to one side, the stately memorial to Thomas Jefferson. The Declaration of Independence flames with his eloquence. And then, beyond the Reflecting Pool, the dignified columns of the Lincoln Memorial. Whoever would understand in his heart the meaning of America will find it in the life of Abraham Lincoln.

Beyond these monuments to heroism is the Potomac River, and on the far shore the sloping hills of Arlington National Cemetery, with its row upon row of simple white markers bearing crosses or Stars of David. They add up to only a tiny fraction of the price that has been paid for our freedom.

Each one of those markers is a monument to the kind of hero I spoke of earlier. Their lives ended in places called Belleau Wood, The Argonne, Omaha Beach, Salerno, and halfway around the world on Guadalcanal, Tarawa, Pork Chop Hill, the Chosin Reservoir, and in a hundred rice paddies and jungles of a place called Vietnam. Under one such marker lies a young man, Martin Treptow, who left his job in a small town barbershop in 1917 to go to France with the famed Rainbow Division. There, on the western front, he was killed trying to carry a message between battalions under heavy artillery fire.

We're told that on his body was found a diary. On the flyleaf under the heading, "My Pledge," he had written these words: "America must win this war. Therefore I will work, I will save, I will sacrifice, I will endure, I will fight cheerfully and do my utmost, as if the issue of the whole struggle depended on me alone."

The crisis we are facing today does not require of us the kind of sacrifice that Martin Treptow and so many thousands of others were called upon to make. It does require, however, our best effort, and our willingness to believe in ourselves and to believe in our capacity to perform great deeds, to believe that together and with God's help we can and will resolve the problems which confront us.

And after all, why shouldn't we believe that? We are Americans.

God bless you, and thank you.

# Ronald Reagan's Economic Plan Address (1981)

President Ronald Reagan became known to the nation as the "Great Communicator" because of his skill, which had been developed during a long career as a movie and television actor and a public speaker, at appealing directly to the people in televised speeches from the Oval Office of the White House. Reagan's first such speech, delivered on February 5, 1981, was one of his most successful. In it the new president urged the American people to support his plan to lift the nation out of what he called "the worst economic mess since the Great Depression." At one point, Reagan dramatized the nation's economic woes by holding up a dollar in one hand and thirty-six cents (which, not carrying any money, he had borrowed from an aide just before going on the air) in the other: the coins represented the reduced value of the dollar since 1960.

In his speech Reagan pointed to a host of problems, including inflation, deficit spending, high interest rates, low productivity, high taxes, and excessive regulation of business. Promising to provide more detail in a speech to Congress on February 18, he offered four major proposals for improvement: cuts in federal spending; reduced federal regulation of business, under the leadership of Vice President George Bush; the encouragement of a "stable monetary policy" by the independent Federal Reserve Board; and dramatic tax cuts of 30 percent over three years for individuals and an accelerated depreciation allowance for business. The proposed tax cuts embodied Reagan's adherence to the unconventional new theory of "supply-side economics," which held that lower taxes would encourage individuals and businesses to be more productive, and, as a consequence, actually pay more in taxes.

Reagan's speech had its intended effect: an unusually large outpouring of letters, telegrams, and telephone calls urging members of Congress to support the president's proposed policies. In June 1981 Congress voted to reduce federal spending on domestic social programs by nearly $40 billion. In August Reagan signed the Economic Recovery Tax Act, which reduced individual tax rates by 25 percent over three years, indexed individual tax brackets to inflation, and provided a host of lucrative tax breaks to business. From the start, the president supported the efforts of Federal Reserve Board chair Paul Volcker to wring inflation out of the economy through tight money policies. Finally, regulatory relief for business was provided through closer scrutiny of proposed new regulations and laxer enforcement of those already on the books.

During the course of Reagan's presidency, inflation, interest rates, and,

*after a severe recession in 1982, unem-
ployment fell. But the combination of
reduced tax revenues and a massive
increase in defense spending caused
the federal deficit to triple to approximately $200 billion per year.*  ~

Good evening. I am speaking to you
tonight to give you a report on the state
of our Nation's economy. I regret to say
that we are in the worst economic mess
since the Great Depression. A few days
ago I was presented with a report I had
asked for—a comprehensive audit if
you will of our economic condition. You
won't like it, I didn't like it, but we have
to face the truth and then go to work to
turn things around. And make no mistake about it, we can turn them around.

I'm not going to subject you to the
jumble of charts, figures, and economic
jargon of that audit but rather will try
to explain where we are, how we got
there, and how we can get back.

First, however, let me just give a few
"attention getters" from the audit. The
Federal budget is out of control and we
face runaway deficits, of almost $80
billion for this budget year that ends
September 30. That deficit is larger
than the entire Federal budget in 1957
and so is the almost $80 billion we will
pay in interest this year on the national
debt.

Twenty years ago in 1960 our Federal
Government payroll was less than $13
billion. Today it is $75 billion. During
these twenty years, our population has
only increased by 23.3 percent. The
Federal budget has gone up 528
percent.

Now, we've just had two years of
back-to-back double digit inflation, 13.3
percent in 1979—12.4 percent last year.
The last time this happened was in
World War I.

In 1960 mortgage interest rates averaged about 6 percent. They are 2½
times as high now, 15.4 percent. The
percentage of your earnings the Federal

Government took in taxes in 1960 has
almost doubled. And finally there are 7
million Americans caught up in the personal indignity and human tragedy of
unemployment. If they stood in a line—
allowing 3 feet for each person—the line
would reach from the Coast of Maine to
California.

Well, so much for the audit itself. Let
me try to put this in personal terms.
Here is a dollar such as you earned,
spent, or saved in 1960. Here is a quarter, a dime, and a penny—36¢. That's
what this 1960 dollar is worth today.
And if the present inflation rate should
continue three more years, that dollar
of 1960 will be worth a quarter. What
initiative is there to save? And if we
don't save we are short of the investment capital needed for business and
industry expansion. Workers in Japan
and West Germany save several times
the percentage of their income that
Americans do.

What's happened to that American
dream of owning a home? Only ten
years ago a family could buy a home
and the monthly payment averaged little more than a quarter—27¢ out of
each dollar earned. Today it takes 42¢
out of every dollar of income. So, fewer
than 1 out of 11 families can afford to
buy their first new home.

Regulations adopted by government
with the best intentions have added
$666 to the cost of an automobile. It is
estimated that altogether regulations of
every kind, on shopkeepers, farmers,
and major industries add $100 billion or
more to the cost of the goods and services we buy. And then another $20
billion is spent by government handling
the paperwork created by those regulations.

I'm sure you are getting the idea that
the audit presented to me found government policies of the last few decades
responsible for our economic troubles.
We forgot or just overlooked the fact
that government—any government—
has a built-in tendency to grow. Now,

we all had a hand in looking to government for benefits as if government had some sources of revenue other than our earnings. Many if not most of the things we thought of or that government offered to us seemed attractive.

In the years following the Second World War it was easy (for awhile at least) to overlook the price tag. Our income more than doubled in the 25 years after the War. We increased our take-home pay in those 25 years by more than we had amassed in all the preceding 150 years put together. Yes, there was some inflation, 1 or 1½ percent a year, that didn't bother us. But if we look back at those golden years we recall that even then voices had been raised warning that inflation, like radioactivity, was cumulative and that once started it could get out of control. Some government programs seemed so worthwhile that borrowing to fund them didn't bother us.

By 1960 our national debt stood at $284 billion. Congress in 1971 decided to put a ceiling of $400 billion on our ability to borrow. Today the debt is $934 billion. So-called temporary increases or extensions in the debt ceiling have been allowed 21 times in these 10 years and now I have been forced to ask for another increase in the debt ceiling or the government will be unable to function past the middle of February and I've only been here 16 days. Before we reach the day when we can reduce the debt ceiling we may in spite of our best efforts see a national debt in excess of a trillion dollars. Now this is a figure literally beyond our comprehension.

We know now that inflation results from all that deficit spending. Government has only two ways of getting money other than raising taxes. It can go into the money market and borrow, competing with its own citizens and driving up interest rates, which it has done, or it can print money, and it's done that. Both methods are inflationary.

We're victims of language, the very word "inflation" leads us to think of it as just high prices. Then, of course, we resent the person who puts on the price tags forgetting that he or she is also a victim of inflation. Inflation is not just high prices, it is a reduction in the value of our money. When the money supply is increased but the goods and services available for buying are not, we have too much money chasing too few goods.

Wars are usually accompanied by inflation. Everyone is working or fighting but production is of weapons and munitions not things we can buy and use.

One way out would be to raise taxes so that government need not borrow or print money. But in all these years of government growth we've reached—indeed surpassed—the limit of our people's tolerance or ability to bear an increase in the tax burden.

Prior to World War II, taxes were such that on the average we only had to work just a little over one month each year to pay our total Federal, state, and local tax bill. Today we have to work four months to pay that bill.

Some say shift the tax burden to business and industry but business doesn't pay taxes. Oh, don't get the wrong idea, business is being taxed—so much so that we are being priced out of the world market. But business must pass its costs of operation, and that includes taxes, onto the customer in the price of the product. Only people pay taxes—all the taxes. Government just uses business in a kind of sneaky way to help collect the taxes. They are hidden in the price and we aren't aware of how much tax we actually pay. Today, this once great industrial giant of ours has the lowest rate of gain in productivity of virtually all the industrial nations with whom we must compete in the world market. We can't even hold our own market here in America against foreign automobiles, steel, and a number of other products.

Japanese production of automobiles

is almost twice as great per worker as it is in America. Japanese steel workers out-produce their American counterparts by about 25 percent.

Now this isn't because they are better workers. I'll match the American working man or woman against anyone in the world. But we have to give them the tools and equipment that workers in the other industrial nations have.

We invented the assembly line and mass production, but punitive tax policies and excessive and unnecessary regulations plus government borrowing have stifled our ability to update plant and equipment. When capital investment is made it's too often for some unproductive alterations demanded by government to meet various of its regulations.

Excessive taxation of individuals has robbed us of incentive and made overtime unprofitable.

We once produced about 40 percent of the world's steel. We now produce 19 percent.

We were once the greatest producer of automobiles, producing more than all the rest of the world combined. That is no longer true, and in addition, the big 3, the major auto companies, in our land have sustained tremendous losses in the past year and have been forced to lay off thousands of workers.

All of you who are working know that even with cost-of-living pay raises you can't keep up with inflation. In our progressive tax system as you increase the number of dollars you earn you find yourself moved up into higher tax brackets, paying a higher tax rate just for trying to hold your own. The result? Your standard of living is going down.

Over the past decades we've talked of curtailing government spending so that we can then lower the tax burden. Sometimes we've even taken a run at doing that. But there were always those who told us taxes couldn't be cut until spending was reduced. Well, you know, we can lecture our children about ex-

travagance until we run out of voice and breath. Or we can cure their extravagance by simply reducing their allowance.

It is time to recognize that we have come to a turning point. We are threatened with an economic calamity of tremendous proportions and the old business as usual treatment can't save us.

Together, we must chart a different course. We must increase productivity. That means making it possible for industry to modernize and make use of the technology which we ourselves invented; that means putting Americans back to work. And that means above all bringing government spending back within government revenues which is the only way, together with increased productivity that we can reduce and, yes, eliminate inflation.

In the past we've tried to fight inflation one year and then when unemployment increased turn the next year to fighting unemployment with more deficit spending as a pump primer. So again, up goes inflation. It hasn't worked. We don't have to choose between inflation and unemployment— they go hand in hand. It's time to try something different and that's what we're going to do.

I've already placed a freeze on hiring replacements for those who retire or leave government service. I have ordered a cut in government travel, the number of consultants to the government, and the buying of office equipment and other items. I have put a freeze on pending regulations and set up a task force under Vice President Bush to review regulations with an eye toward getting rid of as many as possible. I have decontrolled oil which should result in more domestic production and less dependence on foreign oil. And I am eliminating that ineffective Council on Wage and Price Stability.

But it will take more, much more and we must realize there is no quick fix. At the same time, however, we cannot delay in implementing an economic program aimed at both reducing tax rates to stimulate productivity and reducing the growth in government spending to reduce unemployment and inflation.

On February 18th, I will present in detail an economic program to Congress embodying the features I have just stated. It will propose budget cuts in virtually every department of government. It is my belief that these actual budget cuts will only be part of the savings. As our Cabinet Secretaries take charge of their departments, they will search out areas of waste, extravagance, and costly administrative overhead which could yield additional and substantial reductions.

Now at the same time we're doing this, we must go forward with a tax relief package. I shall ask for a 10 percent reduction across the board in personal income tax rates for each of the next three years. Proposals will also be submitted for accelerated depreciation allowances for business to provide necessary capital so as to create jobs.

Now, here again, in saying this, I know that language, as I said earlier, can get in the way of a clear understanding of what our program is intended to do. Budget cuts can sound as if we are going to reduce total government spending to a lower level than was spent the year before. This is not the case. The budgets will increase as our population increases and each year we'll see spending increases to match that growth. Government revenues will increase as the economy grows, but the burden will be lighter for each individual because the economic base will have been expanded by reason of the reduced rates.

Now let me show you a chart I've had drawn to illustrate how this can be. Here you see two trend lines. The bottom line shows the increase in tax revenues. The red line on top is the increase in government spending. Both lines turn upward reflecting the giant tax increase already built into the system for this year 1981, and the increases in spending built into the '81 and '82 budgets and on into the future.

As you can see, the spending line rises at a steeper slant than the revenue line. And that gap between those lines illustrates the increasing deficits we've been running including this year's $80 billion deficit.

Now, in the second chart, the lines represent the positive effects when Congress accepts our economic program. Both lines continue to rise allowing for necessary growth but the gap narrows as spending cuts continue over the next few years, until finally the two lines come together meaning a balanced budget.

I am confident that my Administration can achieve that. At that point tax revenues in spite of rate reductions will be increasing faster than spending which means we can look forward to further reductions in the tax rates.

Now, in all of this we will of course work closely with the Federal Reserve System toward the objective of a stable monetary policy.

Our spending cuts will not be at the expense of the truly needy. We will, however, seek to eliminate benefits to those who are not really qualified by reason of need.

As I've said before, on February 18th, I will present this economic package of budget reductions and tax reform to a joint session of Congress and to you in full detail.

Our basic system is sound. We can, with compassion, continue to meet our responsibility to those who through no fault of their own need our help. We can meet fully the other legitimate responsibilities of government. We cannot continue any longer our wasteful ways at the expense of the workers of this land or of our children.

Since 1960 our government has spent $5.1 trillion; our debt has grown by $648 billion. Prices have exploded by 178 percent. How much better off are we for all that? We all know, we are very much worse off.

When we measure how harshly these years of inflation, lower productivity, and uncontrolled government growth have affected our lives, we know we must act and act now.

We must not be timid.

We will restore the freedom of all men and women to excel and to create. We will unleash the energy and genius of the American people—traits which have never failed us.

To the Congress of the United States, I extend my hand in cooperation and I believe we can go forward in a bipartisan manner.

I found a real willingness to cooperate on the part of Democrats and members of my own Party.

To my colleagues in the Executive Branch of government and to all Federal employees I ask that we work in the spirit of service.

I urge those great institutions in America—business and labor—to be guided by the national interest and I'm confident they will. The only special interest that we will serve is the interest of all the people.

We can create the incentives which take advantage of the genius of our economic system—a system, as Walter Lippmann observed more than 40 years ago, which for the first time in history gave men "a way of producing wealth in which the good fortune of others multiplied their own."

Our aim is to increase our national wealth so all will have more not just redistribute what we already have which is just a sharing of scarcity. We can begin to reward hard work and risk-taking, by forcing this government to live within its means.

Over the years we've let negative economic forces run out of control. We've stalled the judgment day. We no longer have that luxury. We're out of time.

And to you my fellow citizens, let us join in a new determination to rebuild the foundation of our society; to work together to act responsibly. Let us do so with the most profound respect for that which must be preserved as well as with sensitive understanding and compassion for those who must be protected.

We can leave our children with an unrepayable massive debt and a shattered economy or we can leave them liberty in a land where every individual has the opportunity to be whatever God intended us to be. All it takes is a little common sense and recognition of our own ability. Together we can forge a new beginning for America.

Thank you and good night.

# Immigration and Naturalization Service v. Chadha (1983)

Since the 1920s Congress increasingly has dealt with complex problems of public policy by writing legislation in broad language and delegating to the executive branch discretionary authority over how to implement the laws in particular cases. To prevent federal agencies (or even the president) from either abusing their discretion or exercising it in ways that Congress disapproves, Congress also has included in many laws a provision that enables it to pass judgment on what the executive branch does. This provision, known as the legislative veto, permits Congress, in some fashion or another, to overturn an executive regulation or action within a prescribed length of time (often ninety days). In all cases, a legislative veto is final—the president, who can veto ordinary bills that are passed by Congress, has no power to overturn a legislative veto.

The first legislative veto provision was written into a 1932 law that empowered President Herbert C. Hoover to reorganize the executive branch, subject to a vote to veto any of his proposals by either the House of Representatives or the Senate. (Other laws were passed with legislative veto requirements that ranged in difficulty from a concurrent resolution of both houses to the objection of a single designated committee in either house.) From 1932 to 1982, one form or another

of the legislative veto was written into more than two hundred laws, including the War Powers Resolution of 1973. (See "War Powers Resolution," p. 387.)

On June 23, 1983, the Supreme Court decided by a 7-2 vote to declare the legislative veto unconstitutional. The case in which it did so, Immigration and Naturalization Service v. Chadha, originated in 1974 when a Kenyan student who had overstayed his student visa received permission from the Immigration and Naturalization Service to stay longer. Relying on the legislative veto provision of the Immigration and Naturalization Act of 1952, the House voted in 1975 to deport the student, whose name was Jagdish Rai Chadha. Chadha sued, challenging the constitutional basis of the House action.

Writing for a majority of justices, Chief Justice Warren E. Burger argued that the legislative veto violated the Constitution's separation of powers in general and, in particular, the presentment clause of Article I, section 7, which says that binding actions emanating from Congress must be presented to the president for signature or veto. Burger wrote, "The Constitution sought to divide the delegated powers of the new federal government into three defined categories, legislative, executive and judicial, to assure, as nearly as possible, that each Branch of *government would confine itself to its assigned responsibility." In a blistering dissent, Justice Byron R. White complained that, having allowed the legislature to delegate substantial authority to the executive branch ever since the legal controversy over the New Deal, the Court was foolish to deny Congress its best tool for overseeing the exercise of that authority. (See the headnote to "Franklin D. Roosevelt's 'Court-packing' Address," p. 270.)*

*Despite the* Chadha *decision, the legislative veto still is in use, albeit in slightly modified form. During the five years that followed the Court's ruling, for example, more than one hundred new laws were passed containing legislative veto provisions that were implemented through informal agreements between Congress and the executive, arcane legislative language, internal congressional rules, and other such devices.*          ~

CHIEF JUSTICE BURGER delivered the opinion of the Court.

## I

... We granted certiorari in Nos. 80-2170 and 80-2171, and postponed consideration of the question of jurisdiction in No. 80-1832. Each presents a challenge to the constitutionality of the provision in § 244 (c) (2) of the Immigration and Nationality Act, 8 U.S.C. § 1254 (c) (2), authorizing one House of Congress, by resolution, to invalidate the decision of the Executive Branch, pursuant to authority delegated by Congress to the Attorney General of the United States, to allow a particular deportable alien to remain in the United States.

Chadha is an East Indian who was born in Kenya and holds a British passport. He was lawfully admitted to the United States in 1966 on a nonimmigrant student visa. His visa expired on June 30, 1972. On October 11, 1973, the District Director of the Immigration and Naturalization Service ordered Chadha to show cause why he should not be deported for having "remained in the United States for a longer time than permitted." Pursuant to § 242 (b) of the Immigration and Nationality Act (Act), 8 U.S.C. § 1254 (b), a deportation hearing was held before an immigration judge on January 11, 1974. Chadha conceded that he was deportable for overstaying his visa and the hearing was adjourned to enable him to file an application for suspension of deportation under § 244 (a) (1) of the Act, 8 U.S.C. § 1254 (a) (1). Section 244 (a) (1) provides:

"(a) As hereinafter prescribed in this section, the Attorney General may, in his discretion, suspend deportation and adjust the status to that of an alien lawfully admitted for permanent residence, in the case of an alien who applies to the Attorney General for suspension of deportation and—

(1) is deportable under any law of the United States except the provisions specified in paragraph (2) of this subsection; has been physically present in the United States for a continuous period of not less than seven years immediately preceding the date of such application, and proves that during all of such period he was and is a person of good moral character; and is a person whose deportation would, in the opinion of the Attorney General, result in extreme hardship to the alien or to his spouse, parent, or child, who is a citizen of the United States or an alien lawfully admitted fro permanent residence."

After Chadha submitted his application for suspension of deportation, the deportation hearing was resumed on February 7, 1974. On the basis of evidence adduced at the hearing, affidavits submitted with the application, and the results of a character investigation conducted by the INS, the immigration judge, on June 25, 1974, ordered that Chadha's deportation be suspended. The immigration judge found that Chadha met the requirements of § 244

(a) (1): he had resided continuously in the United States for over seven years, was of good moral character, and would suffer "extreme hardship" if deported.

Pursuant to § 244 (c) (1) of the Act, 8 U.S.C. § 1254 (c) (1), the immigration judge suspended Chadha's deportation and a report of the suspension was transmitted to Congress. Section 244 (c) (1) provides:

> "Upon application by any alien who is found by the Attorney General to meet the requirements of subsection (a) of this section the Attorney General may in his discretion suspend deportation of such alien. If the deportation of any alien is suspended under the provisions of this subsection, a complete and detailed statement of the facts and pertinent provisions of law in the case shall be reported to the Congress with the reasons for such suspension. Such reports shall be submitted on the first day of each calendar month in which Congress is in session."

Once the Attorney General's recommendation for suspension of Chadha's deportation was conveyed to Congress, Congress had the power under § 244 (c) (2) of the Act, 8 U.S.C. § 1254 (c) (2), to veto the Attorney General's determination that Chadha should not be deported. Section 244 (c) (2) provides:

> "(2) In the case of an alien specified in paragraph (1) of subsection (a) of this subsection—
> if during the session of the Congress at which a case is reported, or prior to the close of the session of the Congress next following the session at which a case is reported, either the Senate or the House of Representatives passes a resolution stating in substance that it does not favor the suspension of such deportation, the Attorney General shall thereupon deport such alien or authorize the alien's voluntary departure at his own expense under the order of deportation in the manner provided by law. If, within the time above specified, neither the Senate nor the House of Representatives shall pass such a resolution, the Attorney General shall cancel deportation proceedings."

The June 25, 1974 order of the immigration judge suspending Chadha's deportation remained outstanding as a valid order for a year and a half. For reasons not disclosed by the record, Congress did not exercise the veto authority reserved to it under § 244 (c) (2) until the first session of the 94th Congress. This was the final session in which Congress, pursuant to § 244 (c) (2), could act to veto the Attorney General's determination that Chadha should not be deported. The session ended on December 19, 1975. Absent Congressional action, Chadha's deportation proceedings would have been cancelled after this date and his status adjusted to that of a permanent resident alien.

On December 12, 1975, Representative Eilberg, Chairman of the Judiciary Subcommittee on Immigration, Citizenship, and International Law, introduced a resolution opposing "the granting of permanent residence in the United States to [six] aliens," including Chadha. The resolution was referred to the House Committee on the Judiciary. On December 16, 1975, the resolution was discharged from further consideration by the House Committee on the Judiciary and submitted to the House of Representatives for a vote. The resolution had not been printed and was not made available to other Members of the House prior to or at the time it was voted on. So far as the record before us shows, the House consideration of the resolution was based on ... Eilberg's statement ... that

> "[i]t was the feeling of the committee, after reviewing 340 cases, that the aliens contained in the resolution [Chadha and five others] did not meet these statutory requirements, particularly as it relates to hardship; and it is the opinion of the committee that their deportation should not be suspended."

The resolution was passed without debate or recorded vote. Since the House action was pursuant to § 244 (c) (2), the resolution was not treated as an Article

I legislative act; it was not submitted to the Senate or presented to the President for his action.

After the House veto of the Attorney General's decision to allow Chadha to remain in the United States, the immigration judge reopened the deportation proceedings to implement the House order deporting Chadha. Chadha moved to terminate the proceedings on the ground that § 244 (c) (2) is unconstitutional. The immigration judge held that he had no authority to rule on the constitutional validity of § 244 (c) (2). On November 8, 1976, Chadha was ordered deported pursuant to the House action.

Chadha appealed the deportation order to the Board of Immigration Appeals again contending that § 244 (c) (2) is unconstitutional. The Board held that it had "no power to declare unconstitutional an act of Congress" and Chadha's appeal was dismissed.

Pursuant to § 106 (a) of the Act, 8 U.S.C. § 1105 a (a), Chadha filed a petition for review of the deportation order in the United States Court of Appeals for the Ninth Circuit. The Immigration and Naturalization Service agreed with Chadha's position before the Court of Appeals and joined him in arguing that § 244 (c) (2) is unconstitutional. In light of the importance of the question, the Court of Appeals invited both the Senate and the House of Representatives to file briefs *amici curiae.*

After full briefing and oral argument, the Court of Appeals held that the House was without constitutional authority to order Chadha's deportation; accordingly it directed the Attorney General "to cease and desist from taking any steps to deport this alien based upon the resolution enacted by the House of Representatives. *Chadha* v. *INS* (CA9 1980). The essence of its holding was that § 244 (c) (2) violates the constitutional doctrine of separation of powers.

We granted certiorari in Nos. 80-2170 and 80-2171, and postponed consideration of our jurisdiction over the appeal in No. 80-1832 . . . (1981), and we now affirm

## II

### [Section A Omitted]

### B
# Severability

Congress also contends that the provision for the one-House veto in § 244 (c) (2) cannot be served from § 244. Congress argues that if the provision for the one-House veto is held unconstitutional, all of § 244 must fall. If § 244 in its entirety is violative of the Constitution, it follows that the Attorney General has no authority to suspend Chadha's deportation under § 244 (a) (1) and Chadha would be deported. From this, Congress argues that Chadha lacks standing to challenge the constitutionality of the one-House veto provision because he could receive no relief even if his constitutional challenge proves successful.

Only recently this Court reaffirmed that the invalid portions of a statute are to be served "[u]nless it is evident that the Legislature would not have enacted those provisions which are within its power, independently of that which is not.' " *Buckley* v. *Valeo* (1976), quoting *Champlin Refining Co.* v. *Corporation Comm'n* (1932). Here, however, we need not embark on that elusive inquiry since Congress itself has provided the answer to the question of severability in § 406 of the Immigration and Nationality Act, 8 U.S.C. § 406 of the Immigration and Nationality Act, 8 U.S.C. § 1101, which provides:

> "If *any* particular provision of this act, or the application thereof to *any* person or circumstance, is held invalid, *the remainder of the Act and the application of such provision to other persons or circumstances shall not be affected thereby.*" (Emphasis added.)

This language is unambiguous and gives

rise to a presumption that Congress did not intend the validity of the Act as a whole, or of any part of the Act, to depend upon whether the veto clause of § 244 (c) (2) was invalid. The one-House veto provision in § 244 (c) (2) is clearly a "particular provision" of the Act as the language is used in the severability clause. Congress clearly intended "the remainder of the Act" to stand if "any particular provision" were held invalid. Congress could not have more plainly authorized the presumption that the provision for a one-House veto in § 244 (c) (2) is severable from the remainder of § 244 and the Act of which it is a part. See *Electric Bond & Share Co.* v. *SEC* (1938).

The presumption as to the severability of the one-House veto provision in § 244 (c) (2) is supported by the legislative history of § 244. That section and its precursors supplanted the long established pattern of dealing with deportations like Chadha's on a case-by-case basis through private bills. Although it may be that Congress was reluctant to delegate final authority over cancellation of deportations, such reluctance is not sufficient to overcome the presumption of severability raised by § 406.

The Immigration Act of 1924, Pub. L. No. 139, § 14, 43 Stat. 153, 162, required the Secretary of Labor to deport any alien who entered or remained in the United States unlawfully. The only means by which a deportable alien could lawfully remain in the United States was to have his status altered by a private bill enacted by both Houses and presented to the President pursuant to the procedures set out in Art. I, § 7 of the Constitution. These private bills were found intolerable by Congress. . . .

Congress first authorized the Attorney General to suspend the deportation of certain aliens in the Alien Registration Act of 1940, ch. 439, § 20, 54 Stat. 671. That Act provided that an alien was to be deported, despite the Attor-

ney General's decision to the contrary, if both Houses, by concurrent resolution, disapproved the suspension.

In 1948, Congress amended the act to broaden the category of aliens eligible for suspension of deportation. In addition, however, Congress limited the authority of the Attorney General to suspend deportations by providing that the Attorney General could not cancel a deportation unless both Houses affirmatively voted by concurrent resolution to *approve* the Attorney General's action. . . .

The proposal to permit one House of Congress to veto the Attorney General's suspension of an alien's deportation was incorporated in the Immigration and Nationality Act of 1952. . . . Plainly, Congress' desire to retain a veto in this area cannot be considered in isolation but must be viewed in the context of Congress' irritation with the burden of private immigration bills. This legislative history is not sufficient to rebut the presumption of severability raised by § 406 because there is insufficient evidence that Congress would have continued to subject itself to the onerous burdens of private bills had it known that § 244 (c) (2) would be held unconstitutional.

A provision is further presumed severable if what remains after severance "is fully operative as a law." *Champlin Refining Co.* v. *Corporation Comm'n.* There can be no doubt that § 244 is "fully operative" and workable administrative machinery without the veto provision in § 244 (c) (2). Entirely independent of the one-House veto, the administrative process enacted by Congress authorizes the Attorney General to suspend an alien's deportation under § 244 (a). Congress' oversight of the exercise of this delegated authority is preserved since all such suspensions will continue to be reported to it under § 244 (c) (1). Absent the passage of a bill to the contrary, deportation proceedings will be cancelled when the period specified in § 244 (c) (2) has expired. Clearly, § 244 survives as a workable administrative mechanism without the one-House veto. . . .

[Sections C, D and E Ommited]

## F
## Case or Controversy

It is also contended that this is not a genuine controversy but "a friendly, non-adversary, proceeding," *Ashwander* v. *Tennessee Valley Authority* [1936] (Brandeis, J., concurring), upon which the Court should not pass. This argument rests on the fact that Chadha and the INS take the same position on the constitutionality of the one-House veto. But it would be a curious result if, in the administration of justice, a person could be denied access to the courts because the Attorney General of the United States agreed with the legal arguments asserted by the individual.

A case or controversy is presented by this case. First, from the time of Congress' formal intervention, . . . the concrete adverseness is beyond doubt. Congress is both a proper party to defend the constitutionality of § 244 (c) (2) and a proper petitioner under § 1254 (1). Second, prior to Congress' intervention, there was adequate Art. III adverseness even though the only parties were the INS and Chadha. We have already held the the INS's agreement with the Court of Appeals' decision that § 244 (c) (2) is unconstitutional does not affect that agency's "aggrieved" status for purposes of appealing that decision under 28 U.S.C. § 1252. For similar reasons, the INS's agreement with Chadha's position does not alter the fact that the INS would have deported Chadga absent the Court of Appeals' judgment. We agree with the Court of Appeals that "Chadha has asserted a concrete controversy, and our decision will have real meaning: if we rule for Chadha, he

will not be deported; if we uphold § 244 (c) (2), the INS will execute its order and deport him."

Of course, there may be prudential, as opposed to Art. III, concerns about sanctioning the adjudication of this case in the absence of any participant supporting the validity of § 244 (c) (2). The Court of Appeals properly dispelled any such concerns by inviting and accepting briefs from both Houses of Congress. We have long held that Congress is the proper party to defend the validity of a statute when an agency of government, as a defendant charged with enforcing the statute, agrees with plaintiffs that the statute is inapplicable or unconstitutional. See *Cheng Fan Kwok* v. *INS* [1968]; *United States* v. *Lovett* (1946).

## G
## Political Question

It is also argued that this case presents a nonjusticiable political question because Chadha is merely challenging Congress' authority under the Naturalization Clause, U.S. Const. art. I, § 8, cl. 4, and the Necessary and Proper Clause, U.S. Const. art. I, § 8, cl. 18. It is argued that Congress' Article I power "To establish a uniform Rule of Naturalization", combined with the Necessary and Proper Clause, grants it unreviewable authority over the regulation of aliens. The plenary authority of Congress over aliens under Art. I, § 8, cl. 4 is not open to question, but what is challenged here is whether Congress has chosen a constitutionally permissible means of implementing that power. As we made clear in *Buckley* v. *Valeo* (1976), "Congress has plenary authority in all cases in which it has substantive legislative jurisdiction, *M'Culloch* v. *Maryland* (1819), so long as the exercise of that authority does not offend some other constitutional restriction."

A brief review of those factors which may indicate the presence of a nonjusticiable political question satisfies us that our assertion of jurisdiction over this case does no violence to the political question doctrine. As identified in *Baker* v. *Carr* (1962), a political question may arise when any one of the following circumstances is present:

> "a textually demonstrable constitutional commitment of the issue to a coordinate political department; or a lack of judicially discoverable and manageable standards for resolving it; or the impossibility of deciding without an initial policy determination of a kind clearly for nonjudicial discretion; or the impossibility of a court's undertaking independent resolution without expressing lack of the respect due coordinate branches of government; or an unusual need for unquestioning adherence to a political decision already made; or the potentiality of embarrassment from multifarious pronouncements by various departments on one question."

Congress apparently directs its assertion of nonjusticiability to the first of the *Baker* factors by asserting that Chadha's claim is "an assault on the legislative authority to enact Section 244 (c) (2)." But if this turns the question into a political question virtually every challenge to the constitutionality of a statute would be a political question. Chadha indeed argues that one House of Congress cannot constitutionally veto the Attorney General's decision to allow him to remain in this country. No policy underlying the political question doctrine suggests that Congress or the executive, or both acting in concert and in compliance with Art. I, can decide the constitutionality of a statute; that is a decision for the courts.

Other *Baker* factors are likewise inapplicable to this case. As we discuss more fully below, Art. I provides the "judicially discoverable and manageable standards" of *Baker* for resolving the question presented by this case. Those standards forestall reliance by this Court on nonjudicial "policy determinations" or any showing of disrespect for a coordinate branch. Similarly, if Chadha's arguments are accepted, § 244 (c) (2) cannot stand, and, since the constitutionality of that statute is for this Court to resolve, there is no possibility of "multifarious pronouncements" on this question.

It is correct that this controversy may, in a sense, be termed "political." But the presence of constitutional issues with significant political overtones does not automatically invoke the political question doctrine. Resolution of litigation challenging the constitutional authority of one of the three branches cannot be evaded by courts because the issues have political implications in the sense urged by Congress. *Marbury* v. *Madison* (1803), was also a "political" case, involving as it did claims under a judicial commission alleged to have been duly signed by the President but not delivered. But "courts cannot reject as 'no law suit' a bona fide controversy as to whether some action denominated 'political' exceeds constitutional authority." *Baker* v. *Carr*. . . .

### III
#### A

We turn now to the question whether action of one House of Congress under § 244 (c) (2) violates strictures of the Constitution. We begin, of course, with the presumption that the challenged statute is valid. Its wisdom is not the concern of the courts; if a challenged action does not violate the Constitution, it must be sustained:

> "Once the meaning of an enactment is discerned and its constitutionality determined, the judicial process comes to an end. We do not sit as a committee of review, nor are we vested with the power of veto." *Tennessee Valley Authority* v. *Hill (1978).*

By the same token, the fact that a given law or procedure is efficient, convenient, and useful in facilitating functions of government, standing alone, will not save it if it is contrary to the Constitution. Convenience and efficiency are not the primary objectives— or the hallmarks—of democratic government and our inquiry is sharpened rather than blunted by the fact that Congressional veto provisions are appearing with increasing frequency in statutes which delegate authority to executive and independent agencies. . . .

JUSTICE WHITE undertakes to make a case for the proposition that the one-House veto is a useful "political invention," and we need not challenge that assertion. We can even concede this utilitarian argument although the long range political wisdom of this "invention" is arguable. It has been vigorously debated and it is instructive to compare the views of the protagonists. . . . But policy arguments supporting even useful "political inventions" are subject to the demands of the Constitution which defines powers and, with respect to this subject, sets out just how those powers are to be exercised.

Explicit and unambiguous provisions of the Constitution prescribe and define the respective functions of the Congress and of the Executive in the legislative process. Since the precise terms of those familiar provisions are critical to the resolution of this case, we set them out verbatim. Art. I provides:

> "All legislative Powers herein granted shall be vested in a Congress of the United States, which shall consist of a Senate *and* a House of Representatives." Art. I, § 1. (Emphasis added).
> "Every Bill which shall have passed the House of Representatives *and* the Senate, *shall,* before it become a Law, be presented to the President of the United States: . . ." Art. I, § 7, cl. 2. (Emphasis added).
> "*Every* Order, Resolution, or Vote to which the Concurrence of the Senate and House of Representatives may be necessary (except on a question of Adjournment) *shall be* presented to the President of the United States; and before the Same shall take effect, *shall be* approved by him, or being disap-

proved by him, *shall be* repassed by two thirds of the Senate and House of Representatives, according to the Rules and Limitations prescribed in the Case of a Bill." Art. I, § 7, cl. 3. (Emphasis added).

These provisions of Art. I are integral parts of the constitutional design for the separation of powers. We have recently noted that "[t]he principle of separation of powers was not simply an abstract generalization in the minds of the Framers: it was woven into the documents that they drafted in Philadelphia in the summer of 1787." *Buckley* v. *Valeo.* Just as we relied on the textual provision of Art. II, § 2, to vindicate the principle of separation of powers in *Buckley,* we find that the purposes underlying the Presentment Clauses, Art. I, § 7, cls. 2, 3, and the bicameral requirement of Art. I, § 1 and § 7, cl. 2, guide our resolution of the important question presented in this case. The very structure of the articles delegating and separating powers under Arts. I, II, and III exemplify the concept of separation of powers and we now turn to Art. I

## B
## The Presentment Clauses

The records of the Constitutional Convention reveal that the requirement that all legislation be presented to the President before becoming law was uniformly accepted by the Framers. Presentment to the President and the Presidential veto were considered so imperative that the draftsmen took special pains to assure that these requirements could not be circumvented. During the final debate on Art. I, § 7, cl. 2, James Madison expressed concern that it might easily be evaded by the simple expedient of calling a proposed law a "resolution" or "vote" rather than a "bill."

The decision to provide the President with a limited and qualified power to nullify proposed legislation by veto was based on the profound conviction of the Framers that the powers conferred on Congress were the powers to be most carefully circumscribed. It is beyond doubt that lawmaking was a power to be shared by both Houses and the President. In The Federalist No. 73, Hamilton focused on the President's role in making laws:

> "If even no propensity had ever discovered itself in the legislative body to invade the rights of the Executive, the rules of just reasoning and theoretic propriety would of themselves teach us that the one ought not to be left to the mercy of the other, but ought to possess a constitutional and effectual power of self-defense." . . .

The President's role in the lawmaking process also reflects the Framers' careful efforts to check whatever propensity a particular Congress might have to enact oppressive, improvident, or ill-considered measures. The President's veto role in the legislative process was described later during public debate on ratification:

> "It establishes a salutary check upon the legislative body, calculated to guard the community against the effects of faction, precipitancy, or of any impulse unfriendly to the public good which may happen to influence a majority of that body. . . . The primary inducement to conferring the power in question upon the Executive is to enable him to defend himself; the secondary one is to increase the chances in favor of the community against the passing of bad laws though haste, inadvertence, or design." The Federalist No. 73 (A. Hamilton).

See also *The Pocket Veto Case* (1929); *Myers* v. *United States* (1926). The Court also has observed that the Presentment Clauses serve the important purpose of assuring that a "national" perspective is grafted on the legislative process:

> "The President is a representative of the people just as the members of the Senate and of the House are, and it may

be, at some times, on some subjects, that the President elected by all the people is rather more representative of them all than are the members of either body of the Legislature whose constituencies are local and not countrywide. . . ." *Myers* v. *United States.*

## C
## Bicameralism

The bicameral requirement of Art. I, §§ 1, 7 was of scarcely less concern to the Framers than was the Presidential veto and indeed the two concepts are interdependent. By providing that no law could take effect without the concurrence of the prescribed majority of the Members of both Houses, the Framers reemphasized their belief, already remarked upon in connection with the Presentment Clauses, that legislation should not be enacted unless it has been carefully and fully considered by the Nation's elected officials. In the Constitutional Convention debates on the need for a bicameral legislature, James Wilson, later to become a Justice of this Court, commented:

> "Despotism comes on mankind in different shapes. Sometimes in an Executive, sometimes in a military, one. Is there danger of a Legislative despotism? Theory & practice both proclaim it. If the Legislative authority be not restrained, there can be neither liberty nor stability; and it can only be restrained by dividing it within itself, into distinct and independent branches. In a single house there is no check, but the inadequate one, of the virtue & good sense of those who compose it."

Hamilton argued that a Congress comprised of a single House was antithetical to the very purposes of the Constitution. Were the Nation to adopt a Constitution providing for only one legislative organ, he warned:

> "we shall finally accumulate, in a single body, all the most important prerogatives of sovereignty, and thus entail upon our posterity one of the most execrable forms of government that hu-

man infatuation ever contrived. Thus we should create in reality that very tyranny which the adversaries of the new Constitution either are, or affect to be, solicitous to avert." The Federalist No. 22.

This view was rooted in a general skepticism regarding the fallibility of human nature later commented on by Joseph Story:

> "Public bodies, like private persons, are occasionally under the dominion of strong passions and excitements; impatient, irritable, and impetuous.... If [a legislature] feels no check but its own will, it rarely has the firmness to insist upon holding a question long enough under its own view, to see and mark it in all its bearings and relations to society."

These observations are consistent with what many of the Framers expressed, none more cogently than Hamilton. . . :

> "In republican government, the legislative authority necessarily predominates. The remedy for this inconveniency is to divide the legislature into different branches; and to render them, by different modes of election and different principles of action, as little connected with each other as the nature of their common functions and their common dependence on the society will admit." The Federalist No. 51. . . .

However familiar, it is useful to recall that apart from their fear that special interests could be favored at the expense of public needs, the Framers were also concerned, although not of one mind, over the apprehensions of the smaller states. Those states feared a commonality of interest among the larger states would work to their disadvantage; representatives for the larger states, on the other hand, were skeptical of a legislature that could pass laws favoring a minority of the people. It need hardly be repeated here that the Great Compromise, under which one House was viewed as representing the people and the other the states, allayed the fears of both the large and small states.

We see therefore that the Framers were acutely conscious that the bicameral requirement and the Presentment Clauses would serve essential constitutional functions. The President's participation in the legislative process was to protect the Executive Branch from Congress and to protect the whole people from improvident laws. The division of the Congress into two distinctive bodies assures that the legislative power would be exercised only after opportunity for full study and debate in separate settings. The President's unilateral veto power, in turn, was limited by the power of two thirds of both Houses of Congress to overrule a veto thereby precluding final arbitrary action of one person. It emerges clearly that the prescription for legislative action in Art. I, §§ 1, 7 represents the Framers' decision that the legislative power of the Federal government be exercised in accord with a single, finely wrought and exhaustively considered, procedure.

## IV

The Constitution sought to divide the delegated powers of the new federal government into three defined categories, legislative, executive and judicial, to assure, as nearly as possible, that each Branch of government would confine itself to its assigned responsibility. The hydraulic pressure inherent within each of the separate branches to exceed the outer limits of its power, even to accomplish desirable objectives, must be resisted.

Although not "hermetically" sealed from one another, *Buckley* v. *Valeo,* the power delegated to the three Branches are functionally identifiable. When any Branch acts, it is presumptively exercising the power the Constitution has delegated to it. See *Hampton & Co.* v. *United States* (1928). When the Executive acts, it presumptively acts in an executive or administrative capacity as defined in Art. II. And when, as here, one House of Congress purports to act, it is presumptively acting within its assigned sphere.

Beginning with this presumption, we must nevertheless establish that the challenged action under § 244 (c) (2) is of the kind to which the procedural requirements of Art. I, § 7 apply. Not every action taken by either House is subject to the bicameralism and presentment requirements of Art. I. Whether actions taken by either House are, in law and fact, an exercise of legislative power depends not on their form but upon "whether they contain matter which is properly to be regarded as legislative in its character and effect."

Examination of the action taken here by one House pursuant to § 244 (c) (2) reveals that it was essentially legislative in purpose and effect. In purporting to exercise power defined in Art. I, § 8, cl. 4 to "establish an uniform Rule of Naturalization," the House took action that had the purpose and effect of altering the legal rights, duties and relations of persons, including the Attorney General, Executive Branch officials and Chadha, all outside the legislative branch. Section 244 (c) (2) purports to authorize one House of Congress to require the Attorney General to deport an individual alien whose deportation otherwise would be cancelled under § 244. The one-House veto operated in this case to overrule the Attorney General and mandate Chadha's deportation; absent the House action, Chadha would remain in the United States. Congress has *acted* and its action has altered Chadha's status.

The legislative character of the one-House veto in this case is confirmed by the character of the Congressional action it supplants. Neither the House of Representatives nor the Senate contends that, absent the veto provision in § 244 (c) (2), either of them, or both of them acting together, could effectively require the Attorney General to deport

an alien once the Attorney General, in the exercise of legislatively delegated authority, had determined the alien should remain in the United States. Without the challenged provision in § 244 (c) (2), this could have been achieved, if at all, only by legislation requiring deportation. Similarly, a veto by one House of Congress under § 244 (c) (2) cannot be justified as an attempt at amending the standards set out in § 244 (a) (1), or as a repeal of § 244 as applied to Chadha. Amendment and repeal of statutes, no less than enactment, must conform with Art. I.

The nature of the decision implemented by the one-House veto in this case further manifests its legislative character. After long experience with the clumsy, time consuming private bill procedure, Congress made a deliberate choice to delegate to the Executive Branch, and specifically to the Attorney General, the authority to allow deportable aliens to remain in this country in certain specified circumstances. It is not disputed that this choice to delegate authority is precisely the kind of decision that can be implemented only in accordance with the procedures set out in Art. I. Disagreement with the Attorney General's decision on Chadha's deportation—that is, Congress' decision to deport Chadha—no less than Congress' original choice to delegate to the Attorney General the authority to make that decision, involves determinations of policy that Congress can implement in only one way; bicameral passage followed by presentment to the President. Congress must abide by its delegation of authority until that delegation is legislatively altered or revoked.

Finally, we see that when the Framers intended to authorize either House of Congress to act alone and outside of its prescribed bicameral legislative role, they narrowly and precisely defined the procedure for such action. There are but four provisions in the Constitution, explicit and unambiguous, by which one

House may act alone with the unreviewable force of law, not subject to the President's veto:

(a) The House of Representatives alone was given the power to initiate impeachments. Art. I, § 2, cl. 6;

(b) The Senate alone was given the power to conduct trials following impeachment on charges initiated by the House and to convict following trial. Art. I, § 3, cl. 5;

(c) The Senate alone was given final unreviewable power to approve or to disapprove presidential appointments. Art. II, § 2, cl. 2;

(d) The Senate alone was given unreviewable power to ratify treaties negotiated by the President. Art. II, § 2, cl. 2.

Clearly, when the Draftsmen sought to confer special powers on one House, independent of the other House, or of the President, they did so in explicit, unambiguous terms. These carefully defined exceptions from presentment and bicameralism underscore the difference between the legislative functions of Congress and other unilateral but important and binding one-House acts provided for in the Constitution. These exceptions are narrow, explicit, and separately justified; none of them authorize the action challenged here. On the contrary, they provide further support for the conclusion that the veto provided for in § 244 (c) (2) is not authorized by the constitutional design of the powers of the Legislative Branch.

Since it is clear that the action by the House under § 244 (c) (2) was not within any of the express constitutional exceptions authorizing one House to act alone, and equally clear that it was an exercise of legislative power, that action was subject to the standards prescribed in Article I. The bicameral requirement, the Presentment Clauses, the President's veto, and Congress' power to override a veto were intended to erect enduring checks on each Branch and to protect the people from the improvident exercise of power by mandating certain prescribed steps. To preserve those checks, and maintain the separation of powers, the carefully defined limits on the power of each Branch must not be eroded. To accomplish what has been attempted by one House of Congress in this case requires action in conformity with the express procedures of the Constitution's prescription for legislative action: passage by a majority of both Houses and presentment to the President.

The veto authorized by § 244 (c) (2) doubtless has been in many respects a convenient shortcut; the "sharing" with the Executive by Congress of its authority over aliens in this manner is, on its face, an appealing compromise. In purely practical terms, it is obviously easier for action to be taken by one House without submission to the President; but it is crystal clear from the records of the Convention, contemporaneous writings and debates, that the Framers ranked other values higher than efficiency. The records of the Convention and debates in the States preceding ratification underscore the common desire to define and limit the exercise of the newly created federal powers affecting the states and the people. There is unmistakable expression of a determination that legislation by the national Congress be a step-by-step, deliberate and deliberative process.

The choices we discern as having been made in the Constitutional Convention impose burdens on governmental processes that often seem clumsy, inefficient, even unworkable, but those hard choices were consciously made by men who had lived under a form of government that permitted arbitrary governmental acts to go unchecked. There is no support in the Constitution or decisions of this Court for the proposition that the cumbersomeness and delays often encountered in complying with explicit Constitutional standards may be avoided, either by the Congress or by the President. See *Youngstown Sheet & Tube Co.* v. *Sawyer* (1952). With all the obvious flaws of delay, untidiness, and potential for abuse, we have not yet found a better way to preserve freedom than by making the exercise of power subject to the carefully crafted restraints spelled out in the Constitution.

## V

We hold that the Congressional veto provision in § 244 (c) (2) is severable from the Act and that it is unconstitutional. Accordingly, the judgment of the Court of Appeals is

*Affirmed.*

JUSTICE WHITE, dissenting.

Today the Court not only invalidates § 244 (c) (2) of the Immigration and Nationality Act, but also sounds the death knell for nearly 200 other statutory provisions in which Congress has reserved a "legislative veto." For this reason, the Court's decision is of surpassing importance. And it is for this reason that the Court would have been well-advised to decide the case, if possible, on the narrower grounds of separation of powers, leaving for full consideration the constitutionality of other congressional review statutes operating on such varied matters as war powers and agency rulemaking, some of which concern the independent regulatory agencies.

The prominence of the legislative veto mechanism in our contemporary political system and its importance to Congress can hardly be overstated. It has become a central means by which Congress secures the accountability of executive and independent agencies. Without the legislative veto, Congress is faced with a Hobson's choice: either to refrain from delegating the necessary authority, leaving itself with a hopeless task of writing laws with the requisite specificity to cover endless special circumstances across the entire policy landscape, or in the alternative, to abdicate its lawmaking function to the executive branch and independent agencies. To choose the former leaves major national problems unresolved; to opt for the latter risks unaccountable policymaking by those not elected to fill that role. Accordingly, over the past five decades, the legislative veto has been placed in nearly 200 statutes. The device is known in every field of governmental concern: reorganization, budgets, foreign affairs, war powers, and regulation of trade, safety, energy, the environment and the economy.

## I

The legislative veto developed initially in response to the problems of reorganizing the sprawling government structure created in response to the Depression. The Reorganization Acts established the chief model for the legislative veto. When President Hoover requested authority to reorganize the government in 1929, he coupled his request that the "Congress be willing to delegate its authority over the problem (subject to defined principles) to the Executive" with a proposal for legislative review. He proposed that the Executive "should act upon approval of a joint committee of Congress or with the reservation of power of revision by Congress within some limited period adequate for its consideration." Congress followed President Hoover's suggestion and authorized reorganization subject to legislative review. Although the reorganization authority reenacted in 1933 did not contain a legislative veto provision, the provision returned during the Roosevelt Administration and has since been renewed numerous times. Over the years, the provision was used extensively. Presidents submitted 115 reorganization plans to Congress of which 23 were disapproved by Congress pursuant to legislative veto provisions.

Shortly after adoption of the Reorganization Act of 1939, Congress and the President applied the legislative veto procedure to resolve the delegation problem for national security and foreign affairs. World War II occasioned the need to transfer greater authority to the President in these areas. The legislative veto offered the means by which Congress could confer additional authority while preserving its own constitutional role. During World War II, Congress enacted over thirty statutes conferring powers on the Executive with legislative veto provisions. President Roosevelt accepted the veto as the necessary price for obtaining exceptional authority.

Over the quarter century following World War II, Presidents continued to accept legislative vetoes by one or both Houses as constitutional, while regularly denouncing provisions by which Congressional committees reviewed Executive activity. The legislative veto balanced delegations of statutory authority in new areas of governmental involvement: the space program, international agreements on nuclear energy, tariff arrangements, and adjustment of federal pay rates.

During the 1970's the legislative veto was important in resolving a series of major constitutional disputes between the President and Congress over claims of the President to broad impoundment, war, and national emergency powers. The key provision of the War Powers Resolution, 50 U.S.C. § 1544 (c), authorizes the termination by concurrent resolution of the use of armed forces in hostilities. A similar measure resolved the problem posed by Presidential claims of inherent power to impound appropriations. In conference, a compromise was achieved under which permanent impoundments, termed "rescissions," would require approval through enactment of legislation. In contrast, temporary impoundments, or "deferrals," would become effective unless disapproved by one House. This compromise provided the President with flexibility, while preserving ultimate Congressional control over the budget. Although the War Powers Resolution was enacted over President Nixon's veto, the Impoundment Control Act was enacted with the President's approval. These statutes were followed by others resolving similar problems. . . .

In the energy field, the legislative veto served to balance broad delegations in legislation emerging from the energy crisis of the 1970's. In the educational field, it was found that fragmented and narrow grant programs "inevitably lead to Executive-Legislative confrontations" because they inaptly limited the Commissioner of Education's authority. The response was to grant the Commissioner of Education rulemaking authority, subject to a legislative veto. In the trade regulation area, the veto preserved Congressional authority over the Federal Trade Commission's broad mandate to make rules to prevent businesses from engaging in "unfair or deceptive acts or practices in commerce."

Even this brief review suffices to demonstrate that the legislative veto is more than "efficient, convenient, and useful." It is an important if not indispensable political invention that allows the President and Congress to resolve major constitutional and policy differences, assures the accountability of independent regulatory agencies, and preserves Congress' control over lawmaking. Perhaps there are other means of accommodation and accountability, but the increasing reliance of Congress upon the legislative veto suggests that the alternatives to which Congress must now turn are not entirely satisfactory.

The history of the legislative veto also makes clear that it has not been a sword with which Congress has struck out to aggrandize itself at the expense of the other branches—the concerns of Madison and Hamilton. Rather, the veto has been a means of defense, a reservation of ultimate authority necessary if Congress is to fulfill its designated role under Article I as the nation's lawmaker. While the President has often objected to particular legislative vetoes, generally those left in the hands of congressional committees, the Executive has more often agreed to legislative review as the price for a broad delegation of authority. To be sure, the President may have preferred unrestricted power, but that could be precisely why Congress thought it essential to retain a check on the exercise of delegated authority.

## II

For all these reasons, the apparent sweep of the Court's decision today is regrettable. The Court's Article I analysis appears to invalidate all legislative vetoes irrespective of form or subject. Because the legislative veto is commonly found as a check upon rulemaking by administrative agencies and upon broad-based policy decisions of the Executive Branch, it is particularly unfortunate that the Court reaches its decision in a case involving the exercise of a veto over deportation decisions regarding particular individuals. Courts should always be wary of striking statutes as unconstitutional; to strike an entire class of statutes based on consideration of a somewhat atypical and more-readily indictable exemplar of the class is irresponsible. It was for cases such as this one that Justice Brandeis wrote:

> "The Court has frequently called attention to the 'great gravity and delicacy' of its function in passing upon the validity of an act of Congress.... The Court will not 'formulate a rule of constitutional law broader than is required by the precise facts to which it is to be

applied.' *Liverpool, N.Y. & P.S.S. Co. v. Emigration Commissioners, supra.*" *Ashwander* v. *Tennessee Valley Authority* (1936) (concurring opinion).

Unfortunately, today's holding is not so limited.

If the legislative veto were as plainly unconstitutional as the Court strives to suggest, its broad ruling today would be more comprehensible. But, the constitutionality of the legislative veto is anything but clearcut. The issue divides scholars, courts, attorneys general, and the two other branches of the National Government. If the veto devices so flagrantly disregarded the requirements of Article I as the Court today suggests, I find it incomprehensible that Congress, whose members are bound by oath to uphold the Constitution, would have placed these mechanisms in nearly 200 separate laws over a period of 50 years.

The reality of the situation is that the constitutional question posed today is one of immense difficulty over which the executive and legislative branches—as well as scholars and judges—have understandably disagreed. That disagreement stems from the silence of the Constitution on the precise question: The Constitution does not directly authorize or prohibit the legislative veto. Thus, our task should be to determine whether the legislative veto is consistent with the purposes of Art. I and the principles of Separation of Powers which are reflected in that Article and throughout the Constitution. We should not find the lack of a specific constitutional authorization for the legislative veto surprising, and I would not infer disapproval of the mechanism from its absence. From the summer of 1787 to the present the government of the United States has become an endeavor far beyond the contemplation of the Framers. Only within the last half century has the complexity and size of the Federal Government's responsibilities grown so greatly that the Congress must rely on the legislative veto as the most effective if not the only means to insure their role as the nation's lawmakers. But the wisdom of the Framers was to anticipate that the nation would grow and new problems of governance would require different solutions. Accordingly, our Federal Government was intentionally chartered with the flexibility to respond to contemporary needs without losing sight of fundamental democratic principles. . . .

This is the perspective from which we should approach the novel constitutional questions presented by the legislative veto. In my view, neither Article I of the Constitution nor the doctrine of separation of powers is violated by this mechanism by which our elected representatives reserve their voice in the governance of the nation.

## III

The Court holds that the disapproval of a suspension of deportation by the resolution of one House of Congress is an exercise of legislative power without compliance with the prerequisites for lawmaking set forth in Art. I of the Constitution. Specifically, the Court maintains that the provisions of § 244 (c) (2) are inconsistent with the requirement of bicameral approval, implicit in Art. I, § 1, and the requirement that all bills and resolutions that require the concurrence of both Houses be presented to the President, Art. I, § 7, cl. 2 and 3.

I do not dispute the Court's truismatic exposition of these clauses. There is no question that a bill does not become a law until it is approved by both the House and the Senate, and presented to the President. Similarly, I would not hesitate to strike an action of Congress in the form of a concurrent resolution which constituted an exercise of original lawmaking authority. I agree with the court that the President's qualified veto power is a critical element in the distribution of powers un-

der the Constitution, widely endorsed among the Framers, and intended to serve the President as a defense against legislative encroachment and to check the "passing of bad laws through haste, inadvertence, or design." The records of the Convention reveal that it is the first purpose which figured most prominently but I acknowledge the vitality of the second. I also agree that the bicameral approval required by Art. I, §§ 1, 7 "was of scarcely less concern to the Framers than was the Presidential veto" and that the need to divide and disperse legislative power figures significantly in our scheme of Government. All of this, the Third Part of the Court's opinion, is entirely unexceptionable.

It does not, however, answer the constitutional question before us. The power to exercise a legislative veto is not the power to write new law without bicameral approval or presidential consideration. The veto must be authorized by statute and may only negative [sic] what an Executive department or independent agency has proposed. On its face, the legislative veto no more allows one House of Congress to make law than does the presidential veto confer such power upon the President. . . .

### A

. . . When the Convention did turn its attention to the scope of Congress' lawmaking power, the Framers were expansive. The Necessary and Proper Clause, Art. I, § 8, cl. 18, vests Congress with the power "to make all laws which shall be necessary and proper for carrying into Execution the foregoing Powers [the enumerated powers of § 8], and all other Powers vested by this Constitution in the government of the United States, or in any Department or Officer thereof." It is long-settled that Congress may "exercise its best judgment in the selection of measures, to carry into execution the constitutional powers of the government," and "avail itself of experience, to exercise its reason, and to accommodate its legislation to circumstances," *McCulloch* v. *Maryland* 420 (1819).

## B

The Court heeded this counsel in approving the modern administrative state. The Court's holding today that all legislative-type action must be enacted through the lawmaking process ignores that legislative authority is routinely delegated to the Executive branch, to the independent regulatory agencies, and to private individuals and groups....

The wisdom and the constitutionality of these broad delegations are matters that still have not been put to rest. But for present purposes, these cases establish that by virtue of congressional delegation, legislative power can be exercised by independent agencies and Executive departments without the passage of new legislation. For some time, the sheer amount of law—the substantive rules that regulate private conduct and direct the operation of government—made by the agencies has far outnumbered the lawmaking engaged in by Congress through the traditional process. There is no question but that agency rulemaking is lawmaking in any functional or realistic sense of the term....

If Congress may delegate lawmaking power to independent and executive agencies, it is most difficult to understand Article I as forbidding Congress from also reserving a check on legislative power for itself. Absent the veto, the agencies receiving delegations of legislative or quasi-legislative power may issue regulations having the force of law without bicameral approval and without the President's signature. It is thus not apparent why the reservation of a veto over the exercise of that legis-

lative power must be subject to a more exacting test. In both cases, it is enough that the initial statutory authorizations comply with the Article I requirements....

The Court's opinion in the present case comes closest to facing the reality of administrative lawmaking in considering the contention that the Attorney General's action in suspending deportation under § 244 is itself a legislative act. The Court posits that the Attorney General is acting in an Article II enforcement capacity under § 244. This characterization is at odds with *Mahler* v. *Eby* (1924), where the power conferred on the Executive to deport aliens was considered a delegation of legislative power. The Court suggests, however, that the Attorney General acts in an Article II capacity because "[t]he courts when a case or controversy arises, can always 'ascertain whether the will of Congress has been obeyed,' *Yakus* v. *United States* (1944), and can enforce adherence to statutory standards." This assumption is simply wrong, as the Court itself points out: "We are aware of no decision ... where a federal court has reviewed a decision of the Attorney General suspending deportation of an alien pursuant to the standards set out in § 244 (a) (1). This is not surprising, given that no party to such action has either the motivation or the right to appeal from it." It is perhaps on the erroneous premise that judicial review may check abuses of the § 244 power that the Court also submits that "The bicameral process is not necessary as a check on the Executive's administration of the laws because his administrative activity cannot reach beyond the limits of the statute that created it—a statute duly enacted pursuant to Article I."

More fundamentally, even if the Court correctly characterizes the Attorney General's authority under § 244 as an Article II Executive power, the

Court concedes that certain administrative agency action, such as rulemaking, "may resemble lawmaking" and recognizes that "[t]his Court has referred to agency activity as being 'quasi-legislative' in character. *Humphrey's Executor* v. *United States* (1935)." Such rules and adjudications by the agencies meet the Court's own definition of legislative action for they "alter[] the legal rights, duties, and relations of persons ... outside the legislative branch" and involve "determinations of policy." Under the Court's analysis, the Executive Branch and the independent agencies may make rules with the effect of law while Congress, in whom the Framers confided the legislative power, Art. I, § 1, may not exercise a veto which precludes such rules from having operative force. If the effective functioning of a complex modern government requires the delegation of vast authority which, by virtue of its breadth, is legislative or "quasi-legislative" in character, I cannot accept that Article I—which is, after all, the source of the nondelegation doctrine—should forbid Congress from qualifying that grant with a legislative veto.

## C

The Court also takes no account of perhaps the most relevant consideration: However resolutions of disapproval under § 244 (c) (2) are formally characterized, in reality, a departure from the status quo occurs only upon the concurrence of opinion among the House, Senate, and President. Reservations of legislative authority to be exercised by Congress should be upheld if the exercise of such reserved authority is consistent with the distribution of and limits upon legislative power that Article I provides....

[Section 1 Omitted]

### 2

The central concern of the presentation and bicameralism requirements of Article I is that when a departure from the legal status quo is undertaken, it is done with the approval of the President and both Houses of Congress—or, in the event of a presidential veto, a two-thirds majority in both Houses. This interest is fully satisfied by the operation of § 244 (c) (2). The President's approval is found in the Attorney General's action in recommending to Congress that the deportation order for a given alien be suspended. The House and the Senate indicate their approval of the Executive's action by not passing a resolution of disapproval within the statutory period. Thus, a change in the legal status quo—the deportability of the alien—is consummated only with the approval of each of the three relevant actors. The disagreement of any one of the three maintains the alien's pre-existing status: the Executive may choose not to recommend suspension; the House and Senate may each veto the recommendation. The effect on the rights and obligations of the affected individuals and upon the legislative system is precisely the same as if a private bill were introduced but failed to receive the necessary approval. "The President and the two Houses enjoy exactly the same say in what the law is to be as would have been true for each without the presence of the one-House veto, and nothing in the law is changed absent the concurrence of the President and a majority in each House.". . .

This very construction of the Presentment Clauses which the Executive branch now rejects was the basis upon which the Executive Branch defended the constitutionality of the Reorganization Act, 5 U.S.C. § 906 (a) (1979), which provides that the President's proposed reorganization plans take effect only if not vetoed by either House. When the Department of Justice advised the Senate on the constitutionality of congressional review in reorganization legislation in 1949, it stated: "In this procedure there is no question involved of the Congress taking legislative action beyond its initial passage of the Reorganization Act." This also represents the position of the Attorney General more recently.

Thus understood, § 244 (c) (2) fully effectuates the purposes of the bicameralism and presentation requirements. I now briefly consider possible objections to the analysis.

First, it may be asserted that Chadha's status before legislative disapproval is one of nondeportation and that the exercise of the veto, unlike the failure of a private bill, works a change in the status quo. This position plainly ignores the statutory language. At no place in § 244 has Congress delegated to the Attorney General any final power to determine which aliens shall be allowed to remain in the United States. Congress has retained the ultimate power to pass on such changes in deportable status. By its own terms, § 244 (a) states that whatever power the Attorney General has been delegated to suspend deportation and adjust status is to be exercisable only "as hereinafter prescribed in this section." Subsection (c) is part of that section. A grant of "suspension" does not cancel the alien's deportation or adjust the alien's status to that of a permanent resident alien. A suspension order is merely a "deferment of deportation," *McGrath* v. *Kristensen* (1950), which can mature into a cancellation of deportation and adjustment of status only upon the approval of Congress—by way of silence—under § 244 (c) (2). Only then does the statute authorize the Attorney General to "cancel deportation proceedings" § 244 (c) (2), and "record the alien's lawful admission for permanent residence. . . ." § 244 (d). The Immigration and Naturalization Service's action, on behalf of the Attorney General, "cannot become effective without ratification by Congress." Until that ratification occurs, the executive's action is simply a recommendation that Congress finalize the suspension—in itself, it works no legal change. . . .

## IV

The Court of Appeals struck § 244 (c) (2) as violative of the constitutional principle of separation of powers. It is true that the purpose of separating the authority of government is to prevent unnecessary and dangerous concentration of power in one branch. For that reason, the Framers saw fit to divide and balance the powers of government so that each branch would be checked by the others. Virtually every part of our constitutional system bears the mark of this judgment.

But the history of the separation of powers doctrine is also a history of accommodation and practicality. Apprehensions of an overly powerful branch have not led to undue prophylactic measures that handicap the effective working of the national government as a whole. The Constitution does not contemplate total separation of the three branches of Government. *Buckley* v. *Valeo* (1976). "[A] hermetic sealing off of the three branches of Government from one another would preclude the establishment of a Nation capable of governing itself effectively."

Our decisions reflect this judgment. As already noted, the Court, recognizing that modern government must address a formidable agenda of complex policy issues, countenanced the delegation of extensive legislative authority to executive and independent agencies. *[J. W.] Hampton & Co.* v. *United States* (1928). The separation of powers doctrine has heretofore led to the invalidation of government action only when the challenged action violated some express provision in the Constitution. In *Buckley* v. *Valeo* (1976) (per curiam) and *Myers* v. *United States* (1926), congressional action comprised the appointment power of the President. See also *Springer* v. *Philippine Islands* (1928). In *United States* v. *Klein* (1871), an Act of Congress was struck for encroaching upon judicial power, but the Court found that the Act also impinged upon the executive's exclusive pardon power. Art. II, § 2. Because we must have a workable efficient government, this is as it should be.

This is the teaching of *Nixon* v. *Administrator of Gen. Servs.* (1977), which, in rejecting a separation of powers objection to a law requiring that the administrator take custody of certain presidential papers, set forth a framework for evaluating such claims:

"[I]n determining whether the Act disrupts the proper balance between the coordinate branches, the proper inquiry focuses on the extent to which it prevents the Executive Branch from accomplishing its constitutionally assigned functions. *United States* v. *Nixon.* Only where the potential for disruption is present must we then determine whether that impact is justified by an overriding need to promote objectives within the constitutional authority of Congress."

Section 244 (c) (2) survives this test. The legislative veto provision does not "prevent the Executive Branch from accomplishing its constitutionally assigned functions." First, it is clear that the Executive branch has no "constitutionally assigned" function of suspending the deportation of aliens. " 'Over no conceivable subject is the legislative power of Congress more complete than it is over' the admission of aliens." *Kleindiest* v. *Mandel* (1972), quoting *Oceanic Steam Navigation Co.* v. *Stranahan* (1909). Nor can it be said that the inherent function of the Executive Branch in executing the law is involved. *The Steel Seizure Case* resolved that the Article II mandate for the President to execute the law is a directive to enforce the law which Con-

gress has written. *Youngstown Sheet & Tube Co.* v. *Sawyer* (1952). "The duty of the President to see that the laws be executed is a duty that does not go beyond the laws or require him to achieve more than Congress sees fit to leave within his power." *Myers* v. *United States* (Holmes, J., dissenting); (Brandeis, J., dissenting). Here, § 244 grants the executive only a qualified suspension authority and it is only that authority which the President is constitutionally authorized to execute.

Moreover, the Court believes that the legislative veto we consider today is best characterized as an exercise of legislative or quasi-legislative authority. Under this characterization, the practice does not, even on the surface, constitute an infringement of executive or judicial prerogative. The Attorney General's suspension of deportation is equivalent to a proposal for legislation. The nature of the Attorney General's role as recommendatory is not altered because § 244 provides for congressional action through disapproval rather than by ratification. In comparison to private bills, which must be initiated in the Congress and which allow a Presidential veto to be overridden by a two-thirds majority in both Houses of Congress, § 244 augments rather than reduces the executive branches' authority. So understood, congressional review does not undermine ... the decisions of the Executive Branch.

Nor does § 244 infringe on the judicial power, as JUSTICE POWELL would hold. Section 244 makes clear that Congress has reserved its own judgment as part of the statutory process. Congressional action does not substitute for judicial review of the Attorney General's decision. The Act provides for judicial review of the refusal of the Attorney General to suspend a deportation and to transmit a recommendation to Congress. *INS* v. *Wang*, (1981) (per curiam). But the courts have not been given the authority to review whether an alien should be given permanent status; review is limited to whether the Attorney General has properly applied the statutory standards for essentially denying the alien a recommendation that his deportable status be changed by the Congress. Moreover, there is no constitutional obligation to provide any judicial review whatever for a failure to suspend deportation. "The power of Congress, therefore, to expel, like the power to exclude aliens, or any specified class of aliens, from the country, may be exercised entirely through executive officers; or Congress may call in the aid of the judiciary to ascertain any contested facts on which an alien's right to be in the country has been made by Congress to depend." *Fong Yue Ting* v. *United States* (1893). See also *Tutun* v. *United States* (1926); *Ludecke* v. *Watkins* (1948); *Harisiades* v. *Shaughnessy* (1952).

I do not suggest that all legislative vetoes are necessarily consistent with separation of powers principles. A legislative check on an inherently executive function, for example that of initiating prosecutions, poses an entirely different question. But the legislative veto device here—and in many other settings—is far from an instance of legislative tyranny over the Executive. It is a necessary check on the unavoidably expanding power of the agencies, both executive and independent, as they engage in exercising authority delegated by Congress.

## V

I regret that I am in disagreement with my colleagues on the fundamental questions that this case presents. But even more I regret the destructive scope of the Court's holding. It reflects a profoundly different conception of the Constitution than that held by the courts which sanctioned the modern administrative state. Today's decision strikes down in one fell swoop provisions in more laws enacted by Congress than the Court has cumulatively invalidated in its history. I fear it will now be more difficult "to insure that the fundamental policy decisions in our society will be made not by an appointed official but by the body immediately responsible to the people," *Arizona* v. *California* (1963) (Harlan, J., dissenting). I must dissent.

# Ronald Reagan's Grenada Invasion Address (1983)

On the morning of October 25, 1983, a nineteen-hundred-member force of U.S. Marines and Army Rangers invaded the island of Grenada, the smallest of the Windward Islands, around ninety miles north of Venezuela. Two weeks earlier, the elected government of Grenada had been taken over in a coup by pro-Soviet, pro-Cuban military officers. On October 23 the U.S. government had received a formal request from five member nations of the Organization of Eastern Caribbean States (OECS) to restore order and democracy to Grenada. The next evening, with U.S. forces already on their way, President Ronald Reagan privately informed congressional leaders that he intended to intervene militarily.

The Grenada invasion, which involved almost six thousand troops within a few days, went well. In the wake of the coup, the Reagan administration had feared for the safety of approximately eight hundred American medical students who were enrolled at St. George's University School of Medicine. The campus was secured, and the grateful students were sent home to the United States on the first day of the invasion. (Several kissed the airport tarmac after their plane touched down.) During the next week, U.S. forces defeated the defending army of Grenadians and Cubans and

arrested the leaders of the military coup. In all, eighteen American soldiers died in combat, compared with forty-five Grenadian and twenty-four Cuban soldiers. A democratic government was restored to Grenada.

Initially, international and congressional reaction to the Grenada invasion was negative. On October 26, for example, a majority of delegates to an Organization of American States meeting condemned the action as unduly aggressive. Democrats in Congress regarded the crisis as overblown and the victory as trivial. The entire 110,000-person population of Grenada, some pointed out, could be seated in the University of Michigan's football stadium.

Reagan gave a televised address to the nation on October 27. Describing the request of the OECS nations, his concern for the American medical students, and his fears of a Cuban takeover of Grenada, the president evoked a strong positive response from the viewing audience at home. A Washington Post/ABC News poll on November 9, for example, showed that 71 percent of the American people supported the invasion.

The Grenada invasion was popular—and, going into an election year, politically potent—for several reasons. The victory, however minor, came just two days after more than 240 U.S.

*Marines, stationed at the airport in Beirut, Lebanon, were killed by a terrorist bomb. It also contrasted sharply with the futility of the government's anti-Communist policies in Nicaragua. (See "Report of the Tower Commission," p. 474.) Finally, the jubilant return of the medical students offered a happy counterpoint to the capture and long custody of the American hostages in Iran four years earlier.* ~

. . . [In addition to Lebanon] another part of the world is very much on our minds, a place much closer to our shores: Grenada. The island is only twice the size of the District of Columbia, with a total population of about 110,000 people.

Grenada and a half dozen other Caribbean islands here were, until recently, British colonies. They're now independent states and members of the British Commonwealth. While they respect each other's independence, they also feel a kinship with each other and think of themselves as one people.

In 1979 trouble came to Grenada. Maurice Bishop, a protégé of Fidel Castro, staged a military coup and overthrew the government which had been elected under the constitution left to the people by the British. He sought the help of Cuba in building an airport, which he claimed was for tourist trade, but which looked suspiciously suitable for military aircraft, including Soviet-built long-range bombers.

The six sovereign countries and one remaining colony are joined together in what they call the Organization of Eastern Caribbean States. The six became increasingly alarmed as Bishop built an army greater than all of their combined. Obviously, it was not purely for defense.

In this last year or so, Prime Minister Bishop gave indications that he might like better relations with the United States. He even made a trip to our country and met with senior officials of the White House and the State Department. Whether he was serious or not, we'll never know. On October 12th, a small group in his militia seized him and put him under arrest. They were, if anything, more radical and more devoted to Castro's Cuba than he had been.

Several days later, a crowd of citizens appeared before Bishop's home, freed him, and escorted him toward the headquarters of the military council. They were fired upon. A number, including some children, were killed, and Bishop was seized. He and several members of his cabinet were subsequently executed, and a 24-hour shoot-to-kill curfew was put in effect. Grenada was without a government, its only authority exercised by a self-proclaimed band of military men.

There were then about 1,000 of our citizens on Grenada, 800 of them students in St. George's University Medical School. Concerned that they'd be harmed or held as hostages, I ordered a flotilla of ships, then on its way to Lebanon with marines, part of our regular rotation program, to circle south on a course that would put them somewhere in the vicinity of Grenada in case there should be a need to evacuate our people.

Last weekend, I was awakened in the early morning hours and told that six members of the Organization of Eastern Caribbean States, joined by Jamaica and Barbados, had sent an urgent request that we join them in a military operation to restore order and democracy to Grenada. They were proposing this action under the terms of a treaty, a mutual assistance pact that existed among them.

These small, peaceful nations needed our help. Three of them don't have armies at all, and the others have very limited forces. The legitimacy of their request, plus my own concern for our citizens, dictated my decision. I believe our government has a responsibility to go the aid of its citizens, if their right to life and liberty is threatened. The nightmare of our hostages in Iran must never be repeated.

We knew we had little time and that complete secrecy was vital to ensure both the safety of the young men who would undertake this mission and the Americans they were about to rescue. The Joint Chiefs worked around the clock to come up with a plan. They had little intelligence information about conditions on the island.

We had to assume that several hundred Cubans working on the airport could be military reserves. Well, as it turned out, the number was much larger, and they were a military force. Six hundred of them have been taken prisoner, and we have discovered a complete base with weapons and communications equipment, which makes it clear a Cuban occupation of the island had been planned.

Two hours ago we released the first photos from Grenada. They included pictures of a warehouse of military equipment—one of three we've uncovered so far. This warehouse contained weapons and ammunition stacked almost to the ceiling, enough to supply thousands of terrorists. Grenada, we were told, was a friendly island paradise for tourism. Well, it wasn't. It was a Soviet-Cuban colony, being readied as a major military bastion to export terror and undermine democracy. We got there just in time.

I can't say enough in praise of our military—Army rangers and paratroopers, Navy, Marine, and Air Force personnel—those who planned a brilliant campaign and those who carried it out. Almost instantly, our military seized the two airports, secured the campus where most of our students were, and are now in the mopping-up phase.

It should be noted that in all the planning, a top priority was to minimize risk, to avoid casualties to our own men and also the Grenadian forces as much as humanly possible. But there were casualties, and we all owe a debt to those who lost their lives or were wounded. They were few in number, but even one is a tragic price to pay.

It's our intention to get our men out as soon as possible. Prime Minister Eugenia Charles of Dominia . . . she is Chairman of the OECS. She's calling for help from Commonwealth nations in giving the people their right to establish a constitutional government on Grenada. We anticipate that the Governor General, a Grenadian, will participate in setting up a provisional government in the interim.

. . . It is no coincidence that when the thugs tried to wrest control over Grenada, there were 30 Soviet advisers and hundreds of Cuban military and paramilitary forces on the island. At the moment of our landing, we communicated with the Governments of Cuba and the Soviet Union and told them we would offer shelter and security to their people on Grenada. Regrettably, Castro ordered his men to fight to the death, and some did. The others will be sent to their homelands.

You know, there was a time when our national security was based on a standing army here within our own borders and shore batteries of artillery along our coasts, and, of course, a navy to keep the sea lanes open for the shipping of things necessary to our well-being. The world has changed. Today, our national security can be threatened in faraway places. It's up to all of us to be aware of the strategic importance of such places and to be able to identify them. . . .

# Transfer of Power from President Ronald Reagan to Vice President George Bush (1985)

Section 3 of the Twenty-fifth Amendment (1967) created a procedure for a disabled president to transfer temporarily the powers and duties of the office to the vice president. It states, "Whenever the President transmits to the President pro tempore of the Senate and the Speaker of the House of Representatives his written declaration that he is unable to discharge the powers and duties of his office, and until he transmits to them a written declaration to the contrary, such powers and duties shall be discharged by the Vice President as Acting President." The section essentially codified the main elements of the informal arrangement that President Dwight D. Eisenhower had made with Vice President Richard Nixon in 1958 and that subsequent presidents had made with their vice presidents. (See "Dwight D. Eisenhower's Presidential Disability Letter," p. 342.)

President Ronald Reagan was criticized for not invoking the Twenty-fifth Amendment after he was shot on March 30, 1981. Although Reagan was conscious and alert before undergoing surgery, several of his close aides decided not to discuss the amendment with him for fear that a disability declaration might create public confusion about who was running the country. In truth, confusion ensued from the decision not to invoke the Twenty-fifth

Amendment. In an unsuccessful effort to calm public fears, Secretary of State Alexander Haig breathlessly (and inaccurately) told the news media and a national television audience that, constitutionally, he was "in control," at least until Vice President George Bush returned to Washington from Texas.

Reagan and his aides later argued that if the need for an acting president had arisen during his surgery or if medical complications had developed, Bush and the cabinet could have invoked section 4 of the amendment. That section (also similar to the Eisenhower-Nixon arrangement) empowers the vice president and a majority of the heads of the departments—voting separately—to declare the vice president to be acting president if the president cannot. (In a departure from the Eisenhower letter, section 4 also empowers the vice president and cabinet to make such a determination if the president is able but unwilling to do so, as in the case of a mentally ill president.)

On July 13, 1985, preparing for cancer surgery, Reagan did transfer power to Vice President Bush, the first such transfer in history. Following the new constitutional procedure, Reagan sent separate letters to the Speaker of the House of Representatives and the president pro tempore of the Senate to announce both the beginning of the *transfer and the end. For eight hours, Bush was acting president. He spent the time at home, playing tennis and chatting with friends.*

*Curiously, although Reagan's transfer of power to Bush clearly fell under the terms of the Twenty-fifth Amendment, his letters to the Speaker and president pro tempore did not invoke the amendment explicitly. Indeed, Reagan stated his view that the amendment was not meant to apply to "such brief and temporary periods of incapacity."*   ~

Dear Mr. President: (Dear Mr. Speaker:)

I am about to undergo surgery during which time I will be briefly and temporarily incapable of discharging the Constitutional powers and duties of the Office of the President of the United States.

After consultation with my counsel and the Attorney General, I am mindful of the provisions of Section 3 of the 25th Amendment to the Constitution and of the uncertainties of its application to such brief and temporary periods of incapacity. I do not believe that

the drafters of this Amendment intended its application to situations such as the instant one.

Nevertheless, consistent with my long-standing arrangement with Vice President George Bush, and not intending to set a precedent binding anyone privileged to hold this Office in the future, I have determined and it is my intention and direction that Vice President George Bush shall discharge those powers and duties in my stead commencing with the administration of anesthesia to me in this instance.

I shall advise you and the Vice President when I determine that I am able to resume the discharge of the Constitutional powers and duties of this Office.

May God bless this Nation and us all.

Dear Mr. President: (Dear Mr. Speaker:)

Following up on my letter to you of this date, please be advised I am able to resume the discharge of the Constitutional powers and duties of the Office of the President of the United States. I have informed the Vice President of my determination and my resumption of those powers.

# Report of the Tower Commission (1987)

In 1984 Ronald Reagan won a forty-nine-state reelection landslide against the Democratic presidential nominee, former vice president Walter F. Mondale. Yet, as with the three other twentieth-century presidents who won comparable victories—Franklin D. Roosevelt in 1936, Lyndon B. Johnson in 1964, and Richard Nixon in 1972—the Reagan administration began its second term by committing a politically self-destructive act. Like Roosevelt's Court-packing scheme, Johnson's rapid escalation of the U.S. role in the war in Vietnam, and Nixon's Watergate coverup, Reagan's involvement in what came to be called the Iran-contra affair was born of an excessive exercise of presidential power by his administration. (See "Roosevelt's 'Court-packing' Address," p. 270; "Johnson's Tonkin Gulf Message," p. 364; "United States v. Nixon," p. 397; "Nixon's 'Smoking Gun' Tapes," p. 410; and "Nixon's Resignation Speech." p. 415.)

The Iran-contra affair included two secret efforts by the Reagan administration: the sale of U.S. weapons to the government of Iran and the diversion of the proceeds from those sales to the contra rebels in Nicaragua, who were fighting a civil war against the Communist Sandinista government.

The secret weapons sales to the Iranian government of the Ayatollah Khomeini, which took place in 1985 and 1986, diverged sharply from the Reagan administration's much-celebrated antiterrorism policy. When evidence of the sales was uncovered by the press in early November 1986, Reagan initially said that they represented a delicate diplomatic effort to cultivate moderate elements in the Iranian regime. Later, the president admitted that he also had hoped to persuade Iran to secure the release of several Americans who were being held hostage in Lebanon.

News of the Iranian arms sales was followed on November 25, 1986, by the revelation that the administration, led by Admiral John M. Poindexter, the president's national security adviser, and, especially, by Lt. Col. Oliver North, a member of the National Security Council (NSC) staff, had been diverting the profits from the sales to the Nicaraguan contras. This diversion was in clear violation of the Boland Amendment, a measure passed by Congress to prohibit the U.S. government from aiding the rebels. What is more, it also was revealed that North had lied to Congress about the secret aid, then shredded official documents that described what had been done.

On November 26, in an effort to dampen the political firestorm that the month's revelations had ignited, Reagan appointed a special three-member commission to conduct a "comprehensive review" of the administration's ac-

*tivities in the Iran-contra affair. The commission was headed by former Texas senator John Tower and included former Maine senator and secretary of state Edmund S. Muskie and former national security adviser Brent Scowcroft, a retired army lieutenant general. On February 26, 1987, the Tower Commission issued its report, which Reagan publicly received and ruefully accepted.*

*The commission report began with a careful review of the NSC as an institution. Although rejecting the idea that the national security adviser should be confirmed by the Senate, Tower and his colleagues urged that the president use the NSC, which was designed as an advisory body, for operational purposes only in highly unusual cases.*

*As for the Iran-contra affair, the commission placed the blame on Reagan's lackadaisical management style and on the willingness of White House staffers, in effect, to make policy on their own. It reported no evidence that Reagan had been personally aware of the secret aid to the contras.*

*In televised hearings conducted during the summer of 1987 by a special committee of representatives and senators, Congress also investigated the Iran-contra affair. So did Lawrence M. Walsh and federal district court judge Gerhard A. Gesell in subsequent trials of Lieutenant Colonel North and others. These efforts added little to public understanding of the affair, although they did raise doubts about the Tower Commission's conclusion that President Reagan had been a relatively passive, disengaged figure. Accusations also surfaced concerning the possible involvement of then-vice president George Bush.*                           ~

## Part I. Introduction

In November, 1986, it was disclosed that the United States had, in August,

1985, and subsequently, participated in secret dealings with Iran involving the sale of military equipment. There appeared to be a linkage between these dealings and efforts to obtain the release of U.S. citizens held hostage in Lebanon by terrorists believed to be closely associated with the Iranian regime. After the initial story broke, the Attorney General announced that proceeds from the arms transfers may have been diverted to assist U.S.-backed rebel forces in Nicaragua, known as Contras. This possibility enlarged the controversy and added questions not only of policy and propriety but also violations of law.

These disclosures became the focus of substantial public attention. The secret arms transfers appeared to run directly counter to declared U.S. policies. The United States had announced a policy of neutrality in the six-year old Iran/Iraq war and had proclaimed an embargo on arms sales to Iran. It had worked actively to isolate Iran and other regimes known to give aid and comfort to terrorists. It had declared that it would not pay ransom to hostage-takers.

Public concern was not limited to the issues of policy, however. Questions arose as to the propriety of certain actions taken by the National Security Council [NSC] staff and the manner in which the decision to transfer arms to Iran had been made. Congress was never informed. A variety of intermediaries, both private and governmental, some with motives open to question, had central roles. The NSC staff rather than the CIA seemed to be running the operation. The President appeared to be unaware of key elements of the operation. The controversy threatened a crisis of confidence in the manner in which national security decisions are made and the role played by the NSC staff.

It was this latter set of concerns that prompted the President to establish this Special Review Board on December 1, 1986. The President directed the

Board to examine the proper role of the National Security Council staff in national security operations, including the arms transfers to Iran. The President made clear that he wanted "all the facts to come out."

The Board was not, however, called upon to assess individual culpability or be the final arbiter of the facts. These tasks have been properly left to others. Indeed, the short deadline set by the President for completion of the Board's work and its limited resources precluded a separate and thorough field investigation. Instead, the Board has examined the events surrounding the transfer of arms to Iran as a principal case study in evaluating the operation of the National Security Council in general and the role of the NSC staff in particular.

The President gave the Board a broad charter. It was directed to conduct "a comprehensive study of the future role and procedures of the National Security Council (NSC) staff in the development, coordination, oversight, and conduct of foreign and national security policy."

It has been forty years since the enactment of the National Security Act of 1947 and the creation of the National Security Council. Since that time the NSC staff has grown in importance and the Assistant to the President for National Security Affairs has emerged as a key player in national security decision-making. This is the first Presidential Commission to have as its sole responsibility a comprehensive review of how these institutions have performed. We believe that, quite aside from the circumstances which brought about the Board's creation, such a review was overdue.

The Board divided its work into three major inquiries: the circumstances surrounding the Iran/Contra matter, other case studies that might reveal strengths and weaknesses in the operation of the National Security Council system under

stress, and the manner in which that system has served eight different Presidents since its inception in 1947....

...[I]t is important to emphasize that the President is responsible for the national security policy of the United States. In the development and execution of that policy, the President is the decision-maker. He is not obliged to consult with or seek approval from anyone in the Executive Branch. The structure and procedures of the National Security Council system should be designed to give the President every assistance in discharging these heavy responsibilities. It is not possible to make a system immune from error without paralyzing its capacity to act.

At its senior levels, the National Security Council is primarily the interaction of people. We have examined with care its operation in the Iran/Contra matter and have set out in considerable detail mistakes of omission, commission, judgment, and perspective. We believe that this record and analysis can warn future Presidents, members of the National Security Council, and National Security Advisors of the potential pitfalls they face even when they are operating with what they consider the best of motives. We would hope that this record would be carefully read and its lessons fully absorbed by all aspirants to senior positions in the National Security Council system....

Our review validates the current National Security Council system. That system has been utilized by different Presidents in very different ways, in accordance with their individual work habits and philosophical predilections. On occasion over the years it has functioned with real brilliance; at other times serious mistakes have been made. The problems we examined in the case of Iran/Contra caused us deep concern. But their solution does not lie in revamping the National Security Council system.

That system is properly the President's creature. It must be left flexible to be molded by the President into the form most useful to him. Otherwise it will become either an obstacle to the President, and a source of frustration; or an institutional irrelevance, as the President fashions informal structures more to his liking.

Having said that, there are certain functions which need to be performed in some way for any President. What we have tried to do is to distill from the wisdom of those who have participated in the National Security Council system over the past forty years the essence of these functions and the manner in which that system can be operated so as to minimize the likelihood of major error without destroying the creative impulses of the President.

## Part II. Organizing for National Security

Ours is a government of checks and balances, of shared power and responsibility. The Constitution places the President and the Congress in dynamic tension. They both cooperate and compete in the making of national policy.

National security is no exception. The Constitution gives both the President and the Congress an important role. The Congress is critical in formulating national policies and in marshalling the resources to carry them out. But those resources—the nation's military personnel, its diplomats, its intelligence capability—are lodged in the Executive Branch. As Chief Executive and Commander-in-Chief, and with broad authority in the area of foreign affairs, it is the President who is empowered to act for the nation and protect its interests.

### A. The National Security Council

The present organization of the Executive Branch for national security matters was established by the National Security Act of 1947. That Act created the National Security Council. As now constituted, its statutory members are the President, Vice President, Secretary of State, and Secretary of Defense. The President is the head of the National Security Council.

Presidents have from time to time invited the heads of other departments or agencies to attend National Security Council meetings or to participate as de facto members. These have included the Director of Central Intelligence (the "DCI") and the Chairman of the Joint Chiefs of Staff (the "CJCS"). The President (or, in his absence, his designee) presides.

The National Security Council deals with the most vital issues in the nation's national security policy. It is this body that discusses recent developments in arms control and the Strategic Defense Initiative; that discussed whether or not to bomb the Cambodia mainland after the *Mayaguez* was captured; that debated the timetable for the U.S. withdrawal from Vietnam; and that considered the risky and daring attempt to rescue U.S. hostages in Iran in 1980. The National Security Council deals with issues that are difficult, complex, and often secret. Decisions are often required in hours rather than weeks. Advice must be given under great stress and with imperfect information.

The National Security Council is not a decision-making body. Although its other members hold official positions in the Government, when meeting as the National Security Council they sit as advisors to the President. This is clear from the language of the 1947 Act:

> "The function of the Council shall be to advise the President with respect to the integration of domestic, foreign, and military policies relating to the national security so as to enable the military services and the other departments and agencies of the Government to cooperate more effectively in matters involving the national security."

The National Security Council has from its inception been a highly personal instrument. Every President has turned for advice to those individuals and institutions whose judgment he has valued and trusted. For some Presidents, such as President Eisenhower, the National Security Council served as a primary forum for obtaining advice on national security matters. Other Presidents, such as President Kennedy, relied on more informal groupings of advisors, often including some but not all of the Council members....

Regardless of the frequency of its use, the NSC has remained a strictly advisory body. Each President has kept the burden of decision for himself, in accordance with his Constitutional responsibilities.

## B. The Assistant to the President for National Security Affairs

Although closely associated with the National Security Council in the public mind, the Assistant to the President for National Security Affairs is not one of its members. Indeed, no mention of this position is made in the National Security Act of 1947.

The position was created by President Eisenhower in 1953. Although its precise title has varied, the position has come to be known (somewhat misleadingly) as the National Security Advisor.

Under President Eisenhower, the holder of this position served as the principal executive officer of the Council, setting the agenda, briefing the President on Council matters, and supervising the staff. He was not a policy advocate.

It was not until President Kennedy, with McGeorge Bundy in the role, that the position took on its current form. Bundy emerged as an important personal advisor to the President on national security affairs. This introduced an element of direct competition into Bundy's relationship with the members of the National Security Council. Although President Johnson changed the title of the position to simply "Special

Assistant," in the hands of Walt Rostow it continued to play an important role.

President Nixon relied heavily on his National Security Advisor, maintaining and even enhancing its prominence. In that position, Henry Kissinger became a key spokesman for the President's national security policies both to the U.S. press and to foreign governments. President Nixon used him to negotiate on behalf of the United States with Vietnam, China, the Soviet Union, and other countries. The roles of spokesman and negotiator had traditionally been the province of the Secretary of State, not of the National Security Advisor. The emerging tension between the two positions was only resolved when Kissinger assumed them both.

Under President Ford, Lt Gen Brent Scowcroft became National Security Advisor, with Henry Kissinger remaining as Secretary of State. The National Security Advisor exercised major responsibility for coordinating for the President the advice of his NSC principals and overseeing the process of policy development and implementation within the Executive Branch.

President Carter returned in large part to the early Kissinger model, with a resulting increase in tensions with the Secretary of State. President Carter wanted to take the lead in matters of foreign policy, and used his National Security Advisor as a source of information, ideas, and new initiatives.

The role of the National Security Advisor, like the role of the NSC itself, has in large measure been a function of the operating style of the President. Notwithstanding, the National Security Advisor has come to perform, to a greater or lesser extent, certain functions which appear essential to the effective discharge of the President's responsibilities in national security affairs.

~ He is an "honest broker" for the NSC process. He assures that issues are clearly presented to the President; that all reasonable options, together with an analysis of their disadvantages and risks, are brought to his attention; and that the views of the President's other principal advisors are accurately conveyed.

~ He provides advice from the President's vantage point, unalloyed by institutional responsibilities and biases. Unlike the Secretaries of State or Defense, who have substantial organizations for which they are responsible, the President is the National Security Advisor's only constituency.

~ He monitors the actions taken by the executive departments in implementing the President's national security policies. He asks the question whether these actions are consistent with Presidential decisions and whether, over time, the underlying policies continue to serve U.S. interests.

~ He has a special role in crisis management. This has resulted from the need for prompt and coordinated action under Presidential control, often with secrecy being esssential.

~ He reaches out for new ideas and initiatives that will give substance to broad Presidential objectives for national security.

~ He keeps the President informed about international developments and developments in the Congress and the Executive Branch that affect the President's policies and priorities.

But the National Security Advisor remains the creature of the President. The position will be largely what he wants it to be. This presents any President with a series of dilemmas.

~ The President must surround himself with people he trusts and to whom he can speak in confidence. To this end, the National Security Advisor, unlike the Secretaries of State and Defense, is not subject to confirmation by the Senate and does not testify before Congress. But the more the President relies on the National Security Advisor for advice, especially to the exclusion of his Cabinet officials, the greater will be the unease with this arrangement.

~ As the "honest broker" of the NSC process, the National Security Advisor must ensure that the different and often conflicting views of the NSC principals are presented fairly to the President. But as an independent advisor to the President, he must provide his own judgment. To the extent that the National Security Advisor becomes a strong advocate for a particular point of view, his role as "honest broker" may be compromised and the President's access to the unedited views of the NSC principals may be impaired.

~ The Secretaries of State and Defense, and the Director of Central Intelligence, head agencies of government that have specific statutory responsibilities and are subject to Congressional oversight for the implementation of U.S. national security policy. To the extent that the National Security Advisor assumes operational responsibilities, whether by negotiating with foreign governments or becoming heavily involved in military or intelligence operations, the legitimacy of that role and his authority to perform it may be challenged.

~ The more the National Security Advisor becomes an "operator" in implementing policy, the less will he be able objectively to review that implementation—and whether the underlying policy continues to serve the interests of the President and the nation.

~ The Secretary of State has traditionally been the President's spokesman on matters of national security and foreign affairs. To the extent that the National Security Advisor speaks publicly on these matters or meets with representatives of foreign governments, the result may be confusion as to what is the President's policy.

## C. The NSC Staff

At the time it established the National Security Council, Congress authorized a staff headed by an Executive Secretary appointed by the President.

Initially quite small, the NSC staff expanded substantially under President Eisenhower.

During the Eisenhower Administration, the NSC staff assumed two important functions: coordinating the executive departments in the development of national policy (through the NSC Planning Board) and overseeing the implementation of that policy (through the Operations Coordination Board). A systematic effort was made to coordinate policy development and its implementation by the various agencies through an elaborate set of committees. The system worked fairly well in bringing together for the President the views of the other NSC principals. But it has been criticized as biased toward reaching consensus among these principals rather than developing options for Presidential decision. By the end of his second term, President Eisenhower himself had reached the conclusion that a highly competent individual and a small staff could perform the needed functions in a better way. Such a change was made by President Kennedy.

Under President Kennedy, a number of the functions of the NSC staff were eliminated and its size was sharply reduced. The Planning and Operations Coordinating Boards were abolished. Policy development and policy implementation were assigned to individual Cabinet officers, responsible directly to the President. By late 1962 the staff was only 12 professionals, serving largely as an independent source of ideas and information to the President. The system was lean and responsive, but frequently suffered from a lack of coordination. The Johnson Administration followed much the same pattern.

The Nixon Administration returned to a model more like Eisenhower's but with something of the informality of the Kennedy/Johnson staffs. The Eisenhower system had emphasized coordination; the Kennedy-Johnson system tilted to innovation and the generation of new ideas. The Nixon system emphasized both. The objective was not interdepartmental consensus but the generation of policy options for Presidential decision, and then ensuring that those decisions were carried out. The staff grew to 50 professionals in 1970 and became a major factor in the national security decision-making process. This approach was largely continued under President Ford.

The NSC staff retained an important role under President Carter. While continuing to have responsibility for coordinating policy among the various executive agencies, President Carter particularly looked to the NSC staff as a personal source of independent advice. President Carter felt the need to have a group loyal only to him from which to launch his own initiatives and to move a vast and lethargic government. During his time in office, President Carter reduced the size of the professional staff to 35, feeling that a smaller group could do the job and would have a closer relationship to him.

. . . [The NSC staff] has remained the President's creature, molded as he sees fit, to serve as his personal staff for national security affairs. For this reason, it has generally operated out of the public view and has not been subject to direct oversight by the Congress.

### D. The Interagency Committee System

The National Security Council has frequently been supported by committees made up of representatives of the relevant national security departments and agencies. These committees analyze issues prior to consideration by the Council. There are generally several levels of committees. At the top level, officials from each agency (at the Deputy Secretary or Under Secretary level) meet to provide a senior level policy review. These senior-level committees are in turn supported by more junior interagency groups (usually at the Assistant Secretary level). These in turn may oversee staff level working groups that prepare detailed analysis of important issues. . . .

## E. The Reagan Model

President Reagan entered office with a strong commitment to cabinet government. His principal advisors on national security affairs were to be the Secretaries of State and Defense, and to a lesser extent the Director of Central Intelligence. The position of the National Security Advisor was initially downgraded in both status and access to the President. Over the next six years, five different people held that position.

The Administration's first National Security Advisor, Richard [V.] Allen, reported to the President through the senior White House staff. Consequently, the NSC staff assumed a reduced role. Mr. Allen believed that the Secretary of State had primacy in the field of foreign policy. He viewed the job of the National Security Advisor as that of a policy coordinator.

President Reagan initially declared that the National Security Council would be the principal forum for consideration of national security issues. To support the work of the Council, President Reagan established an interagency committee system headed by three Senior Interagency Groups (or "SIGs"), one each for foreign policy, defense policy, and intelligence. They were chaired by the Secretary of State, the Secretary of Defense, and the Director of Central Intelligence, respectively.

Over time, the Administration's original conception of the role of the National Security Advisor changed. William [P.] Clark, who succeeded Richard Allen in 1982, was a long-time associate of the President and dealt directly with him. Robert [C.] McFarlane, who replaced Judge Clark in 1983, although personally less close to the President, continued to have direct access to him. The same was true for VADM [Vice Admiral] John [M.] Poindexter, who was appointed to the position in December, 1985.

President Reagan appointed several additional members to his National Security Council and allowed staff attendance at meetings. The resultant size of the meetings led the President to turn increasingly to a smaller group (called the National Security Planning Group or "NSPG"). Attendance at its meetings was more restricted but included the statutory principals of the NSC. The NSPG was supported by the SIGs, and new SIGs were occasionally created to deal with particular issues. These were frequently chaired by the National Security Advisor. But generally the SIGs and many of their subsidiary groups (called Interagency Groups or "IGs") fell into disuse.

As a supplement to the normal NSC process, the Reagan Administration adopted comprehensive procedures for covert actions. These are contained in a classified document, NSDD-159, establishing the process for deciding, implementing, monitoring, and reviewing covert activities.

## F. The Problem of Covert Operations

Covert activities place a great strain on the process of decision in a free society. Disclosure of even the existence of the operation could threaten its effectiveness and risk embarrassment to the Government. As a result, there is strong pressure to withhold information, to limit knowledge of the operation to a minimum number of people.

These pressures come into play with great force when covert activities are undertaken in an effort to obtain the release of U.S. citizens held hostage abroad. Because of the legitimate human concern all Presidents have felt over the fate of such hostages, our national pride as a powerful country with a tradition of protecting its citizens abroad, and the great attention paid by the news media to hostage situations, the pressures on any President to take action to free hostages are enormous. Frequently to be effective, this action must necessarily be covert. Disclosure would directly threaten the lives of the hostages as well as those willing to contemplate their release.

Since covert arms sales to Iran played such a central role in the creation of this Board, it has focused its attention in large measure on the role of the NSC staff where covert activity is involved.... [I]n many respects the best test of a system is its performance under stress. The conditions of greatest stress are often found in the crucible of covert activities.

## Part III. Arms Transfers to Iran, Diversion, and Support for the Contras

The Iran/Contra matter has been and, in some respects, still is an enigma. For three months the Board sought to learn the facts, and still the whole matter cannot be fully explained. The general outlines of the story are clear....

### Section A: The Arms Transfers to Iran

Two persistent concerns lay behind U.S. participation in arms transfers to Iran.

First, the U.S. government anxiously sought the release of seven U.S. citizens abducted in Beirut, Lebanon, in seven separate incidents between March 7, 1984, and June 9, 1985. One of those abducted was William Buckley, CIA station chief in Beirut, seized on March 16, 1984. Available intelligence suggested that most, if not all, of the Americans were held hostage by members of Hizballah, a fundamentalist Shiite terrorist group with links to the regime of the Ayatollah Khomeini.

Second, the U.S. government had a latent and unresolved interest in establishing ties to Iran. Few in the U.S. government doubted Iran's strategic importance or the risk of Soviet med-

dling in the succession crisis that might follow the death of Khomeini. For this reason, some in the U.S. government were convinced that efforts should be made to open potential channels to Iran.

Arms transfers ultimately appeared to offer a means to achieve both the release of the hostages and a strategic opening to Iran....

### Section C: The NSC Staff and Support for the Contras

Inquiry into the arms sale to Iran and the possible diversion of funds to the Contras disclosed evidence of substantial NSC staff involvement in a related area; private support for the Contras during the period that support from the U.S. Government was either banned or restricted by Congress.

There are similarities in the two cases. Indeed, the NSC staff's role in support for the Contras set the stage for its subsequent role in the Iran initiative. In both, LtCol [Oliver L.] North, with the acquiescence of the National Security Advisor, was deeply involved in the operational details of a covert program. He relied heavily on private U.S. citizens and foreigners to carry out key operational tasks. Some of the same individuals were involved in both. When Israeli plans for the November HAWK shipment began to unravel, LtCol North turned to the private network that was already in place to run the Contra support operation. This network, under the direction of Mr. [Richard] Secord, undertook increasing responsibility for the Iran initiative. Neither program was subjected to rigorous and periodic inter-agency overview. In neither case was Congress informed. In the case of Contra support, Congress may have been actively misled.

These two operations also differ in several key aspects. While Iran policy was the subject of strong disagreement within the Executive Branch, the President's emphatic support for the Contras provoked an often bitter debate with the Congress. The result was an intense political struggle between the President and the Congress over how to define U.S. policy toward Nicaragua. Congress sought to restrict the President's ability to implement his policy. What emerged was a highly ambiguous legal environment.

On December 21, 1982, Congress passed the first "Boland amendment" prohibiting the Department of Defense and the Central Intelligence Agency from spending funds to overthrow Nicaragua or provoke conflict between Nicaragua and Honduras. The following year, $24 million was authorized for the Contras. On October 3, 1984, Congress cut off all funding for the Contras and prohibited DoD, CIA, and any other agency or entity "involved in intelligence activities" from directly or indirectly supporting military operations in Nicaragua.

The 1984 prohibition was subject to conflicting interpretation. On the one hand, several of its Congressional supporters believed that the legislation covered the activities of the NSC staff. On the other hand, it appears that LtCol North and VADM Poindexter received legal advice from the President's Intelligence Oversight Board that the restrictions on lethal assistance to the Contras did not cover the NSC staff.

Confusion only increased. In December 1985 Congress approved classified amounts of funds to the Contras for "communications" and "advice." The authorization was subject, however, to a classified annex negotiated by the Senate and House intelligence committees. An exchange of letters, initiated the day the law passed, evidences the extreme difficulty even the Chairmen of the two committees had in deciding what the annex permitted or proscribed.

The support for the Contras differs from the Iranian initiative in some other important respects. First, the activities undertaken by LtCol North with respect to the Contras, unlike in the Iranian case, were in support of the declared policy of at least the Executive. Second, the President may never have authorized or, indeed, even been apprised of what the NSC staff was doing. The President never issued a Covert Action Finding or any other formal decision authorizing NSC staff activities in support of the Contras. Third, the NSC staff's role in support of the Contras was not in derogation of the CIA's role because CIA involvement was expressly barred by statute....

## Part IV. What Was Wrong

The arms transfers to Iran and the activities of the NSC staff in support of the Contras are case studies in the perils of policy pursued outside the constraints of orderly process.

The Iran initiative ran directly counter to the Administration's own policies on terrorism, the Iran/Iraq war, and military support to Iran. This inconsistency was never resolved, nor were the consequences of this inconsistency fully considered and provided for. The result taken as a whole was a U.S. policy that worked against itself.

The Board believes that failure to deal adequately with these contradictions resulted in large part from the flaws in the manner in which decisions were made. Established procedures for making national security decisions were ignored. Reviews of the initiative by all the NSC principals were too infrequent. The initiatives were not adequately vetted below the cabinet level. Intelligence resources were underutilized. Applicable legal constraints were not adequately addressed. The whole matter was handled too informally, without adequate written records of what had been considered, discussed, and decided.

This pattern persisted in the implementation of the Iran initiative. The NSC staff assumed direct operational control. The initiative fell within the traditional jurisdictions of the Departments of State, Defense, and CIA. Yet these agencies were largely ignored. Great reliance was placed on a network of private operators and intermediaries. How the initiative was to be carried out never received adequate attention from the NSC principals or a tough working-level review. No periodic evaluation of the progress of the initiative was ever conducted. The result was an unprofessional and, in substantial part, unsatisfactory operation.

In all of this process, Congress was never notified.

... [T]he record of the role of the NSC staff in support of the Contras is much less complete. Nonetheless, what is known suggests that many of the same problems plagued that effort as well. ...

## A. A Flawed Process

**1. Contradictory Policies Were Pursued.** The arms sales to Iran and the NSC support for the Contras demonstrate the risks involved when highly controversial initiatives are pursued covertly.

*Arms Transfers to Iran.* The initiative to Iran was a covert operation directly at odds with important and well-publicized policies of the Executive Branch. But the initiative itself embodied a fundamental contradiction. Two objectives were apparent from the outset: a strategic opening to Iran, and release of the U.S. citizens held hostage in Lebanon. The sale of arms to Iran appeared to provide a means to achieve both these objectives. It also played into the hands of those who had other interests—some of them personal financial gain—in engaging the United States in an arms deal with Iran.

In fact, the sale of arms was not equally appropriate for achieving both these objectives. Arms were what Iran wanted. If all the United States sought was to free the hostages, then an arms-for-hostages deal could achieve the immediate objectives of both sides. But if the U.S. objective was a broader strategic relationship, then the sale of arms should have been contingent upon first putting into place the elements of that relationship. An arms-for-hostages deal in this context could become counterproductive to achieving this broader strategic objective. In addition, release of the hostages would require exerting influence with Hizballah, which could involve the most radical elements of the Iranian regime. The kind of strategic opening sought by the United States, however, involved what were regarded as more moderate elements.

The U.S. officials involved in the initiative appeared to have held three distinct views. For some, the principal motivation seemed consistently a strategic opening to Iran. For others, the strategic opening became a rationale for using arms sales to obtain the release of the hostages. For still others, the initiative appeared clearly as an arms-for-hostages deal from first to last.

Whatever the intent, almost from the beginning the initiative became in fact a series of arms-for-hostages deals. The shipment of arms in November, 1985, was directly tied to a hostage release. Indeed, the August/September transfer may have been nothing more than an arms-for-hostages trade. By July 14, 1985, a specific proposal for the sale of 100 TOWs to Iran in exchange for Iranian efforts to secure the release of all the hostages had been transmitted to the White House and discussed with the President. What actually occurred, at least so far as the September shipment was concerned, involved a direct link of arms and a hostage.

The initiative continued to be described in terms of its broader strategic relationship. But those elements never really materialized. ... Even if one accepts the explanation that arms and hostages represented only "bona fides" of seriousness of purpose for each side, that had clearly been established, one way or another, by the September exchange.

It is true that, strictly speaking, arms were not exchanged for the hostages. The arms were sold for cash; and to Iran, rather than the terrorists holding the hostages. Iran clearly wanted to buy the arms, however, and time and time again U.S. willingness to sell was directly conditioned upon the release of hostages. Although Iran might claim that it did not itself hold the hostages, the whole arrangement was premised on Iran's ability to secure their release.

While the United States was seeking the release of the hostages in this way, it was vigorously pursuing policies that were dramatically opposed to such efforts. The Reagan Administration in particular had come into office declaring a firm stand against terrorism, which it continued to maintain. In December of 1985, the Administration completed a major study under the chairmanship of the Vice President. It resulted in a vigorous reaffirmation of U.S. opposition to terrorism in all its forms and a vow of total war on terrorism whatever its source. The Administration continued to pressure U.S. allies not to sell arms to Iran and not to make concessions to terrorists.

No serious effort was made to reconcile the inconsistency between these policies and the Iran initiative. No effort was made systematically to address the consequences of this inconsistency—the effect on U.S. policy when, as it inevitably would, the Iran initiative became known.

The Board believes that a strategic opening to Iran may have been in the national interest but that the United States never should have been a party to the arms transfers. As arms-for-hostages trades, they could not help but create an incentive for further hostage-taking. As a violation of the U.S. arms embargo, they could only remove inhibitions on other nations from selling arms to Iran. This threatened to upset the military balance between Iran and Iraq, with consequent jeopardy to the Gulf States and the interests of the West in that region. The arms-for-hostages trades rewarded a regime that clearly supported terrorism and hostage-taking. They increased the risk that the United States would be perceived, especially in the Arab world, as a creature of Israel. They suggested to other U.S. allies and friends in the region that the United States had shifted its policy in favor of Iran. They raised questions as to whether U.S. policy statements could be relied upon.

As the arms-for-hostages proposal first came to the United States, it clearly was tempting. The sale of just 100 TOWs was to produce the release of all seven Americans held in Lebanon. Even had the offer been genuine, it would have been unsound. But it was not genuine. The 100 TOWs did not produce seven hostages. Very quickly the price went up, and the arrangements became protracted. A pattern of successive bargained exchanges of arms and hostages was quickly established. While release of all the hostages continued to be promised, in fact the hostages came out singly if at all. This sad history is powerful evidence of why the United States should never have become involved in the arms transfers.

***NSC Staff Support for the Contras.*** The activities of the NSC staff in support of the Contras sought to achieve an important objective of the Administration's foreign policy. The President had publicly and emphatically declared his support for the Nicaragua resistance. That brought his policy in direct conflict with that of the Congress, at least during the period that direct or indirect support of military operations in Nicaragua was barred.

...[N]o serious effort appears to have been made to come to grips with the risks to the President of direct NSC support for the Contras in the face of these Congressional restrictions. Even if it could be argued that these restrictions did not technically apply to the NSC staff, these activities presented great political risk to the President. The appearance of the President's personal staff doing what Congress had forbade other agencies to do could, once disclosed, only touch off a firestorm in the Congress and threaten the Administration's whole policy on the Contras.

**2. The Decision-making Process Was Flawed.** Because the arms sales to Iran and the NSC support for the Contras occurred in settings of such controversy, one would expect that the decisions to undertake these activities would have been made only after intense and thorough consideration. In fact, a far different picture emerges.

*Arms Transfers to Iran.* The Iran initiative was handled almost casually and through informal channels, always apparently with an expectation that the process would end with the next arms-for-hostages exchange. It was subjected neither to the general procedures for interagency consideration and review of policy issues nor the more restrictive procedures set out in NSDD 159 for handling covert operations. This had a number of consequences.

*(i) The Opportunity for a Full Hearing before the President Was Inadequate.* In the last half of 1985, the Israelis made three separate proposals to the United States with respect to the Iran initiative (two in July and one in August). In addition, Israel made three separate deliveries of arms to Iran, one each in August, September, and November. Yet prior to December 7, 1985, there was at most one meeting of the NSC principals, a meeting which several participants recall taking place on August 6. There is no dispute that full meetings of the principals did occur on December 7, 1985, and on January 7, 1986. But the proposal to shift to direct U.S. arms sales to Iran appears not to have been discussed until later. It was

considered by the President at a meeting on January 17 which only the Vice President, Mr. Regan, Mr. Fortier, and VADM Poindexter attended. Thereafter, the only senior-level review the Iran initiative received was during one or another of the President's daily national security briefings. These were routinely attended only by the President, the Vice President, Mr. Regan, and VADM Poindexter. There was no subsequent collective consideration of the Iran initiative by the NSC principals before it became public 11 months later.

This was not sufficient for a matter as important and consequential as the Iran initiative. Two or three cabinet-level reviews in a period of 17 months was not enough. The meeting on December 7 came late in the day, after the pattern of arms-for-hostages exchanges had become well established. The January 7 meeting had earmarks of a meeting held after a decision had already been made. Indeed, a draft Covert Action Finding authorizing the initiative had been signed by the President, though perhaps inadvertently, the previous day.

At each significant step in the Iran initiative, deliberations among the NSC principals in the presence of the President should have been virtually automatic. This was not and should not have been a formal requirement, something prescribed by statute. Rather, it should have been something the NSC principals desired as a means of ensuring an optimal environment for Presidential judgment. The meetings should have been preceded by consideration by the NSC principals of staff papers prepared according to the procedures applicable to covert actions. These should have reviewed the history of the initiative, analyzed the issues then presented, developed a range of realistic options, presented the odds of success and the costs of failure, and addressed questions of implementation and execution. Had this been done, the objectives of the Iran initiative might have been clarified and alternatives to the sale of arms might have been identified.

*(ii) The Initiative Was Never Subjected to a Rigorous Review below the Cabinet Level.* Because of the obsession with secrecy, interagency consideration of the initiative was limited to the cabinet level. With the exception of the NSC staff and, after January 17, 1986, a handful of CIA officials, the rest of the executive departments and agencies were largely excluded.

As a consequence, the initiative was never vetted at the staff level. This deprived those responsible for the initiative of considerable expertise—on the situation in Iran; on the difficulties of dealing with terrorists; on the mechanics of conducting a diplomatic opening. It also kept the plan from receiving a tough, critical review.

Moreover, the initiative did not receive a policy review below cabinet level. Careful consideration at the Deputy/Under Secretary level might have exposed the confusion in U.S. objectives and clarified the risks of using arms as an instrument of policy in this instance.

The vetting process would also have ensured better use of U.S. intelligence. As it was, the intelligence input into the decision process was clearly inadequate. First, no independent evaluation of the Israeli proposals offered in July and August appears to have been sought or offered by U.S. intelligence agencies. The Israelis represented that they for some time had had contacts with elements in Iran. The prospects for an opening to Iran depended heavily on these contacts, yet no systematic assessment appears to have been made by U.S. intelligence agencies of the reliability and motivations of these contacts, and the identity and objectives of the elements in Iran that the opening was supposed to reach. Neither was any systematic assessment made of the motivation of the Israelis.

Second, neither Mr. [Manucher] Ghorbanifar nor the second channel seem to have been subjected to a systematic intelligence vetting before they were engaged as intermediaries. Mr. Ghorbanifar had been known to the CIA for some time and the agency had substantial doubts as to his reliability and truthfulness. Yet the agency did not volunteer that information or inquire about the identity of the intermediary if his name was unknown. Conversely, no early request for a name check was made of the CIA, and it was not until January 11, 1986, that the agency gave Mr. Ghorbanifar a new polygraph, which he failed. Notwithstanding this situation, with the signing of the January 17 Finding, the United States took control of the initiative and became even more directly involved with Mr. Ghorbanifar.... [N]o prior intelligence check appears to have been made on the second channel.

Third, although the President recalled being assured that the arms sales to Iran would not alter the military balance with Iran, the Board could find no evidence that the President was ever briefed on this subject. The question of the impact of any intelligence shared with the Iranians does not appear to have been brought to the President's attention.

A thorough vetting would have included consideration of the legal implications of the initiative. There appeared little effort to face squarely the legal restrictions and notification requirements applicable to the operation. At several points, other agencies raised questions about violations of law or regulations. These concerns were dismissed without, it appears, investigating them with the benefit of legal counsel.

Finally, insufficient attention was given to the implications of implementation. The implementation of the initiative raised a number of issues: should the NSC staff rather than the CIA have had operational control; what were the implications of Israeli involvement; how reliable were the Iranian and various other private intermediaries; what were the implications of the use of Mr. Secord's private network of operatives; what were the implications for the military balance in the region; was operational security adequate. Nowhere do these issues appear to have been sufficiently addressed.

The concern for preserving the secrecy of the initiative provided an excuse for abandoning sound process. Yet the initiative was known to a variety of persons with diverse interests and ambitions—Israelis, Iranians, various arms dealers and business intermediaries, and LtCol North's network of private operatives. While concern for secrecy would have justified limiting the circle of persons knowledgeable about the initiative, in this case it was drawn too tightly. As a consequence, important advice and counsel were lost.

In January of 1985, the President had adopted procedures for striking the proper balance between secrecy and the need for consultation on sensitive programs. These covered the institution, implementation, and review of covert operations. In the case of the Iran initiative, these procedures were almost totally ignored.

The only staff work the President apparently reviewed in connection with the Iran initiative was prepared by NSC staff members, under the direction of the National Security Advisor. These were, of course, the principal proponents of the initiative. A portion of this staff work was reviewed by the Board. It was frequently striking in its failure to present the record of past efforts—particularly past failures. Alternative ways of achieving U.S. objectives—other than yet another arms-for-hostages deal—were not discussed. Frequently it neither adequately presented the risks involved in pursuing the initia-

tive nor the full force of the dissenting views of other NSC principals. On balance, it did not serve the President well.

*(iii) The Process Was Too Informal.* The whole decision process was too informal. Even when meetings among NSC principals did occur, often there was no prior notice of the agenda. No formal written minutes seem to have been kept. Decisions subsequently taken by the President were not formally recorded. An exception was the January 17 Finding, but even this was apparently not circulated or shown to key U.S. officials.

The effect of this informality was that the initiative lacked a formal institutional record. This precluded the participants from undertaking the more informed analysis and reflection that is afforded by a written record, as opposed to mere recollection. It made it difficult to determine where the initiative stood, and to learn lessons from the record that could guide future action. This lack of an institutional record permitted specific proposals for arms-for-hostages exchanges to be presented in a vacuum, without reference to the results of past proposals. Had a searching and thorough review of the Iran initiative been undertaken at any stage in the process, it would have been extremely difficult to conduct. The Board can attest first hand to the problem of conducting a review in the absence of such records. Indeed, the exposition in the wake of public revelation suffered the most.

*NSC Staff Support for the Contras.* It is not clear how LtCol North first became involved in activities in direct support of the Contras during the period of the Congressional ban. . . . In the evidence that the Board did have, there is no suggestion at any point of any discussion of LtCol North's activities with the President in any forum. There also does not appear to have been any interagency review of LtCol North's activities at any level.

This latter point is not surprising

given the Congressional restrictions under which the other relevant agencies were operating. But the NSC staff apparently did not compensate for the lack of any interagency review with its own internal vetting of these activities. LtCol North apparently worked largely in isolation, keeping first Mr. McFarlane and then VADM Poindexter informed.

The lack of adequate vetting is particularly evident on the question of the legality of LtCol North's activities. . . .

If these activities were illegal, obviously they should not have been conducted. If there was any doubt on the matter, systematic legal advice should have been obtained. The political cost to the President of illegal action by the NSC staff was particularly high, both because the NSC staff is the personal staff of the President and because of the history of serious conflict with the Congress over the issue of Contra support. For these reasons, the President should have been kept apprised of any review of the legality of LtCol North's activities.

Legal advice was apparently obtained from the President's Intelligence Oversight Board. Without passing on the quality of that advice, it is an odd source. It would be one thing for the Intelligence Oversight Board to review the legal advice provided by some other agency. It is another for the Intelligence Oversight Board to be originating legal advice of its own. That is a function more appropriate for the NSC staff's own legal counsel.

3. **Implementation Was Unprofessional.** The manner in which the Iran initiative was implemented and LtCol North undertook to support the Contras are very similar. This is in large part because the same cast of characters was involved. In both cases the operations were unprofessional, although the Board has much less evidence with respect to LtCol North's Contra activities.

*Arms Transfers to Iran.* With the signing of the January 17 Finding, the Iran initiative became a U.S. operation run by the NSC staff. LtCol North made most of the significant operational decisions. He conducted the operation through Mr. Secord and his associates, a network of private individuals already involved in the Contra resupply operation. To this was added a handful of selected individuals from the CIA. . . .

Because so few people from the departments and agencies were told of the initiative, LtCol North cut himself off from resources and expertise from within the government. He relied instead on a number of private intermediaries, businessmen and other financial brokers, private operators, and Iranians hostile to the United States. Some of these were individuals with questionable credentials and potentially large personal financial interests in the transactions. This made the transactions unnecessarily complicated and invited kick-backs and payoffs. This arrangement also dramatically increased the risks that the initiative would leak. Yet no provision was made for such an eventuality. Further, the use of Mr. Secord's private network in the Iran initiative linked those operators with the resupply of the Contras, threatening exposure of both operations if either became public.

The result was a very unprofessional operation. . . .

The conduct of the negotiators with Mr. Ghorbanifar and the second channel were handled in a way that revealed obvious inexperience. The discussions were too casual for dealings with intermediaries to a regime so hostile to U.S. interests. The U.S. hand was repeatedly tipped and unskillfully played. The arrangements failed to guarantee that the U.S. obtained its hostages in exchange for the arms. Repeatedly, LtCol North permitted arms to be delivered without the release of a single captive.

The implementation of the initiative was never subjected to a rigorous review. LtCol North appears to have kept VADM Poindexter fully informed of his activities. In addition, VADM Poindexter, LtCol North, and the CIA officials involved apparently apprised Director Casey of many of the operational details. But LtCol North and his operation functioned largely outside the orbit of the U.S. Government. Their activities were not subject to critical reviews of any kind.

After the initial hostage release in September, 1985, it was over 10 months before another hostage was released. This despite recurring promises of the release of all the hostages and four intervening arms shipments. Beginning with the November shipment, the United States increasingly took over the operation of the initiative. In January, 1986, it decided to transfer arms directly to Iran.

Any of these developments could have served as a useful occasion for a systematic reconsideration of the initiative. Indeed, at least one of the schemes contained a provision for reconsideration if the initial assumptions proved to be invalid. They did, but the reconsideration never took place. It was the responsibility of the National Security Advisor and the responsible officers on the NSC staff to call for such a review. But they were too involved in the initiative both as advocates and as implementors....

*Congress Was Never Notified.* Congress was not apprised either of the Iran initiative or of the NSC staff's activities in support of the Contras.

In the case of Iran, because release of the hostages was expected within a short time after the delivery of equipment, and because public disclosure could have destroyed the operation and perhaps endangered the hostages, it could be argued that it was justifiable to defer notification of Congress prior to the first shipment of arms to Iran. The plan apparently was to inform Congress immediately after the hostages were safely in U.S. hands. But after the first delivery failed to release all the hostages, and as one hostage release plan was replaced by another, Congress certainly should have been informed. This could have been done during a period when no specific hostage release plan was in execution. Consultation with Congress could have been useful to the President, for it might have given him some sense of how the public would react to the initiative. It also might have influenced his decision to continue to pursue it.

*Legal Issues.* In addition to conflicting with several fundamental U.S. policies, selling arms to Iran raised far-reaching legal questions. How it dealt with these is important to an evaluation of the Iran initiative.

*Arms Transfers to Iran.* ... The Arms Export Control Act, the principal U.S. statute governing arms sales abroad, makes it unlawful to export arms without a license. Exports of arms by U.S. government agencies, however, do not require a license if they are otherwise authorized by law. Criminal penalties—fines and imprisonment—are provided for willful violations.

The initial arms transfers in the Iran initiative involved the sale and shipment by Israel of U.S.-origin missiles. The usual way for such international retransfer of arms to be authorized under U.S. law is pursuant to the Arms Export Control Act. This Act requires that the President consent to any transfers by another country of arms exported under the Act and imposes three conditions before such Presidential consent may be given:

(a) the United States would itself transfer the arms in question to the recipient country;
(b) a commitment in writing has been obtained from the recipient country against unauthorized retransfer of significant arms, such as missiles; and
(c) a prior written certification regarding the retransfer is submitted to the Congress if the defense equipment, such

as missiles, has an acquisition cost of 14 million dollars or more. 22 U.S.C. 2753 (a), (d).

In addition, the Act generally imposes restrictions on which countries are eligible to receive U.S. arms and on the purposes for which arms may be sold.

The other possible avenue whereby government arms transfers to Iran may be authorized by law would be in connection with intelligence operations conducted under the National Security Act. This Act requires that the Director of Central Intelligence and the heads of other intelligence agencies keep the two Congressional intelligence committees "fully and currently informed" of all intelligence activities under their responsibility. 50 U.S.C. 413. Where prior notice of significant intelligence activities is not given, the intelligence committees are to be informed "in a timely fashion." In addition, the so called Hughes-Ryan Amendment to the Foreign Assistance Act requires that "significant anticipated intelligence activities" may not be conducted by the CIA unless and until the President finds that "each such operation is important to the national security of the United States." 22 U.S.C. 2422.

When the Israelis began transfering arms to Iran in August, 1985, they were not acting on their own. U.S. officials had knowledge about the essential elements of the proposed shipments. The United States shared some common purpose in the transfers and received a benefit from them—the release of a hostage. More importantly, Mr. McFarlane communicated prior U.S. approval to the Israelis for the shipments, including an undertaking for replenishment. But for this U.S. approval, the transactions may not have gone forward. In short, the United States was an essential participant in the arms transfers to Iran that occurred in 1985.

Whether this U.S. involvement in the arms transfers by the Israelis was lawful depends fundamentally upon whether the President approved the transactions before they occurred. In the absence of Presidential approval, there does not appear to be any authority in this case for the United States to engage in the transfer of arms or consent to the transfer by another country. The arms transfers to Iran in 1985 and hence the Iran initiative itself would have proceeded contrary to U.S. law. . . .

The Board was unable to reach a conclusive judgment about whether the 1985 shipments of arms to Iran were approved in advance by the President. On balance the Board believes that it is plausible to conclude that he did approve them in advance.

Yet even if the President in some sense consented to or approved the transactions, a serious question of law remains. It is not clear that the form of the approval was sufficient for purposes of either the Arms Export Control Act or the Hughes-Ryan Amendment. The consent did not meet the conditions of the Arms Export Control Act, especially in the absence of a prior written commitment from the Iranians regarding unauthorized retransfer.

Under the National Security Act, it is not clear that mere oral approval by the President would qualify as a Presidential finding that the initiative was vital to the national security interests of the United States. The approval was never reduced to writing. It appears to have been conveyed to only one person. The President himself has no memory of it. And there is contradictory evidence from the President's advisors about how the President responded when he learned of the arms shipments which the approval was to support. In addition, the requirement for Congressional notification was ignored. In these circumstances, even if the President approved of the transactions, it is difficult to conclude that his actions constituted adequate legal authority.

The legal requirements pertaining to the sale of arms to Iran are complex; the availability of legal authority, including that which may flow from the President's constitutional powers, is difficult to delineate.... Nevertheless, [the evidence] was sufficient for the Board's purposes to conclude that the legal underpinning of the Iran initiative during 1985 was at best highly questionable.

The Presidential Finding of January 17, 1986, formally approved the Iran initiative as a covert intelligence operation under the National Security Act. This ended the uncertainty about the legal status of the initiative and provided legal authority for the United States to transfer arms directly to Iran.

The National Security Act also requires notification of Congress of covert intelligence activities. If not done in advance, notification must be "in a timely fashion." The Presidential Finding of January 17 directed that Congressional notification be withheld, and this decision appears to have never been reconsidered. While there was surely justification to suspend Congressional notification in advance of a particular transaction relating to a hostage release, the law would seem to require disclosure where, as in the Iran case, a pattern of relative inactivity occurs over an extended period. To do otherwise prevents the Congress from fulfilling its proper oversight responsibilities.

Throughout the Iran initiative, significant questions of law do not appear to have been adequately addressed. In the face of a sweeping statutory prohibition and explicit requirements relating to Presidential consent to arms transfers by third countries, there appears to have been at the outset in 1985 little attention, let alone systematic analysis, devoted to how Presidential actions would comply with U.S. law. The Board has found no evidence that an evaluation was ever done during the life of the operation to determine whether it continued to comply with the terms of the January 17 Presidential Finding. Similarly, when a new prohibition was added to the Arms Export Control Act in August of 1986 to prohibit exports to countries on the terrorism list (a list which contained Iran), no evaluation was made to determine whether this law affected authority to transfer arms to Iran in connection with intelligence operations under the National Security Act. This lack of legal vigilance markedly increased the chances that the initiative would proceed contrary to law.

**NSC Staff Support for the Contras.** The NSC staff activities in support of the Contras were marked by the same uncertainty as to legal authority and insensitivity to legal issues as were present in the Iran initiative. The ambiguity of the law governing activities in support of the Contras presented a greater challenge than even the considerable complexity of laws governing arms transfers. Intense Congressional scrutiny with respect to the NSC staff activities relating to the Contras added to the potential costs of actions that pushed the limits of the law.

In this context, the NSC staff should have been particularly cautious, avoiding operational activity in this area and seeking legal counsel. The Board saw no signs of such restraint.

### B. Failure of Responsibility

The NSC system will not work unless the President makes it work. After all, this system was created to serve the President of the United States in ways of his choosing. By his actions, by his leadership, the President therefore determines the quality of its performance.

By his own account, as evidenced in his diary notes, and as conveyed to the Board by his principal advisors, President Reagan was deeply committed to securing the release of the hostages. It was this intense compassion for the hostages that appeared to motivate his steadfast support of the Iran initiative, even in the face of opposition from his Secretaries of State and Defense.

In his obvious commitment, the President appears to have proceeded with a concept of the initiative that was not accurately reflected in the reality of the operation. The President did not seem to be aware of the way in which the operation was implemented and the full consequences of U.S. participation.

The President's expressed concern for the safety of both the hostages and the Iranians who could have been at risk may have been conveyed in a manner so as to inhibit the full functioning of the system.

The President's management style is to put the principal responsibility for policy review and implementation on the shoulders of his advisors. Nevertheless, with such a complex, high-risk operation and so much at stake, the President should have ensured that the NSC system did not fail him. He did not force his policy to undergo the most critical review of which the NSC participants and the process were capable. At no time did he insist upon accountability and performance review. Had the President chosen to drive the NSC system, the outcome could well have been different. As it was, the most powerful features of the NSC system—providing comprehensive analysis, alternatives and follow-up—were not utilized.

The Board found a strong consensus among NSC participants that the President's priority in the Iran initiative was the release of U.S. hostages. But setting priorities is not enough when it comes to sensitive and risky initiatives that directly affect U.S. national security. He must ensure that the content and tactics of an initiative match his priorities and objectives. He must insist upon accountability. For it is the President who must take responsibility for the NSC system and deal with the consequences.

Beyond the President, the other NSC principals and the National Security Advisor must share in the responsibility for the NSC system.

President Reagan's personal management style places an especially heavy responsibility on his key advisors. Knowing his style, they should have been particularly mindful of the need for special attention to the manner in which this arms sale initiative developed and proceeded. On this score, neither the National Security Advisor nor the other NSC principals deserve high marks.

It is their obligation as members and advisors to the Council to ensure that the President is adequately served. The principal subordinates to the President must not be deterred from urging the President not to proceed on a highly questionable course of action even in the face of his strong conviction to the contrary.

In the case of the Iran initiative, the NSC process did not fail, it simply was largely ignored. The National Security Advisor and the NSC principals all had a duty to raise this issue and insist that orderly process [b]e imposed. None of them did so.

All had the opportunity. While the National Security Advisor had the responsibility to see that an orderly process was observed, his failure to do so does not excuse the other NSC principals. It does not appear that any of the NSC principals called for more frequent consideration of the Iran initiative by the NSC principals in the presence of the President. None of the principals called for a serious vetting of the initiative by even a restricted group of disinterested individuals. The intelligence questions do not appear to have been raised, and legal considerations, while raised, were not pressed. No one seemed to have complained about the informality of the process. No one called for a thorough reexamination once the initiative did not meet expectations or the manner of execution changed. While one or another of the

NSC principals suspected that something was amiss, none vigorously pursued the issue.

Mr. Regan also shares in this responsibility. More than almost any Chief of Staff of recent memory, he asserted personal control over the White House staff and sought to extend this control to the National Security Advisor. He was personally active in national security affairs and attended almost all of the relevant meetings regarding the Iran initiative. He, as much as anyone, should have insisted that an orderly process be observed. In addition, he especially should have ensured that plans were made for handling any public disclosure of the initiative. He must bear primary responsibility for the chaos that descended upon the White House when such disclosure did occur.

Mr. McFarlane appeared caught between a President who supported the initiative and the cabinet officers who strongly opposed it. While he made efforts to keep these cabinet officers informed, the Board heard complaints from some that he was not always successful. VADM Poindexter on several occasions apparently sought to exclude NSC principals other than the President from knowledge of the initiative. Indeed, on one or more occasions Secretary Shultz may have been actively misled by VADM Poindexter.

VADM Poindexter also failed grievously on the matter of Contra diversion. Evidence indicates that VADM Poindexter knew that a diversion occurred, yet he did not take the steps that were required given the gravity of that prospect. He apparently failed to appreciate or ignored the serious legal and political risks presented. His clear obligation was either to investigate the matter or take it to the President—or both. He did neither. Director Casey shared a similar responsibility. Evidence suggests that he received information about the possible diversion of funds to the Contras almost a month

before the story broke. He, too, did not move promptly to raise the matter with the President. Yet his responsibility to do so was clear.

The NSC principals other than the President may be somewhat excused by the insufficient attention on the part of the National Security Advisor to the need to keep all the principals fully informed. Given the importance of the issue and the sharp policy divergences involved, however, Secretary Shultz and Secretary Weinberger in particular distanced themselves from the march of events. Secretary Shultz specifically requested to be informed only as necessary to perform his job. Secretary Weinberger had access through intelligence to details about the operation. Their obligation was to give the President their full support and continued advice with respect to the program or, if they could not in conscience do that, to so inform the President. Instead, they simply distanced themselves from the program. They protected the record as to their own positions on this issue. They were not energetic in attempting to protect the President from the consequences of his personal commitment to freeing the hostages.

Director Casey appears to have been informed in considerable detail about the specifics of the Iranian operation. He appears to have acquiesced in and to have encouraged North's exercise of direct operational control over the operation. Because of the NSC staff's proximity to and close identification with the President, this increased the risks to the President if the initiative became public or the operation failed.

There is no evidence, however, that Director Casey explained this risk to the President or made clear to the President that LtCol North, rather than the CIA, was running the operation. The President does not recall ever being informed of this fact. Indeed, Director Casey should have gone further and pressed for operational responsibility to be transferred to the CIA.

Director Casey should have taken the lead in vetting the assumptions presented by the Israelis on which the program was based and in pressing for an early examination of the reliance upon Mr. Ghorbanifar and the second channel as intermediaries. He should also have assumed responsibility for checking out the other intermediaries involved in the operation. Finally, because Congressional restrictions on covert actions are both largely directed at and familiar to the CIA, Director Casey should have taken the lead in keeping the question of Congressional notification active.

Finally, Director Casey, and, to a lesser extent, Secretary Weinberger, should have taken it upon themselves to assess the effect of the transfer of arms and intelligence to Iran on the Iran/Iraq military balance, and to transmit that information to the President.

### C. The Role of the Israelis

Conversations with emissaries from the Government of Israel took place prior to the commencement of the initiative. It remains unclear whether the initial proposal to open the Ghorbanifar channel was an Israeli initiative, was brought on by the avarice of arms dealers, or came as a result of an American request for assistance. There is no doubt, however, that it was Israel that pressed Mr. Ghorbanifar on the United States. U.S. officials accepted Israeli assurances that they had had for some time an extensive dialogue that involved high-level Iranians, as well as their assurances of Mr. Ghorbanifar's bona fides. Thereafter, at critical points in the initiative, when doubts were expressed by critical U.S. participants, an Israeli emissary would arrive with encouragement, often a specific proposal, and pressure to stay with the Ghorbanifar channel. . . .

It is clear, however, that Israel had its own interests, some in direct conflict with those of the United States, in having the United States pursue the initiative. For this reason, it had an incentive to keep the initiative alive. It sought to do this by interventions with the NSC staff, the National Security Advisor, and the President. Although it may have received suggestions from LtCol North, Mr. [Michael] Ledeen, and others, it responded affirmatively to these suggestions by reason of its own interests.

Even if the Government of Israel actively worked to begin the initiative and to keep it going, the U.S. Government is responsible for its own decisions. Key participants in U.S. deliberations made the point that Israel's objectives and interests in this initiative were different from, and in some respects in conflict with, those of the United States. Although Israel dealt with those portions of the U.S. Government that it deemed were sympathetic to the initiative, there is nothing improper *per se* about this fact. U.S. decision-makers made their own decisions and must bear responsibility for the consequences. . . .

## Part V. Recommendations

. . . Whereas the ultimate power to formulate domestic policy resides in the Congress, the primary responsibility for the formulation and implementation of national security policy falls on the President.

It is the President who is the usual source of innovation and responsiveness in this field. The departments and agencies—the Defense Department, State Department, and CIA bureaucracies—tend to resist policy change. Each has its own perspective based on long experience. The challenge for the President is to bring his perspective to bear on these bureaucracies for they are his instruments for executing national security policy, and he must work through them. His task is to provide them leadership and direction.

The National Security Act of 1947 and the system that has grown up under it affords the President special tools for carrying out this important role. These tools are the National Security Council, the National Security Advisor, and the NSC Staff. These are the means through which the creative impulses of the President are brought to bear on the permanent government. The National Security Act, and custom and practice, rightly give the President wide latitude in fashioning exactly how these means are used.

There is no magic formula which can be applied to the NSC structure and process to produce an optimal system. Because the system is the vehicle through which the President formulates and implements his national security policy, it must adapt to each individual President's style and management philosophy. This means that NSC structures and processes must be flexible, not rigid. Overprescription would ... either destroy the system or render it ineffective.

Nevertheless, this does not mean there can be no guidelines or recommendations that might improve the operation of the system, whatever the particular style of the incumbent President. We have reviewed the operation of the system over the past 40 years, through good times and bad. ... With the strong caveat that flexibility and adaptability must be at the core, it is our judgment that the national security system seems to have worked best when it has in general operated along the lines set forth below.

### Organizing for National Security

Because of the wide latitude in the National Security Act, the President bears a special responsibility for the effective performance of the NSC system. A President must at the outset provide guidelines to the members of the National Security Council, his National Security Advisor, and the National Security Council staff. These guidelines, to be effective, must include how they will relate to one another, what procedures will be followed, what the President expects of them. If his advisors are not performing as he likes, only the President can intervene.

The National Security Council principals other than the President participate on the Council in a unique capacity. Although holding a seat by virtue of their official positions in the Administration, when they sit as members of the Council they sit not as cabinet secretaries or department heads but as advisors to the President. They are there not simply to advance or defend the particular positions of the departments or agencies they head but to give their best advice to the President. Their job—and their challenge—is to see the issue from this perspective, not from the narrower interests of their respective bureaucracies.

The National Security Council is only advisory. It is the President alone who decides. When the NSC principals receive those decisions, they do so as heads of the appropriate departments or agencies. They are then responsible to see that the President's decisions are carried out by those organizations accurately and effectively.

This is an important point. The policy innovation and creativity of the President encounters a natural resistance from the executing departments. While this resistance is a source of frustration to every President, it is inherent in the design of the government. It is up to the politically appointed agency heads to ensure that the President's goals, designs, and policies are brought to bear on this permanent structure. Circumventing the departments, perhaps by using the National Security Advisor or the NSC Staff to execute policy, robs the President of the experience and capacity resident in the departments. The President must act largely through them, but the agency heads must ensure that they execute the President's policies in an expeditious and effective manner. It is not just the obligation of the National Security Advisor to see that the national security process is used. All of the NSC principals—and particularly the President—have that obligation.

This tension between the President and the Executive Departments is worked out through the national security process described in the opening sections of this report. It is through this process that the nation obtains both the best of the creativity of the President and the learning and expertise of the national security departments and agencies. . . .

### The National Security Advisor

It is the National Security Advisor who is primarily responsible for managing this process on a daily basis. The job requires skill, sensitivity, and integrity. It is his responsibility to ensure that matters submitted for consideration by the Council cover the full range of issues on which review is required; that those issues are fully analyzed; that a full range of options is considered; that the prospects and risks of each are examined; that all relevant intelligence and other information is available to the principals; that legal considerations are addressed; that difficulties in implementation are confronted. Usually, this can best be accomplished through interagency participation in the analysis of the issue and a preparatory policy review at the Deputy or Under Secretary level.

The National Security Advisor assumes these responsibilities not only with respect to the President but with respect to all the NSC principals. He must keep them informed of the President's thinking and decisions. They should have adequate notice and an agenda for all meetings. Decision papers should, if at all possible, be provided in advance.

The National Security Advisor must also ensure that adequate records are kept of NSC consultations and Presidential decisions. This is essential to avoid confusion among Presidential advisors and departmental staffs about what was actually decided and what is wanted. Those records are also essential for conducting a periodic review of a policy or initiative, and to learn from the past.

It is the responsibility of the National Security Advisor to monitor policy implementation and to ensure that policies are executed in conformity with the intent of the President's decision. Monitoring includes initiating periodic reassessments of a policy or operation, especially when changed circumstances suggest that the policy or operation no longer serves U.S. interests.

But the National Security Advisor does not simply manage the national security process. He is himself an important source of advice on national security matters to the President. He is . . . perhaps the one most able to see things from the President's perspective. He is unburdened by departmental responsibilities. The President is his only master. His advice is confidential. He is not subject to Senate confirmation and traditionally does not formally appear before Congressional committees.

To serve the President well, the National Security Advisor should present his own views, but he must at the same time represent the views of others fully and faithfully to the President. The system will not work well if the National Security Advisor does not have the trust of the NSC principals. He, therefore, must not use his proximity to the President to manipulate the process so as to produce his own position. He should not interpose himself between the President and the NSC principals. He should not seek to exclude the NSC principals from the decision process. Performing both these roles well is an essential, if not easy, task.

In order for the National Security Advisor to serve the President adequately, he must have direct access to the President. Unless he knows first hand the views of the President and is known to reflect them in his management of the NSC system, he will be ineffective. He should not report to the President through some other official. While the Chief of Staff or others can usefully interject domestic political considerations into national security deliberations, they should do so as additional advisors to the President.

Ideally, the National Security Advisor should not have a high public profile. He should not try to compete with the Secretary of State or the Secretary of Defense as the articulator of public policy. They, along with the President, should be the spokesmen for the policies of the Administration...

The NSC principals of course must have direct access to the President, with whatever frequency the President feels is appropriate. But these individual meetings should not be used by the principal to seek decisions or otherwise circumvent the system in the absence of the other principals. In the same way, the National Security Advisor should not use his scheduled intelligence or other daily briefings of the President as an opportunity to seek Presidential decision on significant issues.

If the system is to operate well, the National Security Advisor must promote cooperation rather than competition among himself and the other NSC principals. But the President is ultimately responsible for the operation of this system. If rancorous infighting develops among his principal national security functionaries, only he can deal with them. Public dispute over external policy by senior officials undermines the process of decision-making and narrows his options. It is the President's responsibility to ensure that it does not take place.

Finally, the National Security Advisor should focus on advice and management, not implementation and execution. Implementation is the responsibility and the strength of the departments and agencies. The National Security Advisor and the NSC Staff generally do not have the depth of resources for the conduct of operations. In addition, when they take on implementation responsibilities, they risk compromising their objectivity. They can no longer act as impartial overseers of the implementation, ensuring that Presidential guidance is followed, that policies are kept under review, and that the results are serving the President's policy and the national interest.

### The NSC Staff

The NSC staff should be small, highly competent, and experienced in the making of public policy. Staff members should be drawn both from within and from outside government. Those from within government should come from the several departments and agencies concerned with national security matters. No particular department or agency should have a predominate role. A proper balance must be maintained between people from within and outside the government. Staff members should generally rotate with a stay of more than four years viewed as the exception.

A large number of staff action officers organized along essentially horizontal lines enhances the possibilities for poorly supervised and monitored activities by individual staff members. Such a system is made to order for energetic self-starters to take unauthorized initiatives. Clear vertical lines of control and authority, responsibility and accountability, are essential to good management.

One problem affecting the NSC staff is lack of institutional memory. This results from the understandable desire of a President to replace the staff in order to be sure it is responsive to him. Departments provide continuity that can help the Council, but the Council as an institution also needs some means to assure adequate records and memory....

We recognize the problem and have identified a range of possibilities that a President might consider on this subject. One would be to create a small permanent executive secretariat. Another would be to have one person, the Executive Secretary, as a permanent position. Finally, a pattern of limited tenure and overlapping rotation could be used. Any of these would help reduce the problem of loss of institutional memory; none would be practical unless each succeeding President subscribed to it.

The guidelines for the role of the National Security Advisor also apply generally to the NSC staff. They should protect the process and thereby the President. Departments and agencies should not be excluded from participation in that process. The staff should not be implementors or operators and staff should keep a low profile with the press.

### Principal Recommendation

The model we have outlined above for the National Security Council system constitutes our first and most important recommendation. It includes guidelines that address virtually all of the deficiencies in procedure and practice that the Board encountered in the Iran/Contra affair as well as in other case studies of this and previous administrations....

**The Board recommends that the proposed model be used by Presidents in their management of the national security system.**

### Specific Recommendations

In addition to its principal recommendation regarding the organization and functioning of the NSC system and roles to be played by the participants, the Board has a number of specific recommendations.

**1. The National Security Act of 1947.** The flaws of procedure and failures of responsibility revealed by our study do not suggest any inadequacies in the provisions of the National Security Act of 1947 that deal with the structure and operation of the NSC system. Forty years of experience under that Act demonstrate to the Board that it remains a fundamentally sound framework for national security decision-making. It strikes a balance between formal structure and flexibility adequate to permit each President to tailor the system to fit his needs.

As a general matter, the NSC Staff should not engage in the implementation of policy or the conduct of operations. This compromises their oversight role and usurps the responsibilities of the departments and agencies. But the inflexibility of a legislative restriction should be avoided. Terms such as "operation" and "implementation" are difficult to define, and a legislative proscription might preclude some future President from making a very constructive use of the NSC Staff.

Predisposition on sizing of the staff should be toward fewer rather than more. But a legislative restriction cannot forsee [sic] the requirements of future Presidents. Size is best left to the discretion of the President, with the admonition that the role of the NSC staff is to review, not to duplicate or replace, the work of the departments and agencies.

**We recommend that no substantive change be made in the provisions of the National Security Act dealing with the structure and operation of the NSC system.**

**2. Senate Confirmation of the National Security Advisor.** It has been suggested that the job of the National Security Advisor has become so important that its holder should be screened by the process of confirmation, and that once confirmed he should return frequently for questioning by the Congress. It is argued that this would improve the accountability of the National Security Advisor.

We hold a different view. The National Security Advisor does, and should continue, to serve only one master, and that is the President. Further, confirmation is inconsistent with the role the National Security Advisor should play. He should not decide, only advise. He should not engage in policy implementation or operations. He should serve the President, with no collateral and potentially diverting loyalties.

Confirmation would tend to institutionalize the natural tension that exists between the Secretary of State and the National Security Advisor. Questions would increasingly arise about who really speaks for the President in national security matters. Foreign governments could be confused or would be encouraged to engage in "forum shopping."

Only one of the former government officials interviewed favored Senate confirmation of the National Security Advisor. While consultation with Congress received wide support, confirmation and formal questioning were opposed. Several suggested that if the National Security Advisor were to become a position subject to confirmation, it could induce the President to turn to other internal staff or to people outside government to play that role.

**We urge the Congress not to require Senate confirmation of the National Security Advisor.**

**3. The Interagency Process.** It is the National Security Advisor who has the greatest interest in making the national security process work, for it is this process by which the President obtains the information, background, and analysis he requires to make decisions and build support for his program. Most Presidents have set up interagency committees at both a staff and policy level to surface issues, de-

velop options, and clarify choices. There has typically been a struggle for the chairmanships of these groups between the National Security Advisor and the NSC staff on the one hand, and the cabinet secretaries and department officials on the other.

Our review of the operation of the present system and that of other administrations where committee chairmen came from the departments has led us to the conclusion that the system generally operates better when the committees are chaired by the individual with the greatest stake in making the NSC system work.

**We recommend that the National Security Advisor chair the senior-level committees of the NSC system.**

**4. Covert Actions.** Policy formulation and implementation are usually managed by a team of experts led by policy-making generalists. Covert action requirements are no different, but there is a need to limit, sometimes severely, the number of individuals involved. The lives of many people may be at stake, as was the case in the attempt to rescue the hostages in Tehran. Premature disclosure might kill the idea in embryo, as could have been the case in the opening of relations with China. In such cases, there is a tendency to limit those involved to a small number of top officials. This practice tends to limit severely the expertise brought to bear on the problem and should be used very sparingly indeed.

The obsession with secrecy and preoccupation with leaks threaten to paralyze the government in its handling of covert operations. Unfortunately, the concern is not misplaced. The selective leak has become a principal means of waging bureaucratic warfare. Opponents of an operation kill it with a leak; supporters seek to build support through the same means.

We have witnessed over the past years a significant deterioration in the integrity of process. Rather than a means to obtain results more satisfactory than the position of any of the individual departments, it has frequently become something to be manipulated to reach a specific outcome. The leak becomes a primary instrument in that process.

This practice is destructive of orderly governance. It can only be reversed if the most senior officials take the lead. If senior decision-makers set a clear example and demand compliance, subordinates are more likely to conform.

Most recent administrations have had carefully drawn procedures for the consideration of covert activities. The Reagan Administration established such procedures in January, 1985, then promptly ignored them in their consideration of the Iran initiative.

**We recommend that each administration formulate precise procedures for restricted consideration of covert action and that, once formulated, those procedures be strictly adhered to.**

**5. The Role of the CIA.** Some aspects of the Iran arms sales raised broader questions in the minds of members of the Board regarding the role of CIA. The first deals with intelligence.

The NSC staff was actively involved in the preparation of the May 20, 1985, update to the Special National Intelligence Estimate on Iran. It is a matter for concern if this involvement and the strong views of NSC staff members were allowed to influence the intelligence judgments contained in the update. It is also of concern that the update contained the hint that the United States should change its existing policy and encourage its allies to provide arms to Iran. It is critical that the line between intelligence and advocacy of a particular policy be preserved if intelligence is to retain its integrity and perform its proper function. In this instance, the CIA came close enough to the line to warrant concern.

**We emphasize to both the intelli-**gence community and policymakers the importance of maintaining the integrity and objectivity of the intelligence process.

**6. Legal Counsel.** From time to time issues with important legal ramifications will come before the National Security Council. The Attorney General is currently a member of the Council by invitation and should be in a position to provide legal advice to the Council and the President. It is important that the Attorney General and his department be available to interagency deliberations.

The Justice Department, however, should not replace the role of counsel in the other departments. As the principal counsel on foreign affairs, the Legal Adviser to the Secretary of State should also be available to all the NSC participants.

Of all the NSC participants, it is the Assistant for National Security Affairs who seems to have had the least access to expert counsel familiar with his activities.

**The Board recommends that the position of Legal Adviser to the NSC be enhanced in stature and in its role within the NSC staff.**

**7. Secrecy and Congress.** There is a natural tension between the desire for secrecy and the need to consult Congress on covert operations. Presidents seem to become increasingly concerned about leaks of classified information as their administrations progress. They blame Congress disproportionately. Various cabinet officials from prior administrations indicated to the Board that they believe Congress bears no more blame than the Executive Branch. However, the number of Members and staff involved in reviewing covert activities is large; it provides cause for concern and a convenient excuse for Presidents to avoid Congressional consultation.

**We recommend that Congress consider replacing the existing Intelli-**

gence Committees of the respective Houses with a new joint committee with a restricted staff to oversee the intelligence community, patterned after the Joint Committee on Atomic Energy that existed until the mid-1970s.

**8. Privatizing National Security Policy.** Careful and limited use of people outside the U.S. Government may be very helpful in some unique cases. But this practice raises substantial questions. It can create conflict of interest problems. Private or foreign sources may have different policy interests or personal motives and may exploit their association with a U.S. government effort. Such involvement gives private and foreign sources potentially powerful leverage in the form of demands for return favors or even blackmail.

The U.S. has enormous resources invested in agencies and departments in order to conduct the government's business. In all but a very few cases, these can perform the functions needed. If not, then inquiry is required to find out why.

**We recommend against having implementation and policy oversight dominated by intermediaries. We do not recommend barring limited use of private individuals to assist in United States diplomatic initiatives or in covert activities. We caution against use of such people except in very limited ways and under close observation and supervision....**

# INF Treaty: Signing Statements and Television Addresses of President Ronald Reagan and Soviet President Mikhail S. Gorbachev (1987)

On December 8, 1987, President Ronald Reagan and Soviet President and General Secretary Mikhail S. Gorbachev met in Washington to sign a treaty that bound each nation to destroy all of its intermediate-range nuclear-force (INF) missiles. The treaty marked the first time in history that the United States and the Soviet Union had agreed to eliminate an entire class of nuclear weapons and to reduce the size of their nuclear arsenals.

The INF treaty was the result of two major developments in U.S.-Soviet relations. First, Reagan established early in his first term, at a time when the only intermediate-range weapons in Europe were Soviet missiles, that the United States would accept nothing less than complete removal of the missiles. When the Soviets balked, Reagan installed several hundred intermediate-range Pershing II missiles in Great Britain and West Germany in November 1983. This was a politically controversial move both in the United States and in Europe, especially after the Soviet Union broke off negotiations with the United States, protesting that the Reagan administration was not interested in peace.

The second important development that set the stage for the INF treaty was Gorbachev's rise to power in the Soviet Union after Soviet leader Konstantin Chernenko died in March 1985. Gorbachev's desire to revive his nation's moribund economy made him more willing than his predecessors had been to jettison expensive weapons programs. By 1987 Gorbachev was ready to accept the U.S. negotiating position on intermediate-range missiles in order to do so.

The INF treaty required that the United States and the Soviet Union destroy all the nuclear missiles in their arsenals with ranges between 500 and 5,500 kilometers—that is, between approximately 300 and 3,400 miles—along with the associated launchers and support facilities. The United States had 830 such missiles (Pershing IIs and ground-launched cruise missiles); the Soviets had 1,752, mainly SS-20s. The treaty also included detailed and thorough procedures for compliance. Each nation was allowed to inspect the other's weapons facilities closely and on short notice.

Reagan and Gorbachev made brief remarks at the treaty-signing ceremony on December 8. Soon after, in televised addresses that were telecast in both countries, the two leaders stressed the magnitude of the accomplishment, the difficulty of the negotiations that brought it about, and the hope that another agreement concerning long-range, or strategic, nuclear missiles could be reached.

The INF treaty helped to restore

*Reagan's popularity, undoing most of the political damage that had been caused by the Iran-contra affair. (See "Report of the Tower Commission," p. 474.) As with President Richard Nixon's opening to China (see "Richard Nixon's China Trip Announcement," p. 382), it was ironic that the conservative, fervently anti-Communist Reagan was the president who made U.S.-Soviet relations more harmonious than at any time since World War II. Yet— again, as with Nixon—perhaps only such a president could have accomplished the breakthrough without bringing down the wrath of his fellow conservative anti-Communists.*  **~**

---

## Signing Statements

**The President:** ... [S]trong and fundamental moral differences continue to exist between our nations, but today, on this vital issue, at least, we've seen what can be accomplished when we pull together.

The numbers alone demonstrate the value of this agreement. On the Soviet side, over 1,500 deployed warheads will be removed and all ground-launched intermediate-range missiles, including the SS-20s, will be destroyed. On our side, our entire complement of Pershing II and ground-launched cruise missiles, with some 400 deployed warheads, will all be destroyed. Additional backup missiles on both sides will also be destroyed.

But the importance of this treaty transcends numbers. We have listened to the wisdom in an old Russian maxim. And I'm sure you're familiar with it, Mr. General Secretary, though my pronunciation may give you difficulty. The maxim is: *Doveryai, no proveryai*— trust, but verify.

**The General Secretary:** You repeat that at every meeting.

**The President:** I like it.

This agreement contains the most stringent verification regime in history, including provisions for inspection teams actually residing in each other's territory and several other forms of on-site inspection as well. This treaty protects the interests of America's friends and allies. It also embodies another important principle, the need for *glasnost*, a greater openness—in military programs and forces.

We can only hope that this history-making agreement will not be an end in itself, but the beginning of a working relationship that will enable us to tackle the other issues—urgent issues before us—strategic offensive nuclear weapons; the balance of conventional forces in Europe; the destructive and tragic regional conflicts that beset so many parts of our globe; and respect for the human and natural rights God has granted to all men.

To all here who have worked so hard to make this vision a reality: Thank you, and congratulations. . . .

**The General Secretary:** Mr. President, ladies and gentlemen, comrades, succeeding generations will hand down their verdict on the importance of the event which we are about to witness. But I will venture to say that what we are going to do—the signing of the first-ever agreement eliminating nuclear weapons, has a universal significance for mankind, both from the standpoint of world politics, and from the standpoint of humanism.

For everyone, and above all, for our two great powers, the treaty whose text is on this table offers a big chance at last to get on to the road leading away from the threat of catastrophe. It is our duty to take full advantage of that chance, and move together toward a nuclear-free world which holds out for our children and grandchildren and for their children and grandchildren the promise of a fulfilling and happy life without fear and without a senseless waste of resources on weapons of destruction. . . .

May December 8, 1987, become a date that will be inscribed in the history books, a date that will mark the watershed separating the era of a mounting risk of nuclear war from the era of a demilitarization of human life.

## Television Addresses

**The President:** . . . Today, I, for the United States, and the General Secretary, for the Soviet Union, have signed the first agreement ever to eliminate an entire class of U.S. and Soviet nuclear weapons. We have made history. And yet many so-called wise men once predicted that this agreement would be impossible to achieve—too many forces and factors stood against it. Well, still we persevered. We kept at it. . . .

In the next few days we will discuss further arms reductions and other issues—and again it will take time and patience to reach agreements. But as we begin these talks, let us remember that genuine international confidence and security are inconceivable without open societies with freedom of information, freedom of conscience, the right to publish and the right to travel. So, yes, we will address human rights and regional conflicts, for surely the salvation of all mankind lies only in making everything the concern of all. With time, patience, and willpower I believe we will resolve these issues. We must if we are to achieve a true, secure, and enduring peace.

As different as our systems are, there is a great bond that draws the American and Soviet peoples together. It is the common dream of peace. . . .

Only those who don't know us believe that America is a materialistic land. But the true America is not supermarkets filled with meats, milk and goods of all descriptions. It is not highways filled with cars. No, true America is a land of faith and family. You can find it in our churches, synagogues and mosques—in our homes and schools. As one of our great writers put it: America is a willingness of the heart—the universal, human heart, for Americans come from every part of earth, including the Soviet Union. We want a peace that fulfills the dream of all peoples to raise their families in freedom and safety. And I believe that if both of our countries have courage and the patience, we will build such a peace. . . .

**The General Secretary:** I am addressing my fellow countrymen, the citizens of the Soviet Union. I am addressing the American people.

President Reagan and I have just signed a treaty which for the first time in history requires the most stringently verified destruction of two whole classes of nuclear arms. The treaty on the total elimination of Soviet and U.S. intermediate- and shorter-range missiles will, I am sure, become a historic milestone in the chronicle of man's eternal quest for a world without wars.

On this occasion, may I be allowed to refer for a moment to history. Not all Americans may know that at the height of a world war, the very first step taken by the Soviet Republic born in Russia in 1917 was to promulgate a degree of peace. Its author, Vladimir Lenin, the founder of our state, said, "We are willing to consider any proposal leading to peace on a just and solid basis." This has been the cornerstone of Soviet foreign policy ever since.

We also remember another concept of his—disarmament, a world without arms or violence. This is our ideal. Today, regrettably, the risk of a nuclear catastrophe persists. It is still formidable. But we believe in man's ability to get rid of the threat of self-annihilation. We are encouraged by the willing awareness in the world of the nature of the existing peril which has confronted humankind with the question of its very survival. . . .

The treaty just signed in Washington is a major watershed in international development. Its significance and implications go far beyond what has actually been agreed upon. Our passage to this watershed was difficult. It took us lengthy and intense arguments and debate, overcoming long held emotions and ingrained stereotypes. What has been accomplished is only a beginning. That is only the start of nuclear disarmament although, as we know, even the longest journey begins with a first step.

Moving ahead from this start will require further intensive intellectual endeavor and honest effort, the abandonment of some concepts of security which seem indisputable today and of all that fuels the arms race. . . .

Most important of all is to translate into reality as early as possible agreements on radical cuts in strategic offensive arms subject to preserving the ABM [antiballistic missile] treaty, on the elimination of chemical weapons and on reductions in conventional armament. On each of these problems, the Soviet Union has put forward specific proposals. We believe that agreements on them are within reach.

We are hopeful that during next year's return visit of the United States President to the Soviet Union, we will achieve a treaty eliminating practically one-half of all existing strategic nuclear arms. There is also a possibility of agreeing on substantial cuts in conventional forces and arms in Europe, whose buildup and upgrading causes justified concern. . . .

# George Bush's Acceptance Speech for the Republican Presidential Nomination (1988)

George Bush constructed his candidacy for president in 1988 on two main pillars: his résumé of experience in government and his association with President Ronald Reagan.

Bush was the son of Prescott Bush, a wealthy Wall Street banker who represented Connecticut in the Senate. After valiant service in World War II and undergraduate studies at Yale University, Bush struck out successfully on his own, building an oil business in Texas. He was elected to the House of Representatives by Houston voters in 1966 and 1968 and ran a strong race for the Senate in 1970, losing to conservative Democrat Lloyd Bentsen. (Senator Bentsen became the Democratic vice-presidential nominee in 1988.) A series of appointive positions followed in the administrations of Presidents Richard Nixon and Gerald R. Ford: ambassador to the United Nations, Republican National Committee chair, U.S. emissary to China, and director of the Central Intelligence Agency. Portraying himself as a moderate Republican, Bush ran a strong campaign for his party's presidential nomination in 1980, finishing second to Ronald Reagan.

Reagan tapped Bush as his vice-presidential running mate at the 1980 Republican national convention. The Reagan-Bush ticket was elected and, in 1984, reelected. Both as a candidate and as vice president, Bush gave his full loyalty to Reagan, avoiding any hint of disagreement or criticism and even adopting the president's conservative political views. In early 1980, Bush had described Reagan's economic theories as "voodoo economics" and taken a pro-choice position on abortion; as vice president, he adopted the president's position on both issues.

The vice presidency is a politically anomalous office. Five of Bush's seven predecessors as vice president had gone on to win their party's nomination for president. Yet no incumbent vice president actually had been elected president since Martin Van Buren in 1836. A vice president's years of loyal service to the president seemed to underlie both political patterns: most party loyalists appreciated the loyalty and would reward it by conferring the party's presidential nomination on the vice president, but the broader electorate saw mainly weakness and subservience and rejected the vice president in the general election.

In the summer of 1988, Bush seemed likely to inherit both political legacies of the vice presidency. He had raced victoriously through the early caucuses and primaries against a strong field of six other candidates, locking up the Republican nomination for president by early March. Yet going into the party's national convention in mid-August, Bush trailed his Democratic rival,

*Gov. Michael S. Dukakis of Massachusetts, by as much as eighteen percentage points in the polls.*

*The evening of August 18 offered Bush his best opportunity to turn the election around: the scheduled delivery of his acceptance speech for the Republican nomination guaranteed him an enormous television audience of voters. Bush, who was not known as an effective speaker, rose to the occasion with a speech that was well-written (by speechwriter Peggy Noonan), was confidently delivered, and included several phrases that resonated throughout the fall campaign and the early part of this administration: "a thousand points of light," "a kinder and gentler nation," and "Read my lips. No new taxes."* ～

Thank you ladies and gentlemen, thank you very, very much.

I have many friends to thank tonight. I thank the voters who supported me. I thank the gallant men who entered the contest for this presidency this year, and who've honored me with their support. And, for their kind and stirring words, I thank Governor Tom Kean of New Jersey, Senator Phil Gramm of Texas, President Gerald Ford—and my friend, President Ronald Reagan.

I accept your nomination for president. I mean to run hard, to fight hard, to stand on the issues—and I mean to win.

There are a lot of great stories in politics about the underdog winning—and this is going to be one of them.

And we're going to win with the help of Senator Dan Quayle of Indiana—a young leader who has become a forceful voice in preparing America's workers for the labor force of the future. What a superb job he did here tonight.

Born in the middle of the century, in the middle of America, and holding the promise of the future—I'm proud to have Dan Quayle at my side.

Many of you have asked, "When will this campaign really begin?" Well, I've come to this hall to tell you, and to tell America: Tonight is the night.

For seven and a half years I've helped the president conduct the most difficult job on Earth. Ronald Reagan asked for, and received, my candor. He never asked for, but he did receive, my loyalty. And those of you who saw the president's speech last week, and listened to the simple truth of his words, will understand my loyalty all these years.

And now you must see me for what I am: the Republican candidate for president of the United States. And now I turn to the American people to share my hopes and intentions, and why and where I wish to lead.

And so tonight is for big things. But I'll try to be fair to the other side. I'll try to hold my charisma in check.

I reject the temptation to engage in personal references. My approach this evening is, as Sergeant Joe Friday used to say, "Just the facts, ma'am."

And after all, the facts are on our side.

I seek the presidency for a single purpose, a purpose that has motivated millions of Americans across the years and the ocean voyages. I seek the presidency to build a better America. It's that simple—and that big.

I'm a man who sees life in terms of missions—missions defined and missions completed.

And when I was a torpedo bomber pilot they defined the mission for us. And before we took off, we all understood that no matter what, you try to reach the target. And there have been other missions for me—Congress, and China, the CIA. But I'm here tonight, and I am your candidate, because the most important work of my life is to complete the mission we started in 1980. And how do we complete it? We build on it.

The stakes are high this year and the

choice is crucial, for the differences between the two candidates are as deep and wide as they have ever been in our long history.

Not only two very different men, but two very different ideas of the future will be voted on this Election Day.

And what it all comes down to is this: My opponent's view of the world sees a long slow decline for our country, an inevitable fall mandated by impersonal historical forces.

But America is not in decline. America is a rising nation.

He sees America as another pleasant country on the U.N. [United Nations] roll call, somewhere between Albania and Zimbabwe. And I see America as the leader—a unique nation with a special role in the world.

And this has been called the American century, because in it we were the dominant force for good in the world. We saved Europe, cured polio, went to the moon, and lit the world with our culture. And now we are on the verge of a new century, and what country's name will it bear? I say it will be another American century.

Our work is not done, our force is not spent.

There are those who say there isn't much of a difference this year. But America, don't let 'em fool ya.

Two parties this year ask for your support. Both will speak of growth and peace. But only one has proved it can deliver. Two parties this year ask for your trust, but only one has earned it.

Eight years ago, I stood here with Ronald Reagan and we promised, together, to break with the past and return America to her greatness. Eight years later, look at what the American people have produced: the highest level of economic growth in our entire history—and the lowest level of world tensions in more than 50 years.

You know, some say this isn't an election about ideology, but it's an election about competence. Well, it's nice of them to want to play on our field. But this election isn't only about competence, for competence is a narrow ideal.

Competence makes the trains run on time but doesn't know where they're going. Competence is the creed of the technocrat who makes sure the gears mesh but doesn't for a second understand the magic of the machine.

The truth is, this election is about the beliefs we share, the values we honor and the principles we hold dear.

But since someone brought up competence . . .

Consider the size of our triumph: A record number of Americans at work, a record high percentage of our people with jobs, a record high of new businesses, a high rate of new businesses, a record high rate of real personal income.

These are facts.

And one way we know our opponents know the facts is that to attack our record they have to misrepresent it. They call it a Swiss cheese economy. Well, that's the way it may look to the three blind mice.

But when they were in charge it was all holes and no cheese.

Inflation—you know the litany—inflation was 13 percent when we came in. We got it down to four. Interest rates were more than 21. We cut them in half. Unemployment was up and climbing, and now it's the lowest in 14 years.

My friends, eight years ago this economy was flat on its back—intensive care. And we came in and gave it emergency treatment: Got the temperature down by lowering regulation, and got the blood pressure down when we lowered taxes. And pretty soon the patient was up, back on his feet, and stronger than ever.

And now who do we hear knocking on the door but the same doctors who made him sick. And they're telling us to put them in charge of the case again? My friends, they're lucky we don't hit 'em with a malpractice suit!

We've created 17 million new jobs [in] the past five years—more than twice as many as Europe and Japan combined. And they're good jobs. The majority of them created in the past six years paid an average—average—of more than $22,000 a year. And someone better take a message to Michael: Tell him that we have been creating good jobs at good wages. The fact is, they talk and we deliver.

They promise and we perform.

And there are millions of young Americans in their 20s who barely remember the days of gas lines and unemployment lines. And now they're marrying and starting careers. To those young people I say, "You have the opportunity you deserve, and I'm not going to let them take it away from you."

The leaders of the expansion have been the women of America who helped create the new jobs, and filled two out of every three of them. And to the women of America I say, "You know better than anyone that equality begins with economic empowerment. You're gaining economic power, and I'm not going to let them take it away from you."

There are millions of older Americans who were brutalized by inflation. We arrested it—and we're not going to let it out on furlough.

We're going to keep the Social Security trust fund sound, and out of reach of the big spenders. To America's elderly I say, "Once again you have the security that is your right, and I'm not going to let them take it away from you."

I know the liberal Democrats are worried about the economy. They're worried it's going to remain strong. And they're right, it is—with the right leadership it will remain strong.

But let's be frank. Things aren't perfect in this country. There are people who haven't tasted the fruits of the expansion. I've talked to farmers about the bills they can't pay and I've been to the factories that feel the strain of change. And I've seen the urban children who play amidst the shattered glass and the shattered lives. And, you know, there are the homeless. And you know, it doesn't do any good to debate endlessly which policy mistake of the '70s is responsible. They're there, and we have to help them.

But what we must remember if we're to be responsible and compassionate is that economic growth is the key to our endeavors.

I want growth that stays, that broadens, and that touches, finally, all Americans, from the hollows of Kentucky to the sunlit streets of Denver, from the suburbs of Chicago to the broad avenues of New York, and from the oil fields of Oklahoma to the farms of the Great Plains.

And can we do it? Of course we can. We know how. We've done it. If we continue to grow at our current rate, we will be able to produce 30 million jobs in the next eight years.

And we will do it—by maintaining our commitment to free and fair trade, by keeping government spending down, and by keeping taxes down.

Our economic life is not the only test of our success. One issue overwhelms all the others, and that is the issue of peace.

Look at the world on this bright August night. The spirit of democracy is sweeping the Pacific rim. China feels the winds of change. New democracies assert themselves in South America. And one by one the unfree places fall, not to the force of arms but to the force of an idea: freedom works.

And we have a new relationship with the Soviet Union. The INF [intermediate-range nuclear-force] treaty, the beginning of the Soviet withdrawal from Afghanistan, the beginning of the end of the Soviet proxy war in Angola, and with it the independence of Namibia. Iran and Iraq move toward peace.

It's a watershed. It is no accident.

It happened when we acted on the ancient knowledge that strength and clarity lead to peace—weakness and ambivalence lead to war. You see, weakness tempts aggressors. Strength stops them. I will not allow this country to be made weak again—never.

The tremors in the Soviet world continue. The hard earth there has not yet settled. Perhaps what is happening will change our world forever. And perhaps not. A prudent skepticism is in order. And so is hope.

But either way, we're in an unprecedented position to change the nature of our relationship. Not by preemptive concession, but by keeping our strength. Not by yielding up defense systems with nothing won in return, but by hard, cool engagement in the tug and pull of diplomacy.

My life has been lived in the shadow of war—I almost lost my life in one.

And I hate war. Love peace.

And we have peace.

And I am not going to let anyone take it away from us.

Our economy is stronger but not invulnerable, and the peace is broad but can be broken. And now we must decide. We will surely have change this year, but will it be change that moves us forward? Or change that risks retreat?

In 1940, when I was barely more than a boy, Franklin Roosevelt said we shouldn't change horses in midstream.

My friends, these days the world moves even more quickly, and now, after two great terms, a switch will be made. But when you have to change horses in midstream, doesn't it make sense to switch to one who's going the same way?

An election that is about ideas and values is also about philosophy. And I have one.

At the bright center is the individual. And radiating out from him or her is the family, the essential unit of closeness and of love. For it is the family that communicates to our children—to the 21st century—our culture, our religious faith, our traditions and history.

From the individual to the family to the community, and then on out to the town, the church and the school, and, still echoing out, to the county, the state, and the nation—each doing only what it does well, and no more. And I believe that power must always be kept close to the individual, close to the hands that raise the family and run the home.

I am guided by certain traditions. One is that there is a God and he is good, and his love, while free, has a self-imposed cost: We must be good to one another.

I believe in another tradition that is, by now, imbedded in the national soul. It is that learning is good in and of itself. You know, the mothers of the Jewish ghettoes of the east would pour honey on a book so the children would know that learning is sweet. And the parents who settled hungry Kansas would take their children in from the fields when a teacher came. That is our history.

And there is another tradition. And that is the idea of community—a beautiful word with a big meaning. Though liberal Democrats have an odd view of it. They see "community" as a limited cluster of interest groups, locked in odd conformity. And in this view, the country waits passive while Washington sets the rules.

But that's not what community means—not to me.

For we are a nation of communities, of thousands and tens of thousands of ethnic, religious, social, business, labor union, neighborhood, regional and other organizations—all of them varied, voluntary and unique.

This is America: the Knights of Columbus, the Grange, Hadassah, the Disabled American Veterans, the Order of AHEPA [American Hellenic Educational Progressive Association], the

Business and Professional Women of America, the union hall, the Bible study group, LULAC [League of United Latin American Citizens], "Holy Name"—a brilliant diversity spread like stars, like a thousand points of light in a broad and peaceful sky.

Does government have a place? Yes. Government is part of the nation of communities—not the whole, just a part.

And I don't hate government. A government that remembers that the people are its master is a good and needed thing.

I respect old-fashioned common sense, and I have no great love for the imaginings of the social planners. You see, I like what's been tested and found to be true.

For instance.

Should public school teachers be required to lead our children in the pledge of allegiance? My opponent says no—and I say yes.

Should society be allowed to impose the death penalty on those who commit crimes of extraordinary cruelty and violence? My opponent says no—but I say yes.

And should our children have the right to say a voluntary prayer, or even observe a moment of silence in the schools? My opponent says no—but I say yes.

And should free men and women have the right to own a gun to protect their home? My opponent says no—but I say yes.

And is it right to believe in the sanctity of life and protect the lives of innocent children? My opponent says no—but I say yes.

You see, we must change, we've got to change from abortion to adoption. And let me tell you this: Barbara and I have an adopted granddaughter. And the day of her christening we wept with joy. I thank God that her parents chose life.

I'm the one who believes it is a scandal to give a weekend furlough to a hardened first-degree killer who hasn't even served enough time to be eligible for parole.

I'm the one who says a drug dealer who is responsible for the death of a policeman should be subject to capital punishment.

And I'm the one who will not raise taxes. My opponent now says he'll raise them as a last resort, or a third resort. Well, when a politician talks like that, you know that's one resort he'll be checking into. And, my opponent won't rule out raising taxes. But I will.

And the Congress will push me to raise taxes, and I'll say no, and they'll push, and I'll say no, and they'll push again. And I'll say to them: Read my lips. No new taxes.

Let me tell you more about the mission.

On jobs, my mission is: 30 in 8. Thirty million jobs in the next eight years.

Every one of our children deserves a first-rate school. The liberal Democrats want power in the hands of the federal government. And I want power in the hands of the parents. And, I will encourage merit schools. I will give more kids a head start. And I'll make it easier to save for college.

I want a drug-free America—and this will not be easy to achieve. But I want to enlist the help of some people who are rarely included. Tonight I challenge the young people of our country to shut down the drug dealers around the world. Unite with us, work with us.

"Zero tolerance" isn't just a policy, it's an attitude. Tell them what you think of people who underwrite the dealers who put poison in our society. And while you're doing that, my administration will be telling the dealers: Whatever we have to do we'll do, but your day is over, you're history.

I am going to do whatever it takes to make sure the disabled are included in the mainstream. For too long they've been left out. But they're not going to be left out anymore.

And I am going to stop ocean dumping. Our beaches should not be garbage dumps and our harbors should not be cesspools.

And I am going to have the FBI trace the medical wastes and we are going to punish the people who dump those infected needles into our oceans, lakes and rivers. And we must clean the air. We must reduce the harm done by acid rain.

And I will put incentives back into the domestic energy industry, for I know from personal experience there is no security for the United States in further dependence on foreign oil.

In foreign affairs I will continue our policy of peace through strength. I will move toward further cuts in strategic and conventional arsenals of both the United States and the Soviet Union and the Eastern Bloc and NATO. I will modernize and preserve our technological edge and that includes strategic defense.

And a priority: Ban chemical and biological weapons from the face of the Earth. That will be a priority with me.

And I intend to speak for freedom, stand for freedom, be a patient friend to anyone, East or West, who will fight for freedom.

It seems to me the presidency provides an incomparable opportunity for "gentle persuasion."

And I hope to stand for a new harmony, a greater tolerance. We've come far, but I think we need a new harmony among the races in our country. And we're on a journey into a new century, and we've got to leave that tired old baggage of bigotry behind.

Some people who are enjoying our prosperity have forgotten what it's for. But they diminish our triumph when they act as if wealth is an end in itself.

And there are those who have dropped their standards along the way, as if ethics were too heavy and slowed their rise to the top. There's graft in city hall, and there's greed on Wall Street; there's influence peddling in Washington, and the small corruptions of everyday ambition.

But you see, I believe public service is honorable. And every time I hear that someone has breached the public trust it breaks my heart.

And I wonder sometimes if we have forgotten who we are. But we're the people who sundered a nation rather than allow a sin called slavery—and we're the people who rose from the ghettoes and the deserts.

And we weren't saints, but we lived by standards. We celebrated the individual, but we weren't self-centered. We were practical, but we didn't live only for material things. We believed in getting ahead, but blind ambition wasn't our way.

The fact is prosperity has a purpose. It is to allow us to pursue "the better angels," to give us time to think and grow. Prosperity with a purpose means taking your idealism and making it concrete by certain acts of goodness.

It means helping a child from an unhappy home learn how to read—and I thank my wife Barbara for all her work in helping people to read and all her work for literacy in this country.

It means teaching troubled children through your presence that there is such a thing as reliable love. Some would say it's soft and insufficiently tough to care about these things. But where is it written that we must act as if we do not care, as if we are not moved?

Well, I am moved. I want a kinder and gentler nation.

Two men this year ask for your support. And you must know us.

As for me, I have held high office and done the work of democracy day by day. Yes, my parents were prosperous; and their children sure were lucky. But there were lessons we had to learn about life.

John Kennedy discovered poverty when he campaigned in West Virginia; there were children who had no milk.

And young Teddy Roosevelt met the new America when he roamed the immigrant streets of New York. And I learned a few things about life in a place called Texas.

And when I was working on this part of the speech, Barbara came in and asked what I was doing. And I looked up, and I said I'm working hard. And she said: "Oh dear, don't worry, relax, sit back, take off your shoes and put up your silver foot."

Now, we moved to West Texas 40 years ago—40 years ago this year. The war was over, and we wanted to get out and make it on our own. Those were exciting days. We lived in a little shotgun house, one room for the three of us. Worked in the oil business, and then started my own.

And in time we had six children. Moved from the shotgun to a duplex apartment to a house. And lived the dream—high school football on Friday nights, Little League, neighborhood barbecue.

People don't see their own experience as symbolic of an era—but of course we were.

And so was everyone else who was taking a chance and pushing into unknown territory with kids and a dog and a car.

But the big thing I learned is the satisfaction of creating jobs, which meant creating opportunity, which meant happy families, who in turn could do more to help others and enhance their own lives.

I learned that the good done by a single good job can be felt in ways you can't imagine.

It's been said that I'm not the most compelling speaker, and there are actually those who claim that I don't always communicate in the clearest, most concise way. But I dare them to keep it up—go ahead: Make my 24-hour time period!

Well, I may not be the most eloquent, but I learned that, early on, that elo-quence won't draw oil from the ground.

And I may sometimes be a little awkward. But there's nothing self-conscious in my love of country.

And I am a quiet man, but I hear the quiet people others don't. The ones who raise the family, pay the taxes, meet the mortgages.

And I hear them and I am moved, and their concerns are mine.

A president must be many things.

He must be a shrewd protector of America's interests; and he must be an idealist who leads those who move for a freer and more democratic planet.

And he must see to it that government intrudes as little as possible in the lives of the people; and yet remember that it is right and proper that a nation's leader take an interest in the nation's character.

And he must be able to define—and lead—a mission.

For 7½ years, I have worked with a great president—I have seen what crosses that big desk. I have seen the unexpected crisis that arrives in a cable in a young aide's hand. And I have seen problems that simmer on for decades and suddenly demand resolution. And I have seen modest decisions made with anguish, and crucial decisions made with dispatch.

And so I know that what it all comes down to, this election—what it all comes down to, after all the shouting and the cheers—is the man at the desk. And who should sit at that desk.

My friends, I am that man.

I say it without boast or bravado.

I've fought for my country, I've served, I've built—and I will go from the hills to the hollows, from the cities to the suburbs to the loneliest town on the quietest street to take our message of hope and growth for every American to every American.

I will keep America moving forward, always forward, for a better America, for an endless enduring dream and a thousand points of light.

This is my mission. And I will complete it.

Thank you.

You know, you know it is customary to end an address with a pledge or a saying that holds a special meaning. And I've chosen one that we all know by heart. One that we all learned in school.

And I ask everyone in this great hall to stand and join me in this—we all know it.

I pledge allegiance to the flag of the United States of America and to the republic for which it stands, one nation under God, indivisible, with liberty and justice for all.

Thank you.

# George Bush's
# Inaugural Address (1989)

In 1988 George Bush became the first incumbent vice president to be elected president in 152 years. Although Bush's twenty-five-year career in public life included service in Congress and in three presidential administrations, his success in winning the Republican nomination for president could be traced mainly to his association with President Ronald Reagan. In the fall campaign, Reagan campaigned ardently, stressing the vice president's contributions to what Reagan generously began describing as the "Reagan-Bush administration." Bush's own campaign oscillated between harsh invective against his opponent, Gov. Michael S. Dukakis of Massachusetts, and calls for a "kinder and gentler nation." On election day Bush won with 54 percent of the popular vote and a 426-111 margin in the electoral college.

Both during the transition period between election and inauguration and in his inaugural address, Bush stressed the "kinder and gentler" theme, pledging his administration "to make kinder the face of a nation and gentler the face of the world." While stressing continuity with the Reagan administration (he even followed Reagan's innovation of holding the inauguration on the West Front of the Capitol), Bush said repeatedly in his address that "a new breeze is blowing" in the United States and abroad. Americans must no longer regard "the sum of our possessions . . . as the measure of our lives." Instead, the new president said, we "must celebrate the quieter, deeper successes that are made not of gold and silk, but of better hearts and finer souls." As for society's problems, "We have more will than wallet; but will is what we need."

Bush pledged his administration to work with the Democratic Congress, seeking bipartisan solutions to the nation's problems. The "Reagan Revolution," although conservative, was in one important respect like the three other landmark presidencies of the twentieth century that dramatically altered the role of the federal government in American society—Woodrow Wilson's "New Freedom," Franklin D. Roosevelt's "New Deal," and Lyndon B. Johnson's "Great Society." Each of these presidents left his successor with unresolved problems born of the rapid changes just undertaken. In Bush's case, the roster of problems he inherited from Reagan included the massive federal budget deficit, the plight of the homeless, environmental despoliation, and a financially unstable savings and loan industry. ～

Mr. Chief Justice, Mr. President, Vice President Quayle, Senator Mitchell, Speaker Wright, Senator Dole, Congressman Michel, and fellow citizens, neighbors and friends.

There is a man here who has earned a lasting place in our hearts—and in our history. President Reagan, on behalf of our nation I thank you for the wonderful things that you have done for America.

I have just repeated word-for-word the oath taken by George Washington 200 years ago; and the Bible on which I placed my hand is the Bible on which he placed his.

It is right that the memory of Washington be with us today, not only because this is our Bicentennial Inauguration, but because Washington remains the father of our country. And he would, I think, be gladdened by this day. For today is the concrete expression of a stunning fact: Our continuity these 200 years since our government began.

We meet on democracy's front porch. A good place to talk as neighbors, and as friends. For this is a day when our nation is made whole, when our differences, for a moment, are suspended.

And my first act as President is a prayer and I ask you to bow your heads:

"Heavenly Father, we bow our heads and thank you for your love. Accept our thanks for the peace that yields this day and the shared faith that makes its continuance likely. Make us strong to do your work, willing to heed and hear your will, and write on our hearts these words: 'Use power to help people.' For we are given power not to advance our own purposes, nor to make a great show in the world, nor a name. There is but one just use of power, and it is to serve people. Help us to remember, Lord. Amen."

I come before you and assume the presidency at a moment rich with promise. We live in a peaceful, prosperous time, but we can make it better.

For a new breeze is blowing, and a world refreshed by freedom seems re-born; for in man's heart, if not in fact, the day of the dictator is over. The totalitarian era is passing, its old ideas blown away like leaves from an ancient lifeless tree.

A new breeze is blowing—and a nation refreshed by freedom stands ready to push on: There is new ground to be broken, and new action to be taken.

There are times when the future seems thick as a fog; you sit and wait, hoping the mists will lift and reveal the right path.

But this is a time when the future seems a door you can walk right through—into a room called Tomorrow.

Great nations of the world are moving toward democracy—through the door to freedom.

Men and women of the world move toward free markets—through the door to prosperity.

The people of the world agitate for free expression and free thought—through the door to the moral and intellectual satisfactions that only liberty allows.

We know what works: Freedom works. We know what's right: Freedom is right. We know how to secure a more just and prosperous life for man on earth: through free markets, free speech, free elections, and the exercise of free will unhampered by the state.

For the first time in this century—for the first time in perhaps all history—man does not have to invent a system by which to live. We don't have to talk into the night about which form of government is better. We don't have to wrest justice from the kings—we only have to summon it from within ourselves.

We must act on what we know. I take as my guide the hope of a saint: In crucial things, unity—in important things, diversity—in all things, generosity.

America today is a proud, free nation, decent and civil—a place we cannot help but love. We know in our hearts, not loudly and proudly, but as a simple fact, that this country has meaning beyond what we see, and that our strength is a force for good.

But have we changed as a nation even in our time? Are we enthralled with material things, less appreciative of the nobility of work and sacrifice?

My friends, we are not the sum of our possessions. They are not the measure of our lives. In our hearts we know what matters. We cannot hope only to leave our children a bigger car, a bigger bank account. We must hope to give them a sense of what it means to be a loyal friend, a loving parent, a citizen who leaves his home, his neighborhood and town better than he found it.

And what do we want the men and women who work with us to say when we are no longer there? That we were more driven to succeed than anyone around us? Or that we stopped to ask if a sick child had gotten better, and stayed a moment there to trade a word of friendship.

No President, no government, can teach us to remember what is best in what we are. But if the man you have chosen to lead this government can help make a difference; if he can celebrate the quieter, deeper successes that are made not of gold and silk, but of better hearts and finer souls; if he can do these things, then he must.

America is never wholly herself unless she is engaged in high moral principle. We as a people have such a purpose today. It is to make kinder the face of the nation and gentler the face of the world.

My friends, we have work to do. There are the homeless, lost and roaming—there are the children who have nothing, no love, no normalcy—there are those who cannot free themselves of enslavement to whatever addiction—drugs, welfare, the demoralization that rules the slums. There is crime to be conquered, the rough crime of the streets. There are young women to be helped who are about to become mothers of children they can't care for and might not love. They need our care, our guidance, and our education; though we bless them for choosing life.

The old solution, the old way, was to think that public money alone could end these problems. But we have learned that that is not so. And in any case, our funds are low. We have a deficit to bring down. We have more will than wallet; but will is what we need.

We will make the hard choices, looking at what we have, perhaps allocating it differently, making our decisions based on honest need and prudent safety.

And then we will do the wisest thing of all: We will turn to the only resource we have that in times of need always grows: the goodness and the courage of the American people.

And I am speaking of a new engagement in the lives of others—a new activism, hands-on and involved, that gets the job done. We must bring in the generations, harnessing the unused talent of the elderly and the unfocused energy of the young. For not only leadership is passed from generation to generation, but so is stewardship. And the generation born after the Second World War has come of age.

I have spoken of a thousand points of light—of all the community organizations that are spread like stars throughout the nation, doing good.

We will work hand in hand, encouraging, sometimes leading, sometimes being led, rewarding. We will work on this in the White House, in the Cabinet agencies. I will go to the people and the programs that are the brighter points of light, and I will ask every member of my government to become involved.

The old ideas are new again because they're not old, they are timeless: duty, sacrifice, commitment, and a patriotism that finds its expression in taking part and pitching in.

We need a new engagement, too, between the Executive and the Congress.

The challenges before us will be thrashed out with the House and Senate. We must bring the federal budget into balance. And we must ensure that America stands before the world united: strong, at peace, and fiscally sound. But, of course, things may be difficult.

We need compromise; we've had dissension. We need harmony; we've had a chorus of discordant voices.

For Congress, too, has changed in our time. There has grown a certain divisiveness. We have seen the hard looks and heard the statements in which not each other's ideas are challenged, but each other's motives. And our great parties have too often been far apart and untrusting of each other.

It's been this way since Vietnam. That war cleaves us still. But, friends, that war began in earnest a quarter of a century ago; and surely the statute of limitations has been reached. This is a fact: The final lesson of Vietnam is that no great nation can long afford to be sundered by a memory.

A new breeze is blowing—and the old bipartisanship must be made new again.

To my friends—and yes, I do mean friends—in the loyal opposition—and yes, I mean loyal: I put out my hand.

I am putting out my hand to you, Mr. Speaker.

I am putting out my hand to you, Mr. Majority Leader.

For this is the thing: This is the age of the offered hand.

And we can't turn back clocks, and I don't want to. But when our fathers were young, Mr. Speaker, our differences ended at the water's edge. And we don't wish to turn back time, but when our mothers were young, Mr. Majority Leader, the Congress and the Executive were capable of working together to produce a budget on which this nation could live. Let us negotiate soon—and hard. But in the end, let us produce.

The American people await action.

They didn't send us here to bicker. They ask us to rise above the merely partisan. "In crucial things, unity"— and this, my friends, is crucial.

To the world, too, we offer new engagement and a renewed vow: We will stay strong to protect the peace. The "offered hand" is a reluctant fist; once made strong, it can be used with great effect.

There are today Americans who are held against their will in foreign lands, and Americans who are unaccounted for. Assistance can be shown here, and will be long remembered. Good will begets good will. Good faith can be a spiral that endlessly moves on.

"Great nations like great men must keep their word." When America says something, America means it, whether a treaty or an agreement or a vow made on marble steps. We will always try to speak clearly, for candor is a compliment. But subtlety, too, is good and has its place.

While keeping our alliances and friendships around the world strong, ever strong, we will continue the new closeness with the Soviet Union, consistent both with our security and with progress. One might say that our new relationship in part reflects the triumph of hope and strength over experience. But hope is good. And so is strength. And vigilance.

Here today are tens of thousands of our citizens who feel the understandable satisfaction of those who have taken part in democracy and seen their hopes fulfilled.

But my thoughts have been turning the past few days to those who would be watching at home—

To an older fellow who will throw a salute by himself when the flag goes by, and the woman who will tell her sons the words of the battle hymns. I don't mean this to be sentimental. I mean that on days like this, we remember that we are all part of a continuum, inescapably connected by the ties that bind—

Our children are watching in schools throughout our great land. And to them I say, thank you for watching democracy's big day. For democracy belongs to us all, and freedom is like a beautiful kite that can go higher and higher with the breeze....

And to all I say: No matter what your circumstances or where you are, you are part of this day, you are part of the life of our great nation.

A President is neither prince nor pope, and I don't seek "a window on men's souls." In fact, I yearn for a greater tolerance, an easy-goingness about each other's attitudes and way of life.

There are few clear areas in which we as a society must rise up united and express our intolerance. And the most obvious now is drugs. And when that first cocaine was smuggled in on a ship, it may as well have been a deadly bacteria, so much has it hurt the body, the soul of our country. There is much to be done and to be said, but take my word for it: This scourge will stop.

And so, there is much to do; and tomorrow the work begins.

And I do not mistrust the future; I do not fear what is ahead. For our problems are large, but our heart is larger. Our challenges are great, but our will is greater. And if our flaws are endless, God's love is truly boundless.

Some see leadership as high drama, and the sound of trumpets calling. And sometimes it is that. But I see history as a book with many pages—and each day we fill a page with acts of hopefulness and meaning.

The new breeze blows, a page turns, the story unfolds—and so today a chapter begins: a small and stately story of unity, diversity, and generosity—shared, and written, together.

Thank you.

God bless you.

And God bless the United States of America.

# Index

# DATE DUE